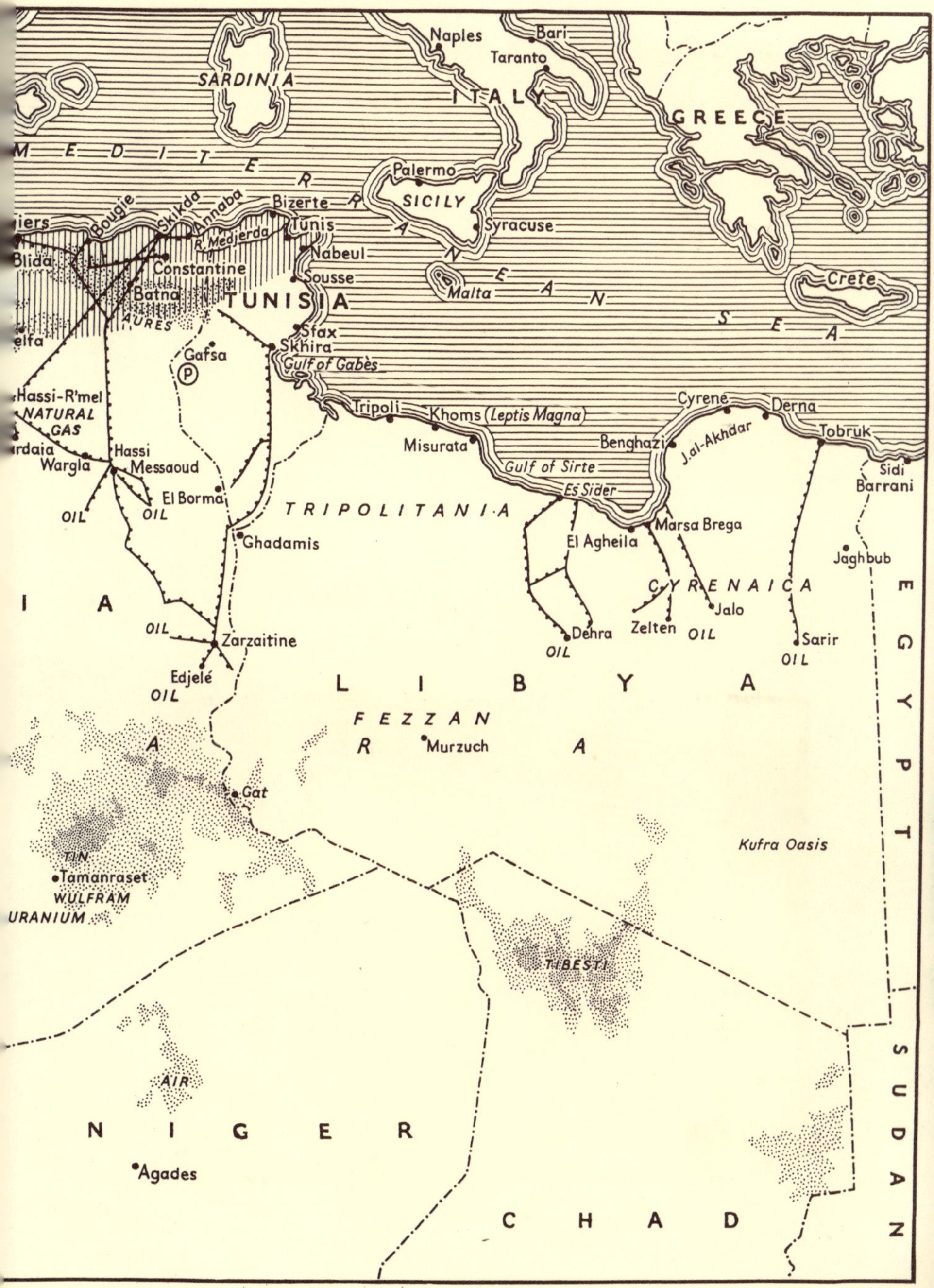
SARDINIA
Naples
Bari
Taranto
ITALY
GREECE
M E D I T E R R A N E A N S E A
Palermo
SICILY
Syracuse
Malta
Crete
Bougie
Skikda
Annaba
Bizerte
Tunis
R. Medjerda
Constantine
Nabeul
Blida
Sousse
Batna
AURES
TUNISIA
Sfax
Skhira
Gafsa
Gulf of Gabès
Hassi-R'mel
NATURAL GAS
Wargla
Hassi Messaoud
El Borma
OIL
OIL
Tripoli
Khoms (Leptis Magna)
Misurata
Cyrene
Derna
Tobruk
Benghazi
J. al-Akhdar
Gulf of Sirte
Es Sider
Sidi Barrani
TRIPOLITANIA
Ghadamis
El Agheila
Marsa Brega
Jaghbub
CYRENAICA
Jalo
Zelten
OIL
Dehra
OIL
Sarir
OIL
OIL
Zarzaitine
Edjelé
OIL
LIBYA
FEZZAN
Murzuch
Gat
TIN
Tamanraset
WULFRAM
URANIUM
Kufra Oasis
EGYPT
TIBESTI
SUDAN
AIR
NIGER
Agades
CHAD

DT   Knapp
185   North West Africa.
K55

DATE DUE

MAY 5 1996			

Subject To Recall After 2 Weeks

**LIBRARY
NORTH DAKOTA
STATE UNIVERSITY
FARGO, NORTH DAKOTA**

DEMCO

North West Africa

WITHDRAWN

North West Africa

A Political and Economic Survey

THIRD EDITION

WILFRID KNAPP

OXFORD
OXFORD UNIVERSITY PRESS
LONDON   NEW YORK   TORONTO
1977

Oxford University Press, Walton Street, Oxford OX2 6DP

OXFORD LONDON GLASGOW NEW YORK
TORONTO MELBOURNE WELLINGTON CAPE TOWN
IBADAN NAIROBI DAR ES SALAAM LUSAKA ADDIS ABABA
KUALA LUMPUR SINGAPORE HONG KONG TOKYO
DELHI BOMBAY CALCUTTA MADRAS KARACHI

ISBN 0 19 215635 7

© Oxford University Press 1977

First Edition published 1959
Second Edition published 1962
(First two editions edited by
NEVILL BARBOUR)
Third Edition 1977

All rights reserved. No part of this publication may be reproduced,
stored in a retrieval system, or transmitted, in any form or by any means,
electronic, mechanical, photocopying, recording or otherwise, without
the prior permission of Oxford University Press

DT
185
K55

Printed in Great Britain by
Ebenezer Baylis and Son, Ltd., The Trinity Press,
Worcester, and London

Contents

	page
Preface to Third Edition	vii
1. Introduction	1
2. Algeria	51
3. Libya	174
4. Mauritania and the Southern Sahara	234
5. Morocco	252
6. Tunisia	341
7. Literature in North West Africa	403
Glossary	421
Statistical Appendix	423
Select Bibliography	437
Index	443

MAPS

The Penetration of Islam into Africa	18
The European Advance into North West Africa	42
European Settlement in North Africa	46
North West Africa	endpapers

The maps on pp. 18, 42, and 46 are reproduced from J. D. Fage, *An Atlas of African History*, London, 1958, by kind permission of Edward Arnold (Publishers) Ltd.

Preface to Third Edition

The present work is a revised version of the survey edited by Nevill Barbour, first published in 1959, second edition 1962. The first edition was thus in preparation as Tunisia and Morocco achieved their independence, and the Algerian War of Independence was in its early stages. In consequence, by far the greater part of the present book is new. It offers an interpretative work of reference covering five states which have come into existence since the Second World War.

The previous editions of this book were published for the Royal Institute of International Affairs by the Oxford University Press. The latter has now taken over entire editorial responsibility for the volume. However, the valuable historical sections of the previous editions have been retained wherever appropriate, and for permission to reproduce these the Editor and publishers are indebted to the RIIA. Thus, the sections Nevill Barbour wrote on the early history of the region and its constituent parts have been kept virtually intact; the more recent history has been written anew with the intention of emphasizing the background to the new states, rather than the policies of France and Italy. An important section by Robert Mabro on the Libyan economy forms an integral part of the whole, while the chapter on North African literature in French and Arabic, by Robin Ostle, is an addition to the survey of politics and economics.

I have received help, advice, and hospitality from many people in my own university, at Durham, and in London; from members of governments and private persons in Libya, Tunisia, Algeria, and Morocco; from Mlle Nicole Grimaud and her colleagues at the Fondation Nationale des Sciences Politiques and the Documentation Française in Paris, and from M. Bruno Étienne and the Centre des Recherches sur les Sociètès Mèditerranèennes at Aix-en-Provence; from M. Abdelmajid Klilib in Algiers; from my graduate students, particularly Mr. Francis Ghilès and Mr. Hugh Roberts; and from members of the British diplomatic service and the United States foreign service and from journalists, especially those of Reuters, the BBC, and *Le Monde*. Their knowledge and insight have been of great value in my attempt to study countries which have little reliable documentation and which lack a free and informed press.

Oxford University Press, particularly as represented by Mr. John Bell, kept the work alive with understanding and encouragement; Miss Anne Charvet and Miss Ena Sheen provided indispensable help with final editing. St. Catherine's College has given invaluable practical support, particularly in providing the typing and secretarial service of Mrs. Jane Macmillan and Mrs. Vera Arthur. Above all my college and university have provided that combination of academic freedom and academic discipline without which objective study is impossible. My wife and our sons have accompanied me on some of the travel and the whole of the intellectual journey which have produced this book.

Like any author I would wish that so much assistance would eradicate error; alas, faults and mistakes no doubt remain. They are my own.

February 1976
Wilfrid Knapp
St. Catherine's College
Oxford

I
Introduction

NORTH WEST AFRICA AND ITS PEOPLE

North West Africa is today divided into four states: Morocco, Algeria, Tunisia, and Libya—together with Mauritania, which can be seen as a link joining North West Africa to black Africa south of the Sahara. The present frontiers of North West Africa date from the Turkish conquest of the three eastern areas rather more than 400 years ago. Before the recent French and Spanish protectorates, however, Morocco had existed as an independent state for 1,000 years; while Tunisia with certain interruptions—principally the 600 years of Roman rule—had been the seat of independent or virtually independent governments for the greater part of the time since the establishment of Carthage in the first millennium before Christ.

Geography

For political reasons, and for the purposes of this book, the eastern limit of North West Africa can be taken as the Libyan-Egyptian and Libyan-Sudanese frontiers. Geographically, however, and to some extent historically, it is more correct to define it as the 300 miles of desert, running right down to the sea, which separate the Libyan coastal province of Tripolitania from the other Libyan coastal province, Cyrenaica.

In the north the area is limited by the Mediterranean Sea; and in the west by the Atlantic. In the south it is defined, east of Mauritania, by the Saharan frontiers dividing Algeria and Libya to the north from Mali, Niger, and Chad to the south. The people of the Sahara, with few exceptions, are Arabic- or Berber-speaking, just as are the people of the coastal states; they derived their religion from the north, not from the south; their way of life has been determined by insufficiency of water, as has that of the people of the countries on their north. Racially the Saharans belong mostly to the white north, not to the black south.

In Arabic North West Africa is known as the Maghreb, or west, and is thereby distinguished from the Arab east, the Mashreq.

Language

More than three-quarters of the population of the whole area speak Arabic as their mother tongue, and one-quarter Berber. But the linguistic heritage of the region has inevitably been affected by the long period of European penetration and domination of which the first sign was the short-lived occupation of certain Tripolitanian and Tunisian coastal towns by the Norman rulers of Sicily in the twelfth century. It was resumed with the Portuguese and Spanish captures of African seaports in the late fifteenth and early sixteenth centuries, almost disappeared in the seventeenth and eighteenth centuries, but revived with the French capture of Algiers in 1830. It culminated with the occupation of the Anti-Atlas and the Moroccan Sahara in 1934, and began to pass away with the independence of Libya in 1951.

The French language and French culture were deeply implanted among the educated classes of Tunisia, Algeria, and the French zone of Morocco, and French became the language of education for Mauritanians. Spanish was spoken in the Spanish zone of Morocco and Italian necessarily became the official language of Libya for a brief period; but Italian culture did not strike any deep roots. In the former French territories the mixture of European culture, including a language of practical value as well as cultural richness, with an indigenous Arabic-North African culture gives a particular character to social stratification and creates important problems for education.

The Two Halves of the Mediterranean World

From the geographical circumstances outlined above, it follows that the majority of the population of the Maghreb belong to the Mediterranean world. This world is distinctive because the Mediterranean is unlike any other sea. It is sufficiently enclosed to have a certain unity, sufficiently small to have some common characteristics of climate, and has been a vital route for communications even when its eastern outlet was over land rather than through the Suez Canal. It is the home of Graeco-Roman civilization, has facilitated the spread of Christianity from its birthplace into Europe and has been the meeting ground of Christian and Muslim civilization. Its shores offer shelter for fishermen and mariners, and for centuries have nurtured the olive and the orange. The customs of people who live on its coasts have appeared to some anthropologists to have more in common than have coastal and inland people of the same nationality.

None the less, the unity of the Mediterranean does not go very far. Although Fernand Braudel has described a continuum of climatic conditions from northern Europe to the Sahara, the critical line in this continuum runs east–west along the Mediterranean separating its northern from its southern shores. While the European shores have an adequate rainfall, equitably distributed throughout the year, the eastern and southern have an inadequate rainfall, except on the actual coast, and the rain falls mainly in the autumn and the spring, often in great momentary excess. The latter areas are therefore characterized by extensive desert regions and by the presence of the desert animal, the camel; and they suffer from extensive erosion of the soil. Linguistically the western and northern shores are inhabited by people who speak some kind of Indo-European language; while Semitic languages prevail on the eastern and southern shores. Where the two areas join, in Spain in the west and Asia Minor in the east, we find intermediate regions, arid but without actual deserts, with languages which are not Semitic but have assimilated a very high percentage of Semitic words. According to the relative attractive force of eastern and western civilization at any given moment these areas are drawn into the orbit of eastern or of western culture. Thus both Spain and Asia Minor have had periods of greatness as representatives at one time of western and at another of eastern civilization. Water, fuel, and wood have been marginally less plentiful upon the southern than on the northern shore. This was of fundamental importance in determining the economic relationship between north and south until the revolutionary change brought by the discovery of oil and gas in the twentieth century. The terrain of the northern and southern shores is also markedly different one from the other. Land communication along the southern shore is relatively easy, at least as far as Morocco, compared with the obstacles presented by the mountainous and indented terrain of the north.

From west to east, the Mediterranean area is also divided, and historical circumstances have added to the divisions which derive from geography. The proximity of Sicily and the north of Tunisia makes a natural break in the Mediterranean Sea: the corresponding break in the southern shore is further to the west where the Gulf of Sirte separates Tripolitania from Cyrenaica. To this must be added the fact that while the advanced technology and political strength of Europe has resulted in intermittent European domination over the whole length of the southern shore, Muslim culture has only advanced from each extremity, halted at Poitiers in the west and at Vienna in the east.

These several factors contribute to the pivotal position which the greater part of North West Africa occupies between the east and the north. The Phoenicians brought the region into their Mediterranean world; the Ottomans too attached North West Africa to the east although the links which they were able to forge remained weak; it was the Arab conquest which established an enduring relationship with the Middle East. None the less, the western Mediterranean has been geographically separate from the east; the north–south relationship in this region has been marked by outstanding periods of culture if not civilization such as the Roman Empire and the Moorish Empire in Spain; while, most important for the present survey, it is at the western end that the southern shore of the Mediterranean has easiest and most direct access to the developed, industrialized heartland of Europe.

Homogeneity and Diversity

For two thousand years political control has spanned the western Mediterranean, so that some part of the southern shore has been ruled from the north, or vice versa. The survival of Spanish enclaves preserves this tradition, but otherwise the advent of independence has been accompanied by a simplification of the political map of North West Africa. Morocco, previously divided between a French and a Spanish zone, has become a unified country although the Spanish enclaves of Ceuta and Melilla remain undisturbed—bringing some benefit to Morocco and evoking some factitious nationalist fervour. On the Atlantic coast the enclave of Ifni was incorporated into the independent state in 1969. But the territory of Spanish Sahara, comprising the Seguiet el-Hamra and the Rio de Oro, remained under Spanish rule until 1976 when it was divided between Morocco and Mauritania, against resistance organized by Polisario and supported by Algeria (see pp. 334-8). (The French attempt in 1957 to separate the Algerian Sahara, with its oil, under an Organisation des Régions Sahariennes, proved abortive, and it became an integral part of the Algerian state.) Tangier lost its international status and was incorporated into Morocco at the time of Independence. A free port of Tangier enjoys a limited commercial success; a free industrial zone has so far failed to develop according to plan, and tourism provides the major contribution to the fraction of prosperity which Tangier has inherited from its former privileged position.

The withdrawal of European political control has been accompanied by the departure of the greater part of the European and Jewish communities. The exodus of the French from Algiers began during the War of Independence and was precipitated by the establishment of the Algerian state. In Tunisia and Libya the departure of the French and Italian communities was accelerated by the nationalization of land in 1964 and 1970 respectively. In Morocco emigration has been more gradual but has accelerated with the increased pace of Moroccanization in recent years. The number of foreigners in Morocco (principally French and Algerians) fell from 396,000 to 112,000 between the two censuses of 1960 and 1971. A large part of the Jewish community emigrated to Israel and to Europe rather than stay as a minority in the new states. The rhythm of emigration has followed the movement towards independence in North Africa and the major events of the Middle East (notably the creation of the state of Israel in 1948 and the war of 1967). The largest Jewish community is in Morocco where the Jewish population in 1971 was 34,000—a diminution from 162,000 in 1960.

The homogeneity of the Arab-Berber population of North West Africa has thus increased markedly (the numerically small but important black population of Mauritania being an exception). The region is also homogeneous in its religion, in contrast to the Arab east. The Malikite rite predominates; there are no indigenous Christian minorities and no important minority Muslim sects, except for the Kharijites of Jerba and the Mzabites of Algeria.

This homogeneity is qualified by the differences between Arabs and Berbers. Berber-speaking groups today form islands of population all the way from the Siwa oasis in Egypt to the Atlantic coast. There are some in Libya and a good many in central and southern Sahara; but very few in Tunisia. There are big groups in the Kabyle country and in the Aurès mountains of Algeria, while the largest concentrations are found in Morocco, the main body being in the central and southern Atlas and a smaller group in the Rif. The position of the Berber language in North West Africa is thus rather like that of the Celtic languages in Britain; it has often survived in place-names after it has ceased to be the locally spoken language. It has in fact provided some of the most characteristic and romantic-sounding names of the Maghreb —Agadir (the fortress), Azrou (the rock), Ifni (the rocky desert), Taourirt (the round peak), Tizi-Ouzou (the rainy mountain pass), Tsettauen (Tetuan, the eyes). Since ancient Egyptian times, the Berbers have called themselves *Imazighen*, which means the free men; and in fact they are distinguished by a great love of personal and group liberty.

But although some Berbers are clearly distinct by language, history, and customs from some Arabs there is no sharp dividing-line between the two peoples. The distinctive quality of the inhabitants of North West Africa (in comparison with those of the Arab east) is not conflict between Arabs and Berbers. It is rather the implantation of Arab Muslim language and culture in an area originally inhabited by Berbers, and the survival of a Berber identity transformed by acceptance of this culture. Berbers have not developed a nationalist movement like that of the Kurds; nor did Christianity survive among Berbers as it did with the Copts in Egypt. Indeed Berbers may be more devout and careful in the practice of the Muslim religion precisely because their language is not that of the Koran and because they cannot claim descent from the homeland, far less the tribe of the Prophet. Spoken Berber is a multiplicity of dialects rather than a single language and this may account for the absence of a written language.

The Muslim religion played a major part in the development of the nationalist movement in North West Africa; its importance at the present time must remain a matter of speculation and judgement, in default of adequate empirical research.[1] When North Africa was under European rule Islam and the sense of an Arab-Islamic identity were important components of the opposition to French rule, even when the objectives of the nationalist movement were equality with France. As Gellner has commented: 'In his heart, the North African knows not merely that God speaks Arabic, but also that modernity speaks French' (Gellner and Micaud, 1973). The newly independent states all accepted Islam as the official religion of the state, Mauritania calls itself the Islamic republic of Mauritania, Libyan legislation is framed in accordance with Muslim law, and the King of Morocco is styled (in the constitution) 'commander of the faithful'. The Tunisian republic introduced a new personal code, giving women rights comparable to those of European women immediately after Independence; but President Bourguiba encountered vigorous opposition to his attempts to 'modernize' the country by ending the practice of fasting during the month of Ramadan. In Algeria the customs which had rooted themselves under the shelter of Islam have made the government reluctant to introduce a new code of personal status; religion serves as a binding force in a nation divided between a modernizing, western élite and a population imbued with tradition. For many North Africans education has made secularism as attractive as it is for Europeans; but at the same time the wealth and importance of such states as Saudi Arabia and Kuwait pulls in the opposite direction.

This is not to say that there are no political divisions within North West Africa based on group loyalties. The notables of Fez excite the hostility and antipathy of many of their countrymen who are Berbers; but this is because they are Fassis, not because they are Arabs, and it is not only Berbers who attach stereotypes to them. The Kabyles (from east of Algiers) have a strong sense of common identity—as long as it is not disturbed by a clannish quarrel among themselves. ('Kabyle' has also been known to be used, by a Kabyle, as an honorific designation of someone he admires.) Thus while some Berbers are clearly identifiable, for the most part the difference between Arabized Berbers, or Arabs living in Berber areas (who may have learned Berber) is neither very obvious nor of political or practical importance.

In the twentieth century the emigration of North West Africans to Europe has acquired a new dimension. The emigration in pursuit of work was an established practice before Independence. Since then, the rapid growth of population south of the Mediterranean and the recep-

---

[1] Recent research in historical studies and in social anthropology has thrown much light on religious practice and belief, and the relation of religion to politics. See in particular the work of Ernest Gellner and Edmund Burke III. For a discussion of Islam in independent North Africa see the essay of 1964 by Leon Carl Brown in Brown, ed., 1966.

tivity of the advanced economies of Europe to men able and willing to fill low-paid, manual jobs, has increased the scale of emigration. The flow phenomenon of migration runs from poorer to wealthier countries in the region, not necessarily between African and European states: thus, while Algeria provides the largest contingent of foreigners in France, Portugal runs a close second, Italian and Spanish immigrants to France rank next before Moroccans, Tunisians, and Yugoslavs. French government statistics showed a rising graph of the number of North Africans in France in 1973; but immigration was stopped by the French government in 1974.

The increased scale of emigration and the changing nature of the societies from which it emerges have brought substantial modifications of character, which are most evident in the experience of Algerians in France. Traditionally, Kabyles would go to France to work, form an enclave in France, and then return to strongly organized society where such deviant habits as they had acquired in Europe would be rapidly shed as they were reintegrated into their homeland. But the size of the Algerian community in France has created obvious openings for a wide variety of classes and professions, from butchers to lawyers (and property owners), so that an alternative Algerian community on foreign land has come into existence.

The departure of the greater part of the European and Jewish communities has enhanced the cultural homogeneity of North West Africa while, at the same time, the exodus and coming and going of North Africans has increased and has acquired its own customs and institutions. (There were, in 1974, nearly as many Algerians in France as there were French in Algeria at the beginning of the War of Independence.) Meanwhile, there remains, for the major part of the populations of North Africa, a material unity which derives from their relationship to the land and to the climate. Affairs of state continue to be the concern of a political and economic élite, living in capital cities. The preoccupation of the majority of the population is still with raising crops and keeping cattle, or grazing sheep and goats wherever pasture may be found.

The lives of the 60 per cent who live on the land still depend on cereals, above all on wheat. This legendary provider of sustenance shows great resilience and rarely fails; but the quantity of its yield remains very sensitive to temporal-climatic conditions—not only on the right amount of rainfall, but on rain at the right time. An excess of rain leaches the soil, taking nutrition below the reach of the roots, so that a wet year exhausts the soil for the following season as well (in contrast to drought, which at least leaves the soil content intact). Yield depends not only on rainfall but on wind which, if it blows too hot during the ripening, may ruin the harvest. Joseph's dream of the seven fat years and the seven lean years is well-founded on statistics available some millennia later. While the importance of wheat, and therefore of climate and soil, has changed little, those living on the land have become subject to demographic pressures as a result of the disappearance of the destructive epidemics of the past. The crude effect of this change is seen in the change from wheat-exporting to wheat-importing economies,[1] or the vigorous efforts that are made to be self-sufficient in wheat; it is also apparent in the movement into the towns. Less immediately apparent is the changing relationship between farmers and herdsmen as the pressure on scant resources is increased. The overall impact of increased population is accelerated as the delicate balance of a rural economy, trading the products of the pasture with those of the town and village, is broken down.

Population growth is associated with movement to the towns. In North Africa, as in other parts of the developing world, urbanization, as a general phenomenon, owes more to demographic pressure in the countryside than to rapid economic growth in the towns. The pattern of urbanization is different in each of the countries of the region. Tunisia has a relatively continuous urban history: the towns which have grown in population and activity are those of historic importance, notably Tunis, Sfax, and Sousse. Kairouan, in contrast, declined from the fifteenth century, yet it survived intact and may owe its present vitality to a tradition of urban living as much as to tourist prosperity.

In contrast, Algeria has little or no urban history. The historic continuity of Tlemsen is exceptional; Roman towns bear no relation to modern urban centres; modern towns were French creations; Algiers had its Casbah rather than a medina. The Moroccan experience falls between the Tunisian and Algerian examples: it has a strong urban tradition, with a modern displacement of urban centres. Volubilis was an outpost of an empire further west, and had no medieval successor of importance. Fez and Marrakesh were towns of wealth and importance which owed their position to agricultural potential and trade routes; whereas Casablanca began its rapid growth because of its connection with France and the outside world, so that one-tenth of Morocco's population now lives in a city with minimal historic antecedents, while the Fassis, who run the government of the country from the new town of Rabat, discuss the possibility of a campaign to preserve Fez, their birthplace (or at least town of origin) from decay.

RELATIONS BETWEEN THE MAGHREB STATES

Neither cultural homogeneity nor the similarity of the basic needs of so large a part of the population has produced political unity. On the contrary, the establishment of four independent states has been followed by the reinforcement of the state system. National govern-

[1] Even when allowance is made, in these statistics, for changes in consumption patterns.

ments have established their single authority over the whole territory under their rule. The development is most obvious in Morocco. National unity was obviously an attractive theme as the division between the *blad al-makhzen* and the *blad as-siba* lost its importance with the spread of modern government, blending bureaucracy and patronage over the whole territory. Local caïds have lost the degree of independence which French rule assured them, while at the same time, the social role of the *sharufa* and the *murabitin* has diminished as the role of the state has increased. In Algeria it has been part of the purpose of the state to eliminate the differences between the rich northern departments and the Sahara, while in Libya the strengthening of the state apparatus has diminished the forces which, at the time of Independence, made federalism appear an appropriate political arrangement.

Meanwhile, politics between the four main states have been characterized by the strengthening of state boundaries as a result of disputes over territory and of accusations made by one state that another is supporting opposition or subversion. Inevitably, the effect of competitive politics of this kind was to strengthen the machinery of state in each country, as a means of self-preservation.

Before Algerian Independence the Tunisian government accused the FLN (Front de Libération Nationale), in concert with Cairo, of supporting Salah Ben Youssef in his struggle for power against Bourguiba; and when Independence was achieved the Algerian government of Ben Bella accused the Tunisians of supporting Ben Khedda. On the one hand, in 1958 Youssefists were arrested in the Algerian Liberation Army; on the other, Bourguiba was charged in 1962 with restricting the movement of Algerian troops loyal to Ben Bella. A temporary amelioration followed when Ahmed Mestiri was nominated ambassador to Algiers in July 1962. But this was immediately followed by an abortive plot to assassinate Bourguiba, when Algeria refused to extradite Tunisians charged with complicity in the affair. In 1963 the crisis between Tunis and France over Bizerte diverted attention from an armed struggle between Tunisia and Algeria over the southern frontier when Bourguiba's government apparently tried to gain control of oil deposits. Algeria held its ground, but the definitive solution of the frontier problem was only resolved by an agreement at the end of 1970.

Moroccan policy towards its borders has been equally activist, as Moroccan governments, and opposition politicians wanting to outdo them, have made claim to a greater Morocco which included, initially, the whole Sahara territory to the south of Morocco. King Mohammed V refused to recognize the state of Mauritania when it became independent in November 1960. For some years the question of Mauritania was central to Moroccan foreign policy. Relations with Tunisia were broken because of the latter's swift recognition of Mauritania; they were resumed following the Arab summit conference of January 1964. In the pursuit of support for its attitude to Mauritania, Morocco became a leading member of the 'Casablanca' group of African states, which asserted its claim to be progressive and revolutionary rather than reformist.

No less important was the dispute between Algeria and Morocco over the frontier area around Tindouf and the iron-bearing mountain, the Gara Djebilet. During the Algerian war, the Moroccan government reached an agreement with the Algerian provisional government supporting the Algerians against French attempts to detach the Sahara from Algeria, but securing recognition that a frontier difference existed between Algeria and Morocco. However, the independent government of Algeria did not confirm the agreement and insisted on the integrity of the frontiers as drawn under the French. The dispute led to frontier fighting in 1963 which had an effect on the internal politics of each country. In Algeria it was used by Ben Bella and Boumediene to tighten their control over Kabylia; in Morocco, the 'plot of 1963' involving Mohamed al-Basri and Ben Barka, included accusations that the defendants had taken the Algerian side in the frontier dispute.

The differences between Morocco and its neighbours moved towards resolution at the end of the 1960s, as Morocco abandoned an increasingly untenable position. A treaty of friendship between Algeria and Morocco was signed at Ifrane in January 1969, establishing a procedure for the settlement of the frontier question. The two heads of state, Boumediene and King Hassan, met at Tlemsen in May 1970—a meeting which was celebrated as symbolic of improved relations. A frontier commission, with help from the National Geographical Institute of Paris (which provided the same service on the Tunisian frontier), opened the way for a frontier agreement which confirmed the Algerian position and was accompanied by an agreement for the joint exploration of the iron ore reserves of the Gara Djebilet.

The improvement in Algerian–Moroccan relations had proceeded unaffected by Algerian recognition of Mauritania in 1967 and it soon became clear that Morocco would accept the existence of its southern neighbour. Mauritania was invited to attend the Islamic conference in Casablanca in 1969, and diplomatic relations were established at the beginning of 1970.[1]

Shortly afterwards the presidents of Algeria and Mauritania, and the King of Morocco, met at Nouadhibou (in September 1970) and again in Rabat (in 1972) to concert policy with regard to the Spanish Sahara—a question of vital importance in relations between the three, especially between Morocco and Mauritania. Algeria appeared to be uninterested in the acquisition of territory, in spite of having a border

[1] The Istiqlal party condemned the recognition of Mauritania and continued to refer to 'the Shinqit, known as Mauritania' (in spite of the fact that a junior member of the Mauritanian embassy attended the 9th party congress in September 1974).

with the Spanish Sahara, and showed a readiness to act as intermediary between the other two.

But at the end of 1975 the question of the Spanish Sahara became inflamed as a result of the successful diplomacy of Morocco (and the political weakness of Spain at the time of Franco's death) in reaching a tripartite agreement transferring control of the area from Spain to Morocco and Mauritania (see below, pp. 334–8). This new development evoked the vigorous opposition of Algeria which, in its search for allies, formed an entente with Libya in support of the Saharan opposition group, the Polisario. The tension between Algeria and Morocco, and the new alignment with Libya, sharpened the ideological differences in the Maghreb, the more so when Tunisia came down on the side of Morocco. In spite of the progress which had been made in the development of good relations with Morocco, on the basis of necessary harmony between nation-states, there were at least some Algerians who began to regret opportunities to intervene in Moroccan affairs which had been lost at the time of the attempts on the life of the king.

Throughout this time Libya had played a distinctive role. As the colony of a power that was defeated in the Second World War, Libya was the first to achieve its independence. The government of King Idris then gave consistent diplomatic support to the efforts of the Maghreb countries to gain their independence. During the Algerian war, Libya readily allowed arms to pass across its territory from Egypt towards Algeria, sought the support of Britain and the United States for a settlement of the Algerian war, and boycotted French imports. In 1962 it acted as host at Tripoli to the Algerian provisional government, although its support for Ben Khedda proved misplaced.

It was appropriate that President Bourguiba should make the earliest approaches to Libya, given the historic relationship between Tunis and Tripoli. As early as January 1957, he evoked the idea of the 'Greater Maghreb' by speaking of the 'unification of North Africa from Soloum to Casablanca'. His approach was obviously related to the strained relations which existed between Tunisia and Egypt under the government of President Nasser. A treaty of friendship was signed between Tunisia and Libya. But here too disputes over the frontier intervened and it was only in 1963 that the treaty of friendship was ratified—the frontier conflict proving less important than that between Tunisia and Algeria. Over the next few years the idea of the Greater Maghreb was kept in the air and gained in attractiveness with the discovery of Libyan oil, which some saw as providing the possible resources for the economic development of the region as a whole. But while Libyan ministers sometimes paid lip service to the idea, they obviously set no store by it, and spoke equally often of Libya as the hyphen between the Maghreb and the Mashreq—the Arab east.

The Libyan revolution brought a more dramatic turn in relations with at least two of Libya's North African partners. Qaddafi's support for revolution and the purity of Islam led him to take a stand against the rule of King Hassan in Morocco. He went beyond normal diplomacy in doing so and set up a powerful radio station to broadcast to Morocco. It was by means of this radio that the inhabitants of Fez first heard of the abortive *coup* against King Hassan at Skhirat. Then, and again in 1972, the Libyan radio exhorted the Moroccan people to side with the rebels against the king. In 1973 the subversives who were active in the Atlas mountains operated from Libya—a fact which provoked Boumediene, who was not prepared for Algeria to be a transit country for this purpose.

Meanwhile, the Libyan government urgently sought union with Egypt as part of a policy which would lead to the strengthening and development of the Arab world. The Tunisian government negotiated a series of conventions with Libya, which appeared to have the purpose of safeguarding Tunisian interests when the union came about. But shortly after the project of union with Egypt had foundered, a new project of union with Tunis was initialled on the island of Jerba. The proposal received no acclaim from Tunisia's neighbours: far from being welcomed as a prelude to the realization, at last, of the Greater Maghreb, it was vigorously resisted by both Algeria and Morocco.

It is true that heads of state have acted as mediators in disputes within the Maghreb: Bourguiba between Algeria and Morocco, Hassan between Tunisia and Algeria, and Boumediene between Morocco and Mauritania. But wider gatherings—an Arab summit conference in Cairo (which brought the restoration of relations between Morocco and Tunisia in 1964), the Organization of African Unity, or the Islamic conference at Casablanca—have also served as meetings of arbitration, or have provided the opportunity for bilateral negotiations to take place without either side having to take any overt initiative towards the other.

There has not been, therefore, any political will to form a serious Maghreb union. Nothing is more respectable, in the language of leaders and governments, than cooperation between Maghreb states, and a proposal to establish a new committee concerned with some aspect of such cooperation is unlikely to be opposed. Such institutional framework as has been established must be judged by the calibre of men and the size of budgets allocated to it.

This absence of political drive has inevitably given shape to the economic relationship between the Maghreb states. Their geographic position gives all of them the same interest in the European market for agricultural produce, traditional exports (such as carpets), and, if possible, industrial products; but their approach to the European Economic Community has been marked by historical differences deriving from Algeria's relationship to France when the Treaty of Rome was signed, and by national rivalries. Libya and Algeria have similar but competitive interests in the sale of hydrocarbons in the world market. It is not surprising, therefore, that intra-Maghreb trade is a small proportion of the trade of each of the Maghreb countries. In spite of the similarity of interest among the several states, having a combined population of less than forty million, competition (or simple disregard of the other Maghreb states) has generally prevailed over community of purpose. The development of a unified electricity grid, or the construction of a fertilizer plant to supply the whole Maghreb, or the creation of a single iron and steel industry—these are projects which come readily to the mind of economists and geographers but are not normally found in the world of nation states. Moreover, the Maghreb has no unified airline.

It is not to be expected, therefore, that any substantial degree of unity would appear in the foreign policies of the Maghreb states. The area has become increasingly less important as the object of strategic competition. Imperial rivalries—always more muted in North Africa than in the Middle East—were no more important than the historic conflict between the Ottoman Empire and Spain. The anxiety shown by the United States at the end of the Second World War over the possibility of communist strength, and similar anxiety, or simulation of it among the French during the Algerian war, is in abeyance. United States' bases in Morocco, important before the development of missiles, have been reduced to a very small scale; British and American bases in Libya had lost their importance before Qaddafi could win prestige by expelling them.

The diminution in strategic competition should not conceal the continuing importance of North Africa as a strategic area. It shares this importance with the whole of the Mediterranean coast; but Morocco is most important of all, controlling as it does the southern side of the Strait of Gibraltar and having an Atlantic coastline. A change of regime in Morocco, especially one which opened the way to a major Soviet presence at the western end of the Mediterranean and on the Atlantic, would constitute an obvious change in the world balance of power and arouse the same alarm (on a larger scale) as that provoked by the visit of the *Panther* to Agadir in 1911. The importance which the United States attaches to stability in the area has been shown by the large amount of aid given to Tunisia, the keen interest in the affairs of Morocco, and the diplomatic attention accorded to Algeria (even when formal diplomatic relations were broken in 1967-74).

The North African states have rightly judged it to be in their interests to remain outside great power conflicts. They participate actively in the Middle East conflict, while remaining, inevitably, minor partners to the 'confrontation states'; Algeria has pressed for active participation in discussions on European security and, with Tunisia, has put forward the concept of a neutral Mediterranean as a 'lake of peace'. But the most distinctive effort of international diplomacy has been that of Algeria in trying to advance its own cause (and that of similar states) in the Organization of Petroleum Exporting Countries and in the United Nations to redress the balance of the world economy towards the developing countries.

HISTORICAL BACKGROUND

Foreign Influences in Antiquity

The original Berber population has, through the centuries, been subjected to five principal foreign influences. The first was Phoenician and Carthaginian, and lasted for some 1,000 years from about 1200 B.C. The second was the period of Roman domination which was firmly established with the destruction of Carthage in 146 B.C. and lasted for about 650 years. There followed the interlude of the Vandals and the Byzantine restoration (429–642). This was succeeded by 1,200 years of Arab predominance in Morocco; and by about 800 in the rest of North Africa, where a Turkish regime established itself at the beginning of the sixteenth century and continued in a modified form until the European occupation in the nineteenth century.

The Carthaginians

The Carthaginians profoundly influenced the whole African shore of the Mediterranean from Tripolitania westwards, and also Sicily, Sardinia, Malta, the Balearic Islands, and south Spain. Carthage, situated on the coast a few miles from the present city of Tunis, was originally a Phoenician colony of Tyre and is reputed to have been founded about 800 B.C. by Queen Elisa (Dido), whom Virgil anachronistically makes a contemporary of the Trojan War. The Carthaginians were distinguished as sailors, as merchants, and as miners. They founded trading settlements at many points of the south Mediterranean and are believed to have explored the coast of West Africa at least as far as the Gulf of Guinea. Their typical settlements were on small and easily defensible peninsulas, such as the hill on which the old Melilla, originally the Carthaginian settlement of Rusadir (Rosh-adir, the Great Cape), is built. The obvious modern parallel is a British settlement such as Hong Kong. The Carthaginian state included the northern portion of modern Tunisia, but extended westward like medieval Tunisia to include the region from Bône to Constantine and eastward to include the Tripolitanian coast. Being interested in trade rather than in imperial expansion or colonization, the Carthaginians appear to have maintained friendly relations with the Berbers (at that time known in general as Libyans; as Numidians in eastern Algeria; and as Mauri in the west) though there was a serious rebellion of those whom they employed as mercenary troops.

Carthaginians and Numidians

Educated Numidians seem to have adopted Carthaginian names, and there was intermarriage between Carthaginians and Numidians, as between Carthaginians and other peoples—the famous Hannibal, for example, had a Spanish wife. Indeed, as a distinguished French historian writes:

> For centuries Carthage alone represented civilization in the eyes of the Berbers. Thus all the Numidian and Moorish *(Maures)* kings who ruled outside the Carthaginian territory adopted the civilization and often the language of their neighbour. . . . Far from becoming fixed as a foreign rule, Punic civilization was, as it were, naturalized and spread by a spontaneous movement in the more evolved portions of the Berber world.[1]

The chief interest of the Carthaginian period today is the extent to which it may have prepared the way for the future Arab conquest. The Carthaginian language, known as Punic, was developed from Phoenician. It is very closely related to Hebrew, and is as near to Arabic as Spanish is to French. The very name of the city of Carthage—*Qart Hadasha* or new city—would be in Arabic *Qariat Haditha*; and the pre-Islamic Arab personal name *Abdshams* was as common in Carthage as in Arabic.

It is certain from the writings of St. Augustine of Hippo (Annaba) that Punic was still spoken in the fifth century A.D. in the eastern portion of what is today Algeria. For the saint, in his capacity as bishop, sought to ensure that Punic-speaking bishops, who would be intelligible to the people, should be appointed in the dioceses concerned. It is true that this still leaves a gap of 200 years till the arrival of the Arabs, but if the language survived the pressure of Roman culture for 600 years, it may well have lasted another 200 after that pressure had been removed and replaced only by the temporary presence of Vandal or Byzantine governors. A more serious objection is that no Punic elements have been found in the modern Arab dialects of North Africa, but our knowledge of Punic is not so extensive that there may not be traces which have escaped the notice of the philologists.[2] However this may be, it is much easier to understand the speed with which Arabic spread

---

[1] H. Terasse, *Histoire du Maroc*, Casablanca, 1949, i. 44.
[2] In the field of anthropology, there seems no doubt that the so-called 'hand of Fatima', universally used in North Africa as a protective device against the evil-eye, is derived from the emblem of a hand which is frequently to be found on Punic funeral monuments.

in Tunisia and with which a flourishing local Arabic culture came into being, if we can assume that the process was facilitated by the fact that the people were talking a kindred language at the time of the Arab invasion and were already impregnated with a Semitic culture. The process would then be exactly parallel to what happened in the Aramaic-speaking territories of Syria and Iraq. It would also help to explain why Berber has disappeared so much more completely from Tunisia than it has from Algeria or Morocco.[1]

The Romans

Six hundred years of Roman domination and an interregnum of 200 years intervened between the fall of Carthage and the coming of the Arabs. The Roman period is familiar to all travellers from the magnificent remains of Roman cities which can be found from Sabratha in Libya to Volubilis near Meknes in Morocco. It was a time of tremendous material development, inspired and directed from Rome as it was throughout the rest of the Empire. Agriculture and forestry, already highly developed by the Carthaginians, were maintained and extended. In addition to the great material monuments, cities, roads, dams, and country houses, whose mosaics are magnificently represented in the Bardo Museum in Tunis, the period of Roman rule left the world a great intellectual monument in the works of St. Augustine, Bishop of Hippo. What St. Augustine was by race is uncertain, though we know that his opponents described him as 'Punic'. Roman rule in North Africa also produced a great Emperor in Septimius Severus, who was born in A.D. 146 near the city of Leptis Magna, for whose monumental character he is responsible, and who died at York in 211. Septimius Severus was certainly African, probably Punic and not Berber. He had to learn Latin as a boy; when his sister came to visit him, as Emperor, in Rome, she made him blush by her inability to speak the language and he persuaded her to return to Africa.

His example proves that at least a minority of Africans were completely assimilated into Roman life, though they may have had a disintegrating influence on it,[2] but we have little direct evidence of how

[1] It has been suggested, e.g. by the late Charles Courtois, that when St. Augustine spoke of Punic, he really meant Libyan or Berber. Seeing that St. Augustine knew at least some Punic and was aware of the close relationship of Punic with Hebrew, this supposition cannot be accepted without the production of evidence which has not so far been forthcoming.

[2] According to a modern Spanish historian, 'Septimius Severus remained an African throughout his life. In his heart of hearts, he always felt—unlike Hadrian—that the two victorious civilizations of the Mediterranean were something alien, and himself adhered to the vanquished civilization of Carthage, a greater admirer of Hannibal than of Scipio. In consequence he had no scruples in doing violence to the prerogatives of Rome' (R. Menéndez Pidal, ed., *Historia de España*, Madrid, 1947–56, ii. xx).

Roman civilization was regarded by the population of North Africa as a whole. A number of writers consider that Christianity in Africa was a religion of the masses and essentially opposed to the influence of Roman civilization. The episode of Tacfarinas the Numidian, who after serving in the Roman legion deserted and became the leader of a rising which went on for years in the Aurès district of Algeria, certainly reminds us of the beginning of the Algerian war; for the latter had its origin in the same area, under the leadership of an Algerian who, like Tacfarinas, had previously had a distinguished record in the army of the ruling power. We may be sure also that a certain nationalist sentiment lay behind the activities of the Numidian kings Massinissa and Jugurtha, though this is not brought out in our historical sources; being entirely Roman, these credit the Numidian kings with no motive other than personal ambition.

The Province of Africa

During the whole of the Roman period and indeed also during the two following centuries, when first the Vandals and then the Byzantines dominated, the centre of power in North Africa remained the former domain of Carthage. The Romans named it the Province of Africa, and this name has been perpetuated in Arabic by the use of the word 'Ifriqiya' to denote the same area. It thus continued to be the most highly civilized portion of North Africa, though Roman rule at its widest extension included the country as far as Volubilis and Salé in Morocco.

The Coming of the Arabs

The next fundamental change was brought about by the coming of the Arabs; these first appeared in Libya in A.D. 642, only nine years after the death of the Prophet Muhammad. It took them very little time to overthrow the Byzantine regime, but about a century more to subdue the resistance of the Berbers. When they had done so they had established not so much the rule of Arabs in North Africa as the rule of the Arabic language and of Islamic culture. The administration which was established was in the material sense inferior to that of the Romans; but it had a quality which Roman civilization had lacked in Africa (though not in Gaul)—that of being assimilable by the mass of the population. The Arab achievement in this respect was very remarkable, and even if we accept the theory of the persistence of Carthaginian influences, remains almost inexplicable unless there was in fact some sort of natural affinity between the Berber and the Arab way of life and thought which did not exist between Berbers and Romans. Much also must be attributed to the effect of the intense religious faith

THE PENETRATION OF ISLAM INTO AFRICA

of the Arabs in the years which immediately followed the prophetic revelation. The sincerity, passionate belief, and rough and ready honesty of many of the early Muslim leaders no doubt had a great effect upon the uncultivated Berber population, even where it was superficially Christian.

The tremendous transformation wrought by Islam in the condition and status of the Arabs themselves can hardly have failed to make a great impression on all who saw it. The change has been described in striking phrases by Ibn Khaldun, the great fourteenth-century North African Arab historian who was of Andalusian origin, though born and brought up in Tunis.

The Arabs in their primitive state are the least adapted of all people for empire-building. Their wild disposition makes them intolerant of subordination, while their pride, touchiness and intense jealousy of power render it impossible for them to agree.... Only when their nature has been permeated by a religious impulse are they transformed, so that the tendency to anarchy is replaced by a spirit of mutual defence. Consider the moment when religion dominated their policy and led them to observe a religious law designed to promote the moral and material interests of civilization. Under a series of successors to the Prophet, how vast their empire became and how strongly it was established!

Ibn Khaldun goes on to describe how a proud Persian, Rustum, amazed at the sight of the serried ranks of Arabs prostrating themselves in prayer behind the Caliph Omar, exclaimed that he could do nothing against a man 'who can turn dogs into civilized beings'.[1]

Arab Imperialism

As the Carthaginians and the Romans, so the Arabs made the former realm of Carthage their base, founding a new capital at Kairouan. Now Arab imperialism in the west (for imperialism it was) differs in certain essentials from Roman imperialism and from the European imperialism which was in time to succeed it in North Africa. There was no settling of colonists who possessed an advanced civilization of their own. We find indeed the establishment of an Arab ruling class; this, however, consisted of the descendants of Arabs whose wives might have been non-Arabs from the moment of the conquest. Thus an 'Arab' of the third generation might already have one only grandparent of pure Arab blood; his father might be only half Arab and his grandmother and mother completely non-Arab. In the case of a great ruling family, the Beni Umayya Caliphs of Córdoba, whose marital connexions are known to us, it has been mentioned by an Arab writer that they had a marked natural preference for blondes, and that the mothers of the

[1] Ibn Khaldun, *Muqaddima*, Beirut, 1900, p. 152.

rulers were almost invariably Christian slaves from the north of Spain.[1] The Spanish orientalist Ribera worked out mathematically that the percentage of Arab ancestry in the Caliph Abd al-Rahman III (912–61) was 0·39 per cent, the remaining 99·61 per cent being Spanish.[2]

In this way, and by large-scale conversion, new civilizations were rapidly produced whose cultural level depended largely upon the contribution made by the original inhabitants of the country, either directly as converts or through the mothers of the ruling classes; for the Arabs themselves brought little in the way of material civilization, but only their language, with all that that involves in ways of thought, and their religion. Thus we find that in Tunisia, where there was an old-established tradition of civilized living, a highly-developed Arab civilization came into being almost at once; whereas in Morocco, which was relatively barbarous in the seventh century, a high level of civilization took much longer to appear. It has to be noted too that in addition to the ruling and assimilating Arabs the conquest also brought with it Arab tribes who might remain in compact masses. These sometimes amalgamated with an existing population, but sometimes remained purely Arab, often constituting a backward and retrograde element. The ruling classes, proud themselves of being Arabs, often refer disparagingly to such tribes as 'Arabs' (as they do at other times to corresponding Berbers) using 'Arab' in the sense of beduin, or primitive Arabs—a double use of the word which can be highly confusing. Taking North Africa as a whole, the effect of the creation of an Arab empire was very rapidly to turn the area into the *Maghreb* or western portion of the Arab world, giving it that typical Arabo-Berber aspect which it has retained ever since. Still basically Berber, its individuality was expressed henceforth through the medium of Islamic civilization and the Arabic language.

Within a century or so the process was so complete that Arab rule was no longer felt as foreign rule. Local princes appeared, who may have been Arab or Berber by race, but whose ways of thought, and language and methods of administration were Arab. Meanwhile the Arab and Berber dislike of central control soon reasserted itself and after a period during which governors were appointed and deposed by the imperial authority in Damascus local dynasties were established. Largely independent, they still sought recognition from the east, however, for reasons of religious or worldly prestige and for the practical assistance which it might bring.

During the whole of this period, until the Turkish predominance in

---

[1] 'Kulluhum majbuluna ala tafdil ash-shaqra' (Ibn Hazm, *Tauq al-Hamama*, Algiers, 1949; Bibliothèque Arabo-française, viii. 72).

[2] Julian Ribera, *Disertaciones y Opusculos*, Madrid, 1928, p. 16. It has, however, to be noted that intermarriage must have become the exception, except for those rich enough to own slaves, once a large distinct Muslim community had been established.

the sixteenth century, Arab culture and political power tended to radiate from two centres. One was in the east, in Ifriqiya; and the other in the west, where it was first situated in southern Spain and later in Morocco. The rulers in Tunisia generally controlled eastern Algeria and Tripolitania, either directly or through tributary rulers in Constantine and Bougie, or in Tripoli, as the case might be. The capital was at first the newly-founded city of Kairouan, then another new city, Mahdiya, on the east coast, and finally Tunis. Western Algeria tended to be subordinate to Morocco.

Ifriqiya

During 800 years of Arab rule, four dynasties succeeded one another in Ifriqiya. The first were the Aghlabids (800–909) with their capital in Kairouan. This dynasty conquered Sicily in the ninth century and made it a Muslim state. The Muslim rulers of the island soon became independent but were themselves driven out by the Normans in the eleventh century. It was at this time also that Malta was first captured and then freed from the Muslims. The next dynasty, the Fatimids (909–69), propagated a heretical form of Islam. After establishing themselves in Tunisia, where they created the new capital, Mahdiya, they moved east, conquered Egypt, and founded Cairo. They then made this their capital, leaving Tunisia to be administered by their tributaries, the Zirids. When the latter became independent, the Fatimid Caliph in Cairo authorized two large and troublesome nomad Arab tribes, who were at the time in Upper Egypt, to attack them and establish themselves in Ifriqiya. These two tribes, the Beni Hilal and the Beni Sulaim, are generally held responsible for causing immense destruction in Ifriqiya, provoking disturbances, and serving as mercenaries in any local fighting. Certainly they caused the ruin of Kairouan, which indeed continued to exist as a holy city, but only—to this day—as a profoundly 'depressed area'. Some scholars attribute a large part in the arabization of the Maghreb to the two tribes. However, they can hardly have numbered more than 150,000, and appear to have had none of the religious fervour of the original invaders. While, therefore, they no doubt increased the proportion of Arab inhabitants by settling in Libya and in the Moroccan plains, it does not appear that they can have made any cultural contribution. Ifriqiya itself had clearly been arabized, as far as culture and administration were concerned, long before their arrival which simply inaugurated a period of anarchy, further increased by the Norman capture of a number of coast towns during the twelfth century. This was ended by the arrival of Almohad forces from Morocco. In the thirteenth century a new dynasty, the Hafsids, arose through the transformation of the Almohad viceroys into an independent reigning family. This family, who were Berber in origin, had been intimately connected with the beginnings of the Almohad movement in Morocco; and they ruled Ifriqiya for over 250 years. Their capital was Tunis and in their time we can discern the rudiments of a Tunisian nationality which can be considered as the forerunner of the present Tunisian state.

Islam on the Defensive

Though the Christian advance in Spain, which had resulted in the capture of Toledo in 1085, was then held up for two centuries; and though the Almohads drove the Normans from Ifriqiya, Islam in the west was on the defensive from the eleventh century onwards. The Hafsid period was itself one of relative peace and of extensive trade relations with Christian Europe. It is true that raids on one another's shipping were not infrequent on the part of Tunis and the Italian maritime republics such as Pisa and Genoa; but there was no serious attempt to change the general balance of power. When the Genoese in 1390 persuaded the Duc de Bourbon and many French knights to lead an expedition against Mahdiya in Tunisia (known at that time to Europeans as 'Africa'), the Muslims were astonished.

This state of affairs was brought to an end about the beginning of the sixteenth century by the Christian Spanish onslaught which had been directed against Ifriqiya as well as against the last Muslim state of Spain, Granada, and against Morocco. In desperation the Arabs of Ifriqiya turned to the Turks, now powerful in the eastern Mediterranean. The latter thereupon drove off the Spanish, whose main efforts were already being diverted to Europe and America; but they then made themselves masters of the territories which they had liberated from the Christians.

But before we consider the Turkish irruption in the east, we must look briefly at the course of events in the west.

Islam in the West

In the early days of the conquest, the chief significance of Morocco (in Arabic geography *al-Maghreb al-Aqsa* or the 'Far West'), was as the starting point for the Arab invasion of Spain. That enterprise, however, cannot be considered as in any way a Moroccan undertaking, even if a number of Moroccan Berbers participated in it, any more than the Allied invasion of Italy during the Second World War could be called an Algerian or Tunisian undertaking on the ground that it started from Tunisia and a considerable number of Algerian troops took part in it. The invasion of Spain was an Arab enterprise, part of the whole great conquest which was at that time still being directed from Damascus; as a result of it Muslim Spain, *al-Andalus*, came to play such an outstanding part in the history of Islam in the west that it cannot be omitted from a survey of the history of the Maghreb.

The Conquest of Spain

Though the early Caliphs had been much alarmed at the idea of occupying territory across the sea, the Strait of Gibraltar appears never to have constituted in itself a very serious obstacle between the countries to the north and to the south. It is difficult, perhaps impossible, to find any moment in history when all the territory to the north of the Strait was in the power of one government and all the territory to the south in the power of another; almost invariably some portion of territory on the one side has been in the power of a government on the other. Climatically, too, there is a close resemblance between northern Morocco and the Iberian peninsula. In fact the French witticism that Africa begins at the Pyrenees can only be held valid if we balance it by saying that Europe begins at the Atlas.

As in North Africa, the invading Arabs put an end to the existing government (in this case Visigothic) with extraordinary ease. They were assisted in this by their fellow orientals, the Jews, who had recently suffered severe persecution at the hands of the Visigothic government, and Jewish garrisons were put in charge of various towns during the advance. Unlike North Africa, however, there was no prolonged resistance to be overcome on the part of the local population, except for the tiny unassimilable area in the extreme north-west which in the course of centuries gave rise to the Christian reconquest. A great number of Spanish were rapidly converted to Islam. The remainder often received extremely favourable terms; and many of the former Gothic rulers retained the greater portions of their estates and privileges, some as converts but others still as Christians. The Arabs at first intermarried freely with the Spanish, the example being set by the Arab ruling classes. Thus the son and successor of the first Arab governor married Egilona, the widow of the last Visigothic king, who was known in Arabic as Um Asim. The lady was shocked that her Arab husband had no such emblem of authority as her former husband had done, and urged him to wear a crown. Unconvinced by his explanation that such a proceeding would be deeply offensive to the democratic spirit of Islam she persuaded him to put on, when at home, a diadem which she had ordered to be made for him. The news got abroad, suspicion was aroused, and the governor assassinated.

Splendour of Muslim Civilization in Córdoba

The population with which the Arabs were mingling in Andalusia had an incomparably higher standard of civilization than the Berbers of Morocco, higher probably than that of the people of Ifriqiya, though they resembled the latter in being the product of Carthaginian and Roman culture. Andalusia had produced one of the greatest of Roman Emperors, Trajan, who was succeeded by another Spaniard, Hadrian.

Apart from another great Emperor, Theodosius, Roman Spain was the home of a host of soldiers, poets, bishops, and philosophers. It was therefore not surprising that it should be in Spain, and particularly in Andalusia, that the Arab imperial system yielded some of its most remarkable results. From about A.D. 800 to 1000, and indeed until 200 years later, *al-Andalus*, or Muslim Spain, was the most civilized area of western Europe, as is shown by a number of picturesque stories recorded by Arab historians or medieval European chroniclers.

The remarkable development of science and learning which took place in the Emirate of Córdoba was commended by an Arab poet in the following verse:

> In four things Córdoba surpasses the capitals of the world—
> Among them are the bridge over the river and the mosque.
> These are the first two; the third is Madinat al-Zahra;
> But the greatest of all things is knowledge—and that is the fourth.

The bridge over the Guadalquiver at Córdoba was built by the Romans and restored by the Arabs; the Great Mosque, still known today as the *Mezquita* (Mosque), was an essentially Arab creation in which much classical material, including many columns from Carthage was used; while Madinat al-Zahra was the famous complex of palace and government offices constructed for Abd al-Rahman III, who of all the Beni Umayya princes was most consciously the creator of a synthesis of Muslim, Christian, and Jewish cultures. The four lines thus introduce the essential elements of the great Muslim capital.

The Muslim City States

Fifty years after Abd al-Rahman III's death the Córdoban state collapsed, for reasons which are not altogether clear, and Muslim Spain broke up into a galaxy of twenty-six little city states. 'Galaxy' seems the appropriate word since some of these little states—Seville, Córdoba, Badajoz, Granada, Almeria, Murcia, Valencia, Mallorca, Saragossa—shone in the medieval darkness with the brilliance of the little Italian states of the Renaissance. In their divided condition, however, they were no match for the less civilized but virile little Christian states of the north. In 1085 Toledo was captured from the Muslims by Alfonso VI of Castile, and in the following year al-Mutamid, the brilliant soldier-poet-king of Seville, decided to invoke the help of the Almoravid sultan, Youssef ibn Tashufin, who had made himself ruler of Morocco and of much of the rest of the Maghreb.

The Moroccan Intervention in Spain

A very clear view of the cultural and political relations between Morocco and Muslim Spain at this period can be gathered from the writings of Arab historians and men of letters. The Moroccan sultan whom al-Mutamid invited to Spain was Youssef ibn Tashufin, the first of the Almoravid sultans. The latter were Berbers from Mauritania. As their name implies, they had been inmates of fortified convents *(ribat)* and came to power as the result of a movement to restore Islam to its primitive simplicity. Youssef ibn Tashufin himself was a fighting monarch and an administrator whose life was based on the simple and austere morals of the early Muslims. Nomad by origin, his principal food was camel milk, camel flesh, and barley bread; his garments were always of wool. His mother-tongue was Berber; although he knew some Arabic, and his correspondence was conducted in that language, he was not able to appreciate the subtleties of the Arab tongue as it was spoken and written in *al-Andalus*. His outlook, at once primitive and austere, did not appeal to the cultivated rulers of Muslim Spain, for whom his assistance was a necessary evil; but they had a strong attraction for some of the Spanish men of religion and for those of the masses who disliked the luxurious living, the scientific and artistic pursuits, the wine-drinking and the hedonism of their upper classes; and, perhaps even more, the taxation which the satisfaction of these tastes involved.

The Moroccan intervention completely changed the military position, for the allies inflicted a resounding defeat on the King of Castile near Badajoz. The Court poets set themselves to flatter Youssef as they had been accustomed to do their own kings. The Almoravids belonged to the Berber tribe of Sanhaja, which had appropriated an Arab genealogy and claimed descent from the Arabs of Himyar; they also observed the habit, still in force today among the Tuareg, of wearing a mouth-muffler. An Andalusian poet utilized these characteristics for a panegyric in which he wrote:

> A king who has the high honour to descend from Himyar.
> If there are tongues which challenge this and whisper 'Berbers',
> Yet they are the people that they are—such people that they first united every virtue in their persons, and then, in modesty, veiled themselves.

It was not long, however, before the poet changed his tone and added a further couplet:

> The Almoravid is not open handed—except to his own relations;
> His features are as ugly as his actions; and therefore he veiled himself.[1]

These verbal pinpricks were the prelude to more serious events. On Youssef's third visit to Spain, he first secured a *fetwa* from the Muftis (religious consultants) condemning the irreligious taxation and practices of the princes and then put an end to the princedoms, taking

---

[1] *Rawd al-Qirtas* al-Shaqundi, *Risala fi fadl al-Andalus*.

al-Mutamid to Morocco as a prisoner. The deposed king finished his days in captivity at Aghmat, in the foothills of the Atlas, a few miles outside the Almoravid capital, Marrakesh. Here, where a river runs out into the plain, amid walnut trees and green vegetation, behind which the high snow peaks rise into the blue sky, al-Mutamid continued to write poems, as moving and melancholy as they had once been gay and vainglorious.

Out of this Moroccan intervention Muslim Spain gained two centuries of reprieve, shielded by the power of Africa. Neither the Almoravids, however, nor their successors, the Almohads, ever made the necessary sustained effort to tackle the Christian menace at its source.

Islam in Morocco

When the Arabs first reached the 'far west', at the beginning of the eighth century, their governors followed the Byzantine practice of making their headquarters in Ceuta or Tangier. Civilization had not spread very far beyond these cities, though the Phoenicians had apparently once had trading posts as far down the coast as Wadi Nun, a few miles short of the present southern frontier of Morocco, and traces of Punic influence and inscriptions have been found at various points of Roman Morocco. The work of introducing civilization into the farther portions of the country was left for the Arab or Arabo-Berber rulers to accomplish. It was not, however, until the coming of the Almoravids in the eleventh century that Morocco acquired a real measure of unity and began to play a part on the stage of world affairs. These rulers united Morocco itself and, besides making themselves rulers of Muslim Spain, also controlled the whole of western Algeria. The next dynasty, the Almohads, annexed also Tunisia, later to become an independent kingdom under the Hafsids who were originally Almohad viceroys.

The Influence of Muslim Spain on Morocco

The Moroccan conquerors of Spain were very rapidly captivated by the civilization of the people whom they now ruled. Architects and engineers were transferred from Spain to the south of the Strait. The architect who built the Giralda tower in Seville had first been brought to Morocco to build the Kutubia tower in Marrakesh and returned later to plan the Hassan tower at Rabat. The extension of Andalusian civilization to Morocco had in fact begun earlier; for in the last days of the Caliphate of Córdoba the rulers of Morocco had owed allegiance to the Caliph. The troubles accompanying the end of the Caliphate intensified the process.

North Africa [says an Arab historian of the eleventh century] may be said to have derived its present wealth and important commerce from Spanish Muslims settling in it. When God was pleased to afflict Spain with the recent disastrous civil war [following the fall of the Caliphate] thousands of Spanish Muslims of all classes and all professions sought refuge on these shores. . . . Agriculture was developed by newly arrived farmers, springs were discovered and used for irrigation; trees were planted; watermills and other useful machinery constructed. . . . Large numbers of educated towns-people did useful work in the administration. The numerous artisans and workmen were particularly valuable. Before their arrival many crafts which are now flourishing were hardly known and it is generally admitted that the immigrants ranked far above the natives in energy and skill [abbreviated].[1]

Influence of Muslim Spain on Christian Europe

Though rather beyond the scope of this survey, it is perhaps worth noticing here that another current of migration, that of the arabized Christians, or Mozarabs[2] was at the same time beginning to move north into the Christian Spanish kingdoms, which were growing in extension and in power as the Muslim power decreased. These arabized Spaniards carried Andalusian civilization with them into northern Spain and it was probably they who were responsible for introducing so many words and terms of Arabic origin into modern Spanish, particularly in the spheres of agriculture and administration, as for example, *alcalde (al-qadi)* for the town mayor. Through the great school of translators set up in Toledo by Alfonso X, Muslim science and learning and Greek scientific works which had been preserved in Arabic were made available to European scholars. The prestige of Arabic as a language of science and administration remained so great that when Toledo was settled with arabized Spanish Christians from the south, after the Christian conquest in 1085, these Mozarabic Spaniards preserved the use of Arabic for legal purposes, such as marriage settlements and the transfer of property, for another 250 years, right into the fourteenth century.

The Segregation of Christians and Muslims

These migrations were, however, also having another effect. Spain was ceasing to be an area consisting of a number of kingdoms, some Christian and some Muslim, in which Christians and Muslims lived together. Fanaticism was increasing. On the Muslim side, this was due to the arrival of the Africans, for whom the sight of a Christian was a novelty and who had no sympathy for them as fellow Spaniards. On the Christian side it was fomented by the crusading spirit which came

---

[1] Quoted in al-Maqqari, *Nafh al-Tib*.
[2] Arabic, *must'arab* (meaning 'arabized').

with the monks of Cluny and the warriors from the north of the Pyrenees. Christians and Muslims were being increasingly sifted out, with all the Christians collected on one side of the frontier and all the Muslims on the other.

By the middle of the thirteenth century the Kingdom of Granada was the only Spanish state still under Muslim rule. It survived for 250 years, during which there was a slow but steady pressure on Muslims remaining in the Christian states of Spain to abandon their faith, emigrate to Granada, or leave Spain altogether.

Granada

The Muslim state of Granada, in spite of being Muslim, was in a sense still accepted as being natural to Spain, though only on conditions of armed coexistence. Periods of peace alternated with periods of war; periods when Granada paid tribute to Castile with periods when it felt strong enough to refuse tribute. On occasions very remarkable treaty arrangements illustrated the nature of this coexistence. In 1456 a general truce was agreed between Castile and Granada with the proviso that fighting was nevertheless permissible on one particular stretch of country—the frontier of the province of Jaen. In 1481 another truce extended to the entire frontier, but fighting was nevertheless declared permissible in the form of operations which must be completed within three days, during which no trumpets must be blown, no flags flown, and no permanent headquarters set up. Under this arrangement the Castilians were able to capture the town of Villaluenga, massacre the inhabitants, do damage in the neighbourhood of Ronda and burn an isolated fortress, all within three days and so without violating the truce. The Muslims for their part retaliated by capturing a town called Zahara and enslaving its inhabitants, also without breaking the truce. This limited degree of tolerance came to an end with the fall of Granada on 2 January 1492. The pressure on the two or three million Muslims remaining in Spain to choose the alternative of conversion or emigration became overwhelming and in 1610 the remaining Moriscos, or forcibly converted Muslims, were simply expelled. (These expulsions led to further settlements by Spanish Moriscos on the North African coast, from Morocco to Tripoli.) This brought into being a new state of armed coexistence in which all the Muslims were to the south of the Strait and all the Christians to the north. It was, however, a long time before this state of affairs was stabilized. In the first flush of the conquest Portuguese and Spanish carried the war on into Africa and early in the sixteenth century we find the Portuguese in possession of Mazagan, Tangier, and Ceuta, and the Spanish of Melilla, Oran, Algiers, Tunis, and Tripoli. The main Iberian effort was, however, diverted elsewhere and the Moroccan dynasties managed, during the late sixteenth and seventeenth centuries to regain all that they had lost, with the exception of Ceuta and Melilla, which remained Spanish, and Mazagan, which was only recovered from the Portuguese in 1790.

The Western Corsairs

Three centuries of raiding by corsairs was the price for the expulsion of the Muslims and for the transference of the war into Africa—justification for which could be found at least in the sixteenth century in Spanish fears of a Muslim counter-attack, backed by the growing power of the Ottoman Turks. The raiding had originally been provoked by the Portuguese policy of carrying the war on into Africa, inaugurated with the unprovoked attack on Ceuta in 1415. In the discussions which preceded the attack, the Portuguese king, John I, pointed out to his impatient, half-English sons that an attack on the Muslims in Africa would be certain to expose south Portugal to constant raids and would also cause the closing of the Strait and the interruption of the valuable Portuguese trade with the Mediterranean in wine, oil, and fruit. The Muslims, far from being aggressors on this occasion, contributed to the success of the unexpected attack by the friendly and unsuspecting welcome which they gave to a spying expedition which was presented to them as a Portuguese embassy on its way to and from Sicily. The assault was followed by the merciless sack of the city and by the slaughter or enslavement of its inhabitants. The later Portuguese attack on Tangier was carried out against the recommendation of the Pope who was consulted by King Duarte in 1437. War should not be made, the Pope said, against countries which were not Christian but at the same time not idolatrous, unless they were aggressive. A king should not expose his people to unnecessary dangers and the proposed war was not one for whose success prayer could be ordered. The consequence of these attacks was that the North African states for centuries waged a war of privateers against any Christian state which had not made a special arrangement with them: this generally involved a cash payment. In the west, the warfare was carried on mainly by Muslim refugees from Spain; they settled in Tetuan and Salé, bringing with them a knowledge of seamanship, which they had acquired in the great days of the Spanish fleets, as well as an intense hatred for the Christian government which had expelled them. Those who settled in Tetuan rapidly became assimilated to the Moroccans; but the 4,000 or more in Salé seem to have been largely Spanish-speaking, with a strong Spanish sentiment, and from 1627 for some time they maintained themselves as an autonomous maritime republic governed by two Alcaldes, one for the town and one for the fortress, who were elected annually. In 1631 those settled in Rabat made approaches to the Spanish king. They were, they said, genuine Christians and had been persecuted for that reason by their Muslim neighbours. If the king would permit them to return to Spain, they would undertake to deliver the place up to him and he could be sure that Moriscos elsewhere would follow their example. The proposal was not accepted, and the use of Spanish by the Muslims died out fairly soon, though many Spanish words passed into the local Arabic dialect. Many Muslims as well as Jews have retained names denoting their Spanish origin—such as Ronda, Mulin, Castillo, Torres, Denia, Bargash (Vargas).

With some difficulty Morocco itself managed to retain its independence at the expense of losing contact with the outer world almost entirely. The result was that its civilization remained medieval, in an ever-increasing state of degeneration.

The practice of privateering was suspended by Sultan Muhammad ibn Abdullah at the end of the eighteenth century and he also released European captives. Raiding was, however, only definitely brought to an end by Maulay Sulaiman in 1817, about the same time as Muslim slavery was abolished in the Kingdom of the Two Sicilies (1815).

The Turks and the Eastern Corsairs

In the central and eastern portions of the Mediterranean the Muslim reaction to Spanish attacks took a similar form to that in the west. Diego de Haedo, Spanish Archbishop of Palermo during the second half of the sixteenth century, in his history of Algeria, notes that a great development of privateering followed the capture of Granada in 1492.[1] In the eastern states, however, the course of events developed differently from Morocco, which always remained primarily a land power. When the Algerians, Tunisians, and Tripolitanians appealed to their coreligionists for help against the Spanish, the people who were in a position to assist them were the commanders of Turkish naval forces in the eastern Mediterranean.

When these had accomplished the task of driving out the Spanish, they established a Turkish regime with themselves as rulers and seem to have thought of their prizes in the first place as naval bases. Thus the ports of Tripoli, Tunis, and above all Algiers, the capital of the richest of the three Ojaks or Regencies into which Turkish North Africa was divided, began to specialize in privateering, while continuing to be centres of trade. 'Privateers' are defined by experts in naval law as 'vessels owned and manned by private persons, but furnished with the authority of their government to carry on hostilities; they were used to increase the naval forces of a State "by causing vessels to be equipped from private cupidity, which a minister might not be able to obtain by general taxation without much difficulty".'[2] In other words, individuals

[1] Ibn Khaldun notes that in his day Bougie was a great centre of privateering.
[2] A. P. Higgins and C. J. Colombos, *The International Law of the Sea*, 3rd ed., London, 1954, p. 389.

received authorization, known in England as Letters of Marque, to equip warships which were then free to attack shipping of any state with which the parent state was at war—a stipulation which seems often to have been interpreted very freely. Thus Sir Francis Drake 'set out on one of his famous voyages to the new world in his "good ship well equipped for war" without a commission of any kind, since "as England and Spain were not then in the best terms of friendship, he thought the general Licence of the Times would be his justification." '[1]

As was to be expected in these circumstances, endless correspondence passed between the chancelleries of the various governments about the rights and wrongs of individual captures and about whether the ships and their passengers had or had not fulfilled the necessary formalities to ensure them the right of unmolested passage. It was equally natural that those who suffered on these occasions rarely hesitated to accuse their aggressors of piracy, though the chancelleries concerned always discussed cases on the basis of the accepted law and practice. The real grievance against the Barbary states was not piracy but the fact that they constantly used small pretexts to threaten a declaration of war. By this means they hoped either to extort monetary concessions, or, if war ensued, to make a profit by privateering.

Any proceeds of such warfare were divided in a legally fixed proportion between the owner, the captain, the crew, and the government. In the sixteenth century English privateers were notorious and much resented by the more organized Spanish navy, just as the Barbary corsairs were later by the European powers. A scene in Shakespeare's *Twelfth Night* is illustrative of this. The Duke, having had the ship's captain presented to him with the words, 'Orsino, this is that Antonio That took the Phoenix and her fraught from Candy And . . . did the Tiger board, When your young nephew Titus lost his leg', addresses him as 'Notable pirate! thou salt water thief!' This it has been suggested may be the echo of some Spanish grandee's words to a captured English privateer. Certainly privateering was in no sense a monopoly of the Muslims.

In 1518 or 1520, for example, it was in a Muslim ship off Jerba that a young Muslim afterwards known as Leo Africanus was captured by a Christian, probably Maltese, corsair; owing to his exceptional intelligence and wide travels, his captors, instead of selling him in the great slave markets of Pisa and Genoa, presented him to Pope Leo X.[2] Malta was in fact a great centre for preying on the shipping of Tunis and Tripoli; in the year 1720 there were 10,000 Muslim slaves held in the island.

---

[1] Quoted in G. Fisher, *Barbary Legend*, Oxford, 1957, p. 140.
[2] E. W. Bovill, *The Golden Trade of the Moors*, London, 1958, p. 121.

European Organization of Privateering

An interesting feature of the corsair period is the very considerable extent to which those concerned were Muslims of European origin. The brothers Barbarossa, who expelled the Spaniards and founded the Algerian state, came from the island of Mitylene and are believed to have been of Albanian origin. The four Turkish governors of Algiers who held office from 1574 to 1586 were all European—a Sardinian, an Albanian, a Hungarian, and a Venetian. When Cervantes was captured in 1575 the privateer captain was a Greek Muslim. In the west, we have seen already that the corsairs were mainly Muslim Spanish.

The Three Regencies

It was in this Turkish period of rule, dating from early in the first half of the sixteenth century, that we first find eastern and central Maghreb divided with the frontiers which exist today. The importance acquired by Algeria at this period was due to the fact that the Barbarossas made it their headquarters and then succeeded in adding the former territories of Tlemsen, Bougie, and Constantine to their domain. For a century or so governors were directly appointed or removed by Istanbul, but later all three Regencies acquired a degree of independence, though they always recognized the suzerainty of the Sublime Porte in some form and contributed naval and military forces when the government in Istanbul required them. In Tripoli and Tunisia hereditary dynasties were founded. That in Tunis originated with a Cretan Muslim, Husain Bey, in 1705 and members of the family continued to reign for 252 years until the last Bey, Amin, was deposed on the proclamation of the Tunisian Republic on 25 July 1957. Though both the Tunisian and Tripolitanian reigning families became largely arabized, the Tunisian court retained to the end a Turkish rather than an Arab aspect in ceremonial and costume. This lingering air of foreign domination was no doubt one factor which enabled the dynasty to be finally removed without raising a ripple on the surface of Tunisian public opinion. Within the Ottoman Empire, the Regencies can in fact be considered self-governing colonies; and their fleets were at the service of the mother country. In Algeria the native population was excluded from the central government, but in general left to go its own way, provided taxes were paid and communications not interfered with. An English visitor in the 1730s remarked that 'the natives of Algiers live extremely happy; for though the government is nominally despotic it is not so in reality'.

In a sense Turkish rule was a westernizing influence, whether direct as in Tripoli or indirect as in Tunisia. The latter country before the French occupation was one of the more advanced Arab countries and was the first Arab state to experiment with a constitution. This was no doubt primarily due to its ancient traditions and connexions.

Algiers

The most original as well as the most powerful of the three Regencies was Algeria. It was here that maritime activity reached its greatest development and in the sixteenth century the Algerian fleet operated against the Spanish possessions in Italy in direct alliance with the French fleet. In the winter of 1543 King Francis I of France handed Toulon city and harbour over to the Algerian fleet as winter quarters. Though Algiers is connected primarily with the corsairs in the memory of Europeans, thanks to the description of the captivity there of Cervantes and to similar narratives, there was in fact a considerable commercial activity. Several powers, including France, which was interested in the coral fisheries, and England, maintained consuls for the purpose of facilitating trade. Wheat was the principal export and went through Bône and Oran as well as Algiers. There were also exports of raisins, figs, dates, woven stuffs, tobacco, leather, and wax. At one period Gibraltar was largely supplied from Algiers. Flourishing local crafts and industries catered for the internal market. The nature of the imports denotes the luxurious life led by the notables in the state's heyday. They consisted mainly of Dutch tiles, Italian marble, silk and velvet from Genoa and Lyons, Venetian mirrors, Bohemian glass, and English clocks; in primary necessities the state was self-supporting.

Unlike the two other Regencies, Algiers became an oligarchic republic. The ruler of the state, the Dey, was elected for life, like the Doge of Venice—the electors in the Dey's case being the Diwan or principal officers of state. Though nominally absolute, his powers were greatly restricted by the insubordination of the ships' captains and the army officers. In fact of twenty-three Deys no less than nine died violent deaths—as opposed to one Venetian doge who was executed. The language spoken in the Diwan was Turkish, and the ruling class consisted of some 20,000 Turkish-speaking people, divided between soldiers and civilians. Here again the European element was prominent and a number of rulers were of known European origin, among them a Venetian.

A very unfavourable picture of the state is given in the mass of tendentious, or as we should say, propaganda literature about Algiers. This was largely inspired, according to a French resident in Algiers in the eighteenth century, by the desire of redemptionist Spanish monks to raise funds to ransom captives. Certainly there exists also a number of much more favourable references, particularly concerning the sixteenth and early seventeenth centuries. A French traveller in 1551 speaks of the good arrangement of the city, of the pleasant private houses, and of the number of baths and eating-houses. The city, he said, was 'very merchant-like' and surprisingly thickly populated for its size. Food was good and cheap, particularly partridges; and he admired the oven-incubators used for hatching chickens.[1] A hundred years later Francis Knight, an Englishman who was there as a prisoner for seven years, describes the city as 'built on the side of a hill ... in form of a top-sail hoised; her houses built stair-like one over the other ...; scarce any house of the city but hath the prospect of the sea; there are in her many stupendious [*sic*] and sumptuous edifices, though outwardly for the major part present themselves but simple and rude'. He too remarks on the teeming population, and also on the great wealth of 'gold, plate [silver], and household furniture' and on the beauty of the women. The gardens around the city were commented on favourably throughout all the three centuries of the regency. Thus Dr. T. Shaw of St. Edmund Hall, Oxford, in the early eighteenth century, wrote:

The hills and vallies round about Algiers are all over beautified with gardens and country-seats, whither the inhabitants of better fashion retire, during the heats of the summer season. They are little white houses, shaded with a variety of fruit-trees and ever-greens; which, besides the shade and retirement, afford a gay and delightful prospect towards the sea. The gardens are all of them well stocked with melons, fruit, and pot-herbs of all kinds.

Another traveller considered the melons to be of 'marvellous goodness and incomparable sweetness'.

No doubt much of the wealth of the city came from privateering but, as has been mentioned, this was at the worst an abuse of a legitimate form of warfare, not given up by England and France until the Conference of Paris in 1856, though fallen out of general use long before that time. At the moment of the conquest the administration of justice was said by an Austrian officer who accompanied the French expedition to have been swift, fair, and efficient;[2] and most observers speak well of the character of the last Dey, Husain.

When the foreign invasion came, it was provoked by the episode when the Dey struck the French consul with a fly-whisk; but the Dey himself appears to have been greatly provoked. In reporting the matter to the Sultan in Istanbul the Dey remarked that the consul first said in an insulting manner that the Dey could not expect the French government to reply to his letters, and then added insulting remarks about the Muslim religion and 'the honour of Your Majesty, the protector of the world'. Whereupon 'unable to bear this affront which passed all tolerable limits, listening only to the natural impulse of a Muslim, I struck

[1] N. N. Daulphinois, in T. Osborne, *Collection of Voyages and Travels*, London, 1745, ii. 559.
[2] *Ruckblick auf Algier*, Vienna, 1837, p. 51. Cf. Shaler, *Sketches of Algiers*, Boston, 1826, p. 23.

him two or three light blows with the fly-whisk which I was holding in my humble hand'.[1]

The Decay of the Corsairs

The great days of the corsair states were the sixteenth and seventeenth centuries. By the eighteenth the growing technical superiority of the European fleets was already reducing the profits from captures. The population of Algiers city diminished and the number of captives fell from 30,000 to a mere hundred at the time of the French attack in 1830.

Islam in the West

When we survey the history of Islam in the west over the eleven centuries from the eighth to the nineteenth, it falls into three clearly marked periods. The first extends from the seventh to the beginning of the eleventh century and is the period of extension and consolidation. Islam comes to be established in nearly the whole of Spain, Sicily, and Malta.

The second period runs from the later part of the eleventh until the beginning of the sixteenth century; this is marked by the advance of the Christian reconquest, first in Sicily and Malta, then in Spain, and finally in Africa. The third is the long period of armed coexistence, in separate continents, which lasted from the beginning of the sixteenth until the beginning of the nineteenth century.

European historians have usually taken a very unfavourable view of the North African or as they called them the 'Barbary' states during this period. It was in fact a time of slow decay for Islam, in the west just as in the east; and it cannot be said that the Barbary states in the Turkish period made any particular contribution to civilization. Still the same could be said of many other countries; the bad reputation of North Africa was primarily a reaction to the privateering. This is often spoken of as mere piracy, and the impression is given that the Barbary states consisted exclusively of pirates living off the proceeds of their ill-gotten gains. This is a very misleading picture; privateering was 'legal'; but the geographical position of the Muslim states and the tradition of enmity between them and the Christian maritime states enabled them to abuse the practice and turn it into a lucrative national profession—as, it is only fair to add, the Elizabethan English did also. The capital cities benefited from this, but the proceeds cannot have affected the economy of the population in the interior.

In so far as Muslim policy was aggressive it was due to the growth of the power of the Turks, and their establishment in the Maghreb which was itself brought about by the Spanish attacks. No doubt the feeling persisted in North Africa that in attacking Christian shipping a blow

[1] 'La Lettre du Dey', *Revue Africaine*, 1952.

was being struck in the Holy War, as well as an opportunity for enrichment being seized. On the whole, however, the North African attitude at this time was defensive, as it had been ever since the loss of Sicily. Privateering was in part a reaction to the declared intention of Christian states to possess themselves of North Africa, and in part to the treatment inflicted on Muslims by the Christian government of Spain. For the west, we have the evidence of an authoritative Spanish writer. 'The people of the Canary Islands [i.e. the Spaniards]', he writes, 'continued their raids on the neighbouring Moroccan coasts throughout the whole sixteenth century; only when the Muslim piracy [*sic*] began to develop, creating a certain danger for them, did they find it necessary to suspend these raids or make them less frequently.'[1] Certainly the accounts of their sufferings, written by Christian captives, are often heart-rending, but if we had accounts written by the Muslim captives in Malta, who were sold in large numbers to the French government as galley slaves, we should no doubt find them just as moving as those of the prisoners in Algiers.

The evidence for the ill-treatment of the Christian captives is, however, much less convincing than might be supposed by those who know only the literature circulated by the Christian agencies concerned with the redemption of slaves and the voluminous literature based on them. A French Marine Commissary who lived in Algiers in the first half of the eighteenth century, while recognizing the relatively 'uncivilized' or unpolished character of life in Algiers, flatly denied that Christian captives were in general badly treated. Having himself been a prisoner of war of the Spanish in 1706, he says that he 'would prefer ten years of slavery in Algiers to one in Spain'. For the period after 1775, when slaves were held only by the state and not by private individuals, we have the testimony of the United States consul, General W. Shaler:

> It is no more than justice to say that their condition was not generally worse than that of prisoners of war in many civilized, Christian countries. Female captives were always treated with the respect due to their sex; the labour required of the men was not excessive; those who could find security that they would not escape, were allowed to go at large on the payment of about 75 cents per month; there were a number of lucrative offices that were always occupied by slaves, in which many enriched themselves; those who were employed in the palace, or attached to the great officers of state, were treated with the greatest mildness; and generally all those who were industriously disposed easily found the means of profiting by it. In short there were slaves who left Algiers with regret, and it is believed that, in the aggregate, they carried away vast sums at their embarkation. That they suffered occasional cruelty and hardship from the caprice or brutality of their keepers and overseers cannot be doubted, for such are inseparable from the unprotected situation of captives of any description.[2]

[1] T. García Figueras, *Marruecos*, Madrid, 1944, p. 303.
[2] Shaler, *Sketches of Algiers*, p. 76.

With regard to the character of the Algerian people, Shaler remarks 'they are a people of very insinuating address, and in the common relations of life, I have found them civil, courteous and humane. Neither have I ever remarked anything in the character of the people that discovers extraordinary bigotry, fanaticism or hatred of those who profess a different religion.'[1] The captives who suffered worst seem to have been the prisoners who were taken to row in the galleys; but this applied equally to the Muslim and the Christian fleets.

In the first part of the period, the Muslim raids on Christian territory were replies to Christian attempts to invade and occupy Muslim territory; in the latter half the Muslim attacks against shipping were their reply to attacks on their own territory, as well as on their shipping. As a student of the subject has written, 'While the Barbary danger had disappeared on the European coast for more than a hundred years the Christian danger existed on the African shores until the end of the eighteenth century.'[2] Nor apparently is it true that the original provocation in the periodical disputes with the Algerian government came normally from the Muslims.

It is too readily assumed that the Pashas and Deys always acted in bad faith in their relations with the Christians. It is very convenient to explain the incidents which brought the European fleets before Algiers in this way; but it is not in accord with the truth. Careful examination of the facts produces overwhelming evidence that in the majority of occasions the first wrongs were committed by the westerners, though it can certainly be granted that the Dey's government was always quick to profit from circumstances where he had any excuse, however small, to break the peace and to begin hostilities which were certain to be profitable to him.[3]

Napoleon Ends a Period

In 1798, when Napoleon captured Malta, he released the 2,000 Muslim slaves whom he found there. In gratitude for this the Dey of Algiers renewed relations with France, and it might have been thought that an era of peaceful Christian and Muslim coexistence, each in their own territory, was about to begin. In fact neither side was ready for such a state of affairs. The technical disparity between Muslims and Europeans was perhaps too great for such a thing to be practicable. The Muslims were still situated, intellectually, in the Middle Ages and it was impossible for them to live in harmony with a post-Renaissance world on the eve of the scientific discoveries of the nineteenth and twentieth centuries. There had to be a further period in which the modern world totally overran the still medieval Islamic countries

[1] Ibid., p. 55.
[2] Godechot, 'La Course maltaise', *Revue Africaine*, 1952.
[3] H. D. de Grammont, *Histoire du massacre des turcs à Marseille en 1620*, Paris, 1879, p. 6.

before there could be created the conditions for a future of mutual respect and comprehension.

The Assault on Algiers

The launching of the assault on Algiers in 1830 was presented to Europe by the French government as an operation to put an end to piracy. By this time Muslim naval activity from the Barbary states was simply an irritating survival. The forces of the Christian powers were by now so superior that Barbary privateering was regarded in Europe as a provocation by states too weak to defend themselves. In this respect the relations of the newly independent United States of America with the Regency are so instructive that it is worth while to outline them at some length.

The American Colonies had established a certain trade with the Levant. Since their shipping was regarded as British, it benefited from the security afforded by British treaties with the Barbary states, and American people and ships were always well received. When the United States became independent, British treaties ceased to apply to American shipping, and the Barbary states in due course let it be known that they would consider themselves free to attack United States shipping (on the grounds of alleged Muslim or Turkish rights in the Mediterranean) unless treaties were negotiated. The United States, which at that time possessed no navy, approached French and other European powers in the hope of getting coverage for American shipping with theirs. The powers concerned, though sympathetic, did not consider this practicable; it would obviously rouse protests and a demand for compensation. The United States then decided to negotiate treaties of their own and a committee was formed for this purpose, composed of John Adams, Benjamin Franklin, and Thomas Jefferson; this was allotted the sum of $80,000 with which to negotiate. In the case of Morocco, which had been the first country to recognize American independence, a treaty was successfully negotiated in 1786, with the assistance of the Spanish government. It was initialled by Thomas Barclay in Marrakesh; the monetary consideration involved, which did not form part of the actual treaty, was agreed in the following year at $10,000. Apart from occasional demands for increased payments, notably in the time of Sultan Maulay Sulaiman, which were successfully resisted, the arrangement worked well and American shipping was not molested in the Atlantic approaches.

The demands of the three Turkish Regencies were very much higher. Negotiations were moreover delayed by the death of Thomas Barclay and then by that of the negotiator appointed to succeed him. Meanwhile Algerian privateers captured two American ships, the *Maria* and the *Dauphin*, in the Strait of Gibraltar (1785) and took twenty-one prisoners. Jefferson tried unsuccessfully to organize a combined front with the European powers; the formation of a small American navy was also authorized, though the construction of the ships was to be suspended if in the meanwhile a treaty were signed with Algiers. The matter became urgent when the Portuguese, who had been at war with the Regency, made peace in 1793; after this the Algerians captured further American ships and took 117 more prisoners. In their indignation, the Americans accused the British of encouraging the Portuguese to make peace and of instigating the Algerians to attack American shipping in order to rid themselves of unwelcome competition. This charge was based on some unhappy remarks made by a Member of Parliament who said that the Barbary states would be 'useful' in limiting American competition. Benjamin Franklin went further and attributed to British statesmen a remark, which had been attributed some decades earlier, in corresponding circumstances, by Spanish statesmen to Louis XIV, to the effect that if Algiers had not existed, it would have been desirable to create it. It was also suggested that the British consul in Algiers had urged the Dey to ill-treat American prisoners.

It was not until the original captives had spent over ten years in Algiers that a treaty was finally signed. This and the accompanying ransom of the captives cost the United States $642,500 in cash and the promise of an annual delivery of $21,600 worth of stores. In 1798 treaties were signed also with Tunis and Tripoli, and consuls proceeded to take up appointments in all three Regencies. One of the former American prisoners, S. L. Cathcart, who had during his captivity been employed as secretary by the Dey, was made consul in Tunis. Another former captive, R. O'Brien, became consul in Algiers and consul-general for the Barbary coast, while the post in Tripoli was given to the fiery William Eaton who had no previous experience of the Mediterranean world. On his way through Algiers to take up his post, Eaton was presented to the Dey by consul-general O'Brien, and emerged in a rage because he had been expected to remove his shoes, according to the Muslim habit on entering a house, and to kiss the Dey's hand. 'Is it not unbelievable,' he said, 'that this elevated brute has seven kings of Europe, two republics, and a continent [sic] tributary to him, when his whole naval force is not equal to two line-of-battle ships?'[1]

Unfortunately relations with the Regencies rapidly deteriorated again, mainly owing to the failure of the United States to make payments and deliver the stores on the appointed dates. In excuse the United States government pleaded their limited resources and difficulties caused for them by French privateers (1799).

Eaton now became the principal advocate of a policy of force. He was infuriated that the European powers should still put up with

[1] J. L. Cathcart, *Tripoli: First War with the United States, Inner History* &c, La Porte, Ind., 1901.

arrangements which had been accepted at a time when the relative strength of the Muslims was very much greater—an historical fact which he ignored.

In 1801 the newly formed American navy was brought into operation against Tripoli and in 1815 against Algiers; in the latter operations the squadron was commanded by Commodore Stephen Decatur who had distinguished himself twelve years earlier in the Tripolitanian operations. American diplomacy, backed by this naval force, was able to secure new treaties. Thereafter relations with Algiers remained undisturbed until the loss of the latter's independence in 1830, thirty-three years after the destruction of the Venetian Republic by Napoleon had shown that the days of small maritime republics were drawing to a close.

In the official 'statement of grievances', which was issued by the French government on the occasion of the invasion of 1830, however, references to piracy occupied a singularly small place. The major grievance was quite clearly the Dey's refusal to continue to allow the French a privileged trading position, based on a fortified *enceinte* ('the Bastion', near Bône), and the serious loss of trade which its loss might involve. In the audience which ended with the blow of the fly-whisk, the Dey had in fact affirmed that he would no longer allow a single French cannon to remain on Algerian soil and that French merchants could for the future only enjoy the same rights as other merchants.

In reality, there is little doubt that the basic motive of the French government was its desire to restore the tottering credit of the regime by a military success; and to win for the restoration government the credit which Napoleon had lost by the evacuation of Egypt. In the event Algiers was duly captured and the achievement inspired a number of laudatory poems throughout Europe including one in the dialect of Genoa, that ancient rival of the Barbary states; but Charles X was nevertheless dethroned. In any case neither his nor the succeeding government was at all clear how to follow their victory up.

The expedition had been accompanied by propaganda to the effect that the French were coming to liberate the Algerians from their Turkish tyrants.

This propaganda had not been entirely insincere; there was a proposal to set up an Arab prince and administration. The age, however, was the age of imperialism and after months and years of indecision it was decided to conquer and colonize the whole country in the high Roman style. According to the standards of today the times were still barbarous and the operation itself was infinitely harder than had been anticipated. In consequence, the sufferings imposed on the Algerian people were very great. Some of their best mosques were taken for churches; Muslim feast-days ceased to be legal holidays; tribal lands were confiscated, and every sort of national symbol was destroyed. The policy of colonization was accompanied by announcements which indicated a changed attitude to the Arab population. 'Soldiers,' said General Bugeaud in 1841, 'you have often beaten the Arabs. You will beat them again, but to rout them is a small thing; they must be subdued.' To civilians he added: 'The Arabs must be reduced to submission so that only the French flag stands up on this African soil.'

The First Pacification

Much of the severity employed was no doubt essential to the success of the military operations; but there was wanton cruelty also, and accounts given in the works of French historians go far to explain the subsequent difficulties of France in Algeria.

After 1880 when the Algerians had been cowed and Algiers became the favourite winter resort for wealthy Englishmen, a book was written about Algeria, entitled *The New Playground*. It may have seemed such to the casual English visitor in search of a pleasant winter climate with an exotic background; but it was full of underlying discontent. In 1905 Budgett Meakin, an Englishman who had an unrivalled knowledge of Muslim life in Morocco a full decade before the occupation and was fully aware of the unfavourable aspects of independent Muslim rule, visited Algeria and Tunisia. He had much good to say of French administration in Algeria, but certain aspects of the regime horrified him. The natives, he wrote,

are despised, if not hated, and despise and hate in return. The conquerors have repeated in Algeria the old mistake which has brought about such dire results in other lands, of always retaining the position of conquerors, and never unbending to the conquered, or encouraging friendship with them. . . . There is actual hatred in Algeria, fostered by the foreigner far more than by the smouldering bigotry of Islam. They do not seem to intermingle even as oil and water, but to follow each a separate independent course.[1]

Of course there was a different side to the picture. There was the comradeship of Frenchmen and Algerians fighting side by side in war; the devotion of doctors to their patients; the affection between teachers and their pupils. A limited number of Algerians undoubtedly absorbed more of the French outlook than those of any other of the North African countries. The leaders of the Algerian revolution were themselves mostly the product of French schools and gained their military experience with the French army in the Second World War or in Indo-China, often with high commendation. Algeria, as a result of French teaching, became a lay state which will admit any existing resident of Algeria to citizenship on equal terms. Yet this could not cancel the memory of the past: the invasion, the series of 'pacifications', the hopes

[1] Budgett Meakin, *Life in Morocco*, London, 1905, pp. 308–9.

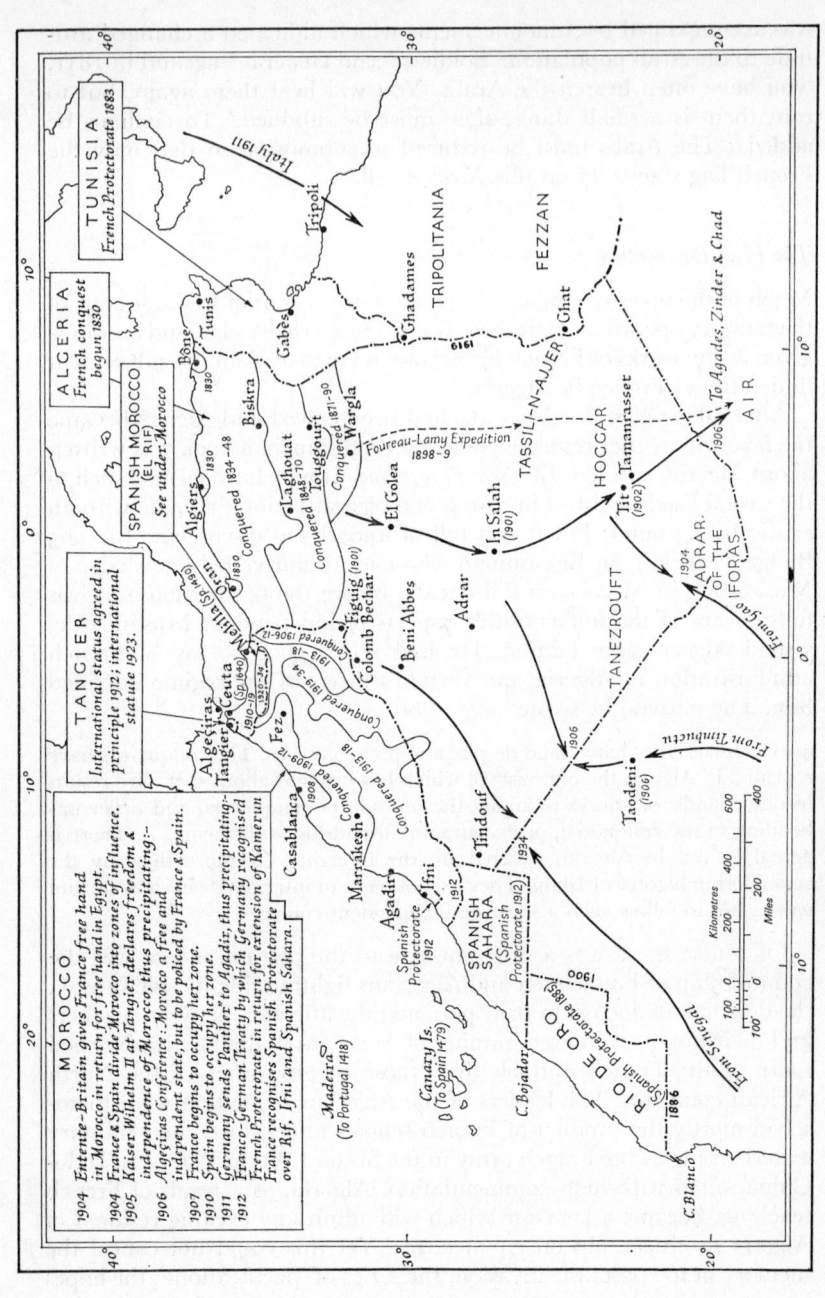

THE EUROPEAN ADVANCE INTO NORTH WEST AFRICA

of equal citizenship which were never fulfilled, the galling contrast in the standards of living of European and of Muslim communities, and the absence of Algerians from any position of high responsibility.

The Extension of European Rule

Once French rule was established in Algeria, it was only a matter of time and diplomacy before France extended her control to the countries on either side. In 1881, a second Arab country, Tunisia, lost its independence; followed, in the east, by Egypt in 1882. By now times had changed; though there was an element of force in the occupation of Tunisia, the operation was more diplomatic than military. The country was not conquered but became a protectorate, retaining its monarchy and something of its former administration, though in practice all authority was soon in the hands of French officials. Budgett Meakin, pursuing his travels to Tunisia, considered the system to be in every respect an improvement on that in force in Algeria even if, as he impishly added, 'the result is a nominally native administration which takes the blame for failures and a French direction which takes the credit for successes'. Though much land passed to the colonists, there was no downright confiscation; mosques were not converted into churches and there were no memories of suffering connected with a long and bitter struggle.

Italy and Libya

The third stage in the European occupation of North Africa was the Italian invasion of Libya in 1911. This was presented to the Libyans in the same way as the attack on Algiers had been to the Algerians, namely as liberation from Turkish government. The policy had the same result; after disposing of Turkish resistance quite easily, the Italians found themselves involved in a long and bitter struggle with the Arab inhabitants, particularly in Cyrenaica. Under Fascism, the subjugation of the Sanusi was achieved by very harsh measures against non-combatants, who were enclosed in concentration camps with a terrible loss of human life. After this operation had been completed, the regime took on a distinctly racialist aspect, though in its material aspects it was highly efficient. However, the Second World War intervened, bringing the experiment to an end before it was possible to judge how Italian–Arab relations were ultimately going to develop.

Marshal Lyautey in Morocco

Finally, in 1912, Morocco was occupied jointly by France and Spain. By this time ideas concerning the government of subject peoples as a sacred trust for humanity were already in the air. As in the case of

Tunisia, the occupation was brought about by diplomatic as much as by military means. Moreover the first French resident-general, Marshal Lyautey, was a man of genius, very humane as well as a great soldier and administrator, a man who appreciated the millenary civilization of Morocco and loved the country and the people. Though convinced that the future of Morocco was henceforth to be indissolubly linked with that of France, he worked with an understanding and sympathy which gave the French regime in Morocco a send-off much more auspicious than that in Tunisia, just as the latter had been more auspicious than that in Algeria. In the incredibly short space of forty-four years, Morocco was brought out of its isolation and freed from the medieval fetters in which it had been bound.

Morocco before the Occupation

It is difficult to realize how great was this transformation unless we first form an idea of what Morocco was like in the first years of the twentieth century. Travellers and residents of several nationalities have left excellent descriptions of the country at the beginning of the century. None failed to be touched with a sense of romance. The long journeys on horse-back or mule-back over almost virgin soil covered in the spring with carpets of wild flowers; the medieval cities with their bustling brightly-coloured markets within the walls, contrasting with the immediate transition to the country outside the city gates; the houses of the rich merchants with their blank walls outside and their tiled courtyards, their fountains and their orange gardens inside—all these made an unforgettable impression on European travellers.

Other aspects of life in the Morocco of that time were less agreeable. The country entered the twentieth century without one engineer, doctor, or chemist; virtually without a road or any wheeled traffic. Indifference to physical suffering in man or beast; inhuman punishments; ignorance of the first notions of modern science; the gory heads of decapitated rebels or criminals nailed over the city gates, these were medieval features which were horrifying to European visitors. In 1909, when the rebel leader Bu Hamara was captured and exhibited in an iron cage (made by the Italian armourer to the sultan) before the eyes of the European diplomats, while his followers were submitted to amputations and other barbarous punishments, it was clear that intervention would not long be delayed; three years later, in 1912, Sultan Maulay Abd al-Hafidh signed the Treaty of Fez.

The Completion of European Control

Though Morocco had been occupied by diplomatic methods and the protectorate established by a treaty signed with the reigning sultan, there were areas in which only the most powerful rulers had been able to exert their authority and where no recognition would be paid to the word of a sultan who entrusted the government of the country to the Christian foreigner.

Two regions, both of them primarily Berber, were particularly involved; one was the Rif, the other the Anti-Atlas. The rising in the Rif was a traditional Moroccan reaction to a weak ruler, such as in the past had often led to the accession of a new dynasty. Taking place when it did, under a leader who had an intimate knowledge of Spain and Spanish administration, it marked a transitional stage on the way to modern nationalism. In the Anti-Atlas, on the other hand, the fighting was never more than the reduction of outlying and stubbornly independent tribes. In 1934 the process was completed and the whole of south Morocco with the Moroccan Sahara beyond it was brought under French (or, in the case of Ifni, Spanish) administration. Since General Graziani had reduced the Sanusi to submission two years earlier, the whole Maghreb had at last been brought under the rule of France, Italy, and Spain, except for Tangier in whose government eight European countries were to participate.

The Nature of European Rule in the Maghreb

European rule, thus established in North West Africa, naturally varied according to whether the rulers were French, Italian, or Spanish; according to the time when the occupation took place; and according to the nature of the country or the portion of the country occupied. If one surveys the picture as a whole, however, it is fair to say that the fundamental conception of both French and Italians was that they were the heirs of Rome, and that they were taking up and carrying on a task which had been interrupted some 1,400 years before. It is true that the Italian government had at first the idea of establishing local parliamentary government; but soon, with the advent of the Fascist regime, ancient Rome became very consciously the model. French methods varied very greatly between Algeria and the two protectorates; but if the method was different, the goal appeared the same. One may go further and say that French and, for the short time that it lasted, Italian rule had the same general effect as Roman rule. The civilization of the metropolis was implanted by administrators and colonists; the latter were backed by armed force, remained 'aliens', and enjoyed a privileged position with regard to the indigenous population. So far as an ultimate end was ever envisaged by the French rulers, it appeared to be not the revival of Arab states in a modernized form but the creation of neo-French states whose civilization would, in some remote future, bear the same relation to French civilization as that of France itself bears to Roman civilization.

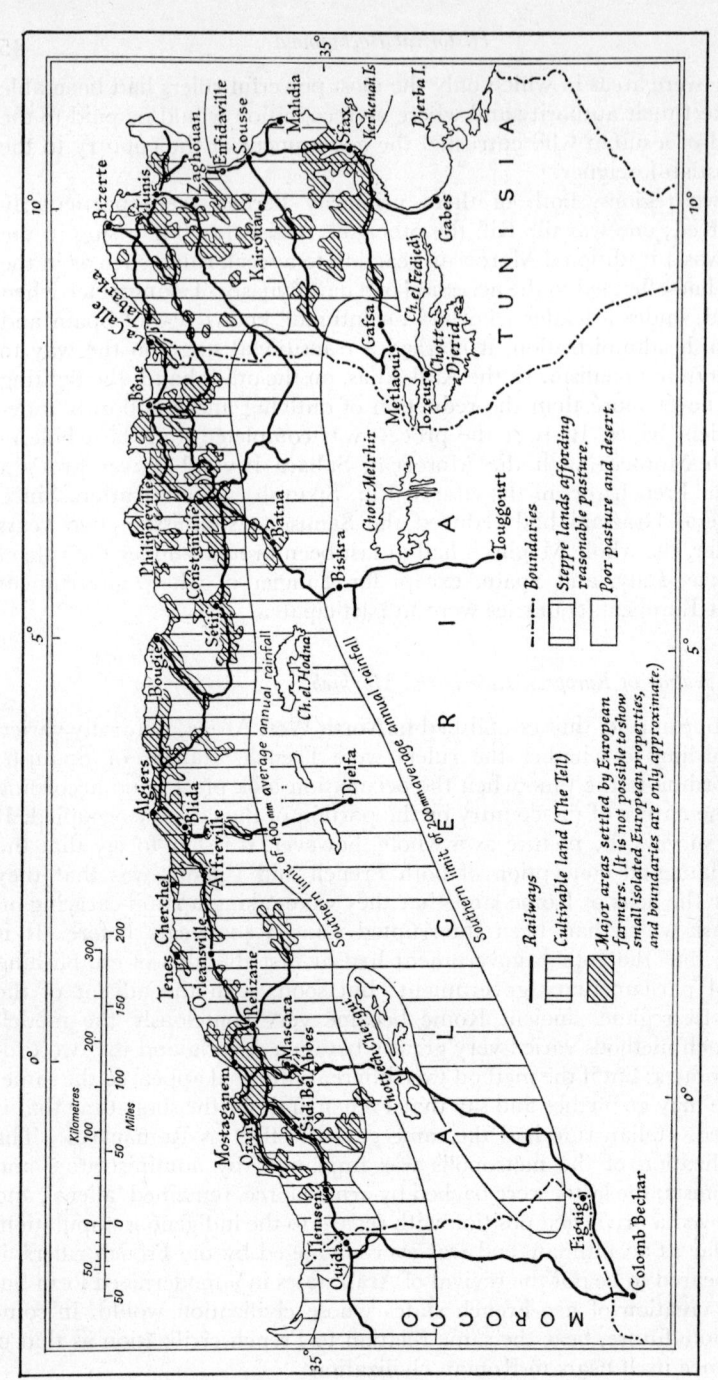

EUROPEAN SETTLEMENT IN NORTH AFRICA

Historical Background

The main difference was perhaps that ancient Rome gave the impression of building for eternity, while there was a certain air of improvisation about the French and Italian constructions, as if they had an uneasy awareness that their domination was not to last very long. The work done was, nevertheless, comparable with that of the Romans.

Certain special problems arose connected with the period in which the colonization took place. The world was being revolutionized by modern science and by its application to human health and industry. Modern hygiene soon produced an enormous growth of the population, just as it had already done in the previous century in Europe. Industry, on the other hand, apart from some mining and a tremendous development in building, remained limited, and thus failed to provide a livelihood for the rapidly expanding population. This did not, however, prevent a repetition of some of the industrial evils of the nineteenth century in Europe, particularly in the creation of enormous *bidonvilles*, or shanty-towns, on the outskirts of every city. In Morocco, in particular, where industry was more developed than in the other areas, its economic basis was the abundant supply of inefficient but cheap labour. Though European experience acquired in the previous decades enabled some remedial measures to be taken, the position was inevitably made worse than in Europe by the fact that the employers were for the most part of a dominant, and the workers of a subject, race. Administrative attempts at improvement came up against local opposition inspired by economic interests. It can hardly be doubted that higher taxation on the employers and industrialists of Casablanca, and the investment of the proceeds in the education and housing of the workers, would in the long run have been advantageous for both Moroccan and French interests, even if it had acted as a considerable brake on industrial development. The *laissez-faire* system which prevailed left the successor governments with problems which make exceedingly difficult both their task within the country and their relations with the former protectors.

In the Spanish zone of Morocco a certain difference was to be noted. Spain had had its own tradition of imperialism, and this had been markedly different from the European imperialism of the nineteenth century. In some respects it was nearer to Arab imperialism. Its essential characteristics had been conquest, followed by an assimilation based primarily on the implantation of the religion and language of the conquerors, assisted by intermarriage. Spanish expansion in Africa in the nineteenth and twentieth centuries, however, came after the 'europeanization' of Spain during the centuries following the Reconquista and its methods were copied from those of France. The Spanish never seemed completely at ease with these. Unable to hope for the assimilation that can only be brought about by religious unity they preferred to adopt a non-assimilationist policy more like the British practice in Arab countries. Influenced by historical memories, the protectorate authorities seemed to be feeling their way toward some cultural ideal which was not entirely Christian Spanish. Thus Tomás García Figueras, a very experienced protectorate official, claimed that Spain envisaged as the goal of the protectorate 'a free and great Moroccan people who will be united with Spain.... A people who will collaborate with her in a magnificent renaissance of hispano-arabic culture.' The precise implications of this ideal are extremely obscure, but it appears to imply a cultural partnership of some sort, not the complete absorption of Morocco into Spanish civilization. It would not be easy to find any parallel French or Italian statement of intention, for which indeed no historical background exists.

The differences which resulted in practice in the Spanish area are described below, p.276. Superficially the administration did not appear very different. In fact it can be said that throughout the whole of North West Africa the most significant result of European occupation in the long run has been the creation of a modern-minded Muslim élite. It is on the qualities of this élite that the future of the area, and of the masses who inhabit it, now depends.

The Growth of Nationalism

Most observers in 1934 must have supposed that European government had been established more or less permanently over all North West Africa. In fact, however, the last resistance of the old type had no sooner been overcome than a new type of nationalism began to develop. The same year 1934, which saw the completion of the occupation, was marked in Tunisia by the birth of a dynamic new nationalist party, the Neo-Destour, under the leadership of the future President of independent Tunisia, Habib Bourguiba; while in Morocco on 8 May 1934 a visit by Mohammed V to Fez was the occasion of a significant nationalist demonstration which prepared the way for cooperation between the nationalists and the monarch and so led to the termination of the French protectorate within twenty-five years. The actual origin of the nationalist movement in Morocco can, however, be dated from eight years earlier, 1926, the year of Abd el Krim el-Khatabi's surrender and of Marshal Lyautey's departure. On the night of 1 August 1926 eight young men from Rabat and two from Tetuan met in a garden outside Rabat. Sitting in the shelter of a mulberry tree and sipping the mint tea which is the national beverage of Morocco, they listened to what one of the party, Mohammed Bennouna of Tetuan, back from the university at Cairo, had to tell them of the growth of the nationalist movement in Egypt. They then went on to draw up plans for a movement of their own. The oldest member of the party was thirty-six, while the youngest but one of them, Ahmed Balafrej, later to be the first foreign minister of independent Morocco, was eighteen. So quickly did things go that the first generation of western-educated young Moroccans were to provide most of the ministers for the first Moroccan cabinet. In the same period, other young men were holding similar meetings in other cities, notably in Fez, the former political capital and centre of Muslim tradition. Among them was the eighteen-year-old Allal al-Fassi, later president of the Istiqlal party and the most original thinker of the movement.

The nationalist movements in Tunisia and Morocco were not very different from those which we have seen develop elsewhere. Their first requests—in Morocco, for example, for the abolition of direct French administration, for equality between Frenchmen and Moroccans, and for the creation of elected municipalities—do not at this distance of time appear so unreasonable and dangerous as to justify treating those who put them forward as agitators, or calling them communists, and eventually imprisoning or banishing them. It is interesting to speculate what would have happened if they had been more sympathetically handled, given by degrees posts of responsibility and allowed to work for the political and technical preparation of their country for renewed independence. It may well be that it would have made little difference to the outcome, but the goal would surely have been reached with less sterile controversy by the way, and without leaving such a heritage of unsettled problems for the newly independent states and between them and their former protectors.

French Policy before 1954

The furthest that the French government before 1954 would ever go in recognizing the goal of independence was to concede that the more advanced of the two protectorates, Tunisia, might eventually enjoy some form of internal autonomy. Of any modification of the protectorate treaties there was no word.

The rising in the Aurès on 1 November 1954 brought a fundamental change. Until that moment successive French governments had persuaded themselves that the promulgation of the Statute of 1947 had ensured the tranquillity of Algeria, whatever might be the case elsewhere. In this idea they were encouraged by one of their greatest Arab experts, the late Robert Montagne. In his *Révolution au Maroc*, published in 1953, the year before the outbreak, he had written (pp. 407, 412):

In Africa only Algeria, thanks to the Statute of 1947, seems to have found a solution leading the various ethnic and religious groups to co-operate in a semi-autonomous regime. . . . Today, in the tempestuous east, only Algeria appears like a rock, from end to end, above which the French flag flies freely, while the troubled seas surge round it.

The shots which shattered the silence of the night of All Saints, 1954, shattered these illusions also and led to a reappraisal of the French position in North Africa. In Morocco the policy initiated by General Juin and carried on by his successor, General Guillaume, had culminated a year earlier in the forcible deposition and banishment of the sultan. Mohammed V had succeeded to the throne as a young man of eighteen, twenty-five years before, and thus belonged to the same generation as the members of the Rabat tea-party. With the years he had developed great diplomatic talents, showing himself persevering, patient, modern-minded, and determined. During the war he had assisted the French, but after the Armistice of 1940 had also protected his Jewish subjects against an attempt to introduce anti-Jewish racial legislation. General Juin, himself of Christian Algerian origin and in some respects the leader of the French North Africans, on becoming resident-general in 1947, decided that the combination of nationalists and sultan must at all costs be broken up; if need be, the sultan must be eliminated. Since the whole system of government in Morocco had been built up on a measure of cooperation between the sultan and the resident-general (officially his foreign minister) this was not an operation to be lightly undertaken. Finally, however, in August 1953, in the time of General Juin's successor, it was put into effect, without the acknowledged or fully conscious approval of the government in Paris, being arranged to appear as far as possible the work of a spontaneous Moroccan movement. By November 1954 it was already clear that the result was not what had been hoped for. The sultan who replaced Mohammed V proved totally ineffective, and the administration did nothing to reconcile Moroccan opinion by the introduction of genuine reforms. The country began to be plagued with terrorism, a thing which had hitherto been unknown in Morocco; and an armed outbreak appeared likely. In Tunisia the position had been greatly eased by the promise of internal autonomy, publicly announced by the prime minister, Pierre Mendès-France, in person at Carthage on 31 July, but negotiations on the terms of the new regime, which it was intended to make extremely restrictive went slowly.

The rebellion which broke out in Algeria on 1 November 1954 opened the War of Independence with a series of explosions. The effect was to hasten the movement to full independence in Tunisia and Morocco. But the juridical relationship of Algeria to France, the presence of a large French settler population, and emotions bred through long years of occupation made the independence of Algeria seem an unacceptable option to the French government. It was eventually achieved after eight years of conflict which in the meantime effected a change of regime in France and substantially altered the political development of the Atlantic world.

II
Algeria
(AL-JAZAIR)

GEOGRAPHY AND POPULATION

ALGERIA (in French *l'Algérie*, in Spanish *Argel*) takes its name from the Arabic words *Al-Jazair*, meaning 'the islands', in this case the little islands in the roadstead of Algiers, the capital city.

Geography

Algeria extends over an area of 2·3 million square kilometres, of which some four-fifths is desert. The coastal region is situated between Morocco and Tunisia, in the centre of that stretch of the North African coast which lies between Tangier and Cap Bon. The coastline is about 1,000 kilometres long while the depth of the country varies from about 350 kilometres at the Moroccan end to about 250 at the Tunisian frontier; the inland cities of Tlemsen and Biskra are on roughly the same latitude. Algeria lies high, having an average altitude of 1,000 metres.

From north to south, the country is divided into two natural regions. These run parallel to the sea; one is the Tell (an Arabic word meaning 'hill', but here perhaps rather a survival from the Latin *tellus*, 'the fruitful earth') and the other the steppes of the High Plateaux. The latter lie between two parallel folds, one known as the Atlas of the Tell, the other as the Atlas of the Sahara, both running from east to west. The great desert, the Sahara, extends southwards from the foot of the Saharan Atlas.

In western Algeria the High Plateaux project to the north; while in eastern Algeria the Tell, in the form of two mountainous masses, the Constantine area and the Aurès, projects almost into the desert. These differences in the configuration of eastern and western Algeria were reflected in the Middle Ages by a political division, the Constantine area going with Tunisia in the east (Ifriqiya) and the Tlemsen area with Morocco in the west.

The Tell is a Mediterranean land; it has a regular annual rainfall of over 400mm., which is the minimum necessary for growing cereal crops, but this is very irregularly divided between autumn and spring.

The total rainfall is actually greater in Algiers city than in Paris; and the occasional flood waters cause an erosion of soil which, on an average, costs Algeria 250 acres of cultivable land every day of the year. The mean annual temperature at Algiers is 64°F (17.8°C). Though its former forests have largely been destroyed, the Tell is naturally a land of trees and of jujube scrub. Except for the Chélif, the water-courses are no more than periodical torrents, the Arab *wadis*, which nevertheless carry away water capable of irrigating a million acres.

The steppes of the High Plateaux, at a greater altitude, have a more continental and a drier climate. When rain falls, it covers the soil with a thin layer of flood water, similar to the sheet-flood of the south-west of the United States. Esparto grass (*stipa tenacissima*), which is commercially exploited, extends over 10 million acres. The High Plateaux also contain immense basins of salt marsh, known as *shott* or *sebkha*.

Algeria north of the Sahara thus forms a narrow and mountainous rectangular pad which rises to 2,500 metres in the Jurjura of the Kabyle country and in the Aurès. Its landscapes resemble those of the south of France, in Provence or Languedoc, at least in the neighbourhood of the sea. This resemblance, aided by proximity and ready access, made it easy to establish settlers of Mediterranean origin.

Population

The population of Algeria was last counted in the census of 1966, which reported a total of 12,101,994 persons. The estimated growth rate is one of the highest in the world, possibly 3·2 per cent. The population has the characteristics commonly found in developing countries: a large proportion (47·9 per cent in 1972) aged less than fifteen; a high marriage rate (an estimated 54–55 per cent of the population aged more than ten being married in 1966); and a small active population, aged between twenty and fifty-nine years (35·2 per cent in 1972). The level of rural unemployment remains high, in spite of migration to the towns (and to France) and in spite of the creation of new jobs by industrialization and regional development programmes.

The population of the country changed profoundly as a result of the War of Independence. The French community left, almost in its entirety. In 1954 the non-Algerian population numbered 984,031 in a total population of 9·4 million. According to the Algerian census of 1966 there were 68,400 French nationals in Algeria, although the French *Journal Officiel* had given the figure of 92,086 the previous year; but of these nearly 30,000 were technical assistance personnel and their families. Moroccans formed the largest non-Algerian group—nearly 100,000, of whom nearly three-quarters were in the Oran department. The Jewish community left with the French, and went either to France or to Israel. The population was not homogeneous, since 17·9 per cent were counted as Berber-speaking (44·5 per cent in the department of Aurès, 40·8 per cent in Sétif, and 81·8 per cent in Tizi-Ouzou). Berber loyalties remained strong, although the Berbers did not form a cohesive political group.

The Algerian war resulted in massive casualties. There are no reliable figures of Algerian casualties, which the Algerian government numbers at between one million and one and a half million. (French casualty figures, released in 1970, were 26,614 killed and 64,985 wounded.) The war was divisive, in that more Algerian Muslims fought as soldiers or *harkis* on the French side than fought in the Algerian army. It was also disruptive in breaking established attachments to a place of birth. This was the experience of men who joined the maquis, and also of families who were forced to move into the regroupment villages which the French established in their war against the guerrillas. French official sources gave the figure of nearly two million persons in regroupment centres in 1961 and it has been estimated that the total was nearer to 2·3 million, or one-third of the rural population. Many of the regroupment centres remained after the war, and some are now being developed as part of the agrarian reform programme.

The upheaval of the war also accelerated the movement into towns. In addition, Algerians moved into flats and houses as soon as their European owners left, and naturally brought their relatives from the country to live with them. Subsequently some towns have continued to increase in size as a result of economic growth. The city of Algiers grew from 450,000 in 1954 to 900,000 according to the 1966 census; Constantine, Batna, Sétif, Médéa, and Tizi-Ouzou are centres of rapid growth, while Oran has only recovered slowly from the departure of the French and the changed status of a port so clearly linked in the old days to metropolitan France. The total urban population changed from an estimated 2·4 million, of whom 1·5 million were Algerians in 1954 to 3·7 million Algerians in 1966; while the rural population increased by only 19 per cent in the same period.[1] However, for those in search of work France and western Europe exercise a powerful rival attraction, so that there were nearly three-quarters of a million Algerians in France in 1972 (462,000 men and 273,000 women) and a million emigrants, or 14 per cent of the Algerian population, in western Europe.

The distribution of population over Algeria was predictably uneven. The northern littoral and the coastal mountains were the most densely populated, the density lessening from there to the Sahara. Within the northern sector the greatest densities are found in urban agglomerations which are centres of modern economic activity; but there are also rural areas, like Kabylia, which remain overpopulated in spite of emigration.

[1] A. Prenant, cited in *Maghreb*, no. 63, May–June 1974, p. 40.

HISTORY AND POLITICS

From Antiquity to the Seventh Century A.D.

The prehistoric period of Algeria remains a mystery. All that we learn from the discovery of stone tools is that there were men in Algeria between the tenth and fifth centuries B.C. It would appear that the Berbers of today are the product of a complicated racial mixture resulting from a succession of invasions and cross-breedings.

From the twelfth century B.C. the Phoenicians used ports on the Algerian coast as staging posts on the route from Carthage to their distant trading establishments; Bône and Philippeville were among their ports of call, and also Algiers, known to them as 'Ikosim', which could mean in Punic 'Owl Island' or perhaps 'Thorn Island'. In this remote period the village seems to have been the unit of settled life, as the tribe was of nomadic life.

After the overthrow of Carthage in 146 B.C. the Romans formed a province of Africa corresponding, more or less, to present-day Tunisia. Simultaneously a Numidian kingdom controlled by the great Berber chiefs Massinissa and Jugurtha for the first time constituted a united and independent realm corresponding to modern Algeria. A little later this was delivered into the hands of Rome through the agency of a more westerly Berber realm, Mauritania.

During the following three centuries Roman provinces in North Africa seem to have coexisted with native monarchies. After that period Roman Algeria no longer included the western High Plateaux. In normal times 30,000 men sufficed to maintain order, and a single Legion, the Third Augusta, was stationed at Lambèse, about 120 kilometres south of Constantine. The *pax romana* was, however, punctuated by revolts and in any case hardly affected the people in the mountain country. The Romans built cities of their own; Caesarea, the modern Cherchell, may have had 40,000 inhabitants. At the eastern end of the country the Romans penetrated as far as the desert. The cultivation of cereals became a source of revenue for the Numidians. In the towns the current speech was Latin. The existence of some twenty bishops in Numidia in the middle of the third century shows that Christianity was widespread and flourishing.

In spite of all this, Berber tribal life continued its separate existence in the High Plateaux of the south-west even in the Empire's greatest days. With the decline of the Empire, the Roman advance was followed by a withdrawal. Meanwhile Roman legionaries had often turned into farmers.

Berber dislike of Roman authority often showed itself in the form of revolts and tribal incursions, and perhaps most strongly of all in the century of Donatist religious schism. In the territories which were evacuated by Diocletian a certain survival of municipal institutions is discernible (though these may be simply an early form of the Berber councils known in modern times by the Arabic name of *jamaa*), and Christianity lingered on in the form of isolated churches. Africa was already rapidly losing its Roman character when 80,000 Vandals arrived during the fifth century. Though they did no more than establish a number of coastal garrisons for a period of about a century or so, they cut Africa off from the imperial and pontifical authority. A number of Christian Berber kingdoms took their place. At the beginning of the sixth century the Byzantines drove out the Vandals but took over only eastern Algeria, leaving the rest in the power of the Berbers.

Though the pagan and Christian civilizations of Rome were at work in the Berber lands of North Africa for nearly 800 years, they have left few traces, apart from the ruins of their cities. There survived the use of the Julian calendar for agricultural purposes, a few Latin words, perhaps a few customs, and the plan of the Roman house adapted to Berber use. The last surviving Christian communities disappeared from Bougie and from Tlemsen in the eleventh century.

Throughout these centuries the love of liberty, indeed the anarchical tendencies, of the Berber population were very evident. At the beginning of the first century A.D. a legionary of Berber origin, called Tacfarinas, deserted from Roman service and summoned the tribes of the Aurès to arms; and was soon joined by people from the south and from the east. For seven years Tacfarinas and his bands held the Romans in check. When in danger, he would retire into the mountains or the desert. When left alone, he would fall upon villages and farms or assault a strongpoint. Finally surrounded near the present Aumale, 124 kilometres south-east of Algiers, he and a great number of his people died fighting.

It may well be asked whether the mass conversion to Christianity, followed by the speedy adoption of heresies, was more a political than a religious phenomenon. Impatient of the burden of Roman civilization and discontented with their existence on great estates (*latifundia*), poverty-stricken peasants may well have welcomed a revolutionary religion which appealed to the weak and the oppressed and undermined the foundations of the old Roman society.

The Middle Ages, from the Seventh to the Fifteenth Century

For 800 years, from the seventh to the fifteenth century, Algeria was no longer a separate land. As its geographical name in Arabic, *al-Maghreb al-Ausat*, or Middle West, indicates, it was the central portion of the Maghreb or Arab west. Its limit on the west was, roughly speaking, the Moroccan frontier of today, but the present eastern province, Constantine, was then normally part of Tunisia. Closely associated with its neighbours, Algeria regarded them with suspicion but bowed to their authority.

The country was at that time a great rural region, with little in the way of towns, inhabited by nomadic shepherds in the west and by peasants, either settled, or semi-nomadic, in the east. The names of two big Berber groups have survived: the Zenata who were mainly nomadic, except in the Aurès; and the Sanhaja who were mainly settled except for the notable exception of the Almoravids. The small Spanish horse known in English as a jennet possibly derives its name from the Zenata horsemen.

In the middle of the seventh century, fifteen years after the death of Muhammad, Arab horsemen appeared in the Berber lands for the first time. They soon put the Byzantine military forces out of action; but the Berbers gave them much trouble. The first centre of resistance was in the region of Tlemsen, not far from the Moroccan border, where they were led by a Christian chief, Kusayla; the next was near Biskra, where the Arab conqueror, Oqba ibn Nafi, died fighting. The natural fortress formed by the Aurès mountains held out for three years under a legendary queen known as al-Kahina or 'the prophetess' who was apparently, like her subjects, a judaized Berber. Her defeat involved submission and the loss of independence; having submitted, the Berbers accepted Islam. Those Berbers who were Christian do not seem to have clung to their faith. They were, moreover, to be arabized, as well as made Muslims.

A French Orientalist, William Marçais, has thus described this event.

In the seventh century, the Berber country broke with the west and attached itself to the east, totally and irremediably, without it seems suffering any interior conflict or any qualm of conscience. Their new lords, the Arabs, soon had no need to exercise power directly. But though they now left the country to itself, they had marked it indelibly. It had been made so thoroughly Arab that the Maghreb, or Arab west, can today be considered almost in its entirety as a distant province of the Arab world, somewhat out of the general orbit.[1]

What is meant by 'making it Arab' has been admirably defined by the same writer. It implied, he says, the adoption of Arabic as the language of civilization and of conversation, and pride in membership of the civilization of which that language is the expression. It implied considering the literary monuments of the Arabs as a glorious inheritance, and taking their masterpieces as examples. In short, it meant wishing to belong to the Arab world and modelling oneself as far as possible upon its standards. In other words it could be defined as 'the intimate association of a certain linguistic condition with a whole body of aesthetic tastes, emotional aspirations and intellectual habits'. For the

[1] W. Marçais, 'Comment l'Afrique du Nord s'est arabisée', *Annales de l'Institut d'Etudes Orientales de la Faculté des Lettres d'Alger*, iv, 1938.

purpose of daily speech, the Berber language has nevertheless remained the mother tongue of nearly a third of the population in certain mountain areas.

A second Arab invasion, that of the Beni Hilal, who came from Upper Egypt in the middle of the eleventh century, devastated the Maghreb. 'Like an army of locusts', wrote the Arab historian Ibn Khaldun three centuries later, 'they destroyed everything in their path.' This invasion, like the first, failed to turn the Berbers of present-day Algeria into Arabs by race. The invasion of the seventh century (according to Marçais) involved about 150,000 fighting men, from which number some must be deducted as casualties but others added in the way of families, merchants, and officials. The second, in the eleventh century, consisted of two big tribes which it would be an exaggeration to estimate at 200,000 souls. Thus the inhabitants of Algeria today, as of the rest of North Africa, are more or less arabized Berbers. Other racial elements must have entered into their composition too—Phoenician, Roman, Vandal, Byzantine, together with an admixture of Iranians from Khorasan who were dispatched to North Africa as reinforcements by a Caliph of Baghdad, and of Persians who formed a kingdom in Tihert, near Tiaret, in the province of Oran in the eleventh century.

In the tenth century the Berbers adhered *en masse* to the egalitarian puritanism of Kharijite Islam; it was among the people of the Little Kabylia that there then arose the power of the Shiite Fatimids who subsequently conquered Egypt. A century later the Almoravids coming from Morocco took possession of the country as far as Algiers; they were succeeded by the Almohads who controlled Tunis also. Tlemsen, the Tremesen of the medieval chronicles, profiting by an influx of refugees from the brilliant civilization of Muslim Spain, became capital of a prosperous Zenata kingdom, which was periodically menaced by its Moroccan neighbours, the Almohads and the Beni Merin, until it was finally annexed by the Turks at the beginning of the sixteenth century.

Algeria under the Turks (sixteenth to nineteenth century)

The three centuries of Turkish domination in Algeria have been little studied by historians. Yet the period was important, for it was then that Algeria received its present frontiers. It was also a time of fusion of the Arab and Berber elements of the population and, by no means least important, it was the moment when Algeria entered history as a distinct entity.

The Turkish arrival in Algiers was not the result of a plan thought out in Istanbul. At least at the start it was a private enterprise on the part of two corsairs, the Barbarossa brothers, Aruj and Khair al-Din. They had first become famous for harassing Christian shipping and for the help which they gave Spanish Muslims expelled from Spain who wished to cross to the shores of Barbary. At the beginning of the sixteenth century the Spaniards occupied several Algerian ports, including Mers el-Kebir, Oran and Bougie, and besieged Algiers itself. The inhabitants invoked the aid of Aruj who subsequently made himself ruler and began to carve out a kingdom, which soon stretched as far as Tlemsen. His brother and successor, Khair al-Din, did homage to the Sultan in Istanbul and was appointed Pasha, extending his rule to Bône and Constantine. In the south, he subdued Biskra, Touggourt, and Wargla. Tlemsen, which was for some time disputed between the Spaniards and the Moroccans, finally fell to the Turks also.

Political control was at first in the hands of Pashas appointed for three-year periods, and then of Aghas of whom there were four, all of whom were assassinated, and finally Deys. Of the latter, who were addressed by foreign powers as 'Very Illustrious and Magnificent Sir', there were twenty-eight. They ruled absolutely, but fourteen of them died a violent death. They had to reckon with two rival powers; on the one hand the corps of Janissaries, called the militia (*ojaq*), who were recruited from the towns and islands of Anatolia and whose numbers fell from 20,000 at the end of the seventeenth century to 5,000 in 1830; and on the other with the Corporation of Corsair Captains (*taifat er-rais*), whose privateering was a principal resource of the Dey's treasury.

No full account exists of the internal organization of the Algerian state. It was divided into three provinces which were the origin of the later French departments—Oran in the west, Médéa or Titteri in the centre, and Constantine in the east. These were governed by Beys, while the district of Algiers formed a separate unit. The three Beys were responsible for the collection of taxes in their respective provinces. All public offices were farmed out by the state. Since the Turkish garrisons were inadequate to maintain order by themselves, the Turkish government ruled by dividing. They relied on certain 'integrated' tribes—like the Makhzen tribes of Morocco or Tunisia—who were used to bring pressure on the remainder. Military colonies around the Kabyle country, for example, ensured the safety of travel. The Turkish government of the Deys appears to have taken little interest in the interior of Algeria. Having arrived by sea, their principal interest was in that element, and the profits from privateering in the Mediterranean became a prime source of revenue. In the seventeenth century there were nearly 35,000 Christian captives in the prisons of Algiers. Military and naval action by Spain, followed by French and British and finally American naval demonstrations and, later, the great advance in European naval construction led to the decline of the corsairs who, in the early seventeenth century, had raided as far afield as Iceland and caused a scare on the coasts of Devon and Cornwall. From the middle of the eighteenth century the population of Algiers city began to fall. In 1816, when Lord Exmouth bombarded it, there were no more than 1,200 captives left in its prisons. By 1830 the population of Algiers, estimated in the seventeenth century at 100,000, had sunk to 40,000.

The immediate pretext of the French expedition of 1830 was the celebrated blow with his fly-whisk which Dey Husain gave the French consul Deval, in an altercation over the unpaid debt of two Algerian Jews who had furnished the French government with large quantities of wheat years before under the Directorate. A more substantial reason was the desire of Charles X's government to win credit by putting an end to the interference with maritime trade which the Barbary states were still capable of causing in spite of their decay. It appears, however, that there was one occasion on which Algeria herself sought French protection, in the middle of the sixteenth century. Simultaneously threatened by Muslim Turks and Spanish Christians after the Battle of Lepanto, certain Algerians (ceulx d'Alger) wrote to Charles IX (according to a letter which he sent to the French ambassador in Istanbul) asking him 'to take and receive them into his protection'. In fact for many years there was a definite alliance between France and Algeria under which French and Algerian fleets jointly attacked the possessions of their common enemy, Spain. A French consul was established in Algiers from 1581 and diplomatic relations continued between the two countries, except in time of war, from that time until 1830. Algeria exchanged diplomatic missions with a number of other countries including England, who also maintained a consul in Algiers. The state coined its own money and the Dey had a council consisting of a foreign minister and minister of marine (*wakil al-kharg*), a minister of war (*agha*), and a minister of the treasury and interior (*khaznagi*).

The French Occupation, 1830–1918

On 25 May 1830 a French fleet, carrying an expeditionary force of 37,000 men, sailed from Toulon. Disembarkation began on 14 June, at Sidi Ferruch. On 5 July Dey Husain signed an act of capitulation with General de Bourmont. Article 5 stated: 'The exercise of the Muslim religion will remain free; neither the liberty of any class of the inhabitants nor their religion, nor their property, nor their commerce and industry will be impaired in any way. Their women will be respected. The Commander-in-Chief gives this undertaking on his honour.' The evening before, Article 2 of the Convention presented to the Dey had declared that 'the religion and the customs of the Algerians will be respected. No soldier of the army will be permitted to enter a mosque.' The word of France was thus pledged, from 1830, to maintain Islam and the customs of the people of Algeria, which must presumably have included their language. These two points were to be specifically reproduced, more than a century later, in the Statute of Algeria of 1947, but were not, even then, to be completely applied.

On the financial side, the Algiers expedition was a rare example of an enterprise entirely covered by the sums 'recovered' on the spot. The Casbah treasury was found to contain 15,500 lb. of gold, worth 25 million francs of the period, and 220,000 lb. of silver, worth 24 million francs—in total 49 million francs, of which 43 million were dispatched to France. With other booty, the entire sum captured was 55 million francs. This covered the 48 million francs which the venture had cost and left a profit of some 7 millions.

At the time when the decision to send the expedition was taken, very little was known in France about Algeria. Eighteenth-century scholars and men of letters had virtually ignored North Africa and recapitulated, in their encyclopedic productions, the accounts of writers as distant as Leo Africanus. The area was too close to Europe, or insufficiently wild, to have the appeal of an exotic world of nature, although a literature of fantasy and imagination had been published on the themes of capture, forced conversion, rape, escape, and rescue (in which Christians were always the victims and stereotyped 'Turks' the villains). The more hardheaded information which European consuls provided was limited to matters of practical concern to traders and European governments, and was unenlightened by any deep knowledge of a community beyond the barrier of language and custom. The information which North Africans provided was virtually nil since they did not travel in Europe, nor did they have an active merchant navy trading there. They did not publish books which could inform Europeans about the society in which they lived, preoccupied as they were with an inferior scholastic theology and not having a developed system of printing presses (see Valensi, 1969; Lucas and Vatin, 1975).

The initial occupation of Algiers was soon followed by the overthrow of the Bourbon government whose declining prestige the invasion had been intended to enhance. But after some four years of indecision and confusion the government of Louis-Philippe decided that the occupation must continue. The need to secure territory already won generated fresh expansion, and in contrast to many other areas of the world Algeria became from the first a land of colonization, where settlers acquired land and constantly wanted more.

In metropolitan France the extension of conquest was set against a general background of indifference, changing, with the passage of time, into an unreflective assumption that Algeria was part of France. Against this general background a small number of persons, whether officially or privately, acquired perceptive and sometimes sympathetic understanding of indigenous society and the effects of French conquest.

A parliamentary committee produced a critical account of the conquest as early as 1833; Tocqueville followed his *Démocratie en Amérique* with an enquiry into the Algerian situation (although it remained unpublished until 1962). The revolt of 1871 was followed by a lengthy parliamentary enquiry which produced the Sicotière report; a further enquiry was held after the Sétif rising, but its circulation was restricted. Towards the end of the nineteenth century a movement for reform in Algeria had the support of men of government like Ferry and Jonnart as well as the members of the Société Française pour la Protection des Indigènes des Colonies, founded in 1881 by Leroy Beaulieu. The twentieth century produced anthropologists like Germaine Tillion.

However, these people, even when acting officially, were a minority and represented no strong interest. The Muslim population of Algeria had neither the impetus nor the education nor the political access to enable them to contribute to knowledge of Algeria or to affect policy. French governments oscillated in their Algerian policies. Policy, like intellectual debate, shifted between the poles of assimilation and association; or was affected by the political premises of successive regimes rather than by knowledge of Algeria. Meanwhile the overwhelming majority of the colonists shared a singleness of purpose in pursuit of their own interests; they kept a monopoly of power in Algeria and were constantly able to assert their influence in Paris.

The Ottoman Regency of Algeria lacked the organization and resources to offer any serious resistance to the initial French invasion. However, the collapse of Ottoman rule left much of the religious framework intact. Muslim and tribal society in Algeria was extensively organized by religious brotherhoods—popular, democratic in their organization although in normal times only a minimal degree of organization was necessary. The largest of these brotherhoods were the Taibia, the Derkaoua, and the Kadria and it was the last of these which in 1832 elected an outstanding leader to resist further expansion by the French. This was Abdel Kader whose political achievement stands out in the history of the nineteenth century. Abdel Kader was a reforming Muslim, and an effective guerrilla commander and political leader. In resisting the French conquest he made it his ambition to establish a Muslim state in the interior of Algeria. He gained the allegiance of the tribes by conquest or persuasion—or by the mistakes of the French— and kept their loyalty temporarily by his military prowess, his devotion to the faith, and the firm determination which stemmed from it.

The first phase of Abdel Kader's resistance began with his election and was brought to an end by the treaty of Tafna in May 1837. The agreement, negotiated by General Bugeaud, was sufficiently generous in the concessions it made to Abdel Kader to excite vigorous criticism in France. Over the next few years he constructed a new state. It was founded on the organization provided by the religious brotherhoods, and the authority he exercised came from his being accepted as a religious leader. But the government which he established was more modern than the moribund structure of the Ottomans. It had a hierarchical order of functionaries, largely drawn from among religious leaders, who were paid stipends. The state issued its own money and established an efficient and equitable system of taxes. Agriculture was organized to provide reserves of grain and a rudimentary industry based on the iron mines of Zaccar. A series of military bases was constructed, the most important being at Tagdempt, west of Tiaret. Dedicated to the purity of Islam and opposed to contact with Christians Abdel Kader none the less kept himself informed of political developments in Paris and Europe; he was sufficiently aware of the limitations of his own power to be ready to negotiate with the French, justifying himself by reference to the ulema of Fez and Cairo. When his state collapsed in the face of the French army it had no successor; but it is interesting to note that it was contemporary with the theocratic state founded by Mohammed Ali el-Senussi, grandfather of King Idris of Libya (see below pp. 182–3).

After Abdel Kader there was no further possibility of the construction of a Muslim state. Equally important was the fact that the religious brotherhoods, although they maintained a large membership until the twentieth century, were gravely weakened. Abdel Kader's rule heightened the conflict between a formalized Islam based on written texts, and the mystical religion focused on saints and nourished by emotional experience, of which the religious orders were the institutional expression.

The bargain struck at Tafna was not the basis for a lasting relationship between Abdel Kader's state and the French colony. On the French side there was pressure for renewed colonization; and in any case Abdel Kader's authority was not extensive enough to guarantee French settlers from attack by Algerians. Dissatisfaction with the treaty of Tafna and the insecurity of the colony led the French government to decide to destroy Abdel Kader's power, by diplomacy and by conquest. Bugeaud was appointed to carry out this task.

General Bugeaud, who became Marshal of France and Duc d'Isly, was almost as distinctive a figure as Abdel Kader. He shocked a wide audience by his social conservatism and the pungency of his views on the rights of victorious soldiers, even before he achieved fame for his victories in Algeria and notoriety for his suppression of working-class riots in Paris. He was opposed to rapid colonization and admired the Carthaginians and Romans for their 'double policy of force and seduction' which could still be employed effectively in the nineteenth century. 'Thus alcohol conquered the Indians, and money should subdue the Arabs.' But whatever his views, his achievement was in commanding the army of 108,000 men sent from France, making them a mobile force with military standards which owed much to his own soldierly dedication, even though his success involved the ruthless devastation of any village which so much as gave hospitality to Abdel Kader. In Bugeaud's own words: 'We have destroyed much. Perhaps I shall be considered a barbarian; but I place myself above the criticism of the press when I am convinced that I am accomplishing a work which is of value to my country.' None the less, it took five years, and the resignation of Bugeaud, in dispute with his government, before Abdel Kader surrendered, in December 1847, on the formal undertaking of General La Moricière and the Duc d'Aumale that he would be given safe-conduct either to Alexandria or to Acre—an undertaking which the French government failed to honour.

The collapse of Abdel Kader's power brought an end to concerted resistance, and the sufferings of the Algerians were augmented until 1851, by drought, locusts, and cholera. Meanwhile in France the 1848 revolution produced the government of the Second Republic which immediately reformed the government of Algeria in the direction of assimilation and civilian rule. Algeria was declared an integral part of French territory and French citizens in Algeria were able to elect deputies to the Assembly in Paris. The coastal region was divided into three departments, like those of France, which, from 1858, elected departmental councils. Elected municipal government was set up in the principal towns. Municipal councils included a one-third Muslim and foreign representation (drawn from non-French settlers), which, for a brief period, was elective—a provision which immediately evoked the practice of administrative control of elections. The principal departments of government were brought directly under the appropriate ministries in Paris. Outside the settled area government remained in the hands of the military. Conquered territory was administered by the *bureaux arabes*. These had been established, following Bugeaud's initiative, between 1841 and 1844. Each bureau was under the command of a lieutenant or captain, with adjutant officers, a caïd and his assistants, and a Muslim secretary—about ten persons in all, French and Muslim. The extent to which they worked as a team, intermediary between the French army and tribal leaders (rather than becoming mere assistants to an army officer), varied from one place to another, but they were universally unpopular with the settlers, whose protests secured the abolition of the central direction of the *bureaux arabes* in 1848, but not the bureaux themselves.

The overthrow of the Second Republic by Louis Napoleon's *coup d'état* in 1851 restored the power of the military over the whole country. General Randon, whom Louis Napoleon appointed governor-general immediately after the *coup*, conquered and subjugated territory to the south (notably with the occupation of Laghouat) and to the east, into Greater Kabylia. Randon believed in the efficacy of a display of force (which usually took the form of destruction of crops and buildings) as a means of establishing French rule—a policy which was likely to evoke desperate resistance from men who saw that there was little to be gained from submission. The fighting was brutal and the aftermath of a battle or punitive expedition no less so. Far from their own civilization and blind to the existence of another, French soldiers and officers were unbridled in their behaviour.

At the same time colonization continued at an increased pace. In 1851–7 the immigrant population grew by 40 per cent from 131,000 to 181,000, of whom 107,000 were French and the remainder other Europeans. Hopes that Algeria would provide an outlet for the French unemployed were realized only to a minor degree, since relatively few of these colonists could make the necessary transition from urban slums to pioneer villages. Randon encouraged colonization and continued the policy of *cantonnement* (see p. 142). An attempt was made to encourage European investment in the development of agriculture, but European companies found it easier to acquire land and rent it without development; while new crops such as cotton and tobacco enjoyed only a brief success before being replaced by wheat, leaving the vine as the only successful innovation.

In spite of the growth of colonization these years were relatively good for the Muslim population, which drew some benefit from economic progress. Moreover the army, harsh as it was in warfare, had an interest in Arab welfare (once the population had made its peace with the French), which the settlers lacked. The *bureaux arabes* took on a new role in trying to develop the area under their control, organizing the digging of wells, building dams, and themselves trying new crops. In 1858 they and the military commanders reacted vigorously against Napoleon III's brief return to a policy of assimilation which benefited the colonists and aroused alarm among the Muslims. It was reversed two years later.

From 1860 Napoleon III became increasingly interested in Algeria. He visited the country, studied it, and became almost as sympathetic towards the Algerians as he was critical of the colonists, whose republican sympathies he had distrusted from the time of his *coup d'état*. He was influenced by Ismaïl Urbain, the illegitimate son of a Marseillais and a mulatto, whose awareness of his birth inspired him with an interest in and understanding of Muslim Algeria. Urbain had been converted to Islam and was *mal vu* if not ostracized by French society, but he was none the less accepted by Napoleon as an adviser. As a result Napoleon became aware of the distinctive character of Muslim Algeria, which suddenly appealed to his romantic sense of nationalism, and he embarked on a new direction, expressed in a letter of 6 February 1863 to Marshal Pélissier (the governor-general) in which he wrote: 'Algeria is not a colony properly so-called, but an Arab kingdom. The indigenous population, like the settlers, have an equal right to my protection and I am as much emperor of the Arabs as emperor of the French.' It followed that the Algerians should be protected from further inroads of colonization and given the opportunity, by the development of private property and civil rights, to develop their own society.

It would have taken many years, and much energy to reverse the process of colonization of the preceding thirty years. The only lasting effect of Napoleon III's rule came from his *senatus-consulte* of 14 July 1865. Its first article provided that: 'the Muslim native is French; nevertheless he continues to be governed by Muslim law. He can be admitted to serve in the armed forces. He can, on his request, be admitted to the rights of a French citizen; in this case he is governed by the civil and political laws of France.' This half-way measure was modified, but not substantially changed until after the Second World War, and provided the legal basis for the subsequent civil and political problems of Algeria, as well as the aspirations of many Algerian Muslims. They became citizens yet not citizens; they had the opportunity to become full citizens of France, if they were prepared to commit the apostasy of renouncing their Muslim status and if the French Conseil d'État would have them; they could and did become soldiers and fight for France, without thereby becoming citizens; as officers they could not (until 1919) rise above the rank of lieutenant. Their Jewish countrymen were accorded the same status by the *senatus-consulte*; but for them it was a rapid transition: by the Crémieux decree of 1870 they became French citizens, with no choice in the matter, except emigration.

The *senatus-consulte* was followed by another period of natural disaster in Algeria—drought, locusts, and cholera—and in France by the collapse of the Second Empire in military defeat. These events combined to produce the last major uprising in Algeria prior to the war of 1954. It was led by Mohammed el-Hadj el-Moqrani who, until then, had followed his father's example of alliance with the French. The decisive factor which induced him to rise against them was probably his fear that the defeat of the French army in the war with Prussia would deny Algerians, ravaged by natural disaster, such protection as the army had offered against further inroads by the colonists. His fear seemed fully justified by the actions of the Government of National Defence, which extended the area of civil administration and suspended Napoleon III's limitation on land acquisition. The campaign he led was further fortified by a call to religious war by an elderly *marabout* of the Rahmaniya order, El-Haddad.

The revolt proved to be a further disaster. It did not touch off, as Moqrani hoped, a widespread uprising, which alone could seriously have threatened French rule, particularly since the attack could not be organized until March 1871, when the French army was no longer engaged against Prussia. The bitter fighting which ensued, over a period of six months, was confined to Greater Kabylia. It ended in defeat and in the death of Moqrani and was followed by French sequestration of the rebels' lands which they then had to buy back at a cost which was frequently ruinous. The colonists exploited it to discredit further the policies of the Second Empire, and won a sympathetic audience in France.

Thereafter uprisings in Algeria were sporadic and minor, while the Third Republic brought political stability to France. In these circumstances French Algeria became firmly established. The colonists behaved like victors in developing the country in their interests, first extending colonization by expropriation of land. The benefit which the Muslim population derived from economic development was outweighed by the loss they suffered from occupation; moreover, the improvement in public hygiene led to a growth in population, putting even greater pressure on the land. They were drawn into the French orbit: Muslims as well as Europeans served in the French armies in 1870, more were to do so in 1914–18; the French language, culture, and state became the sole route towards modernity, self-betterment and power. French dominance was too short to transform Algeria to the extent that Spain reshaped Latin America; but it was long enough to effect a permanent change.

The colonists believed that they created the prosperity of Algeria. They had the evidence of their eyes to persuade them, as towns and roads were built, trees planted along village streets, vineyards laid out and carefully tended, water piped, and drains dug. The harsh and dangerous existence of pioneers gradually gave way to the lulling comforts of colonial life while the underprivileged, the inadequates, and the delinquents who formed a large proportion of the early immigrants were succeeded by a generation with the sense of status and achievement precariously enjoyed by poor whites. An increasing number of settlers were attracted to the small towns, whose essentially French character was modified by the Algerian environment and by the fusion of diverse European immigrants. (A law of 1889 gave French citizenship automatically to the children of non-French settlers unless they refused it.) It was easy to believe that Muslims were better off as workers than they had been as minimal landowners (some were), and that continuing poverty, as obvious to the eyes as French improvements, was attributable to population increase and the endemic laziness of Arabs.

In fact there was a widespread impoverishment of Muslim society.[1] The great families who had given an *éclat* to traditional Arab and

[1] There was much diversity, and many exceptions were individually important. For a detailed examination see C.-R. Ageron, *Les Algériens musulmans et la France (1871–1919)*, Paris, 1968.

Berber society were reduced to medium landowners. Peasant proprietors gained little from the modern sector of the economy. They could sell their grain in good years instead of storing it, but their traditional extensive agriculture could not be made more productive without a degree of knowledge and capital not available to them. Many sold their land and became labourers or moved to the towns.

At the same time French colonization provided opportunities and employment in the towns and villages. A new class emerged of small businessmen, small proprietors, owners of small factories for flour or oil. This class was to become more important in the interwar years, although the development of a system of representative government did not keep up with it. In contrast the class of officials remained relatively impoverished. Men who accepted office of this kind had already lost their individual wealth and did not acquire large salaries; but the payment they received was important to them, as was the social prestige and the power which came from being the means of access to the administration.

In 1881 the appointment of Albert Grévy as governor-general was followed by the extension of the territory governed, locally, by elected municipal councils. In the most settled zone the form of administrative unit was the *commune de plein exercice*, the number of which was increased to 209 in 1884. They were run by municipal councils, which included a maximum of one-third Muslim representation, but, from 1884, they were only partly elective. Where there was little European settlement the territory remained under military command, which slowly developed a few native councils. In the intervening area the communes were *communes mixtes*. In these communes the Muslims had a majority in the local council, but it had only advisory power and government was in the hands of administrators. The natural tendency, with increasing colonization, was for the *communes de plein exercice* to increase in number and size, so that there were 261 in 1900. This was of direct benefit to the Europeans. The creation of a *commune de plein exercice* gave control to the local European community while the extension of the boundaries of a commune enabled it to collect taxes from neighbouring villages thus incorporated into its jurisdiction, without any corresponding increase in expenses.

The absence of equitable representation of Muslims was the more important since they had an inferior status in other respects too. Conquest was followed by the sequestration of land, which had the effect of imposing the heavy financial burden of repurchasing the land on any tribe which suffered this fate. This was a temporary phenomenon. But until 1919 Muslims continued to pay traditional taxes like the *achour*, a Koranic tithe on cereals. They not only paid French taxes as well, but the medieval Islamic taxes were subject to the modern French device of 'additional centimes' when added revenue was needed. The result was that they paid a disproportionate part of the country's taxes, especially as a large part of government expenditure was directed towards the modern, European sections of towns and did not flow back to the Muslims in rural improvement or education.

Muslims were subject to a legal code of their own, the *code de l'indigénat* which covered a range of offences from attending unauthorized meetings to failing to fight forest fires. The *code de l'indigénat* which remained in force until after the Second World War was applied by justices of the peace, without right of appeal, or (in the *communes mixtes*, from 1881) by administrators. The punishments awarded under the code were not harsh; but they were numerous, burdensome, and inequitable.

Finally, the Muslim population gained little (though the gain was significant) from French education. The expansion of schools for Muslims was limited by the opposition of the colonists to Muslim education (which they thought would be subversive) and by Muslim reluctance to send children to non-Muslim schools (thereby strengthening the case for French parsimony). Thus the proportion of Muslims in school grew, in a period of reform, from 1·73 per cent in 1892 to 5·7 per cent in 1918. The distribution of schools was very uneven, in part because school building depended on local action in spending money from the national budget, in part as a result of the policy favouring Kabylia in a rather half-hearted attempt at *divide et impera*. Where there were schools there were some French teachers dedicated to a liberal and humanitarian ideal, who educated Algerians in the same tradition, seeking a synthesis of the best in two civilizations (fully justifying, thereby, the anxieties of the colonists).

The stability of Algeria and of the Third Republic provoked a movement of reform which eventually produced limited results at the end of the First World War. The Europeans in Algeria sought greater control over Algerian affairs; but in France there were men like Jules Ferry, Jules Cambon, and Jonnart (both the latter served as governors of Algeria) who believed that (in Jonnart's words): 'The settlers are guided by legitimate and reputable preoccupations. But their horizon is inevitably a limited one. To leave the fate of 3,500,000 Arabs in their hands would mean exposing the native to a denial of justice and to a kind of exploitation (I cannot avoid that word) which even though it is based on the law is none the less profoundly immoral and likely to retard if not compromise the spread of our influence.' (Confer, 1966, p. 34.)

The immediate outcome of the reform movement was to give greater autonomy to Algeria, but only limited gains to the Muslims. In 1896 the French government reversed once again the policy of assimilation, by which the Algerian administration had been attached directly to government departments in Paris, and transferred power to the governor-general. (However, education and justice remained under the French ministries, though paid for out of the Algerian budget.) Meanwhile the laws of 1898 and 1900 gave Algeria financial autonomy, by the creation of Délégations Financières, an elected body which voted the Algerian budget when it had been prepared by the governor-general (although the budget did not become effective until it had also been voted in Paris). At the same time the Conseil Supérieur de l'Algérie, an advisory council for the whole of Algeria which until then had been of little importance, was strengthened and given a majority of Muslim members. The governor-general had by this time become an office of considerable power and prestige. The days when the office might be filled by a general were long past. Appointments were made by the French government, on the recommendation of the minister of the interior, the appointment being either from among the ranks of prefects and governors of colonies or from among politicians. The governor-general had to work with the elected bodies in Algeria which, on issues affecting their interests, closed their ranks.

With the approach of war in 1914 the French government legislated for conscription in Algeria. The measure was welcomed by a small number of educated Algerians, who had created an embryonic nationalist movement of Jeunes Algériens, and was vigorously opposed by settlers and their representatives—the two sides hoping and fearing respectively that conscription would give a greater 'droit de cité' to Algerians. During the war conscription was not universally applied; but it did bring some 173,000 Muslims into the French services, with only a few insurrectionary protests against it. Labour was mobilized, and 119,000 Algerians were recruited to work in France. Some 25,000 Muslims and 22,000 Europeans from Algeria lost their lives.

In recognition of the part played by Algerians in the war, Clemenceau proposed measures of reform to improve their status. Inevitably the proposals met with strong resistance from the Europeans, with the result that the reform measures were severely attenuated. None the less the law and decrees of 1919 greatly increased the Muslim electorate in Algeria, increased Muslim representation on municipal and departmental councils, and restored the right of Muslim municipal councillors to participate in the election of mayors (a right they had enjoyed but briefly under the legislation of the Second Republic). There were now some 420,000 Muslims who were *demi-naturalisés*: they were electors, and, no doubt more important to many of them, they were exempt from the *code de l'indigénat*.

The creation of this massive Muslim electorate was to some extent deceptive.[1] More than three-quarters of the electors only voted in elections for the relatively unimportant councils of *communes mixtes*.

[1] For a full discussion see Ageron, op. cit., ii. 1217–21.

Although the total of European voters, some 140,000, appeared small in relation to the Muslims, they continued to control the communes of major settlement, where the increase in the number of Muslim representatives only brought them from one-quarter to one-third of each council. Moreover, the Muslims, as voters, were kept separate from the Europeans[1]—a segregation which the Europeans sought to defend with every means in their power when, after the Second World War, they could not prevent the further extension of political rights to Muslims. Second class voters in Algeria, the Muslims were denied access to the French parliament in Paris, where they had no representatives and no right to vote. The effect of this limitation was immediately obvious since growing opposition to Algerian reform prevented legislation being passed to allow Muslims to become officers in the armed services. Although a bill giving equal military pensions was passed, the proposal to open ranks beyond lieutenant was not.

Meanwhile it was still possible for Muslims to attempt to escape, individually, from their inferior status by seeking French citizenship. But to do this they were obliged to give up their Muslim status. Under Muslim law this constituted apostasy, annulling marriage and making property subject to confiscation. Even for those who were free enough to ignore Muslim law it constituted a major break from family and immediate social background. Nor was an applicant assured that citizenship would be granted: it was conceded as a privilege not a right. In 1899–1909 some 551 requests for citizenship were made and of these 214 were granted. The attempt by French reformers to facilitate the procedure of naturalization was reversed by administrative obstruction. In the interwar years the number of naturalizations increased, but remained politically insignificant; there were, in 1936, a total of 7,635 naturalized Algerians.

The condition of Muslims improved as a result of the First World War and its aftermath. On balance the war economy and restricted food imports appear to have enriched rather than impoverished rural suppliers and Muslim commercial classes. Reform, for all its limitations, had increased civil and political rights. Government posts were more widely open to Muslims, in a way that increased employment, even though it was not on a sufficient scale to create an indigenous bureaucracy. There was a general shortage of labour in agriculture. The effect of military or industrial service in France was, for the majority, an increase in status and self-respect. A few Algerians were sufficiently aware to become increasingly nationalist as they became conscious of the discrimination which they suffered as officers. But ordinary soldiers were impressed by what they saw, and returned home proud of having fought a campaign, possibly of having won a medal.

[1] An Algerian Muslim who was accorded French citizenship lost the right to represent Algerian Muslims, although French citizens by birth could do so.

In the years between the wars no further substantial reforms were carried out. The next great reform movement in France, the Popular Front, lost its momentum before Blum's proposal for extending French citizenship in Algeria could be fought through to legislation.

Algerian Reaction to French Rule, 1919–54

Algeria was slow to develop a nationalist movement. Tribal resistance had been conquered and defeated, leaving a society which lacked those classes of persons who in other countries (and eventually in Algeria) produce nationalist movements. The group of people who formed the governing class in Tunisia, largely of Ottoman descent, had no parallel in Algeria. The limited availability of education delayed the growth of a new indigenous bourgeoisie of businessmen who would resist the dominance of French trade, or schoolteachers with a sense of national pride, or lawyers who, in defending individuals in the courts, would at the same time make a case for their nation. Representatives of these groups could easily be found; but only after the Second World War were they likely to become numerous and powerful enough to constitute an effective nationalist movement; and by that time they were overtaken by revolution. The dominance which France enjoyed was based on the weakness of any modern opposition in succession to traditional tribal revolt. It was also a positive form of dominance, in that many of the most nationalist Algerians would share de Gaulle's sentiment: 'Toute ma vie je me suis fait une certaine idée de la France', and would nurture a strong loyalty to that idea.

At the same time the power, the wealth, and the modernity of France became objects of admiration, particularly among those Muslim notables whose sense of self-importance was enhanced by participation in local and Algerian government, however slight their influence on the course of events. From this class emanated a series of tributes to the benefits of French rule, coupled with demands that they should be given full equality with European citizens of Algeria. Their repeated assertion of their high regard for France no doubt encouraged the comforting illusion among the French that the policy of assimilation, cloaking as it did their own dominance, would endure. With supreme self-confidence the French celebrated the centenary of their occupation with a series of demonstrations and banquets—including a special celebration on 14 June 1930 of the disembarkation at Sidi Ferruch. No mention was made of the part which Muslim Algerians had played in the development of their own country since that date, nor was there any reference to the political demands which they now made. Muslim notables were thus placed in the dilemma of whether to condemn the conquest, and therefore the whole work of colonization, or to keep quiet and so betray their constituents. They generally resolved their problem by reiterating their demands, and at the same time praising the French. Thus Ben Larbey, a municipal councillor of Algiers, denied that the invasion had met with armed resistance: the Algerians had recognized that the French were the bearers of 'the treasures of modern civilization' while Haj Hammou, speaking for the teachers in mosque schools, praised Allah for sending the French 'today our friends and brothers, delivering us from ignorance' (Kaddache, 1970, p. 192).

Not all Algerians were equally vocal or enthusiastic in their acclaim of French civilization. But those who were most outspoken in the demands they made for Algerians were greatly inspired and influenced by French culture. This was particularly true of the small group of educated people, some of them French citizens by choice, who formed the movement of Jeunes Algériens at the beginning of the century. They modelled themselves on the Jeunes Tunisiens more than on the Young Turks. But the Jeunes Tunisiens were drawn from an upper class of Turkish descent which had survived the French protectorate and remained an integral part of Tunisian society; whereas the Jeunes Algériens had taken a decisive step away from their traditional Muslim background, were attracted by the republican ideals of France, and were ambitious to pursue a political career in a French environment, rather than to be the vanguard of a Muslim Algerian movement.

A different tone was given to the Jeunes Algériens movement by the alliance it made with Emir Khaled, grandson of Abdel Kader. Khaled was commissioned in the French army after attending St. Cyr in 1893–6. He served in Morocco, where he distinguished himself as a soldier but proved an embarrassment because of his family and his political interests. He became increasingly active in support of the Jeunes Algériens until the outbreak of the First World War, which brought a return to active service.

With the end of the war he returned to political activity, pursuing a campaign which was more nationalist than that of the Jeunes Algériens, as might be expected from his family roots in Algeria, but which was none the less strongly committed to France. He presented himself, in 1919, as a Muslim candidate for election, refusing to sacrifice his Muslim status to acquire French citizenship. He appears to have toyed with the idea of Algerian independence at the time of the Versailles peace conference, but he sought above all that Muslims should have equal rights with the French, without having to sacrifice their personal status. In a letter addressed to Herriot in 1924 the demands he made included representation in the French parliament, suppression of those laws and administrative jurisdiction which fell on Muslims not on French citizens, and the application to the Muslim religion of the law on the separation of church and state.

Khaled and his colleagues had no difficulty in winning popular election to the municipal council of Algiers, the departmental council, and the financial delegation. But it was impossible for him to construct an effective political base. He was temperamentally unsuited to doing so, and his constituency was very limited. His election was at first invalidated by the Algerian government because he had not given up his personal status. Later he took his seat; but resigned, sensing that it was useless to take part in Algerian politics without being able to affect government in Paris. Meanwhile he continued to publicize his ideas in the journal *Ikdam* ('Valour'), but in 1923 he was either expelled from Algeria or left voluntarily. He went first to Egypt, then, after the success of the left in the French elections of 1924, to Paris. In Algeria the movement he inspired was split between his supporters and those Jeunes Algériens who sought full and secular assimilation with France.

In Paris Emir Khaled was active among Algerian students and workers and joined the Étoile Nord-Africaine, becoming its vice-president. In this way he formed a personal link between the Jeunes Algériens and a new political movement of a quite different kind. For the Étoile Nord-Africaine was a nationalist movement which acquired its initial impetus among Algerians in France, who were living in conditions which, events proved, were more propitious to the growth of nationalism than was the case in Algeria itself, where the movement gained ground a decade later.

The Étoile Nord-Africaine was the creation of Hadj Ali Abdel Kader, who became known as Messali Hadj, a man whose character tended towards the mystical, whose ideas were likely to run to extremes, and who in the end remained ineffective through his preoccupation with his own position in the movement he had created rather than with the purpose for which it existed—a shortcoming which must be attributed in part to his constant harassment by the French government.

Messali Hadj fought in the ranks in the First World War, stayed in France, married a Frenchwoman, and joined the French communist party, attending the communist school at Bobigny. The foundations of the Étoile in March 1926 must have seemed to offer great possibilities to the French communist party. But Messali limited his alliance with the communists in pursuit of his nationalist and radical programme. It included, as early as 1927, the independence of Algeria, the withdrawal of French troops, the creation of a national army, and the nationalization of large estates.

It is scarcely surprising that the Étoile was constantly under attack by the French government. It was dissolved in 1929; Messali went to Moscow to attend an international congress, and returned to found his nationalist newspaper, *El-Oummah*. In 1933 he was jailed for two years; but in 1935, unsubdued, he founded the Union Nationale des Musulmans Nord Africains. Moreover, harassment by the French produced its own unexpected results. Seeking refuge in Geneva, Messali came into contact with Chekib Arslan, a Druze emir who made himself a nodal point of Arab nationalism, publishing (in French) *La Nation arabe* and keeping up a voluminous correspondence with Arab nationalists. This intellectual contact, together with the fact that a return to Algeria was permitted by the Blum government, renewed his roots in the Arab world. It marked a decisive turning towards Algerian nationalism and away from left-wing thought, which became definitive when, in 1937, he broke with the communists and saw the Étoile Nord-Africaine dissolved, without protest from the communists in the French chamber. In March 1937 he formed the Parti du Peuple Algérien.

Meanwhile the enlargement of Muslim representation by the reforms of 1919 inevitably prompted further demands, while providing a limited degree of organization to achieve them, and an outlet for personal ambition. Thus in 1934 Dr. Mohammed Salah Benjelloul founded the Fédération des Élus Musulmans in the department of Constantine. Le Tourneau wrote of Benjelloul that he was 'clever, brilliant, adept at all the finesse of local politics; he appeared more concerned with his personal future than with Algeria and demonstrated a tenacious opportunism' (Le Tourneau, 1962, p. 316). But the Fédération was copied, though with less *éclat*, elsewhere. The demands emanating from the Fédération were that Muslims should enjoy the same rights as the French in Algeria, while remaining members of their own Muslim community. They sought access to French citizenship without renunciation of Muslim status, not so much because they were devout as because such renunciation constituted a major break with family and society (a fact of which the Algerian settlers were well aware). Apart from the question of citizenship they demanded (for the educated Muslim élite from which they were drawn) representation in the French parliament; administrative equality including the reform of the *communes mixtes* into *communes de plein exercice* in which Muslims would exercise power; equality in military and civil service; and the suppression of legislation discriminating adversely against Muslims.

The Fédération des Élus provided the framework for the early career of Ferhat Abbas, who distinguished himself both by the forthrightness of his assimilationist views in this early period, and the stamina with which he pursued a different objective during and after the Second World War. Ferhat Abbas was born in 1899 at Taher (a *commune mixte*) south-east of Djidjelli, in the Constantinois. His grandfather had lost his lands to the French after the conquest; but this did not prevent his father from becoming a *bachaga* in the service of the French, with the rank of Commander of the Legion of Honour. His father's great desire was that his children should receive a French education, with the result that Ferhat Abbas learned French, but spoke only halting Arabic. He inevitably remained conscious of his Muslim and Algerian background, the more so when he encountered the European attitudes of superiority which marked so large a part of colonial society. He served in the army as a conscript, then went to the University of Algiers, studied chemistry, and became an active student leader. He qualified as a pharmacist in 1932 and set up a chemist's shop in Sétif. There he divorced his Muslim wife, whom he had married by family arrangement and married the divorced wife of a local doctor, against the vigorous opposition of her settler family.

Established at Sétif, he was elected departmental councillor in 1933, municipal councillor the next year, and financial delegate in 1936. At this time he was firmly assimilationist. The whole purpose of his political activity was to secure equality for Muslims (which would open the way for him to become a member of the French Chamber). While the object of his ideals and ambitions thus lay in France, the obstacle to their achievement was found in the colonial system in Algeria. He wanted Algeria to cease to be a colony and to become a province and it was in this context that he argued, in a passage so often quoted since:

If I had discovered the Algerian nation, I would be a nationalist and I would not blush for it as a crime. Men who die for a patriotic ideal are honoured and respected. My life is not worth more than theirs. But I would not die for an Algerian fatherland because such a fatherland does not exist. I cannot find it. I questioned history. I questioned the living and the dead. I search through the cemeteries: nobody could speak to me of it. You cannot build on air.

As Abbas differed from Messali Hadj, so the contrast between the two of them and the Muslim theologian Ben Badis illustrates the diversity of Algerian nationalism. Abd al-Hamid b. Muhammad al-Mustafa b. Makki Ibn Badis was born in Constantine in December 1889. His family claimed descent from one of the great Berber families belonging to the Sanhaja tribe. Although proud of his Berber origins, Ben Badis's cultural and religious loyalty were entirely Arab. On the other hand, his family had accepted, in recent times, the addition to their prestige which the French occupation offered, so that Ben Badis's grandfather had received a decoration from Napoleon III in 1864 and his father had been a member of the Conseil Supérieur de l'Algérie.

His education was Arabic, religious, and traditional. He went to the Zitouna mosque in Tunis for four years and then undertook a pilgrimage to Medina and Mecca, stopping at Cairo on his return, and thus avoiding military service (for which he may not have been physically fit in any case). On his return he decided to set himself up as a teacher —in a minor mosque in Constantine, the Green Mosque, since teaching in the great mosque came under the control of the state. From this starting point he built up, with financial contributions from Muslims, a large group of free religious schools and established a Ben Badis Institute in Constantine to train Muslim teachers.

The Ben Badis movement was directed towards religious reform and had some elements in common with the Wahhabite movement of Saudi Arabia. Ben Badis's principal colleagues were Sheikh Taieb el-Okbi, who was born in the Biskra region but spent twenty-five years in the Hejaz before settling in Algiers, and Sheikh Brahimi Si el-Bachir (also known as Taleb el-Bachir) from the Constantinois, who spent several years in Egypt and Syria and then established himself at Tlemsen, from where 'he controlled the whole Oran region with his cold lucidity' (Julien, 1972, p. 102).

The iniquities which they sought to eradicate were those which had grown up in the popular practice of religion—the great underworld from the viewpoint of an educated clergy, where religion borders on superstition and magic, where local 'saints' provide a warmer religious experience than is to be found in an austere mosque, a world where divine, or supernatural power reaches down to the people through faith-healers, midwives, and sellers of charms so that the people respond by worshipping, meditating, or just dancing round tombs, shrines, relics, or rocks.[1]

The power and influence of the *murabitin* and the membership of religious brotherhoods had been in decline for a number of years before Ben Badis took up the offensive, but the need for reform was no less imperative for a man of his temperament. In addition, his movement sought to restore the Islamic community of Algeria to its unity and strength, particularly through the medium of religious education. Sunnis and schismatics, Arabs and Berbers were to forget their differences in a return to the purity of the faith.

On both counts Ben Badis was opposed to the dominance of France. He accused the French of having cultivated the ignorance and superstition of the brotherhoods by exercising their authority through their organization, and at the same time he condemned any Algerian who was ready to take up a non-Muslim nationality. Consistently, therefore, he accompanied his religious organization with intense political activity. In the early 1930s he created the Ulema's Association, which was inspired by his principle: 'Islam is my religion. Arabic is my tongue. Algeria is my country.' He directly contradicted Ferhat Abbas, asserting: 'We too have searched history and questioned the present and we have established that the Muslim Algerian nation is not France, cannot be France, and does not want to be France. It is impossible for it to be French, even if it wants assimilation.'[2]

He pointed out that nations less developed than Algeria were already independent and argued that Algeria could look forward to a period of change and further development at the same time as France changed its

---

[1] For a description of a comparable society see Keith Thomas, *Religion and the Decline of Magic; studies in popular beliefs in sixteenth and seventeenth century England*, London, 1971.
[2] *Ech-Chihab* (The Meteor), April 1936, quoted by Le Tourneau, p. 319.

colonial policy. Then: 'France will treat Algeria as England treated Canada, Australia, South Africa. Algeria will then enjoy a large degree of independence and France will be able to count on her as a free country can count on another. This is independence as we think of it, and not the bloody and incendiary independence which our criminal adversaries depict. It is on this independence that we can count, with time and the good will of France.'[1]

Having established the Ulema's Association Ben Badis became increasingly concerned with political questions rather than with Islamic reform, so that he is reported as saying repeatedly: 'Before being a religious personality, I am a native Algerian; and nothing which concerns Algerians leaves me indifferent' (Kaddache, 1970, p. 247). The distinctive quality of Ben Badis's thought was that his concern with the problems of Islam provided an immunity from French civilization, so central to the ideas of many of his contemporaries, even when they reacted against it, while his contribution to the development of nationalist opposition increased the importance of Islam as part of Algerian identity.

Subsequently the richness of his thought and the heterogeneity of his following have been subject to gross oversimplification by an Algerian government which has given Ben Badis a place of honour in the advance guard of the Algerian revolution (his death in April 1940 making his place in the Pantheon more secure). The primacy of the religious over the political, and the importance which Ben Badis attached to the participation of Muslims in constant meeting and consultation, have little part in the official ideology of the Algerian republic, for all the frequency with which Ben Badis's name is invoked in the press. Moreover the Ulema's Association embraced a wide range of opinions, from those who, like Ben Badis, were reformist in their theology as well as in their politics to those who were puritanical and doctrinaire. But in spite of the weakness which this heterogeneity implied, the Association was of major importance in the nationalism of the interwar years.

With few exceptions there was little intermeshing of European and Muslim politics in Algeria. The communist party was the most successful in becoming a mixed party of French, Jews, and Muslims. Purely French at its formation, it was at first vigorously opposed to any form of Algerian nationalism and this instinctive racism was slow to die. But the directives which the party received from France were that it should form a common revolutionary front and from 1935 it was successful in recruiting Arabs not only to membership but to important posts in the party—notably Ouzegane Amar and Ben Ali Boukhort. At this time, the party was a branch of the French party, but in 1937 an autonomous Algerian communist party was formed.

[1] *Ech-Chihab*, June 1936.

However, for ideological and tactical reasons, its success was limited. There were few Algerian Muslims or Frenchmen who wanted to make common cause against French imperialism; the mixed character of the party proved a disincentive to many Muslims, and in general the sense of nationalism was stronger than that of class. The closest allies of the communists were the followers of Messali. But the alliance was always one of convenience rather than affinity and was subject to the vindictiveness of opportunistic allies who found themselves outmanoeuvred by their partners.

Apart from the communists, the socialists too sought to adapt their electoral programme to appeal to Muslims; but they did so from a strong basic commitment to a policy of assimilation which the North African sections had long been intent on advocating in the councils of the party as a whole. The extreme right in French Algeria—the Parti Social Français and the Parti Populaire Français—also made efforts to gather Muslim votes and to enlist Muslim notables who would embroider their lists of members; but their success was minimal.

In general, the ideas and demands of Muslims were of little interest to the Europeans in Algeria. Theirs was a community which, in spite of its extreme sensitivity to any proposals affecting their interests, was little politicized, developed political activity at election time and for the most part remained within the bounds of its European preoccupations.

Nor, in the interwar years, did the various strands of the Algerian nationalist movement receive mass support, in spite of the multitude of grievances which accumulated in the hearts and minds of so many Algerians.[1] The impact of French culture on some educated people was such that their sense of nationalism was complex—a combination of loyalty to an imperial power with a sense of national identity, of which there are many other examples in the Middle East and India; some who came to speak French far better than Arabic none the less retained all their reserve towards France, but they were still cut off from their indigenous roots. The number of Muslims who participated in municipal government and were politically active in centres like Algiers, Oran, and Constantine remained a small proportion of the whole. The practice of voting, representation, and attention to political ideas lacked any tradition among Muslims (and certainly received no encouragement from the French), so that the pull of administrative favour on elected representatives was far stronger than that of their minimal political base.

The mass of the Muslim population never came to be infiltrated by a political party like the Neo-Destour in Tunisia; but equally it

[1] In 1911 the sense of grievance among the townspeople of Tlemsen was strong enough to induce 800 of them to emigrate to Syria. For the catalogue of their grievances which the subsequent enquiry revealed see Julien, 1972, p. 95.

remained little touched by France even though the system of local government and minor officialdom brought it into the French orbit. Julien cites one religious brotherhood which met every year to elect its head, who then immediately stepped down in favour of the leader appointed by the native affairs bureau; but every member of the brotherhood understood the division of responsibility between them: one leader had spiritual *baraka*, the other administrative (Julien, 1972, p. 94). No doubt many French settlers, anxious as they were at the possibility of being overwhelmed by this growing and still uncomprehended population, were comforted by the way in which the peasants retained their religious faith and continued their customary lives. Only a sensitive observer would see, as Le Tourneau has done, the complexities of the Muslims' feelings:

The Muslims had no fewer complexes. The first was of inferiority. They had been conquered and continued to suffer the consequences of their defeats of the nineteenth century, with all that that involved in external humility, often coupled with duplicity and cunning. Confronting the Europeans, they lacked confidence and thus forfeited much of their strength. But at the same time, ill-informed as they were about their own past, they knew that their distant ancestors had been able to win victories and to behave as masters. In the depths of their hearts they were aware of a natural pride, sometimes scarcely concealed behind an external humility—pride of Arabs for so long conquerors and overlords, pride of Berbers who, in the mountains of Kabylia or the Aurès, were able to hold out against so many invaders and safeguard their independence. To that was added the sentiment of the natural superiority of the Muslim community over all others, since it alone had received the Truth in all its integrity. It was this community which would lead the world to salvation: it was unjust that it should be brought down to its present state and this situation could not last for long. For the moment it had no choice but to accept its fate, but the day would come when events would resume their normal course. (Le Tourneau, 1962, p. 309.)

It was this substratum of Muslim feeling on which the events of the next twenty years were to have their impact; for with the passage of time, the dominance of France gradually lost its automatic acceptance. This process was forwarded by the demographic, economic, and social development of the country; and by more specific events: the failure of the Popular Front to carry out reform, the experience of the Second World War, and the failure to reform after the war.

In the twentieth century the European population of Algeria grew at the rate of about 1 per cent per annum, from 883,000 in 1926 (of which 657,000 were French born or naturalized and the remainder, non-French) to 984,000 in 1954. This slow growth in population was accompanied by a concentration of agricultural property and a diminution of the number of agricultural proprietors. Mechanized large-scale agriculture accounted for 38 per cent more of the European total in

1954 than in 1930 and the number of owners diminished from 35,000 to 17,000 in the same period. Only 14·4 per cent of the European population was engaged in agriculture, 28·6 per cent in industry, and the remainder in the service-commercial sector of the economy. Productivity meanwhile increased vigorously, with the result that European agriculture accounted, in 1954, for some 55–65 per cent of the total recorded agricultural output of the country.

In contrast the Muslim population began the demographic surge which still characterizes it at the present time, rising from 5·1 million in 1926 to 8·4 million in 1954 (figures from Ageron, 1966). There were no empty lands on which this population could settle. The concentration of agricultural property, which affected the larger Muslim, as well as the European, holdings and the mechanization which went with it, increased yet further the number of landless and unemployed Muslims, and statistics show a substantial fall in agricultural output and in the total of cattle and sheep (owned by an increased number of people). The Muslim population, like the European, moved into the towns. But whereas the Europeans moved into service industries or commerce, possibly with capital saved from farming, the Muslims crowded into the existing Muslim quarters or *bidonvilles* on the edge of big towns. In Algiers the Casbah was increasingly constricted by the growth of the European city around it; yet in the decade 1921–31 the Muslim population, concentrated in the Casbah, grew from 47,669 to 76,804 (Kaddache, 1970, p. 11).

It was against this background that the diverse strands of Algerian resistance to France gained in strength and became increasingly nationalist. But nothing illustrates so vividly the fragility as well as the force of Algerian nationalism, and the obstinacy of the European community, as the events surrounding the French Popular Front government of 1936–7. In order to encourage the French government to move in the desired direction a First Muslim Congress, ranging from the Ulema's Association to the communists and including the Fédération des Élus, was convened at the beginning of June 1936. Messali was not invited, but managed to address the congress none the less. The demands of the congress were for the attachment of Algeria to France, with representation of Muslims in the French parliament, a single electoral college, abolition of discriminatory laws, and access to French citizenship without loss of Muslim status. The congress was an unprecedented demonstration of unity; but it was followed by Messali's final break with the communists, who joined with the Ulema's Association to exclude Messali from a second conference the following year.

The reform which Blum proposed, with the advice of Senator Violette (a former governor-general of Algeria), was more modest than the demands of the congress. It provided for the exercise, by Muslims of certain categories, of the political rights of French citizens, without renunciation of Muslim status. The categories included former officers and non-commissioned officers; those decorated in the war; those with university qualifications; official representatives of commerce and agriculture; workers holding a work-medal; and trade union secretaries with a minimum of ten years' service. These persons, of whom it was calculated there might be some 20,000–25,000 would be added to the existing European electorate (ten times that number) to elect deputies to the French parliament: one deputy for every 20,000 registered electors.

Although the reform was welcomed by the participants in the First Muslim Congress—and even more by a wide constituency of Algerians likely to benefit from it—its effect was inevitably divisive. It was denounced by Messali as an 'instrument of colonization which would create an élite class of Algerians' (his hostility provided the grounds for the alliance of the congress against him). It ran counter to the Islamic nationalism of the Ulemas, although they made no haste to express their reservations.

However, the decisive response to Blum's proposal was from the Europeans in Algeria. Insensitive to the divisions among Algerian nationalists they saw only the threat to their position, and their reaction had sufficient support in Paris for the proposal to be dropped without even being discussed in the French parliament.

The Second World War brought no immediate crisis between the French and Muslim nationalists. The Vichy government took 'the revenge of the anti-Dreyfusards' in its anti-Jewish policies, repealing the Crémieux decree and restricting Jewish admission to the university (a policy which General Giraud continued and was only reversed at the end of the war). Both Messali's party and the communist party were banned; the death of Ben Badis left the leadership of the Ulema's Association to Sheikh Brahimi who, for all his spiritual authority, lacked the political dynamism of Ben Badis.

As a result Ferhat Abbas became the sole representative of a steadily growing nationalist opinion. Sensitive to the period of flux in which Algeria found itself he addressed a series of appeals from the Muslim community, first to Marshal Pétain then (after the Anglo-American landing) to the 'responsible authorities' and thirdly, at the end of March 1943, to the governor-general (Peyrouton) appointed by the French Committee of National Liberation.

The series of appeals show a rapid progression from the deference of the first to the proud insistence of the last; they also show the development of Ferhat Abbas's sentiments away from the assimilationist views of the 1930s. The appeal of March 1943 was called the Manifesto of the Algerian People; it represents a turning-point in the growth of Algerian nationalism and became a charter for a new political movement. In the manifesto and its subsequent elaboration 'the Algerian people' demanded liberty and equality in their own country, in language, education, and worship; the abolition of colonization plus agrarian reform; full and immediate participation of Muslims in the government of their country; recognition of the political autonomy of Algeria as a sovereign nation; and the possibility in the future of a North African federation. As political activity continued to centre on Ferhat Abbas, his movement called itself the Amis du Manifeste.

The French Committee of National Liberation, the provisional governments and the governments of the Fourth Republic which followed were committed to reform in Algeria. But (as appears inevitable at the beginning of a period of decolonization), the movement of French opinion did not keep pace with Algerian nationalism; and reform enacted in Paris was thwarted by the French administration in Algeria. The defeat of France, the modernity of the United States, and the interest shown in Algerian nationalism—notably the conversations which the American representative in Algiers, Robert Murphy, had with Ferhat Abbas—together with news from the Middle East, where Syria and Lebanon were moving towards independence and the Arab League established, all contributed to the growing effervescence of nationalist feeling and the breakdown of submission and deference.

The first reform was announced by de Gaulle in his Constantine speech of December 1943 and was embodied in an *ordonnance* of March 1944. The decree met the demands which had been made twenty-five years earlier by Emir Khaled and others. It gave equal rights to both Muslims and French, removing discriminatory legislation and opening civilian and military careers. It opened the second electoral college to all Muslim males over twenty-one and enlarged the first college by admitting to it (in addition to the French) sixteen new categories of the Muslim élite, along the lines of Blum's proposal of 1936; and it increased Muslim representation on municipal councils from one-third to two-fifths.

This was followed by the introduction of the constitution of the Fourth Republic, which gave Algerians the representation at Paris which they had so long sought. These changes, together with the liberal policy of the governor-general, opened up a brief period in which Algerian parties were able to participate in the active political life which stems from relatively free elections. They were ill-prepared to do so. They lacked electoral organization and they hesitated between the advantages of participation and the efficacy of boycott. None the less the success of Ferhat Abbas's party in elections to the French Assembly and of the Messalists in municipal elections testified to their popular support—sufficiently for the French administration to ensure thereafter that elections were better managed.

The second reform within Algeria came in 1947, with the enactment of the Algerian statute by the government of the Fourth Republic. In an assembly dominated by the communist and socialist parties it won a narrow majority: 320 votes out of 624, with the fifteen Muslim deputies (elected under the provisions of the 1944 *ordonnance*) abstaining in protest against its limited character. The essence of the new statute was the creation of an Algerian assembly, having wide powers in financial matters and some influence over administration. It was composed of 120 deputies, elected in equal numbers by two electoral colleges. The first was composed of Europeans and assimilated Muslims, numbering 370,000 and 60,000 respectively; the second was composed of 1,300,000 Muslim voters, from which women were, for the time being, excluded, though the statute decreed their inclusion. The Algerian Muslims were to become French citizens, with the title of Muslim French, while keeping their personal Muslim status. The statute provided also for the progressive disappearance of the military territories of the south, and of the *communes mixtes* which were to be assimilated to the *communes de plein exercice*. The statute in fact returned to the original pact of 1830, reaffirming the independence of the Muslim religion vis-à-vis the state and arranging for the teaching of Arabic at all levels.

The end of the war brought a dramatic outburst of nationalist feeling in Algeria, which produced incidents symptomatic of suppressed emotion, which in turn gave a new direction to events. In Algiers a mixture of relief at the end of the war and an expression of hope for the future brought a massive Muslim demonstration on 1 May 1945, which was controlled and pushed back into the crowded Casbah with roughness and force.

A week later a far more catastrophic outbreak occurred in the small town of Sétif, in the Constantinois, where the mayor authorized a Muslim demonstration to celebrate the Allied victory. Some of the participants arrived with green flags bearing the crescent, and banners bearing the slogan of Algerian independence. It seems that as the police tried to take the flags and boards away, a shot was fired. Most of the crowd dispersed; but a few battled with the police, then went through the town killing or savaging French citizens (the local communist leader having his two hands severed by an axe). The mayor, known for his liberal attitude to the Muslim population, was shot. The passions of conflict were released: rumour spread that revolt had broken out throughout Algeria (and, indeed, there were smaller uprisings in other parts of the country). In the countryside the domestic bonds were broken as servants turned, sometimes savagely, on their masters.

The French armed forces counteracted. Senegalese and foreign troops carried out unrestrained reprisals while villages were attacked from the air and cruisers bombarded the outskirts of Kerrata. This was accompanied by an outburst of savagery by the Europeans towards Muslims, which was only slowly brought under control. Nearly a hundred Frenchmen were killed and the same number injured. The official figure for Muslim victims was 1,500; the nationalist figure was 50,000; in confidence army officers gave figures of 6,000–8,000.

Subsequently many of those who joined the Algerian revolution dated their espousal of the nationalist cause from the shock of Sétif. Ferhat Abbas, for all his experience of political activity, said: 'The 8th May brought us back to the crusades, with this worsening feature that, as far as the French in Algeria were concerned, it was a part of their élite which for weeks tortured in cold blood and murdered innocent people. This was possible because the Arab had always been considered a different being, an enemy, an inferior man.'

In speaking thus Ferhat Abbas accurately diagnosed one aspect of French dominance, of which the obverse was that Algerians accepted their inferior position with the supposition that 'we are not like them'.[1] In spite of the political reforms which opened employment to Muslims, the pattern of European economic and social dominance remained unbroken and often unchallenged, on the assumption that it was idle to try to occupy positions held by the dominant French, since such an objective was obviously unattainable. Alternatively, inferior status, measured by an ordinary economic indicator, was accepted because the way of life of the less well-off was itself attractive; the sense of community, the compactness, and the familiarity of the Casbah, for example, constituted advantages which largely compensated for the unattainability of the pleasures and privileges of the dominant group.

An incident like that of Sétif, coming at a time when the people, whether literate or not, were in an exceptionally sensitive mood, could break the bonds which had bound together so disparate a society. Moreover this enhanced sensitivity among the Muslims (some of whom listened to the BBC, while others learned by word of mouth of the formation of the Arab League) was reinforced by the return of men who had fought in the war or worked in France, who reacted sharply against the contrast between the relative equality they had known abroad, and the subordination they were expected to accept on their return. In these circumstances resentment erupted. Thus Courrière (1968) tells of the outburst, albeit restrained, which met the French anthropologist, Jean Servier, in the small town of Arris, at the end of October 1954. In asking for a ball-point pen, Servier used the word *bic*, which is the French equivalent of 'biro', but also one of the numerous derogatory colloquialisms for an Algerian. The shopkeeper stiffened, then relaxed as he saw Servier's surprised innocence: 'No doubt we should be used to being called *bic, melon, crouillat*! But I can't stand it any longer.' Such resentment, once released, evokes the natural fear of the dominant group for its own security, which is seen as depending

---

[1] For the development of this idea see Philip Mason, *Patterns of Dominance*, London, 1970.

on the continuation of its dominance. Each group is then likely to lower its expectation of the way in which its adversary will behave, and therefore to act increasingly from fear and resentment until callousness and brutality become commonplace.

French dominance was not overt outside the areas of colonization; in the mountains, in Kabylia and the vast ranges of the Aurès, French government scarcely penetrated and a traditional economy continued to support a customary society. Anthropologists like Servier or Germaine Tillion studied an unchanging way of life and were made deeply aware of its values and attractiveness. But here, once conflict began, the countryside could offer every advantage to guerrillas familiar with the terrain and the people; and the dominant power would put in its first major appearance in military, not civilian, form.

In 1947 it was the hope of reformers that a middle group of Algerian moderates and French liberals would develop and hold together a political system which would de-fuse violent nationalism—a hope which was sustained long after the Algerian war broke out. In practice, however, those who might have played this role faced almost every possible obstacle. The most important was the obstinate resistance of the European community in Algeria, and the influence which they were able to exercise on governors who, sent from Paris to implement a French policy for Algeria, would leave covered with flowers for their receptivity to the ideas of the French Algerians. Such was the experience of Naegelen, who was appointed to give the new direction indicated by the statute of 1947, but who supervised elections, under that statute, in which every device was used to secure a majority for those amenable to the European minority.

Both Ferhat Abbas and Messali Hadj reconstituted their political parties at the end of the war. Ferhat Abbas changed the Amis du Manifeste into the Union Démocratique du Manifeste Algérien (UDMA) while Messali transformed the Parti du Peuple Algérien into the Mouvement pour le Triomphe des Libertés Démocratiques (MTLD). However, neither of these parties was likely to fill the role which optimists hoped for, and there were no other parties of importance. The Ulema's Association had ceased to be effective as a political organization after the death of Ben Badis. The communist party (which in any case could scarcely play the part of a liberal group) was mistrusted by Muslims for reasons of faith, by the bourgeois for reasons of ideology and interest, and by the Messalists who were best acquainted with them.

The UDMA under Ferhat Abbas's leadership was not a mass party. The qualities which made it most attractive to some of the French friends of Algeria separated it from the Algerian people, in whose eyes it was too bourgeois and secular. Its membership would need time to grow downwards, and would only do so as the Muslim community improved its lot, producing a larger number of educated, relatively well-to-do people, who would form the cadres of the party.

The weaknesses of the MTLD were the obverse of these. Messali had always struck a sympathetic chord among the Algerian proletariat, first in France and then in Algeria itself. He has been described as 'the great Marabout who can be more persuasive than any political leader because he is a master of the art of mixing—with a typically Algerian finesse—verses from the Koran and direct appeals to the people' (Courrière, 1968, p. 51). In addition he had learned about the organization of political parties from his alliance with the communists. On the other hand the MTLD lacked a pragmatic political programme and gave much space to rhetoric, exploiting the evocative principles of independence, Islam, and class interest.

The passage of time might have produced such pragmatism, had it been widely encouraged in Algeria by men like the liberal mayor of Algiers, Jacques Chevallier, rather than restricted and constrained by the imprisonment or confinement to France of men like Messali. But it was best with internal divisions which presaged those which were to weaken the revolutionary movement during the War of Independence. In April 1953 a secret congress of the MTLD, held near Algiers, attacked Messali's leadership without actually naming him—and without his being able to defend himself since the French government kept him in France. It also elected a central committee which was thus, for the first time, independent of Messali instead of being appointed by him. As a result the party was deeply split, suffering the fate of other revolutionary parties acting partly in exile, with the added ingredient of mutual antagonism endemic in the Berber-Arab society of Algeria. For the MTLD in the spring of 1954 the split between Messalists and Centralists (of whom the foremost was Hocine Lahouel) became the dominant issue.

Meanwhile, it was inevitable that the political conditions of Algeria during and after the Second World War would incite some men to seek effective means of direct action against the French. Both the legal repression of the Parti du Peuple Algérien and the subsequent frustrations of an organization so preoccupied with its internal divisions had this effect; but nothing was more influential than the way in which political expression was blocked by electoral trickery, or the numerous indignities and affronts which individuals suffered thereby. At the same time, the war had left behind a small but important source of small arms for a revolutionary movement.

A small group of members of the MTLD in consequence established, soon after the war, an 'Organisation Secrète'. Officially it was part of the MTLD and used the MTLD organization to establish its own network. But in spite of the great personal prestige of Messali, it became in effect an independent organization, for it was the great weakness of

Messali that, having preached revolution for so long, he could neither go underground himself nor accommodate himself to the fact that others, taking the risks of direct action, were escaping from his control. The original group of the OS included Mohamed Belouizdad, Ahmed Ben Bella, Aït Ahmed, and Ali Mahsas. They were joined by Ben Boulaïd, a miller from the Aurès; Larbi Ben M'Hidi from the Oran region; Rabah Bitat from the Constantinois; Mohamed Khider, elected deputy from Algiers in November 1946, who became the treasurer of the movement; Mourad Didouche; and Mohamed Boudiaf, at thirty-five the oldest of them. From Kabylia came Krim Belkacem, son of a caïd, whose respect for his father was overtaken by a sense of revolt against the way in which his father was used to manipulate elections and who therefore took to the maquis rather than accept the inducements the sub-prefect offered him.

In 1948 a few members of the OS, led by Ben Bella, succeeded in robbing the Post Office at Oran and getting away with over three million old francs (about £2,300 at that time). This constituted the original capital of the Algerian revolution (which now resides in a Swiss bank, see below pp. 112, 116n). The affair was regarded by the police as simple robbery until 1950, when a member of the OS named Rhaim turned informer. The police were then able to round up the organization, although their success in doing so was marred by the fact that Ali Mahsas and Ben Bella succeeded in escaping from the Blida prison and Ben Boulaïd and Zirout from that at Bône.

The OS was thus broken up. It had become an embarrassment to the leadership of the MTLD and was formally disbanded. But its members had only been dispersed—to Paris, Cairo (where Mohamed Khider joined Ben Bella just before his parliamentary immunity expired), to the mountains of Kabylia, and the Casbah of Algiers. It was a matter of time before the revolutionaries would regroup, as they did in the spring of 1954. Boudiaf, Didouche, Ben M'Hidi, Ben Boulaïd, Bitat, and a newcomer, a friend of Didouche, named Zoubir Bouadjadj (whose father had been gassed in the French army in the First World War and never recovered) set up a successor to the OS which they called the Comité Révolutionnaire d'Unité et d'Action.

At the end of July this group recruited a 'committee of twenty-two' to a meeting in a villa of the Clos Salembier[1] and agreed that in spite of shortage of arms, money, and popular support—and the fact that many of them were meeting each other for the first time—they should attempt to organize a revolution. Among those present at this meeting were Lakhdar Ben Tobbal, Abdelhafid Boussouf, Boudjemaa Suidani,

[1] No records were kept of these days of clandestine and improvised planning and the memories of those participants who survived the War of Independence became confused and contradictory as to detail. For the best sources see Courrière, 1968–71, and Quandt, 1969.

and Youssef Zirout. Krim Belkacem was not present, but his leadership of the Kabyles was recognized. The five were confirmed as a directing committee, and Krim Belkacem was added to them in August. Two others, the Kabyle Abane Ramdane and Dr. Lamine Debaghine joined them soon after the revolution began.

The War of Independence, 1954–62

On 10 October 1954 the six directing members of the Comité Révolutionnaire d'Unité et d'Action—Krim Belkacem, Rabah Bitat, Ben Boulaïd, Larbi Ben M'Hidi, Mohamed Boudiaf, and Mourad Didouche[1]—changed the name of their movement at the same meeting at which they decided to launch the revolution on 1 November. The change had a symbolic importance: they would enter the war under a new etiquette, and one which would have greater simplicity and appeal than the cumbersome title of their improvised committee. Henceforth they would be the Front de la Libération Nationale and would achieve, by that alone, a propaganda success as a revolutionary movement beyond their expectations.

Their task from then on was exacting enough merely in terms of military or guerrilla warfare. But in addition they had to establish their own authority. Their survival first and their success subsequently would depend on their ability to command the support of the Muslim population and on making good their claim to be the sole representatives of the Muslims vis-à-vis the French. More than that, they took as their aim from the start the independence of Algeria, which could only mean the reversal of the pattern of domination, giving the numerically superior Muslims a decisive voice over the European minority.

The launching of the revolution was an initial success. Co-ordinated attacks were made over the whole of the country north of the desert, at Ouillis and Cassaigne in the Oran region; at Batna, Arris, Biskra, and Khenchela in the Aurès; in Kabylia; and in the Algiers district. The nature of the attacks varied, as did the degree of success: an electric transformer station blown up at Khenchela; attacks on police stations and barracks; telephone wires cut; barns full of recently gathered cork and tobacco burnt in Kabylia; an attack on a barracks between Boufarik and Blida which went off at half-cock; bomb explosions in Algiers itself. On the road between Biskra and Arris a bus was held up and the caïd Hadj Sadok was challenged to respond to the FLN's appeal to join the revolution. His attempt to draw his gun was prevented by a burst of fire which killed him and the first innocent European victims of the war, the schoolteacher Guy Monnerot and his wife. Elsewhere casualties were few: the object of the attacks was to establish the

[1] These six, together with Ben Bella, Aït Ahmed, and Mohamed Khider, who were in Cairo, became known as the nine 'chefs historiques' of the revolution.

existence and the power of the FLN, not to inflict casualties—civilian casualties being strictly forbidden.

In the following months the resources of the French police and security seemed entirely adequate to deal with the small-scale outbreak of 1 November. Zoubir Bouadjadj and the whole FLN network in Algiers were arrested. Rabah Bitat was taken in the Casbah in March 1955 (he escaped from his prison in Constantine in November); Ben Boulaïd was arrested in February 1955 on the frontier between Libya and Tunisia, carrying papers which showed the scale of operations in the Aurès. Larbi Ben M'Hidi went to Cairo in search of arms.

In fact the French were not able to deal with the outbreak. The action which the French government was bound to take to repress the rebellion inevitably kept it alive. While it took three or four months to capture the FLN leaders who knew they were pursued, the leaders and militants of the MTLD were rounded up the day after the events of 1 November. They were released in May 1955 and made contact with the FLN. In the countryside, particularly in the Aurès and in Kabylia, the FLN could continue their guerrilla attacks, and the response of the French forces, taking the form of punitive raids was bound to be to some extent indiscriminate and drive villagers into the maquis. On many occasions such raids were far worse and included excesses committed against the Muslim population. The FLN themselves were not gentle with the Muslim population. Their reports of activity in these months include a high number of 'executions' of traitors or informers. But the adverse effect of their terrorism was countered by that of their adversaries. The daily toll of victims included many more Algerians than French (Lebjaoui, 1970, p. 47).

Moreover the political approach of the government in Paris encountered, as it always had, the opposition and resistance of the settlers in Algeria. Mendès-France and his successor Edgar Faure sought to apply the statute of 1947. Jacques Soustelle was appointed governor-general of Algeria. He arrived with a plan for pacification which included firm repression of the leaders of the rebellion, coupled with the application of the statute, including the teaching of Arabic and the reform of the *communes mixtes*. He was able, initially, to establish a new feeling of confidence among some Algerians, and he appointed Germaine Tillion, a progressive anthropologist with a close knowledge of the Chaouia tribes, to his personal cabinet. He set up special administrative sections of the army, staffed by officers among whom there were many with a commitment to the realization of French republican ideals in Algeria for Algerians. Their task was to eliminate insurrectionaries and to bring assistance and progress to the mass of the population. But in spite of the partial success of these measures, they came too late to halt the momentum of the insurrection; nor could they stop the appeal of some form of independence, once the revolt had opened up the possibility of it. Sixty-one elected representatives passed a motion (26 September 1955) stating that 'the immense majority of the population is now committed to the national Algerian idea', and that they would 'direct their action towards the attainment of this aspiration'.

By this time the second legislature of the Fourth Republic was approaching its term. In preparation for the forthcoming elections a 'Republican Front' was formed between the socialists under Guy Mollet and the radicals under Mendès-France. It appeared to be a powerful combination and those who supported it did so in the expectation of a more liberal policy towards Algeria. Ambiguously, Guy Mollet spoke of an Algerian personality, although he never suggested that his first step would be other than the control of the rebellion. Liberal and progressive opinion in France looked for reform in Algeria which would give it a form of autonomy in which Muslims could participate fully, while retaining its close association with France. At most, independence was seen as a matter for the distant future.

A decisive turning point came at the beginning of 1956. The temper of the Europeans in Algeria showed itself when Albert Camus addressed a meeting organized jointly by a group of European liberals and representatives of the FLN. Their purpose was to initiate a civil truce and to build up a community of understanding between Europeans and Muslims, with the modest objective of protecting the civilian population: 'the Arab movement and the French authorities without having to meet or to commit themselves to anything else, declared simultaneously, that during the present troubles the civilian population will always be respected and protected.'

The meeting itself, with both Europeans and Muslims, including Ferhat Abbas, on the platform, was a success. But it was extremely difficult to find a hall where the participants would be relatively undisturbed; and as Camus spoke the cries of 'Camus au poteau', 'Mendès au poteau' could be heard coming from outside.

The resistance of Europeans to any concession to the Muslim cause organized itself further when Guy Mollet visited Algiers, as prime minister, on 6 February (an historic date, the twenty-second anniversary of the Stavisky riots, when Daladier's government resigned in the face of right-wing demonstrations in the Place de la Concorde). Mollet's investiture as prime minister on 31 January had coincided with the departure of Soustelle from Algiers—a departure which was marked by enthusiastic demonstrations on the part of the Europeans in Algiers, who, whatever their earlier hostility to Soustelle's policy, saw the new government as a threat to the security of 'l'Algérie française'. Their anxieties and hostility increased when it became known that Mollet had appointed General Catroux, a liberal born in Algeria, distrusted for his activities in Syria and Morocco, to succeed Soustelle. It was Mollet's intention to instal Catroux in Algiers at the end of his visit.

Opposition to reform thus built up momentum. The first clash occurred when Mollet arrived in Algiers, and he and his colleagues were pelted with tomatoes and anything else to hand. He took refuge from the crowd and drove to the Palais d'Été, while the demonstration continued through the town. Mollet telephoned Paris and accepted the resignation of Catroux. Instead he appointed Robert Lacoste.

Mollet's collapse in the face of the demonstration made clear that he lacked the will and the authority to impose a policy of reform radical enough to undercut support for the FLN (supposing that were possible), against the opposition of the European population. His defence, and that of his supporters, was that he ceded not to violence but to the obvious patriotism of the Europeans, including postal workers and 'little men' who turned out with their wartime medals and who were good members of the socialist trade union, the Force Ouvrière. Mollet, patriot himself, would not desert these men; the more so because of his erroneous belief that the rebellion in Algiers owed much to support and stimulus from Egypt. Even had his response to the situation in Algeria been different, it would have been impossible for him to implement an effective policy of reform, far less to move towards independence. Neither the climate of opinion in France nor the structure of authority in the Fourth Republic would have allowed such a course of action. The problem was one which only time, much suffering, and a change of regime in France could resolve.

Meanwhile, the FLN had made important progress as a political movement, whatever its weaknesses as an effective military and guerrilla force. Ferhat Abbas had made contact with the FLN in May 1955. While continuing to plan an open political role he had promised his support to the insurrection and had every reason to be sceptical of successful negotiation with the French. There was no similar move on the part of Messali Hadj; instead, Messali renamed the MTLD the Mouvement National Algérien (MNA) which remained an intransigent, though unsuccessful, rival to the FLN. The Algerian communist party decided, in July 1955, to join the rebellion, keeping its organization intact. Three months later, in September, it was declared illegal. But the FLN was not prepared to negotiate an alliance with the communists. By the summer of 1956 they arrived instead at an agreement whereby individual communists could join the FLN, and would receive their orders and postings without regard to their communist party groupings. For practical purposes the party ceased to exist and the FLN had no rivals on the left—a result which came about the more readily since the communist party in France gave no practical support to the FLN and in March 1956 voted in the French National Assembly for special powers to be given to the government.

Within Algiers the FLN also gained ground. By the end of 1955 two men, Yacef Saadi and Amar Ali, known as Ali la Pointe, controlled the

Casbah. Yacef Saadi was the son of a baker, whose shop in the middle of the Casbah was of major strategic importance. He had been a member of the Organisation Secrète at the age of eighteen and was introduced to the Comité Révolutionnaire d'Unité et d'Action by his friend Zoubir Bouadjadj. Ali la Pointe (who took his nickname from the house on Pointe-Pescade where, from Miliana, he had come to live) was a poor boy who lived in the streets of the Casbah, where his education bore little relation to school studies. Together he and Saadi fought and won a rough battle with the French, who had thought of penetrating the Casbah through its demi-monde and so establish a network of informers. Yacef Saadi and Ali la Pointe acted quickly to kill the underworld bosses Hacène le Bônois and Budd Abott and to establish their own dominance. For the next year the Casbah was a safe fortress for the FLN, and its underworld paid subscriptions to the cause. Outside the Casbah the battle for the allegiance of the Muslim population continued—allegiance which, if it was not forthcoming from patriotism, would be inculcated by fear as the FLN killed rival leaders of the MNA, or exploded bombs in cinemas with a tiny Muslim audience, as a demonstration of force.

Important initiatives were also taken outside Algeria. In the summer of 1955 the first serious attempt was made to win over to the FLN the Algerian workers in France, who in large majority were Messalists. Mourad Terbouche, who had been prominent in the MTLD but had gone over to the FLN with the outbreak of the rebellion, undertook a successful initial mission. At the beginning of 1957 he was followed by Mohamed Lebjaoui, a prosperous merchant and shopkeeper in the rue Bab Aznoun who had joined the FLN soon after 1 November, through the intermediary of H'Didouche, brother-in-law of Yacef Saadi. Lebjaoui was arrested shortly after his arrival in Paris. But in a few weeks he had succeeded in taking further the organization of the Algerians in France in support of the FLN, making inroads into their allegiance to Messali. An important part of this organization was the system of subscriptions which went with it, which was to constitute a factor of major importance in financing the war and the provisional government. Meanwhile the external leaders of the revolution—Ben Bella, Aït Ahmed, and Mohamed Khider—were established in Cairo. Their prime tasks were to secure arms and recognition for the FLN. They received hospitality from President Nasser, who extended the practice already established under Farouk of supporting Arab nationalist movements. But they felt considerable frustration, since Algeria seemed remote from the Middle East and their revolution was not at first taken seriously by the Egyptians; moreover, Nasser had personal reservations towards Ben Bella.

In 1955 Aït Ahmed and Mohamed Yazid, who had joined the Cairo group, travelled to Asia in the hope of securing recognition from the neutralist conference at Bandung. They attended the preliminary meeting at Bogor, and Ahmed remained for the conference itself. But they were unable to persuade Nehru or the Colombo powers to include Algeria in the conference communiqué. None the less their initiative showed the importance which the FLN attached to international recognition. In addition the external group were best placed to take advantage of contacts with the French government whenever possible.

Both in Cairo and in Algeria the revolution kept up its momentum. The French government meanwhile sought to carry out Mollet's programme for a settlement of the 'Algerian problem'. It carried forward some of the reforms included in the Soustelle plan, particularly the transformation of all *communes* into *communes de plein exercice*, with full elective councils. It provided for economic and social reform, including land reform involving the expropriation of large estates and assistance to Muslims to purchase land. A new organization was set up to develop the resources of the Sahara; under its aegis oil was discovered in 1956.

At the same time the French government sought an end to the war by negotiation. Mollet publicly offered a cease-fire without conditions, to be followed by elections and negotiations which would recognize the equality of Muslims. He was prepared and anxious to initiate conversations in any way to facilitate a movement towards peace. His policies had critics on the left in France, who argued that he was not vigorous enough in pressing forward with reform which would enlist the confidence of the Muslims; and on these grounds Mendès-France resigned from the government in May 1956, thus breaking the Republican Front alliance. But the major obstacles came from within Algeria, where an inconclusive guerrilla war in the countryside, violence in the towns, and French reprisals increased the gulf between the Muslim and the European communities and left Lacoste isolated.

The political organization of the FLN took major steps forward. In June 1956 the first issue of the FLN newspaper, *El-Moujahid*, appeared, roneotyped, in French and Arabic editions. The name, 'The Crusader', was derived from *jihad* or holy war. The first editorial was careful to point out that this did not imply any religious intolerance, even though it was the case that 'Islam was the last refuge in Algeria of those values hunted down and profaned by an outrageous colonialism'.

Even more important was the summoning of the first conference of the FLN since the beginning of the war. It opened in a house in the valley of the Soummam on 20 August 1956, and dispersed three weeks later, on 10 September.

The conference drew up a formal plan of organization, took certain important decisions of principle, and agreed on a political programme. The direction of the FLN was put in the hands of a national council, to be called the Conseil National de la Révolution Algérienne (CNRA) composed of seventeen full members and seventeen alternatives. The council included men who had belonged to earlier political organizations and who had rallied to the Front. They were now given full recognition, with the intention of strengthening the claim of the FLN to be the sole representative of the Algerian people. Thus the full members included in their number Ferhat Abbas and El-Madani Tawfik from the Ulema's Association. Dr. Ahmed Francis, Ferhat Abbas's brother-in-law and right-hand man (one of the four men with whom Soustelle had conferred on his appointment), was named an alternate member (he was later one of the negotiating team at Evian).

The conference also established a committee of coordination and execution (CCE), composed of five men. This committee was to be the directing body of the revolution, taking its decisions by unanimity and exercising authority over the different zones of operation. They met in Algiers, although *Moujahid* merely announced that they would meet 'somewhere in the maquis, in Algeria'. The former zones of operations were restyled *wilayas*, each of which was divided into zones and then regions. Algiers was now separated from the Algerois *wilaya* and established as an autonomous zone. The whole organization was based on two principles: that political authority had primacy over military, and that the 'interior' had primacy over the 'exterior', notably, Ben Bella and his colleagues in Cairo.

The 'platform of Soummam' was a proud and important document. The military achievements of the Armée de Libération Nationale were referred to as the 'Algerian miracle'. The political achievements of the revolution were contrasted with the bankruptcy of other political movements—the MNA and the MTLD being moribund forces existing only in France through the presence of Messali and through immigrants' ignorance of events in Algeria. The worthwhile members of the UDMA and the Ulema had joined the FLN and the remnant of the UDMA had been dissolved. Most rigorous was the denunciation of the Algerian communist party, whose subjection to the French communist policy it condemned as beni-oui-ouisme—a term of abuse (Mr. Yes-man-ism) previously reserved for Algerian notables who collaborated with the French. The platform also defined conditions for a cease-fire. The most important of these were the recognition of the 'indivisible Algerian Nation', the independent sovereignty of Algeria in all areas, including foreign policy and defence, and of the FLN as the only organization representing the Algerian people (in return for which the FLN would ensure the observance of a cease-fire). Again, peace negotiations following a cease-fire would be on the condition that 'the sole negotiating party for Algeria remains the FLN. No interference with this fact on the part of the French government is admitted.'

The congress showed both the strengths and weaknesses of the FLN as it stood in the late summer of 1956. It was a major achievement to have held the conference, bringing together the leaders of the revolution in the relative security of Kabylia.

But their security was fragile: as the members of the congress met they learned of the death of Mustafa Ben Boulaïd in the Aurès, victim of a booby-trapped radio dropped by parachute by the French;[1] scarcely had they dispersed when Youssef Zirout was killed in an encounter with French troops. The congress reached agreement. It brought together men who were isolated from each other by the physical conditions of the war: Lakhdar Ben Tobbal and Youssef Zirout from the Constantinois met Krim Belkacem and Abane Ramdane for the first time, and renewed acquaintance with Larbi Ben M'Hidi whom they had not seen since the meeting of 25 July at Clos Salembier. There were vigorous rivalries which festered with suspicion. For the time being they were kept in check in the pursuit of a constructive unity; but while the congress could agree on a platform and an organization, it brought into prominence dissensions which were at the root of subsequent struggles for power.

The first of these rivalries was between the internal and the external leaders of the revolution. Ahmed Ben Bella, having directed the Organisation Secrète from its earliest days expected to retain his leadership. But while he was in Cairo the revolution had taken shape within Algeria, and it was there that men's lives were at stake.

The Soummam conference took place after tentative discussions had opened up between FLN members and the French government. The first contact had been made by Christian Pineau in Cairo, through the intermediary of the Egyptian government. The discussions were renewed when Mohamed Yazid and Ahmed Francis met Pierre Commin (as Mollet's representative) in Belgrade in July 1956. A further meeting was arranged to take place in Rome at the beginning of September, so that when the Soummam conference opened it was explained that an invitation had been sent to the leaders of the external FLN, but that they were held up in Italy. Inevitably anxiety arose. The fact that the discussions were taking place and that the participants on the FLN side included 'liberals' rather than 'revolutionaries' inevitably aroused anxiety within Algeria.

The discussions produced no result. Meanwhile, the decisions of the Soummam conference that the interior should have primacy over the exterior was intended to tie the hands of the men in Cairo; and the very success of the conference established the primacy of the internal group. It is scarcely surprising that Ben Bella was, subsequently, critical of the decisions which had been reached at Soummam.

---

[1] The report of his death was not confirmed at the conference and he was nominated to the CNRA—partly no doubt because of the difficulty of finding a replacement among the factious contenders of the Aurès. See Courrière, 1969, pp. 371ff. and Quandt, 1969, p. 102.

The second of the rivalries which the conference had done little to subdue was that between the zones of operations—the newly named *wilayas*. The establishment of the CCE (committee of coordination and execution) and the insistence on the primacy of the political over the military (meaning that a politically determined strategy should regulate the tactical considerations of local commanders) was intended to give cohesion to the revolution as a whole. In practice there was nothing to prevent the *wilayas* becoming to a greater or lesser extent the personal fiefs of the leaders. At the same time the subordination of the military leaders to a political directorate proved, in the long run, impossible to sustain.

Finally, important personal rivalries simmered at Soummam. The preparation and organization of the conference was attributable in large part to Abane Ramdane. He originated from Kabylia but had made his career in Algiers. He had joined the revolution after the Clos Salembier meeting and was not one of the original twenty-two; but the early casualties, by death and imprisonment, in 1955 had opened the way for his rise to power. He had achieved a commanding position in Algiers, and the establishment of Algiers as the future meeting-place for the CCE obviously accorded with his objectives. Subsequently, he was able to assert himself as a sort of secretary-general of the committee, even though decisions were taken unanimously. In the meantime, at Soummam, he evoked the resentment of Krim Belkacem and others, in spite of the success of Larbi Ben M'Hidi in smoothing relations between them. As Courrière conjectures: 'These conversations of August 1956 were, no doubt, the origin of the alliance between Krim and Ben Tobbal, later joined by Boussouf which later took over the leadership of the revolution, Abane being "eliminated" and the headquarters established at Tunis' (Courrière, 1969, p. 373).

However important these dissensions, the fact remained that the improvised insurrection of 1954 had now been given a structure and a command. Shortly afterwards French action brought about a decisive change in the balance of power. On 22 October the French authorities in Algeria ordered the French crew of an aircraft, on hire from a private company to the King of Morocco, to land at Algiers instead of following its route to Tunis. Its passengers, Ben Bella, Mohamed Khider, Aït Ahmed, Mohamed Boudiaf, and Lacheraf, were arrested.

The event was a major miscalculation. It discredited Mollet, who supported the action of Lacoste and the Algerian military command, although they had diverted an aeroplane out of international airspace without his authority. Moreover the French government gained nothing from the affair. They had succeeded in capturing only those who, being external representatives, had least part in the actual conduct of the war. The anxieties which the internal members of the CNRA had about the trustworthiness of Ben Bella and his associates in Cairo were put to rest, since they were no longer competitors for the leadership. There was no longer any question of discreet peace-feelers. The King of Morocco and President Bourguiba of Tunisia, who had no choice but to tread a delicate path between France and Algeria, were affronted, the more so since the arrested men were on their way to a Moroccan–Tunisian–FLN conference in Tunis.

The miscalculation on the part of the military in Algiers is readily understandable. They saw the chance, by a swift if irregular *coup*, to capture some of the leaders of the rebellion they were fighting. Mollet's misjudgement followed in part his exaggeration of Egypt's role in the Algerian war, and he therefore overestimated the importance of the exterior leadership. Cairo was perceived as the centre of a virulent and contagious Arab nationalism, threatening to undermine western interests. The French government's first preoccupation, following the nationalization of the Suez Canal on 20 July 1956, had become the diplomatic and military preparations for the Suez expedition, which landed on 5 November. The capture, three weeks beforehand, of a consignment of arms from Egypt on board the *Athos*, confirmed the French in their estimate of Algerian dependence on Egypt.

The new year, 1957, produced a further important and dramatic change in the sequence of events generally called 'the battle of Algiers'. The intensity of terrorist attacks in the city had increased during the previous autumn. In August 1956 a bomb was placed by French counter-terrorists in the rue de Thèbes, in the Casbah. On 30 September Yacef Saadi and the Casbah took their revenge; three girls, who could leave the Casbah with less risk of being searched, planted bombs in the Milk Bar and the Cafétéria—two of the most frequented cafés of the town—and in the Mauretania building. The first two went off, causing damage and casualties; the third remained unexploded. On 28 December Ali la Pointe shot and killed, for effect, Amédée Froger, mayor of Boufarik and president of the Federation of Mayors.

These were isolated incidents, attributable to a few terrorists. In January 1957, the CCE decided to call a general strike in Algiers of eight days duration. Their purpose was to demonstrate the solidity of the people of Algiers behind the FLN; thereby to draw attention to the revolution at the new session of the General Assembly of the United Nations, where Mohamed Yazid was ready, in any case, to exploit the affair of the Moroccan aeroplane; and in this way to bring encouragement and support to the men in the field, increasingly hard pressed by the arrival of French reinforcements.

The strike was a serious challenge to French authority. It was met decisively and ruthlessly. The civilian police were inadequate to deal with it and Lacoste therefore had recourse to the military, over whom a new commander had just been appointed, General Jacques Massu, who replaced Lorillot. Under the command of Massu and of Colonel

Bigeard the paratroopers occupied the Casbah. When the strike began on 28 January they forced the inhabitants to open shops, to go out to work. The strike was broken, and so was the network of authority which the FLN, especially Larbi Ben M'Hidi and Yacef Saadi, had constructed. Ben M'Hidi was captured and interrogated (not tortured) by Colonel Bigeard in a remarkable confrontation between combatants on opposite sides. Ben M'Hidi was then summarily executed in March 1957, although it was officially stated that he had hung himself. Another six months passed before Yacef Saadi was taken and Ali la Pointe allowed himself (and twenty-one other people) to be blown up in the house in which he had taken refuge, rather than surrender.

The battle of Algiers was a decisive victory for the French. The FLN control of the Casbah and its ability to terrorize the city from a safe sanctuary was destroyed. However, the victory had been achieved by asking the army to take over from civilian authority; and it had employed the extensive use of torture, with the consequent resignation of Paul Teitgen (a member of the Catholic Mouvement Républicain Populaire) from the post of secretary-general and a growing sense of revulsion in metropolitan France. Moreover, the victory was won in Algiers, not Algeria. Of the five members of the CCE only Larbi Ben M'Hidi had been executed. Krim Belkacem, Ben Khedda, Abane Ramdane, and Saad Dahlab succeeded in making their escape.

More important was the fact that the French government was unable to exploit, politically, the advantage which it had gained in Algiers. Mollet's ministry came to an end with his resignation after a financial debate in May 1957. He was succeeded by Bourgès Maunoury. The policy of the government was modified in detail but remained substantially the same; it was to propose reforms in Algeria which would be sufficiently attractive to the insurgents to persuade them to agree to a cease-fire. There would be a framework law which would establish elected local government and a single Algerian assembly. But the attempt to legislate such proposals rapidly descended into the ineffectiveness of French parliamentary politics. The government was attacked by a growing minority of critics on the left—Mollet in particular—minority socialists who broke from the party in 1958 to set up the Parti Socialiste Autonome. But opposition from the right, with the support of the settlers in Algeria, was more damaging. It brought the defeat of a framework law for reforms in Algeria and the fall of the Bourgès Manoury government on 30 September. The French government lacked any continuing authority in the Assembly and the will to impose its policy on the settlers in Algeria. The 'third force' in Algeria, although it existed, exemplified by such men as the liberal Jacques Chevallier, was not sufficient to provide leverage to the government.

However, the French success in the battle of Algiers had decisive repercussions for the Algerian leadership by driving out Abane Ramdane and destroying his political organization in the city. Following their escape, Krim Belkacem, Ben Khedda, and Saad Dahlab made their way to Tunis, from where they could travel easily to Cairo for the second meeting of the Conseil National de la Révolution Algérienne. There and again in Tunis on their return Abane Ramdane had to face the concerted attack of the five colonels in charge of the *wilayas*: Krim, commanding Kabylia; Abdelhafid Boussouf, the Oran region; Ben Tobbal, the Constantinois; Ouamrane, an old colleague of Krim's, the region round Algiers; and Mahmoud Cherif, the Aurès. Inevitably Ramdane carried the blame for the débâcle in Algiers—Ben M'Hidi having paid with his life. The colonels also resented the political control which had been established at Soumman and asserted their own claims, as the men responsible for the conduct of the guerrilla war. Boussouf for his part was in continuous communication with the imprisoned Ben Bella, whose antipathy to Ramdane had not diminished. Finally the alliance was cemented by a strong sense of revolt against Ramdane's personal dominance, so that Krim could accuse him of aspiring to be a Führer. Ramdane's overbearing manner and harsh tongue were in no way softened by the pain of stomach ulcers; but he made no concessions and refused to take himself off to Switzerland for a rest cure.

Krim Belkacem took the lead in insisting that Ramdane be put under restraint, or simply killed; Ben Tobbal firmly resisted summary execution. As a result Ramdane was taken by Krim and Mahmoud Cherif to Morocco, where Boussouf was after returning from Cairo. Their plan, which Ramdane began to suspect en route, was to imprison him there. But when they arrived Boussouf ordered his execution, which was carried out by strangling on 27 December 1957.[1] The following May, *Moujahid* carried a full-page photograph with black margins and explained that he had died on the field of honour; in this way he became a hero of the revolution and his death continued to be so described in the Algerian press long after it had become common knowledge that he had been eliminated by his rivals.

The leadership of the revolution was now gravely diminished. The CCE was reconstituted to include the five colonels, plus Ferhat Abbas, Lamine Debaghine. Abdelhamid Mehri; while five 'historic leaders' in French prisons (Aït Ahmed, Ben Bella, Bitat, Boudiaf, and Khider) were honorary members. But of the other four of the historic nine only Krim Belkacem was still alive and he shared effective power with Ben Tobbal and Boussouf, whose second in command, Houari Boumediene, was beginning to make himself known. French military pressure was taking effect: the success in Algiers sent many young men into the

[1] The above account follows that of Courrière, 1970, pp. 183-9.

countryside; but as the French sealed the Tunisian frontier by the construction of the fortified Morice line the supply of arms became increasingly hazardous. Defenceless and demoralized, these new maquisards were easily rounded up. The conflict with the MNA continued to take its toll; and the French army became increasingly successful in psychological warfare, intelligence operations, and in setting Algerians against each other.

In these circumstances, as the Algerian colonels had asserted themselves against Ramdane because he appeared too dictatorial, so the French military again asserted their independence of the politicians, whom they found divided and irresolute. In February 1958 the local military commanders ordered an air attack across the Morice line. Their target was an FLN base on Tunisian territory, at the Tunisian village of Sakiet Sidi Youssef. From the base attacks were mounted into Algeria: an ambush of French troops and the shooting down of a reconnaissance aircraft were the immediate provocation for the French attack. The military acted without authorization from Lacoste or the French government, which was once again presented with a *fait accompli*.

The Sakiet incident was the precipitating factor in a series of events which, on 13 May 1958, brought de Gaulle back to power in France. The Tunisian government brought the attack on its territory before the Security Council. The British and United States governments, in order to escape a difficult choice between their ally, France, and Tunisia, offered their 'good offices' as mediators; with the result that Robert Murphy and Harold Beeley (who had long experience of Middle Eastern diplomacy and was deputy representative at the UN) were appointed to act for them. The conflict between Paris and Algiers was thereby sharpened.

Military operations were at a stalemate. Algiers had been pacified and the revolution in the country appeared to have been brought under control. Increasingly the European community was prepared to take to the streets in an effort to create a strong government, in Algiers and if possible in Paris. At the same time the cumulative effect of European war, the war in Indo-China, and the apparent possibility of the repetition of civilian betrayal in the Algerian war brought a similar readiness within the army to take over the authority of government, or establish a government of its own design. Thus, whatever the divisions in Algiers, the demand for action mounted—from the European poor represented by Robert Martel, the wealthy settlers whose spokesman was Alain de Sérigny (editor of *L'Echo d'Alger*), the students led by Pierre Lagaillarde, and the *lycéens* eager to outbid them.

The growing crisis of authority was watched carefully by de Gaulle, and also by those loyal to him who were willing to act independently, in the Gaullist interest. Chaban-Delmas, as minister of defence, sent his *chef de cabinet* Léon Delbecque to establish an 'antenna' in Algiers. Having made contacts in the army through Commandant Jean Pouget he established a vigilance committee which was intended to lead and control the *coup* which everyone saw approaching in Algiers.

The first mass demonstration, in which some 30,000 people participated, occurred on 26 April—a dress rehearsal for the second, on 13 May. Initially both demonstrations converged on the area which had become the traditional site for such gatherings: the war memorial at the top of what is now the Boulevard Khemisti. The momentum increased from one manifestation to the next as emotions rose against a government in Paris which seemed on the point of betraying French Algeria to its Muslim population, or to the Americans, or to the left. The movement was further accelerated by the determination of various groups not to be overtaken in the race, or see their demonstration captured by their rivals. Equally significant was the fact that Lacoste left Algiers for Paris on 10 May, while General Salan wrote formally to General Ély expressing the anxiety of the army for the interests of the Europeans in Algeria, and for those Muslims who had given their support to France. He asked that his letter be brought to the attention of the president, saying: 'The French army would unanimously feel that the surrender of this patrimony is an outrage. One could not predict its desperate reaction.'

On 13 May the second mass demonstration moved from the war memorial to the 'Forum', in front of the Gouvernement-Général. The crowd was of overwhelming size, made up (as any such demonstration is bound to be) of diverse groups; Pierre Lagaillarde's group held, initially, the tactical initiative. It was a demonstration against the government of the Fourth Republic but the demonstrators had no candidate of their own to replace it: their immediate objective was to bring the army to power in Algiers. Civilian power was inadequate to control the crowd, even had the will been present. Since early 1957 the coercive power had been in the hands of the parachutists; and now General Massu was the popular hero of the crowd. Massu, for his part, sympathized with the objectives of the demonstration, although he held some of its leaders in contempt and was not prepared to act for them against the authority of his immediate superior, General Salan.

It was these circumstances which led to the creation, within the Gouvernement-Général, of a committee of public safety, in response to the crowd outside. A half-rebellion had occurred: a communiqué was issued on 14 May stating that General Salan was provisionally taking over civilian and military power; yet Salan remained in telephonic communication with Paris, where Pierre Pflimlin had been invested as prime minister. Order was thus assured in Algiers; but no one had a clear idea of the next moves, except Léon Delbecque and the Gaullists. Overtaking Lagaillarde, Delbecque had secured a place for himself as vice-president of the committee for public safety, a position from which he appears to have been decisive in turning the committee towards de Gaulle and persuading Salan to reply to the crowd's *Vive l'Algérie française* with *Vive de Gaulle* as de Gaulle, in France, expressed his readiness to 'assume the powers of the Republic'. Meanwhile, the Muslim population of Algiers had stayed at home. On 16 May a small number of army officers organized a manifestation by Muslims to demonstrate Muslim loyalty and the possibility of integration. In spite of careful supervision against the possibility of violence as at Sétif, it generated its own mood of genuine fraternization with Europeans. But it was unlikely to carry the day against the quite different policies of the committee of public safety.

The committee, having opened up the line to de Gaulle, had still to maintain its momentum. A diversion was arranged by the arrival in Algiers of Pascal Arrighi, a Gaullist deputy from Corsica, who was prepared to lead a Corsican insurrection in support of Algiers. He received the blessing of the committee and returned to establish a Corsican committee of public safety.

There was an element of comic-opera in the Corsican affair; but it was alarming to the metropolis since it appeared as a prelude to the invasion of France by the paratroopers—an invasion which was indeed in preparation, under the code-name 'Resurrection'. It was forestalled by a tactical move of great skill and masterly ambiguity by de Gaulle who announced on 27 May that he had 'begun the regular process needed to establish a regular government'.

The sequence of events by which de Gaulle came to be appointed prime minister of the Fourth Republic on 1 June 1958 and elected the first President of the Fifth Republic has often been recounted and needs no rehearsal here. The ambivalence of his position has also been made clear: he appeared as the one man able to save France from civil war and to find a solution to the Algerian problem, and yet he had to frame a policy which would keep his authority intact among the European integrationists in Algeria as well as the political parties and formations on whose support he depended constitutionally.

In this situation de Gaulle made use of ambiguity and camouflage in pronouncements concerning Algeria. Initially his policy was to move towards a situation in which Algerians would accept a settlement keeping Algeria closely linked to France, in some ill-defined way—a settlement which required the emergence of a body of moderate men, both Muslim and European, to make it workable. In pursuit of this objective he made clear, from the moment of his first visit to Algeria in June 1958, that he was not the prisoner of those who had set up committees of public safety in Algiers and Oran, while concealing his intentions behind such carefully chosen phrases as *Je vous ai compris*. He re-established civilian government in Algeria in December 1958, appointing Paul Delouvrier as delegate-general. General Salan was replaced by General Challe, an air-force general, in order to remove the political character of the command (some 1,500 officers were retired or transferred from Algeria). Moreover, de Gaulle was confident of Challe's military abilities. In a press conference de Gaulle made an immediate and dramatic appeal to the FLN to lay down their arms in a 'peace o the brave'.

In October 1958 de Gaulle had outlined, at Constantine, a plan for Algerian development, raising wages, distributing land, developing Algerian oil and gas, and setting up 'great metallurgical and chemical complexes' (a plan which, elaborated and partially implemented, was inherited and put into effect by the Algerian Republic).

Assuming the presidency in January 1959, he spoke of 'a pacified and transformed Algeria, developing her own personality in her own way and closely linked with France' having a 'place of choice' in the new French community. Important steps were taken towards the objective of developing an Algerian political and bureaucratic community. Early in 1959 some 7,000 suspects were released from internment camps, 180 persons condemned to death were reprieved, Messali Hadj was allowed to live in a Paris flat, and Ben Bella and his four colleagues were transferred from the Santé prison to the Île d'Aix. A steadily increasing number of Muslims were appointed to administrative posts (the number rising from 21,000 to 37,000 between 1957 and 1960) and to commissions in the army and the reserve (an increase from 198 to 386 and 25 to 244, respectively, in the same period). Local elections were held, bringing in some 11,000 Muslim councillors (figures from Pickles, 1963, p. 66).

However the most decisive development in de Gaulle's policy was his announcement in a broadcast address of 16 September 1959, of 'recourse to self-determination', since 'we can now look forward to the day when the men and women who live in Algeria will be in a position to decide their own destiny'. The choice would be offered to Algerians 'as individuals' and it would be a choice between three possibilities: secession (which 'would carry in its wake the most appalling poverty, frightful political chaos, widespread slaughter, and, soon after, the warlike dictatorship of the communists'); out-and-out identification with France (when the French people would, 'in effect spread from Dunkirk to Tamanrasset'); or a Federal Algeria (French, Arab, Kabyle, Mzabite), governed by Algerians 'backed up by French help and in close relationship with her, as regards the economy, education, defence, and foreign relations'. The promise of a free referendum was followed by an invitation to Algerian representatives to come to Paris, secretly or publicly, to negotiate.

This clear-cut announcement (which was ratified in a referendum on the principle of self-determination in January 1961) inevitably provoked the opposition of those who had contributed to de Gaulle's return to power in the belief that he would follow a single policy of integrating Algeria with France. In January 1960 the dismissal of General Massu (following the latter's interview with a Munich newspaper) sparked off a great demonstration, with the setting up of barricades in Algiers; in April 1961 a more serious plot among senior officers, involving Generals Challe, Zeller, Jouhaud, and Salan, sought to repeat the experience of May 1958 and halt the progress towards negotiation and an 'Algerian Republic', a phrase which de Gaulle used for the first time on 4 November 1960. De Gaulle's authority and self-confidence were sufficient to crush both challenges, and it became clear how wide the gap had grown between the French in Algeria (including the ultras of the army, but not the conscript soldiers) and those in France.

Meanwhile two distinct developments were taking place among the Algerian combatants. On the military side, the success of the French in the conduct of the war steadily increased the importance of the Algerian armies on the frontiers. Soon after the formation of the second CCE a Military Operations Command was established with two branches, eastern and western—the former at Ghardimaou in Tunisia and the latter at Oujda in Morocco; subsequently the two were combined in a single État Major Général. Meanwhile in September 1958 the second CCE was dissolved and a provisional government of the Algerian republic (GPRA) established. These developments greatly increased the institutional strength of the revolution; but they also produced a triangular conflict between the GPRA, the internal forces, and the army of the frontiers.

The provisional government made a fine display of wide-ranging consensus. The president was Ferhat Abbas, with Ben Bella and Krim Belkacem as vice-presidents; the old centralists of the MTLD were represented by Ben Khedda and Mohamed Yazid, and the UDMA (Ferhat Abbas's party) by Ahmed Francis. Even the Ulema's Association was given a place, since El-Madani Tawfik was included.

The creation of the government opened a new front in international politics where its representatives were able to advance with talent and skill, without revealing the dissensions and conflicts in their own movement. The GPRA secured diplomatic recognition from the Arab states and then from those states sympathetic to the Algerian cause or willing to earn some political capital from appearing so. It aroused the covert opposition of Nasser's government, because of its independence; but this made more cordial the welcome given by Bourguiba, so that the GPRA established itself in Tunis.

Since 1955 the FLN had run an information office in New York headed by Mohamed Yazid; in September 1955 the UN General Assembly first agreed to put the Algerian question on its agenda. The recognition of the GPRA, particularly by the increased number of

African and Asian members, strengthened its hand, which was played with great skill by Abdelkader Chanderli, who proved singularly adept at diplomatic initiatives as well as public relations. Mohamed Yazid, meanwhile, had become minister of information in the GPRA. In December 1958 the French delegate walked out of the political committee in protest and a General Assembly resolution recognizing the right of the Algerian people to independence failed by only one vote to win the necessary two-thirds majority.

The conflicts within the leadership went through a new phase in a long series of meetings in a house in the rue Parmentier in Tunis, from October 1959 to January 1960. The meetings resulted from the initiative of Krim Belkacem, whose animosity towards the provisional government was only increased by the growing effectiveness of the French offensive against the forces of the interior. It was his intention to impose the supremacy of interior military leaders in the determination of a single military and political strategy, by setting up a new national council of the Algerian revolution to supersede the provisional government.

The attempt failed; the alliance of the 'three Bs' who shared complicity in the execution of Abane Ramdane (Boussouf, Ben Tobbal, and Krim Belkacem) showed no cohesion and Krim, who held the post of minister of armed forces in the first provisional government became minister of foreign affairs—a change which he accepted with as much grace as he could command. Ferhat Abbas remained at the head of the newly constructed provisional government, in spite of Krim's offensive against him; but El-Madani Tawfik became ambassador to Cairo and Ben Khedda was appointed a roving ambassador. Lamine Debaghine, who was suffering from a nervous depression, was removed from office.

Krim devoted characteristic energy to the conduct of the provisional government's foreign relations from the ministry's office in Cairo (while government remained in Tunis). New ambassadors were appointed, including Benhabyles (who was to become director-general of the foreign ministry after Independence) to Japan and Lakhdar Brahimi (subsequently ambassador to Cairo and then to London) to Indonesia. Chanderli remained at the UN. A diplomatic mission was undertaken to a number of foreign capitals, including Moscow (which had not recognized the GPRA) and Peking, where the warmth of the welcome and the promise of aid confirmed the support given to an earlier mission in 1958. A major contribution was added to the growing diplomatic success of the revolution, compensating for its military losses.

But in internal politics the most important outcome of the rue Parmentier meetings was the enhanced position of Boumediene. His prestige and authority had grown since the spring of 1959, when he had presided over a tribunal which condemned to death a Colonel Lamouri and his principal colleagues for having attempted an abortive *coup* against the GPRA from their base in Tunisia; and he had established a reputation for his effectiveness in organizing the army of the frontiers. He was now given command over the État-Major Général. His erstwhile superior officer, Boussouf, remained minister for armament and communications in the GPRA, and Boumediene was free to exploit the independent power which his command gave him.

The armies which Boumediene helped construct made a major contribution to military operations without being engaged in the murderous guerrilla activities of the interior. By crossing the fortified line which the French had built down the Tunisian frontier, whenever conditions allowed, they kept a massive French force tied down. From Morocco the Algerians were able to listen in to French radio communications and so guide guerrilla operations across the frontier to maximum effect. At the same time, Boumediene was able to appoint officers who were loyal to him, and who shared his belief that the political future of Algeria should take a socialist direction, and that this was no less important than military victory.

It was against this background that the first abortive contacts between French and Algerians took place. Early in 1960 the success of Challe's campaign had so demoralized some of the guerrillas that they were prepared to enter into peace discussions. Contact was established between three leaders, known as Si Salah, Si Mohamed, and Si Lakhdar, and the French through the intermediary of a caïd of Médéa. By the end of March a tacit cease-fire agreement had been worked out and at the beginning of June the three leaders of *wilaya* 4 (surrounding Algiers) were brought to Rambouillet, where they met de Gaulle. Together they discussed plans which would have led to a progressive laying down of arms, the combatants being allowed to return home unmolested or join the French army. The leaders returned to Algeria, and in a speech of 14 June 1960 de Gaulle renewed his appeal to 'the leaders of the insurrection'. 'We are waiting for them here,' he said, 'in order to seek with them an honorable end to the fighting that is still going on. . . . After which, everything will be done so that the Algerian people may express their views in a calm atmosphere. The decision shall be theirs alone.' The plan misfired. When the three returned to Algeria not only were they unable to persuade their fellow combatants, but one of them, Si Mohamed, changed his mind. Si Lakhdar was then executed; Si Salah was to have been tried at Tunis but was killed in battle with the French, as was Si Mohamed, in August 1961.

Meanwhile de Gaulle's speech of 14 June had brought a response. From Tunis, within hours of the speech, had come an announcement that the provisional government was prepared to negotiate a meeting between a delegation presided over by Ferhat Abbas and de Gaulle. At the end of the month the preliminary party, led by a Maître Boumendjel was brought to Melun. But the meeting proved abortive.

The Algerians sought to arrange a meeting which would imply a virtual recognition by de Gaulle of the provisional government; Ferhat Abbas was to be free to hold press conferences, establish contact with foreign embassies, and concert with Ben Bella and his fellow prisoners on the Île d'Aix. For de Gaulle the proposal went too far and offered too little. The meeting was brought to an end after four days.

The final sequence of negotiations opened in Evian in May 1961—the site being chosen so that the Algerian delegates could enjoy the security of the Swiss frontier. By that time the balance of forces had changed. De Gaulle's suppression of the colonels' revolt had shown that he had won and would keep authority to negotiate self-determination; the acceptance of the referendum on self-determination showed the support of the French people for his policy. At the same time, the European population of Algeria had forfeited its claim to special consideration in the negotiations. Those, who in the early days of the revolt, had tried to keep lines of communication open with the Muslim community were now overwhelmed in the violent resistance of the Organisation de l'Armée Secrète.[1] On the Algerian side, the power of the Oujda group had steadily increased.

But the first round of negotiations at Evian was inconclusive. De Gaulle still hoped at this stage to retain control over the Sahara and its reserves of oil. Its importance for French policy was considerable. It would increase French independence vis-à-vis the major oil companies and it would enhance French influence in Africa. De Gaulle argued that the Sahara had only been brought into Algeria for the administrative convenience of France, and that the oil should be shared with the African countries. By himself, Krim Belkacem might have reached agreement with the French but the purists of the nationalist movement, Boumediene chief among them, were less prepared to compromise. For them, the Sahara was an integral part of Algerian territory, the oil was part of the heritage of Algeria, and the French community an alien people whose departure they would welcome. But although the talks of 1961 were broken off they were not abandoned. It had become less essential for de Gaulle to settle Algeria so that France could play the part he envisaged in the world; while the FLN were within sight of independence.

Inevitably the negotiations sharpened the division within the FLN camp. But at a series of meetings at Tripoli, Mohammedia (outside Rabat), and at the château d'Aulnoy, where the French allowed the participation of Ben Bella, and again at Tripoli a semblance of unity was maintained. Limited concessions were made to the intransigent position of the État Major: the GPRA was once again remodelled, at

[1] Even though, in the last moment before Independence, Krim and the OAS leader, Jean-Jacques Susini, signed an agreement of mutual amnesty.

the national council meeting at Tripoli in August 1961, and Ben Khedda replaced Ferhat Abbas as president.

Finally, however, the successful outcome of the negotiations was assured by the activity of the Europeans in Algeria and the rebellious army officers—Salan, Godard, and others—who had formed the OAS and set up a Council of National Resistance under Georges Bidault. Their objective was to render life in Algiers impossible and to prevent an agreement with the FLN by creating havoc and disorder. The effect was the opposite. They eliminated one possible obstacle to a settlement; had the Europeans without the OAS made a bid to stay in Algeria with political rights as a community, dissension on the Algerian side would have been much greater and an agreement more difficult.

The Evian talks were resumed in March 1962. The État Major maintained its criticism of the GPRA and the negotiators at Evian to the end, contesting the clauses concerning French rights and the surrender of oil revenue. The fact remained that the objectives of the revolution had been achieved and Krim could challenge his critics to show how they would expel the French army. Failure to agree at Evian would prolong OAS violence and leave de Gaulle no option but to appoint an Algerian government of his own nomination backed by the French army. But although Krim Belkacem's arguments carried the day, he alone signed the Evian agreements on 18 March 1962.

The essence of the Evian agreements was to open the way to the complete independence of Algeria by means of a referendum, and to offer continued cooperation with France. There was to be an immediate cease-fire, and safeguards for the interim period up to the referendum, which produced the expected overwhelming majority in favour of independence on 8 April 1962. Thereafter Algeria took control of its own affairs, including foreign policy and defence. The rights of the French were safeguarded (they could retain French citizenship and enjoy full Algerian civic rights for a transition period of three years, when they must choose between French and Algerian citizenship) as if a large number was expected to remain in Algeria, but without their being accorded special protection as a community within the Algerian state.

France accorded to Algeria a privileged financial position, with a promise of continued economic and technical assistance. In return, Algeria confirmed all the rights given by the French government for the development and transport of Algerian oil, and set up a joint enterprise, with parity between France and Algeria, for further exploration. All French troops were to be withdrawn, but France retained the use of the Mers el-Kebir base for fifteen years, as well as certain air bases. (Withdrawal from Mers el-Kebir was in fact completed in January 1968.)

The French government thus saw a long, costly, and emotional war brought to an end. Free from the burden of Algeria, de Gaulle could endeavour to restore France to its position of greatness in Europe and the world, while at the same time attaching great importance to co-operation with Algeria—an area of foreign policy which continued to occupy the president's close personal attention. On the Algerian side Ben Khedda, as president of the GPRA, welcomed the agreements in that they conceded four points of major importance: the territorial integrity of Algeria, without any 'amputation' of the Sahara; independence, including defence and foreign policy; the unity of the Algerian people, without any 'community' structure; and recognition of the GPRA as the only representative of the Algerian people.

As a spokesman for the FLN Ben Khedda had reason to be pleased, even though his personal future was limited. The success of the FLN inside Algeria was not solely in military action against the French. It had engaged in constant political activity to break down the influence of Messali's following, which never succeeded in creating a military force but retained the allegiance of Algerians, especially in the towns. It also combated the attempts of the French to win a significant show of political support, by discouraging participation in elections and by mobilizing crowds in order to demonstrate its control and authenticate its claim to be the sole representative of the Algerian people. Little has so far been written of this aspect of the war and the Algerian government has had little incentive to conduct research into events which are inconsistent with the myth of national unity and popular uprising. Some glimpses are to be found in the published diary of Mouloud Feraoun.

The successful outcome of the war thus constituted a major political victory for the FLN. Its troops inside Algeria had ceased to be an effective fighting force, even though they retained the potentiality of hardened guerrilla units. They numbered some 6,000 to 7,000 men, harassed by the French, their *wilaya* units cut off from each other and with little incentive to fight once the process of negotiation had begun. The armies on the frontiers were more important, being a force of some 40,000. But the whole Algerian army was outnumbered by the Algerians who had continued to serve with the French. These men, of whom there were some 80,000, sought the best future they could find as the war ended. Some were murdered; others were able to return to their villages and were absorbed back into the community. A large number went to France and lived in camps until they could find a way out, with minimal help from the French government. In 1975 their children, returning to Algeria, ran the risk of being detained by the Algerian government.

Political Developments, 1962–75

The successful outcome of the war brought great prestige to Algeria, giving it a heroic stature which it was soon to share with Castro's Cuba.

But it had little else. The provisional government had effectively pressed the Algerian case in foreign capitals and at the United Nations, but its legitimacy was not accepted and it had no territorial base, in the sense of areas liberated in the course of the war, from which to operate.

Nor did the nationalist movement develop any coherent ideology or body of political ideas. The conditions of French rule had not encouraged the growth of a large intelligentsia, and the circumstances of the war had given little place to the development of ideas. The most thoughtful class of Algerians was the product of the French system of education—they were schoolmasters, or sons of schoolmasters, who were responsive to the ideals of French radical socialism and would have sought a freethinking, anticlerical new state. But too often they found themselves intermediaries between France, to which they owed much in terms of education and freedom of mind, and Algeria, which they recognized as their own country. Boumediene regarded political education as an integral part of the military effort; but the impact of his ideas was necessarily limited. In general, internal divisions and rivalries within the nationalist movement were too great and the struggle for independence too hazardous for a political consensus to emerge.

The struggle for power which had characterized the war years continued after Independence. The three obvious contestants for power were the provisional government, the *wilaya* commands, and the army of the frontiers. However, a dramatic change had occurred in the provisional government as a result of the release of Ben Bella. He was no longer forced, by his imprisonment, to be a sleeping partner. Instead he enjoyed the prestige which stemmed from his early leadership of the revolution and he was eager to regain primacy in the movement. At the same time the exhausted *wilaya* armies were unlikely to be a match for those of the frontiers. The result was that in a surprisingly short time many wartime leaders, in the interior army and the provisional government, were eclipsed as Ben Bella and Boumediene rose to pre-eminence.

The first round in the post-war struggle was fought at the Tripoli congress of May 1962. Its purpose was to determine a programme for the future and to elect a political bureau. The congress succeeded in voting a Tripoli charter, which committed Algeria to a socialist plan for the future. But the charter also condemned the wartime provisional government for its failure 'to keep feudalism out of certain levels of its own organization'. This constituted a victory for Ben Bella and his following. They also proposed a list of members of the political bureau; but this was not brought to the vote.

The competing factions then returned to Algeria. Significantly Ben Bella entered the country from Morocco, via Tlemsen—the area of his childhood and the region where Boumediene was strongest. His opponents, under Ben Khedda's leadership, established themselves at Tizi-Ouzou. But Ben Bella and his group kept the initiative. On 22 July they published the Tripoli charter for the first time; and they announced that the political bureau which they had proposed at Tripoli would take office.

Their initiative had the support of Boumediene and the army of the frontiers, moving towards Algiers. The Tizi-Ouzou group capitulated —although the commanders of the *wilayas* furthest from the frontiers (Kabylia, Northern Constantinois, and Algiers) did not. Only after severe fighting did Boumediene enter Algiers, on 9 September, thus making possible the holding of elections to a national assembly and the constitution of Ben Bella's first government.

Ben Bella had thus established a substantial lead over his opponents because he was supported by Boumediene, who had the strongest command over the army. His claim to leadership was naturally contested by those who had been able to play a more active role in the nationalist struggle. Lacking adequate political authority he constructed, as the best substitute, a series of alliances. In this way he retained his pre-eminence in civilian government, while the armed force of the state remained under Boumediene's control.

Meanwhile legislation was passed in the form of decrees, and administration was more or less effectively carried out by the bureaucratic machinery constructed by the French. In these circumstances the decree laws affecting the economy—notably the March decrees (1963) establishing self-management in agriculture and industry and the nationalization of property—were issued as moves in the struggle for power, but they none the less had an important effect on the development of the country's economy.

The first casualties in the civilian struggle for power were Ferhat Abbas and Mohamed Khider. In keeping with his earlier political career Ferhat Abbas took his stand on the rights of the national assembly, of which he was president, and argued against the dominance of the party and the 'Marxist–Leninist socialism' of Ben Bella. He resigned from his presidency on 12 August 1963 and thereby sacrificed the limited political power he enjoyed. He was arrested in 1964, held in confinement in the south of the country, released in 1965 as Ben Bella sought to strengthen his hand against Boumediene, and now lives in retirement from politics.

Mohamed Khider's battle, in contrast, was within the party. He had shared capture in 1956 with Ben Bella, and sided with him in 1962. Then as secretary-general of the party he urged the pre-eminent rights of the party, as a mass organization, in the government of the country, while seeking to build up his following among party officials and planning a party congress without reference to Ben Bella. But in April 1963 he appears to have decided that Ben Bella's followers were more numerous than his own, and resigned. Ben Bella was immediately, if irregularly, elected to succeed him. Two months later Khider left for Switzerland and arranged for the transfer of party funds, amounting to twelve million dollars, from Lebanon to Switzerland—funds which had been collected during the war and were under his personal control. In spite of this he was able to return to Algiers during the remainder of 1963. He then moved back to Europe to undertake the organization and financing of opposition to Ben Bella. He was tried in absentia and condemned to death in April 1965. He was assassinated in Madrid in January 1967.

Other opponents of Ben Bella and Boumediene were more important, since they commanded military force, or were allied to military commanders, and had a territorial base. Mohamed Boudiaf was allied with the Kabyles Colonel Mohand ou el-Hadj and Krim Belkacem in an opposition group calling itself the Union pour la Défense de la Révolution Socialiste. Their plan to overthrow Ben Bella was discovered, and Boudiaf was imprisoned. This did not end Kabyle opposition, in which Aït Ahmed, Mohand, and Krim Belkacem were the leading figures. Together they formed a new movement, the Front des Forces Socialistes. But they did not hold together. Partly because a frontier clash with Morocco could be represented as a national challenge, Ben Bella was able to negotiate an agreement with Colonel Mohand (who was nominated to the political bureau in April 1964), thus splitting a movement that was in any case only loosely tied together. Aït Ahmed continued to lead an armed insurrection in Kabylia, while at the same time Colonel Chaabani opened a separate revolt in the area of his command on the edge of the Sahara. Both of these movements had been mastered by the army by the autumn of 1964. However, Boudiaf's Parti de la révolution socialiste survived as a refugee opposition group in Europe.

Throughout this period Ben Bella held the limelight; he occupied the leading positions in the government and party, toured the country, made speeches, travelled abroad, and attracted attention as the ruler of a prestigious new state. The fact remained that he owed his position, initially, to the army, and that the successful action which had been taken against the opposition strengthened the army, without any corresponding reinforcement of the civilian institutions of the state.

Boumediene was intent on building the army into an effective, modern, and united force. Subsequently he was proud to say—and justified in saying—that the Algerian army was not an army 'confined to its barracks' but one which had an active social role to play. First, however, it had to be brought under sound military organization and discipline and officered by men skilled in modern military science, rather than by guerrilla leaders, however much their bravery and resilience might compensate for lack of education. Boumediene therefore abolished the *wilaya* commands of the war and reorganized the army into military regions. As he did so he was called on to combat the forces of Aït Ahmed and Chaabani, and his success strengthened the army further.

Moreover the alliance between Ben Bella and Boumediene had given the latter important positions of strength within the government. Boumediene was himself minister of defence; Ahmed Medeghri, who had been a major in his command, was minister of the interior in the governments of 1962 and 1963. Abdelaziz Bouteflika was at first given a minor post in the 1962 government but then became foreign minister (the first holder of the office, Mohamed Khemisti, had been shot and killed in the street by an unbalanced youth without political motives). Cherif Belkacem, who was at the head of the western command at the end of the war became minister of orientation and education in the 1963 government and Ahmed Kaïd was made minister of tourism.

Ben Bella's team in these governments held the economic ministries: Ali Mahsas was minister of agriculture, Bachir Boumaza was minister of national economy, and Mohamed Nekkache was minister of social affairs. The minister of justice, Hadj Smain, was also one of Ben Bella's men. Ahmed Francis, Ben Bella's brother-in-law joined the first government; so did Rabah Bitat, although he broke with the second government immediately after it was formed.

The public evidence is that Ben Bella moved, in the second half of 1964, to reduce the influence of Boumediene and that Boumediene had no choice but to react or see his own power decisively curtailed. Ben Bella took over the appointment of prefects from Medeghri, and accepted the resignation which Medeghri offered as a result. He remodelled his government in December 1964, demoting Cherif Belkacem and dismissing Ahmed Kaïd altogether. He strengthened his alliance with the Algerian communist party and with the trade union organization, as if making sure of his allies on the left before moving against the army, while at the same time insisting that he had no intention of turning Algeria into a Muslim state.

In response to these moves Boumediene and a small handful of close supporters—Abdelaziz Bouteflika, Ahmed Kaïd, Cherif Belkacem, Ahmed Medeghri, and Taher Zbiri—carried out their *coup* in the early hours of 19 June 1965, on the eve of the Afro-Asian conference which was to meet at the newly built Club des Pins, on the coast just outside Algiers. It was a peaceful *coup*; Ben Bella was woken, and was arrested. There was no opposition from within the army, and Boumediene had the support of Major Ahmed Draia, commanding the Compagnie Nationale de Sécurité and of Major Mahmoud Guennez, controlling the people's militia.

There is no way of knowing whether Boumediene would have so

acted had he not been alarmed by the moves which Ben Bella had made against his supporters. He was in almost every respect different from Ben Bella. He was much closer to the native soil of Arab North Africa. He had less French education than Ben Bella, who spoke French more readily than Arabic. Born in 1932, he was due to serve with the French army after the Second World War, but when he was conscripted he sought refuge in Tunis, then enrolled at Al-Azhar University in Cairo. He was nationalist and conservative in social and cultural matters, while Ben Bella was open to foreign influence and sought importance in the Afro-Asian world.

Ben Bella must have seen the possibility of a *coup* from Boumediene but he clearly did not suspect any immediate danger. By this time he probably exaggerated his own popularity. Nothing the government had done since 1962 had served to improve conditions of life for the ordinary people. Government action had at best laid the basis for future growth, and had often been motivated by political rivalry rather than constructive intention. But Ben Bella was still greeted by enthusiastic crowds when he travelled outside Algiers, and he interpreted this as a demonstration of popular support for himself and the work of his government rather than natural enthusiasm for the success of the War of Independence.

Since his regime was established by *coup d'état* in June 1965, Boumediene has modified his public style. Having taken power, he remained a recluse. His initial speech was broadcast over radio and on television, but without any picture, the screens remaining intentionally blank. He was scarcely seen in public. Subsequently he began to take part in public occasions. In 1972 it was noticeable that he had begun to smile in public and to act in an informal manner—a change which occurred when Fidel Castro visited Algeria, and when Boumediene had undergone dental surgery at the hands of a French dentist. None the less he remained a mysterious figure. It was not known whether he was married. It was believed that he led a relatively pure and simple personal life; certainly he was free of the ostentation which characterizes many political leaders. Whether he actually prefers seclusion or whether he deliberately cultivates a sense of mystery is unknowable. He continues to give evidence of being a far-sighted and hard man.

Taking power, he was not popular, nor was his regime. Conservatives who looked to the security of Islam as a brake against the onslaught of communism welcomed his *coup*. The communist party, which Ben Bella had manipulated successfully—accepting its support when there was little risk of its making a bid for power—saw its future in danger. Youth organizations—the students' union and the youth organization of the FLN—demonstrated in the streets, supported by the communist party, and thus created the only vigorous opposition to the new order which had to be forcibly suppressed. Boumediene's was a nationalist appeal; but it was a nationalism without glamour, which meant little to the mass of the population and less than nothing to those youthful enthusiasts who saw the governments of the Third World decide to adjourn *sine die* the Afro-Asian conference which Ben Bella had prepared. Only later did national self-assertion begin to have an important positive appeal: in the stand which Boumediene took over the war in the Middle East in June 1967; in the 'battle for oil' in 1971; and in a renewed bid for Third World leadership.

In the first years of the new regime Boumediene was obliged, as Ben Bella had been before him, to consolidate his power. None the less, over the years which followed the *coup*, the regime showed a remarkable degree of stability and continuity, even when allowance is made for attempts against it. This stability was in part the result of the development of the army and the security forces. But it owed much also to the close cohesion of Boumediene's closest colleagues, who were known as the Oujda group. There was much similarity in the geographical and social origins of this group—although in the latter respect they differed sharply from Boumediene. Abdelaziz Bouteflika (from Tlemsen), Ahmed Kaïd (from Tiaret), Cherif Belkacem, who grew up in Morocco, Ahmed Medeghri (from Saïda), and Tayebi Larbi (from Sidi-bel-Abbès, the headquarters of the foreign legion), all came from the west of the country. They all sprang from middle class or well-to-do urban families. The family of Ahmed Kaïd owned considerable estates as a result of their position as caïds and Ahmed Medeghri was related by marriage to the wealthy Othmani family. Unlike Boumediene, they were all educated in French schools. All of them joined the nationalist movement during the Algerian war, and only Ahmed Kaïd had joined the FLN in 1954. They represented a new generation (Bouteflika joined the FLN as a result of his participation, at the age of nineteen, in the student strike of 1956) and had little in common with the now legendary 'chefs historiques' of the revolution.

Those who had lost in the struggle for power constituted a number of opposition groups with impressive names: the Mouvement Démocratique du Renouveau Algérien, which Krim Belkacem founded in October 1967; the Front des Forces Socialistes of Aït Ahmed. A left-wing organization called the Organisation de la Résistance Populaire was formed by Mohamed Harbi, Boualem Makhouf, and Hocine Zahouane, together with the former communist Bachir Hadj Ali, but it was sufficiently harassed for the minister of information, Bachir Boumaza, to declare that it was 'completely dismantled' in September 1965. However, in October 1966, Bachir Boumaza was dismissed, in the company of Ali Mahsas and Hadj Smain (all close colleagues of Ben Bella), and went to Europe to found the Organisation Clandestine de la Révolution Algérienne.

But these opposition groups formed no common front and had no effective means of action in Europe. The opposition in Algeria was contained by the coercive forces of the state, carrying out arrests and sometimes trials, about which very little information was available. On the other hand, four of the participants in the Kabylia rebellion of 1963–4 were pardoned and released from prison. They included Mohamed Ben Ahmed, known as Major Si Moussa, who had been sent as an emissary to Kabylia by Boumediene without Ben Bella's knowledge. The opposition was further weakened when Mohamed Khider was assassinated.[1] Krim Belkacem, who had been condemned to death in absentia, was assassinated in Frankfurt in October 1970.

To some extent these conflicts resembled the personal and tribal rivalries which had dominated Algerian politics during and immediately after the War of Independence. But the outcome was the establishment of a distinctive alliance and an important choice of objectives. While political power was concentrated in the hands of Boumediene and his supporters, the choice for economic development was one of efficient, capital-intensive modernization under the direction of effective economic managers such as Belaïd Abdesselam as minister of economy, Smaïl Mahroug as minister of finance, and Ahmed Ghozali at the head of Sonatrach. The populist programme of self-management was allowed to atrophy and no radical redistribution of wealth was put into effect. On the contrary a state bourgeoisie enjoying privilege as well as wealth quickly established itself. In theory, this class was 'open to the talents' and the government was anxious to educate skilled managers: in practice the way to the top was inevitably easier for those who started with an educational advantage, which in turn depended on social class.

Obviously, the Algerian élite had come far since the beginning of the war. The army, the security services, and the bureaucracy were parts of a state apparatus which bore no resemblance either to terrorism or to the guerrilla tactics of the maquis, while none of the powerful economic administrators had participated in the Algerian nationalist movement. (Rabah Bitat's membership of the Council of Revolution therefore constituted an important, though nominal, link with the past.) The distinctive quality of Boumediene is the more striking. He had created an Algerian order without belonging to it—a society in which his army played a central part but one in which his sense of obligation to the North African peasant class from which he had sprung remained unfulfilled.

There was relatively little opportunity for the accumulation of private wealth in the modern industrial sector of the economy, but it

---

[1] The Algerian government fought a series of court actions to recover the FLN funds which he had taken with him, but, in 1974, the Swiss court ruled against them on the grounds that the only contract was between Khider and his bank.

was possible to add an administrator's income and perquisites to ownership of land. It was not possible to purchase freedom, since the perquisites of office—house, car, servants, and travel—constituted a tied cottage on a grand scale, but the distance between such a person and the *fellah* was immense.

From 1971 Boumediene initiated a new turn in Algerian policy. It included the nationalization of the oil industry—a bold venture of national self-assertion but one which continued the existing direction of powerful state industrial organizations. In contrast, land reform, and the populist manner in which it was carried out, including the mobilization of student activists, represented a more radical development of the regime which appeared to run counter to the interests of those enjoying power and position. At the same time the Oujda group broke up. Ahmed Kaïd was relieved of his post at the head of the party; Ahmed Medeghri was killed in a car accident which, rumour said, was contrived because of his ill-health and his differences with Boumediene. In straitened economic circumstances the political stability of the regime came increasingly under strain.

The Structure of Government

The consolidation of power meant the strengthening of the existing institutions of government. Boumediene had no interest in reviving a parliamentary assembly at this stage. His strategy was to construct a political system from the base, developing popular institutions locally and regionally as a prelude to the establishment of national institutions. Without this process of political education, an assembly would only be a parody, a western institution with no roots in the political life of the country.

In accordance with this strategy, communal assemblies were set up by a decree of January 1967, and came into existence as a result of elections held the following month; *wilaya* assemblies were set up in May 1969. Both have subsequently been renewed: the Assemblées Populaires Communales by elections held in February 1971 and the Assemblées Populaires de *Wilaya* in May 1974.

Although the language of the decrees establishing the assemblies and the propaganda surrounding the elections include the best phrases of Algerian politics, the institutions themselves bear a strong resemblance to French local government, except that they lack political life. The communes are similar to French communes, the *wilayas* to French departments—indeed, until 1974, the *wilaya* divisions corresponded very closely to those inherited from the French, with the addition of two Saharan *wilayas*, until an administrative reform in July 1974 increased the number of *wilayas* from fifteen to thirty-one. The assemblies elect executive committees, rather than a single mayor or president.

The closest similarity is in the system of *tutelle* which is exercised by the prefect or *wali*. The decree establishing the *wilaya* assemblies defines the *wilaya* as having political, economic, social, and cultural functions and, at the same time, being an administrative constituency of the state. 'The *wilaya* is administered by a popular assembly elected by universal suffrage and by an executive nominated by the government under the direction of the *wali*.' Thus, while the Assemblées Populaires de *Wilaya* discuss the budget, regional planning, agrarian reform, and a wide range of other questions, they do so within a framework determined by the central government and administered by the prefect. The same is true of the Assemblées Populaires Communales, although the enlarged versions of these have played some part in the programme of agrarian reform. To the control of a French style *tutelle administrative* there is added, in the Algerian case, the presence of the army, which has supervisory roles through a hierarchy of military districts paralleling the civilian administration, while at the same time a number of civilian posts are held by army officers.

Thus, although elections have been held and an increasing number of electors have voted in elections (78·27 per cent in the *wilaya* elections of 1974), there are many obstacles to the growth of political life through the assemblies. The elections permit choice between candidates, all of whom are nominated by the FLN—there being, systematically, twice as many candidates as seats to be filled. There is no competition between parties. Nor do candidates engage in an electoral contest, since campaigning is the work of members of the Conseil de la Révolution, ministers, and notables of the FLN and the trade union organization.

Moreover, the FLN has consistently disappointed the hopes of those who expected it to play a part in stimulating political activity or in the 'mobilization of the masses'. There is no lack of slogans to describe the role which the FLN is expected to play in the politics and development of the country, although the grandiloquence of the rhetoric inevitably makes it suspect.

The party being the organized formation of the sovereignty of the people and the reflective expression of its sentiments and aspirations is the central and directing institution of the revolution. By reason of its historical significance, its popular, political and ideological content, its structure, its mission which is limited neither in time nor space, and by the fact that it safeguards objectives to be realized, it represents authority and the revolution at one and the same time.[1]

In practice, the party has atrophied. The heavy hands of the state and the army have not allowed it any independent political activity. It is unattractive to young people with an educated and intelligent

---
[1] Ahmed Kaïd, 'Aspects essentiels de la révolution culturelle', interview with *Révolution africaine*, issued by the Département de l'Orientation et Information du Parti, Algiers, 1971, p. 21.

interest in politics, since they are required, as members, to be more conformist than non-members are. They see no attraction in stifling their natural readiness to talk among themselves, in small groups bound by family, local, or even political ties, and to adopt instead the party line.

The party may serve as a springboard for some ambitious men in pursuit of power; but it is not the obvious or only route to the top. The state, the army, and the national companies offer far greater rewards and do not call for party adherence, while the more political networks follow a clan system of personal patronage independent of the party. The party has not grafted itself on to existing patterns of local leadership as in Tunisia; nor has it developed spoils and rewards for its humbler adherents.

There have been frequent attempts to bring the party to life. Ahmed Kaïd tried to make 1968 a 'year of the party' and to carry out a renewal of its personnel. On 1 November 1972, Boumediene spoke of the necessity for the party to fulfil its mission as the 'moteur révolutionnaire efficient et dynamique'. The same theme was repeated in 1974 when Boumediene visited the *wilaya* of Constantine and emphasized his objective to 'Faire du parti un instrument de contrôle à la hauteur des exigences de la révolution'. But the enduring obstacles to a revitalization of the party were at this time enhanced by the atmosphere of uncertainty about political change which pervaded the summer months of 1974.

Whatever the shortcomings of the FLN, it has retained such a dominant position that no national organization, whether it be the union of students or the union of Algerian women, has enjoyed an independent role. The most resistant organization is that of the trade unions, the Union Générale des Travailleurs Algériens (UGTA). It was founded in February 1955 in order to secure independence from the French and the communists. None the less, the vigour which the trade union movement retained derived from traditional militancy, which was strongest among railway workers.

The UGTA never had the opportunity to take industrial action or press wage demands. Its role was at best to act as a channel of communication for workers' grievances; more often it was an ancillary instrument for the government in running the economy and, in any case, it had no autonomous role outside the state and party. In spite of this, it retained considerable life of its own, and with the added impetus which the state seemed to be giving to the development of socialism, it appeared at its fourth congress, in April 1973, to be entering on a new role.

Like its predecessors, the fourth UGTA congress was organized under the supervision of Cherif Belkacem, representing the party, and Said Mazouzi, minister of labour and social affairs. None the less, as one experienced observer of Algeria reported, it was possible that the congress represented a turning-point in the history of the organization.[1] It was, for the first time, held in public; the reports from *wilayas* were alert and critical; the average age was thirty-two. Of seventy-five members of the new executive committee, only thirty-nine were incumbents (for the first time four seats were reserved for women), and the smaller secretariat of eleven members included five newcomers. The secretary-general, Abdelkader Benikous, was re-elected but a new post of assistant secretary-general was created, to which Aziz Abdelmagid, a railway worker, son of a *fellah* from the Aurès, was elected.

The obvious opportunity open to the UGTA derived from the importance attached, in the course of 1971, to worker participation in management which, together with agrarian reform and the cultural revolution was to shape the new Algeria. The participants at the congress showed their readiness to engage in such activity and to take a more active part in building a socialist state. The *wilaya* of Blida provided a picturesque metaphor of the role of the UGTA when it reported:

The entrepreneur who directs the working masses (who have elected him to this management) keeps in view the realization of the objectives and has, as one of his duties, to point out irritating consequences, errors, overloading, if there are any in order to allow the architect to restudy his plans and find the necessary variations following the suggestions of the working masses.

There remained, however, many obstacles in the way of achieving this objective. The political problem of the activity of an independent or autonomous trade union movement remained unresolved; participation in trade unions remained relatively low; and the organization had totally inadequate resources of its own for the education and training of men who might participate in management. Finally, the ministers, Abdesselam chief among them, who gave priority to the technically efficient development of industry, were in the ascendant, and there was no evidence that worker participation commended itself to the management of the national companies.

THE ECONOMY

Economic Strategy

The economy of Algeria is a matter of politics, even more than that of most countries. This is only partly the result of deliberate decisions to bring the economy within the direction of the state; geography and history combine to give the economy its political character. Geographically and historically close to France, yet endowed with a natural

[1] Nicole Grimaud, on whose article the following passage is based; *Maghreb*, no. 57, May–June 1973, pp. 26, 30.

resource (oil and gas) which opens up possibilities of world-wide trade, and with a major part of its population living on the land, in conditions deeply affected by French colonization, Algeria has no choice but to take political decisions affecting the economy, while the growth of the economy in turn affects its social structure and its political stance.

The range of the economy can be seen as stretching from the oil and gas industry to subsistence (or less than subsistence) agriculture. The oil and gas industry is modern—the technology of gas liquefaction has been developed since Independence—and requires highly developed skill in manufacturing, marketing, and finance. It will remain extremely remunerative until, at some time in the foreseeable future, supplies are exhausted. Agriculture has only been modernized to a limited extent in the most fertile areas, has not developed agricultural marketing or financial skills to any large degree, and occupies, or fails to occupy, a population which has an alarmingly high birth rate.

Geographically Algeria's obvious trading partners are the countries of western Europe. In spite of the long delays which impeded the conclusion of a revised agreement between Algeria and the EEC, in 1972 the Community absorbed 58 per cent of Algeria's exports and provided 61 per cent of its imports. But while oil and gas could be sold anywhere in the world (accounting for 93 per cent of exports in 1974) other Algerian products did not find an easy market in competition with the developed industrial and agricultural products of Europe, in spite of geographical proximity.

It was the more important, therefore, that in January 1976 agreement was at last reached with the European Community. It followed delays consequent on EEC insistence that Algeria should not discriminate against European firms and governments trading with Israel. Algeria finally accepted a non-discrimination clause, in a compromise formula subordinating it to 'considerations of national security'. The agreements, like those signed at Lomé the previous year, provided for substantial financial aid ($120 million over five years). Tariffs on agricultural products were reduced. The major beneficiary was likely to be viticulture, following an 80 per cent reduction in the tariff on ordinary wine. The duty on petroleum products was to be progressively removed over a period of five years.

When Algerians took over the government of their own country they were in a more advantageous position than many new states, given the potential value of the oil and gas reserves. They inherited a sound infrastructure of roads, railways, and ports, and they took over the fixed assets of French industries. But they lacked skilled men, whether managers or technicians, whether in modern industry or in the tending of vines. They also appeared to lack markets. The purchasing power of the internal market was immediately reduced by the departure of the French settlers. Few agricultural products had an assured market abroad: wheat, even if a surplus could be produced, would compete unfavourably in Europe; wine had depended on special privileges in the French market. Industrial products would have to be sold either internally or in Europe, given the small size of the Maghreb as a whole and the difficulty of communication with other African states.

The independent government entered a political and economic situation of great confusion. The result of the departure of the French was that some industrial concerns, as well as farms, were taken over by self-constituted management committees, acting either through a common-sense wish to get machines working, or through more ideological motives. The confusion was increased by the political struggle for power as Ben Bella established his authority; and by the ideological debate, to which foreign advisers, rejoicing in the possibilities of building a new world, readily contributed.

The early years saw the establishment of two institutions, both impeccably socialist, but in conflict with each other, and neither concerned with an overall strategy of development. By decree, in March 1963, the government ruled that vacant industrial and mining enterprises as well as agricultural concerns were to manage their own affairs. But while individual factories were to be self-managed, industries were nationalized, and given a centralized, appointed management. In agriculture, state management inhibited and restricted the self-management of farms, but nevertheless allowed it to survive as an important part of the modern sector. In industry, the requirements of economic efficiency and large-scale organization, the centralizing tendencies of the Algerian state, and the establishment of government or party control over the trade union movement, all mitigated against the development of self-management. When new national companies were set up no provision was made for self-management and when existing enterprises were grouped within a national company the institutions of self-management were weakened or disappeared.

When Boumediene took over the government the pattern of state companies was established, and was developed further thereafter. The commitment of the government to the participation of workers in industry was not abandoned, but it had no more than verbal importance until 1971, when a new attempt appeared to be under way to give it greater reality.

With greater political stability there came also a strategy for economic development. This strategy gave priority to industrial over agricultural development and, within the industrial sector, to basic industries so as to produce an accelerator effect, bringing the creation of secondary industries in their wake.

Without doubt, Algerian economic growth owes much to this long-term strategy. It was not outstandingly original, indeed the French Constantine plan had stressed the importance of basic industry in saying:

Without doubt these heavy industries employ directly only a small local workforce, in proportion to the cost of investment involved. But they will have not only a multiplying effect, but above all they will act as a test case to be followed by other investment decisions in manufacturing industry.

On the other hand, the strategy had intellectual coherence, strengthened by the ideas of Professor Destanne de Bernis who, working with Ahmed Ghozali, developed the theme of *industries industrialisantes*. De Bernis has argued that the economic situation of Algeria, breaking its way into a world that is already industrialized, is like that of the newly unified Germany in 1870, and that the best inspiration for Algerian economists is to be found in List, not in Adam Smith. He also argued that an agricultural revolution has always followed, never preceded, an industrial revolution—a view which, whether generally valid or not, fits the Algerian case. The rural population of Algeria cannot be supported at a reasonable standard of living on the limited agricultural land available, and must therefore find employment in industry, which in turn will provide machinery and fertilizers for agriculture as well as furnishing a market for an improved and increased agricultural output.

Intellectual coherence and a sense of direction have made it easier for the government to accept and impose restraint and self-discipline. In the implementation of its plans the government has controlled the investment of outside capital. Where possible it has used internal financing, and when it has invited either capital or expertise from outside it has retained its own majority control over it. At the same time this austere and planned development has been assisted by several autonomous factors. The most important is the rising market for oil and gas, which has given this most important basic resource greater value than was foreseen. Secondly, the problem of limited employment in the capital-intensive industries which have been given priority has been mitigated by the availability of jobs for some half-million Algerians in France, while Algeria has continued to receive substantial aid from France. Finally, the population has accepted the restrictions implicit in this plan of development, from the absence of substantial improvement in traditional agriculture to the shortages in consumer goods and the limitation on travel in coastal towns looking towards France.

In this overall economic strategy several minor themes were of importance. First, it called for a major effort in education. Official figures show education as absorbing some 20·4 per cent of the operating budget in 1967, rising to 23·5 per cent in 1971. The proportion of the equipment budget going to education has been more variable, but the proportion of the total budget for 1971 was virtually the same as the operating costs, 23·6 per cent. These figures are the more important since administrative costs remain high in an over-centralized and clumsy bureaucracy. The return on the investment in education is incalculable, since the returns are still to come; meanwhile the urge to invest in education has come from the desperate need for trained men rather than from a sophisticated analysis of cost-benefit.

The development of the armed forces has gone hand in hand with that of the economy. But a major part of the military strategy is concerned with basic training rather than the purchase and use of expensive equipment; the army is put to work on productive enterprises like the construction of the trans-Saharan highway; and the conscript soldiers undoubtedly include a large number who would be unemployed or underemployed in civilian life. However, the Sahara crisis was the occasion, if not the cause, of a major (23 per cent) increase in the defence budget for 1976 'to safeguard the revolution'.

Finally, the strategy of development has given minimal importance to the development of tourism. A few 'tourist complexes' have been created (meaning hotels with bungalows, shops, and other facilities) and, in 1973, the tour operators were able to increase their activities. But if the ministry of tourism calculated that the number of Germans and Belgians entering the country had more than quintupled between 1964 and 1971, the totals for 1971 were only some 16,000 and 5,000 respectively. Out of 226,000 'travellers' entering Algeria in 1971, 78,000 came from France and 59,000 from Morocco and Tunisia combined. The social problems consequent on invasion from societies with high levels of leisure and consumption have thus been avoided.

The implementation of economic strategy was begun under the headings of two plans. The first was the 'pre-plan' of 1967–9. As a planning exercise it was modest, although its importance for the economy was great. It followed the main lines of the French Constantine plan, and detailed figures were only published when the magnitudes of actual expenditure could be foreseen. But during this period the structure of state-directed industry was built up, with the creation of major national companies, purchasing and marketing agencies, cooperatives, and other institutions. Special development programmes were also begun during this period. These programmes had considerable importance in the effort which has been made to improve the economy and living standards of regions which are naturally underendowed and distant from major centres of production. They have also been of obvious political importance, in contributing to a sense of national unity and in strengthening, by the expenditure of money in the development of a region, the articulation of the state and party machine over the country as a whole. The *wilayas* of Oasis, Aurès, and Greater Kabylia were the first to benefit from these programmes, in 1966, 1968, and 1969, with allocations rising from 300 million to 550 million dinars.

The next plan was a four-year plan running from 1969 to 1973. The most important feature of the plan, as the strategy would suggest, was massive investment in industry, which was to receive 45 per cent of a total investment of 27,740 million dinars. Agriculture was allocated 15 per cent of this investment, education and infrastructure 10 per cent and 8 per cent respectively. The proportion going to immediate improvement in the condition of the people was correspondingly small, only 5 per cent of the investment plan being allocated, for example, to housing, in spite of a rapidly growing population. Within the industrial sector, steel and, above all, oil and gas were to take the largest share.

Oil and Gas

Algeria's reserves of oil are of major importance to the Algerian economy, although they are relatively small on the world scale; the same is true of the annual flow of oil, in terms of quantity of oil going to the industrialized world and annual income. Its reserves were estimated, in 1969, at just over 1,000 million tons (Libya has 4,000 million and Saudi Arabia 18,600 million). Its output in 1969 was nearly 44 million tons, being about 2 per cent of the world output, only one-tenth of United States or Saudi Arabian production and less than a third of that of Libya. Algeria planned the production of 60 million tons of petrol by 1975; but although 51·1m. tons were produced in 1973 output fell back in 1974 and again in 1975, to 42·6m. tons.

In its supply of gas Algeria's place on the world scale is higher than for oil. Reserves are variously estimated at between 3,000 and 4,000 billion cubic metres, which is in the region of half the reserves of the United States and competing with Iran for third place behind the US and the Soviet Union. The production of gas is still being developed. Only three billion cubic metres were produced from the major Hassi-R'Mel field in 1971 but this should rise to 40 billion cubic metres in 1978. The thermic value of gas in relation to petrol is approximately calculated at a thousand cubic metres of gas for one ton of petrol.

Both oil and gas in Algeria are of a high quality. The oil has a low sulphur content; the gas is rich in methane (84 per cent) and has only 6 per cent inert constituents. The gas is also rich in condensate, providing 220,000 tons of condensate per billion cubic metres of gas—the condensate being a raw material for the petrochemical industry.

Oil and gas reserves, with the possibility of exports of this magnitude, are of obvious importance. There are substantial differences between them, and their exploitation has been undertaken in significantly different periods of history. Oil was prospected and exploited by private companies with their home base in that part of the world (principally the United States) which was politically, as well as industrially and commercially, strong. Moreover the natural characteristics of oil are such that it is most conveniently exploited if its flow is interrupted as little as possible—from the ground, through the refinery, to the consumer. The development of gas as a major source of energy outside the United States has been subsequent to that of oil because of the cost and difficulty of transportation (so that gas accompanying oil, as in Iran, has normally been burned uselessly on the spot). In consequence the development of gas, particularly in the Algerian case, has occurred in the post-colonial period, under the direction of an Algerian government which, for this purpose, has been politically as strong as any government in the economically developed world. The problems of production and marketing have been at least as great as with oil since the technological solution to the problem of transport across the sea is by liquefaction, which confines the transport to a limited number of liquefying and deliquefying points of entry and exit.

The exploitation of oil and gas provides a reliable and increasing source of revenue—the sharpest single increase coming with the quintupling of world oil prices in 1973. It ensures a flow of cash to the government independent of taxation (62 per cent of revenue in the 1976 budget coming from oil and gas) and has enabled the government to build up reserves of foreign currency. However, the effect is to provide the opportunity for investment in industry and education for a relatively large population, rather than to bring immediate riches. This is the more so since gas, which forms such an important part of the total hydrocarbon resources, calls for lengthy and heavy investment. Algeria is therefore a heavy borrower in the international (especially European) money market, and depends on external loans for the development of the gas and other industries. Inevitably the government is particularly sensitive to inflation in the industrialized world. The heavy demands on hydrocarbon revenues have been reflected in the Algerian insistence, within OPEC, on the maintenance of a high price for oil, in the negotiation of loans from European banks in 1975, and in the Algerian role in Third World politics.

The economic and social importance of the industry within Algeria stems from the fact that it is, by its very nature, élitist. Oil and gas do not call for a large labour force; they require expert management, characterized by foresight and the ability to marshal substantial financial resources and take long-term investment decisions. The élite responsible for this development are members of the government and the directors of the national companies. The rhetoric of the Algerian government concerned with the participation of workers in the management of their own industries has little relevance to the practical development of this prime source of the country's wealth.

The Political History of Algerian Oil

The development of the oil industry in Algeria followed a distinctive course. France had played little part in the exploration for oil which preceded the Second World War. It lacked both the imperial influence which gave Britain access to Middle Eastern oil (and the Dutch to the oil of Indonesia) and the indigenous resources and financial combination which produced the great American companies. The only French company of substantial importance was therefore the Compagnie Française du Pétrole (CFP) which held a minority interest in the predominantly British Iraq Petroleum Company.

In consequence it was the French state, rather than private oil companies, which took the leading part in financing the exploration for oil in the Sahara during the War of Independence. The development of the oil represented the possibility of greater French self-sufficiency, at a time when France was weak in relation to the United States, the German Federal Republic, and even Britain. The vision at this time was of a prosperous Algeria, still part of a France made more powerful by the possession of natural resources developed by the French and not by the multinational majors of the oil industry. This vision passed with Independence. But, as we have seen, cooperation between France and Algeria in the oil industry was a central part of the Evian agreements.

The Algerian view was in some respects a mirror image of the French, and drew its strength from Algerian nationalism. The Algerians, during the War of Independence, were immediately aware of French exploration and French plans for the development of the Sahara. The wartime *Moujahid* contains frequent references to French activity in oil exploration, and awareness of the possibilities of an oil industry increased the insistence of the FLN on the unity of Algerian territory.

With the advent of Independence oil came to occupy an important place in Algerian political emotions. There was a strong sense that the natural resources of Algeria belonged to the Algerian state—a combination of a peasant-like attachment to the land, a French legal tradition which gives legal ownership of the subsoil to the state, and a French Jacobin view of the state itself. To this was added the aspiration to economic independence and resistance to 'neo-colonialism'. As Boumediene subsequently argued, Algeria had disbursed an advance on its own resources in order to fight the War of Independence; the acquisition of independence must be followed by economic independence, which would give access to wealth for future development.

Algerian Control of Oil and Gas

The starting point of Algerian oil policy was thus the predominant French interest in exploration, production, and marketing. The most important producer was a new company financed as to 80 per cent of its capital from public funds—the Entreprise de Recherche et d'Activité Pétrolières, selling through the ELF network and consequently known as ELF–ERAP. It had several subsidiaries, of which the most important was the Compagnie de Recherche et d'Exploitation des Pétroles Sahariens, in which Royal Dutch Shell was a minority shareholder. This group produced, in 1969, approximately 18 million tons annually. The second most important producer, CFP, with its subsidiary Omnirex, produced approximately 12 million tons. Together these two companies accounted for 90 per cent of production.

British and American companies accounted for the remainder. French policy, and the potential of other possible fields, had made Algeria relatively unattractive to them. The companies most heavily involved were Royal Dutch Shell and Phillips. These, together with minor Italian and German concerns, were nationalized after the Middle East war of 1967. Mobil, Getty, and El Paso were also present, and were not nationalized at this time. The French government had no wish to open Algerian oil to the big American and international companies who for their part, after Independence, saw no great attraction in further exploration in Algeria.

The Evian agreements confirmed the rights of the French companies, while giving the Algerian government the right to determine future concessions. At the same time a joint Franco–Algerian organization, with equal participation by the two countries, was established to play an advisory role with regard to certain technical matters and new concessions.

The rights of the French companies therefore remained intact. They continued to extract and market the oil. One of the most important wells, at Hassi Messaoud, was developed, with two base camps in the desert which were irrigated with artesian water; trees were planted and even a nursery for animals was installed under the newly grown trees. In essence this was no different from a similar American colony in Saudi Arabia, or from the renowned British refinery at Abadan. But the fact that the French government had played so large a part in opening up the Algerian fields added to the sense of continuing colonial occupation, while the size of the exploitation was large enough to be worth capturing, yet not so large that an Algerian government would be afraid of touching it for fear of bankruptcy from a retaliatory boycott.

Only eighteen months after the Evian agreements the Algerian government moved towards gaining control of the oil within its territory. It claimed a major part in the construction of a new pipeline, in spite of the existing agreement under which the companies had the right to transport the oil. The French companies were only prepared to give a 10 per cent, then a 20 per cent share. In consequence the Algerian government raised its own finance and commissioned a British company, the CJB group, to construct the new pipeline and train Algerian technicians. The Algerian company which took responsibility for the pipeline was the Société Nationale des Transports des Hydrocarbures (Sonatrach). This was a decisive intrusion of Algerian activity into the oil industry.

The insistence of the Algerian government on its part in the new pipeline provoked fresh negotiation with the French government which led to a new agreement, in July 1965, from which Algeria drew further advantages. The agreement confirmed the existing oil concessions in the hands of French companies. It gave Algeria a more favourable fiscal arrangement, though one where the tax was based on a price of $2·08, compared with the posted price of $2·35 on which the other oil companies in Algeria were paying tax. Sonatrach purchased an additional share in SNREPAL, to become half owner, equal with the French company.

In addition the agreement established a new cooperative association (known as Ascoop) which was to undertake research and exploration over an additional area—each company, one Algerian and one French, working independently and sharing costs and profits over fifty years (but with the French making an advance of money to the Algerian company). Equally important for the future was a clause of the agreement which separated gas from oil: gas was to be purchased at the wellhead by the Algerian government at a price related to the capital cost of research and production, from which point the Algerian companies could exploit it as they wished. At the same time the French government agreed a programme of aid to Algeria of 400 million francs a year, to be managed through an industrial cooperation organization (OCI). Finally, the agreement provided for a revision of its fiscal terms in 1969, and of the whole in 1970.

The agreement won little support in France, where the government had difficulty in securing its acceptance by the senate. In Algeria by contrast the government was well aware of the advance which the agreement represented; while the way in which it was welcomed showed clearly that the government would look for further advance in the same direction as soon as the opportunity presented itself. Speaking on 19 March 1966—at the inauguration of the third oil pipeline on the anniversary of the Evian agreements—Boumediene emphasized that 'The moment of truth which follows accession to Independence lies in the question whether peoples previously colonized have the ability to exploit, by themselves and in accordance with the standards of a modern economy, the richness of their own country.' In this context he welcomed the equality between France and Algeria which the agreements established—in SNREPAL and Ascoop and the gas agreement, whereby 'l'intervention de l'Algérie va prendre une dimension jamais enregistrée jusqu'à ce jour'.

The cooperation which the 1965 agreement envisaged proved extremely difficult to achieve in practice. It was made more difficult by the involvement of the French state. Initially the French government had taken on a major responsibility for the exploitation of the oil of Algeria as the only way of keeping the big international companies out. But under the new agreement the problems which arose compounded inter-governmental difficulties with those of a commercial transaction. The French oil companies were bound to act like other oil companies in the pursuit of profits and the control of their own investment, even though ERAP was a state company, while the state was inevitably brought into difficulties which it might have avoided, could it have left oil disputes more fully in the hands of purely commercial companies.

Moreover the political economy of oil in the world as a whole changed rapidly in the quinquennium which the 1965 agreement was intended to cover. The most important single event in its various repercussions was the Middle East war of 1967. It had the effect of limiting the supply of oil, temporarily, as a result of the closure of the Suez canal, and giving an advantage to Mediterranean oil. This occurred at a time when the demand for oil in the industrialized world was increasing rapidly, while political awareness of the national advantages of possessing oil resources in the producing countries was heightened. In Algeria the 1967 war had a direct repercussion in that the British and American companies were nationalized. Those interests were too small for their nationalization to be a major issue in itself, but they may have provided an additional incentive to Paul Getty to sign an agreement with the Algerian government which the latter could proclaim as a new step forward in the relation between governments and oil companies in the Arab world (a claim unjustified in the event, since the Getty agreement proved an isolated incident). The most important aspects of the agreement, from the political (and financial) point of view, were that it gave Sonatrach a 51 per cent share in the joint company (although decisions of the board of the company were to be taken by three-quarters majority) and it committed Getty to reinvesting 75 per cent of its 'Algerian' profits in Algeria.

In addition, the nationalization of the US interests made it easier for the Algerian state companies, notably Sonatrach, to develop a purely contractual relationship with American companies by which the Algerians bought expertise and capital. Following the precedent established in the contract with Britain for the third pipeline, the purchase of sophisticated equipment was accompanied by technical training, while joint US-Algerian companies were established, with the Algerians always retaining the major part, for research and development.

This manner of cooperation was very pragmatic. It was the beginning of a growing range of commercial contacts with the United States, in spite of the rupture of diplomatic relations as a result of the Middle East war. At the same time an important school for oil technicians was established as a result of an agreement (1964) with the Soviet Union. (The Soviet Union, it can be supposed, gained from the oil-knowledge which its experts were able to acquire in contact with western oil companies; and it purchased a small quantity of oil from Algeria at a lower price than Algeria received on the world market.) Inevitably difficulties arose in day-to-day operations, since the French personnel were cooperating with Algerians who relied on both American and Russian training.

Against this background Algerian–French cooperation in accordance with the 1965 agreement gave rise to numerous difficulties and disagreements. The long-term perspective was, for the Algerians, very encouraging. Above all the supply of gas meant that, whatever happened to oil, there would be an assured export to an energy-hungry world and a supply of energy for Algeria's own industry. However, the Algerians sometimes acted as if the Sahara was an eldorado of wealth, whereas the French companies (more accurately, as it appears to date) were sceptical of its further resources. The Algerians took advantage of collaboration with the French, which was indispensable to them at this stage, while seeking to escape from the constraints of collaboration as soon as possible. They were pragmatic, but not necessarily conciliatory, in seeking the advantages of protective state agreements and of free commercial exchange, according to the needs of the situation. Finally, the young men responsible for the conduct of business on the Algerian side saw themselves as the defenders of the interests of a new state, against the combined resources of the oil industry and the Quai d'Orsay, neither of which was renowned for giving away points in any negotiation.

It was in this spirit that the Algerians accused their French partners of undertaking too little exploration in Algeria. They were awkward collaborators in the industrial cooperation organization, with a certain tendency to resent any reaction from their French colleagues other than straightforward approval of what they proposed. Subsequently (in the White Book relating to the negotiations for the revision of the 1965 agreement) they accused the French government more generally of pursuing an Algerian policy in French interests. In the words of the Algerian White Paper:

It is indeed notorious that, within the framework of the fifth French plan, the share of French supply coming from Algeria was fixed at 33 per cent, a percentage determined for entirely French reasons, and it was as a function of this objective, entirely foreign to Algeria and the Algerian sub-soil, that the French companies who controlled oil production in Algeria regulated the exploration and exploitation of the sub-soil of this country. [*Documents sur les relations* . . ., p. 12.]

It was against this background that the negotiations were begun which were to be affected abruptly, in February 1971, by the nationalization of Algerian oil and gas. The opening round of talks was concerned with the posted price (and then the reference price) on which payments to Algeria were calculated. These discussions could have started, according to the agreement of 1965, on 1 January 1969. In the event they did not begin until November 1969, when the French government was free of domestic preoccupations.

The Algerian government did not wait for the negotiations to open before informing the companies that new posted prices would operate from 1 January 1969. The current posted price was $2·08. The new posted price which they proposed was $2·65, equivalent to a tax reference price, under OPEC procedures, of $2·85. They justified this price by comparison with the prices of Libyan and Middle East oil, with adjustment made for distance of transport and quality.

In reaction, the French government made an initial tactical mistake, in proposing a reduction of four cents in the existing price. This had a bad psychological effect which they soon regretted. They then proposed a posted price of $2·35, which was, understandably, rejected by the Algerian government. By the summer of 1970 the negotiations on price had reached deadlock. President Pompidou therefore proposed that the negotiations should be widened to permit the conclusion of a more comprehensive agreement on Franco–Algerian relations, covering such questions as wine, immigrant labour, investment and development aid from France to Algeria, and other outstanding topics. His proposal was welcomed by the Algerian government.

The French government now made an important strategic miscalculation. It underestimated the extent to which the balance of oil politics was tipping towards the producing countries, and it misjudged the determination of the Algerian government to gain control of its own oil and gas. The bargaining strength of the oil producers was demonstrated, in 1971, by the successful negotiation of the Tehran agreement, followed by the acceptance of Libyan demands at Tripoli. But in the previous year it was possible to underestimate the growth in demand for oil, and to regard the existing sellers' market as a temporary result of the closure of the Suez canal. The logic of this position for the French government was that it need not hurry to settle with the Algerians, as long as the companies were still paying on the old posted price.

It is difficult to know how Algerian strategy was determined over the same period. Clearly the loss of revenue as months passed without a new agreement was an important factor, although the government was undoubtedly aware that any brusque action would almost certainly produce at least a temporary further reduction. At the same time self-confidence increased, with the development of indigenous oil capability and in the atmosphere of rising hopes among oil producing countries. Evidence of the probable intentions of the Algerian government was provided when Ahmed Ghozali and collaborators visited Paris in February 1970. More strikingly, Boumediene, speaking at Skikda on 16 July 1970, expounded the bases of his policy in a characteristic combination of rhetoric and pragmatism. He said:

Certain groups have been unable to understand that Algeria is today an independent country. They persist in believing that oil questions are not a matter of complete and total Algerian sovereignty but a sort of co-sovereignty. We say to them: No. The oil is ours, as is the gas, since they are well and truly found in Algeria. We were opposed in the recent past to the colonialists who tried to separate the Sahara from the Tell.

If we were able to analyse Algerian oil, we should discover that the blood of our martyrs is one of its constituents, because the possession of this wealth was paid for with our blood. Moreover, foreign capital which was invested in the exploitation of our oil has for the most part been recovered and remunerated.

Boumediene's speech was a clear indication of determination. When negotiations with France were resumed there was no lack of inventiveness on the French side or of activity to reach agreement on the Algerian. But the positions each side adopted remained far apart, and the Algerian negotiators—the foreign minister Bouteflika, with the minister of economy, Abdesselam, supporting him—were a match for their partners in firmness and negotiating skill. The French government offered a comprehensive plan of cooperation in the production and marketing of oil and gas in Algeria and France, which the Algerians rejected. Instead they offered to purchase French interests in Algerian oil, giving the Algerians the majority share and accepting the French companies as minority partners. The gap remained wide; the French sought a break in the negotiations while the Tehran discussions proceeded, and at the same time secured the payment, by the companies, of 675 million francs towards the arrears which would have accrued by the time an agreement was reached. The negotiations had not degenerated into an acrimonious dispute; but neither did they promise an early solution. In these circumstances therefore the Algerian government decided to act, and on 24 February 1971 Boumediene announced the nationalization of oil and gas, in a speech to the UGTA. The terms of the announcement remained moderate. He said:

We are sovereign, and we can take any decision which follows naturally from the normal exercise of sovereignty.

Nationalization is a right of the Algerian state, recognized by the United Nations; we announce officially, moreover, that we shall compensate all the companies affected by these measures on the same basis as companies which have previously come under state control.

Another decision is to be noticed; we will continue to supply the French market with Algerian oil on the basis of the market price. It has been reported before today that the price of our oil is too high; in this case it is sufficient not to take it. But as long as France requests it, its market will be supplied by us.

The reaction of the French government was equally moderate: although it protested against the unilateral action of the Algerian government, it insisted only on proper indemnities and did not dispute the right, in principle, to nationalize. Negotiations between the two governments were resumed on this basis—the question of oil still being associated with other questions, especially wine and development aid. However, the Algerian government now pressed its demands to the point where the French government broke off the discussions. The Algerians may have regretted having pushed their luck too far, or they may have intended to enhance the political show of their victory over the French. Negotiations were now in the hands of the companies, who began by strengthening their own bargaining position by means of an embargo on Algerian oil. A settlement was none the less reached relatively quickly—with the Compagnie Française du Pétrole on 30 June and with ERAP in December 1971.

The settlements consisted essentially of agreement on the amount of compensation and the amount of debt arrears. In the case of the Compagnie Française du Pétrole some $35 million was due to the company, which was to be paid over seven years. With ERAP the balance was in favour of the Algerians, so that ERAP handed over part of its assets in Algeria as a final settlement. This left the French companies holding minority interests, with Sonatrach as the majority partner. Their minority interest gave them the right to a proportion of the oil produced, totalling 13 million tons (compared with 35 million tons before nationalization), subject to fiscal charges in line with OPEC and to contractual obligations concerning research, investment, and the repatriation of profits. The minor companies (Eurafrep, Coparex, Omnirex, and Francarep) decided that it was not worth continuing operations in Algeria and made a settlement which balanced compensation and debt-arrears so that they could withdraw from the field. In 1975 ELF–ERAP decided not to renew its five-year production agreement with Sonatrach (although it continued to share in exploration) while CFP signed a new agreement covering investment and production.

The importance of the 'oil battle' was obvious. It enhanced the popularity of Boumediene's government and added to its prestige in the Third World. Victory in the oil battle became a constantly recurring theme in Boumediene's speeches, associated with cultural and agrarian reform. Yet the battle had, outside the rhetoric, been very subdued. Emotions were strong on both sides, but did not override a sense of pragmatism. Both sides made miscalculations, but in the end a settlement which the companies found satisfactory was reached, leaving the Algerians with their great prize of oil ownership intact. The French government might have made a more imaginative leap forward in what could be thought of as the last phase of decolonization;

instead it moved somewhat bureaucratically, judging Algerian demands by the criterion of existing practice rather than taking the initiative in offering a new status. None the less, it remained flexible in its negotiations and did not abandon its policy of good relations with Algeria and the Arab world. Both the dynamism of Algerian militancy in the pursuit of a new deal for raw material producers and French policy in such areas as a European Arab dialogue were to be seen in embryo in these events.

Meanwhile the development of Algerian gas resources underwent a revolution of a different kind. The principle of Algerian ownership of its natural gas was proclaimed by Ben Bella without giving rise to great dispute—for the technical reason that the transport of gas was still in the developmental stage. From the Algerian point of view the possibilities of large-scale export were not fully realized and it seemed obvious that gas should provide the energy for Algerian industry. Correspondingly the French policy of securing an energy source independent of the American oil companies had left gas out of account, and the companies had not constructed downstream operations and outlets for the sale of gas as they had for petrol. In consequence the agreement of 1965 giving separate treatment to gas, and the nationalization in 1971 of the extraction of gas from the ground excited far less attention than was the case with oil. On the other hand, Algeria lost possible contracts in Europe against competition from Libya and Russia—a fact which emphasizes the value, to Algeria, of established outlets through the French companies for its oil.

Algeria has, however, taken a leading part in all aspects of the application of gas technology, with the result that it can look forward to a period of massive export of gas coupled with its use for domestic industry. The first plant for the liquefaction of gas on a commercial scale was begun at Arzew before Independence, in 1961, by the Compagnie Algérienne de Méthane Liquide (Camel), which was then composed of Anglo-Dutch (Shell), American (Continental), and French interests, and in which Sonatrach became the majority partner in 1971, with Conch (Shell plus Continental Oil) retaining 40 per cent. The plant came into production in 1964 and the first contract for its product was signed with the British Gas Council, taking delivery of one billion cubic metres at Canvey Island; it was followed by a French contract, in 1965, for half that amount.

Since then further contracts have been signed on a growing scale, necessitating the construction of new liquefaction plants, pipelines, and special gas tankers. The liquefaction centres are at Arzew and Skikda and the pipelines which bring gas from the fields have branches to supply Algiers and all principal towns. New pipelines are under construction to meet the slightly more complex need of the gas and condensate which comes from the Hassi Messaoud field. Stage by stage Algeria has increased the proportion which its own indigenous resources of materials and skill play in this endeavour. (The second pipeline from Hassi-R'Mel, for example, was constructed with steel pipes partly manufactured by the National Steel Company at Annaba.) Contracts for the sale of gas which have been concluded since the first, with the British Gas Council, show a rapidly ascending order of magnitude. These include contracts with the Gaz de France to deliver gas to Fos, and a two-phase contract with Alocean-Distrigas to supply to Boston, Mass. The most important contracts were signed with American companies and had to run the gauntlet of the United States Federal Power Commission. An initial contract with El Paso, signed in 1971, was cancelled two years later and it was only in 1975 that a new contract with El Paso and another with Panhandle were finally settled. The contract with El Paso was for the supply of 10,000 cubic metres a year from 1981, and that with Panhandle for 4,500 cubic metres a year from 1980. The lengthy negotiation of these contracts bridged the period of the rapid increase in oil prices and as a result the final version indexed the price of the gas supplied to changes in the price of other energy sources. Another contract, with Distrigas, which had also fallen foul of the FPC in 1971 was negotiated in 1975. A further contract was signed with the Spanish company, Empresa Nacional del Gas (Enagas). It included provision for tied and untied loans to Algeria, and for the delivery of the gas to Spain in Algerian ships.

The development of the natural gas industry has depended on skilled and imaginative management and financing. Sonatrach has been responsible for the planning and management of pipelines and liquefaction plants (and has a majority position in Camel). It has been necessary to negotiate very large credits and construction contracts. Thus the initial estimate for the new liquefaction plant at Arzew, to meet the contracts with the United States and Europe, was of the order of some 2 milliard francs (say £200 million). The pipeline from Hassi-R'Mel to Skikda was constructed by French and Italian companies (Sofregaz and a subsidiary of SNAM-Progetti) with steel pipes supplied from France, Italy, and Japan.

Algeria as a supplier of gas is thus in the forefront of a new world industry. The most dramatic aspects of the development have been in technology; the most taxing is the battle which El Paso has fought, with the support of the Algerians, before the Federal Power Commission of the United States to establish a precedent in the United States regulation of natural gas, hitherto entirely supplied domestically. Moreover a further stage of the technological adventure is being planned: the construction of pipelines under the Mediterranean, to Italy via Tunis and Sicily, and to Spain, either under the Strait of Gibraltar or directly from Mostaganem to Carthagene and then on to the industrial areas of northern Europe.

The development of natural gas has been economically worthwhile as a result of the growing demand for energy, which has increased the price consumers are prepared to pay and has justified capital expenditure in the industry. Even so, the scale of Algerian development is outstanding in itself. It has been achieved thanks to the financial ability of such men as Smaïl Mahroug and Abdesselam and the experience and skill of Abdelkader Chanderli. No less outstanding is the achievement of Sonatrach itself, under the direction of Ahmed Ghozali. In 1968 it already had an annual budget of £1·5 million and matched the most modern companies in the industrialized world in its equipment, its ability to make good use of foreign service industries, and in its management structure.

Shipping

Algerian development plans have given major importance to shipping. These plans are being implemented with a combination of political will and commercial energy. The company responsible, the Compagnie Nationale Algérienne de Navigation (CNAN) is regarded as the most complete and progressive Arab shipping company. The objective is for Algeria to play a predominant role in the transport of methane, and to carry at least 50 per cent of Algeria's seabourne trade. CNAN is directed by Mohamed Guendouz, with the intention of ensuring the commercial success of the company when the whole range of its operations is taken into account.

In 1975 CNAN owned two oil tankers and had further tonnage on order. It is a member of the Arab Maritime Petroleum Transport Company, set up in January 1973 by eight members of the Organization of Arab Petroleum Exporting Countries to own and manage a tanker fleet, part of which will sail under the Algerian flag. Following the signature of the major gas contracts, which included options open to Algeria for the transport of gas, CNAN ordered five methane carriers from France.

In contrast to the tanker fleets of the Arab oil producers, CNAN spans the whole range of shipping and has been given particular importance in the plan of 1973–7. It is not an offshoot of the oil industry. In 1975 it owned thirty ships in addition to its two tankers and one small methane carrier. It has succeeded in tough negotiations with France and the Soviet Union for a 50-50 sharing of shipping and has developed an important liner capacity, carrying 70 per cent of the 300,000 passengers (mainly emigrant workers) between Algeria and France. It has set up a joint Algerian–Mauritanian company which operates a full liner service to North European ports with two ships, and plans a joint company with Libya to carry hydrocarbons and dry cargo. It has a monopoly of coastal trade, brokerage, and towing (with twenty modern tugs) which ensures a substantial return, subsidizing some of the international operations which are more competitive and have to bear the cost of amortization on loans.

Industrial Development

Second to the oil and gas industry, Algeria has developed its metallurgy —an industry which was included in the Constantine plan. It is essentially a base industry and is attractive to a country seeking to industrialize itself and acquire a degree of self-sufficiency. The most important steel mill is at Annaba, constructed with Soviet assistance and the participation of the army engineers. It is the responsibility of the Société Nationale de Sidérurgie, which also directs other steelworks, including the tube factory at Geghaia, taken over from the French company Vallourec. (SN Métal is responsible for processing metals.) Part of the supply of iron ore comes from within Algeria, which in 1962 produced some two million tons of ore, virtually all of it exported. In 1971 production of ore had risen by 50 per cent and nearly all of this was used domestically (1972: 3·6 million tons). A major untapped source of ore is known to exist at Gara Djebilet, some hundred miles south of Tindouf. The reserve is estimated at two billion (2,000 million) tons of which half can be exploited by open-cast mining. But the ore is also rich in phosphate and, more important, is extremely remote so that its exploitation will require very heavy investment.

To some extent an internal market for steel already existed. It has grown with the construction of the Annaba complex, and investment has been undertaken in the *industries de transformation,* under SN Métal and the Société Nationale de Constructions Mécaniques (Sonacome, as well as Sonelec—electricity and electronics). The state, has, in two successive stages, taken over the Berliet enterprise which was established before Independence, and the factory at Alger-Rouiba is being enlarged; while an agreement with Renault provides for the assembly of cars. There are similar arrangements with Beutz for the supply of tractors, of which 50,000 were produced in 1972 (Sonarem also produced 300 railway wagons in 1972).

The Annaba complex includes a fertilizer plant, and Algeria can be expected to maintain increasing output of fertilizers, based on indigenous resources of phosphates, oil, and gas. The principal phosphate mine is at Djebel Onk, with reserves estimated at 500 million tons; annual production in 1972 was half a million tons, of which half was exported and the remainder processed at Annaba.

In these areas of heavy and medium industry, the national companies left little room for private enterprise. In textiles, private firms remain, together with self-managed enterprises. These are relatively small concerns, operating within the framework of state purchasing and marketing companies. In addition, private enterprise is now active in some new industries, notably plastics (while the Mzabite community has established a privately-owned radiator factory at Ouargla). The older small private and self-managed firms are generally more labour-intensive. Algerian figures show that the total labour force in the non-agricultural sector has grown from about 200,000 in 1966 to 300,000 in 1970. During that period, the share of private industry, in numbers employed, fell from 52 per cent to 34 per cent while the public sector rose from 35 per cent to 58 per cent; the remainder (13 per cent falling to 8 per cent) being in self-managed enterprises.

In contrast to Tunisia and Morocco, Algeria has done relatively little to develop tourism. There were 20,000 hotel beds in 1970 and 35,000 at the end of 1973 (a figure which appears unbelievably large to those who go to Algiers for business or pleasure and look for a hotel room).

The overall strategy of industrial development and growth shows impressive and encouraging results. The state has kept to its intention to invest heavily in major industries, and resources have become available at an unforeseen level as a result of rising oil prices. The level of investment, which averaged 3·1 milliard dinars during the three-year plan 1967–9, rose to an average of 8·5 milliard dinars during the four-year plan, 1970–3. Gross domestic product rose sharply, except during 1971, when the nationalization of oil limited production and export. The percentage increase was 11·6 per cent in 1970; it dropped to 2·7 per cent in 1971 and rose again to 16·6 per cent in 1972. Internal resources provided the high proportion of 73 per cent of total public investment in the period 1969–73.

Encouraging as these statistics are, they do not conceal the economic and social problems which have persisted or increased during the four-year plan. The new industries are capital-intensive, in a country with a rapidly expanding population, and industry remains concentrated in specific centres. The high level of investment is related to low consumption expenditure because a large proportion of the population is used to being poor—too poor, for example, to pay 10 dinars (£1) for the installation of meters required for rural electrification. None the less, investment has been directed to regional development (Tlemsen, Sétif, and Saïda being the beneficiaries of the 1970–3 plan). Towns like Tizi-Ouzou and Sétif, which previously were no more than centres for impoverished rural areas, have been transformed by industrial development.

Agriculture
Omar was terribly hungry, always, and there was hardly ever anything to eat in the house; he was hungry to the point where on some occasions the foam of his saliva hardened in his mouth. To subsist, in consequence, was for him the sole preoccupation.

Yet he became accustomed to never being satisfied; he had established a private relationship with his hunger. Overall, he could treat it with the friendship due to someone close; and he allowed himself every indulgence with it. Their relationship came to be established on the basis of a reciprocal courtesy which was attentive and full of delicacy, of a kind which can only come about with the full understanding which exists between two people who first judge each other without making any concession and then recognize each other as worthy, the one of the other.[1]

The French colonization of Algeria involved settlement on the best land. It thus disrupted and impoverished an existing society, which nevertheless increased rapidly in number.

Settlers and Algerian nationalists inevitably had different views of the history of colonization. The emotion of the settlers owed much to the belief that French colonization had brought life and prosperity to the land—that the agricultural wealth of the country owed its origin and growth to French investment and hard work. The nationalist view was that the French had taken the best land by force and driven the Algerians on to poor land. This latter view is correct; but it has sometimes blinded Algerians to the importance of the increase of the Muslim population to its present level of 15 million—a burden on the land which remains after the departure of its one million Europeans.

At the time of the French conquest, Algeria supported between two and three million inhabitants, as far as is known. The most prosperous part of the countryside was that adjoining the towns, to the extent that many of the first arrivals among the French were dazzled by the fertility of the land, and passed rapidly from supposing the land to be barren to exaggerating and romanticizing its possibilities. One French officer recorded: 'This land, which people had told us was wild and uninhabited, is covered with pretty country cottages and houses surrounded by gardens; they are all built on the tops of hills whose gentle contours are in complete contrast to the aridity of the slopes of Provence.'[2]

Similar remarks are recorded about the surrounds of such towns as Blida, Médéa, Mostaganem, Mascara, Cherchell, Djidjelli, and others, where the land benefited from and added to the wealth of the military, governmental, and merchant classes living in the town. The imaginative observer can easily reconstruct the scene around the country lanes of Hydra and Ben Aknoun, and will be able to do so for a few more years before development blots out the past.

The best land a little further from the towns was no doubt cultivated in a system of *latifundia*, using paid or sharecropping (*khammes*) labour,[3] a form of cultivation to be found in most fertile parts of the Mediter-

[1] Mohammed Dib, *La Grande Maison*, Paris, 1952, pp. 109–10.
[2] See Lacoste, Nouschi, Prenant, 1960, p. 202.
[3] The commonest form of sharecropping in North Africa is one where the labourer receives, traditionally, one-fifth of the crop, hence khammès, from the Arabic for 'five'.

ranean basin. Farms such as these were devoted to growing grain and raising cattle. In the words of recent French historians:

> In the Mitidja, for example, so often described as a pestilential marsh recovered by French endeavour, many estates comprised, in 1830, vast farms rented by tenants or by *khammes*, themselves employing local wage earners living in tents, or immigrant mountain people lodged in shacks; the major part of their land was given over to sheep raising, whether the herds of the Beylik or of private owners and their workers; the surrounds of the farm were planted and made into gardens, and a bit further out were divided between biennial fallow and grain crops; contemporary observers calculated this cultivated zone as being between one-eighth and one-twelfth of the total area.[1]

On less fertile and more mountainous land, cultivation was less intensive, since the population was smaller and less fixed. The ownership of the land was complex and traditional. It included various forms of tribal ownership (*'arch*) which included common grazing or a communal system of redistribution of land on inheritance; private ownership (*melk*) which might be mixed with tribal customs; and larger estates belonging to the state (*azel*), to an individual, or to a religious foundation (*habbous*), with diverse arrangements associating the ownership of the land to the people working it.

French conquest and European colonization imposed itself on the land of Algeria at the expense of the indigenous population. During the first half-century of occupation the French acquired land primarily by conquest, with the marginal added advantage that indigenous speculators—often Jews, or through Jewish intermediaries—were eager to sell land. The resistance of Abdel Kader and the revolt of Moqrani were as calamitous in their outcome as they were tenacious in their opposition. Each successive wave of conquest, and each revolt suppressed, meant that more members of the indigenous population were killed in battle or died as a result of illness and starvation, and their lands taken over by European settlers—a form of conquest and colonization neither new nor unique in the world's history, but distinctive in the form it took, and its outcome, in Algeria. The existing system of law and custom in landownership was defenceless against European invasion. Inevitably, unsuccessful resistance forfeited legal rights in the eyes of the successful colonizers. Existing rights of ownership were little understood or respected by the colonizers, and the indigenous population lacked any system of laws or any legal class which could defend them. Legislation was, as always, a civilizing influence; but only, in this instance, among the settler community, at the expense of the original inhabitants, their laws, and customs.

The growth of the European colonization went through its first rapid expansion in the 1840s, with the introduction of the *ordonnances* of 1844 and 1846 (increasing the domain of the state at the expense of

[1] Lacoste, etc., 1960, p. 205.

tribal land) and the submission of Abdel Kader in 1847. In 1841 there were some 27,000 settlers, in 1950 there were 112,000. This was followed by the application of a policy of *cantonnement* based on the comfortable supposition that tribes occupied land wastefully, in their nomadic way, so that if they were restricted to a more limited area they would be obliged to use it more intensively. Meanwhile part of their land could be added to the state domain and thus be made available to settlers.

The decade 1863–73 was even more decisive in changing the balance. It opened with the *senatus-consulte* of 1865 and closed with the law of 1873. Both of these measures favoured individual property in the French fashion to the detriment of the existing land system. The intervening years were marked by the suppression of the Moqrani rebellion (1870–1), followed by the sequestration of the lands of the losers, and a period of drought in 1866–70, together with invasions of locusts. These scourges of nature bore hardest on the Muslim population in the immediate starvation they caused, and in making landownership even more vulnerable to the inroads of private purchase, for which the settlers almost alone had the resources. In 1871–80 some 400,000 hectares, it is estimated, became available to the settlers (compared to only 480,000 in the period 1830–70). This quantitative change was accompanied by the break-up of the tribal system of landownership.

The remainder of the nineteenth century saw a continuation of the same process, with an additional encroachment into the forests of Algeria. These forests were always subject to fire, but would grow afresh afterwards. With the spread of colonization, however, the effect of fire was detrimental to the life of the Algerian *fellah*. Legislation had protected the forests and the rights of the Algerians in them. But in the latter part of the nineteenth century a forest fire was followed by the sequestration of forest land, or its being made available for purchase to settlers, while the remainder of the forest was protected by legislation which weighed heavily on peasants (and for the enforcement of which the French developed a class of minor civil servants in the *garde-champêtres*). The reduction of forest land was taken further in the First World War, when trees were cut to provide timber and additional losses were caused by military action during the War of Independence.

The fact that the Europeans came as colonizers in the wake of conquest did not diminish the pioneering spirit of those, French for the most part, who developed the land, particularly on the higher plains, away from the coast. They saw themselves as opening up new lands, not readily accessible, or remote from easy communication. They were confident of their own virtues, proud of their education, readiness to work, and ability to plan ahead.

There was a limit to their achievements, and a social cost to the rest of the community. They transformed the indigenous agriculture by growing two major crops for export, wheat and wine. The limitation of the environment became obvious, as the years passed, in the production of wheat. Traditional Algerian agriculture had produced a relatively low wheat crop. On the best land near the coast wheat was commonly grown as part of mixed farming. On the Tell a simple form of farming was practised. The ground was disturbed little in rudimentary tilling and the crop was, by European standards, poor. Moreover the ground was cropped only every other year, with an intermediary year fallow.

Initially French colonists followed the traditional pattern, which differed little from medieval practice in Europe. They then began to increase the working of the soil, as they became more established and better equipped and as they could sell grain to the towns and for export to France. At first the return on this increased working of the soil was excellent and many farmers dispensed with the year's fallow. But their success was attributable to the accumulated humus which rudimentary tillage had conserved over the years. The Algerian climate made it impossible to replace this humus quickly, since summer crops of fodder or vegetables did not grow on the Tell. As the humus was exhausted crops fell. There was a return to fallow. Then dry farming was introduced; the soil was worked (and worked to increasing depth as tractors were introduced) during the fallow year, to aerate the soil and accelerate the degradation of organic matter. The long-term effect was, however, a continued exhaustion of the soil, whose resources were not replenished either by intermediary crops or by fertilizers, which were scarcely used in Algeria before Independence. As Mazoyer has said in summary: 'In Europe mechanical intensification would have had the same result, but it was compensated by the cultivation of root crops and by use of fertilizers which prevented the soil from being impoverished. In a Mediterranean climate mechanical intensification, by itself, leads to the ruin of the soil.'[1]

Agricultural development in Europe, and even more in North America and Australia, was possible because new land could be opened up for farming. It was possible to feed a growing population at a higher standard of living and still have an export surplus. But in Algeria the cultivable land was already largely exploited and use of marginal land led to a diminution of the arable area through soil erosion.

The development of vineyards by the French colonization was, by some criteria, much more successful than that of wheat. It was a new industry to which the climate and resources of some parts of Algeria are well suited. Initially the culture of vines lent itself readily to small-scale cultivation. But the inroads of phylloxera, aggravated in Algeria by a succession of bad years (1887–92), produced a crisis and transformation in the industry similar to that in France. The small producer was vulnerable to the loss of production, especially when he still owed

[1] Marcel Mazoyer, *Agriculture et Développement en Algérie* . . ., Algiers, 1970, p. 15.

debts to the Bank of Algeria. Land was sold to companies or wealthy individuals, who alone could afford to replant the vineyards with stock resistant to phylloxera—an economic transformation which was associated with radical right-wing protest and anti-Semitism in politics.

Subsequently Algerian wine had to compete with French wine, which it could not do on favourable terms. In the long run, however, with the growth in the demand for wine in industrialized Europe and elsewhere, viticulture had marked advantages for the Algerian economy. In spite of mechanization it remained relatively labour-intensive in a country which had an excessive supply of labour. As wages rose in Europe the advantages of the Algerian wine industry increased, and the vineyards could continue to offer employment.

It was ironic that the industry should, after Independence, be ill regarded by Algerian leaders. Alcohol was unacceptable to Islam, and the vineyards in Algeria were seen as a symbol of colonization. Some French critics of the colonization of Algeria (Aron, ed., 1962, p. 215) were susceptible to a kind of romanticism which is alien to economic thought when they wrote: 'The natural vocation of the land is to nourish its inhabitants. But the best Algerian lands were used for the cultivation of produce for export.' One could expect the emotions of Algerians to be even more hostile to viniculture and, in the decade after Independence, many acres of vineyards were taken up. However, a sense of pragmatism has held its ground and wine continues to be produced and exported, in spite of the shortage of expertise in production in a Muslim country and the delay with which the state has sought alternative outlets away from France.

The result of agricultural development under colonization was to leave Algeria with a dual agricultural economy and a legend concerning that economy; to which was added, immediately after Independence, an attempt to introduce a new system of agricultural enterprise —self-management and state marketing—accompanied by its own ideology.

The 'modern' sector of the economy occupied the best land, employed machinery, and produced for the market. It was dominated by Europeans. Muslims were active in the modern sector, but they were a small proportion of the agricultural Muslim population (some 20,000–25,000 out of 532,000); they spent a small proportion of the total wage bill in agriculture, used few tractors (only 418 out of 19,509 in 1954), and handled proportionately little agricultural credit (in 1952 the Crédit Agricole Mutuel, with 50,000 members, equally divided between Europeans and Muslims, loaned 16 million old francs to 16,316 Europeans, and only 2·6 million francs to 8,400 Muslims.

European agriculture had been subject to considerable concentration. There were a few large individual property owners, notably Borgeaud, Blachette, and Gratien Faure, owning many thousands of hectares; there were no Muslim landowners on such a scale, though there were some six hundred who owned more than 500 hectares. There were also massive agricultural companies—the Compagnie Algérienne, with 100,000 hectares, the Compagnie Génévoise with 15,000 hectares in the Sétif region, and the Trappist property of Staoueli, sold to Borgeaud after the separation of church and state.

The War of Independence itself brought a transfer of land to Algerians. Some land was bought or acquired by Algerians. The conditions of the war and the dedication of the French settlers to 'Algérie française' limited such transfer and it is virtually impossible to determine its extent. The private ownership of land, in the hands of the Algerian political élite, became the most sensitive area of later land reform.

The major transfer took place at the time of Independence when land in the modern sector passed to Algerians in a process of 'reconquest', which in some respects was as confused as that of the French conquest. Many French landowners departed, leaving their lands empty; many were encouraged to leave by the arrival of armed Algerians ready to take over their land; in other cases, a foreman was left to look after the land, which was then taken over by the state in the nationalization of 1963. The total area involved was 2·6 million hectares.

In practical terms, this often meant that French estates were left without direction in the middle of the agricultural year. This situation was met first by local action, necessarily subject to little coordination, and then, in 1963, by central decree with little or no reference to local conditions. Locally, whoever was able to take the initiative in organizing farm workers did so, through whatever institution was closest, the army, the FLN, or a group of trade union militants. In this way farm work was carried on, although with obvious limitations consequent on the disruption of markets.

In 1963 the organization of all production was in theory made subject to the 'March decrees', which established the practice of self-management, or *autogestion*, in agriculture as well as industry and mining. Although self-management already existed in Yugoslavia, the decrees were a major innovative step in their attempt to set up a new system of popular participation in production. They were issued, and immediately took the force of law, without any kind of public discussion, either in the press or in the national assembly, or by consultation of the workers whose rudimentary institutions of self-management they legalized and developed. This combination of local participation with centralism was, moreover, embodied in the decree legislation. On the one hand it established the institutions which were to run the farms, and on the other it gave to the Office National de la Réforme Agraire the task of 'organizing the management of farms abandoned by their proprietors'. Thus while work on the farm was the responsibility of the local institutions, everything that determined the limits within which the farm could operate—marketing, credit, equipment, purchase of seed and fertilizer—lay outside their control.

Self-management cannot be said to have prospered in Algeria. In the industrial field, as we have seen, this was because many enterprises were removed from the scope of self-management, while in the important new concerns—oil, gas, and metallurgy—the requirements of skilled entrepreneurship left little room for amateurism, and were not brought within the domain of the March decrees. In agriculture the experience of the first decade was that the institutions of self-management on the farms failed to come to life, in part because only a small minority of workers showed the initiative or had the level of education necessary to make them work, and in part because of the involvement of outside bodies, even if these were cooperatives. Agriculture remained a relatively neglected sector of the economy until 1971, in spite of periodic preoccupation with the problems of *autogestion* (leading particularly to the 1969 'enrichment' of the decree of 1963) and constant verbal reference to 'agrarian reform'. With certain exceptions, farms were thus allowed to stagnate, neither increasing their productivity nor proving to be vital centres of participation.

The complex provisions of the March decrees establishing the institutions of self-management are unsuited to practical implementation by uneducated, predominantly illiterate farm workers.

The basic institution of a self-managing farm is the general assembly, composed (under the 1963 decree) of all permanent (not seasonal) workers. The assembly 'adopts' the development plan, annual programmes, and arrangement of work, and 'approves' the final accounts. It also elects a council of workers if the general assembly is larger than thirty members. The assembly must meet at least every three months.

The workers' council, which must meet at least once a month, adopts the internal regulations of the enterprise, decides on purchases, sales, and loans required under the general plan, examines the accounts, and 'elects and controls' the management committee.

This committee is given overall responsibility for management of the enterprise and, more specifically, draws up the development plan and the annual programmes, establishes the internal organization of work, and draws up the accounts. It too must meet at least once a month.

The management committee elects, annually, a president from among its own number, who presides over the management committee and also over the council of workers and the general assembly. He countersigns cheques. In addition he represents the enterprise in external relations before the law, on the authorization of the management committee.

The enterprise also has a director. He is appointed by the *organisme de tutelle* on the advice (*agrément*) of the Conseil Communal d'Animation de l'Autogestion, a body designed to coordinate the activity of self-managed enterprises, made up of presidents of management committees together with representatives of the party, the trade unions, the army, and the communal administrative bodies. The director has two distinct functions. He is representative of the state, with responsibility for supervising the legality of farm operations and their consistency with the national plan, as well as proper accounting and records of minutes. At the same time he is a director with the normal responsibilities of an executive officer, with the task of ensuring, under the authority of the president, daily operations in accordance with the decisions of the management committee and the council of workers. He signs cheques and is treasurer responsible for cash.

This careful design, with its sophisticated distinctions between institutions and their responsibilities, was launched into a rural world which was bound by tradition and which lacked educated personnel.[1] As a result, those who worked the farms were able to safeguard estates, and hold a balance between their deteriorating completely on the one hand and passing into private ownership on the other. But not only did they not develop, they did not reach the level of production they had known under the French. They were hindered in their operation by the restraints of a centralized state, but they did not themselves pass under state control or become state farms. In particular the directors, who might, under the text of the decrees, have been the instruments of strict state control, possessed neither the competence nor the means to achieve this result. As Claudine Chaulet has commented: 'These "directors" whose role should have been of the first importance, according to the text of the legislation, were in practice young men, often full of goodwill but crushed by their responsibilities. Moreover, they were badly paid, they had no statutory tenure, they were often moved from one post to another, they rarely lived on the site, and did not always have any means of transport.'[2]

The restraints which the state, state banks, and cooperatives imposed on the farms limited the possibility of self-government. An overall plan can scarcely be made in full independence when sales must be directed through state monopolies, and day-to-day decisions depend on coordination with outside bodies. In addition the natural tendency in an organization, even of the kind which the decrees envisaged, would be for control and privilege to be concentrated at the top, and this tendency has been exaggerated by the strength of tradition. In the

---

[1] The most useful study of farm self-management from which much of what follows is drawn, is a survey of the Mitidja area: Claudine Chaulet, *La Mitidja autogérée*, Algiers, 1971. It provides a perceptive insight into rural life as well as a scientific study of its main subject.

[2] Ibid., p. 150.

Mitidja the self-governing farms took over French estates; they are the successors of the private Algerian or Turkish estates which the French admired (and acquired) at the time of the conquest. It is easy to understand that many workers see the president of the management committee as the replacement of the *colon* who was 'patron', and that some presidents readily act out the role attributed to them, inheriting a paternalist attitude to their workers.[1]

The presupposition of this arrangement was, in the first place, that the farms should be commercially viable; they were to produce and sell their produce in order to make a profit and the profit would then be divided between a state levy, provision for deterioration and investment on the farm, and a distribution of bonuses. Initially very few farms made a profit, and in these conditions remuneration came to be indistinguishable from a wage payment, even though it was, nominally, an 'advance'. The scale of advances extended from eight dinars a day for an ordinary worker to twenty dinars for a mechanic.

The different standards of living which this wage differential produced were exaggerated by other factors. Thus the more skilled workers —and particularly those who enjoyed a directing position in the enterprise—worked all the year, except for holidays, while the lower paid could only be found work for some two hundred days, plus twelve days of paid holiday. There were extra non-monetary rewards: the availability of crops at cost price, or their availability by a sharing out without any accounting. Lodging was sometimes free, when it was available on the farm, either in simple buildings or as a result of dividing up the former *colon* home, with all the absurdities, and inadequate sanitation which a crude division produced. But these non-monetary rewards usually worked in the same direction as the inequalities of wage payment: in favour of the better paid. Nor did rudimentary social services redress the balance.

However, in 1968 the financial achievement of some of the self-managing farms showed an improvement, partly real, partly the result of improved accounting. On 11 June 1968 Boumediene and his minister of agriculture, Tayebi Larbi, distributed the profits of the preceding year to the workers on the self-managing farm of Menzel Chouhada, at El-Khemis (in the department of El-Asnam). The profit was of the order of £100 per worker, and of this he received two-thirds, the remaining third going into the social fund of the farm. This was the first of such ceremonies, which in 1968 extended to 572 farms, or about one-third of the total. At the same time a fresh effort was made to improve and revivify the whole system of farm self-management. A

---

[1] 'Le Président donne des ordres ... c'est le patron du domaine comme l'était le colon' and 'Un ouvrier, c'est comme un enfant, on lui donne un morceau de sucre, il se taît. C'est comme ça, l'ouvrier'—are among the comments collected by Chaulet's survey, p. 170.

committee, drawn from the party and led by Ahmed Kaïd, put forward proposals for changes in the constitution of the farms and in the institutions with which they worked. These proposals were put into effect in the *ordonnance* and decrees of the following year. The *ordonnance* clarified the legal position of the self-managing farms: the land was described as belonging to the state, and put at the disposal, for a limited time, of collectivities of workers. It also guaranteed the rights of the workers, individually and collectively, in such matters as social security.

The main effect of the decrees was to shake up the existing internal structure of the farms. Seasonal workers were brought into the collectivity (it was now sufficient to have worked 200 days on a farm of polyculture, 160 on a farm of monoculture, to qualify), with the result that the general assembly was increased in size, sometimes by as much as 50 per cent. Henceforth the president was to be elected by the general assembly and was given supervisory powers over the director. At the same time a complicated balance was established in the nomination of candidates to the presidency between members of the farm and a 'communal committee', with representatives from the party, local government, the ministry of agriculture and agrarian reform, and the trade union—a balance designed to protect the electors from the imposition of a candidate supported by a dominant clique, and from the imposition of an 'official candidate' from outside. The council of workers (now required when the farm had more than fifty members) and the management committee remained, with fresh provisions intended to ensure their genuine renewal by election and with limitations on membership among members of the same family. The role of the director was modified to make his post more clearly executive (he was no longer a member of the management committee, but only an observer). A further decree reformed the system for the distribution of the revenue of the farm. It limited the share going to the state and local government to 30 per cent and then provided for a distribution to the investment fund and the social fund of the farm, together with a new system of 'points' to be collected during the year determining the individual reward to members.

Outside the farms themselves corresponding changes were introduced, designed to improve the conditions in which they operated. A new agricultural bank was established, together with new cooperatives responsible for the supply of seeds and equipment and for marketing, of which the OFLA—the Office des Fruits et Légumes d'Algérie— was the most effective. At the same time important powers which affected the detailed running of the farms were confirmed in the ministry of agriculture and agrarian reform, while others were attributed to departmental government. The immediate effect of the changes of 1969 was to produce an important series of elections which, at least in the Mitidja, were marked by great liveliness and freedom of choice. In some cases this resulted in a major change in elected personnel, but in others the incumbents were confirmed in office. In common with the national congresses drawn from the agricultural sector the elections indeed showed that, whatever the shortcomings of the system of self-government, it still permitted and encouraged the emergence of talent and awareness among its participants—a fact which is confirmed by Chaulet's enumeration of individual examples, qualitatively important if numerically restricted.

No systematic survey of the working of farm self-management has been carried out since the reforms of 1969. In the long run it may prove an effective way of running the modern sector of agriculture. But the practices which showed themselves in the first five years are deep-rooted in Algerian society. This is particularly true of centralization. Aït Amara has commented on the early period: 'From the start in 1963 the system of centralized direction made a nonsense of the responsibilities given to the institutions of management. Directors were reduced to the carrying out of decisions taken by superior administrative organizations. A dense network of instructions, directives, post-facto controls, and prior authorizations was woven between the farms and the central and regional administrations, transforming the supervisory power into hierarchical power.'[1] That some improvement was effected by the reforms of 1969—as well as by the growing experience of an active minority on self-managing farms—cannot be in doubt. The official account describes the increased frequency of meetings and the reality of elections which, together with decentralization 'depuis le redressement du 19 juin 1965' has restored the prerogatives of the collectivities of workers. But the restraints within which the farms have to operate derive in part from bureaucracy, which does not disappear automatically, even if the bureaucratic unit is local rather than national. Moreover the proliferation of cooperative organizations may complicate the life of the farm if it is dependent on a series of outside bodies, in different towns each some fifteen or twenty kilometres from the farm, for supplies and marketing. This is a shortcoming which is no doubt reflected in the government's recognition of the need to 'deepen the relationship between farms and administrative organs, both in advance of production and following it.'[2] The frustration of one farmer was vividly expressed at the congress of self-managing farms held in April 1973:

A good part of our crop has been declared second choice by the marketing services. Just take tomatoes as an example. This same service about a year ago asked us from its Oran office to grow tomatoes. Naturally, that's what we did. Result, our tomato crop rotted and we were obliged to throw it away. It was not a matter of kilos, it was not a matter of quintals, but of tens and tens of

---

[1] *Archives Internationales de Sociologies de la Co-opération et du Développement*, supplement of Jan.–June 1971.   [2] *La Réforme agraire*, préambule, p. 11.

quintals. How, my brother, in these conditions, can you make a profit? But that's not all, and anyway, if it was only a question of tomatoes—you can read the account book if you want—at least a half is pushed back at us.

The facts he related indicate that many of the problems of the early period remain, while the discussion of them in *Moujahid* indicated a new readiness to bring such problems into the open, at least for the time being. Moreover the question of self-management was by this time put in a new perspective with the implementation of the four-year plan and with the introduction of agrarian reform.

Whatever the achievements of self-managing farms, they brought little or no benefit to the 'traditional' sector of French agriculture, which remained relatively unchanged. The self-managing farms provided no better leaven than they had when the French owned them. For example seasonal workers, returning to their villages from the vineyards of self-managed farms, found conditions so different that any agricultural practice they may have learned was inapplicable.

The most serious incubus on the traditional sector was the growth of population, unaccompanied by any increase either in employment or in food supply. The links between the traditional sector and the towns continued to be disrupted as the towns were provided with industrial goods at the expense of the artisanal products of the country. Some areas—notably Kabylia—lost much of their traditional life as the result of the war and population increase, while young men went to work in France, sending home remittances which provided a better source of income than the olive or nut trees had done. However, specific areas, like oases close to the oil wells, benefited from a spin-off from oil production, and more substantially, the infrastructure of whole regions was improved by programmes of regional reform adopted by the government.

The Algerian census of 1964–5 showed that 25 per cent of land in the private sector was in holdings of more than 50 hectares while it was estimated independently that 650,000 peasants and sharecroppers worked holdings of less than 10 hectares. The Algerian statistics show:

    16,500 holdings of above 50 hectares
    147,000 between 10 and 50 hectares
    114,000 between 5 and 10 hectares
    310,000 less than 5 hectares

To the problem of uneven distribution was added that of absentee landowning, which accounted, according to one estimate, for one-fifth of the privately owned agricultural land, in a country where improving landlords scarcely exist.

The Tripoli programme of 1962 had outlined principles of agrarian reform, but for nearly a decade it was not more than an oft-repeated slogan. Meanwhile, the areas of the country that had borne the heaviest brunt of the War of Independence witnessed industrial development and growth of towns (to which, as always, the rural population was attracted) with little corresponding improvement in the countryside. To some extent, this was the result of deliberate policy rather than simple postponement. Boumediene, in a speech which, although self-justificatory, is close to the truth, said on 26 May 1970:

> We did not want to hurry the application of the agrarian revolution for the simple reason that priority was given to self-management and to the restructuring of the economy in a general manner, the re-establishment of security and stability over the whole of the territory and the development of the industrial revolution. In a word, it was a question of organizing on a healthy and lasting basis the whole apparatus of the state.

It is likely that Boumediene was aware of the upheaval which land reform must cause in the countryside, and the extent to which some of his colleagues' personal interests would be affected—for the War of Independence had not been led by landless peasants. In addition, the programme of Algerian economic development gave primacy to industrialization, as a means of providing capital for investment in agriculture and an outlet for agricultural products. Of total national investment in 1973, industry was to take 47 per cent, agriculture only 16 per cent; but increased revenue and prices raised the actual proportion for industry to 60 per cent.

However that may be, a decisive measure of agrarian reform was at last enacted by *ordonnance* on 8 November 1971. The first article is striking in its simple enunciation of principle:

> The land belongs to those who work it. Only those who cultivate it and bring it into use have any right over it.
> The agrarian revolution has as its aim the elimination of the exploitation of man by man.
> The agrarian revolution aims at the radical transformation of the conditions of life and work in the countryside.

A particularly notable example of what had come to be seen as 'the exploitation of man by man'—the system of *khemassat*, or crop-sharing—was abolished outright by Article 89.

The *ordonnance* set up a Fonds National de la Réforme Agraire. This was a national depository for land while it was being transferred to new ownership. Before the reform could be fully implemented, this fund became the centre of propaganda and publicity since a large number of landowners were encouraged or pressured into giving land to it. While the organs of publicity claimed that these gifts were unprecedented, the aura which surrounded them had something in common with the cession of lands in France on the night of 4 August, as depicted by some historians of the French Revolution—although in the Algerian case, the 'gifts' were spread over a long period, and it was widely known that, for example, higher civil servants and diplomats endeavoured to ensure their future careers and promotion by handing over a minimum parcel of land to the fund. None the less, it was reported that 1,232 individuals had given 60,000 hectares to the fund.

The decision to implement agrarian reform was of major political importance. Against any revolutionary change it could well be argued that agrarian reform had not succeeded anywhere in the world—least of all in neighbouring Tunisia—and that economic development and agricultural improvement along sound technological lines should continue until greater national prosperity had been achieved. Moreover, those who argued in this way were themselves landowners, including such men as Ahmed Kaïd, on whom the implementation of agrarian reform would depend. Boumediene was an exception in coming from a poor peasant family. He pressed the question to an issue and carried the revolutionary council reluctantly with him, at least in the short run. He insisted on the full scope of reform, including expenditure to give unprecedented standards of living to peasants in cooperatives and in socialist villages, thereby committing himself to the extent of running considerable political risks.

The political arrangements for the reform were designed to minimize the dead hand of bureaucracy and maximize popular participation, while at the same time the government retained tight control over an operation of great political sensitivity. The Assemblées Populaires were enlarged to enable them to supervise the operation. They co-opted local representatives from the party and from local branches of local organizations—from the mayor's office, veterans' organization, UGTA, the Union Nationale des Femmes Algériennes, the newly formed agricultural trade union (Union Nationale des Paysans Algériens), and the FLN youth movement. Technical committees were set up, and newly appointed executives sent from Algiers to activate the local agents of the ministry, lest they be too close to vested interests or too buried in paper work. Students from agricultural colleges participated in preparing the census of land, and students and conscripts were sent to spread the gospel of land reform. The consequent agitation and publicity was reported to have some effect in undermining local inertia and resistance, although the dialogue between students and peasants did not always lead to enhanced mutual respect. The party was thus given a minimal role in the project, which was carried out at a time when it was at a low ebb (Ahmed Kaïd having been relieved of his office, the direction of the party fell to Cherif Messaadia).

Before redistribution could begin a census of land had to be carried out, as there was no adequate cadastral survey or land register. This work was done by a vast team of officials and students from agricultural colleges, using questionnaires, enquiry, and local knowledge to establish details of ownership as accurately as possible.

Redistribution was then carried out in three parcels. The first was from public land, to which had been added the small area of land from religious trusts. Five million hectares of land were surveyed and one million judged arable; it was distributed to about 55,000 beneficiaries. The second parcel was of land in absentee ownership (with exception made, for example, where absenteeism resulted from death or injury in the War of Independence). The scale of this operation was limited by the fact that many absentee owners had already given land to the Fonds National de la Réforme Agraire.

The third parcel was obviously the most difficult: it consisted of the limitation of landholdings and the compulsory transfer of any excess. The principle which the *ordonnance* laid down (in Article 65) was that the maximum holding should be that which (taking account of local fertility and climate) would provide an income three times that of a man employed 250 days on a self-managed farm, i.e. 9,000 dinars (£900) per year, plus 50 per cent in the case of a family. The *ordonnance* also required *fourchettes*, maxima and minima, to be decreed for different types of land-use; when this had been done, specific limitations, or narrowly separated *fourchettes* (which had to be within the range of the national *fourchettes*) were decreed for each locality. The national limits, and two local examples are shown in the following tables:[1]

Property limits for private holdings

Land use type	land would be expropriated above the following limits	
	minima (ha)	maxima
1. Cropland		
Irrigated	1·00	5·00
Dry-farmed	5·00	110·00
2. Plantations and fruit-tree groves		
(a) Irrigated:		
Clementines	1·50	3·50
Other Mediterranean fruit trees	3·00	9·00
Stone-fruit trees	2·00	13·00
Pip-fruit trees	1·50	7·50
Olive groves and other hardy trees	10·50	35·00
(b) Dry-farmed:		
Stone-fruit trees	4·00	6·00
Pip-fruit trees	2·50	4·50
Olive groves and other hardy trees	11·50	45·00
Vines for wine	4·00	18·00
Vines, for table grapes	3·50	7·00

Source: *Journal Officiel de la République Algérienne*, no. 59, 24 July 1973

[1] Quoted by K. Sutton: 'Agrarian reform in Algeria—The conversion of projects into action': *Afrika Spectrum*, Hamburg, 1974, no. 1.

Property limits for private holdings in the wilaya *of El Asnam*

Land use type			zones (ha)			
	1.	*2.*	*3.*	*4.*	*5.*	*6.*
1. Cropland						
(a) Irrigated	1—2	2—3	2—4	2—4	2—4	2—4
(b) Partly-irrigated	2—3		5—7	5—7	5—7	5—7
(c) Dry-farmed	6—9	7—12	30—50	35—50	20—27	50—80

2. Plantations and fruit-tree groves
   (a) Irrigated: all zones
       Clementines without pips, Montréal
       Satsuma, Wilking   2—2·5
       Other Mediterranean fruits   3·5—6
       Stone-fruit trees   2·5—3·5
       Pip-fruit trees   2—3
       Pomegranates   4·5—6

   (b) Dry-farmed:
       Almond-trees   5—7
       Fig-trees   5—7
       Olive-trees   15—20
       Stone-fruit trees   5
       Table grape vines   5
       Vines, for wine (plains)   7—9
       Vines, for wine (slopes and hills)   5—7

Source: *J.O.R.A.* no. 65, 14 August 1973, p. 722

Property limits for the date-palm holdings in the wilaya *of Aurès*

	zones				
	1.	*2.*	*3.*	*4.*	*5.*

Deglet nour variety
1. In full production: No. of palm-trees:
   (a) Water valorisée   110—140 150—180 180—220 270—320 270—320
   (b) Water
       non-valorisée   90—110   130—150 155—180 225—255 225—255
2. Production in decline:
   (a) Water valorisée   145—160 220—270 220—270   —   —
   (b) Water
       non-valorisée   125—145 180—220 180—220   —   —

Source: *J.O.R.A.* no. 65, 14 August 1973, p. 744

The excess land has been expropriated and compensation paid in 2·5 per cent Treasury Bonds, redeemable over fifteen years (the amount being based on land tax prior to agrarian reform).

But the purpose of the reform is not only to effect a change of ownership. The reform is described as an agrarian revolution which is intended to be 'an intervention (in the economy) of a general character and a "long haul operation"'. The mode of distribution of expropriated land follows the same form as the principles of the limitation of landholding, except that the size should be such as to provide a revenue equal to that of a farmworker (instead of triple that amount). But the recipients do not become individual owners; they must belong to cooperatives. A variety of cooperatives is provided for, with the intention of covering every aspect and every phase of agricultural production. Thus, there are pre-cooperatives, for example, where the land has been disused and has to be brought into production; there are Coopératives Agricoles de Production which are more fully organized cooperatives; and there are looser Coopératives d'Exploitation en Commun, where peasants work (and draw income from) their own plot according to a cooperatively agreed crop plan. Finally, there are service cooperatives, of which the most important are Coopératives Communales Polyvalentes de Services. They are intended to provide services for existing veterans' cooperatives, self-managed estates, and private owners, as well as for the more recent beneficiaries from the land reform. They provide seeds, fertilizers, and machines and organize marketing as well as performing supervisory functions over the new cooperatives. Some 600 units are planned, of which forty-seven were reported as near completion at the end of 1973.

Land reform and the establishment of the cooperatives will have an effect on the standard of living of peasants, especially in poor areas, only over a period of time (even though the programme provides 150 dinars a month in cash and 100 dinars a month in food during a 'settling in' period up to the first harvest). A more ambitious programme is, therefore, envisaged—again with strong personal impetus from the president—for the establishment of 'a thousand villages'. They are designed to rehouse peasants and provide clinics, schools, and social services in new buildings. The standard of building is high— a different order of quality to that to which peasants have been accustomed. Although a first phase of one hundred villages was planned for 1973, only a slow start was made. Twenty-six were completed by 1975 and a further fifty-six were under construction. Those which had been built (for example, at Ras Bouira) immediately became showpieces.

The degree of success of Algeria's agrarian revolution will only be seen over a period of years. In the meantime there are indications of its possible future course. The expropriation of land has been carried through without effective opposition. Some of the losers have, no doubt, access to new wealth in the government or the national industries, some are content to remain private owners of substantial pieces of land; most are docile towards government action. The government is investing considerable sums in the agrarian reform programme and, although the proportion of investment going into industry and agriculture (43·5 per cent, 15 per cent) is not markedly different in the new four-year plan, the increase in oil revenues should safeguard the cooperatives from the financial shortage of the Tunisian attempt.

The reform of agriculture has initiated a major alteration of structures, without, so far, implementing any revolutionary changes in the basket of produce which the countryside provides for domestic consumption and for export. Wheat, grown on the uplands of the Tell and the High Plateaux, constitutes the major crop; and inevitably it remains vulnerable to the same vicissitudes of climate as the rest of the Maghreb. Thus the 1975 wheat harvest, at 700,000 tons, was 150,000 tons below the 1974 level, because of bad weather. Viticulture, which is possible along a belt up to a hundred kilometres from the coast (and is particularly developed around Oran) has survived the ideological attitudes of those who saw it as an 'imperialist' crop, and the possibilities for export are good. Citrus fruits—about half of them oranges—continue to be grown in the coastal zone, many of the former French estates having been taken over by Algerians who had served a successful apprenticeship with their former owners. The Saharan oases are famous for their dates and the date palm has been the centre of the life of Saharan villages since time immemorial—both in the practical advantage to be drawn from the palm tree and in the ancient ceremonies that surround the fertilization of the flowers. It remains to be seen how much survives the impact of agrarian reform. Surprisingly, the oases have also seen a new development in the culture of tomatoes—although the main area for their production is still in the north. As we have seen, the production of tomatoes is particularly sensitive to the delays of bureaucracy in a socialist economy, and the growers in the south have resorted to private enterprise in a way that self-managed farm producers find more difficult.

Some amelioration of agriculture is possible by the construction of dams and by irrigation; but the paucity of rainfall away from the coastal area and the difficult terrain limit the possibilities. However, an important land reclamation project, with Bulgarian assistance, was put under way in 1975 in the Mitidja, near Algiers. The dam is intended to irrigate some 70,000 acres. A contract has also been signed with an American company for the supply of water drilling equipment for the steppe and the desert areas. These are large-scale projects involving massive capital investment for long term rewards. At the other end of the scale is the 'plastic revolution'—the development of simple plastic cloches to improve the quality (and advance the season) of early vegetables—a traditional export to France.

Finally sheepherding has been a traditional part of the Algerian landscape and provides the minimal amount of meat which sometimes accompanies couscous, as well as the sheep which are slaughtered (even on the balconies of flats in the city of Algiers) for the great Muslim feasts. The pastoral sector of the agricultural economy is now being brought into the agrarian revolution. Over twenty million hectares have been used by 170,000 herdsmen to provide for eight million animals; but fifty per cent of the livestock is owned by five per cent of the herdsmen. The government intention is to buy sheep, reallocate them and group them into cooperative units. The first model village based on sheep farming was opened at Debbagh Maghoura in July 1975.

The difficulties of the 'long haul' are obvious. The growth in population is rapid, and there are no reserves of unused land to be brought into cultivation. The natural response is movement into the towns; but there is still a shortage of work in the towns. On the other hand, there are too few young men with the ambition to become agricultural extension agents: once educated, they seek jobs in the town, preferably in the government. There is even a need for skilled men in humbler trades—glaziers and plumbers to maintain the 'socialist villages' once they are built. Yet the need for such men is the greater, since peasants do not readily understand that, as beneficiaries under the agrarian revolution, they must work in cooperatives.

Conclusion

We have seen that the economic development of Algeria was set in train by a political decision in favour of industrialization which superseded the socialist experiment of self-management. The programme of industrialization, with the hydrocarbon industry as its base, was substantially similar in its early years to that envisaged by the French in the last years of their rule. It gave pre-eminence to technical skill and entrepreneurial ability, called for great effort from those responsible for exacting work and responsibility, but provided substantial rewards in return.

From 1971 President Boumediene gave a new leftward direction to the agricultural sector by a programme of land reform which included an attempt to mobilize students and peasants. This directly affected some members of the governing class who gave up land, and it introduced a current of activism which could not easily be reconciled with the meritocracy of the industrial sector. At the same time the resources of the country were severely strained as inflation increased the cost of the exploitation of gas resources and the construction of the base. Agricultural production did not immediately increase as a result of land reform and food imports placed an additional burden on the balance of payments. As a result there was little room for manoeuvre in the economy in the recession years around 1975, at a time of political experimentation, both in connection with land reform and the development of new political institutions.

ARMED FORCES AND SECURITY

Throughout the political upheaval of the end of the war and its aftermath Boumediene was able to pursue without interruption the construction of a national army (which changed its name from Armée de la Libération Nationale to Armée Nationale Populaire in 1963). In the Ben Bella years, when Boumediene was minister of defence, the task was of some urgency. It was imperative to bring the maquis into an organized and disciplined force which could be relied on to obey a single command. The army was used to establish control of Kabylia and in the frontier war with Morocco.

Military assistance was provided by the Soviet Union in the supply of tanks and aircraft and the provision of instructors; subsequently aircraft have also been purchased from France. Both the Soviet Union and France have provided training missions working in Algeria, and Algerian officers have gone to France and to the Soviet Union for advanced training. By 1970 the total armed forces numbered about 60,000 men, plus a gendarmerie of 8,000. The air force and navy (responsible for coastal defence) accounted for about 3,000 men each in the total strength.

After Independence the training which Boumediene had undertaken in the frontier camps could be placed on a more professional footing in military schools. One of the first to be founded, in 1963, took over the former French École Militaire Interarmes at Cherchell—in effect a military academy. In 1969 Commandant Yahyaoui was appointed its director in succession to Commandant Abderrahmane. No less important is the École du Génie at Hussein Dey. While these two are particularly outstanding, they form part of a large system of military education rendered imperative by the low standard of education on which the government sought to construct a modern specialized army. An École Militaire d'Administration was set up at Beni Messous and an École des Cadres de la Logistique (originally the École des Cadres du Matériel) at El Harrach—these fused into the more prestigious EFTAL—École de la Formation Technique et Administrative de la Logistique (at El Harrach) in September 1971. Cadet schools have also been set up, at Guelma, Kolea, and Tlemsen; initially with the intention of providing an education for the orphaned sons of *moujahidine*[1] they are open to other boys, and places are eagerly sought after.

The distinctive quality of the schools consists in their combination of traditional, élitist style with political education. During the war the Armée de la Libération Nationale gave great importance to the work of political commissars in the army, not in controlling and directing

[1] *Moujahidine*: members of the ALN or of the civilian organization of the FLN who had engaged in the fight for liberation before the cease-fire of March 1962.

officers, but in providing political instruction. The political commissariat has its own organization and its own training school, set up in 1962. The accounts of the activity of the military schools which appear regularly in the army magazine *El Djeich* invariably include reference to political education as part of the curriculum—together with general education, specialist training, and organized leisure and sport.

But while political education is related to the needs and demands of a socialist society, the quality and style of military training and promotion do not differ from those of historic military schools. This is perhaps particularly true of the Cherchell academy, where the passing-out parade, with the striped trousers of dress uniform, the speeches, and the conferment of commission follow a familiar pattern. Selection and advancement depend on achievement measured in examinations, and success necessarily carries an élitist prestige.

Training for the armed forces is not confined to the army. An air force has been built up almost from nothing. Initially a few pilots went to Syria and Egypt to train on MiGs. Then a pilot training school was established at Tafaraoui, a technical training school at Blida, and a third school at Bousfer. In the words of *El Djeich*: 'The air force is an élite arm which cannot permit laxity in the recruitment and selection of personnel' (December 1971). The first promotion of officers from Tafaraoui occurred in January 1970 at an obviously moving ceremony described in *El Djeich*, February 1970:

Then came the swearing of the oath pronounced in a vibrant voice by an officer of the school and repeated in a choir by the new officer swearing to defend the fatherland and to hold high the flame of the popular revolution.

The Major of the promotion, the standard bearer, advanced to the front of the official tribute followed by a group of the outgoing promotion and facing the new pupils waved the national flag.

In comparison with the air force the navy has received less attention —a technical training school exists at Tamanfoust (previously La Pérouse) but higher officers have, since Independence, been able to receive training in France.

A third stage in the growth of the armed forces was precipitated by the Middle East war of 1967. A detachment of troops was sent to the Middle East and although the speed of the campaign deprived them of the chance to engage in fighting, they remained on the Suez front until the summer of 1970, when the acceptance of the Rogers plan provided the pretext for their repatriation.

More important for the development of the army was that the Middle East crisis provoked the recruitment of students (including girls) on emergency reserve, and this was followed by the institution of two years military service for men. The result was to increase substantially the effective strength of the army, and to permit its further development as a pioneer corps. The École du Génie in any case undertook important projects of civilian construction, such as the University of Constantine, the zinc factory at Ghazaouet, and part of the steel complex at Annaba. With the advent of national service, men were available to work on the construction of the trans-Saharan road and on rural development.

The political and social importance of this innovation has been very considerable. 'The mobilization of the masses', so important in the doctrines of the left, is partly achieved by military conscription. The recruits receive, as in any army, instruction and military training, with all the advantages of systematic work and organization. In addition they receive political training and the experience of developing their country.

The integration of national servicemen into the military schools and their deployment in the country owed a great deal to Abdelkader Chabou, secretary-general of the ministry of defence (in addition to Boumediene himself). Chabou's career was in many respects characteristic. He grew up at Médéa and Batna, joined the French army in 1947 and attended the military schools of Boussaada and Cherchell before going to Saumur. He was commissioned in a tank regiment and fought in Indo-China. Having been posted back to Algeria he fought in the War of Independence, joined Boumediene's staff, became secretary-general of the armed forces of the provisional government and for a time was *chef de bataillon* on the eastern front. He became secretary-general of the ministry of defence immediately after Independence and headed the commission responsible for national service as well as the national aeronautical council, coordinating military and civilian aviation. He was killed in a helicopter crash on 1 April 1971.

Under his direction the army extended its activities both in the economy and as a social institution. During the War of Independence supply units were established, especially on the Tunisian frontier. At Independence these were developed into army cooperatives, formally established under a Direction Nationale des Coopératives/Armée Nationale Populaire in 1963. They have become sufficiently important to supply the army with its needs in some areas, and to sell outside the army, as well as to engage in building construction. The army cooperatives run a furniture factory, a publishing and printing business for the Éditions Populaires de l'Armée, a shoe factory, and a light engineering complex, among other enterprises. The army has its own cinema laboratory, its own social security, and a collection of holiday camps for soldiers' children.

In these respects the army enjoys a position of importance and pre-eminence. It performs economic and social functions for itself, and for the country as a whole, of a non-military kind. It provides its own political education through the political commissariat; it has its own publications and cinema and it is not subject to outside control, except that of the government, and even then its own officers take a leading part. Reports in *El Djeich* of military ceremonies such as annual passing-out parades have only rarely included a representative of the FLN in the list of those on the platform (usually made up of the president, secretary-general of the ministry of defence, commander of the military region, director of the school), and when an FLN representative is included he appears low in the list. In the battle for accommodation which dominates much of life in Algiers soldiers have priority over civilians. The hunting of deer in the Sahara is forbidden, but not, it appears, to the minister of defence.

The armed forces guarantee internal order in time of crisis or major change—as, for example, the introduction of the second phase of land reform in 1973. In more normal times, order is maintained by the Gendarmerie Nationale under the command of Colonel Bencherif. It has its own Écoles de Gendarmes, the first at Bel Abbès and others, for officers, at El Harrach and at Sidi M'Hamed and follows French procedures, having benefited from French training. The same is true of the Sûreté Nationale, which is directed by Ahmed Draia.

Recruitment into the Gendarmerie was easy in the first instance, since its personnel were drawn from wartime combatants. To that extent, the need to provide employment for veterans coincided with the requirements of a substantial police force which, like everything else in independent Algeria, started from a very narrow base.

However, this is only part of the considerable effort which the government has undertaken to look after the *anciens moujahidines*, numbering, according to the membership of the Association d'Anciens Moujahidines, some 90,000 in October 1969. A Ministère d'Anciens Moujahidines was created by the Ben Bella government in June 1965; some 30,000 were given employment in public service; a further 10,000 participated in 395 agricultural cooperatives and were provided with housing and stock by the government. Licences for cafés, taxis, and tobacco kiosks have been distributed to the widows of former combatants and to the combatants themselves.

A serious effort has also been made to provide education for *moujahidines*. A special university examination has opened the way for some to pursue or resume university education (an important number of students had taken part in the school and university strike of May 1956 and, unable or unwilling to resume their studies, then joined the resistance). University classes are held at times which allow veterans in employment, especially in the civil service, to attend and to work towards a university certificate (an arrangement which gives the classes themselves an attractive diversity). For children orphaned, or having suffered the loss of a father, children's homes have been created with schools attached.

The Military Balance

The distinctive quality of the Algerian army lies in the way it has been developed as part of political and even civil society. At the beginning of 1976 it appeared that it might be called on to undertake the prime task of an army—to fight a war. For this purpose the army could command 65,000 men, plus a possible 40,000 from the security forces. It was reported that the Soviet Union had modernized the tank forces of the Algerian army, so that there were 400 modern Soviet tanks, together with about fifty French light tanks. These were supported by Soviet fighters (MiG 15, MiG 17, and MiG 21) and by light fighter bombers. To these might be added Mirages from Libya, if these were made available as a result of the newly formed entente between the two countries.

FOREIGN RELATIONS

In any conventional analysis of international relations, Algeria ranks as a small power. It has a population of 15 million; its industrial base is minimal, in spite of its resources of oil and gas; and its armed forces are not capable of conducting a major war. But as Boumediene's regime became more firmly established and as the second decade of independence approached, Algeria began to play an increasingly active and diplomatically successful part in world affairs. It has done so as part of a deliberate effort to play an exemplary role. Whereas, during the war and early years of independence, Algeria had an exemplary role thrust upon it by the new left, it chose its own exemplary path ten years later. Algeria, as Bruno Étienne has said, *se veut exemplaire*.

Algerian ministers have frequently expressed a grand concept of Algeria's role in the world. Thus, Abdelaziz Bouteflika, as foreign minister, has described Algeria as the central country of the Maghreb, on the borders of the Mediterranean, with a double attachment to Africa and the Arab world and, thus, ideally placed to be the crossroads of three continents: Europe, Africa, and Asia. In another context, the government has given itself a central place in relationships between the producers of energy, industrialized consumers, and the Third World.

Algeria enjoys security, flanked as it is on each side by its Maghreb neighbours, and protected by the sea in the north and the desert in the south. In the early days, its neighbours disputed the delimitation of the desert frontiers—a historical sequel to the fact that the great medieval kingdoms of the Maghreb were in modern Tunisia and Morocco, but that French conquest (and the drawing of the frontier) came first to Algeria. These disputes have now been settled, to the advantage of Algeria since the Algerian principle of the permanence of the imperial frontiers has been accepted. However, Algeria remains vitally interested in the Sahara question. The joint Moroccan–Mauritanian annexation evoked its vigorous opposition and rekindled an intense ideological rivalry with Morocco (see below, p. 338).

While enjoying security for geopolitical reasons, Algeria has made the pursuit of security an important part of its diplomatic effort. It does so as a non-aligned state, although making little use of the old rhetoric of non-alignment. In consequence, Boumediene has actively supported the idea that the Mediterranean should become a 'lake of peace' by the withdrawal of the Soviet and US fleets so that its affairs are managed undisturbed by the Mediterranean powers themselves. The Algerian government has also insisted, successfully, that Algeria should be heard in the European security conference, as a country whose security depends on that of Europe.

The areas of world diplomacy in which Algeria has carried most weight are those of the oil producers and the non-aligned states. Algeria joined OPEC in 1969. It remains a minor producer and, until 1975, derived minimal benefit from its hydrocarbon resources as a whole, because of its limited production of oil and the need for large-scale investment before the gas resources can be exploited. Within OPEC, Algeria has therefore consistently argued for the maintenance of high prices for oil. It has also argued the importance of the European relationship, being foremost in pressing for the removal of the embargo on export of oil to Holland and Denmark in 1974. It sought an Arab–European axis as a counter to that between the United States and Saudi Arabia and resisted United States efforts to effect a reduction in oil prices. But in external relations OPEC drew advantage from the readiness of Belaïd Abdesselam to accompany Zaki Yamani to Europe and the United States in explanation of the Arab states' oil policies during and after the Middle East war of 1973.

But Algerian nationalization of its own oil industry and the policies it has been able to pursue as part of the OPEC cartel, are the most important ways in which Algeria wishes to be an exemplar to the world. In consequence, it has brought fresh groupings of national states into active cooperation, albeit in a preliminary, verbal way, and it tries to revivify existing institutions. This policy gathered momentum at the fourth conference of non-aligned countries held in Algiers in September 1973, which brought together seventy-six full members, observers, and three guest countries, together with representatives of the United Nations, OAU, the Arab League, and the African, Asian, and Latin American Solidarity Organization. Many countries were represented by their heads of state, ranging from King Faisal of Saudi Arabia to Fidel Castro. Boumediene, addressing the conference, spoke of the common bond of the non-aligned countries in being undeveloped and having suffered imperial domination, and urged that, in future, the non-aligned world should count on its own strength to become 'the motor of history'. Although non-aligned, the conference was not neutral on many of the disputes in course round the world, and found time to support liberation movements in Africa.

The non-aligned conference, which attracted attention to Algiers by the *éclat* of its numerous representatives and the smooth efficiency with which it was conducted, was followed by a Special Session of the UN General Assembly, summoned at the request of Algeria, in April 1974. Boumediene addressed the Assembly, under the presidency of Bouteflika, and the Algerian government prepared an extensive memorandum with supporting documents, entitled Petroleum, Raw Materials, and Development. The argument was replete with condemnation of the manner in which the developed industrialized countries conducted the affairs of the world to their own advantage and to the detriment of developing countries. It followed that developing countries must count on themselves and not on the will of the rich. OPEC was taken as an example of the possibilities open to raw material countries, and Algeria was an example of the possibilities of development:

Relying on themselves and on their own means constitutes the only way open to the developing countries. The example of Algeria: the struggle for development is the extension of the struggle for liberation. . . . The measures that it has taken (mines, land, petroleum) following the struggle for liberation show that Algeria is able to accept the necessary combats, battles, struggles and sacrifices in order to recover or defend a right. . . .

The battle for the recovery of natural resources leads directly into the battle of prices. Several Third World countries have joined the battle for the recovery of natural resources. Yet the final materialization of this recovery will not effectively take place if the mechanisms of transfer in favour of the rich are maintained. . . .

The argument approaches the quality of a mystique as it urges the generative impact of nationalization as a means to development:

Nationalization in itself constitutes an act of development. When nationalization brings us face to face with the realities and the responsibilities of complex industrial operations, it locates the conditions for the acquisition of practical management experience. When it tears down the barrier which a foreign company erects between us, as producers, and our clients and suppliers, it brings us immediately into the play of international relations. Thus the desire for development gives way to demands for development, and then to action to bring about development.

These themes have been carried forward and repeated at all the major conferences in which Algeria has taken a leading role. It has sought to give fresh impetus to UNIDO, notably at its conference at Lima in

1975 (Abderrahmane Khene, a former minister in the Algerian government, having been appointed secretary-general on the termination of his tenure of the same post with OPEC). In the world diplomacy concerning energy, it has sought acceptance of its thesis that discussions should be extended to the larger area of the supply and control of raw materials and their prices.

The abrasiveness of the Algerian approach has inevitably aroused some antipathies: among the developed countries which find that the rhetoric does less than justice to their own policies towards the Third World and among developing countries which resent the ubiquitous assertiveness of the Algerians. Members of the United Nations concerned with population growth also found puzzling the aggressive opposition to birth control of the Algerian representative at the Bucharest conference on world population in 1974, notwithstanding the Algerian contention that economic development was the sole remedy for a growing population. None the less, the success of the Algerian government in mobilizing the non-aligned world, the 'seventy-seven' developing countries, the United Nations, and OPEC in support of its essential themes, was incontrovertible. In 1976 the achievements were still diplomatic rather than practical; it was not immediately evident that other products were susceptible to the same degree of successful cartelization as oil (particularly when world depression posed the question of whether the OPEC cartel would hold together), and there were obvious differences in the manner in which differently endowed developing countries could be inspired, if at all, by the Algerian example. But the mystique had been created—a mystique which drew a veil over the shortcomings of Algeria's inequalities and shortcomings and gave the country a prestige far in excess of its power.

The militancy of Algeria's rhetoric with regard to foreign relations has naturally led to its taking a strong stand on questions of Middle East politics. But its influence has probably been greater within the framework of Third World politics than in the Middle East, except for the consistent support which it has given to the Palestinian cause. It was particularly notable, for example, that the Algerians won the support of such conservative monarchs as the Shah of Iran and King Faisal for their policy of linking the question of energy, in relation to the industrialized world, to that of raw materials. The conference held in Algiers in 1975 also made it possible for Boumediene to continue the work of mediation, which had begun in Cairo, between Saddam Hossein of Iraq and the Shah, leading to a settlement between those two countries of their longstanding dispute over the mouth of the Tigris and Euphrates, together with the termination of Iranian support for the Iraqi Kurds. Possibly as a result, Algeria was ready to act as mediator in the Lebanese civil war of 1975, and, at the time of writing, to participate in an Arab peacekeeping force.

In many respects Algeria had greater political affinity with Syria than with other Arab countries of the Mashreq. They shared a commitment to some form of socialist revolution, and a support for the Palestinian cause which was not allowed to threaten the authority of their own state. A certain sentimental attachment between the two countries has moreover remained from the participation of Syrian doctors in the FLN during the War of Independence.

Syria was also the principal beneficiary, in the heat of battle, from the assistance which Algeria made to the Arab states fighting Israel in October 1973. It is not known whether Boumediene was forewarned of the outbreak of the conflict (he remained silent when Qaddafi and Bourguiba complained that it broke out without their knowledge). It is also uncertain how much aid Algeria sent to the conflict. Algerian planes landed at Cairo on 7 October and it has been suggested that some 25,000 troops were sent—those on the Syrian front participating in the battle, while those sent to Egypt were incorporated into the Egyptian army too late to go to the front. The assistance sent continued after the war was over; it appears to have taken the form of the supply of petrol and a major contribution of Soviet armament. On all these questions official Algerian sources remained silent.

Relations with Egypt were very close while Ben Bella was Head of State. His overthrow inevitably led to a period of strained relations while Nasser was in power. During the Middle East war of 1967 Algerian planes were despatched east; but the short duration of the war and logistical shortcomings prevented their taking any effective part. The assistance which Algeria provided in 1973 might have established the foundation for renewed close collaboration; but the Algerian government had little in common with the conservatism of Sadat or the pursuit of Egyptian interests at the expense of the Palestinians.

Algeria played a leading part in promoting the Palestine Liberation Organization as the representative of the people of Palestine. The Palestinians are seen as a militant people, able to continue a long political and military campaign until they achieve recognition and victory, as did the FLN. Al-Fatah in particular has received the support of the Algerian government, and has always had access to Algerian radio; but the violence of extremist organizations has received no support. It remains the case that the Palestinian leaders resort more readily to Riyadh, Damascus, or Baghdad for haven and support than they do to distant Algiers.

Algerian influence in the Middle East, in spite of the inspiration which militants have received from the War of Independence, remains comparatively limited. Even the important degree of cooperation which exists in the strategy of oil diplomacy is modified by differences of interest (as well as political disposition) between Algeria and Saudi Arabia, or between Algeria and Iraq.

In African politics (as distinct from those on non-alignment into which African states enter) Algeria has played an even less direct part. Its position on such questions as Rhodesia and Angola has been radical and this has shown itself in votes in the Organization for African Unity. But it has been less active in that organization than the Moroccans, and has not engaged in the same activist (and moneyed) diplomacy as the Libyan government.

Seeking support among the developed countries for its worldwide diplomacy, Algeria gave priority to the region of closest proximity and economic interest, western Europe. In comparison the relationship with the super-powers and with China remained at a lower level. The United States was of major importance in economic diplomacy as it provided a potential market for natural gas; in addition, the Algerian government was more pragmatic than its rhetoric would suggest and was, therefore, aware of the advantages to be gained from relations with the country whose actions in Latin America, the Middle East, and Vietnam it so readily denounced. Diplomatic relations between the two countries were broken off after the Middle East war of 1967, but the United States conducted its affairs under the shelter of the Swiss embassy quietly and with good effect. Kissinger's policy in the Middle East after the war of 1973 and the withdrawal from Vietnam opened the way to improved relations; Kissinger found it advantageous to stop in Algiers on his way to the Middle East and diplomatic relations were formally resumed in November 1974.

In spite of the anxieties so readily felt in France and the United States that Algeria would become an outpost for the Soviet Union in the eastern Mediterranean, there has, in the event, been little ground for close cooperation between the two countries. The Soviet Union has equipped the Algerian armed forces and the Czechs have provided advice and training for the security services. But Algeria, in the pursuit of non-alignment, has no incentive to offer bases to the Soviet Union, while the technology required for industrial development is more readily found in western Europe and the United States than in the eastern bloc.

To the extent that the Algerian government makes a choice within the communist bloc, the attachment of sentiment is undoubtedly to China rather than to the Soviet Union. The experience of the War of Independence is not forgotten—a time of mortal danger when the French communists, still in the Stalinist mould, voted full powers to Mollet's government and the Soviet Union was slow to recognize the provisional government, while the Chinese welcomed a delegation from the FLN with calculated warmth and provided small-scale but tactically important financial aid. Boumediene has visited both the Soviet Union and China, and appears to have found the Chinese ambience much more congenial than that of Moscow; and the example of Chinese development is one with which the Algerian government can readily empathize. But China is geographically distant, trade is minimal, and aid small (though impressive, both at Blida and at the Chinese staffed hospital near Algiers).

Europe, and especially western Europe, therefore, remains a strong point of focus in Algerian foreign policy. Algerian policy has sought a diversification of its western European contacts, while western countries have seen the possibility of outlets in Algeria. Trade with the German Federal Republic has increased substantially and Willy Brandt visited Algiers shortly before his chancellorship came to an end. Britain offers particular advantages to Algeria as a source of education, especially in English. British trade with Algeria enjoyed an initial success of major importance in the participation of a British company in the construction of the oil industry. London became an important centre for loans to finance industrial development.

Relations with France remained particularly intense. There is no other example in the history of empire of one country densely colonized, over a period of more than a century, which is so close geographically as to permit a constant and continuous interaction after independence had been secured. From the Algerian side the French connexion, following Independence, was indispensable for reasons of language, technical and cultural assistance, and the continuity of habits unbroken by the harsh experience of the eight-years' war. The French government responded with flexibility which stemmed from the value of Algeria in the repertoire of presidential and Quai d'Orsay policies. De Gaulle miscalculated the possibilities of Franco–Algerian cooperation, underestimating both the speed with which the Algerians would be ready to take control of their own economy, especially the oil industry, and the force of nationalism directed towards the achievement of economic autonomy. None the less, he took a close personal interest in Algerian affairs (relatively minor matters were taken from the Quai d'Orsay direct to the Elysée), and saw Algeria as providing a connecting link between France and the Third World. His departure from the presidency in 1969 was followed by the crescendo of the oil negotiations, leading to Algerian nationalization in February 1971; but the trauma was shortlived and was followed by an accommodation under which France continued to benefit from the availability of Algerian oil and Algeria retained a market, while still diversifying its hydrocarbon outlets. Communal relations between Frenchmen and Algerian immigrants were not always harmonious, nor were they made easier by the recruitment of former *pieds noirs* in the French police force; and at least one bomb incident (at the Marseilles consulate in the summer of 1974) seemed attributable to Algerian internecine quarrels being extended to French territory. But state relations were not unduly disturbed and President Giscard d'Estaing, a vigorous supporter of

'Algérie française' in his early days, made a state visit to Algeria in 1975.

His visit evoked a complex mixture of nostalgia mingled with anger among the Algerian population. It was followed by a sudden worsening of relations between the two countries. The Algerian government bitterly reproached the French for their attitude to the Saharan question, which was interpreted as support for the conservative government of Morocco and the imperial interests of the United States. They also reproached France for the adverse balance of trade between the two countries. The arguments brought by the Algerians stemmed in part from the presuppositions of a socialist economy (urging that agreements should be signed like those between France and the countries of eastern Europe) and in part from the sense of a 'special relationship'—reproaching French oil companies for buying from the Gulf rather than Algeria.

Differences of this kind owed their intensity to the close and historic relations between the two countries. Once they gave rise to tension, other grievances concerning the well-being of Algerian workers in France or the activities of *harkis* assumed an enflamed importance.

SOCIETY AND EDUCATION

Nowhere was the deprivation of French rule in Algeria more obvious than in the lack of skilled and educated manpower with which Algeria emerged to Independence. A decree of 1883 extended the principles of Jules Ferry's educational laws of 1881 and 1882 to Algeria. The subsequent development of free primary education transported much of the spirit of French education to a small proportion of the Algerian population. The École Normale at Bouzarea trained schoolteachers with the puritan austerity of the French educational system (while keeping Muslim students separate from French) and the teachers, in turn, transmitted many of the ideals of the French Third Republic—the pursuit of scientific knowledge and the possibility of upward social mobility through education.

The number of Muslims brought into the educational system remained small: less than 23,000 out of a potential school population of 680,000 in 1898. At the outbreak of the War of Independence in 1954, some 14 per cent of Algerian (non-European) children between the ages of six and fourteen were in school; there were only 6,000 in secondary school and 589 in higher education. During the war the French government greatly increased its educational budget as part of the attempt to 'kill home rule by kindness'. None the less, the war ended with a minimal number of men trained for the top positions in society; of these, the majority were doctors, lawyers, and pharmacists rather than engineers (of whom there were, perhaps, ten). To fill semi-skilled jobs there were sufficient men with bare literacy, while basic trades, such as those of bus driver, clerk, and electrician had been so dominated by European settlers that Muslims had not acquired the skill required. A single Algerian had reached the level of Préfet—Belhaddad, of Constantine, in the late 1950s.

Algerian governments have attempted to remedy the lack of education by a massive onslaught on all fronts. This has included a high proportion of the general budget attributed to education (23·5 per cent in 1971, 19·6 per cent in 1972, but this latter figure does not include higher education and research); the recruitment of foreign teachers (the French playing a major part, including financial support, so that there were 6,500 teachers in 1969–70); the creation of new institutes and the adoption of traditional French establishments; finally, the arabization of state education, with traditional Koranic instruction continuing to play a minor (but not diminishing) role in separate schools under a separate ministry.

The salient characteristics of the main body of state education ten years after Independence are indicated by the fact that, in the school year 1971–2, 62 per cent of those eligible were in elementary school, including a much higher proportion of boys (76 per cent in the Algiers *wilaya*, against the lowest *wilaya* figure of 44 per cent for Médéa). The disproportion between boys and girls was more striking in secondary education, for which the aggregate figure was 287,000 in all kinds of secondary education, of whom only 83,084 were girls. In university education Algiers retained the lead with some 16,000 students, while the new universities of Constantine and Oran counted 3,500 and 4,600 respectively.

It was easy to extrapolate from these figures towards the rapid achievement of universal elementary education, and a target of 100,000 students in higher education by 1980. But the expansion of education was required to keep up with a very high rate of population growth which imposed a continuing strain on buildings and teachers. These problems were not alleviated by the process of arabizing education, ending the use of French as a language of instruction progressively in primary and secondary education, increasing the availability of courses in Arabic at the university, and requiring a knowledge of Arabic in examinations.

Although the language of education was changed, the structure and method remained essentially that of France, with its strong emphasis on annual programmes and examinations. The weaknesses in the system, therefore, showed themselves in the number of students obliged to repeat a year's work, thus increasing the size of classes and prolonging the school course, unless, as was frequently the case, the pupil dropped out.

While the major part of the educational system followed these traditional lines, an attempt was also made to provide vocational training for specific tasks. On the one hand, this meant the continuation of institutions modelled à outrance on French experience, notably the École Nationale d'Administration, preparing higher civil servants, and the military academies. To make provision for the direction of the oil industry, students were sent, from 1963, to the United States. But in 1964 the Centre Africain des Hydrocarbures et des Textiles was established with Soviet assistance in 1964 and the Institut Algérien de Pétrole set up by the French the following year. A further step was taken as the first four-year plan showed the urgent need for trained cadres, and Instituts de Technologie were set up. They dispensed with paper requirements for admission, were established in buildings already available or quickly constructed, and set out to train men and women for specific jobs—with varying degrees of success.

The commitment of the government to this massive programme of education, as part of the equalizing ideology of socialism and in order to provide trained manpower, was slow to produce results (as any educational policy must be) and created its own problems. Scarcity of certain skills continued to exist side by side with a growing number of educated young men with nowhere to go. Moreover, the economic and political structure of the country—the emphasis on industrialization, the importance of trade with western Europe, and the modern requirements of the armed forces—meant that power, status, income, and influence were to be found in occupations requiring western skills. A modern version of a Mamluk class thus dominated the country.[1]

The traditional world of Islamic learning and the network of social influence and importance, characteristic of Islamic society, was kept in being. The minister of traditional education (*enseignement originel*) and religious affairs, Mouloud Kassim, retained an important role and a secure platform. A distinct role was given to religious education, the teaching of Arabic, the acquisition of scientific skill within the framework of Muslim education and in the training of religious cadres. Six new religious schools were added, in 1971–2, to the twenty already in existence and plans drawn up for 'faculties' at Algiers, Constantine, and Oran for comparative studies based on Islamic law and religion and Arabic literature.

The numbers involved in religious education remained small: just over one thousand pupils qualified for a certificate (*al-Ahliya*) in 1970.

[1] Cf. the description by Ira M. Lapidus of fourteenth-century Mamluk Syria: 'The populations of Damascus and Aleppo fell into three broad classes: the Mamluk military élite which commanded the armies and administered the state; the local notability distinguished by some measure of political power, religious learning, and wealth which included the ulama, merchants, and professional; and the majority of the populace who possessed none of the crucial values.' 'Muslim Urban Society in Mamluk Syria' in A. H. Hourani and S. M. Stern eds., *The Islamic City*, Oxford, 1970, p. 195.

But religion and tradition continued to play a far more extensive role in Algerian society. It provided a unifying ideology and practice, relating 'revolutionary' Algeria to its past and incorporating the modern sector into a national whole. The contribution of Ben Badis to Algerian nationalism, the observance of Ramadan,[1] the austere sermons of Mouloud Kassim printed in *Moujahid*, and the slaughter of sheep on the balconies of Algiers flats for the great feast, all play an important part in maintaining at least an outward cohesion in a divided society.

It followed that 'modernization' made very little progress among the mass of the population in personal matters, particularly concerning women. This was the more striking because the participation of women in the War of Independence led to expectations of their full emancipation. But in 1976 a personal code revising the rights of women and the family has yet to be enacted. Women's education, as we have seen, progressed more slowly than that of men, with adverse effects on the supply of schoolteachers, secretaries, and typists. Birth control, rejected on the platforms of world conferences as a fruitless distraction from the imperatives of economic development, was inadmissible (in 1972 contraceptives were included in the list of forbidden goods which was given to incoming travellers at the frontier). The separation of men and women, the vulnerability of women who broke the code of behaviour, and the mixed bawdiness and romanticism of male society, remained characteristic of Algeria outside its most westernized segments.

Finally, the traditional society was one which Boumediene was not prepared to abandon. He did not want to transform Algeria into an Arab Sweden, or to allow the indefinite existence of a society divided between a traditional mass and a modernized élite. His ambition was to maintain intact the culture and authenticity of the Algeria in which he had grown up, while raising the standards of the whole country, internationally and internally, by means of economic development.

The National Charter

In circumstances of economic stress and in face of a felt need for political renewal the government embarked, in spring 1976, on a great campaign, leading up to a national referendum in June, centred on the 'National Charter'. The draft of the Charter—a lengthy document covering all aspects of Algerian achievement, government, and aspirations for the future—was made the subject of debate in party, trade unions, and meetings of the burgeoning peasants' association. On 27 June 1976 it was approved by a referendum in which (according to the official figures) 98·51 per cent voted Yes, in a poll of 91·36 per cent.

[1] On the other hand, the suggestion that Friday be taken as the day of rest was rejected since it would effectively cut Algerian industry and commerce from Europe for four days each week.

III
Libya

GEOGRAPHY AND POPULATION
Geography

Libya has a common frontier in the west with Tunisia and, further south, with Algeria. Across its southern border, over 1,000 kilometres from the Mediterranean, lie Chad and Niger. Its eastern frontier is with Egypt and Sudan. The Mediterranean coastline is nearly 2,000 kilometres long, although the direct distance is less than 1,300 kilometres. The total area is 1,759,540 square kilometres—smaller than Algeria, but almost twice the size of Egypt, five times that of France, and one-third of the United States.

Its geography lacks those characteristics which distinguish the countries of the Maghreb. To the west the Atlas mountains provide a series of folds which capture the north-west winds and provide a shelter against the desert, so that the country is relatively favourable to human life some 300 to 400 kilometres from the coast. The whole of Libya lies further to the south (Tripoli and Benghazi are on roughly the same latitude as the Algerian desert towns of Touggourt and Ghardaia) and the platform of the Sahara comes directly into the Mediterranean zone. The coastal strip is less than 100 kilometres wide and disappears altogether along the Gulf of Sirte, where Tripolitania and Cyrenaica are 'cleft in two by the 650 kilometres of dreary waste—an abomination of desolation which must be one of the most marked natural and human frontiers in the world' (Monroe, 1938). It is also the location of Libya's oil reserves. Before the discovery of oil, agriculture employed 70 per cent of the labour force and contributed 30 per cent to gross domestic product; but there are only some 10 million hectares of productive land in Tripolitania, of which at least 8 million are pasturage; in Cyrenaica there is a further 4 million, of which 3·6 million are pasturage. The desert region of Fezzan supports only nomadic life outside the oases.

The traditional economy of Libya was always constrained by the shortage of water. The settled agricultural zone of Tripolitania is bounded by the line of 150mm. average rainfall (barley and olives, the principal crops, require a minimum of 200mm. annual rainfall). Rainfall has long been supplemented by irrigation from wells which tapped the Phreatic water table of the Jefara; by using motor pumps the Italians were able to exploit a Quaternary aquifer and expand the area of their farms southwards. In the east the 'Green Mountain'—Jabal Al-Akhdar—rises to 800 metres. It leaves a coastal plain to the west, around Benghazi, but only a thin strip of coast to the north and east. Unlike the mountains of the Maghreb the Jabal Al-Akhdar is a high limestone massif, part of the Saharan platform. Permeable, it prevents the accumulation of sedimentary water; fractured and dissected, it hinders the movement of animals. There are no perennial rivers; but wadi farming is possible on the south slope. However, like most of Libya it is subject to hot desert winds which may raise the temperature to 122° F. (50° C.). The economy of the desert depends on some artesian wells and sedimentary water which feed the oases and are accessible by shallow wells. One spectacular deposit of fossil water has been discovered at Kufra. But the extent of underground water, its salinity, and the degree to which it is replenished are matters of constant study.

Libya boasts no great cities and there are virtually no great monuments more recent than the magnificent Roman ruins in the west and Greek Cyrene in the east. None the less there has been a continuous urban history. The towns have always served as centres for foreign settlement, nodal points for a restricted rural hinterland, government centres, and trading posts for the trans-Saharan trade (including gold dust and slaves), the export of agricultural products and, in recent times, the import of food and material. In the west Tripoli has survived on the site of one of the three Roman towns from which it takes its name. Tripoli has always been a more important town than Benghazi —more open to foreign influence, serving a larger hinterland, and having a larger population. To the east of Tripoli, Khoms and Misurata are the only towns of any substance before Benghazi, since Marsa Brega (on the Gulf of Sirte) serves as an oil terminal without having developed into a town. In contrast to the dominance of Tripoli over Tripolitania, the urban life of Cyrenaica is shared between Benghazi and the smaller but important outlets of Derna and Tobruk. Under King Idris the federal capital was established at Baida because of its importance for the Sanusi order and it remains an important centre of Islamic education.

The Italian occupation and subsequent economic development have inevitably affected population growth and distribution. The settlement of Italian colonists produced a migration abroad, and into the towns. After Independence the movement to the towns continued, and the development of oil brought increased importance to Benghazi. The Libyan government has used the revenue from oil to construct flats to house the immigrant population. It has also confronted, with much success, the problem of unemployment and shortage of trained labour existing side by side. However, the development of the economy still depends on foreign workers, Egypt and Tunisia being the main sources of supply.

Population

The 1973 census showed a total population of 2,259,497. Population censuses taken in 1954 and 1964 returned 1,088,889 and 1,564,369 inhabitants for the respective years. Libya is the smallest country of North Africa in population size and among the least populated countries of the continent, though the fourth largest in area. The UN estimated the population density in 1969 as one person per square kilometre of the total area and 70 persons per square kilometre of arable land (54 persons for the rural population on arable land). The population is concentrated primarily in and around Tripoli and Benghazi, on the northern highlands in both eastern and western provinces, and around a few oases scattered in the desert. In 1964, the census recorded the following regional distribution: Tripolitania, slightly above 1 million (65 per cent of the population), Cyrenaica, 451,000 (29 per cent), and the Fezzan some 79,000 (5 per cent). Small population size and low density do not necessarily imply that Libya is a labour-short economy. For the economic concepts of labour shortages and labour surpluses refer to the relationship between manpower and other resources rather than to the absolute size. Libya, like many developing countries, suffers in fact from structural imbalances in employment (and in the composition of manpower resources), that is from the co-existence of excess supplies for certain jobs and activities and shortages of a wide range of skills required for other occupations.[1]

Vital statistics and comparisons of the two available censuses suggest very high rates of population growth in the past twenty years (mid-1950s to mid-1970s). In 1964, the annual rate of population growth was estimated at 3·6 per cent, and most demographic studies and expert reports on Libya put average growth rates for these twenty years in the range 3·1–3·7 per cent per annum. These estimates are inevitably subject to error because vital statistics are both incomplete in coverage and unreliable; under-reporting seems to have affected population censuses to a greater degree perhaps in 1954 than in 1964. Yet an analysis of the age structure in the censuses, sample data on crude birth and death rates collected by UN demographers, and other partial evidence tend to support the view that the Libyan population has been growing recently at a fast rate, comparable to the rates of growth in Algeria, Morocco, Tunisia and the Sudan (all in the 3·2–3·5 range in 1970–5) but higher than in Egypt (2·8–3·0) and higher than the average aggre-

[1] See R. Mabro, 'Labour Supplies and Labour Stability: a Case-Study of the Oil Industry in Libya' in *Bulletin*, Oxford University, Institute of Economics and Statistics, 32, no. 4, November 1970.

gate rate in Africa (2·8).[1] It seems that crude birth rates have remained high since the late 1940s at around 46–48 per thousand while death rates though still high by international standards, may have declined to 16 per thousand by the early 1970s. Such a situation is precisely what is meant by a population explosion as it involves both high and accelerating population growth. International migration may have also contributed half a percentage point to annual increases. At Independence and in the following years, many Libyans returned to the country from Egypt, Tunisia, and Chad. The oil boom in the 1960s attracted Arab migrants to the tune of 5,000–7,000 a year. The inflows were probably larger after the 1969 Revolution when Libya attracted considerable numbers of Egyptians from the highly skilled professional to the unskilled construction worker. Immigration was partly compensated for by the departure of Italians, many of whom left the country in 1970 after the nationalization of their farms and businesses and by the emigration of the Jewish community, numbering 30,000 in 1954 and now reduced to a handful of residents.

A high and increasing rate of population growth poses different problems to a poor, and to a rich, developing country. Pre-oil Libya had her economic difficulties compounded by the demographic expansion (the natural increases rather than the absorption of migrants). Post-oil Libya has the means to carry the social burdens initially entailed by a fast growing population—heavy dependency ratios, educational and social welfare costs. These population increases are followed after a lag of fifteen to twenty years by increases in the number of entrants to the labour force. This could help restore the balance between the abundant financial resources of the oil economy and the scarce supplies of complementary factors; but much depends on the educational and investment policies pursued during the interval. The past experience of older oil-exporting countries—the Gulf States or Venezuela—leaves us without much ground for optimism. Oil countries generally fail to take advantage of the period of grace afforded by oil revenues to correct the structural imbalances which affect their economies. Their policies often tend to aggravate the disequilibria.

The Libyan population is youthful, a consequence of the demographic characteristics discussed above. The median age of the population was twenty-two years in 1954, and nineteen years in 1964. Approximately 44 per cent of the 1964 population were less than fifteen years old. This proportion might have slightly increased since. The apparent sex ratio reported by the census is implausibly high (108 males for every 100 females). A high mortality rate in child-birth may explain part of the abnormal excess in the proportion of males; under-reporting of females is however suspected by most observers.

[1] See UN Economic Commission for Africa, *Demographic Handbook for Africa*, April 1975, Table 5.

The Libyan population is homogeneous in certain respects. Thus, Libyan Muslims constitute the overwhelming majority of the population. In other respects dualism and sharp differentiation tend to prevail. First, there is an important minority of aliens. The proportion of non-Libyans in the total population, estimated at between 6 and 10 per cent in the early 1970s, is in fact much smaller than in the oil-producing countries of the Gulf and in Saudi Arabia. The problems of absorption are less acute and the threat to the national identity is not felt as strongly in Libya as in these other countries. Secondly, the Libyan population is divided between sedentary settlers and nomads or semi-nomads. The proportion of the latter groups seems to have declined from 26 per cent in 1954 to 22 per cent in 1964, and the downward trend has been continuing ever since. Thirdly, there are regional and tribal differences in culture and social modes of behaviour. These features however should not be unduly exaggerated. Fourthly, the urban-rural dichotomy—sharp differences in amenities, social infrastructure, incomes, employment opportunities, modes of living, etc., —is a feature of the economy which Libya shares with most of the Third World.

These socio-economic differentiations are often associated with population movements. International migration, which was mentioned earlier on, is one example. The settlement of nomads and semi-nomads, consistently encouraged by the government under both Monarchy and Revolution, is another interesting movement characteristic of post-war developments. The most significant phenomenon however is the considerable movement of population away from rural areas to the towns. Internal migration has assumed major proportions since the early 1950s. The statistical data unfortunately are very inadequate and there is a dearth of studies on migration. It seems that a combination of push factors—drought and impoverishment in agriculture—and pull factors —employment opportunities in the early days of petroleum exploration—initiated the movement in the 1950s. The towns continued to attract migrants despite the stagnation of employment in the petroleum industry. (This stagnation always takes place when the industry completes the exploration and development phase and becomes mainly engaged in production.) The expansion of the urban service sector (including government services), the development of a welfare state which initially favours the towns, the stagnation of agriculture, and the spread of education, all contribute to attract rural migrants to the main urban centres. In the 1960s the population of both Tripoli and Benghazi grew at around 7 per cent per annum, twice as fast as the rate of natural increase.

Finally, a word on the qualitative features of the human stock. These relate mainly to health and education. At the time of Independence the Libyan population was not only poor but largely illiterate and plagued by diseases and a high rate of infant mortality. The 1954 census put the rate of illiteracy (population aged six years and over) at 73 per cent. In 1950–1, Libya had only four preparatory and secondary schools with an aggregate of 300 students.[1] A number of serious diseases were then endemic in the country though their incidence—with the exception of tuberculosis, trachoma, and intestinal parasites—was probably low. Some authorities estimate that as many as 75 per cent of the population may still suffer from trachoma. An IBRD mission reported in 1959 a very high rate of infant mortality—close to 50 per cent—largely attributable to gastro-enteritis, deficient nutrition, and tetanus.[2]

Considerable progress has been achieved on all these fronts in the 1960s and early 1970s. Yet much remains to be done in the eradication of disease. In 1971, the average life expectancy was still as low as thirty-seven years and the infant mortality rate was close to 300 per thousand live births.

HISTORY AND POLITICS
In Antiquity

North Africa was first linked to the civilized world—then in the Bronze Age—by Phoenician traders seeking shelter from the storms of the Mediterranean. About 700 B.C., Tripolitania was colonized by their countrymen who founded three cities—Oea, Sabrata, and Leptis—known collectively as the *emporia*. Cyrenaica was first settled by Dorian Greeks, who are said to have founded Cyrene in 631 B.C. Subsequently they built Euesperides (eventually to become Benghazi), Barce, its port of Teuchira, and Apollonia. The five cities, known as the Pentapolis, flourished culturally and commercially and became a part of the empire of Alexander the Great. In 320 B.C. they passed into the hands of his successors in Egypt, the Ptolemies, to whom they were even more closely bound by the marriage to Ptolemy III, in 246 B.C. of Queen Berenice, whose father had made himself independent ruler of Cyrenaica.

Both Tripolitania and Cyrenaica eventually came under the control of Rome. The former was gradually absorbed after the destruction of Carthage in the second Punic war, and the latter was left to Rome by the will of Ptolemy Apion, King of Cyrene in 96 B.C. The two countries were administered separately, Cyrenaica being linked with Crete and Tripolitania becoming the province of Africa Nova, which was finally united with its western neighbour Africa Vetus, by the Emperor Augustus. The Romans occupied Libya for nearly five centuries and brought a prosperity which the country has never since known. They penetrated the Fezzan, far to the south; and went even further, to places not seen again by Europeans until the nineteenth century. They

[1] See *Statistical Abstract of Libya 1958–1962*, Tripoli, 1963, pp. 145–6.
[2] IBRD, *The Economic Development of Libya*, Baltimore, 1960, p. 253.

left aqueducts, cisterns, milestones, theatres, and Christian churches, whose ruins still proclaim the greatness of their achievements. They exported corn, olive oil, ivory, gold-dust, and even wild animals for the amphitheatre at Rome. The prosperity of Cyrenaica was checked by a great Jewish rebellion in A.D. 115, but probably Tripolitania was at the height of its glory in the reign of the Emperor Septimius Severus, who was born in Leptis Magna in A.D. 146 and died in York in 211.

The decline of the Empire brought both religious and political discord, and in Tripolitania ended in disaster. In 429 the Roman governor allied himself with King Genseric of the Vandals against the Empress Placidia. Genseric crossed the Strait of Gibraltar, and eventually conquered Tripolitania. His barbaric armies destroyed the civilization which had been built up and put nothing in its place. They were finally expelled by Belisarius, who reconquered Libya for the Byzantine Emperor Justinian. The country, however, never regained its former peace and prosperity, though some of its cities were rebuilt and re-fortified. It remained a shadow of its former self, and was quite unequal to checking the advancing forces of Islam, then mustering in Egypt.

The Arab Conquest (642) to the Italian Occupation (1911)

In A.D. 642 Arab armies reached Cyrenaica and swept steadily westwards, overwhelming the Byzantine colonies without much difficulty. Libya was controlled first by the Umayyad Caliphs of Damascus, and then by their successors the Abbasids, whose most famous member, Harun al-Rashid, in 800 appointed the Aghlab family as viceroys, with their capital in Tunisia. They remained in power until superseded by the Fatimids, the Shia founders of modern Cairo, whose original capital was Mahdiya in Tunisia. In their turn, the Fatimids appointed the Ziri family as their viceroys in the west; the latter, however, soon rose against their overlords. To punish their bid for independence the Caliph loosed upon them the large and warlike beduin tribes of the Beni Hilal and Beni Sulaim, who completely engulfed Cyrenaica and the greater part of Tripolitania. This second Arab invasion in the eleventh century had much more profound effects than the first on the ethnic composition of Libya and reduced the area to chaos. Tripoli alone of the Libyan cities of antiquity remained an inhabited town. In Cyrenaica, settled life virtually ceased.

During the confusion of the following century the Norman King Roger of Sicily invaded Tripoli, with the intention of extending his empire across the Mediterranean. This brief European intervention was brought to an end after twelve years by the Almohad rulers of Morocco, who moved east in 1158 in order to put an end to Christian rule in North Africa.

For the next 350 years Tripolitania was ruled from the west, from Tunis and Fez, first by Almohad Caliphs, directly, then by their vassals and successors, the Hafsids; while Cyrenaica remained under the influence of Egypt, ruled by the Fatimids and later their successors the Seljuk Turks. As the power of the Hafsids waned, Tripolitania entered an obscure and confused period in her history which Ibn Galbun,[1] the eighteenth-century Tripolitanian historian, dismisses in a few lines.

Spanish expansion in the reign of Ferdinand and Isabella brought renewed European intervention. In 1510 Count Peter of Navarre captured Tripoli in a night attack. The Spaniards added considerably to the fortifications of the city but did not retain it long for themselves. In 1530 the Emperor Charles V granted Tripoli, Malta, and Gozo to the Knights of St. John who had been forced out of Rhodes by the Ottoman Turks. They retained Tripoli, with extreme difficulty, until 1551 when the Turkish Admiral Darghut Pasha seized it for Sulaiman the Magnificent, then at the height of his power. From then until modern times Libya, like Tunisia and Algeria, became a part of the vast Ottoman Empire, which stretched from Iraq to the eastern frontier of Morocco.

The power of the Porte, however, rapidly became little more than titular. In Tripolitania a succession of Janissaries and renegade adventurers from Greece, Italy, and the Mediterranean islands, ruled by force and cunning in the name of the sultan. They were independent in internal affairs, though paying tribute to Constantinople. In Cyrenaica the sultan's authority was not acknowledged at all until 1640, when Mohammed Sakesli, a Greek from Chios, and the outstanding ruler of the century in Tripoli, established one of his followers as bey of Benghazi, and built there a strongly fortified castle. Under these adventurers, privateering, which had always flourished on the Barbary coast, was greatly extended. War which was the legal pretext for these operations was frequently declared and produced reprisals in the form of bombardments of Tripoli. Consulates were established to further trade interests and to conduct diplomatic relations.

Early in the eighteenth century the Caramanli family became hereditary and virtually independent rulers in Tripoli. Ahmed Caramanli (1711–45) secured his position by massacring most of his rivals, both Turkish and Tripolitanian, at a banquet, and dispatching a large tribute to Constantinople, the property, it was said, of his victims. He was, however, an able ruler who extended his control over the Tripolitanian hills, the Fezzan, and parts of Cyrenaica, and brought an unwonted stability to his conquests. His successors continued his ruthless methods, preying upon the commerce of the smaller maritime powers with great success. The last effective ruler of this house, Youssef, was a supporter of Napoleon, to whom he rendered services during the

[1] Ettore Rossi, *La Cronaca araba tripolina di Ibn Galbun*, Bologna, 1936, p. 66.

Egyptian campaign. On the other hand he came into conflict with the United States when the latter, which had negotiated a treaty to secure the free passage of their shipping, refused a demand for increased 'protection money'. Youssef declared war by cutting down the flagpole in the American consulate, on 14 May 1801. This war lasted until 4 June 1805. In 1803 the Americans lost the frigate *Philadelphia* in Tripoli harbour, her captain and crew of 300 being taken prisoner. In 1804 the captured frigate, which was being repaired by the Tripolitanians for their own use, was successfully destroyed in a daring raid by Lieutenant Stephen Decatur. Another remarkable episode of this war was a march from Alexandria of the American consul in Tripoli, William Eaton, with a motley international force of some 400–500 men, including some US Marines. The object of the expedition was to replace Youssef by a rival claimant to the throne of Tripoli. The latter's name was Hamed and he and his supporters formed the bulk of the expedition. On arriving at the Gulf of Bomba, the expedition, now in desperate straits, was saved by three American naval vessels with whose aid they succeeded in capturing Derna (13 May 1805) where they were then besieged until peace was declared a month later. This episode was the origin of the line 'from the halls of Montezuma to the shore of Tripoli' in the US Marine Corps ballad, Derna being regarded as a dependency of Tripoli though in fact it lies 1,000 miles further east than the capital.

Youssef's maritime activities were henceforth gradually curtailed by the increasingly superior technical qualities of the European navies and by the French seizure of Algiers in 1830 and the British occupation of Malta. Faced with ruin, he abdicated in 1834, and thus precipitated a civil war between his heirs, in which Turkey intervened. In 1835 the Turkish fleet removed the whole Caramanli family, and appointed a new governor, directly responsible to Constantinople. The change was welcomed by the European powers, as promising a more stable government and the end of piracy.

The return of the Turks at this moment was far from popular in Libya, and made little difference to the chronic unrest prevailing in Cyrenaica. It was soon overshadowed by the rise of a great religious leader who gave a sense of unity, at least to Cyrenaica. In 1843 Sayyid Mohammed Ali el-Senussi (Sanusi), grandfather of King Idris I, founded the Sanusi sect, to which all the Arabs of Cyrenaica and many in eastern Tripolitania still adhere. He called for a return to the purity and spirituality of Islam at the time of the Prophet Muhammad, finding a ready response from the independent tribesmen of Cyrenaica who for centuries had lacked clear and strong guidance. Sayyid Mohammed Ali had great gifts of organization, and the country was soon covered with a network of lodges *(zawiya)* of the order; half schools, half centres of meditation and work, and wholly fortresses, these had clear analogies in function with the Christian monasteries of the Middle Ages. Like the latter, the *zawiyas* were clearly a by-product of a weak and unpredictable central authority. The analogy must, however, not be carried too far, because celibacy has no place in Islam. These lodges unified the country under the will of the founder and rescued it from the anarchy of centuries. Such activity, although most salutary and impressive in its effect upon the Arabs of Cyrenaica, was not acceptable to the Sublime Porte, and the Sayyid prudently withdrew to the remote oasis of Jaghbub near the Egyptian border. His son, Sayyid Mohammed el-Mahdi el-Senussi, saw the movement reach the apex of its influence, with over fifty lodges, and sought the fastnesses of Kufra to escape from alien contact and influence. In fact the movement did not increase the difficulties of Turkey in Libya, since after the French had seized Tunis in 1880 it was generally felt that the sultan's rule was preferable to that of an infidel power. By this time, however, the Porte was in such financial straits that it was unable to take advantage of its fortuitous popularity. Its administration, if congenial, was neither progressive nor efficient. In seventy-five years Libya had thirty-three governors, all except one of whom are held to have enriched themselves at the country's expense. When at last the Young Turks put an end to the tyranny of Abdul Hamid, in 1908, a vigorous effort was made to improve conditions in North Africa. But it was too late. Italy struck before the Empire could be reorganized.

From the Italian Occupation (1911) till Independence (1951)

On 3 October 1911 the Italians launched an attack on Tripoli; and subsequently landed troops at Derna, Khoms, Misurata, and Tobruk. They employed large forces, both naval and military, and met with little opposition, since their invasion was well-timed. Though they had little difficulty in establishing bridgeheads, their progress inland was slow. They had only advanced a dozen miles from their base when the sultan, alarmed by the threat of war in the Balkans, began to negotiate for peace. In October 1912 he signed the Treaty of Ouchy (or Lausanne) by which he gave up his rights in Libya; he did not, however, recognize Italian sovereignty but by a curious diplomatic device granted the Libyans 'full autonomy'. For their part the Italians had already proclaimed in 1911 their sovereignty as conquerors of the country. By the spring of 1914 they had completed their military occupation, although the Sanusi almost immediately began to attack their outposts in the Fezzan. The outbreak of the First World War weakened Italy's position; and when she joined the Allies she automatically came into direct conflict with Turkey at a time when she could ill spare troops for Africa. The Sanusi, supplied with Turkish and German arms and ammunition, attacked the British in Egypt, while the Tripolitanians turned upon their Italian masters. By 1917 the Italians held only the towns of Khoms, Tripoli, Zuara, and the Cyrenaican ports, and were on the verge of losing their new possession altogether.

At the end of the war the Tripolitanian leaders, advised by Abdurrahman Azzam, later first secretary-general of the Arab League, felt strong enough to proclaim a republic. To counter this the Italians offered to set up locally elected parliaments in Tripolitania and Cyrenaica, under Italian governors. For two years the Italian government negotiated with the Libyans, who continued to press for self-government, finally offering the Emirate of united Libya to Sayyid Idris el-Senussi. The Sayyid's followers had always been the backbone of opposition to Italian rule, and he alone could unite the country. In July 1921 the Italian government took a decisive step by appointing the dynamic Giuseppe Volpi (later Count Volpi of Misurata) to be governor of Tripolitania. He proceeded to subdue the Tripolitanians by force of arms, without reference to the liberal and hesitant ministers in Rome. The advent of Fascism a year later strengthened his hand. By vigorous and ruthless action he and his military commander—Graziani—reconquered northern Tripolitania by the end of 1923. Fighting continued intermittently for the next six years, by which time even the Fezzan had been reoccupied. Graziani then passed on to Cyrenaica and reduced it to exhausted quiescence, which he called 'Pax Romana', by the end of 1932. His success was achieved by herding the civilian population into concentration camps and so depriving the Sanusi fighters of supplies and auxiliaries. The subsequent loss of life among human beings and livestock was very heavy. By the time the 'pacification' was completed, the numbers of the population had been very greatly reduced. The inhumanity of these methods caused a bitterness which outlived the Italian regime.

As soon as the Italian occupation was secure, the Italian government turned its thoughts to colonization. Count Volpi proposed to grant large concessions of land to wealthy Italians who could develop the resources of the country. Mussolini, however, favoured the establishment of large numbers of peasant proprietors, thinking more of rural overpopulation in Italy than of the economic aspect of the schemes. Libya was to become the 'fourth shore of our sea'. But there were innumerable difficulties and by 1933 it had become clear that if the government wanted to people North Africa with metropolitan peasants within a reasonable time it would have to do so out of state funds. Accordingly the many small-scale schemes for assisting colonists were finally abandoned, and plans for mass emigration of peasant families were adopted. In 1938 20,000 persons in family groups from the most densely populated rural areas in Italy left Genoa in a blaze of publicity. In 1939 10,000 others left more quietly from Venice. They were settled on the Jefara plain of Tripoli and the Green Hills of Cyrenaica, in small, neat houses, in which everything down to a box of matches was provided before their arrival. The fields were already sown, and the animals in the stalls. The plan provided for hire-purchase of the farm by the peasant tenant who could become his own master after twenty years. The outbreak of the Second World War prevented a third mass migration, and made it impossible to judge the success of the earlier ventures.

When Italy declared war in June 1940, there were large military forces in Libya under the command of Marshal Graziani. With great circumspection they moved to attack the British in Egypt, only to be promptly driven back by General Wavell who captured Benghazi in February 1941 and cut off the retreating mass of the army on the coast road south of the city. Thereafter the war ebbed and flowed over Cyrenaica until, in the autumn of 1942, the British Eighth Army swept the Axis forces out of Libya for ever. On 23 January 1943 the British forces captured Tripoli city and passed rapidly on to link up with the Anglo-American forces in Tunisia. From the beginning of the war Sayyid Idris el-Senussi had supported the Allied cause and on his initiative a Libyan Arab force had been raised in Egypt and trained to fight beside their British allies.

The end of the war was followed by six years of tortuous diplomatic activity concerning the future of Libya, ending, through an unusual conjunction of circumstances, in the recognition of Independence.

Prelude to Independence

Libya, as it emerged to Independence, differed sharply from its neighbours to the west, still engaged in the process of decolonization. Italian settlement had thrown down no permanent roots; state-supported colonization had ended with the outbreak of war. The long years of conquest and the attempts at settlement had evoked a strong and lasting sense of nationalist animosity towards the invader, but the nature of Libyan society, and the absence of the liberal example, had not produced a well-organized nationalist movement. Italian rule was overthrown by the Allied armies, not by the armed resistance of the Libyans, nor by the dialectic of nationalism and a liberal metropolitan government which was so important further west.

The effect of the Second World War was to create a limited alliance between Emir Idris and the British. Idris succeeded in dominating those of his countrymen who were alarmed at the dangers of antagonizing the Italians and resisted the reproaches of those who argued that the alliance should only be made on the basis of a promise of independence. Under British organization and command a Sanusi force was recruited, eventually numbering some 10,000 men, to take part in the Libyan campaign (and to welcome those Libyans who deserted from the Italian army).

Idris repeatedly pressed the claim for his country's independence. But at the end of the war the British government had only committed itself (in a statement by Anthony Eden on 8 January 1942) to preventing Cyrenaica ever returning to Italian rule. After the war Ernest Bevin proposed (at the Council of Foreign Ministers in 1946) that Libya should be given complete independence; but by that time the intertwined issues of the disposal of the former Italian colonies and access to so important a piece of territory on the Mediterranean coast inhibited any Draconian settlement.

As the Axis armies were defeated Libya was placed under British and French military administration—the British responsible for Cyrenaica and Tripolitania, the French for Fezzan. But the disposition of Libya (as of the other Italian colonies) rested with the Council of Foreign Ministers whose other members not only did not necessarily support Britain and France but had plans and aspirations of their own —the United States for the continuance of its wartime air base (Wheelus Field) outside Tripoli and the Soviet Union hoping to acquire influence and bases in the Mediterranean. And as Italy became a respectable and accepted power in the post-war world, its interests regained their legitimacy, at least with Britain and the United States. When the peace treaty with Italy was signed in 1947, Italy renounced all claim to its colonies; beyond that the treaty provided for the continuation of the existing order only for the time being; but the Council of Foreign Ministers agreed that the problem should be taken to the General Assembly of the United Nations if no settlement were agreed within a year of the treaty coming into effect (by September 1948).

Meanwhile, Libya posed an obvious problem even to those most genuinely concerned with the future of the country. The Libyan desire for independence was indisputable, as a four-power commission (set up by the Council of Foreign Ministers) reported after a lengthy visit in spring 1948; but the resources for independence were minimal—a poor country, with an estimated 94 per cent illiteracy rate, only a handful of Libyan graduates, no doctor of medicine, and no confirmed source of wealth to permit the construction of a new state.

In the short run the manner in which Britain and France administered Cyrenaica and Fezzan contributed appreciably to the solution of these problems. Idris returned to Cyrenaica in July 1944. His authority was strong, although it was challenged by younger nationalists (whose political organization Idris suppressed). Had Cyrenaica alone been in question the way would have been open for the development of self-government under British tutelage, the British maintaining their bases and providing financial and administrative support for Idris's rule. Similarly the French governed Fezzan through the old enemies of the Italians—the Saif al-Nasir family. The British (many of whom came to Libya from the Sudan service) reopened schools for Libyans and recruited them into the administration (in 1951 80 per cent of civil servants in Cyrenaica and 71 per cent in Tripolitania were Libyan) while the French carried out a programme of hygienic improvement, curing malaria and reducing the incidence of trachoma; they opened schools and improved working conditions.

To some extent, therefore, the immediate problem was concentrated on Tripolitania. In the ferment of the post-war years and under the tolerant rule of the British military administration, political activity in Tripoli was exceptionally vigorous. The opposition to Idris, with its various strands of republicanism, Arab nationalism, and antipathy to Libyan federalism was organized particularly within the Omar Makhtar Sports Club—a disguised political club established in 1942 under Idris's patronage. But while political parties multiplied they neither attracted a mass following nor formed a united bloc strong enough to be a rival centre of power to Idris. Meanwhile, as the British established their position in Cyrenaica and the French in Fezzan, Tripolitania was left without tutelage—an obvious anomaly in the fertile minds of the leaders of great powers. The Soviet Union proposed a ten-year trusteeship for Tripolitania (exciting the same alarm as when Alexander I offered to participate in controlling the Barbary pirates). Even more intrepid, Ernest Bevin and his Italian counterpart, Carlo Sforza, proposed a joint trusteeship for ten years—Italy being responsible for Tripolitania, Britain and France for Cyrenaica and Fezzan respectively. The plan provoked widespread and massive demonstrations in Libya and was defeated in the UN General Assembly by the adverse vote of the Haitian delegate, Emile St. Lot, who was rewarded by having his name bestowed on a Tripoli street.

With the failure of this final Anglo-Italian bid to settle the Libyan question outside the hurly-burly of the world community, the United Nations took responsibility for Libya. In November 1949 the General Assembly adopted a resolution that Libya should become independent not later than January 1952 under a constitution to be agreed by a Libyan constituent assembly, with the assistance of a UN Commissioner (Adrian Pelt, a Dutchman, being appointed to this post).

Resistance to Libyan independence now evaporated. Libyan opposition, rivalry between the European partners, and UN votes had prevented an imperial division under the guise of a trusteeship. Soviet claims lost even the scant attention accorded to them before the intensification of the cold war. British interests appeared secure. They were reinforced by the continuing alliance with Idris, which produced an agreement for Cyrenaican independence shortly before the UN vote of October 1949 and by the support which ensured Idris's primacy in the constitutional discussions which followed. The United States continued to be a lessee of the Wheelus base.

It remained for the Libyans to construct a constitution, in accordance with the United Nations resolution. The process inevitably gave plentiful scope for the expression of the dissident political opinion which had come into the open in the previous years. The task of constitution making was given to an appointed National Assembly, which was representative of the three regions of Libya but whose legitimacy, because it was appointed, was not universally accepted. The demand, notably from Tripolitania, for a unitary state continued to be pressed; but it was unacceptable to Idris, who remained in control.

Libya under King Idris

The independence of the United Kingdom of Libya was proclaimed in December by its first hereditary ruler, Sayyid Mohammed Idris el-Senussi. Its constitution established a federal bi-cameral system of government; elections were held in early 1952 and the first parliament met in March. It was more difficult to foster the kind of political life which such a constitution presupposed. There existed a wide gap between the traditional classes of Libyan society, both rural and urban, and a small number of more instructed men living in the towns who had broken away from a traditional environment. Their numbers were few and they had no organization to enable them to grow roots back into the society from which they had emerged.

The decisive contest in the elections of March 1952 was between these members of a new class, organized in the Tripolitanian National Congress Party, and the traditional order of tribal society. The result was an outstanding victory—44 seats out of 55 in the lower house—for Idris's government. It was challenged by the National Congress party, which claimed that the election had been manipulated and which, therefore, took to the streets in a demonstration which developed into a riot. As a result the National Congress party was dissolved, and other parties forbidden. Party leaders were arrested; Bashir Sadawi, a consistent opponent of the regime was deported to Egypt (he died in exile in the service of King Saud).

Thereafter King Idris succeeded in maintaining, for more than a decade, a balance between competing claims, both inside the country and in foreign policy, which provided stability but did not integrate or absorb the forces of change within society. Moreover political stability facilitated the development of the country's oil resources—a most powerful factor of unintended subversion.

Internally the game of politics consisted in balancing the claims of regions, tribes, and families. No doubt, modern political organization would have been slow to develop in the best of circumstances—but the ban on political parties meant the reinforcement of the traditional ties of geographical origin and family relationship, which remained strong even after migration into the towns. It was symptomatic that the second major crisis of the regime, in 1954, arose from a family quarrel over the succession to the throne when a young Sanusi prince, Al-Sharif, murdered the king's principal adviser Ibrahim al-Shalhi. Idris remained childless but, determined that his side of the family should remain on the throne, he named his brother Mohammed al-Rida as his heir, who was succeeded, as heir apparent, by his second son, Emir Hasan al-Rida when he died in 1955.

The formal apparatus of the government consisted of ministries, a cabinet, and the legislative assemblies. In practice the crisis of 1954, like that of 1952, reinforced the power of the monarch, who succeeded in balancing the demands of tribal leaders with those of the bourgeois families of the littoral. Premiers and cabinet ministers were appointed to conciliate the rival claims of regions; on several occasions the resignation of the prime minister was provoked by the intervention of the king, ruling by decree. The royal diwan remained the centre of power, and the king insisted on control over the key ministries—finance and petroleum, defence and interior—which were kept in the hands of the tribal notables from Cyrenaica, so that the system of government support was closely related to that of the Sanusi order. Political activity flourished: it consisted of competition for advantage and position, the formation of alliances, and bidding for support. But the system was not one which encouraged initiative, and the king was obviously more intent on conserving a mobile balance of forces than devising a strategy for development. Increasingly he retired from political life to his palace at Tobruk.

Libya remained a poor country, and the king's foreign policy sought to maintain a balance between, on the one hand, Britain and the United States who provided financial support, and the Arab world on the other. In February 1953 Libya joined the Arab League, and in July 1953 signed a twenty-year alliance with Britain. The accompanying agreements gave Britain 'facilities within the territory of Libya for military purposes' (provided Libyan sovereignty was not compromised). The major advantage for Britain was to provide alternative bases to the Suez base in Egypt (although on a much smaller scale) and to ensure staging posts at Idris airport near Tripoli and El-Adem near Tobruk for air routes to East Africa and the Far East. In return Britain made annual grants (totalling initially £3·75 million) for budget support and development. Britain became a major supplier of arms to Libya—an advantageous position which facilitated the negotiation of the sale of an air defence system shortly before the revolution of 1969 (at a time when oil revenues had eliminated Libyan need for British financial support and strategic and economic developments had reduced the importance of the British bases in Libya).

The United States was similarly successful in negotiating the continuation of the lease of its base at Wheelus Field, for which a payment of $42 million over the period 1954–71 was agreed, together with immediate aid in the form of wheat valued at $3 million. Diplomatic relations were established with the Soviet Union (in 1955) but that country was always held at arm's length and was used as a lever with which to bargain for increased aid from Britain and the United States. The Libyan prime minister, Bin Halim, welcomed the Eisenhower doctrine and received visits from Vice-President Richard Nixon and Eisenhower's special representative, James P. Richards.

Of the three powers most concerned with Libya at the end of the Second World War only France was unsuccessful in negotiating a new defence agreement satisfactory to itself. The opposition which was frequently expressed in the Libyan parliament to the alignment with Britain and the United States was much stronger with regard to France, because of the war in Algeria. In return for a contribution of 500 million francs France received only limited air and surface transit rights; all troops were withdrawn from Fezzan by the end of 1956 and the way was open for Libya to become a supply route for arms from Egypt to Algeria. At the same time relations with Italy were settled. The Italian government made a contribution to Libyan development and the position of Libyan colonists was clarified—they became owners of their land, but many took advantage of the provision made for them to sell their land to Libyans and return home with the capital so acquired. Their decision proved wise, since those who stayed were expropriated and expelled by Qaddafi in 1970.

The delicate path between the interests of these powers which were increasingly regarded as 'imperialist' (at a time when decolonization gained momentum) and the Arab states, inspired by Nasser, was a difficult one to tread. But for a time Idris succeeded. The British were denied the use of their bases in Libya during the Suez campaign of 1956; but relations with Britain and France were maintained.

The balance, internal as well as external, was maintained at the cost of allowing economic, social, and, therefore, political currents to gain strength, without the possibility of outlet or expression. These forces grew even in the days of Libya's poverty; they were greatly strengthened with the beginning of serious exploration for oil. Under Idris the government of the country retained its traditional mould. But the economy of the country was distorted by the influx of cash—modest in comparison with subsequent oil revenues, but substantial in comparison with any previous experience. Foreign military establishments spent over £6m. in 1955 and official economic aid, to a country of some two million inhabitants, increased from less than £1·5m. in 1951 to £10m. in 1955. Education was expanded as a means to economic and social development, a Libyan university was founded at Benghazi and schools established, bringing a five-fold increase in the school population.

This transformation of Libyan society occurred at a time when Arab political consciousness was rapidly sharpening. Libya was open to the major currents of political excitement coming from the east. The expansion of education depended to a large extent on Egyptian teachers; but their influence was exceeded by that of Cairo radio—especially as transistor radios became available. The most important subversive force of all was the development of the country's oil resources; the first concessions were granted in November 1955, the Esso strike at Bir Zelten was made in 1959 (quickly followed by others in the same year); and an export of 6·6m. barrels was achieved in 1961.

The exploitation of oil brought great wealth to Libya and gave the government that overwhelming source of money, independent of taxation, which is characteristic of oil-producing states. But the administration responsible for directing the country had a tradition of minor corruption which was inflated into gross corruption; and although the government drew up development plans, it lacked the administrative resources or the political energy to accelerate their implementation. A decade after Independence it was easy to identify every form of opposition to a regime which made so little provision for political change in the face of overwhelming economic and social upheaval.

Libyans increasingly shared a sense of identification with Nasser's Egypt—whether in the heyday of Nasser's prestige or in the stupefaction of the defeat of 1967. The Ba'athist party recruited members in spite of police pressures, so did the Muslim Brothers. A cousin of the king, Abdullah Abd el-Senussi, formed a 'party of the people' drawn from rich commercial classes seeking power for themselves on a programme of closer collaboration with Egypt. Not least important, those Libyan graduates, many of them educated abroad, who were most eager to participate in the development of the country could not readily find a place in an administration where clientele relationships and corruption played so large a part. The movement of the towns in search of new money produced a discontented working class which erupted in major riots in 1962, 1964, and 1967.

Police suppression, the arrest of leaders, and the despatch of dissident students abroad failed to restore any real stability. It became a commonplace expectation, especially after 1967, that Idris's regime would be overthrown. The problem for those outsiders most directly concerned with the fortunes of Libya—the oil companies and the British and US governments—was rather to identify where the most successful action was likely to originate. The army was an obvious candidate; but when the *coup* of September 1969 was carried out—during the absence of the king in Greece—the men responsible were younger, more junior, and less known than had been expected.

The Coup of 1 September 1969

The *coup* which succeeded, against minimal opposition and without bloodshed, on 1 September 1969 was inspired and led by Muammar Qaddafi. Subsequently a legend was created around the *coup* and the preparation for it—a legend encouraged by Qaddafi, nurtured by official publications, and ornamented by western admirers. But like all good legends it is based on a fundament of truth.

Qaddafi was born in 1942 in the desert region of the Syrte, in the border area between Tripolitania and Fezzan. Little is known about his father; but he belonged to a tribe owing allegiance to the traditional dominant tribes of Fezzan, the Saif al-Nasir. Muammar went to a secondary school at Sebha, apparently at the expense of an uncle who worked in the police administration there. His education was in Arabic. He was not a docile pupil, and got into trouble for organizing political activity among the other boys in the school in the excited days of the Suez expedition and Nasser's increasing prestige. As a result he was sent to continue his education at Misurata.

He was admitted to the University of Libya in 1962 but after one year he left without graduating and went into the army. He was commissioned in the Signals in August 1965 and went on a course at Beaconsfield in England (he is said to retain affectionate respect for his English teacher, and to like the English countryside). He held the rank of captain when he organized the *coup*.

His desert origins have contributed an important part to the legend, and undoubtedly his early youth at Sebha was of major importance in the formation of his character and in the emergence of the revolutionary group, several of whom were his companions at school. Less attention is normally given to the years spent in the commercial town of Misurata, with its 350,000 inhabitants. In spite of his brief expedition on a training course to England he remained ignorant of the outside world; his own romanticism could the more easily be centred on Gamal Abdel Nasser, and his view of politics be shaped by Cairo radio. The Libyan *coup* was thus consciously modelled on that of the Egyptian free officers. Subsequently Qaddafi attached considerable importance to the difference between a *'coup' (inqilab)* and a 'revolution' *(thawrah)*. A *coup*, he said, was a casual event occurring at the pleasure of senior officers, whereas a revolution is something of which it is impossible to determine precisely the date of origin:

A revolution is the opposite, even if the practical application of the idea partakes of the same appearance as a military *coup*. A revolution is a vital necessity which grows naturally in the consciousness of the society as a whole ... the necessity for a complete and radical change ... produces ... a man of revolution, a man of comprehensive and complete change, a man who is as born again in a new age.[1]

[1] Qaddafi, *Story of the Revolution*, quoted by Ruth First, *Libya: The Elusive Revolution*, London, 1974, p. 101.

Not all of the original group of young men at Sebha joined the army; but although Qaddafi has referred, in his own account, to the civilian side of his movement, the civilians played no active part. Whether for practical reasons, or in emulation of the Egyptians, the group planning the *coup* was confined to those who had joined the army—Qaddafi instructed some of his friends to enter the Military Academy and as one of them, Mahaichy, commented on the first anniversary of the revolution: 'we supported Nasser's ideas ... we decided the military was the best means to achieve revolution'.[1]

However that may be, the central committee of the Free Officers met regularly for the next five years. It is not clear what took place at these meetings, but they undoubtedly succeeded in building up a sense of participation in a great venture. Ascetism was made a rule of conduct; it included a ban on alcohol, gambling, and the night clubs which flourished in oil-rich Libya.

The officers took the obvious step of trying to discover the sympathies of their superiors; but it was only in the last months, between March and September 1969, that two colonels were recruited to the plot. They were Colonel Adam Hawwaz, who played a political role in relation to foreign embassies, and Colonel Musa Ahmed. The latter's participation was of key importance. When the *coup* took place he immobilized the headquarters of the Cyrenaican defence force and thus played a vital part in ensuring the success of the *coup*.

The timing of the *coup* was determined by the fact that several of the officers were due to be posted overseas from 2 September. On the previous night the officers acted, with that combination of planning, improvisation, and daring which is successful provided it is also lucky. In Cyrenaica Musa Ahmed's personal authority, and the tribal authority he exercised, neutralized the royal army; Tripoli was taken by armoured car regiments; and Fezzan offered no difficulty. The successful plotters used the army's new signals system for their communications and Qaddafi, following the best traditions, secured the radio station in order to announce the rule of the new regime. Qaddafi and his colleagues had forestalled discovery of their plot, not because a *coup* was not expected but because the warnings had been so numerous. (Colonel Abdul Aziz Shalhi, who was later reported to have attempted a *coup* against Qaddafi, was the favourite runner.)

The Republic of Libya

The regime which came to power had certain clear objectives, some of which were easily achieved; it produced an ideology, which remained ill defined and confused, but was a source of inspiration to many Arabs outside Libya who looked for some distinctive ideological purity rather

[1] Transcript of television interview, quoted ibid., p. 103.

than for the compromises of politics. It had most difficulty in developing a cohesive system of government. The revolutionary leaders made an alliance with those young technocrats who had found the old regime alien to them; but its greatest problem (one shared with many new regimes in the Arab world and elsewhere) was in creating a political organization which would be in some sense representative of the people, and serve as a transmission belt for the policies of the government.

The supreme governing body was (and is still at the time of writing) the Revolutionary Command Council—the group of officers who had made the revolution and who were bound together by the common bond of daring enterprise which they had successfully accomplished together. (For the first years at least the RCC continued to live in army barracks and to share a single large room in which the business of government was conducted.) The exceptions were Adam Hawwaz and Musa Ahmed, who were accused and tried within a few months of the establishment of the new order. They were sentenced to death but the sentence was not carried out.

Qaddafi remained the leading figure of the Council; in a group of eleven captains and one lieutenant he was promoted to the rank of colonel. Qaddafi's authority was not sufficient to allow him to impose his wishes on his colleagues; but they for their part could not dispense with him as their principal. The RCC thus acted as a collective body, in which contentious issues were fought out to some sort of conclusion. Failure to agree might result in silence and an absence of policy over an extended period; or Qaddafi might resign from his office without, apparently, destroying the balance he held with his colleagues—since his resignation was never final, nor, as far as is known, did it enable him to overrule the Council. External policy appears to have provoked the most important disputes of this kind, e.g. the prelude to the eventual decision to seek union with Egypt, and oil policy before the Tripoli negotiations of 1971.

Qaddafi remained the spokesman and chief ideologist of the regime. It quickly became apparent (to him as well as to others) that he had a gift for communication with his people. He gained a reputation for simplicity and charm which outside observers, impressed by the chauvinism and aggressiveness of many Libyan policies, were reluctant to credit. He showed a talent for conducting large meetings, both addressing crowds and arguing with members of the audience; and he was adept in television interviews. It was a role to which he attached central importance; for he retained a suspicion of intermediaries between the leadership and the people (notwithstanding his attempts to develop popular participation in government). There was thus no one to replace Qaddafi in conveying the decisions of the government to the people and in providing the leadership, or at least the rhetoric, to accompany them. He broadcast the collective wishes of the RCC; and it must be presumed that this role increased his leverage with his colleagues, who were unlikely to disavow him.

At the same time he developed a simple and relatively coherent view of the world which he wished to be known as a 'third theory', a third way between Marxism and the philosophy of the western democracies and Marxism or (and this new theme seemed to predominate at the beginning of 1976) 'military fascism'. In the meantime the main outlines had been made clear, even if the shape which the state was taking, and its relations with the outside world, seemed to have little connexion with an ideology which began to appear to be the hobby of the principal architect of the new regime. However, the philosophy was not static; in the comparatively short life of the regime it showed distinct developments, particularly between the first, formative period 1969-72 and the subsequent years which were marked by the 'popular' or 'cultural' revolution.

The major tenets of Qaddafi's philosophy are proclaimed as being those of Islamic socialism. The Islamic content is closely related to the Koran, and Qaddafi has frequently expressed the view commonly held by devout Muslims that all wisdom is to be found in the Koran. Modernity is not antipathetic to Islam; for although Islamic theology has shown none of the innovation which has characterized modern Christian theology it is claimed that modern scientific knowledge and technology have always been contained in the Koran, lying unperceived until the present time. It is consistent with this view that Libyan legislation embodies Koranic principles and traditional Islamic punishments such as the ban on alcohol and the levying of an alms tax (*zakat*). At the same time the economy is pressed forward in the pursuit of modernity.

It might appear that Qaddafi's political and religious view shares much with that of the Muslim Brothers; but in practice he has expressed his strong dissent from their ideology and his practical opposition to their political role. He charges them with their lack of Arab nationalism and he accuses them of organizing a sect or party which would be an undesirable impediment between the government and the people. In this context Arab nationalism is probably the prior emotion for Qaddafi, rather than something that stems from an interpretation of Islam; but it is readily accommodated in a view of Islam which takes the Koran in a fundamentalist sense of being the word of God—written in Arabic—and the Arabs as a chosen people. Thus he is reported as saying that if the Muslim Brothers were allowed to return to Libya they would form a party which would soon have the 'upper hand' over the people; that from the moment they promote Islamic unity they are bound to oppose Arab unity and that it is well known that the CIA finances the Muslim Brothers.[1]

[1] Mirella Bianco, *Kadhafi, messager du desert*, Paris, 1974, p. 167.

Qaddafi's attachment to Islam and to nationalism often rejects intolerance and fanaticism, except with regard to Israel. Since 1973 he has attached more importance to religion and piety within the framework of any religion than to Islam. He has argued that the 'divine concept' of Islam, as distinct from its interpretation by man, is one which embraces all religions.

'It is a mistake to follow Muhammad and not Jesus, or Jesus and not Muhammad, for the divine concept is much more profound than the human concept of Islam' (speech of 8 February 1973). In this new religious philosophy all the prophets should be believed and followed—anyone who does so and believes in a single God is thereby Muslim, and the only distinction which God makes between men is according to the degree of their piety.

Similarly his pronouncements on Arab nationalism avoid intolerance, sometimes at the cost of consistency. As we have seen, the claim of the Arabs to be chosen people rests on the fact that they have been the propagators of Islam, because of the Prophet's Arab birth and because of the Arabic language. The claim is for a religious, civilizing mission—not that Arabs are racially superior, but that they are especially honoured, and therefore have a special duty. Christian Arabs need be no less Arab than Muslims—though they must recognize the greatness of Islam. 'The best among you,' he said in a speech of 19 November 1971 'is not he who belongs to the Arab race. That would be a racist criterion. . . . The best in God's view is the most pious.' Qaddafi's nationalism also claims to be tolerant of other nationalisms. But his world has no place for Zionism; Zionism is condemned as an aggressive form of nationalism like Nazism, and relations with Israel are inadmissible since the Koran forbids any relationship with those who fought you and your religion and expelled you from your home (speech of 19 November 1971).

The other stand of Qaddafi's 'third theory' is that of socialism. In developing his socialist view Qaddafi has no difficulty in referring to egalitarian passages of the Koran or to verses enjoining charity and he insists that the major tenets of socialist doctrine were written there centuries before Marx and Lenin. In addition he rejects many of the central presuppositions of Marxism—its materialism, which is contrary to religion, and the notion of the class struggle, which is destructive of the Islamic idea of the community.

The ideal world which emerges from Qaddafi's speeches is one of simple, utopian socialism: social justice above all, absence of exploitation, a fair sharing of the labour of society and of the products of that labour. The difference between this socialism and Marxism—and even more the difference between this ideal world and the repressive, bureaucratic regime of the Soviet Union—is easy to draw. Much less attention is given to explaining the values of Islamic socialism in relation to the capitalist world; its vices are assumed to be self-evident, and Qaddafi probably has no sense of the value of individualism and liberal democracy, which have never had any important place in Arab radical thought.

The Political System

Qaddafi himself has retained the instincts and style of tribal democracy and has neither assumed the panoply of power nor sought to enrich himself in office. He continues to lead an austere life and is driven in a jeep without escort. He can pick olives to help peasants in their work, without affectation.

However, the construction of a political system consistent with Qaddafi's view of society has proved difficult. To some extent domestic politics have been subordinated to external relations; Qaddafi probably saw the elimination of 'imperialist' positions as a contribution to internal democracy, and the country lived for some time in the expectation of union with Egypt, which would have created new requirements for political organization. Predictably it has proved easier to construct the administrative branch of government—the establishment of ministries and the appointment of civil servants—than to stimulate political activity in a political party or in mass organization. This has produced the paradoxical result that while Qaddafi's ideology attaches minimal importance to the nation state, Libya has acquired greater administrative unity than at any time in its history.

The first initiative was taken in June 1971—the anniversary of the 'liberation' of Libya from US troops—with the establishment of the Arab Socialist Union. It clearly followed the example of Egypt (the headquarters of the party in Tripoli was still decorated, in 1975, with fresh portraits of Nasser) and the decree setting up the party denounced insular parties (like those of Lebanon), foreign importations (communism), and parties working clandestinely like the Ba'ath. Instead the ASU was to be the vehicle of Arab nationalism, acting by persuasion.

No doubt the intention of the RCC was to establish a political structure which would facilitate the political and economic initiatives of the immediate future. The first years of the revolution had sustained their own momentum; but members of the RCC who had toured the country to explain their actions and to communicate government intentions to the people met with little response. It appeared politic therefore to create an organization which would enhance the claim of the new regime to be founded on popular participation, and would give the government the possibility of manipulating popular support when its policies encountered the resistance or apathy of the bourgeoisie. Thus the party was to be based on an alliance of the 'active popular forces', which included peasants, workers, soldiers, intellectuals, and non-exploiting capitalists; and peasants and workers were to form not less than 50 per cent of the members of any branch of the party. The structure of the party followed, on paper, a simple organization, with provincial congresses which would elect committees, from whom the RCC would appoint a national congress.

The ASU provided a rudimentary political organization, and took some root where habits of political organization already existed. Trade unions were brought into the party (although strikes were made illegal in April 1972) and the combination of trade union tradition with the new ASU structure in such areas as the Tripoli docks or the oil industry produced a force of some importance. In 1974 the reconstruction of the government followed a resolution of the national council of the ASU calling for government changes to accelerate the economic and social development of the country.

In general, however, the achievement of the ASU proved disappointing. It was easier to restrict public debate by closing independent newspapers and forbidding the establishment of other political parties (made punishable by death in May 1972).

A second initiative was undertaken, by Qaddafi, in February 1973. The political atmosphere was tense, since the shooting down of a Libyan Boeing aircraft over Egypt had provoked vigorous demonstrations against the proposed union with Egypt. Qaddafi appears to have become suddenly aware of the strength of feeling among his own countrymen against Egypt, at the same time as his own idealized view of that country was clouded by the realities of Sadat's regime.

Whatever the motives, in April 1973 he proclaimed, in a speech at Zouara, five principles of a new stage in the revolution: the suspension of all the laws then in force; expulsion of all the adversaries of the revolution; the arming of the masses so that they could attain the objectives of the revolution (namely liberty, unity, and socialism); the purging of the administration together with a struggle against a bourgeois democratic attitude in the administration; and a cultural revolution directed against everything contrary to the Koran.

Much of this programme remained a dead letter. The Zouara speech was followed by upheaval and effervescence which failed to produce any important structural results. The police carried out a series of arrests among intellectuals—university teachers, lawyers, and professional people—and among the bourgeois families. It was at one time estimated that a thousand people (a substantial proportion of Libya's small educated class) were taken into temporary confinement. At the same time popular committees came into existence. The number of these committees was reported to have grown from about 400 in April 1973 to 2,400 by August. They showed some spontaneity, and many grievances were no doubt given free expression; but the committees were manipulated by the administration, or the ASU, or the police in a natural struggle for power.

The storm blew itself out at the same time as the possibility of union with Egypt evaporated—one of the last great 'popular' movements was a great 'unity convoy' of some 5,000 vehicles which crossed the Egyptian frontier and destroyed the Egyptian tourist bureau at Mersa Matruh with the expressed intention of pressing on to Cairo and forcing Sadat to sign an instrument of union. (The convoy was halted by an empty train at a level crossing, and neither the march nor Qaddafi's announcement of his resignation had the desired effect.) Since then the idea of popular committees, in residential areas and in workplaces, has not been allowed to die, but it has not taken any substantial form. In May 1975 Qaddafi returned to his theme in a major broadcast address. He explained the means by which the whole people would elect people's committees which would interact with a general national congress. Once again the proposal emphasized the sovereignty of the people, which would express itself in the congress, without the distortions of party, class, or group. However, it was generally agreed among those involved in the government of the country that Qaddafi's plans for the realization of the 'third theory' were still in a formative stage.

Young technocrats have an important part in the practical government of the country. Defence and foreign policy remain the exclusive preserve of the RCC, and domestic and economic planning are shaped in broad outline under its control. Decisions are taken either in the RCC, or in a supreme planning council, which combines the RCC and the council of ministers under Qaddafi's chairmanship. But ministers, and the small number of trained cadres in the ministries, prepare plans for the RCC and often have a decisive role in the implementation of decisions taken by the RCC. A part of comparable importance is played by young technocrats who have assumed responsibility for the nationalized oil companies.

It follows that ministers and executives seek the support of members of the RCC for their projects. This relationship has given particular importance to Abdesselam Jalloud who has, without doubt, played the second most important role in Libya after Qaddafi. His origins are similar to those of Qaddafi: they were at school together at Sebha and were fellow conspirators in organizing the 1969 Revolution. As a young officer he attended courses in Britain and the United States, where he abandoned the austerity which Qaddafi still retains.

Jalloud's function has been to direct production and commerce. He has been responsible for major negotiations concerning the purchase of arms and oil; and he has collaborated closely with the technocrats in the implementation of economic planning, and in gaining acceptance of their projects. In this way he has built up an important clientele within the regime.

The conflict between Qaddafi's ideological approach to politics and the more pragmatic concerns of some of his colleagues sharpened in the summer of 1975. Major al-Mahaichy, a leading member of the Revolutionary Command Council and minister for planning, fled the country after an unsuccessful *coup*. The most plausible explanation of the event seemed to be that Mahaichy represented the pragmatists in the government (including the young technocrats in his own ministry) and had the support of an important group of army officers. They were opposed to the rhetoric and political upheaval of Qaddafi's socialism, and were at the same time committed to the construction of Libya, rather than the pursuit of the chimera of Arab unity.

Al-Mahaichy escaped to Tunisia, where the government refused to extradite him to Libya; he then went to Egypt where he was given political asylum. His colleague al-Hawadi, also a member of the RCC and minister of the interior, was arrested and spent two weeks in prison. He was then released but at the time of writing his name had not reappeared in the press.

The failure of the *coup* was followed by decrees extending state control over business. The import of cars and lorries was nationalized; certain sectors of industry were confined to joint-stock companies, and others restricted to state-owned companies.

At the same time Qaddafi pressed ahead with the attempt to construct a political system. In January 1976 there appeared the first volume of a long-awaited 'Green Book' in which Qaddafi had promised he would elaborate the principles of popular government. The Green Book was an amplification of the political ideas of Qaddafi—including the familiar criticism of political parties and parliamentary assemblies and the necessity for popular participation in government. 'The authority of the people cannot be fragmented, and can only be achieved by the adoption of people's congresses and popular committees, for there is no democracy without their existence.'[1] At the same time the Green Book and the congress seemed to indicate a turn to the left in Qaddafi's rhetoric. Popular democracy was still represented as the single middle path, but fascist military dictatorship replaced communism as the evil to be avoided. Similarly it was reported that in a colloquium discussing Islam and Christianity Qaddafi refused to be drawn into a condemnation of communism.

The publication of the Green Book coincided with the summoning of an elected 'National Congress' which met in Tripoli in January 1976. The debates at the congress were stated to 'mark a new political system in the Libyan Arab Republic'. It appeared to be the case that the composition of the assembly showed a fresh attempt to mobilize political activity, rather than building on the cadres of the Arab Socialist Union or the popular committees. The congress listened to an address by Qaddafi, which included a reminder that this was the third

[1] The Green Book is not available in England at the time of writing; extracts are taken from the Libyan Embassy publication, *Arab Dawn* (February 1976).

anniversary of the declaration of Jerba, 'which established the Arab Islamic Republic between Libya and Tunisia'. Major Jalloud, as prime minister, played an equally prominent part and appeared to have survived successfully the tensions of the regime, especially those of the previous summer.

THE ECONOMY
(by Robert Mabro)

History and natural endowments define, at any given moment of time, opportunities for and constraints on economic development. On emerging from the colonial era and the Second World War, Libya faced an intractable development problem; and neither history nor nature could provide economic comfort. There had been no significant accumulation of capital under the Ottoman and the Italian rule. The darkest aspect of colonization was the educational policy which left most Libyans illiterate and prevented the emergence of an educated élite by obstructing access to secondary schools and universities. The fierce repression of heroic resistance movements took a heavy toll of lives and drove many Libyans into exile. The displacement of the local population off the best tracts of land by Italian settlers, the dislocation of the infrastructure, and famines during the war debilitated further the human stock. At Independence Libya found herself very poorly endowed with skilled and educated manpower, a most important product of accumulation over time and a crucial resource for economic development.

Before the oil era, nature seemed to be as unkind as history. Libya is essentially an immense desert with scattered settlements—coastal strips, oases, and the northern plateaux including the Jabal Akhdar in Cyrenaica and the mountains of Tripolitania. This geographical configuration has been likened to an archipelago consisting of a few small islands widely dispersed in a vast sea of sand. The distances which separate the Fezzan and the settlements around Benghazi and Tripoli from each other run into hundreds of miles. This is a limiting factor on economic development: the costs of the infrastructure needed to link these various areas are considerable and the benefits of economies of scale are denied to most enterprises and activities located in small and isolated settlements.

Nature has been generous with oil and niggardly in all other respects. Mineral resources—other than petroleum and gas—are either non-existent or not yet proven.

The Libyan economic predicament is better understood against this background. Before the oil era, economic development appeared to be an almost impossible task: the paucity of both human and natural resources, the constraints on agricultural progress, and the peculiarities of the geography all seemed to pose insuperable obstacles. As late as 1959, unaware perhaps of the significance of oil finds, Benjamin Higgins wrote that if there is hope for the poorest and most destitute economy of the world, there might be some hope for Libya. But the question to which we may address ourselves is whether oil, in spite of all the immediate benefits it bestows on the economy, is a significant agent of long-run development. Oil has released a single, though important constraint on Libya's economic development—the availability of finance. All other constraints—and the list is formidable—still operate today and they are likely to restrict the pace of economic development for many years to come. And oil is a depletable resource which may not sustain for more than two decades the level, not to mention the rate of growth, of income to which Libya has become accustomed. The old predicament was how to break away from the vicious circles of poverty and backwardness. Oil has transformed Libya within ten years from a poor to a fairly rich country through a short-cut which by-passed the long and hard route to income growth—economic development and accumulation of human and productive capital. The present predicament is how to use oil wealth in ways that would achieve the old objective—a decisive breakthrough from the constraints of backwardness—and thus prevent stagnation, fall in incomes, or even the recurrence of poverty after the oil era.

Resources

Libya's major economic resource before the discovery of oil at the end of the 1950s was agriculture. This sector still retains its importance, not as a major source of income or of exports but as a large employer of labour.

Agricultural resources are located in two coastal zones—one in the western and the other in the eastern region of the country—and in the oases. The two coastal zones which are the most productive agricultural areas of Libya are separated by the Gulf of Sirte. In Tripolitania a series of oases punctuate the coast which stretches over some 320 kilometres from the Tunisian border to Misurata. The Jefara plain lies between this narrow coastal band—8 to 15 kilometres in width—and the Jabal Nafusah. The plain is some 320 kilometres long and 130 kilometres in width. In Cyrenaica, the Al-Marj plain covers a very small area and the coastal oases are few in number. The Jabal Al-Akhdar which lies behind the plain is a high plateau covered with tree groves. Behind the Jabal Nafusah there is a poor grazing belt. The main groups of oases, deep inland, are the Fezzan, Kufra, Ghadamis, Jalo, and Al-Jaghbub.

Water supply is scarce, and in areas where the main source is rainfall, the supply is very irregular. Mean annual precipitation varies between

100 and 600mm. in the different areas of the coastal agricultural zones. The highest average rainfall is in Jabal Al-Akhdar (600mm.). In the western region, the mean is around 350mm. in Tripoli and less than 275mm. in the Jefara region. The variability—deviations from annual averages—is significant. In the agricultural zone, variations of 20 per cent or more have occurred in 23 of the 40 years for which records are available. When the annual precipitation is below average to such an extent, serious damage affects grain-crops. In Libya, seven in any twenty-year period are expected to be drought years.

Underground water which has its origin in rainfall is tapped from artesian and perched aquifers as well as from the general water table. This is the major source of water supply for Libyan agriculture. Several springs exist in certain regions (Garian, Jabal Al-Akhdar, etc.) but their potential is still unknown.

Ground water resources have been seriously damaged in Libya by intensive and uncoordinated use. Near the coast, where the best agricultural land lies, the lowering of the water table leads to salinization of the aquifers. Salinization of soils occurs where aquifers are at shallow depths and when heavy demands are placed on them. Salts are flushed down again into the aquifer and their concentration in the water tends to increase. But the most worrying phenomenon is the increasing rate of decline of the water level, especially in Tripolitania.

The discovery in 1968 of a huge underground reservoir of pure water at Kufra has initiated a major agricultural development project in this remote and isolated oasis. But the economic usefulness of this discovery is not evident because of the almost insuperable transportation problem. The water situation in Libya has not been improved by the Kufra find, though its characteristics have been modified. There is imbalance—surpluses where water may not sustain an economically viable project and shortages where it is most needed—rather than general scarcity.

Table 1: Land Use in 1960

	hectares (000s)	percentage
(a) Arable land (for field crops):	2,265	100·0
crops	883	39·0
meadows	78	3·4
vegetables and flowers	26	1·2
fallow	1,278	56·4
(b) Orchards and fruit plantations	134	
(c) Grazing land	8,000	

Sources: Libya, Ministry of Planning and Development, *Agriculture in Libya and a Plan for its Development*, Tripoli (?), n.d., pp. 41–2, and J. A. Allan *et al.* (eds.), *Libya, Agriculture and Economic Development*, London, 1973, p. 61 (estimates of grazing land).

Libya can increase water supplies by erecting desalinization plants. Several projects have been studied. The existence of a technological solution does not negate the fact that water is scarce, a term which simply means that the costs of incremental supplies tend to rise very sharply.

Libyan agriculture consists of three main activities: field crops, trees, and livestock. Dualism is a pervasive feature. Dichotomies run along several lines—irrigation/dry farming, settled/shifting cultivation, traditional/modern farms—and tenure systems vary from collective forms of tribal ownership to private property.

The shares of the three main activities in land use, according to data gathered in 1960, are presented in Table 1. The area devoted to trees may be understated because scattered trees, which exist in significant numbers, were probably not taken into account. The data clearly reveal that land is not used intensively. Some 40 per cent of the arable land was cropped in 1960 and the total area under field and tree crops amounts to slightly over one million hectares. The cultivated area represented 0·6 per cent of Libya's total territory.

The crop pattern was as follows:[1]

	hectares (000s)	percentage
cereals	945	84
vegetables	26	2
industrial crops	12	1
fodder crops	5	1
trees	134	12
total	1,122	100

Three features are worth noting. First, the very high share of cereals in land use which is the result of climatic conditions and of the general underdevelopment of agriculture. Second, the small share of industrial crops, which reveals the absence of potential linkages with manufacturing outside the food sector. Third, the insignificant share of fodder crops, which reflects on the quality of livestock husbandry.

In 1960 the irrigated area was estimated at 121,000 hectares, some 10–11 per cent of cultivated land. The poverty of agricultural resources becomes apparent here. Not only is the cultivated area small but some nine-tenths is under dry farming, depending on erratic and insufficient rainfall. Cereal yields which are very low in Libya compared to other North African countries, even on irrigated land, are extremely poor in areas under dry farming. Thus in 1960 the yield per hectare was 1·45 quintal for wheat and 1·57 quintal for barley in non-irrigated land.

In 1960, again, 58 per cent of the area defined as agricultural land

---

[1] See *Agriculture in Libya* ..., op. cit., pp. 41 and 45.

by the census[1] (3,868,000 hectares, an estimate which excludes a large proportion of the grazing land) was privately owned; 35 per cent was under tribal tenure; 3 per cent was held by cash tenants; and the rest was under other forms of tenure. Share-cropping, which seems to have been significant at the time, does not appear in this classification. The extent of tribal ownership is underestimated but this form of tenure generally relates to grazing land and shifting cultivation.

Marked differences in techniques, modes of organization, market orientation, and other production characteristics exist between farms. Farms established during the Italian occupation—mainly between 1911 and 1939—are sometimes defined as modern and are distinguished from older farms where traditional methods of cultivation still prevail. The distribution of land holdings is also very uneven. This feature, combined with technological dualism, suggests that the distribution of agricultural incomes is characterized by great inequalities. The nationalization of holdings owned by foreigners—all 'modern' though not necessarily large farms—may have reduced the degree of inequality. It is impossible, however, to make firm statements on this topic, because of the dearth of statistics. Tribal ownership is often blamed for sustained damage to Libya's agricultural resources. Land suitable for field crops is used for grazing. Little is invested in improvements and soil conservation because of lack of private incentives. It is true that erosion, a secular problem in Libya, has caused significant loss of soil fertility. But the relationship between agricultural malpractices and tenure is not amenable to simple generalizations. Settled farmers, operating in a market economy and enjoying private rights of ownership, are also causing considerable environmental damage in Libya through excessive and uncoordinated demands on ground water resources.

The agricultural output mix includes a wide range of fruit and tree crops and, by contrast, very few field crops. Olives, dates, and almonds are the most important fruits; citrus were largely introduced after the war and seem to have a promising future; finally Libya grows temperate fruit such as apples, pears, grapes, apricots, peaches, and plums as well as semi-tropical fruit such as pomegranates and bananas. Fruit yields are low compared to world averages—half to a third of world average for olives and dates, a quarter to a sixth for citrus. The main cereals are barley and wheat; the main vegetables, potatoes and tomatoes; and the main industrial crop, groundnuts.

Animal wealth essentially consists of sheep, goats, and camels. The livestock economy is associated both historically and sociologically with nomadism. Shifts towards sedentary agriculture over the past century

---

[1] The 1960 agricultural census, the main source of these data, failed to cover adequately grazing land. The figure of 8 million hectares in Table 1 is an estimate of the ministry of agriculture which seems more in line with earlier data than the census estimate.

have transformed the livestock economy—it has become more transhumant and less nomadic.[1] Grazing activity tends to be concentrated on the margins of cultivated areas. Some historical data on Libya are presented in Table 2. The material is probably defective because recording all transhumant and nomadic herds inevitably poses problems. However, the apparent fluctuation in numbers reflects a true situation. The variability of climatic conditions affects animal wealth from year to year in at least two ways: first, through the availability of feed on grazing land and, second, through the impact of changes in incomes and relative prices (field crops/livestock products/other goods) on the rate of slaughtering.

Table 2: Livestock in Libya

Year	Sheep	Goats	Cattle	Camels
1945	n.a.*	570,494	38,717	130,781
1955	1,471,000	1,142,000	135,000	152,000
1960	860,000	950,000	80,000	153,000
1965	1,461,221	1,338,726	108,634	286,427
1970	2,163,200	1,234,400	106,820	163,430

Note: *I did not reproduce here the figure given in the source because it seems suspiciously low.
Sources: (1945–65) J. A. Allan et al. (eds.), op. cit., p. 62; (1970) Ministry of Planning, *Statistical Yearbook 1971*, Tripoli, 1973, p. 118.

We have surveyed agricultural resources at some length because oil economies place great expectation on this sector for long-term development and because outside experts tend to focus on agriculture when they volunteer judgments and advice. It is important to stress that agriculture—the major non-oil resource in Libya—has very little to offer in its present state. One option is to create a very capital-intensive, industrialized, agriculture, an option which may take much time to implement because of the shortage of domestic skills. Such options are never viable commercially or economically in the short run. They could make sense as a gamble with a pay-off in the very long term and may be worth studying in this perspective.

Resources other than oil and agriculture include the coastal waters, a few minerals, and potential tourist attractions. Fishing is underdeveloped despite the existence of sponge beds and fishing grounds containing tuna, sardines, red mullet, and other varieties. These beds are more actively exploited by foreign fleets—Greek, Italian, and Maltese—than by Libya. Mineral resources other than a large iron-ore deposit in the Wadi al-Shati (Fezzan), gypsum, salt, and limestone are either insignificant or yet unproven. The mineral inventory of the country is far from having been properly and comprehensively compiled. The future may still hold one or two major surprises. Libya has

[1] See J. A. Allan et al. (eds.), op. cit., pp. 60–1.

two main tourist attractions: beautiful beaches and archaeological sites. But the resource is untapped. The development of a tourist industry on a large scale involves social diseconomies which many countries like to avoid. A rich oil economy can put a high negative value on these diseconomies and decide against a significant expansion of the tourist industry. Libya would be at a considerable disadvantage if she chose to compete with other countries for tourists; wage and price levels are high, alcoholic drinks are prohibited, and social amenities are in need of considerable improvement.

The Economic Structure

The following snapshots reveal interesting features of the economy before and after oil, as well as features of change. In the early 1950s, agriculture engaged more than one-half of the labour force; this proportion fell to 36 per cent in 1964 and 30 per cent in 1972. This structural shift, common to all developing countries, was accelerated in Libya by both the impact of oil and the unfavourable conditions prevailing in agriculture. The structural shift in the composition of the labour force increased the share of construction (from say 5 per cent in the early 1950s, to 8 per cent in 1964, and 11 per cent in 1972) and services, which occupied in 1972 some 40 per cent of the work force. The shares of petroleum and manufacturing did not increase. The paradox of an oil economy is that petroleum generates a vast income and hardly any additional employment. The task of creating jobs falls squarely on governments which receive the oil revenues. Hence the expansion of construction and services noted above which reveals that governments are more inclined (or perhaps find it easier) to build and administer rather than to engage in productive activities.

Official estimates of gross domestic product at factor costs by industrial origin for 1959 and 1967 are presented in Table 3. In 1959 oil revenues had already had an impact on the economy through large-scale expenditures on exploration and development; hence the large share of the tertiary sector in the GDP estimate. In 1967 Libya was nothing but an oil economy, with petroleum accounting for some 55 per cent of GDP. The indirect contribution of petroleum to other sectors is also considerable: their apparent growth reflects little more than the expenditure of oil revenues. The structure of non-oil GDP is of some interest. The drop in the percentage contribution of both agriculture (from almost 27 per cent to 8 per cent) and manufacturing (from 12·3 to 4·8 per cent) remains very significant when the petroleum sector (whose product can be treated, to a large extent, as an export tax) is removed from the accounts. The dramatic increases in the contribution of construction and services revealed by employment data appear in a glaring light.

Table 3: Gross Domestic Product at Factor Costs, 1959 and 1967 (current prices)

	1959 £ (million)	%	%	1967 £ (million)	%	%
Agriculture	13·8	26·7	24·5	30·9	9·0	4·1
Manufacturing	6·4	13·3	11·4	16·4	4·8	2·2
Construction	2·0	3·9	3·5	66·2	19·3	8·9
Transport	4·0	7·7	7·3	31·6	9·2	4·2
Other services	25·5	49·4	45·6	198·9	57·6	26·6
sub total	51·7	100·0	92·3	344·0	100·0	46·0
Petroleum	4·3		7·7	403·8		54·0
total	56·0		100·0	742·8		100·0

Note: Totals may not add up because of rounding.
Sources: (1959) Statistical Office, Ministry of the Economy; (1967) Ministry of Planning, *National Accounts 1962–1971*, Tripoli, 1972, Table 1.

Exports provide yet another indicator of structural change. In the 1950s, the value of Libyan exports fluctuated between £3·5 million and £4·8 million.[1] They consisted of esparto grass, groundnuts, olive oil, almonds, sponges, live animals, animal hides, and metal scrap. Oil was not then on the export list. Since 1961, the value of exports has been increasing to very high levels, reaching almost Libyan dinars[2] 1,000 million in 1971. But the value of non-oil exports measured at current prices began to decline in 1960. It fell from £3,111,000 in 1960 to LD526,000 in 1971. The drop in export volume was probably much more significant. The inflationary impact of oil revenues, structural changes, and a lack of incentives have drastically affected the export performance of all sectors other than petroleum. That the share of non-oil exports should become insignificant is in the order of things; that the current price value of these exports should fall by so much raises interesting questions about the prospects of long-run developments.

Oil

The nature and prospects of the Libyan economy changed drastically with the discovery around 1960 of important oil reserves.

The history of the oil industry in Libya had its significant beginning with the enactment of the First Petroleum Law in June 1955.[3] True, the Italians had made a few attempts at exploration in the 1930s but

[1] Value of Libyan exports in £(000s): 1954, 3,668; 1955, 4,265; 1956, 3,805; 1957, 4,752; 1958, 4,312; 1959, 3,659; see Bank of Libya, *Economic Bulletin Statistical Supplement*, July 1967.
[2] The currency was renamed dinar after the 1969 Revolution with no change in value.
[3] Royal Decree No. 25 of 1955. On that law, see Abdul Amir Q. Kubbah, *Libya, Its Oil Industry and Economic System*, Beirut, 1964, pp. 64–72.

were unsuccessful, and the Second World War abruptly interrupted these activities. As soon as the British military authorities established themselves in the country in 1943, the Western powers became interested in possible oil finds. The US state department sought an assurance that American companies be given equitable treatment in Libya in any exploration programme.[1] In 1947 and 1948, Esso (now Exxon) carried out some preliminary work. After Independence the Libyan government responded promptly to this interest and issued in late 1953 reconnaissance permits.

The 1955 Petroleum Law was an important event on two counts. First, it enabled a large number of companies to engage in the systematic exploration of large tracts of land, an activity which soon rewarded both the country and the companies with significant oil finds. Secondly, the law departed from the usual system of concession-granting in the Middle East. The repercussions on the structure of the oil industry, largely unforeseen at the time, later proved to be considerable. The conventional system usually led to the establishment of a single concessionnaire in the exporting country—e.g. Aramco in Saudi Arabia, Anglo-Iranian in Persia, etc. Through this system, the major oil companies—the famous Seven Sisters—virtually controlled all oil production outside the United States and the communist bloc. Libya departed from this pattern because she wanted fast exploration and development at a time of plentiful oil supply. To encourage competition between large and small oil companies was rightly thought to be the appropriate method. The Law was designed to attract as many firms as possible by combining favourable inducements with provisions on the maximum number of plots and the maximum area to be held by any one firm and further stipulations on the surrender of plots left unexplored after five years.

The major consequence of the 1955 Law for the world oil industry was the entry of the Independents in an area hitherto denied to them. The Independents are petroleum companies which competed with the Majors in the oil product markets but did not control sources of crude petroleum outside the Middle East. Now, some independent companies—Occidental, Amerada, Continental, and Marathon for example—had preferential access to oil in a privileged location close to the expanding European markets. They increased their share of oil products sales during the 1960s at the expense of the Majors. Another consequence of the 1955 Law which became apparent many years later, in 1970, was the weakening of the company front vis-à-vis the exporting countries. Certainly, that front was never as monolithic and rigid as the legend would have us believe. But the Independents introduced a particularly weak link. They were dependent on oil supplies in Libya (while the Majors enjoyed diversification of sources) and

[1] See FO 371/976, 25 March 1943 in the London Public Record Office.

hence were fairly vulnerable to pressures exerted by the host government. Their existence helped to some extent—though it did not determine or provide an explanation for—the Libyan success in obtaining higher taxes in 1970, the first of a series of significant events which changed the rules of the oil game in favour of OPEC.

Let us now turn to the sequence of oil developments in Libya which followed the 1955 Law. Between 1955 and the end of 1958, seventy-seven concessions were granted to fourteen companies, many of which were consortia of Major and Independent oil firms. These concessions covered some 55 per cent of the Libyan territory. By the end of 1961, the number of concessions had increased to ninety-five and several companies entered the scene either as partners of old concessionnaires or as new operators.[1] Achievements were both rapid and significant. Libya distinguished herself in the history of the oil industry as the country in which exploration, development, and production proceeded at very fast rates. Indeed, the first major oil discovery was made by Esso on 10 June 1953—the Zelten field—less than four years after the granting of the concessions; and the first exports left the shores on 12 September 1961, not much more than two years later. The task was not always easy—minefields remaining from the Second World War had to be cleared and an infrastructure of roads, pipelines, and terminals had to be built to enable first exploration and then production and shipments. The discovery of Zelten was rapidly followed by others: several smaller fields were found in 1959,[2] Esso Sirte drilled a promising well in Raguba and British Petroleum had its first success with the important Sarir field in 1961; finally Occidental turned out to be the luckiest of all in 1967, drilling a well in Idris with a tested production rate of 43,000 barrels a day and another (D1-103) with almost 75,000 b/d. A new batch of concessions was granted in 1966,[3] raising the number to 136. At the end of 1967, there were forty-two concession holders in Libya: twenty-two Americans, six West Germans, three each Anglo-Dutch, French, Italian, and Swiss, one British, and one Spanish.[4]

Libya's petroleum policies and legislation did not remain static in the face of these developments. The eager and immediate response of oil companies to the inducement of the 1955 Law revealed that its provisions were perhaps too generous. As early as November 1957, the government began to insist on better terms in negotiating the grant of new concessions. The deflation and other allowances were reduced in agreements signed in 1958 and completely eliminated in subsequent

---

[1] See Ministry of Petroleum Affairs, *Libyan Oil 1954–1967*, n.d., Table 16.
[2] Greater Mabruh (Esso Sirte), Emgaget (Gulf), Beida (Amoseas), Bir Talacson (Shell), Amal (Mobil), Dahra and Waha (Oasis). Some of these fields had little or no commercial value.
[3] None was granted in the five years between April 1961 and March 1966.
[4] *Libyan Oil*, op. cit., Table 13.

contracts. New concessionnaires—e.g. Elwerath and CORI in 1959—were requested to pay a bonus. A novel principle was also introduced: an undertaking to spend a fixed minimum amount on exploration over a specified period of time. This principle has since gained wide currency. Libya, however, refrained from requesting the retroactive application of these terms from old concessionnaires.

The discoveries of 1959–60 further revealed that Libya had important oil reserves and that very large supplies would soon become available. Libya found a typical problem, similar to that of the British government with the North Sea, the predicament of the 'dissatisfied landlord'.[1] The landlord initially concedes terms which may have been necessary to induce the companies to invest in exploration. If no oil is found, the companies would have wasted their money and both partners are disappointed. But if a rich discovery is made the landlord is also dissatisfied. He knows that the tenant is acquiring a much larger rent than necessary to keep him producing. The landlord will inevitably want more.

Libya amended the 1955 Law by promulgating a new legal instrument on 3 July 1961. But the changes were not very radical. The new decree defined certain concepts—company profits, reference prices for tax purposes, allowable expenses—with much greater precision than hitherto. But the basic 50/50 principle of taxation was not altered. The legislation was not made retroactive but old concessionnaires were advised to accept the new terms. And more interestingly, the Libyan practice of allowing sales or marketing discounts from posted prices was not discontinued at this stage.

This practice, perhaps the most significant inducement provided by Libya to the pioneers, had implications for the oil industry in Europe. Companies with access to Libyan oil enjoyed clear advantages over other competitors in the European markets. The Independents— which accounted for almost half of Libya's output in the mid-1960s— offered high discounts (and hence paid less taxes per barrel) than the Majors which tended to stick to the posted prices or to remain close to them in transferring oil to their affiliates.[2]

Libya joined OPEC in June 1962. In 1964 OPEC arrived at an agreement with the oil companies which involved the expensing of royalties and which fixed the allowable discounts from posted prices at a uniform rate ($8\frac{1}{2}$ per cent on the first year declining by one percentage point in the second and third year). Libya was asked to adopt this system. It suited her as it implied higher revenues per barrel without disincentive for further exploration and production by the companies. Libya was now a major oil exporter and the bargaining power was vested in her. In 1965 she adopted the OPEC agreement and pressed

[1] See M. Adelman, 1972, p. 42.
[2] See E. T. Penrose, 1968, pp. 201–6.

the concessionnaires to accept the new terms. The Independents which benefited most from taxation on the basis of realized prices objected strongly. The Majors were not unhappy with a return to a uniform system and expected to weaken the competitive Independents and to re-establish an 'orderly' market, the euphemism for oligopolistic domination. Indeed, some major companies might have encouraged Libya to introduce the 1965 legislation. But such actions are never the real determinants of change. The real forces were the increasing power of oil-producing countries and the competition of oil companies.

Libya's position strengthened further after the 1967 Middle East war. Production and exports continued to increase at a fast rate. By 1969 Libya was supplying some 25 per cent of Europe's oil. The entry of Occidental, an Independent, which obtained concessions in March 1966 and which after a short lapse of time became a significant producer, introduced another weak link on the company side. The closure of the Suez Canal 'heaped an acute tanker shortage atop the chronic shortage of the preceding seven years'.[1] The Nigerian civil war delayed the emergence of a significant competitor. That oil prices,[2] measured in real terms, continued on the downward slide which had begun in 1957, might indicate that the short-term demand/supply situation was still not favourable to the exporting countries. But Libya, enjoying an increasingly strong position in the market for her own crude—because of the enhanced freight advantage, the increased attractiveness of sulphur-free petroleum induced by new worries about pollution, and the growing dependence of Europe on Libyan supplies—could not but feel that real prices were both too low and moving in the wrong direction.

In 1970 a combination of favourable events enabled the Libyan government to press for and obtain a higher price for oil. First, the 1969 Revolution brought into power young officers who were less inhibited in their approach to the oil companies than the government of the old regime. The significance of this factor, however, should not be overstated. We have seen that Libya always played her hand in the oil game with skill and acumen. The style under the Monarchy was perhaps different from that under Qaddafi: persuasion rather than confrontation, the carrot rather than the stick. But Libya, like any other country, whatever the ideological colours of the regime, always tried to realize the potential advantages of a situation as soon as they were perceived.[3] Secondly, the sabotage of Tapline in Syria in May 1970

[1] M. Adelman, 1972, p. 121.
[2] Net-back prices from Rotterdam to the Gulf.
[3] Many oil analysts and commentators fail to see this point. They tend to believe that politically conservative regimes are less militant and that they are easier to accommodate. That is not true. The Shah of Iran has always been a powerful—and often successful—force behind price rises. And it is the conservative Saudi Arabia which initiated the participation talks and the 1973 embargo.

enhanced the monopolistic position of Libya in the Mediterranean. Thirdly, the spot tanker rate shot up in 1970 to more than 2·5 times the average 1969 level, signalling a short-term shortage of tankers. The existence of such bottlenecks weakens the bargaining power of companies as they cannot counteract the threat of confrontation and cutbacks in one country with swift shifts to other sources of supply. Tankers for carrying additional oil from the remote shores of the Gulf in the event of a Libyan cut-back were just not available at the time.

The Libyan government perceived that the situation was extremely favourable. In May 1970 it pressed Exxon and Occidental to raise the posted price by 50 US cents and the lax rate from 50 to 58 per cent. Occidental, the most vulnerable company, was ordered to reduce production from some 680,000 to about 500,000 barrels a day. Occidental gave in, soon followed by others. By October 1970, most companies had fallen in line. Libya gave OPEC its first major success. The 1970 settlement led to the Tehran–Tripoli agreements of 1971, which raised the posted price of marker crude from US$1·8 to US$2·18 and the lax rate from 50 to 55 per cent. Libya increased her take per barrel by some 80 US cents because of quality premia. The agreements involved escalation clauses and were supposed to last five years. They lasted until October 1973 when the Gulf producers, taking advantage of a favourable market situation, decreed substantial price increases.

Table 4: Oil Exports and Oil Revenues, Libya, 1961–1974

Year	Oil exports in million barrels	Government revenues in million US dollars	Oil production in million tons
1961	5·2	3·2	
1962	65·5*	38·5	8·7
1963	167·2	108·8	22·4
1964	313·7	197·4	41·4
1965	442·6	371·0	58·9
1966	547·4	476·0	72·3
1967	627·1	631·0	84·0
1968	945·0	952·0	125·5
1969	1,131·5	1,132·0	149·8
1970	1,187·6	1,294·8	159·8
1971	988·9	1,766·0	133·1
1972	812·9	1,548·0	108·2
1973		2,100·0†	104·9
1974		6,600·0†	73·5

Notes: * Adjusted according to Libyan sources.
† Estimates.
Sources: Oil exports: *Arab Oil and Gas Directory*, the Arab Petroleum Research Centre, Beirut, pp. 445–6. Oil revenues: Petroleum Information Foundation. For 1973 and 1974 see Shell, *Information Handbook 1975–6*, p. 154. Oil production: B.P. *Statistical Review of the World Oil Industry*, several issues.

Table 4 shows the development of exports and oil revenues between 1961 and 1974. Several features deserve comment. First, the very steep climb of production and exports in the first few years. In 1966 Libya was already the fourth largest producer in the Middle East/North Africa region, by-passing Iraq and accounting for more than 12 per cent of production in that region. She became the third largest producer in 1968, increasing her share to 17 per cent; and in 1969, for a passing moment, she was the second largest producer, slightly ahead of Saudi Arabia[1] and surpassed only by Iran. Her share of the regional production peaked then at 17·5 per cent.

The second feature is the decline of production after 1970 which reflects a combination of factors. In the late 1960s, Libya became increasingly concerned with conservation, partly because she began to realize that the life of her reserves at the going rates of production might turn out to be too short relative to the time horizon of desired economic development; and partly because she became suspicious of technical malpractices on the part of companies eager to produce as much as they could immediately, irrespective of the long-term damage to future recoverable reserves. The interests of an operating company tend to conflict with those of the host country, especially when the former is very uncertain about its future.[2] But the fall in production in 1971–3 also reflects the consequences of such events as the nationalization of BP and the enforcement of the cut-backs and embargoes decreed by Arab oil producers in October 1973 during the Middle East war. Thus, in 1972 and 1973 Libya's oil production was below the level attained in 1968 and one-third down from the 1970 peak. These lower rates of production—say 2–2·5 million barrels a day—are close to the 'optimum' rate for Libya given the nature of her oil reserves, the characteristics of oil fields, prices, revenue needs, and the time horizon of economic development. Most observers recognize that to continue producing at the rate of 3–3·5 million b/d, as in 1969 and 1970, would have been undesirable for both technical and economic reasons. Lower rates of production were associated with higher revenues because of successive price increases secured since 1970. Indeed, an interesting feature of Table 4 is the continuous growth of oil revenues. Between 1961 and 1974, government income from oil rose every year (with a single exception in 1972) above the level attained in the preceding year.

Finally, note the considerable drop in average production which occurred in 1974. In that year Libya took a disproportionate share of the aggregate fall in OPEC production. In September 1973, just before the Middle East war and the Arab cut-back, OPEC total production

---

[1] Excluding output from the Neutral Zone.
[2] In economic jargon, the company and the country apply very different rates of discount to the future.

was 32·4 million b/d.[1] Average OPEC production in the second half of 1974 (July–December) fell to 29·15 million b/d, that is 10 per cent below the September 1973 level. But this reduction was not evenly distributed between the various producers. Libya suffered the largest proportional fall—46·7 per cent. In fact, Libya, whose share of OPEC production was only 7 per cent in September 1973, accounted for a third of the total fall in output that occurred in the second half of 1974.

The interpretation of this phenomenon reveals interesting aspects of the oil market—a market in which Libya has always assumed a special role because of the specific characteristics of her petroleum. It also throws some light on the rules of the oil game played after the dramatic price increases of late 1973. Libyan crude enjoys three advantages over Gulf or Arabian petroleum: low sulphur content, high degree of API gravity (which means higher yields of the valuable light products), and proximity to European markets. These advantages carry premia over the price of marker crude (Arabian light) which serves as a reference. OPEC fixes only the marker price, and individual members have substantial freedom in determining and varying the premia.

Ideally, premia should be set at levels which equalize the attractiveness of different varieties of crude to buyers. In other words, they should reflect exactly the value to the buyer of the quality differential with reference to the marker crude. Before 1970 Libya was selling her full-capacity output at prices which involved lower premia than market conditions warranted. She incurred a loss of potential income. In 1974 she was operating well below capacity and exports were continually declining because the premia were much higher than the market value of the quality differentials. Tanker freight rates had collapsed wiping away much of the locational advantage. Excess capacity in the refining industry and changes in the structure of demand for oil products reduced the attractiveness of lightness and low sulphur content. Failure to reduce the price differential by the correct amount drove Libyan exports in early 1975 below one million b/d. The move back to two million b/d was achieved in mid-1975 through a price cut which seems to have exceeded the desired objective. The oil market in the second half of 1974 and during 1975 was characterized by a series of significant shifts in supplies from one exporting country to another, leading in most cases to delayed and often incorrect adjustments of price differentials. These shifts, and the erosion of the price structure, did not seriously threaten the solidarity of OPEC or lead to the undermining of the price floor. But there are disadvantages in an administered system of price differentials: it does not have the ability to respond rapidly to changing market conditions, not simply because of inevitable bureaucratic rigidities but because of a lack of economic

[1] See R. Mabro, 'Can OPEC hold the line?' in *Middle-East Economic Survey*, XVIII, no. 19, February 1974.

sophistication and detailed market information. Libya has suffered most from it, and in trying to recover losses, it may have inflicted some strains on the Organization. Some observers believe that the issue of price-differentials will turn out to be significant for the future of OPEC. This highlights the role of Libya: though a small producer, her actions may well have more than a marginal effect on OPEC. They did in 1970 by inaugurating a series of successes. They could in other circumstances erode and strain, though probably not break, the producing country front.

Economic Development

The distinction between income growth and economic development, always important and yet often glossed over, is of particular relevance to the analysis of oil economies. Oil revenues are like manna from heaven. They accrue in a way and at a rate which bear little relationship to the actual contribution of domestic factors of production. During the 1960s and early 1970s, Libya, like most OPEC members, enjoyed extraordinary income growth thanks to the discovery of oil and increases in world demand and prices. But growth in the main was neither the manifestation nor the reward of economic development. In an oil economy, the usual order of things is reversed. Social and economic development does not precede or accompany income growth but is expected to follow from large-scale investment programmes and other policies which governments, freed from financial constraints, try to implement and pursue in earnest.

Libya adopted a first five-year plan (1963–8) soon after her emergence as an oil-exporting country. As oil revenues grew faster than originally expected, the plan was continually expanded through additional allocations. Initially, planned expenditures were set at £169 million but the final version budgeted £460 million. Actual expenditures, however, did not exceed £336 million. The failure to meet investment targets is not uncommon in oil economies as planners and governments always tend to underestimate the real constraints on implementation: manpower, infrastructure, and institutional limitations. The emphasis in the first plan (1963–8) rested heavily on public works and utilities, transport and communications, and housing. These sectors absorbed 54 per cent (including 11 per cent for housing) of actual expenditure. This may be compared with the 10 per cent share absorbed by agriculture, 9 per cent by education, 5 per cent by industry, and 4 per cent by public health.[1]

The 1963–8 plan was followed by a second five-year plan (1969–74) which was scrapped by the Revolution. The new government wanted to revise priorities and objectives and establish a new institutional frame-

[1] See *Maghreb: Études et Documents*, XL and XLVI, Paris, 1969–71.

work. *Ad hoc* investment programmes were adopted in the fiscal years 1970–1 and 1971–2 (April to March) and a three-year development plan (1972–5) was issued thereafter. The latter budgeted LD1,168 million. The early emphasis on transport and communications gave way to increases in the investment shares of agriculture (14 per cent), manufacturing (15 per cent), and electricity (9 per cent). Petroleum appeared as a separate category with a large share (10 per cent), a reflection of the desire to transform Libya from a raw material exporter to an industrial country specialized in the processing of the main primary product. This objective stems from a profound aspiration to industrialize, common to all developing countries. The technical and economic difficulties which bedevil the implementation of such an objective are considerable.

Macro-economic developments in Libya can be gauged from a revised set of national accounts published by the ministry of planning in 1972 and 1974. These accounts, which suffer from a number of weaknesses candidly acknowledged by their authors, cover the period 1962–73. They correspond to the first oil era beginning in 1962, the year which saw the significant start of oil exports, and ending in 1973, the year of the dramatic oil price increases. Despite inevitable defects, the accounts are worth analysing. They provide broad but interesting indications of the development of the oil economy.

Let us first look at gross national expenditure (Table 5) which is perhaps a more meaningful aggregate than gross product for an oil economy. The interesting question is not 'where does income accrue from?' since we know that it accrues directly and indirectly from oil, but 'how are oil revenues spent?' Table 5 suggests that gross national expenditure almost trebled in real terms in the ten years 1962–71. As in most oil economies, public consumption tends to grow faster than any other expenditure aggregate (index in 1971 = 665 with 1962 = 100). This trend was not affected by the change of regime: it started under the Monarchy and continued under the Revolution. The underlying determinants are the fast expansion of public employment (a privileged method for redistributing oil revenues), defence expenditures (a common phenomenon in oil economies which reflects the desire to translate abstract financial power into military strength and perhaps the need to protect the new riches from envious neighbours), and the welfare state. Though classified as public consumption, current expenditures on education, health, and social services may be construed, in part at least, as investment in human capital. The share of private consumption declined under the Monarchy but seems to have increased very fast after 1969, for at least two years. The investment share increased at the beginning of the oil era to some 35 per cent of gross national expenditure, and remained remarkably constant until 1968. The very marked fall in 1970 and 1971 which compensates for the rise in both private and public consumption, reflects the early uncertainties of the Revolution about investment priorities, projects, and plans inherited from the old regime. As mentioned before, the second five-year plan was scrapped and the implementation of a number of projects was either cancelled or deferred. The fall in the investment ratio seems to have been temporary and is entirely attributable to the government deciding to revise priorities and to define a new economic strategy. The national accounts for 1971–3, though available only at current prices, suggest a resumption of previous trends: public consumption continued to rise but the shares of both private consumption and investment seemed to have been moving back towards the pre-1970 level.

GDP data by industrial origin (at constant 1964 prices) confirm a number of generalizations about an oil economy. First, little growth occurs in agriculture. The contribution of this sector to GDP fluctuated between LD16·4 million and LD22·5 million during 1962–71 with no apparent trend. These variations are characteristic of an agriculture depending so heavily on irregular rainfall. The absence of an upward trend suggests that investment has either been misdirected or that it involved long gestation lags. Second, manufacturing tends to grow faster than agriculture although from a small base. The manufacturing contribution to real GDP appears to have doubled from LD10 million in 1962 to some LD27 million in 1971. This rate of increase, although high, is not very impressive considering the very small size of the sector in the initial year. Absolute increments to a small initial output need not be very large to yield high rates of growth. We are inclined to believe that little industrial development has taken place in Libya in the first decade of the oil era. Third, the oil boom is always associated with a construction boom because of considerable increases in investment and because infrastructure and housing generally occupy a significant place in the investment pattern. Gross value added in construction increased by a factor of 4·3 between 1962 (LD12·7 million) and 1968 (LD54·6 million), and we have seen earlier that the expansion would have appeared more dramatic if 1959 had been taken as the base year. Finally, considerable growth takes place in the services. Public administration and defence increased their contribution to GDP from LD17·2 million in 1962 to LD74·0 million in 1971; education from LD5·6 million to LD31·8 million; and health services from LD2·3 million to LD14·0 million. All these sectors expanded much faster than non-oil GDP (1971 = 238 with 1962 = 100), and some faster than total GDP. Here again, the usual order of things is reversed by oil. Usually economic development entails a sequence in which agriculture gives way to industry while industry in a second phase induces the expansion of the services. In the oil economy, development starts in the tertiary sector; and the question is whether this sector can be expected to transmit growth to agriculture and industry. There are reasons for scepticism. The sectoral links are weak in an oil economy. The main link which operates through imports is with the rest of the world. Growth in demand does not elicit strong supply responses from the domestic sector of the economy because of innumerable constraints and bottlenecks; and the inducement is stolen away by the trading partners. There is no easy solution to that problem. To curtail imports would lead to inefficient investment, inflationary pressures, and widespread frustration which most governments are unwilling or unable to accept. The task—and it is a long and painful task—is to implement with care a development programme designed to increase the supply of scarce factors. The scarcest factor, of course, is human skills.

Table 5: Gross Expenditure of the Libyan Economy (selected years)

(a) *LDmillion. Constant 1964 prices*

	1962	1964	1966	1968	1970	1971
1. GNP at market prices	187·7	306·1	489·9	653·4	806·3	747·3
2. Net borrowing and transfers from abroad	57·8	8·5	−35·3	−38·2	−158·7	−38·6
total	245·3	314·6	454·6	615·2	647·6	708·7
3. Private consumption	146·1	159·0	218·4	271·2	325·9	355·3
4. Public consumption	28·5	45·0	73·4	125·1	177·7	190·2
5. Gross fixed capital formation	68·9	109·0	159·2	213·6	151·9	157·4
6. Changes in stock	1·8	1·6	3·6	5·3	2·1	5·8
total	245·3	314·6	454·6	615·2	647·6	707·8
index	100	134	180	250	262	289

(b) *Percentages*

	1962	1964	1966	1968	1970	1971
3. Private consumption	59·6	50·5	48·1	44·1	48·8	50·1
4. Public consumption	11·6	14·3	16·1	20·3	27·4	26·9
5. Gross fixed capital formation	28·1	34·7	35·0	34·7	23·5	22·2
6. Changes in stock	0·2	0·5	0·8	0·9	0·3	0·8
total	100·0	100·0	100·0	100·0	100·0	100·0

Source: Ministry of Planning, *National Accounts 1962–71*, Tripoli, 1972, Table 23.

Benjamin Higgins, writing about Libya in the mid-1960s, had one piece of advice to offer: 'when in doubt, educate!' The advice sounds sensible and seems in line with our earlier argument, yet it is too short. It is not sufficient to educate. If that were enough Libya would have no cause for worry. Like all oil economies and many developing countries, Libya can boast of an impressive record in that field. The expansion of schooling began well before the oil era. Between 1950–1 and 1960–1 the number of pupils increased from 32,741 to 146,725 and the number of schools from 208 to 751.[1] In 1971–2, the number of pupils in all schools increased to 473, 865 and that of schools to 1,718.[2] In that year 6,312 students were enrolled at the University of Libya. The rapid growth of public expenditure on educational services has already been noted.

But educational developments cannot be properly appraised in terms of numbers only. In 1971–2 86 per cent of all pupils were receiving primary education, a sign of recent expansion which may pose insuperable problems in the near future. A considerable demand for secondary education is likely to emerge when these large cohorts of pupils reach the end of the primary cycle. The quality of secondary education, which in any case leaves something to be desired, may never recover from a hurried attempt to accommodate this large increase in demand.

As in all developing countries, the secondary cycle is dominated by classical education. In 1971–2, less than 6 per cent of students in secondary schools were receiving technical or vocational training. Teachers, the essential input of educational services, were in short supply. The ratio of pupils was 1:24 in that year. Some 20 per cent of all teachers had no other qualification than a primary certificate of education.[3]

The fundamental problem faced by an oil economy is that the employment policy pursued cancels many of the benefits imparted by education. The educated aspire to income and status and the government obliges by offering jobs in its ever-expanding bureaucracy. The motivated will continue to improve his skills and realize his potential. But the motivation is weak because jobs are secure, promotion is often more related to age (and in some instances to political patronage) than to performance, and income and status objectives are achieved fairly rapidly. The government has little option but to educate and employ, because the oil boom unleashes strong expectations for betterment which any regime, irrespective of its professed ideology, has to satisfy. Betterment means education, the privileged ladder for social mobility. Betterment means income through the redistribution of oil revenues. Merchants, intermediaries, and entrepreneurs in the private sector get their cut—in socialist Libya as in capitalist Saudi Arabia, though the proportions and the magnitude are different. But the numbers involved are small. Redistribution on a larger scale entails either the doling

[1] See *Statistical Abstract of Libya, 1958–1962*, op. cit., pp. 145–6.
[2] *Statistical Abstract 1971*, Tripoli, 1973, p. 97.
[3] Ibid., pp. 97, 102, and 106.

out of a subsidy or the provision of a disguised subsidy in the form of a government job. As neither the donor nor the recipient prefers the first method, there is little option but to adopt the second. The links between education, employment, and the redistribution of income continually reinforce the demand for each. Governments find that their freedom to vary policy becomes more restricted.

Yet the development of the economy gradually opens up job opportunities in the private sector—construction, manufacturing, commerce, etc. The public employment policy initially designed to compensate for a deficiency in the demand for labour, ends up by creating artificial shortages. Libya imports foreign labour, not merely because of specific shortages of skilled manpower but because government policy has created structural imbalances. Unskilled labour is absorbed in the public sector where many remain underemployed while contractors, farmers, and industrialists have to import unskilled workers from Tunisia and Egypt.[1] The educated manpower is not correctly deployed. Teachers are in short supply while secondary school leavers and arts graduates seek clerical jobs in government offices, some of which are already crowded with redundant employees. Far-reaching policies are called for to redress these imbalances. The task is not easy, the results may not be conspicuous, the social and political difficulties lying in the way may seem insuperable. Yet, Higgins's message, suitably paraphrased, remains the most urgent. Human capital is the most important resource for economic development. The abundance of capital may prove to be of little use in the long term unless the period of grace afforded by the oil era is devoted to building up manpower resources. But this implies more than building schools. Incentives have to be kept alive; the rewards should go to the skills which the economy needs most; the vital nexus between production and distribution, unfortunately missing in the oil industry, should be strengthened in all other economic sectors.

Conclusion

Economic development in Libya is handicapped by considerable obstacles: paucity of resources, a late start, and an unfavourable geographical configuration. The population and the area of the country are too large to enable the adoption of a Kuwait or Dubai strategy: i.e. the development of a *rentier* city-state which may be able to ensure its future as a financial centre. The natural resources are too limited and the population too small to allow for significant development on conventional lines, that is, through agriculture and industry without very considerable inputs of skills and technical innovations.

Libya may continue to enjoy riches in the next two or three decades.

[1] See R. Mabro, 'Labour Supply and Labour Stability . . .' op. cit.

She may succeed in improving the distribution of these riches which still remains extremely unequal and leaves pockets of poverty in both rural areas and towns. She may accumulate some financial reserves abroad. She may enter the post-oil era with a good transport infrastructure and not too many uneconomic projects. But the long-term prospects of sustained growth are not good. Apart from the many natural handicaps, Libya, like most oil countries, is the prisoner of a contradiction which mars many endeavours. Oil gives these countries a precious gift—a fairly long period of time which could enable them to implement difficult objectives gradually. But oil also robs them of this advantage. The sudden accrual of wealth breeds impatience and shortens the time horizon. By wanting too much development too early they may end up getting none.

FOREIGN RELATIONS

Muammar Qaddafi and his colleagues regarded the *coup* of September 1969 as the starting-point of Libyan independence. In consequence they gave priority to the removal of foreign bases, and the elimination of what were considered to be vestiges of imperialism. By the end of October 1969 the opening démarches with the British and US governments had been made, and an anti-British demonstration brought the crowds on to the streets of Tripoli. The Libyan demands met with a ready compliance from both Britain and the United States. The British bases at Tobruk and Al-Adam would in any case have been unlikely to survive the Treasury's demand for economy; the breaking of a contract with Idris's government for the supply of an air defence system and other *matériel* remained a much greater source of contention between Britain and Libya. The Wheelus Field, although very useful to the United States, was expendable. The British withdrawal was complete by the end of March 1970 and the American three months later. There was some popular enthusiasm at this liberation of the national territory and the legitimacy of the new regime was enhanced, although neither Egyptians nor Algerians were likely to regard Qaddafi's national struggle as comparable to their own.

The expulsion of the British and Americans was followed by the expropriation of Italians and Jews. Italian land and property was taken over by the government. Some 3,000 farms, representing 100,000 hectares, were distributed to individual Libyans; expropriated shops were put on sale; Italians were allowed to work only if they had a permit from the RCC. Jewish property was confiscated in two stages: first that belonging to Jews who had emigrated, and then the property of Jews in Libya, although in this case with the right to compensation.

At the same time banks, insurance companies, and companies trading in oil and oil products were nationalized. (The oil companies were subject to different legislation; see above, pp. 208–16.) Private companies operating in Libya were required to 'libyanize' their management. The assertion of the national identity took a more visible form in the requirement that all shops and hotels should, like the streets, be designated only in Arabic. In 1973 the government required an Arabic translation in the passports of foreign visitors and all visa and airport formalities were conducted in Arabic alone.

But in contrast to the governments of many new states, the new Libyan government sought, not to reinforce the borders of the national state, but to promote a union into which Libya would be absorbed. The obvious first partner in such an arrangement was Egypt, for both geographical and ideological reasons. The attractiveness of Egypt stemmed in part from the prestige of Nasser; but the experience of the abortive union with Syria from 1958 to 1961 made Nasser extremely cautious of any fresh adventures. Initially President Sadat was less shy of a compact which would provide additional strength for Egypt in the effort to recover from the defeat of 1967. Two unions were adumbrated in 1971: between Egypt, Libya, and Syria, and between Egypt, Sudan, and Libya (an attractive combination, bringing together labour, land, and capital). Neither went further than paper and rhetoric.

None the less, union with Egypt remained a constant preoccupation for Qaddafi, and it commended itself for obvious practical reasons to many of his colleagues. Many members of the Libyan élite saw Libya as a country which could better realize its full potential if it joined another Arab state which would complement its resources with those of manpower, education, and importance in international politics. There were thus practical reasons on the Libyan side corresponding to those which, initially, made the idea attractive to Sadat, who welcomed the possibility of Libyan capital at the disposal of Egypt, together with a 'new frontier' for his people across the western desert. For Qaddafi the idea had a much more important ideological content: he saw union with Egypt as the first step towards a larger Arab union, pursuing the proper objectives of the defeat of Israel, and the return of the Arabs to their earlier grandeur as a chosen Muslim people.

In consequence, it was Qaddafi who made the running, suggesting a 'total fusion' of Libya and Egypt to Sadat in February 1972 and speaking publicly of the plan for union in a speech to students at Misurata in July. The plan, to which Sadat acceded in principle, was for a political union which would be put to the people of the two countries in a referendum on 1 September 1973. There was to be a single capital, Cairo, and one president elected by universal suffrage, who would in the first instance be Sadat, given Egypt's numerical superiority. In order to give detailed shape to the union some 300 Egyptians and Libyans, in equal numbers, spent long months in a series of committees.

As they did so, Sadat's foreign policy developed in a direction which left little room for union with Libya. He made a working alliance with King Faisal of Saudi Arabia in preparation for the limited war of October 1973. The wealth and the oil of Libya could not rival that of Saudi Arabia, and the volatile Qaddafi was not a man with whom Sadat would want to go into the trenches in Sinai. Meanwhile the differences between Egypt and Libya, which in grand terms made them seem complementary, presented very thorny problems under detailed examination. Reservations on the Egyptian side grew stronger, although they were not expressed publicly: and they were matched among the Libyans who were less ideologically minded than Qaddafi. Both Jalloud and the foreign minister, Mansur Kikhia, were known to be hesitant; while many young technocrats, in spite of being attracted by the resources of Egypt, were equally aware of the added complications of trying to develop their own country as part of a union.

The summer and autumn of 1973 proved bitter for Qaddafi. It must be assumed that the ideal vision of Egypt which he had constructed when he listened to Nasser and the voice of the Arabs broadcast from Cairo became increasingly tarnished. (It is not known how his view of an Islamic union accommodated itself to the existence, in Egypt, of a larger number of Christians than there were Muslims in Libya.) But the political development of Libya, particularly in the promotion of the 'cultural revolution' apparently in response to differences between the two countries, made the possibility of union less and less attractive to Sadat. Qaddafi was not party to the negotiations which Sadat was conducting with Saudi Arabia, Qatar, the Ba'athist regime in Syria, and King Hussein (whom Tripoli radio designated as the king-agent of imperialism), but he was aware of something in the wind and went twice to Cairo, once to conduct a stormy interview with Sadat and then (on the anniversary of Nasser's death) to ignore him.

The referendum of 1 September 1973 never occurred, and there has been no union with Egypt. The collapse of the proposal was followed shortly afterwards by the war of October 1973 and relations between the two countries fell to a very low level. Accusations and counter-accusations abounded over the next two years—notably when the Egyptians accused Qaddafi of plotting to overthrow the Sadat regime and to pay for the assassination of Sadat.

The failure of the union with Egypt was followed by one further abortive venture when Qaddafi and President Bourguiba signed a proclamation announcing their decision to join Libya and Tunisia into a single 'Islamic Arab Republic'. From the Libyan point of view such a union was free from some of the objections against union with Egypt since, in population and resources, the two countries were more nearly equal. But while the Egyptian union broke down in the long period of detailed negotiation, the new proposal carried an air of improbability since it was to be submitted to referendum a week after the Jerba meeting. Even in so short a time however the opposition mobilized itself in Tunisia (see below, pp. 389–90) and the plan was postponed *sine die*. But relations between Libya and Tunisia remained close; Tunisian workers continued to make a major contribution to Libyan development (and to the budgets of their families at home) and practical cooperation between the two countries was uninterrupted. In August 1975 the Libyan minister of the interior, Commandant el-Hamidi, made an official visit to Tunis and declared his government's intention of reinforcing links with Tunisia. The status of Tunisian workers in Libya and of Libyans in Tunisia was discussed, along with problems concerning the common frontier; it appeared therefore that Libya had accepted the Tunisian view of cooperation as a means to possible subsequent union, rather than the reverse process.

Under Qaddafi's presidency the Libyan government is uncompromising towards Israel and supports, without discrimination, Palestinian revolutionaries. Qaddafi has condemned Zionism as an aggressive nationalism like Nazism and stated that 'the racial Zionist entity must be completely liquidated, and this makes us refuse any shape of truce, acceptance, or negotiations with this aggressive enemy. We are not fighting for territorial adjustments or better borders. It is a ferocious war between an established nation and an aggressive enemy who plans to uproot it once and forever' (speech of 4 February 1974). In a simplistic view of the origin of Israel Qaddafi recognizes that Jews went to Palestine to escape from Nazi oppression, but that this came to an end with the defeat of Germany in 1945. Since then Jews are not oppressed anywhere in the world (not even in the Soviet Union). It follows that Jews who emigrated to Palestine before 1948 should have the right to stay in a Palestine which would not practise any form of discrimination, to which Arab refugees would naturally return. Libya would welcome back Libyan and other Arab Jews, and the European countries and the United States should do the same. ('This is the only just and final solution for this problem.')

This 'solution' of the problem of Israel forms part of Qaddafi's dream of a greater Arab world, in which the Arab states unite in a national and populist campaign. In practice Libya has played less part in the formation of policy towards Israel than almost any other Arab state (except in its support for Palestinians) and, paradoxically, popular reaction towards Israel has been muted, in contrast to the demonstrations which took place under King Idris in 1967.

As we have seen, the shooting down of a Libyan Boeing prompted demonstrations against Egypt. Qaddafi replied by setting up centres where Libyans could volunteer to join the battle against Egypt—an invitation which evoked very little response. Qaddafi's awareness, in the following months, of Egyptian negotiations with the other Arab states did not forewarn him of the impending war of October 1973. His reaction to the conflict was critical of its character (since it was not an Arab 'national battle') and of the battle plan. But the announcement of a cease-fire was met with vigorous denunciation and condemnation —of the United States and the Soviet Union for 'imposing' the cease-fire, of the Egyptians and Syrians for accepting it, and of the European states for not coming to their aid.

Libya sent no troops to the battle area. Its military contribution was presumably confined to the despatch of Mirage aircraft, before the war broke out. A condition of their sale by France was that they should be used by Libya for defensive purposes; but there were reports that they had been transferred to Egypt and in October 1973 Israel made an official protest to the French government that 'French' Mirages had taken part in attacks on targets in Israel—an allegation that was denied by the Libyan government the following day.

Libya was similarly eclipsed in the embargo on oil exports. In 1967 popular reaction and a strike of oil workers had prevented the export of oil, and the Libyans had talked of the use of an oil weapon in the event of a war against Israel during the conflict over prices in 1970-1. But in 1973 the oil policy was led by Saudi Arabia. The Libyan government had taken nominal control of 51 per cent of production; but it had no practical control over output or export or even the resources to check the rumour that Libyan oil, after passing through Italian refineries, was the main fuel source for the US sixth fleet in the Mediterranean.

Libyan support for Palestinians has been consistent. In Qaddafi's ideology they have the double merit of conducting a battle against Israel and of being revolutionary. The full extent of active support is difficult to determine. The aspect which has attracted most international publicity has been the readiness of Libya to provide a haven for terrorists, like those belonging to Black September who in September 1972 negotiated their release after an operation at Munich which resulted in the death of several Israeli athletes. In 1974 Jalloud gave a press conference in Tripoli in which he condemned Palestinian action outside Palestine, and condemned all hijackings. But in 1975 members of the Japanese Red Army who had held the US ambassador hostage in Kuala Lumpur were given sanctuary in Libya, presumably because of the action which other members of their organization had undertaken at Lod airport.

It is reported by Pierre Rondot that there are two Al-Fatah guerrilla training camps in Libya, one at Tawqarah, near Benghazi, which has been in operation since 1971, and the other at Ras Hilal, fifty miles from El-Baida on the Egyptian border, where Al-Fatah frogmen are trained (by instructors who include a number of British mercenaries). Qaddafi has declared Libya's willingness to help Palestinian volunteers, has offered training sites in Libya, and the assistance of Libyan embassies to Palestinians making their way to Libya.

The extent of aid, whether financial or of any other sort, to the Palestinians remains a matter of sceptical speculation and cannot be accurately established. Moreover Qaddafi's policies have to some extent been overtaken by the support which Arab governments gave to the Palestine Liberation Organization after the October war. Qaddafi was not present (although he was represented) at the Rabat summit conference in October 1974 when the Arab states recognized the PLO as the representatives of the people of Palestine and the PLO itself is bound to seek the support of a broad range of Arab states rather than turn to the isolated government of Libya.

Consistently with his policy towards the Palestinians Qaddafi has expressed great hostility towards Jordan. King Hussein is regarded as the executioner of the Palestinians because of the action of the Jordan army against the *fedayeen* in September 1970, after the Palestinians had shown their defiance of Hussein's government by landing hijacked planes on Jordanian territory. In November 1972 the Jordanian security forces accused the Libyan government of financing a plot led by Rafei Hindawi to assassinate Hussein, and some forty Jordanians accused of receiving money from Libya were arrested.

Finally the Libyan government has worked actively to counter Israeli influence in black Africa by offering aid and assistance in the expectation that diplomatic relations with Israel will be broken. This policy appears to have been successful with Burundi, Togo, and Chad —where Libya at first supported the insurrection of the Muslim Toubbou tribes and then (in April 1972) abandoned the rebels in favour of the government, which in November broke relations with Israel. President Bokassa of the Central African Republic was less susceptible to Qaddafi's persuasion, and his government severed diplomatic relations with Israel only when the October war and the oil embargo provided a greater inducement to do so. A promising relationship with Uganda ran into difficulties as the Libyans grew anxious about the possible misdirection of the financial aid they had given to President Idi Amin—who made a series of complaints about Libyan behaviour, eventually saying that they were 'like all Arabs—undependable and untrustworthy'.

In spite of scanty knowledge of the world, beyond what could be learned from the radio, Qaddafi appeared willing to use Libyan resources to support the Arab cause wherever it appeared to be at risk; to support Muslims; and to support revolutionary movements. He welcomed news of the attempt against King Hassan of Morocco and for two years Tripoli radio kept up a vigorous campaign against his rule. It appears likely that the Moroccan subversion of 1973 received aid from Libya (see below, pp. 310–11). However, the radio campaign halted after the October war (in which Moroccan troops took part). The Libyan government supported the Moroccan case against Spain over the Sahara and the Spanish principalities, but subsequently took the Algerian side against Morocco.

South Arabia and the Gulf are areas where Qaddafi has sought to act against dangers to the Arab world. Libya was the only Arab country to react to Iranian seizure of the islands of the Tumbs and Abu Musa when Britain withdrew from the Gulf. The reaction was directed against Britain (Libyan funds were removed from London banks and BP was nationalized). Subsequently Qaddafi was reported as being willing to act with Iraq and South Yemen in order to remove the 'intolerable' presence of Iran in Oman, where Iranian forces were supporting the sultan against the insurrection of Dhofar. At the same time he has sought to reconcile the differences of the governments of the two Yemens, in order to end a wasteful conflict between Arabs and lessen the possibility of Russian and Chinese intrusion. On the other side of the Bab el-Mandab the Eritrean Liberation Front has sought support from Libya and it is reported that financial and arms aid has been given; while at the same time Libya has sought to ally with Somalia and also to diminish the status of Ethiopia in the Organization of African States. In principle support has also been offered to the Muslims in the Philippines and to Black Muslims in the United States.

The extent of support which has actually been delivered is difficult to discover in most of the cases where it has been offered, or where Libya has been accused of providing it. But it is one of the paradoxes of Qaddafi's Libya that the single most decisive intervention may be one that restored a government rather than overthrowing it. In July 1971 left-wing officers initiated a *coup* against President Numeiry of Sudan. The *coup* quickly gained the support of the Sudanese communists. The Libyan government ordered a British civilian aircraft carrying two of the new junta to land at Benghazi. The two officers were returned to Khartoum and shot. However, this successful intervention did not make for prolonged good relations. Sudan was reproached for not taking the union with Egypt and Libya seriously; and Sudanese rebels appear to have looked for aid in Libya.

The volatility of Libyan foreign policy under Qaddafi's direction has prevented the development of close and stable relations with other Arab states or with such potential regional partners as Morocco. It is understandable that relations with most of the major powers should also have been turbulent. British relations with Libya in the early years were complicated by the previous connexion with Idris's regime and by Qaddafi's view of the British record in the Middle East, dominated by the Balfour declaration and the Suez expedition. To these political and ideological factors (on the Libyan side) were added practical questions concerning the arms contract or the British airliner—

problems which dragged on because of the sporadic attention which the Libyan foreign ministry gave to questions of practical detail. The British embassy, in common with the American and Soviet embassies, was reduced in size at the request of the Libyan government and found itself working under enclosed and difficult conditions.

Meanwhile Libya found a new source for dissension by offering support to the Irish Republican Army. Libyan relations with the Irish provide an unusual story of inconsequentiality. In 1972-3 the explicit verbal support which Qaddafi gave to the IRA appeared to be backed up by the supply of arms when, in August 1973, the navy of the Irish Republic arrested the SS. *Claudia* carrying five tons of arms, ammunition, and explosives, of Russian origin, which was thought to have come from Libya. This did not prevent the Libyan government opening negotiations to buy arms from Britain. The following year the Ulster Defence Association sent a delegation to Libya to outflank the IRA, and appeared to interest the Libyans in their plans for Northern Ireland. Finally, the government of the Irish Republic has actively pursued relations with Libya, no doubt with the intention of dissuading the Libyan government from interfering in Irish affairs. In April 1975 an Irish delegation of parliamentarians, led by a junior minister, visited Libya and relations seemed to be moving along more pragmatic lines.

Among the countries of western Europe France has found itself to be Libya's most politically favoured partner, in part because of the Middle East policy which France has pursued since 1967, in part because the relatively minor participation of France in Libyan affairs before Independence left no outstanding problems. When King Idris's arms contract with the British became a casualty of the September *coup* the Libyan government turned to France for the purchase of 110 Mirages, and there have been subsequent discussions about the purchase of sophisticated French weapons. In November 1973 Qaddafi, instead of attending the Algiers summit of Arab leaders, went to Paris, where he had a long interview with Pompidou and then took part in a colloquium organized by *Le Monde*. In February 1974 Jalloud went to Paris to sign an 'oil-for-aid' agreement similar to one which France had signed with Iran. It guaranteed the supply of Libyan oil to France (the share of Libya in the French oil market having fallen from 14 to 5 per cent in the previous year) in return for industrial aid and exports and cooperation between banking and financial institutions. Subsequent contracts implementing this framework followed in the next year. In February 1975 the French ministers of agriculture and foreign trade visited Libya; Libyan declarations of admiration for France's independent policy and the rhetoric of the Euro-Arab dialogue took practical shape as French agricultural exports to Libya rose from 87 to 200 million francs between 1972 and 1974.

Meanwhile Italy has returned to a position of major importance in trade and investment. The political atmosphere was improved in 1975 by an agreement on compensation for Italians in Libya, and Libya took first place in Italy's export drive to the Arab world.

It would be consistent with Qaddafi's 'third theory' for Libya to maintain an equal, and substantial, distance from both the United States and the Soviet Union. In practice relations with the United States have indeed been distant, while the forces of international politics appear to be stronger than Qaddafi's anti-communism in creating a limited partnership with the Soviet Union. The United States has been the object of vigorous verbal attack, a US military aeroplane was attacked by Mirage fighters in an isolated incident in March 1973 and the Libyan embargo on the export of oil to the United States was maintained until January 1975. In recompense there have been no important areas for cooperation between the Libyan and US governments. American oil companies have had to accept partial or complete nationalization and Libya has led the way in a price policy which the United States tried to oppose. This has not prevented the employment of a large number of US citizens, particularly in oil and construction industries and a modest amount of trade between the two countries.

As we have seen, Qaddafi's ideology shows a resistance to Marxism which is unusual amongst Arab socialists, while his world view rejects the hegemony of great powers. In 1972 events appeared to be moving in the right direction: Egypt expelled its Russian advisers and projects of union between Arab states were under discussion. The Arab nation appeared to be asserting its greatness, at the expense of Soviet intrusion. But the Soviet Union, with an obvious interest in naval power in the Mediterranean, cultivated the new government of Libya, to the extent that Qaddafi was awarded the Order of Lenin 'in appreciation of his efforts for world peace'. At the same time Jalloud took a more pragmatic view of relations with the communist world. He visited Moscow in March 1972 and was able to implement policies which were more his own than Qaddafi's by signing agreements for technical and economic cooperation in the oil industry, at a time when the East European market enabled Libya to dispose of the output from the nationalized BP field.

The October war was followed by increased contacts between the Libyan and Soviet governments. In May 1974 Jalloud made a five-day visit to the Soviet Union, while Qaddafi was reported as saying that 'we have always regarded the Soviet Union as a friend, and relations are now better than ever before'. The outcome of Jalloud's visit was the signature of an agreement for the purchase of arms to the value of 800–1,000 million dollars. The Soviet Union was also reported as agreeing to provide Libya with an 'atomic centre' including a nuclear reactor with an eventual capacity of 10 million watts. At the end of 1975 a leftward turn in Qaddafi's domestic policy, at the same time as the conflict over the Sahara, seemed to give added importance to these links with the Soviet Union.

Ideology, volatility, and improvisation have thus played a larger part in Libyan foreign policy than in that of most other countries. The normal conduct of state-to-state diplomatic relations has been given little institutional basis and has often been impeded by Qaddafi's practice of making unannounced visits to the neighbouring Arab countries (so that on one occasion President Boumediene met Qaddafi at Hassi Messaoud in order to avoid the impropriety of such improvisation). In the early years after the revolution there was little room in foreign affairs for technically able young men to influence development as there was in economic planning. Initially the foreign minister was also minister for 'unity'. This post was held by Salah Boweisir. In July 1972 Mansur Kikhia, a career diplomat who had been undersecretary for foreign affairs, became foreign minister; but he resigned in April 1973, probably through a mixture of ill health and disagreement with the upheaval of the cultural revolution, as well as scepticism about union with Egypt. (He was subsequently appointed Libyan representative at the UN.) Abdel Ati el-Obeidi, minister of labour, was given responsibility for foreign affairs; but this was stated to be a temporary arrangement, and it was known that el-Obeidi was fully occupied with his own ministry. However, no fresh appointment was made until Commandant Abdel Moneim el-Houni, a member of the RCC and close colleague of Qaddafi, was appointed minister of foreign affairs in November 1974.

Throughout this time Abdesselam Jalloud engaged in a continuous process of negotiations leading to practical agreements on matters of economic cooperation. He gave little evidence of interest in pan-Arabism, the struggle against communism, or Islam, and was much more concerned with practical results.

The failure of the union with Egypt and the isolation of Libya at the time of the October war left a vacuum in the more ambitious and theoretical aspects of Libya's foreign relations which coincided with the withdrawal of Qaddafi from the forefront of the political scene. The years 1974-5 were correspondingly marked by more modest initiatives, more likely to bear fruit over a longer period. These included the reconciliation with Morocco and the practical relationship with Tunisia. The Cyprus conflict opened up favourable possibilities for Libya, since Libya supported Turkey in its conflict with Greece. Jalloud visited Turkey in January 1975 and a wide range of cooperative ventures was worked out based on Libyan oil and money in return for Turkish expertise and labour, with the possibility of Turkish training for the Libyan troops. Similar cooperation could be expected to develop with

Malta, following the agreements already made in 1971–2 and the readiness of Dom Mintoff to strengthen his hand in negotiations with the NATO powers.

This growing pragmatism in the conduct of foreign policy, and the pre-eminent role of Jalloud, were further exemplified by the part Libya tried to play during the Lebanese cataclysm of 1976. However, the crisis over the Sahara which broke out with the signature of the three-power agreement of November 1975 opened the way for active and ideological involvement in Maghreb politics. Qaddafi offered his backing to Algeria and to Polisario. It was an alliance which would put Libyan financial resources behind Algerian support of Polisario against the Moroccan army, but one which Boumediene was likely to regard with some caution, in view of the earlier relationship between the two countries.

EDUCATION AND SOCIETY

Libyan society inevitably reflects the recent history and politics of the country. Since the 1969 Revolution Qaddafi has endeavoured to maintain or construct an Arab-Islamic society; while at the same time the needs of a developing economy call for rapid advance in education and technical training. Islamic law and custom permeate civil law and practice, to more or less effect. The total ban on alcohol (which extends to foreign diplomatic missions) is symptomatic of a general puritanism. As the state has accepted responsibility for social welfare, in the provision of health services, lodging, and social insurance, it has legislated for the state collection of the *zakat*, or alms tax—an innovation of rather symbolic importance. In October 1972 a Koranic law prescribing amputation as a punishment for theft was reintroduced—apparently as a deterrent. (It evoked considerable excitement outside Libya, but there are no reports of the punishment having been inflicted in this rather gentle society.) Religious holidays are given more importance than civil holidays; Qaddafi has customarily delivered a partly religious, partly political sermon at the end of Ramadan and Commandant Bachir Hawadi has presided over a committee designed to ensure that civil law is in accordance with Koranic law. The status of women is protected by a new personal code, although women remained unequal to men in such matters as the giving of evidence. In 1974 there were six women in employment for every 100 men.

The RCC has made important efforts to fill the gaps in Libyan education. In 1972 the Libyan educational system had produced only 2,300 students holding a diploma or advanced degree. In consequence the government has made a major drive to develop all levels of instruction. Education accounts for 28 per cent of the national budget; the number of primary schools increased from 1,032 to 1,311 in the first two years after the revolution, with a 50 per cent increase in the number of pupils. The universities of Tripoli and Benghazi have been expanded—the new university of Benghazi promising to be one of the more interesting architectural achievements of the region. Education in Arabic is free from the complexities of a dominant European language, as is the case in the neighbouring countries of the Maghreb. It remains under strong Egyptian influence—there were 2,600 Egyptian teachers in Libya in 1972 and school books were being drawn up in accordance with Egyptian practice. The teaching of Islam has an important part in general education, while political influences are also evident in the importance given to French as a foreign language.

At the same time a rapid effort has been made to meet the immediate needs of technical skill. Expertise in oil has been given a high priority: students have been sent to the United States and Algeria for technical training, others have gone to the Institut Français du Pétrole in Paris and a local oil institute is being established in Libya. The problem of labour supply has been the object of careful study under the direction of the energetic minister of labour, Abdel Ati el-Obeidi, and as a result of his initiative institutes for technical and professional training are being established to meet the needs for skilled and semi-skilled workers.

IV
Mauritania and the Southern Sahara

GEOGRAPHY AND POPULATION

For the purpose of this survey the Southern Sahara may be defined roughly as the vast region lying between the 25th and 15th parallels of latitude. It is limited in the west by the Atlantic, in the north by the southern frontiers of the Algerian and Libyan Saharan areas, in the east by that of the Sudan, and in the south by no administrative boundary but by the human borderland where white and black Africa (*blad al-bidan* and *blad as-sudan*) intermingle. The region embraces the whole of Mauritania, together with the northern part of Mali, most of Niger, and the northern portion of Chad.

Geography

The region is one of vast plains which, however, present varied characteristics: steppes covered here and there with a meagre vegetation of stunted shrubs and tufts of harsh grass, sandy wastes called *regs* which, if hard, are ideal for camel travel but are devoid of water and plant life. These must be differentiated from those agglomerations called *ergs*, composed largely of shifting dunes. The monotony of these plains is relieved by dried-up river valleys, rocky plateaux, and by rare oases formed where underground water is accessible. The character of the meagre vegetation reflects these topographical differences. The most important of the high plateaux and mountain masses *(adrar)* which divide the plains are, from west to east, Adrar Tmar in the north and Tagant in the south-east of Mauritania; Iforas in Mali; Air in Niger; and Tibesti in Chad. Their relief assures them a regular season of rains and, possessing permanent water and pasture grounds, they are among the more favoured regions. The principal villages, such as Shinqit and Atar in the west and Agades in the centre (Air), owe their existence to relatively good pastures, date-palm groves, or previous importance in trans-Saharan traffic. The first mentioned, Shinqit (of Soninke origin), is the Arabic name of the area, possessing a certain linguistic and racial unity, to which many Europeans, in modern times, confusingly gave the name Mauritania, so that its inhabitants, the Shanaqta, are known in French as *Maures* (Moors). It is a *zawiya* centre, now decadent, which earned a certain reputation in the Islamic world because of the frequent pilgrimages of its inhabitants.

The desert character of the region, the extreme poverty of vegetation, and the rarity of animal life are due not to the nature of the soil but to the aridity of the climate, marked by the irregularity or absence of rain, aided by high temperatures and intense evaporation. Two climatic bands may be distinguished: the south-Saharan proper from approximately 25° to 18° N.; and the Sahilian from 18° to 14° N. As will be seen from a climatic map these divides are wavy and variable; for instance, in the plain *(tenere)* between Tibesti and Air the Sahara advances southwards to 16°. These areas belong to the southern watershed in that the rains fall during the summer and not, as in the northern Sahara, during the winter. The southern Sahara is much less desolate than the northern portion; most years it rains nearly everywhere, though irregularly, and great herds of camels and sheep can find pasturage, even if oases are rare and poor compared with those of the north. The Sahilian (Arab. *sahil*, 'borderland') is distinguished from the Saharan climate in that it rains regularly to the extent of 200–500mm. each year between July and September. The feature which distinguishes it from the Sudanese climatic band, which follows it, is that the rains are insufficient to allow for cultivation without irrigation. The Niger itself flows through 500 km. of desert in the big sweep, the so-called Niger bend, which it makes to the north, reaching its apex at the caravan port of Timbuktu. Though there are a few black African villages in the dry valleys, the area is Saharan rather than Nigerian. The Sahara is traversed from north to south by caravan routes which avoid the *ergs* and keep to the rocky or gravel desert.

Population

In spite of its aridity human beings can live in parts of these wastes. The population of the definitely Saharan area is about 320,000 of whom some 140,000 are Mauritanians; but it must be remembered that white Saharans also inhabit the Sahel. The state of Mauritania has a population of about 1·2 million of whom the majority are white. Similarly the majority of the Tuareg are located in parts of the Sahel because any increase in population is impelled there by the barren nature of their homeland. Apart from French officials, the dominant inhabitants, all Muslim, are Moors in the west, Tuareg in the centre, and Teda in the east. At the beginning of the Christian era black Africans were the dominant race in the southern Sahara and they still form an important part of the population; they are scattered all over the region but are now subordinate to new dominant groups. Speaking either Arabic or Tamahaqq, they belong culturally more to the Saharan than to the black African world. Their former culture, however, reveals itself in their superstitions and in their enjoyment of drum and dance rhythms. They are an important element in the life of the Sahara, because its agricultural economy is wholly dependent upon them, and they have made a deep racial imprint upon many groups of whites. There are two types of blacks: oasis cultivators (Arab. *haratin*, Tam. *ikawaren*), to be clearly differentiated from the descendants of slaves (Arab. *abid*, Tam. *iklan*), who cultivate favourable valleys, tend herds, and act as servants of the whites.

The Teda (or Tubu) form a distinct and homogeneous people; though dark and speaking a Sudanese language, they are not black Africans but probably descend from an old Saharan race. They number about 100,000 (44,000 in Niger and 56,000 in Chad) and are scattered over a vast area of the eastern Sahara from Hoggar in the west to the Libyan desert in the east, and from Fezzan in the north to the Chad in the south. Their main groups live in the mountainous regions of Tibesti, Borku, and Ennedi, the Kawar group of oases, and parts of Kanem and Waday.

In the west, the Moors are the dominant people; in the centre, the Tuareg. The Moors (who range across the frontiers of Mauritania, Senegal and Mali) occupy all habitable country between the Atlantic and the Iforas mountains. Of Berber origin, they are now Arabic-speaking and call themselves 'whites' (Arab. *bidan*) as opposed to the 'blacks' *(sudan)*. In the south of Mauritania, the Trarza, Brakna, and Kunta are the most important tribes; in the north the great nomadic tribe of Riqaibat, part of whom are in Rio de Oro; in the Saharan parts of the Sudan such as Hawd and Azawad we find smaller tribes including the Barabish, Kunta, Idaw Aish, Ahl Tishit, Awlad Mubarak, Mashduf, and Awlad Delim. The ruling clans of Arab origin such as the Beni Hassan are sometimes mixed with and sometimes juxtaposed to their Berber tributaries or *zanaga*. Arabization has had a variable effect upon the social organization of the Moorish groups but nowhere has it obliterated the Berber foundation. Thus the Riqaibat speak pure Hassaniya Arabic with Berber admixtures, but their social organization is basically Berber. Women, as with all Saharan nomads, play an important role. Monogamy is universal. Women are masters of the tent, receiving and entertaining visitors. The assembly *(jamaa)* is the governing body; *cadis* are tolerated, but only as advisers if someone invokes Islamic law, not as judges.

The Tuareg domain stretches from In-Salah in the northern Algerian Sahara to Hombori within the Niger bend in the south, and from Iforas in the west to Tahoua in Niger. They speak a particular Berber dialect, known as Tamahaqq, and have preserved a Libyan script called *tifinagh*. The northern group, who live in the mountainous area of the central Sahara beyond the limits of the area we are considering, are small in numbers. The main groups live north and south of the Niger bend and in Air, and these through living in a different physical environment and in contact with black Africans have been modified in physical characteristics, mode of life, and customs. Most of them have lost their camels, which could not stand the change of climate. Noble clans have sometimes retained their racial purity owing to the matrilineal reckoning of descent; thus the son of a noble and a serf woman would not be a noble but belongs to his mother's class. In fact the Tuareg display every gradation of type from Berber to black African. The southern Tuareg have increased in numbers, whereas the pure nomads are kept at a constant level by a lower birth-rate and by migration.

Besides the above there are in Chad Arab tribes known as the Shoa or Shuwa who have penetrated from the east. Some are camel-nomads *(abbala)*, but the majority are semi-nomadic cattle-breeders *(baqqara)* who occupy fixed villages during part of the year. They speak their own Arabic dialect, their social organization is quite different from that of Saharans, and they belong more properly to the Sudan. A distinct Arab group of camel nomads are the Awlad Sulaiman who migrated from the Fezzan after expulsion by the Turks in 1842 into the Teda area north-west of Chad. They live and speak like Tripolitanian Arabs.

HISTORY

The history of the south Sahara during the past 2,000 years is composed of three interwoven strands: the migrations and struggles of nomad tribes, the control of the routes and tribes by black states in the Sahel and Sudan, and, throughout the whole period, the steady pressure of the white Saharans upon its black inhabitants. From the fourth century A.D. the multiplication of the camel resulted in the formation of powerful Berber groups and the gradual reduction of Sahara blacks to the status of slave cultivators. Nevertheless the great black empires of the Sudan continued to dominate the southern Sahara, controlling its trade routes and exploiting deposits of salt, until the Moroccans conquered the Songhay state in 1591. This intervention was exceptional; in general, relations with North African states were almost entirely economic, apart from the occasional exchange of a diplomatic mission. Arab geographers and historians, our chief source for this period, testify both to the security of the trade routes under the black empires and to the accompanying spread of Islam. The rise of the Almoravid dynasty in the wastes of Mauritania in the eleventh century and its conquest of the Maghreb and Muslim Spain had as an offshoot the conquest of the capital of the Ghana empire in 1076. But though Almoravid rule strengthened the hold of Islam over the western Berbers, its major effort was directed towards the north. It never gained control of the Sahel and its influence as an islamizing factor can be exaggerated.

In the fourteenth–fifteenth centuries an Arab tribe, the Maaqil, advanced into Mauritania. They were a branch of the Beni Hilal whose unleashing upon North Africa by the Fatimids in the middle of the eleventh century was a cause of its further arabization. Their dominion led to a transformation in the life of the western Berbers and to their adopting the Arabic language. They gave up the custom of wearing the mouth-muffler (Arab. *litham*, Tam. *taghelmuzt*), a characteristic feature of all Saharan Berbers which is still retained by the Tuareg. Many arabized Berbers had regained their independence by the nineteenth century. Arab tribes also pressed on the Berbers of the Hawd (Sudan) but were repelled, though Arab sections like the Kunta established themselves peacefully, and these tribes also became arabized. In the central Sahara the Tuareg resisted both Arab penetration and arabization. The destruction of the Songhay state by the Moroccans led to Tuareg expansion and control over the Niger bend (completed by 1770) and finally the whole Sahil from Timbuktu to Chad. This Tuareg supremacy lasted until the French conquest. On the other hand the Teda in the Sahara north of Lake Chad resisted Tuareg pressure and remained independent.

The French Occupation

French control of the whole area grew out of their occupation of the Sudan at the end of the nineteenth century. The nomads remained undisputed masters of the southern Sahara up to 1900. In 1890 the French and British agreed that the region situated south of Algeria and Tunisia should be regarded as a French sphere of influence as far as a line running from Say on the Niger to Baroua on Lake Chad. Modifications were made in 1898, 1904, and 1906. After Kitchener's conquest of the Eastern Sudan in 1898 another agreement defined the boundary with that country and brought Tibesti, Borku, and Waday into the French sphere. Farther west, Senegal was first relieved from the pressure of the Moors by Governor Faidherbe (1851–65). After he left further expansion was not encouraged from Paris and it was only in the present century, after the occupation of Sudan, that the western caravan routes and south Mauritania were brought under control through operations which were completed in 1934 when the assumption of the protectorate over Morocco enabled expeditions from the south to be joined by others from the north.

After posts were established along the Niger bend (1899) control was gained over the Ullemmeden Tuareg and the Moorish tribes of the Sudan. Farther east, after the defeat of Rabih in the Chad region (1900), action was taken against the Sanusi, leading to the establishment of control over Waday, Borku, and, finally (1914), Tibesti. The position was not changed by the important Sanusi rising of 1916–17.

During this time it was important for France to exclude any other major power from control of the Shinqit area but it did no more than establish administrative control, based on Senegal. Moreover, the administration kept the tribal system intact and governed through it. Thus, French rule neither destroyed the traditional basis of society by imposing a modern administrative structure upon it (although the governor of Senegal, Poirier, and his Senegalese allies, including Senghor, would have done so): nor did it evoke a modernizing independence movement in resistance to colonial rule (although the Entente Mauritanienne of Horma Ould Babana might, in time, have developed into such a movement).

The whole of west Africa was governed in an administrative federation of eight territories, under a single high commissioner. The area, together with French West Africa, was promoted to independence by the French government as part of a policy of decolonization, motivated by a search for a political settlement for black Africa and accelerated by de Gaulle's advent to power. Of the states which emerged from this process only Mauritania is the concern of this survey, since it is unique in its attachment to the north as well as the south.

POLITICAL DEVELOPMENT

The Islamic Republic of Mauritania, which became independent on 28 November 1960 had no prior history as a nation state. It has natural frontiers to the west and south—the Atlantic and the Senegal river; but the border with Mali resulted from French administration (as did, from an earlier period, that with Algeria), while the northern border with Spanish Sahara was defined by the Franco-Spanish convention of 1900. Since the country before Independence was a tribal community, of which the French administration was centred at St. Louis, there was no capital city; Nouakchott was chosen for the purpose. The separation of the new state from its neighbours was initially resisted by the Union Nationale Mauritanienne, representing black Moors and Africans from the south-east who sought union with Mali (a less attractive cause when the Mali Federation dissolved into Mali and Senegal), while others looked for union with Morocco, whether for its own sake or for their own immediate political advantage. Morocco resisted the creation of the new state, and Moroccan political parties (as distinct from the government) have not abandoned their claims to a greater Morocco which includes Mauritania as well as the Spanish Sahara. But the dominant Mauritanian party under the leadership of Moukhtar Ould Daddah prevailed. Mauritania became independent (1960) and was recognized by the United Nations (1961) and by the community of states, including Morocco (1969).

The political direction of Mauritania has retained a remarkable simplicity. The president, Moukhtar Ould Daddah, is secretary-general of the only party in the state, the Parti du Peuple Mauritanien. Moukhtar Ould Daddah was born in December 1924 at Boutlimit, in the Trarza district. He was educated at the local primary school, at the École des Chefs in St. Louis (Senegal), and then in Paris. There he studied law and was politically active among the handful of Mauritanian students.

He aligned himself with the Mauritanian deputy to the assembly of the Fourth Republic, Sidi el-Moukhtar N'Diaye, eight years his senior, the son of a Wolof, also educated at the École des Chefs. N'Diaye's party, the Union Progressiste Mauritanienne, had the support of traditional chiefs and of the French administration. It was thereby assured of success against its rival, the Entente Mauritanienne, whose leader, Horma Ould Babana, had been put up by socialists in Senegal (French and Senegalese) to enjoy a temporary success in the first French national assembly of 1946. Defeated in 1951 and again in 1956 by N'Diaye, Horma went into voluntary exile in Senegal and then sought his fortune with Allal al-Fassi and the exponents of the idea of Greater Morocco. He subsequently continued to serve as a rallying point for Mauritanians discontented with the party of N'Diaye and Ould Daddah, without achieving any substantial political success.

N'Diaye gracefully ceded the leadership of the UPM to Ould Daddah, who became president of the executive council, which the French set up under the framework law of 1956, providing for colonial devolution. (N'Diaye faithfully supported his younger partner's policies as president of the territorial assembly.) It remained for Ould Daddah to establish the unity of his country as it moved towards independence, and the supremacy of his own political following. He did so in part with the support of the French who (in agreement with the Spanish government) ended the activities of both the Moroccan irregulars of the Armée de la Libération and their supporters among the Riqaibat tribes in the north, by a successful police operation in February 1958. By successful political manœuvring, and with the advantages of French favour, he carried through the union of his party with the remnants of Babana's Entente Mauritanienne, naming the consequent merger the Parti du Regroupement Mauritanien (May 1958). He successfully resisted several breakaway movements: notably the youthful Nanda al-Wataniyya al-Mauritaniyya led by Bouyagi Ould Abadine and Ahmed Baba Ould Ahmed Miske; the Union Nationale Mauritanienne created by Souleyman Ould Shaikh Sidiya, which advocated membership of the Mali federation; and the Union Socialiste des Musulmans Mauritaniens of Ahmed Ould Kerkoub. Although the opposition to Ould Daddah appeared sufficiently serious to justify several arrests in 1960, it was unable to challenge successfully the combination of tribal and popular support, party organization, and growing entrenchment in the administrative machine which ensured all of the forty seats in the first national assembly (May 1959), and Moukhtar Ould Daddah's election to the presidency, by 373,962 out of 399,295 votes cast (August 1961).

In 1965, Mauritania became a single-party state, the party now being named the Parti du Peuple Mauritanien (PPM) and claiming some 400,000 members. The Bureau Politique National (BPN) is the effective organ of government, the assembly and the council of ministers having ceremonial functions. Thus, the party rules of 1966 read: 'The government and administration merely carry out strictly and completely the directives and programme of the party . . . the first qualification for appointment to any responsible post (territorial command, administration, government) is unconditional attachment to the party.'

Ministers and regional governors are members of the Bureau Politique and thus participate in the construction of the policy they execute. Key posts have been kept in the hands of an 'old guard' of Ould Daddah's friends,[1] but a serious and constant effort is made to open the government and party to younger men, and Ould Daddah has said that his mission is to ensure the peaceful coexistence of the generations. In the new government of December 1972 ten posts went to men with university diplomas and an average age of thirty-three. The party rules have to some extent been liberalized, to permit greater freedom of election. Initially, the administration was able to absorb easily the relatively small number of young men returning from education abroad, principally in France. Far more supporting cadres could be absorbed than have so far been educated—there were only seventy-eight secondary school graduates (with baccalauréat) in 1971 and sixty in 1972, while Senegal, having only three times the population, produced twenty-five times as many.

The Parti du Peuple Mauritanien has thus had relatively little difficulty in dominating the politics of Mauritania; but the establishment of large-scale enterprises, financed mainly by foreign capital, has given rise to a trade union movement with its own independent base and with considerable frustration and emotion behind it. In 1968 a strike for higher wages coupled with a demonstration against the privileged and segregated conditions of European employees at Zouerat was met by troops who fired on the crowd, killing eight and wounding forty (according to official figures). There were further strikes in the following years, the most important being in September 1971, when 90 per cent of the working class in the mining and fish industries stopped work. The impact of the strike can be assumed to have been

---

[1] In the 1972 government: interior, Ahmed Ould Mohamed Salah; national defence, Sidi Mohamed Diagana; foreign affairs, Hamdi Ould Mouknass; public works and labour, Baro Abdoulaye. The party chairman is Abdoul Aziz Sall, former minister of the interior and *directeur de cabinet* of the president.

felt over a wide section of the country, since the industrial working class maintains close links with family and tribal relations in the pastoral economy. It also received sympathetic support from students.

The security forces have contained worker discontent. At the same time, the party has carried out a lengthy, and so far successful, campaign to bring the trade unions under party control and to establish a new Union des Travailleurs Mauritaniens (the fifth congress of the old UTM, held in April 1972, became the first congress of the new 'integrated' UTM). The supremacy of the party was achieved by means of a massive campaign of information and persuasion across the country, which resulted in the acceptance of the party themes and the adhesion of 11,000 out of the statistical 15,000 workers to the new UTM. The trade unions were given representation in the national party organizations and were promised representation in all governmental institutions; but the party was given responsibility for determining national policy, the trade unions were given the right to advise the government and state their demands within the framework of government policy; and the government was recognized as the guarantor and executor of the law. The ideological themes of the old UTM were rejected by Ould Daddah who stated: 'We are a long way from crushing the rights of workers, who in any case are denied no rights, particularly the right to strike. But we are a long way too from a syndicalism based on concepts such as class. For there to be classes, and thus exploitation, there has to be a national fund of capital. But this scarcely exists.'

As a result, opposition in Mauritania no longer has any obvious legal outlet, since the PPM is the only party allowed to exist, and associations have to be authorized by ministerial decree. That opposition should exist is inevitable, particularly in a developing country with an indispensable door open to France. In 1972 the minister of the interior admitted for the first time the existence of a clandestine opposition movement, calling itself the Mouvement Démocratique National, which had been created in 1968. It was said to embrace various secret organizations, including the Union Générale des Étudiants et Stagiaires Mauritaniens, which can readily organize itself in Paris. The main activity of opposition activists in Mauritania appears to be the distribution of tracts and the inscription of political *graffiti*, the slogans being of a left-wing, anti-imperialist kind, directed particularly against the economic exploitation of foreign mining concerns. The formation of a new opposition party, Le Parti de la Justice de Mauritanie, was announced in Paris in July 1974.

None the less, the extent of the opposition remains limited and in 1976 the regime of Moukhtar Ould Daddah appeared secure. In spite of the communication between industrial workers and their families, political opposition had little meaning for nomadic tribes suffering the extremities of drought conditions. A small number of educated Mauritanians protested vigorously against the concentration of power in the hands of Ould Daddah and the party hierarchy; but the development of the bureaucracy and to some extent, the economy, provided outlets for educated young men; the small community of Nouakchott, with its population of 100,000, was not in danger of becoming impersonal or faceless; and the president distinguished himself by the simplicity and absence of luxury in his personal life.

THE ECONOMY

Mauritania provides an outstanding example of a dual economy: 90 per cent of the population live by traditional agriculture and stock-raising, scarcely entering the market economy, while a small minority are employed in modern mining and fisheries, for which the bulk of the capital has come from abroad.

There has been little change in the rural economy as a result either of French rule or of independence. The changes which have occurred, of which the drought of the 1970s has been the most important, have impoverished rural society instead of promoting development.

For the greater part, the traditional economy is pastoral. But the southern edge of the country runs along the Senegal river and permits settled agriculture dependent on the flooding of the river. Millet is the most important crop, planted when the river subsides in December or January and harvested in April or May. Smaller quantities of beans, corn, yams, watermelons, groundnuts, barley, and rice are also grown. Millet cultivation also takes place in the plateau regions which receive rain (Tagant, Adrar, Assaba Hodh, and Brakna), where the peasants construct small dams to hold the water; but the yield is extremely low compared with that of the river valley. Even in the river valley the drought was so severe that in 1972 the river failed to flood, so that salt water from the sea came up the valley in January instead of April; there was no millet crop and the peasants were occupied in making reserves of fresh water.

The high plateaux also provide reservoirs of water sufficient for the cultivation of date-palms. Production is estimated to be in the region of 15,000 tons, of which nearly all is consumed locally or sold within the country. There has been little incentive to develop efficient marketing, and Senegal normally imports dates from Algeria rather than from its immediate neighbour across the river.

For the rest the population is nomadic and pastoral, and has recently suffered grievously from famine. No reliable estimates of the losses exist; but it is suggested that by 1973 the stock of cattle had fallen from 2·3 million to 1·6 million, and the stock of sheep and goats from 7 to 6 million, the losses in the most heavily affected areas amounting to some 60–80 per cent of the total stock.

The economy of the nomadic areas has been adversely affected by the decline in trans-Saharan caravan trade. Such trade provided the most obvious attachment of the Sahara to a market economy and constituted an essential part of a balanced arrangement in which the supply of caravans, especially of camels, provided cash income. In addition the French administration pacified the area, ended raiding and slave-trading, and officially abolished the keeping of slaves.

The social structure of nomadic and rural society remains hierarchic —and this social hierarchy is superimposed on racial distinctions which give superiority to whites over blacks. The decline of both raiding and the practice of religion nevertheless left intact the social distinction and economic advantage enjoyed by warriors and priests. Traditional Saharan society, of which the greater part of the Mauritanian population forms an integral part, has been sharply divided into classes; and although slavery has ended, former slaves have not returned home nor, for the most part, have they found work in the modern sector. At the summit of the Moorish hierarchy are the Hassan Arabs who constitute the noble warrior class. Next come the clerical or maraboutic class of arabized Berbers who, as tributaries of the nobles, do not bear arms but tend the herds of Arab clans and perform religious duties. Many of these are now free from Arab tutelage. Another class of Berber origin are the *zanaga* who also are tributaries and pay dues to the Arabs. Below them come sedentary black peoples (*haratin* and *abid*). There are also rigid caste groups of smiths, hunters, and bards. Tuareg and Teda society is divided on similar lines.

The administration of independent Mauritania has been grafted on to this traditional hierarchy. Tribal leaders thus form the administrative class of a state aspiring to modernization. They accumulate both public appointment and private wealth without, at the present time, acquiring position in a modern market economy.

The Mauritanian government has begun to interest itself actively in the possibility of constructing heavy industry on the basis of the country's supposed mineral resources. A decree of July 1972 provided for the establishment of a Société Nationale Industrielle et Minière (SNIM) with a capital of just over 2 billion francs CFA[1]—although the greater part of this capital is made up of the state's share in Miferma and Somima (see below), transferred to SNIM and topped up with 400 million francs from the state budget. The first director of SNIM is Ismaël Ould Amar— born in 1940, educated in Paris, and ready to see Sonatrach as an example of the possibilities for Mauritania.

SNIM plans the development of mineral resources, proven in whole or in part, including iron ore close to the copper mines of Akjoujt, sulphur, phosphates at Aleg and Kaëdi, and an important reserve of gypsum near Nouakchott, which can be rapidly exploited for export by

[1] 50 CFA = 1 French franc.

lorry to Senegal. It also has plans for industrial development, particularly in relation to the existing mining industry—an explosives factory and a small steel works. Further in the future is a plan for a large steel works based on the ore to be extracted from Akjoujt.

These are important plans for development, which will depend on the validity of assumptions about mineral resources, availability of finance, and above all on the speed with which a skilled labour force can be brought into existence. In the meantime the modern sector of the economy consists almost exclusively of iron and copper mining and of fishing, in the development of which foreign companies have played the major part. Iron ore is mined near Idjil (formerly Ford Gouraud) near the border of Spanish Sahara and brought to the sea at Nouadhibou. The enterprise was in the hands of an international company, Société des Mines de Fer de Mauritanie (Miferma) in which European firms participated (Denain-Nord-Est-Longry from France, British Steel Corporation, the Italian Italsider, and Thyssen). Annual investment in 1972 and 1973 averaged nearly 6·5 billion francs CFA compared with a total state budget of 10·4 billion. Miferma was nationalized in 1974, and replaced by the Complexe Minier du Nord (Cominor). Compensation was paid, and management remained largely in the hands of Europeans. By this time output had risen from 1·3 million metric tons (1963) to 11·7 million (1974).

In its first decade Miferma had relatively little impact on Mauritania as a whole, except in the provision of tax revenue (the total tax revenue, including income tax on employees, was calculated at 3,189 million francs in 1972). The construction of port installations, transport facilities, and equipment for crushing the ore has not provided infrastructure of long-term value; and the payment of salaries has resulted in an increase in imports rather than in providing a stimulus to the Mauritanian economy. The company employed, in 1973, 4,386 persons, including 679 Europeans. Non-European labour came from neighbouring African countries as well as from Mauritania itself. The company provided training facilities, particularly in literacy. A total of 3,560 persons had received such training (including 400 Mauritanian foremen) by 1973. The mining is open-cast and highly mechanized; on the other hand, conditions of work, wages, and welfare facilities for Mauritanians are bad compared with many other countries.

Copper mining is on a much smaller scale. The Société Minière de Mauritanie (Somima) had a 22 per cent Mauritanian holding (thanks to assistance from the World Bank and the International Development Association), the majority belonging to Charter Consolidated. It is centred at Akjoujt, and the ore is exported through Nouakchott—again necessitating the construction of a new town at Akjoujt and a road to the port. The ore is of a low quality and extraction difficult. The industry suffered excessively therefore from the world glut in 1974, and it was in these circumstances that it was nationalized in February 1975.

The Mauritanian fishing industry made a bad start when the government purchased trawlers which could not operate in Mauritanian waters. It sold them at a loss and for the next few years sold licences to fish in Mauritanian waters (which are exceptionally rich) in order to repay the debt incurred. Repayment was completed in 1972 and in the same year the territorial waters were extended to a 20-mile limit. In consequence the government has adopted a new policy of issuing licences with conditions attached (in addition to payment) concerning the employment of a certain number of Mauritanian crew and the unloading of a proportion of fish at Nouadhibou to supply the Mauritanian industry. Licences have been given to individual French fishing concerns since the revision of the Independence treaty with France (which gave French and Mauritanian fishers reciprocal rights in each others' waters), and an agreement has been concluded with the Soviet Union.

The onshore fishing industry consists of the Industries Mauritaniennes de Pêche (Imapec) with capital provided by the Spanish government; the Société des Frigorifiques de Mauritanie (Sofrima) financed as to 30 million by the Mauritanian state, 35 million by a Japanese company, and 15 million by private Mauritanian and French capital (the president being Mauritanian and the director Japanese); and the Mauritanian Fishing Company (Mafco) wholly owned by Japanese companies (Mafco freezes squid and octopus, supplied by Japanese ships, for export to Japan). There is also a Compagnie Mauritanienne pour l'Armement, la Pêche, l'Industrie et le Commerce (Comapic) which produces fish flour and oil and has a minority (5 per cent) Mauritanian holding.

In brief, the Mauritanian economy remains very poor, while the manner in which its small riches were being developed had become a matter of major political controversy in which a small number of Mauritanian activists and French intellectuals participated. The companies which operate in mining and fishing are obvious targets for left-wing criticism. The mining companies provided bad conditions for workers and the money they paid to the government went into the salaries of bureaucrats rather than into the improvement of working conditions. Nationalization provides an obvious political answer to these criticisms. But it does not offer an easy solution to the problem of how to spread revenue through the economy as a whole; nor does it postpone the predicted early exhaustion of the country's mineral resources.

For the government, and for the young technocrats like the director of SNIM, the international companies were a *pis aller* to provide, in the short term, the revenue to construct the infrastructure of the state.

Plans exist for the development of a country so poorly endowed by nature that its flat linear coastline, lacking natural inlets and subject to shifting sands, provides no natural port (so that a Chinese team has undertaken a prolonged survey of the possibilities of replacing the wharf with a deep water port at Nouakchott). There are also plans for the development of agriculture, which have largely given way to emergency attempts to safeguard the countryside against the ravages of drought. There are obvious possibilities for the development of settled agriculture along the Senegal river; but political primacy has always been with the desert tribes, and their pastoral economy is even less susceptible to government intervention. The countries of the Maghreb are faced with the problem of developing areas which were unattractive to French settlers as well as keeping up agricultural improvement on former settler land; but whereas in the north the French at least found part of Morocco to be *le Maroc utile*, Mauritania, seen from Senegal, was *le pays vide*.

FOREIGN RELATIONS

Mauritania maintains close links with France, in spite of the fact that the Mauritanian government provoked a minor political crisis in the course of the negotiated revision of the 1961 independence agreements. In its relations with France and the European Economic Community it has been closely linked with the states of black Africa, not with the Maghreb. It was a signatory to the Yaoundé association agreement of 1965 and it joined with the other eighteen African states (including Madagascar) in the defence of their common interests at the time of British entry to the community in 1972. Until 1970 the dispute with Morocco inhibited the development of the northern connexion, in spite of Moukhtar Ould Daddah's view of his country as the hyphen between north and south. Desert routes and tribal movement have traditionally provided important links with Libya, which have to some extent been brought up to date by economic cooperation; and the Mauritanian government has looked further afield, notably to China, for economic development.

The move towards greater monetary and economic independence began a decade after Independence, and two years after Moroccan recognition of Mauritania, when in November 1972 it was announced that Mauritania would withdraw from the West African Monetary Union in order to create its own currency, while in the meantime the government sought a revision of the existing treaty arrangements with France. The subsequent negotiations with France (conducted on the Mauritanian side by the president's brother, Ahmed Ould Daddah) led to partial agreement in February 1973. The French government, anxious for the future of the franc zone, refused to provide reserve backing for the new Mauritanian currency. The West African Monetary Union had pooled its reserves and they had been guaranteed by France, in return for a fixed parity free exchange between the French franc and the CFA franc. Mauritania's withdrawal from the arrangement had therefore represented an important bid for independence (Moukhtar Ould Daddah stating that Mauritania would willingly abandon its new currency if there were an independent West African currency). When the French government refused to provide backing or to print the new bank notes the gap was filled by Algeria and Libya, with promises of support from Saudi Arabia and the Gulf states, while the banknotes were designed in Algeria and printed in Yugoslavia. The new currency was named the *ouguiya* and its unit value fixed at five francs CFA, or one-tenth of a French franc.

The agreements which the French government made with newly independent Mauritania covered all aspects of assistance, fishing, and military cooperation. Over the period 1959–72 France provided financial aid totalling 600 million French francs, including 240 million francs in investment; in 1972 there were 282 French technical assistants in Mauritania, of whom 152 were teachers.

Apart from the monetary question, the revision of these agreements provided no serious obstacle, since French interests in Mauritania were insubstantial (there being neither military base nor large-scale investment). They none the less proceeded slowly, because the French negotiator, Billecocq, was engaged in the French election, the Quai d'Orsay was concerned about implications for other territories, and those concerned with protocol were reluctant to accept the suppression of the French ambassador's automatic right to be doyen of the diplomatic corps at Nouakchott. These delays provided the opportunity for Moukhtar Ould Daddah to make a well publicized speech stating (shortly before agreement was reached) that Mauritania would henceforth consider the old conventions out of date.

The new agreements provided a greater sense of independence. Mauritania sacrificed some of the privileges in its relations with France, such as automatic recognition of educational qualifications. The agreement on economic cooperation was in form similar to those with other countries, and provided the framework for specific arrangements for French participation in economic development. (At the time of the signature of the agreement France was providing emergency aid of food for the relief of famine.) The French government made provision for continuing technical assistance, and the agreement also provided for the schooling of French children in Mauritania, covering the important differences in the two educational systems. The old agreement on military cooperation, which gave (among other provisions) reciprocal rights to the French and Mauritanian air forces to fly over each other's territory was not replaced as no agreement was reached.

Defining a role for Mauritania in African politics Moukhtar Ould Daddah has frequently reiterated the theme that his country links Moorish North Africa with the black centre of the continent. A statement of 1963 is characteristic: 'Do not forget that Mauritania is a summary of Africa, its north being peopled by Moors and its south by blacks. By its geographical position, and its economic and historical position it forms a hyphen between the Maghreb and Central Africa.' In practice Mauritania's most active role to the south and west has been in cooperation with its neighbours, Mali and Senegal. It withdrew from the Organisation Commune Africaine et Malgache (OCAM) immediately after its formation in 1965, although the organization held its first meeting (as successor to the Union Africaine et Malgache de Coopération Économique) in Nouakchott and Moukhtar Ould Daddah was its first president (he later characterized the withdrawal as a 'choice for austerity and independence'). Mauritania has participated actively in the Organization for African Unity (and now regards OCAM as an unnecessary rival to the OAU). It was under the presidency of Moukhtar Ould Daddah that in June 1971 the OAU adopted its most severe resolution (up to that time) in condemnation of Israel, describing the continued occupation of Arab territories as 'a serious threat to the regional peace of Africa'.

The states on the banks of the Senegal formed an association (the OERS, or Organisation des États Riverains du Sénégal) with ambitious political and economic objectives which came to nothing. In 1972 three of the four members of OERS, Senegal, Mali, and Mauritania formed a new body, the Organisation pour la Mise en Valeur du Fleuve Sénégal. Guinea, the fourth member of OERS, was left out, although the door was kept open for it to join, and the new organization concentrated on the development of the single river basin. The new organization was based at Dakar, but Moukhtar Ould Daddah was the first president, and the secretary-general, Mohamed Ould Amar, was also Mauritanian. In 1974 the organization adopted an ambitious development programme designed to extend over forty years, providing dams, canalization, river ports, and improvement of the sea port of St. Louis, together with a less important agricultural programme. The estimated total cost was 800 billion francs CFA (16 billion French francs) which it was hoped would be raised from the World Bank, the European Fund, and various national governments. The distinctive quality of the plan is that it proposes joint, tri-national ownership and administration of the infrastructure.

The northward connexion of Mauritania—a connexion which distinguished it from the other peoples of the south Sahara—could not be developed until the relationship with Morocco was clarified. The Moroccan government and Moroccan political parties laid claim to a 'greater Morocco' including Mauritania. (Tunisian recognition of

Mauritania after Independence provoked a crisis in relations with Morocco.) The Moroccan claim could find some justification in the fact that the Entente Mauritanienne of Horma Ould Babana sought union with Morocco, and the Riqaibat tribe ranges across the frontier into Morocco.

The recognition of Mauritania by Morocco in September 1969 and the exchange of ambassadors in January 1970 opened the way to cooperation with the Maghreb states. Initially the rapprochement with Morocco remained vulnerable to disagreement between the two countries over the Spanish Sahara (see pp. 334–6). Moroccan interest in the Sahara was undoubtedly a major reason for King Hassan to settle with Mauritania—for the sake of bilateral relations, and to enhance the Moroccan position in a wider international environment. (It has even been suggested that recognition was accorded on the understanding that Mauritania would not press claims to the Sahara.) President Boumediene has played an active role in promoting a common position (as well as in safeguarding Algerian interests), and the heads of the three states met at Nouadhibou (September 1970), Nouakchott (May 1973), and Agadir (July 1973). The communiqués and comments which emerged from these meetings were serene, and there was obviously no difficulty in arriving at a common position against continued Spanish rule. But when, in 1974, King Hassan heated the Sahara question, for internal political advantage and to regain the initiative from Spain, the Mauritanian foreign minister announced that Mauritania regarded the Spanish Sahara as an integral part of its national territory, and echoed the Spanish thesis by reference to self-determination in the spirit of the United Nations.

This important and major source of difference did not prevent Mauritania constructing a closer relationship with the countries of the Maghreb and participation in various organizations and committees for Maghreb cooperation. This was the more so as long as Algeria had an interest in strengthening its hand vis-à-vis Morocco by its relationship with Mauritania. Some 150–200 Mauritanian students annually have been studying in Algeria in recent years; Algerian university teachers and planning experts go to Mauritania; the Algerian government has financed hospitals and health centres, it has provided doctors to run them; and it has supplied material for the Mauritanian armed forces. Finally, Algeria supported the Mauritanian currency and assisted the security forces.

Relations with Libya have been of less practical importance in building bonds between the two countries—although the two presidents have exchanged official visits and Libya has made substantial loans for road building and for the construction of an Islamic institute at Boutlimit and a mosque at Nouakchott. The Libyan government, like the Algerian, has contributed to the reserve of the *ouguiya*, and one of the national Libyan banks has joined with the Mauritanian state in the establishment of a Banque Arabe Libyenne Mauritanienne pour le Commerce Extérieur et le Développement, with a 51 per cent Libyan share in the 250 million franc CFA capital, and a Mauritanian director.

China has come to be regarded as the most important foreign country participating in Mauritanian development, after France. Ould Daddah visited Peking in February 1967 and negotiated a credit of a billion francs CFA (expendable solely on purchases from China). An important number of Sino-Mauritanian projects have been carried out, of which the most interesting is the establishment of the state farm of M'Pourie (4,000 hectares) with 800 hectares of rice fields. Water has been brought to Nouakchott, a cements works established, initially to provide for the aqueduct; there is a provision for an electric power station. There were thirty-three Chinese doctors in Mauritania in 1971, medicaments have been provided against cholera, and an agreement on health and hygiene assistance was signed in 1972. The Chinese Embassy is one of the most important buildings in Nouakchott; comparable to it are the Maison des Jeunes and the Maison de la Culture, provided by the Chinese. The New China News Agency was, in 1973, one of the three permanent correspondents in the capital, along with Tass and Agence France Presse.

V
Morocco
(AL-MAMLAKAT AL-MAGHREBIYA)

GEOGRAPHY AND POPULATION
Geography

Morocco's geographical position gives her a special and privileged place among the countries of North Africa, to which she definitely belongs since there is no break in continuity between Morocco and Algeria in the spheres of geography, climate, botany, or the human way of life. Morocco's strong individuality comes from her being the only country in North Africa which has an Atlantic façade and is thus at the same time oceanic and Mediterranean. When the Algerian ranges reach Morocco their east–west alignment is interrupted; the Atlas bends to the south-west and opens out like a fan towards the ocean, thus winning from the desert a wide belt of land; for Marrakesh is on the same parallel as the Algerian oasis of Wargla.

In fact, however, this vast maritime façade has played a less significant role in the life of the country than might have been expected. This is due to both natural and human factors. The Mediterranean shores, as well as the Atlantic, are inhospitable. The former are lined by the Rif mountains which drop sheer to the sea; the latter are rendered dangerous to navigation by the 'bar'. Add to this that Moroccan Berbers are not a people who have ever taken to maritime activities, and we understand why the sea has generally held a secondary place in Morocco's relations with the rest of the world. This is, however, no longer the case, now that modern techniques have made possible the construction of artificial ports such as Casablanca.

In the north, Morocco projects in the form of the Tangier peninsula as if reaching out to meet Europe and the Iberian peninsula at the point of Tarifa, only nine miles away across the sea. This double role, as the southern shore of a strait which is one of the most important and frequented waterways of the world, and as an outpost of Africa at the gateway of Europe, marks Morocco out as an intermediary and as a point of union. A bridge between two continents, situated between the main continent of Africa and a headland of Europe, she forms a junction where their two civilizations can meet; while her position at the extreme west of the Muslim world, of which she was once an outpost, looking across at Christendom, make her one of the possible junctions of east and west.

This privileged position is also one of strategic importance, a quality which can bring danger with it. In the case of Morocco, it was responsible for the establishment of Portuguese and Spanish outposts on her shores when the Reconquista was nearing completion. The shores of the strait have provoked the covetousness of great powers with the result that Tangier has often been in the hands of strangers, and Ceuta still is. In modern times they made the entire country the stakes of a great international power struggle. The protectorate of 1912 was the final outcome of the triangular rivalry of England, Germany, and France. In 1942 the Americans made Morocco their springboard for the liberation of Europe.

Geologically, the soil of Morocco can be divided into three principal zones; these differ in age and structure. Northern Morocco is a detached fragment of Europe, and the Rif an Alpine range which prolongs the Andalusian Cordillera. The extreme south belongs to the ancient primary continent known as the 'Saharan shield', Central Morocco is intermediary in age as well as in position. The Hercynian fold constituted the base on which deposits settled during the secondary and the beginning of the tertiary eras, while folds of jurassic type were added later in the tertiary.

The country has a strongly marked relief. Several peaks in the High Atlas reach 4,000 metres while Tubkal (4,213) is the highest in all North Africa. It has been pointed out that if the level of the sea were to be raised by 300 metres the general outline of the country would still be the same. High plains and plateaux work their way into the heart of the main ranges.

The latter are like a jaw, opening towards the west. The more northerly branch, the Rif, which is prolonged by the Beni Snassen mountains to the east of the Muluya, runs along the Mediterranean. The lower branch is separated from the former on the east by the narrow Taza corridor, forms the circle of an arc, north-east and south-west, and ends at the edge of the Atlantic. This branch is more complex than the other. Three ranges can be distinguished: the High Atlas, which runs beside and then accompanies the Middle Atlas range to the north, beyond the valley of the upper Muluya; and in the south the Anti-Atlas, which is joined to the High Atlas by the footbridge-like Sirua mountain.

This mountain framework has had important consequences—some of them happy, others less so. As has been mentioned, Morocco lies wide open to the ocean to whose beneficent influences she is subject. The two arms of the pincers enfold the fertile plains of the Gharb, the Chaouia, and the Sus, which are the heart and the wealth of the country. Almost all the great cities are to be found there: Fez, Meknes,

Rabat, Casablanca, Marrakesh. The Rif on the other hand cuts Morocco off from the Mediterranean, which has only played a substantial part in the life of the country by means of the strait. In the north, Tangier and Tetuan are the only large cities. The High and Middle Atlas themselves cut off a vast zone from the Atlantic plain and bring it under the influence of the desert, all the way from the mouth of the Dra on the Atlantic to that of the Muluya on the Mediterranean. This is the Morocco of the pre-Saharan steppes, and of the High Plateaux of eastern Morocco, the domain of nomads and of extensive stock-breeding. This outer Morocco, as we may call it, has always been incompletely connected with the other Morocco, but it has nevertheless weighed upon it very heavily in the course of the centuries, periodically casting out hungry warriors to seek their destiny in the rich plains of the north-west. It is no accident that the majority of the great movements which have convulsed the country, as well as the majority of the dynasties which have ruled over it, have emerged from this arid Morocco of the deep south.

The High and Middle Atlas form a true central mountain block, difficult to penetrate, where sturdy mountaineers were long able to defy the central power and to threaten communications between the provinces.

They are also the reservoir of Morocco. From them, a number of vigorous watercourses emerge in various directions: the Muluya, which empties itself into the Mediterranean; the Sebu and the Um er-Rebia, which run towards the Atlantic; and the Saharan wadis—the Dra, which the breath of the desert dries up before it can reach the ocean; the Ziz and the Gheris, which lose themselves in the sands of the Sahara after watering the palm groves of Tafilalet. The Sebu and the Um er-Rebia, both more than 300 miles along, are the most important rivers of North Africa. The Dra with its 745 miles would rank as the longest, if it were not intermittent in its lower course.

The presence of this compact mountain block in the centre of Morocco renders communications between certain regions difficult. The prolongation of the Middle Atlas towards the ocean causes the main road from Fez to Marrakesh to pass by the coast. This is the line followed by the principal railway, connecting Marrakesh with Casablanca, Rabat, Kenitra (Port Lyautey), Meknes, Fez, and Oujda and continuing beyond that to Algiers and Tunis, with its 1,860 miles of permanent way. From this principal axis there branch off the Tangier–Fez line (which is the oldest of them); a line joining Casablanca to Oued-Zem, whose principal function is to serve the phosphate deposits of Khouribga; and a line Safi–Louis Gentil which carries the phosphates from the latter centre. The total length of the railway network is 1,150 miles.

The principal road axis follows much the same route as the railway, though since the completion of the occupation, a direct road has joined Fez with Marrakesh, crossing the Middle Atlas and running along the foot of the High Atlas. The cities of the plain are connected across the Atlas with the oases of Tafilalt (Erfoud), of the Dra (Goulimin), and of south-east Morocco (Figuig). The existing road network extends over 30,000 miles and has been substantially improved in recent years, especially along the coast.

There are connexions with the exterior by land (railway and road to Algeria), by sea, and by air. Regular lines of steamships connect Casablanca with Marseilles and Bordeaux in one direction and with Dakar and black Africa in the other. Interior air lines serve Agadir, Marrakesh, Casablanca, Tangier, Meknes, Fez, and Oujda; while the international airports of Casablanca and Rabat are served by the major airlines, providing connexions to the Maghreb and Africa, Europe and America.

Population

The vast majority of the Moroccan population belongs to the white race; on a linguistic basis, which does not necessarily correspond with their racial origin, they can be divided into those who speak Arabic and those who speak Berber.

The Berbers who formed the population of all North Africa at the dawn of history are the oldest-established inhabitants of Morocco. As in Algeria and the Sahara, Berber is still spoken in Morocco, and by a higher percentage (possibly 30 per cent). The Arabs arrived later, in two main waves; the first, at the time of the Muslim conquest in the eighth century; the second during the twelfth and thirteenth centuries with the coming of the Beni Hilal and the Maaqil. Many tribes which are today Arabic-speaking were not so originally, but are Berbers who have been arabized. The process of arabization, which is not yet complete, has continued at an increased rate since Independence.

Generally speaking, the process has gone furthest in the towns, the plains and plateaux, and in the pre-Saharan regions. The mountain areas have remained Berber-speaking except for the Jabala, east of Tangier, which has long been arabized through its position as a much frequented passage between Muslim Spain and Morocco.

The population includes a small minority of blacks, of diverse origin. In the towns their presence can be explained by the former existence of slavery, particularly of black concubines who were very popular with the well-to-do citizens of the towns. In the southern oases, however, all along the edge of the Sahara, there is a particular type of black population known as *haratin* (in the singular *hartani*). Some of them are no doubt the result of a crossing with Sudanese blacks, imported by the nomads to cultivate the oases. But it is possible that as a whole they represent a former black population of the Sahara whom the *periplus* of Hanno calls Ethiopians and describes as existing at the mouth of the Dra.

The Jewish population, reduced to some 50,000 since the creation of the state of Israel and the advent of Independence in Morocco, were in part the descendants of Jews expelled from Spain after the Reconquista; these settled by preference in the coastal towns. But the majority, who called themselves Plishtim (Palestinians), claimed that their forbears came directly from Palestine. History, however, tells us nothing of mass Jewish migration from Palestine and North Africa. It is more probable that the 'Palestinians' were the remnants of former Berber tribes converted to Judaism and then conquered and dispersed by the Muslim conquest, which they resisted desperately.

Morocco conducted a census in July and August 1971, which revealed significant changes in size and composition. From the time of the previous census (1960) the population grew from 11,626,000 to 15,379,000, being an increase of 3,753,000 persons or 32·28 per cent. The population became more homogeneous at the same time, as a result of the departure of Europeans and Jews. The character of the population was shown to be typical of developing countries: a high proportion of young people, a low percentage of active population (and therefore high level of unemployment), predominance of the primary sector, marked natural increase in population, and rapid urbanization.[1]

Of the total population, 26 per cent was regarded as active (44 per cent of the male population and only 8 per cent of the female),[2] and of this part some 56·4 per cent was in the primary sector (almost entirely in agriculture except for between one and two per cent in mining). But although such a high proportion continued to be engaged in agriculture, a disproportionate part of the total increase in population was to be found in the towns: 58·4 per cent urban increase against only 21·4 per cent rural. The urban increase was not evenly distributed: a high proportion of urban immigrants went to the towns of the central Atlantic area, Casablanca having pride of place and being, with 1·5 million inhabitants, the third town of Africa, after Cairo and Alexandria. In contrast certain towns grew more slowly than the natural increase; but these were often country or coastal towns (Ouezzane, Chaouen, Maulay Idriss, Essaouira). Thus while the statistical division between town and country tends to exaggerate the proportion of truly urban societies (since many 'towns' are centres of rural habitation rather than urban communities), the same is not true of the statistics for the increase in urban population, since this has been concentrated

[1] R. Fosset, 'Les Caractères démographiques et géographiques de la population du Maroc en 1971', *Maghreb*, no. 57, May–June 1973.
[2] These are statistics requiring careful interpretation. Thus the difference between the activity of men and women in the countryside is less than the figures would suggest.

in the most urban of the towns and cities. The distinction between town and countryside is also blurred by partial migration to commercial activity in the towns, the revenue thus gained being spent in improving domestic property in the village (in the manner described by J. Waterbury in *North for the Trade*, 1972). It follows from the above that there is a high level of urban unemployment, poverty, and squalor. In spite of this urban increase, 65 per cent of the population lives in the country. Many of those who emigrate to the towns do so because of demographic pressure on limited resources, and there is reason to believe that the rural population in the dry areas has grown absolutely poorer.

Family Planning

In the face of this rapidly growing population the government has given some attention to the possibilities of family planning, to little effect. Serious attention was first given to population growth and birth control in 1966, partly in response to the prompting of the Ford Foundation, whose North Africa office in Tunis deployed a major part of its activity in this direction. Pilot schemes of family planning were instituted, a survey of popular attitudes to family planning was carried out, and national and local committees set up. A royal decree changed the penal code prohibiting propaganda in support of birth control, and the way was thus opened for mass action.

Consistently with these early initiatives the five-year plan (1968–72) gave some importance to family planning. Noting that the natural increase of the population was one of the highest in the world and that 46 per cent of the population was less than fifteen years old, the plan aptly commented: 'less numerous generations of adults must nourish, maintain, and educate young generations in continuously increasing numbers. In addition the adult generations are undereducated and undertrained and do not command a sufficient range of productive employment. The burden of the younger generations represents one of the obstacles to saving and in consequence to a high level of investment. As long as demographic growth is not controlled it imposes a heavy mortgage on the economic and social development of the country' (Plan, 1968, i. 86).

The plan therefore provided a programme with a budget of 6·1 million dirhams. The intention was that the programme should work within the framework of the public health system as a whole—the expansion of which was also an important part of the plan. The family planning programme was set out with a style and numerical precision that can exist only on paper. The objectives of the programme were to include making available to families the choice between different kinds of contraception; meanwhile, the intra-uterine device was accepted as the most suitable for a generalized programme and a timetable for the insertion of 500,000 devices over a period of five years was set out, together with an educational programme and the training of family planning advisers.

However, family planning in Morocco has been inhibited by the deficiency in modern resources for its development and an excess of traditional and religious resistance. In December 1971 the Moroccan minister of public health presided over a conference on Islam and family planning, attended by representatives of twenty-two African and Asian countries. *Al-Amal*, the Istiqlal party's Arabic newspaper, commented that birth control went against Islam and against the legitimacy of marriage (adding that there are inoffensive methods of reducing the number of pregnancies, such as withdrawal at the moment of coition), and that the economic crisis was not due to demographic growth but to industrial backwardness. In addition: 'Muslims, today, have a greater need to procreate and multiply than ever before because Islam is threatened in its principal positions and has to confront a Zionist and imperialist war, with the character of a crusade. This war will continue and many Muslims will die on the field of honour.' A month later *Al-Amal* took up an editorial from the Ulema journal *Al-Mithaq* which gave particular point to this last theme: 'In relation to Morocco, we notice that Spain, which dominates authentically Moroccan territories in the north and the south, has a population of 15 million souls. When will we be able to conquer and grasp these lands if Spain does not stop increasing in numbers and we do not stop decreasing?'[1]

This degree of obscurantism was not shared by many of the educated or by those women in the countryside who had already borne several children. The progress made by the family planning programme is briefly set out in the new plan (1973–7) which reviews the achievements of the previous five years:

> The credits allocated to family planning ought to make possible the attainment of the objective of the insertion of 500,000 intra-uterine devices and the instruction of 600 male and female attendants during the five-year period, but these credits have been transferred to the construction of a National Centre for Family Planning.
>
> The number of insertions of intra-uterine devices had reached only 68,500 by 31 December 1972 and the programme of instruction of attendants has been abandoned. This delay is explained by the absence of a programme of information and education among the population with the participation of all the ministries concerned.

Thus, while the plans for public health in general fell sadly behind schedule, the programme for family planning collapsed. Nothing in

[1] *Al-Amal*, 31 December 1971 and 30 January 1972; quoted in *Revue de Presse*, Algiers.

the new plan offers hope for the future. The literary and numerical imagination of its predecessor has given way to bureaucratic phraseology describing a programme of information, motivation, and education to be undertaken by all the ministries concerned, notably, interior, national education, youth, and sports; while the medical part of family planning will be an integral part of the activities and provisions of the public health service.

HISTORY AND POLITICS TO 1956

From the Earliest Times to the Death of Maulay al-Hassan (1894)

The prehistory of Morocco is only just coming to be known. Man seems to have been present in Morocco from the Chellean age. Many traces of his activities remain from the palaeolithic and neolithic eras, principally chipped or polished stones and rough pottery.

When the curtain rises on history, the country was inhabited by Berbers. All that we know of the history of ancient Morocco, however, is that of the foreign settlements. The Phoenicians were the first to land on the coasts of Morocco; in the twelfth century B.C. Rusadir (Melilla) was a staging post for them on the way towards Gadir (Cadiz) and Tartessos. Carthage followed and had a chain of trading factories on the Moroccan coast, of which the principal were Lixus (opposite the modern Larache), Thymiaterion (Mahdiya), Sala (Salé), and Karikon Teichos (Mogador). Punic civilization had, however, only a limited influence on Morocco in general.

In the Roman period 'Moorish' princes *(Mauri)* enter history. We learn that during the Jugurthan war the Moorish prince Bocchus abandoned Jugurtha to become the ally of Rome; but we still hear nothing about the life of Morocco. The Romans themselves did not penetrate western Mauritania until the time of Augustus. Juba II, though a faithful vassal of Rome, was killed by order of Caligula, and the annexation of his kingdom proclaimed in A.D. 40. The province called Mauritania Tingitana was not very extensive; the *limes* passed a few kilometres south of Rabat, and a little to the south of Meknes and Fez. The governor generally resided at Volubilis, whose ruins have been excavated and have revealed noteworthy monuments. In 285 B.C. the province was reduced in size; Diocletian ordered the evacuation of the southern portion and attached the rest to the Spanish dioceses. Christian evangelization began in the third century and there were sufficient Christians to justify the creation of four bishoprics.

In some cities the Latin and Christian way of life survived the fall of the western empire. In the eighth century the Arab conquerors found some Christian tribes still existing and certain Latin inscriptions in Volubilis are dated as late as the seventh century. As far as we are concerned, however, Morocco during this interregnum is lost in almost complete obscurity.

Muslim armies raided Tunisia in 647 and are commonly held to have reached Morocco in 684. But the expedition of Sidi Uqba, the founder of Kairouan, was not followed up and it was Musa ibn Nusair who reduced Morocco to the allegiance of the Umayyad Caliph in Damascus at the beginning of the eighth century. The Berbers who were mostly pagans rallied readily to Islam and took part in the conquest of Spain and the invasion of Gaul. Morocco was not, however, destined to remain long within the empire of the Caliphs. With the rest of the Berber lands, it participated in the Kharijite schismatical revolt of the eighth century and in consequence became for ever detached from any political allegiance to the east.

Islamization, at first superficial, soon spread and strengthened its hold in the course of a confused and little-known history. Heretical kingdoms, for the most part Kharijite, divided the country among them, until an Oriental prince, Idris, a descendant of the Prophet, fleeing from the Abbasids, found refuge at Oualili, the former Volubilis. Chosen by Berber tribes as their leader, he was able to establish a kingdom whose religion conformed with orthodoxy. His son founded the city of Fez, which was destined to play a leading role in the diffusion of Islamic religion and culture.

Morocco was nevertheless unable to escape the backwash of the struggles between two great Berber tribes, the Sanhaja and the Zenata. The nomad Zenata, repelled by their opponents, penetrated Morocco by the Taza corridor and founded a number of principalities, without succeeding in forming an empire.

This was to be the work of their rivals the Moroccan Sanhaja, true nomads from the western Sahara. Converted to the austere Islamic rite of Malikism by a Muslim religious lawyer, they hurled themselves on Morocco to spread their doctrine. Emerging from a fortified monastery *(ribat)* on the Mauritanian coast, their rulers were destined to found Marrakesh and create the first great Moroccan dynasty, that of the Almurabitun or Almoravids—'the people of the *ribat*'—who reigned for a century from 1053 to 1147. Their power spread beyond Morocco and the first sultan, Youssef ibn Tashufin, ruled as far as Algiers. Summoned by the Spanish Muslims to put a stop to the reconquest he halted it effectively, but followed this success up by deposing the Spanish princelets and annexing their territories, while Andalusian civilization began at the same time to dominate the cities of Morocco.

Exhausted by the effort which they had made, the Sanhaja succumbed, after three generations, before the mounting force of another race, the Masmuda, long-established sedentary people from western Morocco. Once again, it was a religious impulse—the preaching of the unitarianism taught by a clerkly Berber, Ibn Tumart, whence the name al-Muwahiddun or Unitarians—which inspired these mountaineers. It was, however, an outsider, a Berber from the neighbourhood of Tlemsen, by name Abd al-Mumin, who succeeded Ibn Tumart as leader, struck down the Almoravids, and captured Marrakesh in 1147. He took over the task of the Almoravids and further enlarged their empire, making it stretch from the frontiers of Castile to Tripoli. In 1162 he assumed the title of Caliph.

His religious reform, however, did not prove durable and the Malikism of the Almoravids survived. The Christian reconquest, too, resumed its progress and finally Almohad princes, divided among themselves, succumbed to a new invasion by the Zenata.

The hour had come for the appearance of the third great Berber clan, led by the Beni Merin. Coming from eastern Morocco they first conquered the north, then took Marrakesh in 1269, and finally made their capital in Fez. They were unable to hold the former Almohad empire together. Several attempts to reconquer the eastern Maghreb failed; for a few years they retained Ifriqiya but could not permanently hold even Tlemsen on the threshold of Morocco.

Meanwhile the consequences of a new factor, the arrival of the beduin Arabs, had begun to make themselves felt. Certain tribes of purely nomadic camel-owners, the Beni Hilal, who had left Arabia and been settled for some time in Upper Egypt, reached Ifriqiya in the eleventh century. They continued their progress towards the west in the following century, only to be totally defeated by Abd al-Mumin at the battle of Sétif. The Almohad sultan, Yaacub al-Mansur, deported some of the more turbulent and, in order to have them more under control, settled them in the Gharb plain in the north, in the Haouz near Marrakesh, and in the Tamesna around Casablanca. In the thirteenth century other beduins, the Maaqil, who came originally from south Arabia, reached Morocco along the northern border of the Sahara. Spreading through the pre-Saharan Moroccan steppes, from the mouth of the Dra to that of the Muluya, they subdued the Berber nomads. With the decadence of the Merinid power, they crossed the passes of the Atlas and began a long odyssey, which finally brought some of them, the Zaer, up to the gates of Rabat. These beduin migrations were responsible for the arabization of the countryside.

The efforts of the Merinids on behalf of religion gave the Moroccan towns a delicate adornment of mosques and *madrasas* (colleges), which they still possess, but did not prevent the implantation in the countryside of a rather degraded form of sufism, or mysticism, which gave rise to an astonishing cult of holy men (marabouts).

In the fifteenth century a new peril threatened Morocco. As the Christian reconquest of the Iberian peninsula drew to its end, the Spanish and Portuguese began to assault the coast, establishing themselves at a number of points. By the beginning of the sixteenth century the Portuguese were masters of Ceuta, Tangier, and Arcila, had founded Agadir and Mazagan, and had captured Safi and Azemmour on the Atlantic.

The Merinids had meanwhile been succeeded by a related Zenata family, the Beni Wattas (1465–1549). When these proved impotent to check the Portuguese, resistance to the infidels was organized out of the popular depths by heads of confraternities, marabouts, or *shorfa* (descendants of the Prophet) who became leaders in the *jihad*. With this multiplication of little local chiefs, characteristic of Berber individualism, the state itself disappeared until new leaders, the Saadian Sharifs, arose and favoured by fortune had little difficulty in disposing of the last Beni Wattas.

This was the end of the Berber dynasties. They had not only lived their hours of glory, and decorated the cities of Morocco with grandiose or delicate and subtle monuments. They had also created the framework of the state, known henceforth as the Makhzen. This framework was solid enough to maintain itself through all the vicissitudes of fate and to surmount the most dangerous moments of decadence.

The Saadians (1549–1654) won their prestige through their successes against the Portuguese, whom they drove from Agadir, Safi, and Azemmour, and through their quality as *shorfa*. But they had no such strong tribal basis as the preceding dynasties and they had therefore to rely on a military force which was principally composed of outsiders. A bold military expedition across the Sahara reduced Timbuktu and Gao and drained the gold of the Sudan towards Morocco. This won them prestige in the eyes of the European powers, with whom they entertained fairly active diplomatic relations. They even took the Spanish as allies in order to counter the Turks who were threatening their eastern frontier. In their day Marrakesh regained its former splendour and was adorned with a new series of decorative monuments.

The maraboutic crisis from which the Saadians emerged was also the cause of their disappearance. While the Moriscos expelled from Spain and installed at Rabat and Salé were creating a veritable corsair republic, holy men like al-Ayashi in the north and Bu Hasan in the Sus were busy carving out fiefs for themselves in the rest of the country. The most powerful of them were the holy men of Dila, a *zawiya* in the Middle Atlas, who captured Fez and Salé and at one moment had the whole of north Morocco under their domination. It looked as if the Sanhaja of central Morocco might be going to repeat the achievement of the Almoravids.

For a moment it seemed so; but then the prospects of the Dilaids were ruined by the extraordinary career of Maulay Rashid (1660–72), a Sharif from Tafilalt who belonged to the Alawite family, that is to say a descendant of Ali ibn Abi Talib, the son-in-law of the Prophet. A new Sharifian dynasty had come into existence, that which is still reigning over Morocco today. Maulay Rashid's successor, Maulay Ismail (1672–1729), displayed enormous energy in the struggle against the Christians and against the Turks. He organized a corps of black troops and held the country with a network of fortresses. But the greatest danger which he had to face was the pressure of the Sanhaja Berbers from the Middle Atlas who were beginning to come down from their mountains and attempting to establish themselves in the Atlantic plains. During his lifetime he held them, but his immediate successors did not have the same energy as himself and his death was the beginning of a long period of anarchy.

Sultans of merit, such as Sidi Muhammad ibn Abdullah (1757–92), Maulay Sulaiman (1792–1822), and Maulay Abd al-Rahman (1822–59) made a sustained effort to keep the country under control and to ward off foreign intervention. Though they could not avert the French irruption of 1844 or the Spanish of 1860, they made skilful use of the rivalries which divided the powers and successfully neutralized England, Spain, France, and later Germany, by playing them off one against the other.

Internally they relied on the Arab tribes; these were treated as *gaish* (army) tribes and exempted from taxation, in return for which they provided the most effective contingents of the army. Conscious of their role as religious chiefs, the Alawite sultans endeavoured to reduce the field of Berber customary law and to replace it by the Koranic law or sharia; to repress the excesses of maraboutism and saint worship, and to establish a purified Islamic worship. The individualism of the tribes nevertheless persisted, and every time that there was a fresh manifestation the dissidence *(siba)* began to spread. One of their greatest weaknesses, as of preceding dynasties, was the difficulty of the succession. No simple and regular rule governed this and in consequence the death of the sovereign was almost invariably the signal for a struggle among the members of the reigning family which gave rise to a serious political crisis.

The last great sultan before the occupation was Maulay al-Hassan (1873–94). More than any of his predecessors, he reduced the area of the *blad es-siba* (country in dissidence). He was also able to make himself respected abroad where he secured the summoning of a convention of Madrid in 1880 in the hope of regulating the excesses of the system by which foreign 'protection' was given to Moroccan subjects, thus virtually withdrawing them from the operation of Moroccan law. He also endeavoured to modernize the country by sending missions of students to study abroad. The change from Moroccan to foreign conditions was, however, so abrupt and the training which the students acquired abroad was so alien to the ways of thought of their environment that when they returned they were unable to apply the knowledge which they had acquired. Morocco's fundamental problem was not solved. The outside world was evolving at an ever-increasing speed; new techniques were being adapted in the immediate vicinity of Morocco. Europe was in the full spate of expansion; its economic and military power and its corresponding demands were growing from day to day. Meanwhile Morocco remained as it had been for centuries, displaying indeed a noble devotion to its traditions, but with its organs of government and its customs suffering a fossilization which rendered them incapable of fulfilling the tasks required of them in the modern world. Maulay al-Hassan was thus unable to accomplish in Morocco the renovation which Peter the Great worked in the somewhat similarly-situated Muscovy of his day.

The Moroccan Crises

On the death of Maulay al-Hassan the Empire was fated to pass into weaker hands. His son and successor, Maulay Abd al-Aziz, was only fourteen years old and for six years he remained the ward of a former slave of his father, Ba Ahmad ou Musa.[1] The latter took the title of wazir and ruled with a rod of iron, in the old traditional way but without introducing new methods or any material reforms. When he died, in 1901, the young sultan decided to govern himself. He was intelligent and anxious to modernize his empire, but did not have a strong will. He made light of the long-established etiquette of the court and surrounded himself with Europeans among whom there were a number of adventurers and salesmen. Fascinated by the products of modern science, he encumbered his palace at Fez with miscellaneous and highly expensive objects. As he was also genuinely trying to reform the state administration, disgruntled conservative circles had no difficulty in discrediting him in the eyes of the public. The discontent, heightened by dislike of the foreigners, began to spread to the tribes.

Agitation was set off by a financial reform which was excellent in principle but unskilfully carried out. The old Koranic taxes, *zakat* and *ashur*, which gave rise to abuses in their collection and to excessive exemptions, were replaced in 1901 by a single tax, the *tertib*; this was calculated on income derived from land and livestock. All those who had been benefiting from the former state of affairs leagued themselves against this reform. When the mistake was made of abolishing the former system before the new one was ready to take its place, many tribes took the chance and paid nothing at all. Morocco entered on the fatal round of deficits and loans, debts and guarantees, which was to deliver its public finances over to the total control of the foreigner.

The tribes of the region of Taza, to the east of Fez, rose at the summons of the Rogui (pretender) Bu Hamara ('the man of the she-

---

[1] 'Ou' is the Berber equivalent of the Arabic 'ibn', meaning 'son'.

ass'), who passed himself off as the Sharif Mohammed, elder brother of the sultan, and as some sort of inspired person. Having raised eastern Morocco, he captured Oujda in 1903. He then marched on Fez with the intention of dethroning Maulay Abd al-Aziz and having himself proclaimed sultan. Though he failed, the troops of the Makhzen were equally unable to dislodge him from Taza. He was not defeated until several years later, by Sultan Maulay Abd al-Hafidh.

This state of affairs within the country was the more dangerous since Morocco, now almost the only African state to remain independent, was exciting the greed of the outside world. Her geographical and strategical position made her an important stake. It is true that mutually contradictory ambitions could to some extent be made to cancel one another out. Maulay al-Hassan had been very successful at this diplomatic game but when his successor tried to continue it the weakening of the central power made it much harder. Moreover competition among the great powers was becoming keener. France, having succeeded in covering her Algerian conquest on the east with a protectorate over Tunisia, wanted to cover it on the west also. In particular she feared the installation or preponderance of the Germans in Morocco; for Germany, having regarded the colonial expansion of France with a favourable eye as calculated to avert her thoughts from the 'blue line of the Vosges', was now becoming disturbed at a partition of Africa in which she had no part and at a French expansion which now appeared to her more dangerous than she had expected.

Great Britain, anxious for the security of the strait, wished to prevent the southern shores from falling into over-powerful hands. Spain did not want to be overlooked in a competition which was being pursued on her doorstep and for a country in which she already had sovereign possessions. Other powers, less directly interested, supported their respective allies.

Morocco thus found herself involved in the major diplomatic crises of the beginning of the twentieth century and her fate bound up with European politics. In 1904 France succeeded in obtaining the recognition by Great Britain and Italy of her preponderance in Morocco, granting them in return a free hand in Egypt and Libya respectively. In the same year she concluded a secret agreement with Spain which delimited two zones of influence, one in the north and one in the south. Germany's opposition, however, still remained and set off three successive crises.

The first was provoked in 1905 by a spectacular visit of the German Emperor William II to Tangier. It brought about the resignation of the French foreign minister, Delcassé, and resulted in the Conference of Algeciras in 1906. The final Act of the Conference (7 April 1906) proclaimed the independence and integrity of the Sharifian Empire and the economic equality of the powers. French preponderance was rather vaguely recognized, as well as a certain Spanish participation, while Morocco became more than ever an international problem. The agreements of 1904 were not affected.

In eastern Morocco, incidents on the very vaguely defined frontier led to the intervention of French troops; these occupied Oujda on 29 March 1907 and the mountains of Beni Snassen in December 1907 and January 1908. At Casablanca the massacre of European workers who were engaged on the construction of a port and the disturbances which followed brought about the landing of a French expeditionary force. Attacks by the neighbouring tribes led little by little to the occupation of the whole of the Chaouia, in spite of the hesitations of the French government at Paris.

The inability of Sultan Abd al-Aziz to prevent these foreign interventions finally discredited him with public opinion. In August his brother Maulay Abd al-Hafidh was proclaimed sultan at Marrakesh. The French expeditionary force which at first resisted the new claimant was later ordered to remain neutral. Maulay Abd al-Aziz's forces were defeated and Maulay Abd al-Hafidh was proclaimed at Fez on 7 June 1908 and recognized by the powers on 5 January 1909.

A second Franco-German diplomatic crisis arose over deserters from the French foreign legion at Casablanca in 1908. It was solved by an agreement in 1909 in which Germany recognized 'France's special interests', Franco-Moroccan agreements, concluded in March 1910, accentuated the French grip on the finances and administration. Further tribal disorder led to new interventions by French troops; and in 1910 the proclamation at Meknes of another pretender led Maulay Abd al-Hafidh to ask for help, whereupon Fez was relieved by a column under General Moinier. In 1911 Spain in application of the 1904 agreement occupied Larache and Alcazarquivir (al-Ksar al-Kebir).

Meanwhile the annoyance caused in Germany by the French advance was manifested in a third diplomatic crisis of which the culmination was the dispatch of a German gunboat to Agadir. Agreement was reached on 4 November 1911. In return for 'compensation' in equatorial Africa, Germany agreed to allow France, who had been supported by her British ally, to undertake the pacification and organization of Morocco, on condition that economic liberty was preserved. Maulay Abd al-Hafidh, now face to face with France alone, had no alternative but to sign, on 30 March 1912, the Treaty of Fez by which a French protectorate was established over Morocco. In a convention with France, signed on 27 November 1912, Spain agreed the limits of her zone. Though both zones were nominally under the sovereignty of the sultan, the Spanish zone became virtually autonomous as the result of a permanent delegation of the sultan's power to his lord lieutenant or khalifa in that region. In principle it was agreed that Tangier should have an international regime but, as the powers had not yet agreed on the terms of this, the Statute of Tangier was not established until the Convention of Paris in 1923.

The French Protectorate

The manner in which the French occupation of Morocco took place was similar to many other examples of imperial expansion. The legal form adopted was that of a protectorate—a theoretical sharing of sovereignty which gave France the same effective power in relation to the Moroccan government as it already enjoyed in Tunisia. But the style of this new expansion was unprecedented in its self-consciousness —understandably since the protectorate was not established until 1912, and the pacification of the country was not achieved until 1934, more than a decade after the mandate system had given a new façade to old empires.

To undertake the extension of empire into Morocco the French government found, in Marshal Lyautey, a successful exponent of imperial rule. Lyautey had learned from his experience in Indo-China, but thought himself particularly suited to the role he was given in Morocco, believing that his own attachment to monarchy, aristocracy, and religion was shared by Moroccans. He believed that he had a place in history and took care, in what he wrote and said, that the record should be kept as he wanted.

The golden age of his rule were the early years. He enjoyed the self-confidence of a man with a clear view of the world; in the conduct of business he was both practical and charming. He worked hard at his task and neglected no opportunity to be seen governing in accordance with his own precepts. He made himself readily accessible, retained an openness in his government, and conducted relations with Moroccans with politeness and courtesy.

In 1926 he left Morocco almost in disgrace, receiving a salute from a British frigate as he passed the Strait of Gibraltar but scarcely any from his own government and people. Their reproaches were ill-founded—he was blamed for military reversals which would not have occurred had his prior advice been followed. His tragedy was in part that his aspirations were based on false premises, and in part that he lacked the power to put his policies into practice.

Lyautey developed a coherent system of ideas about the conquest of empire and about the character that empire should take once it was established. He believed that authority rested on coercion, but that coercion should not normally be invoked—in the words of his oft-quoted aphorism: 'show force in order to avoid using it'. Power, he believed, derived from God and should not be abused; its rightful use permitted the development of the creative force of society: 'the grandeur and the beauty of colonial war is that, the very day after the battle, it creates life'.

In practice it was unlikely that such a neat pattern of 'pacification' could be followed. Lyautey was fortunate in that parts of Morocco had already been brought under French control before he arrived as resident-general in April 1912, as a result of the military action in the regions of Oujda and Casablanca. The settled areas of the Fez region were quickly subdued. Lyautey then sought the alliance of the great caïds of the south against the resistance of a tribal leader, al-Hiba, who occupied Marrakesh and laid claim to the throne. But the alliance was only effected after al-Hiba had been defeated by French troops, and was an impromptu, very practical move to secure the south at a time when French military and administrative strength was limited. Thereafter alliances with the caïds became a permanent feature of colonial policy in Morocco and were used to justify the claim that indigenous institutions were kept intact.

But the great caïds were not representative of the mass of the country outside the plains of Fez and the coast, which remained to be overcome. The conquest of these tribes followed Lyautey's departure; but it is unlikely that he would have been able to apply his ideas successfully. His intentions were based on the assumption that the allegiance of tribal leaders could be won, and the support of the tribe thus ensured. But it was characteristic of the greater part of Moroccan tribal society that authority was very weak. The tribes were and are segmented, so that as French conquest proceeded (after Lyautey's departure), it was frequently constrained by the fact that a man assumed to exercise authority over a wide area would prove to have no enduring authority, and that, while enjoying the rewards of having himself submitted, he could not secure the hoped-for submission of a 'tribe'. For while the French administration understood much about the nature of Moroccan society, they failed to comprehend the degree of segmentation amongst Berber tribes, and the nature of their leadership. Subsequent research, poineered by Gellner, has shown that division and sub-division makes the counting of 'tribes' meaningless and has revealed the nature of elective annual chieftancy.

Imperial rule, in Lyautey's philosophy, should recognize (as he did) the values of the indigenous society over which it was established and should respect its institutions, religion, and customs. Consistently with this view, French towns were built outside the existing towns (Fez still provides the most striking example) and conquest was followed by the establishment of a *souk* or market. In this way, it was hoped, Moroccan life would proceed uncorrupted and protected, in both town and countryside. This society should not only be preserved, but developed in association with France. In a memorandum of 1920 Lyautey urged the establishment of schools for the sons of notable Moroccan families who would thus be educated to form an élite combining the best of Moroccan and French culture. This élite should be brought to participate increasingly in the administration of the country.

The schools and colleges which Lyautey planned were duly founded. But Morocco was not a closed society where such schools would exercise a dominant influence. Before and during the First World War Morocco was sensitive to the growth of pan-Islamic feeling. Geographically, it was indeed remote from Cairo and Istanbul; but not so remote as to prevent the contagious influence of the pilgrimage to Mecca nor so enclosed as to shut out the spread of ideas which were themselves pervasive, for all that they lacked organizational support to back them up. The products of Lyautey's schools included the first Moroccan nationalists.

In addition Lyautey's view of the imperial relationship idealized his own position as a pro-consul. He was not the ruler of France, nor independent of its power and authority. When he was brought into the French government during the First World War his immediate experience of his lack of influence helped undermine his own self-confidence. He could not control the immigrants who came to Morocco nor the capital which was invested there, so that the French protectorate could not leave Moroccan society intact, nor release its creative force undiluted by the impact of French expansion. Finally, Morocco was governed by an administration which was increasingly resistant to Lyautey's vision of empire. Lyautey's successors paid lip service to his principles while abandoning much that he advocated; but the power of the administration as a bureaucratic force was established before he left.

Spanish Morocco

Spanish rule in the north of Morocco contrasted sharply with Lyautey's empire. It was the successor to centuries of Spanish occupation of the ports of Tangier, Ceuta, and Melilla—enclaves on the coast, served from Spain, without any connecting communication by road and without any pretension to dominate the hinterland. The impulse for the new expansion came from France, and nothing in contemporary Spanish history suggests that the Spanish political economy would have produced imperialist ambition were it not for the activism of its neighbour across the Pyrenees. It followed that while Lyautey developed his policies of controlled, deliberate, and self-conscious expansion, the Spaniards acted in their area of responsibility as men who had acquired an estate and thought some action imperative, ill-prepared as they were, both morally and militarily, to undertake it. They sought to enlarge the area of effective control, pushing forward into the Jabala and the Rif; although the army they deployed was ill-paid, underfed, and led by officers who left their troops in the field and sought the comparative comfort of the town.

The Resistance of Abd el Krim

The first and most substantial modern resistance to imperial expansion was organized against Spanish rule. It emerged as a result of the exceptional leadership of Mohamed Abd el Krim el-Khattabi and his brother, who bore a different mode of the same name, Mhammed, members of the Beni Urriaguel tribe. They were the sons of an ambitious and aspiring father with the result that they received an education which enabled them to live in the Spanish orbit. Mhammed won a Spanish government scholarship and studied mineralogy and military engineering in Madrid, enjoying unqualified success. Mohamed, the elder brother, who became known to the world as Abd el Krim, had already distinguished himself at the Spanish school in Melilla, and then went to the Qaraouiyine university at Fez. In 1906 he was made editor of the Arabic supplement of *El Telegramma del Rif* (in Melilla) and then became a secretary in the Bureau of Native Affairs, where he soon became concerned with titles to iron deposits in Beni Tuzin territory, bordering the lands of his own tribe (Woolman, 1969, p. 76).

The result was that while, in other circumstances, Spanish moves to extend the area of effective control might have led merely to sporadic tribal resistance, it evoked in the 1920s the emergence of a Rifian republic under Abd el Krim. The response of the Rifian tribes to Spanish encroachment was one of alarm and resistance; but the achievement of Abd el Krim in mobilizing an alliance and keeping it in being, creating a rudimentary civilian and military order, was outstanding. Moreover, in the earliest days of the rebellion, his forces scored a dramatic victory at Anual (July 1921). The immediate provocation was the construction by the Spanish commander, General Sylvestre, of a new post at Igueriben,[1] three miles in advance of Anual. Abd el Krim, who had already tested Spanish strength by a skirmish at Abarran, launched a successful attack against Igueriben and then overran Anual, his men massacring the garrison, including Sylvestre, and capturing supplies and arms (20,000 rifles, 400 machine-guns, and ammunition) to supply the rebellion. In retrospect, it appears that if the attack had been sustained, Melilla would have fallen; but Abd el Krim's men entered the city and then withdrew—some, no doubt, to fetch in the harvest.

Abd el Krim's objectives were limited, revolutionary as the impact of the Rifian republic was. It was not his intention to extend the area of his rule outside the Rif since his authority was based on a system of alliances between tribes and on his personal fame—neither of which

[1] His action was contrary to the policy of caution decided on by the minister of war and the high commissioner, Berenguer. He apparently had the support of the king, Alfonso XIII, and the discovery of letters purporting to be written to him by the king added to the discredit of the monarchy and thus indirectly to the *coup* of Primo de Rivera.

was likely to be effective among the people of the central area around Fez. It is uncertain whether, if he had been able to contain the area of the republic, it could have survived, given the wish in Spain to 'avenge Anual' and regain prestige in the eyes of the European powers. In the event, he came into conflict with France as well as with Spain and was defeated by their combined forces. Between two protectorates, the Spanish and the French, it had been easy to draw a line of division (albeit one which cut arbitrarily through tribal divisions), since there was no conflict between the two and the authority which each claimed over the tribes was limited. But to the extent that Abd el Krim replaced the Spaniards, and in so doing sought the allegiance of the tribes—in this case to cover his southern flank—conflict with the French became likely. It was not Abd el Krim's intention to provoke such a conflict; he frequently expressed admiration for France, in contrast to his enmity towards the Spanish, and was aware of the limitations of his own political strength and the hazards of confronting France. On the French side, only so exceptional an administrator as Marshal Lyautey would be likely to make an alliance with Abd el Krim; and even Lyautey is quoted as saying: 'Nothing would be so bad for our regime in North Africa as the installation near Fez of an independent Musulman State, modernized and supported by the most warlike tribes, with a morale exalted by success against Spain . . . in short, the most serious kind of menace, which should be dealt with at the earliest possible moment.'[1]

The movement towards conflict intensified during 1924 when the French government authorized a military advance across the Wergha river into the land of the Beni Zerwal—a classic imperialist forward move, designed to make the settled area of the protectorate more secure, and risking, even provoking, counter-attack. The Rifians, whose overtures to the French to settle a dividing line were rejected, accepted the challenge which, it appeared, might jeopardize their authority and the credibility of their tribal alliances. Early in 1925 the decision to attack was taken and the plan of campaign decided—it was to strike a decisive blow at Fez, presumably in the hope that France would then accept the existence of the limited Rifian state in return for withdrawal from Fez.

The initial attack was launched against the Wergha forts in April 1925, and merciless fighting brought disaster for the French defences, as Lyautey, who had constantly asked unavailingly for reinforcements, had predicted. Fez was, indeed, threatened. But the inevitable strategic effect was to produce a Franco-Spanish alliance and concerted mobilization against the Rifian republic—at a time when the Spanish government of Primo de Rivera had eliminated the worst faults of

[1] In a letter to the French government, December 1924; H. Jaques, 'L'Aventure riffaine et ses dessous politiques', p. 64, quoted in Woolman, 1969, pp. 169–70.

maladministration. In September 1925 Spanish forces carried through a successful landing operation at Alhucemas Bay as French troops advanced along the Wergha line. The Rifians were unable to survive the winter and in May 1927 Abd el Krim and his family escaped the possibility of humiliation by the Spaniards and vengeance from his own defeated followers, by surrendering to the French. He was deported to Réunion, where he lived with his family until 1947. He was then allowed to return and live in France; but slipped boat at Port Said and settled in Cairo, enjoying the hospitality of King Farouk (and subsequently of President Nasser) and playing an active, if ineffective, political part until his death in February 1963.[1]

The short-lived political and military organization which Abd el Krim had created, reaching the apex of its power in early 1925, was of major importance, though of little permanent advantage to the Rif. It was a despotic, even cruel, regime constructed on segmented tribal society unused to submitting to authority, where bravery and victory in battle were the prime virtues and treachery was an accepted mode of behaviour as long as it was successful. None the less, Abd el Krim extended the area under his effective control until it covered the whole interior of Spanish Morocco. He collected taxes—although the main source of finance for the war may well have come from German businessmen. He treated with foreign envoys as a head of state, and evoked the interest of the French communists and the Comintern. He enforced and interpreted Koranic law, introducing a degree of austerity and observance in excess of previous habit. Tribal custom was irreversibly changed by his rule. As David Woolman has commented:

the Rifian government indirectly helped the Blad al-Makhzen by doing its work for it, so that instead of having to conquer the Rif peacemeal, the Blad al-Makhzen could take over *en bloc*. As a result, until 1956, Spain governed her Moroccan zone on a pattern laid down not by her own administrators, but by Abd el Krim (Woolman, 1969, p. 210).

The Completion of French Rule

After the subjugation of the Rif French rule was extended stage by stage over the Middle Atlas, the Tafilalt, the Jabal Saghro, and finally the Anti-Atlas and the deep south. Lyautey's maxim of showing force in order not to use it came readily to the lips of those responsible for the conquest; but the intensity of the war is better measured by French casualties. Between 1907 and 1935 these numbered 27,000 dead and 15,000 wounded.

The subjection of the whole of the French protectorate to a single central authority brought about a permanent change in the structure of

[1] His brother, Mhammed, returned to Morocco in 1967 but died of a heart attack a few months after arriving in Rabat.

Moroccan government. The old distinction between the *blad al-makhzen* and the *blad as-siba* disappeared, as did the Makhzen government in its traditional form. In spite of Lyautey's aspirations, the quality of French rule had much in common with that in Algeria. The government was one of direct administration in which traditional native administrators were entirely subordinate to French officials, operating a colonial service to which virtually no Moroccans were recruited. At the head were three Grandes Directions, of interior and political affairs, finance, and public works. Outside the formal structure of government the settler community created its own important centres of power in the presidencies of the chamber of agriculture and the chamber of commerce and industry, to which were allied the independent banker, Yves Mas, owner of two daily newspapers. Vestiges of the traditional government remained, to the extent that the French used the great caïds of the south and the religious brotherhoods as instruments of their rule; but in doing so they deprived them of power and importance.

Moroccan Reaction to French Rule

The conquest of Morocco was contemporaneous with the ferment of reform and nationalism which spread from the Middle East across North Africa. It is scarcely surprising that as young men emerged from school in the late 1920s they should be inspired by the same ideas. In this way the Moroccan nationalist movement began to take shape. Its members were well-educated young men from bourgeois families. They did not (until the Second World War) seek a mass following, but remained a small élite movement. The principal channels for the spread of their ideas were free schools, which they established or inspired to promote Arabic and religious instruction, and organizations of students in France. They included Allal al-Fassi, Mohammed Lyazidi, Ahmed Balafrej, M'Hammed Bennouna, and others who were to become the leading politicians of the independent government.

The cause of religious reform played an important part in the origin of the movement. The ideas of Jamal ad-Din al-Afghani and Muhammad Abduh found their way to Morocco, where the principal exponents of their Salafist doctrine were Abdullah Ben Driss Senoussi and Bouachib Doukkali. Their desire for puritanical reform was directed principally against unorthodox religious practices and the worship of saints. Like their counterparts in Algeria the reformers sought to diminish the influence of the brotherhoods.

There was little that was nationalist in these ideas. But it was inevitable that the pursuit of Islamic reform and the attempt to return to the piety of early Islam should also provoke resistance to the imposed rule of an alien civilization—particularly one which was ready to look for allies in the brotherhoods. There was in addition a direct personal link from Doukkali through Maulay al-Arabi al-Alawi, who was the student of Doukkali and tutor of Allal al-Fassi.

The most important stimulus to the growth of a nationalist movement was provided by the French. In 1930 they introduced a new decree, in the form of a *dahir*—the normal method of legislation used by the sultan in non-religious matters. The *dahir* recognized the civil jurisdiction of the tribal courts applying Berber customary law and placed the bulk of the tribes under French criminal law. Far from being a new departure, it continued and legislated for previous practice, which was to foster Berber customs, language, and culture. Lyautey himself had written: 'It is not our business to teach Arabic to populations which have hitherto got on without it. Arabic is a factor of Islamization, because it is acquired with the Koran. It is our interest to make the Berbers develop outside the framework of Islam.' Following Lyautey, many French officials and military men had cultivated a mythology of a Berber identity distinct from that of the Arabs and susceptible to French seduction away from the Arabs of the plains and the towns. The constituent elements of the mythology were the pre-Islamic origins of the Berbers, including their attachment to Christianity and Judaism, and the fighting spirit of mountain men. For some French administrators and scholars the distinction formed part of an even more exotic flowering of Cartesian rationality as Moroccan society was interpreted in the terms of a threefold dichotomy—the *blad al-makhzen* as opposed to the *blad as-siba*, the spiritual as opposed to the temporal authority of the sultan, and Berber civilization as contrasted with Arab.[1] This deceptive symmetry had its limitations as an intellectual hypothesis, and was an even poorer guide to political action.

Consistently with the suppositions about the potentiality of a Berber policy Berber schools were established, a Berber college was set up at Azrou, and Berber law was recognized by the administration. But the Berber *dahir* went further. It touched a sensitive point, providing a group of young Moroccans with the possibility of winning support for their opposition to the French. The decree could easily be depicted as an attack on Islam, an attempt to divide the country, and a derogation from the duty accepted by the French of protecting Moroccan institutions. The means of opposition were at hand: the form of prayer, known as *latif*, used in time of trouble or sorrow, was said in the great mosque of Salé and repeated in several mosques throughout the country. The protest grew in volume and proved sufficient for the protectorate to retreat, so that the judicial system of the country was reunified by a decree of April 1934.

[1] See Edmund Burke III, 'The Image of the Moroccan State in French Ethnological Literature: a new look at the origin of Lyautey's Berber policy', in Gellner and Micaud, 1973.

By that time fresh impetus had been given to the nationalist movement. Earlier in the year the sultan visited Fez and was greeted by such ovations that the French cancelled the sultan's visit to the mosque on Friday and rushed him back to Rabat, thus provoking violent demonstrations. The experience stimulated an informal committee of ten people (including Omar Abdeljalil, Mohamed Douiri, Allal al-Fassi, Mohammed Lyazidi, and Mohammed Hassan al-Wazzani) to draw up a nationalist programme. It came to be known as the plan of reforms, and was presented to the sultan, the French prime minister (Pierre Laval), and the resident-general in December 1934. The plan began by rehearsing the terms of the protectorate and then urged that these terms should be respected: that the protectorate should be a form of control not of direct administration; that Arabic be used as an official language, and economic measures be undertaken to raise the standard of living of the Moroccan people.

In spite of its moderation, the plan of reforms marks, in retrospect, a significant turning-point in the development of Moroccan nationalism. It belongs to the period when imperial rule appeared at its apogee, but was in fact crumbling. From then until the outbreak of the Second World War, the nationalist movement in the French protectorate established its strength as a political force. It was subject to every kind of weakness and impediment, being obliged to act clandestinely, save for a moment of liberalism in 1936–7; but it paved the way for the future.

The movement split as a result of personal differences between Allal al-Fassi and al-Wazzani. The criticism which al-Wazzani brought against al-Fassi was that his Arabic background and his weakness in French must hinder him in negotiations with the French. To the outside observer, the qualities of the two men, the one with his roots deep in the scholarly élite of Fez, and the other a graduate of the École Libre des Sciences Politiques in Paris, appear complementary—as they did to Chekib Arslan and the Tunisian Destour leader, Abdel Aziz Taalbi, both of whom intervened to try to effect a reconciliation. But conflict of personality, or desire to defend a patrimony, were too strong. When al-Fassi was elected chairman of the executive committee of the Committee for Action in January 1937 al-Wazzani refused the post of secretary-general. He formed his own group, which never grew into a large party, with mass following; while Ahmed Balafrej took the post which al-Wazzani had declined.

The movement was also subjected, from 1937 onwards, at fairly frequent intervals, to 'decapitation' by the French—a process which is comprehensible only on the assumption that the French gravely misinterpreted or misunderstood the growth of nationalist sentiment. Mild repression was initiated in early 1937; it was intensified as the result of riots near Meknes. The persistent pressure of the arrival of the French, their acquisition of land, and their plans for a Catholic pilgrimage suddenly became intolerable when a project was announced for the diversion of the Sebu river for the benefit of settler lands. The Meknes riots caused many deaths and were followed by demonstrations in other major towns. Troops occupied the medina at Fez, surrounding the Qaraouiyine university. Nationalist leaders were arrested; al-Fassi and al-Wazzani were sent into exile; others, like Omar Abdeljalil and Ahmed Balafrej, went abroad voluntarily in order to be free to engage in nationalist activity in Europe.

As a result the nationalist movement remained deceptively small and lacking in organization. Its central core continued to be the élite of Fez and Rabat. But its distinctive feature was the degree of commitment to the nationalist cause among the élite, including the sultan; and the fact that the Moroccan élite retained an influence over society relatively undisturbed by conflicting social aspirations. A superficial view gave the impression that the movement would collapse if its leaders were removed—a policy which was eventually taken to its logical conclusion in the deposition of Sultan Mohammed Ben Youssef. But national opposition to the French had taken root in an élite society in which the authority of leadership was weak; the movement could survive because it was not dependent on the pressure of a few leaders. It was also fortified by the growing understanding between the sultan and the nationalists. Communication between them remained excellent, so that they could play their different roles at least in the knowledge of each others' intentions and often in concert.

At the same time, a nationalist movement developed its own life and organization in the Spanish zone. It enjoyed certain advantages, but lacked the vigour of the southern party. Like the movement in the south it was subject to internal division. The principal groups were the Islah (National Reform) party of Abdessalem Bennouna and Abdel Khalek Torres and the Maghreb Unity party of Mekki Naciri—a refugee from the French zone.

Successive Spanish leaders sought the support of the Moroccans: General Franco enlisted some 130,000 Moroccan troops to fight in the Spanish Civil War. The Spanish government could afford to be tolerant, and it took advantage of the divisions and weaknesses of the northern nationalists. The centre of nationalist feeling and organization at Tetuan lacked the prestige of Fez or Rabat. The sultan's representative in the north, the khalifa, was prepared to cooperate with the Spanish authorities. Important concessions were made to the Moroccans in cultural matters, with the teaching of Arabic in schools, the establishment of Islamic cultural centres in Granada and Córdoba, and the construction of a Morocco House in Cairo. Before the Second World War there was relatively little cooperation between the northern and the southern nationalists; but the north provided some sort of haven, the security of which depended on the vagaries of Spanish policy.

The Second World War had a substantial psychological and social effect on the nationalist movement. In September 1939, the Moroccan nationalists and the sultan declared their support for France in the war; but the defeat of France and the arrival of American troops in Morocco destroyed much of the prestige which the French had enjoyed. Paradoxically, the most visible sign of the vulnerability of French authority was the deposition of a liberal, humanitarian resident-general, General Noguès, because of his Vichy loyalty. He was replaced by the Gaullist General Puaux, who was known for his suspension of constitutional government in Syria and Lebanon at the outbreak of the war. The war economy increased national feeling in Morocco as in many other countries; specific hardships were blamed on the French, while the upheaval of war broke down traditional loyalties.

The war also produced a significant meeting between President Roosevelt and Sultan Mohammed Ben Youssef. The United States offered a banquet in the sultan's honour during the Casablanca conference in January 1943, inviting Crown Prince Maulay Hassan, Elliott Roosevelt, and General Noguès (before his replacement). The meeting opened Mohammed's eyes. He was sufficiently imaginative as a person and skilled as a politician to see the possibilities which the changing world balance of power might open for Morocco.

During the year that followed, while tension mounted between the hopes awakened by American victories and the unbending rule of General Puaux, the nationalist leaders, notably Ahmed Balafrej and Mohammed Lyazidi, resumed their activity. At the end of 1943, they collected signatures to an independence manifesto which was presented, on 11 January 1944, to the governments of France, the United States, Britain, and the Soviet Union. It referred to the contribution of the Moroccans to the cause of Free France during the war, as well as to the commitment of the allies to the Atlantic Charter and their sympathy towards the Moroccan people; and it went on to solicit the independence of Morocco in its territorial integrity under the rule of Mohammed Ben Youssef. In this way, the Istiqlal (or Independence) party came to be formally constituted.

Over the next twelve years the nationalist movement gained in strength. The understanding and the alliance between the Istiqlal and the sultan grew closer as a result of French policy. In January 1944 the sultan was forced to disavow the Istiqlal publicly—pressure which proved counter-productive. He respected de Gaulle and was impressed, even seduced, by the visit to France which was organized for him in 1945; but his conversations with de Gaulle were followed by the latter's resignation in January 1946. His growing and obvious popularity with the Moroccan people, and the harsh action of the French security service against them, created unusually strong bonds between monarch, party, and people.

The movement towards independence was punctuated by violent outbursts and dramatic changes of direction. In 1946 the sultan secured from de Gaulle the retirement of Puaux; the Gouin government implemented the decision and named Erik Labonne in his place. Immediately, Allal al-Fassi and al-Wazzani were allowed to return from exile. An important programme of reform was proposed. But it met two obstacles: it was resisted by the Istiqlal and by the sultan who sought independence before reform; and it was resisted, possibly even sabotaged, by French officials and the settler community in a manner that was to characterize the succeeding years. In return for agreement to sign the reform decrees, the sultan secured the permission of the French government, as well as the Spanish government, to travel through the Spanish zone and visit Tangier (with the consent of the British and US governments, in addition to those of Spain and France): the first time that a Moroccan sovereign had done so since 1899. His departure was marred by a bloody incident in Casablanca when Senegalese troops, after a brawl, ran amok and shot Moroccans, while the French forces of order did little or nothing to stop them. The sultan's journey through the Spanish zone resounded with the popular acclaim of Moroccans. In Tangier, on 10 April 1947, he made a speech to Moroccan notables, French and Spanish officials, and representatives of the diplomatic corps. He departed from his text by omitting the tribute it contained to French achievements in Morocco; Labonne's gamble on a policy of reform to outflank the hostility of the European community was thereby ruined and Labonne was replaced by General Juin.

There followed a period of increasingly sharp hostility between the nationalists and the administration. On the other hand, the nationalist movement gained from developments in the Spanish zone. The momentum of the southern nationalists drew the northerners along with it. Their limited cooperation with Franco's government, which had included a certain amount of falangist organization, was discredited by the defeat of the Axis, and was in any case a *pis aller* which would be abandoned if there were a prospect of independence. From 1947 the Istiqlal and the Islah cooperated closely and in 1951 a National Front brought together the rival parties of both north and south—the Islah and the Maghreb Unity parties, the Istiqlal and the Democratic parties. The Spanish government continued its policy of tolerance towards the nationalists, partly in order to embarrass France. The haven thus provided increased in value with the growing intensity of confrontation in the south.

The strength of the movement in the French protectorate continued to lie in the participation of the sultan, who exercised authority and leadership throughout Moroccan society, and in the growing international support which the nationalists received in Cairo, from the Arab League, and in the United Nations. At the same time, the movement acquired additional strength, and became increasingly threatening for two different reasons. In the towns, and particularly in Casablanca, urban workers began to organize and were ready, through strikes and by terrorism, to support the nationalist cause; while in the countryside the tribal sectors of society were willing to show, by armed force, their support for the sultan.

The action of the local French administration contributed much to these developments. The most outstanding miscalculation, for which General Guillaume was responsible, was to build up the position of the great caïd al-Glaoui and then, in August 1953, to depose Mohammed Ben Youssef and replace him on the sultan's throne by Ben Arafa, propped up by the support of al-Glaoui and the French administration. The substitution was planned in Morocco, and Mohammed Ben Youssef was put in the position of having to write to the president of the French Republic in a vain attempt to prevent his own overthrow; but when the *coup* was successfully engineered, the government in Paris accepted the *fait accompli*, exiled Mohammed to Madagascar, and exercised its 'protectorate' over and through the new ruler. He was not recognized by the Spanish government.

But meanwhile Casablanca was coming to life. It was a new city, with none of the tradition of Fez, where the specifically Moroccan form of nationalism had established its roots. Casablanca was a creation of the French, owing its existence to a seaborne occupation and its economic development to French industry. Almost its entire population was immigrant; it had a French bourgeoisie with its roots in France and a working population drawn from the Moroccan countryside. During the decades of its growth, the city remained quiet (except for the outburst of 1947), in spite of economic and social conditions—inequality, hardship, and overcrowding—which might be expected to produce violent outbursts. The fact of recent arrival, the geographical division of the town into quarters, European and Moroccan intersecting each other, and the strength of a police force designed to protect European society, no doubt all contributed to quiescence. None the less, nationalist emotions, ideas, and organization spread easily. They came from the Fassi (i.e. coming from Fez) bourgeoisie, who had established shops and warehouses in the rue de Strasbourg, as well as from French schoolteachers; and Moroccan political parties set about organizing this large urban population. To some extent the way was prepared for them by the French Confédération Générale du Travail. The law did not allow the formation of Moroccan trade unions; but by 1948 some 40,000 Moroccan workers had been brought into the CGT. The challenge to the Istiqlal was obvious and in 1949 Abderrahim Bouabid and Tayyib Bouazza (a former miner who had left the communist party to join the Istiqlal) set about organizing a national trade union movement.

The quiet of Casablanca was broken by the news of the murder by French nationalists of the Tunisian trade union leader, Ferhat Hached. The event was denounced by the Istiqlal press. It had struck a direct blow at trade union leaders, to whom Ferhat Hached was a well-known figure, at least by reputation. But the scale of the riot which followed, on 7 and 8 December 1952, seemed disproportionate: it resulted from the ripening of communal and national feeling, together with the escalation of violence which springs readily from the skirmishes between an unprepared police force and an excited population, stimulated further by the culpable alarmism of the French press. In the fighting four European civilians and three *mokhzanis* were killed; the figure for Muslim dead was not less than the French official count of thirty-four.

The outbreak was followed a few months later by the *coup* against Mohammed Ben Youssef. Whatever the complex of emotions that had produced the 1952 riots, the deposition of Mohammed was felt as a direct attack on Islam and a legitimation of violence. The next two years were, therefore, characterized by continuing urban terrorism, not only in Casablanca, but in other major towns, including Port Lyautey, Fez, and Marrakesh. Casablanca alone saw some 2,276 acts of violence and sabotage between September 1953 and September 1955, with 66 Europeans and 406 Moroccans killed.

The course of these events was of major significance both for the movement to independence and for the subsequent history of Morocco. The removal of Mohammed Ben Youssef was seen to be counter-productive, not only in the resistance of the Moroccans but in the counter-terrorism it provoked among the European population (albeit a slender foretaste of the subsequent action of the OAS in Algeria). The tradition of insurrection among some Moroccans remained (Mohamed al-Basri began his career of armed resistance in these years). But the movement remained nationalist, the communists losing the little support they had been able to command among urban citizens. Inevitably, the legend grew up that the working class had won the battle for the liberation of Morocco; but in fact the population of Casablanca and other towns was too heterogeneous for this to be the case. In Casablanca the militant leaders were from diverse backgrounds while a sample of persons arrested shows some 42·5 per cent of the 'troops' coming from a traditional artisanal and commercial background. Finally, the events of 1953–5 gave Casablanca its 'droit de cité' in Moroccan nationalism. In the words of its biographer:

Casablanca effaced the stigma of being a foreign creation. By making itself 'the capital of the resistance' it conquered its title to nobility, one is almost tempted to say, it acquired its naturalization papers. In the speech which he delivered in the city on 19 October 1956 Allal al-Fassi, after having accused the French of having created Casablanca to 'destroy the towns of Fez, of Marrakesh and of Meknes, the towns which incarnated the glory of the country', celebrated also the role of Casablanca in the liberation of Morocco and cried: 'How great is the glory of Casablanca'. (Adam, 1970, ii. 548.)

In Paris, the advent to power of Pierre Mendès-France brought a change of policy towards Tunisia and Morocco. He was forced out of office before being able to negotiate a settlement; but his policy was continued by his successor, Edgar Faure. Both men were sensitive to the force of Moroccan nationalism, and realized the dangers which must ensue as French authority—and the authority of the men whom the French had put into office—began to crumble. Subsequently, Pierre July, whom Faure appointed minister of Tunisian and Moroccan affairs, wrote: 'we were reaping what we had sown. We had too often replaced authentic leaders who imposed themselves on their tribes thanks to their personal ascendancy, by civil servants without any deep attachment to the areas they were responsible for controlling. The deposition of the sultan, the Youssefist propaganda, the distance which separated the youth of the countryside from the old leaders aggravated further the tension between the tribes and their administrators.' (July 1974, p. 177.)

The outbreak of the Algerian war increased the urgency to find a settlement in Morocco. But two major sets of problems presented themselves. The first followed from the fact that the French state had given its authority to the deposition of Mohammed Ben Youssef and had put Ben Arafa in his place. Ben Arafa governed Morocco no further than the walls of his palace; but the government was not prepared to drop him or al-Glaoui unceremoniously. Secondly, violence continued in Morocco; and while for the government in Paris this increased still further the necessity for negotiations, its impact was not always the same in Morocco. This was particularly true of the tragic and almost calamitous riot of Oued-Zem—a rising in the medina of the town, supported by tribes from outside, when the rioters ran amok, killing and mutilating. Moreover, the government encountered singular misfortune in the choice of Residents, all of whom proved susceptible at best (like Gilbert Gradval) to indiscretion and wilfulness, at worst to a *folie de grandeur*.

In the face of these difficulties, the Faure government succeeded in bringing together, in August 1955 (immediately after the 'massacre' of Oued-Zem), a conference with Moroccans at Aix-les-Bains. The Moroccan representatives included the grand vizir, Mohammed Ben Abdesselam el-Mokri (an extraordinary veteran who, in 1870, had led the Moroccan volunteers to assist the French in suppressing the Algerian revolution). Representatives of the Jewish community also participated. The conference proved successful, reaching agreement on five points covering the departure (without abdication) of Ben Arafa and the establishment of a throne council, with a government of national union to negotiate with France. No one insisted that Mohammed Ben Youssef should be restored to his throne.

The success of the Aix-les-Bains conference opened the way to negotiations with Mohammed Ben Youssef himself. Meanwhile, armed uprising increased in the rural areas of the country and an army of liberation was formed under the leadership of Khatib and Ahardan—an army that was not only loyal to Ben Youssef, but determined to rescue him from the intrigues of the Istiqlal. The army flourished, especially in the north, thanks in part to the tolerance of the Spanish—so that the new Resident, General Boyer de la Tour, saw a fresh, impending Rif war, while his government was the more anxious to end the conflict by pressing forward with its policy before it was undermined in the national assembly. Only in this way could the slide into war—'notre hantise permanente' as Pierre July described it—be avoided.

Eventually, Mohammed Ben Youssef imposed himself. General Catroux was sent to Antsirabe to secure his acceptance of the agreement of Aix-les-Bains; but he was not prepared to sacrifice his throne so readily and as he was brought to France, it became clear that he could claim a legitimacy open to no other government. On 25 October, al-Glaoui declared his allegiance to Mohammed, stating that his return to the throne alone could 'unite minds and hearts'. Four days later Ben Arafa abdicated. Mohammed Ben Youssef returned to rule as Mohammed V, king of an independent Morocco, including the Spanish zone to which Franco's government conceded independence.

GOVERNMENT AND POLITICS, 1956–1975

Until the brutal interruption of the two abortive *coups* of 1971 and 1972 Moroccan politics appeared to have developed its own peculiar amalgam of institutions comparable to those of western Europe together with political behaviour deriving from the indigenous sources of Moroccan society.

On the surface it seemed that political life might move towards the system which, in western Europe, has developed into constitutional democracy based on party rivalry. Constitutional government was slow to arrive; the constitution gave medieval powers to the king, and was suspended after a few years. None the less, political parties engaged actively in politics, even when harassed by the state; they constituted and strengthened their party organization and their system of patronage, and seemed to develop a recognizable pattern of inter-party dispute and intra-party dissension. The press was more diverse and showed a certain degree of freedom.

Political freedom as it appeared on the surface was real and important.

It ensured a degree of political discussion in the press greater than was to be found in any other contemporary Arab country except Lebanon and Kuwait. The limitations on freedom of expression were no less significant. Political discussion was permitted as long as it kept within bounds and emanated from acceptable sections of opinion, and it was acceptable as long as it was relatively uninformed. There was little of the free enquiry which forms an integral part of a genuinely free press. The Maghreb Agence Presse, which once functioned as an independent agency was brought under government direction; while the concern of the Istiqlal press for factual enquiry was not such as to embarrass the government.[1] For all that, enough freedom of expression existed to be prized by those who were committed to the establishment of an enlarged freedom, yet were aware of the exceptional advantages they enjoyed in Morocco, in contrast to a wide range of repressive regimes, of which Algeria was the example closest to hand.

But active party politics, and even more the reading of newspapers, remained the concern of a minority of the population of whom some 75 per cent were illiterate. For the mass of the population the only source of publicly available information was the radio, a monopoly whose propaganda value the government readily exploited. In the absence of free elections it remained impossible to make any serious assessment of the awareness or sentiments of the mass of the people; not only because votes were not freely cast but because ordinary citizens have too strong a sense of survival to take a clear stand when no practical alternative is open to them.

This limited degree of freedom within which national politics can be conducted is not the only, nor indeed the fundamental, distinguishing feature of Moroccan government. The continuity of monarchy and the brevity of the French protectorate are no less important. The monarchy not only survived: it acquired an unprecedented lustre in resistance to French rule, to which, at the same time, it owed increased governmental authority. Around the monarchy the élite class—those holding government posts, or posts in banking, commerce, and the army—remained small and was closely linked by family ties and shared experience. Within the nationalist movement conflicts between generations scarcely had time to develop; conflicts of class, which the economic impact of a more prolonged occupation might have evoked, remained nascent. In consequence, the nationalist revolution saw none of the regional redistribution of power which characterized the success of Bourguiba's Neo-Destour party and it was neither accompanied nor followed by a social revolution.

---

[1] As was shown when *L'Opinion* published a series of articles calling for the independence of the Chatterton Islands before becoming aware of the hoax that had been perpetrated. Nor, outside the area of the daily press, did there exist any publication of empirical enquiry comparable to the *Revue Tunisienne des Sciences Sociales*.

The shared experience of those in important posts in the first decade after Independence thus reached back beyond the nationalist struggle. The bonds formed by participation in the nationalist movement, whether among graduates of the Qaraouiyine university or in the more popular agitation in Casablanca, were important. But Moroccan nationalists grew up under the old sultanate; their relationships with each other were formed under the old order or derived, in many cases, from family relationships reaching back for centuries. And although this society had important connexions with the Arab east—possibly far more extensive than historians have so far recorded—it remained relatively closed to outside influence, and almost entirely so to the influence of Europe (as it had been to Rome and to the Ottomans).

The close network of relationships has produced a sense of national cohesion among participants in national politics, and a sense of belonging to a specifically Moroccan society (which is sometimes substituted for effective political contact with the majority of the people). It facilitates nationalist appeals on the part of the regime, the campaign for the Sahara being an example. It reinforces the belief of all but a minority of Moroccans engaged in politics in the need to pursue a distinctively Moroccan course, both to safeguard the values of the past and to provide a solid foundation for change.

Another effect of this network of family relationships is to modify political and party antagonisms by adding to the dimensions of individual loyalty, and by maintaining lines of communication invisible and inaudible from the outside. Thus a family occasion may well bring together a member of the royal cabinet and leaders of the Istiqlal and its rival, the Union Nationale des Forces Populaires (UNFP); and although family relationships do nothing to safeguard the unknown militants of the UNFP from the police, UNFP leaders are better informed about the activity of ministries than most opposition parties (although they cannot normally get news of the whereabouts of their arrested colleagues).[1]

There is no better study of the distinctive pattern of Moroccan political behaviour than the sensitive and informed account by John Waterbury.[2] He has described an essentially conservative society, marked by continuous competitive tension but held together by the

[1] More recently the cement of family relations has broken down in the case of Anis Balafrej, arrested for complicity in the events of March 1973. Anis, declaring himself a Marxist revolutionary, resisted the efforts of his father Ahmed Balafrej on his behalf (unless his friends were given the same relief), in spite of his need for medical attention to a kidney ailment, and it is not clear, therefore, how responsive the king would have been to Ahmed Balafrej's intercession. But at the time of writing this appears to be an aberration rather than a new style in Moroccan politics.
[2] J. Waterbury, *The Commander of the Faithful*, London, 1970. See pp. 108–9 for an example of the interlocking of family and political relationships. The present work owes much to Waterbury's analysis as well as to the factual information supporting it.

overriding desire of its participants to defend their positions in a system of stable equilibrium, neither destroying their rivals nor seeking to initiate any great movement of change. Amongst Waterbury's comments on élite behaviour it is particularly useful to cite the following:

> A Moroccan's use of political power is essentially defensive and the idea of bold initiatives is repugnant to him. . . . While the Moroccan may wish to extend the scope of his power in order better to protect or expand his patrimony, he goes about this with great caution. His major concern is conservation rather than expansion . . . outright conflict is avoided for it could spell defeat for one side or the other with the victor swallowing the patrimony of the vanquished. Defeat, then, may bring about disequilibrium, a state that Moroccans generally seek to avoid.

This pattern of behaviour Waterbury relates to the durable habits and assumptions formed in tribal society. Moroccan tribes (as Gellner has shown) are internally segmented, the component groups living in a sustained state of balance and tension, since without tension the group would fall apart like a cricket team without any fixtures. 'Thus the system worked to guarantee tension in order to invigorate the group and ultimately to maintain equilibrium among the groups' (Waterbury, pp. 6, 7).

The history of politics in independent Morocco must be interpreted with the specific characteristics of Moroccan government and society in mind. The monarch called the play in a game of which he determined the rules. Several of the important pressures to which political parties in a democratic system of government have to respond were therefore absent. Moroccan political parties had little incentive to develop sustained competitive activity to enlarge their electoral base, nor were they faced with the necessity of choice and decision which confronts a party leadership brought into office by a diverse but expectant electorate. In the absence of these forces, and given the smallness and interlocking nature of the political élite, it is understandable that divisions between and within parties should often be factional splits, subsequently justified by a rearrangement of a selection from the current repertoire of slogans and pronouncements. It is sometimes important to discern the real differences of interest and opinion which were muffled or distorted by the froth of politics as well as by the restraints of the regime.

The Constitutional Experiment

For four years of the period 1956–75 national politics were conducted within the framework of a constitution. The first constitution was introduced in 1962 and suspended in 1965; the second, introduced in

1970, collapsed with the Skhirat *coup* of the following year; the third was drawn up, and (like its predecessors) accepted by popular referendum, in 1972. The second abortive *coup* intervened before the institutions which it provided for could be set up.

While there are important variations between the constitutions, they all have the intention of establishing a form of constitutional government in which the king is entitled commander of the faithful as well as king, and is given power appropriate to a country where, before the protectorate, the structure of government was medieval. The first constitution established a bi-cameral legislature; however, the second chamber disappeared from the texts of the two succeeding constitutions. In the 1972 constitution the single 'chamber of representatives' is elected, two-thirds by universal direct suffrage and the remaining third by an electoral college chosen by local governments and professional and employees' organizations. The government is made responsible both to the king and to the chamber of representatives. The powers of the latter in regard to legislation and in relation to the government are similar to the example of the Fifth French Republic. The government may be obliged to resign by a vote of no confidence or a vote of censure initiated from the chamber; but the conditions under which such votes can be taken (including a three-day delay and the requirement of absolute majority of all members of the chamber) are strictly defined.

The king has always held the power of dissolution; he presides over the council of ministers and over the planning council and the supreme council of magistrature; he is supreme commander of the armed forces and makes civilian and military appointments; he also appoints judges on the proposal of the supreme council of the magistrature. He has the right of pardon and the right to proclaim a state of emergency (under Article 35, which was invoked in 1965).

The texts of the three constitutions thus give a clear indication of the general character of the regime, while at the same time they admit the latitude of interpretation usually to be found in such documents. Thus the first two articles of the constitutions of 1970 and 1972 describe Morocco as a 'constitutional, democratic, and social monarchy', and attribute sovereignty to the nation (which exercises sovereignty directly by referendum and indirectly through constitutional institutions). But Article 19, concerning the monarchy, reads: 'The king, commander of the faithful, supreme representative of the nation, symbol of its unity, guarantor of the continuity of the state, watches over respect for Islam and the constitution. He is the protector of the rights and liberties of citizens, social groups, and collectivities.' In practice the powers given to the king have been far more important, even under constitutional government, than the 'sovereignty of the nation' and the whole manner in which government is conducted has shifted power away from the elected representatives and party leaders.

Under the constitution Islam is recognized as the religion of the state, which guarantees the free exercise of religion. Although the representatives are protected from arrest and prosecution for anything they say in the exercise of their office, exception is made in the case of opinions which 'concern the monarchy or Islam, or which show disrespect towards the king' (Article 37). Finally, each constitution provides the starting point, but only the starting point, for the solution of the central problem of constitutional monarchy (at least from the king's point of view) of ensuring a majority ready to support the king's government in the elected assembly.

All three constitutions have included an article which prohibits a single-party system: a clause to which Ahmed Reda Guedira, in drafting the constitution of 1963, attached particular importance as a means of combating the monopoly of the Istiqlal. No constitution has provided for an assembly elected solely by universal suffrage. The 1970 constitution was more flexible than that of 1972 since it left the distribution of seats between the different modes of election to be determined by law; but it created a threefold division of those elected by direct suffrage, those elected indirectly by local government, and those elected indirectly by professional and employees' organizations; and the electoral law attributed only ninety seats to direct election, and ninety and sixty seats respectively to the other two classes. The 1972 constitution thus swings the balance to the other side, by providing for two-thirds election by direct suffrage.

Political Parties

As the objective of political action changed from the struggle for independence to the establishment of national government, the Istiqlal party was unrivalled as a political organization. Its leadership included representatives of most of the important families of Fassi origin; its early lead in the nationalist cause ensured that new generations of Paris-educated students would join the Istiqlal; and to this dominance of the urban bourgeois class it had added the development of an organizational strength outwardly similar to that of a European political party. It had a large budget (estimated at £500,000 in 1964), one French and one Arabic newspaper (*L'Opinion* and *Al-Amal*), and social organizations dependent on the party.

The section of the Istiqlal which broke away in 1937, under the leadership of al-Wazzani, formed itself into a Parti Démocratique de l'Indépendance (PDI) in 1946. Its differentiation from the Istiqlal is better explained in terms of personal following than of consistent doctrinal or strategic questions, although it was reproached by the Istiqlal for being ready to compromise with the protectorate. It was sufficiently important to participate in the conference of Aix-les-Bains. But its organization diminished rather than developed after Independence and it remained a group linked by personal and habitual ties rather than party allegiance.

While the Istiqlal thus dominated the political scene it also faced innumerable problems, some of which were the reverse side of the sources of its strength. Although it had succeeded in recruiting the Casablanca leadership and had the trade union organization, the Union Marocaine du Travail, under its banner, its success was limited to creating a coalition rather than a united party. It had engaged in mass recruiting in the period 1947–52, and had received a flood of applications for membership at Independence; but it lacked the cadres to muster the vaguely directed enthusiasm of this mass adherence, so that units and regions of party membership lived in relative ignorance of each other. It enjoyed an uneasy relationship with the armed resistance (Allal al-Fassi being the only Istiqlal leader to condone Moroccan terrorism).[1] Finally, its leadership was sharply divided between individuals and groups.

The man for whom it was most important to assess the potential strength of the party was King Mohammed V, who returned from his two years' exile to lead the country to independence, bring armed resistance groups under government control, and retain a free hand in politics as befitted his conception of a king—or a president since he was justifiably confident that he would win a presidential election under a republican form of government.

Whatever the weakness and problems of the party, it was solidly established, and there was every reason to suppose that a leader would emerge strong enough to limit the king's freedom of action.

Within a few years the leadership was secured by Allal al-Fassi. Initially his position was weak, as a result of his having spent nineteen years prior to Independence in exile: in Gabon from 1937 until 1946, and in Cairo from then until 1956. His exile enhanced his prestige as a symbolic leader of the nationalist movement but left the competition for effective leadership still to be won—his major rivals being his contemporary Ahmed Balafrej, spokesman for the Rabat Istiqlal, and the younger recruits to the movement—Mehdi Ben Barka, Abderrahim Bouabid, and Abdullah Ibrahim. But he had already given fresh lustre to the distinction of his family, which could claim links with Oqba ibn Nafi and had grown into an important dynasty in Andalusia by the time it transferred to Fez shortly before the fall of Granada. Allal's father, Abdelwahid al-Fassi, was mufti of Fez, member and secretary of the Council of Ulemas, curator of the library of Qaraouiyine university, and preacher in the royal mosque.

The platform of the party was, under the protectorate and in the early years of independence, vigorous in its simplicity; it was national-

[1] Waterbury, 1970, p. 174.

ist to the extent that Allal al-Fassi opposed the independence agreements because they did not provide for a great Morocco (including Mauritania) or disengagement from France. It supported the throne and a political order based on divine rather than popular authority, and it had a strong commitment to Islam. (In 1962 Allal al-Fassi, as minister of Islamic affairs, initiated a legal process against Bahais in Morocco, thus laying himself open to charges of instituting a new Inquisition.)[1]

The role which the Istiqlal could hope to play in national politics in these early years was still indeterminate, and the manner in which it should conduct itself proved a major source of division. Initially Istiqlal leaders served under Sidi M'Barrek Bekkai; when he resigned in May 1958, a new ministry was formed under the premiership of Ahmed Balafrej. But throughout, the dependence of ministers on the king's wish, and the fact that the party could not impose itself on the king or determine the composition of a ministry, were irritants to the younger activists. No national elections were held at this time, but local elections took place in May 1960. The preparation for elections accentuated divisions in the party since they called for efficient organization, which in turn affected the balance of forces within the party.

It was in these circumstances that the Istiqlal party split, the secession from the Istiqlal leadership forming the Union Nationale des Forces Populaires. Waterbury has drawn attention to the specifically Moroccan aspects of the split, which was brewing for some three years, became effective in January 1959, and definitive with the establishment of the UNFP in September 1959. But in many respects the split was what one could expect to find in any political grouping in similar circumstances. The struggle for independence had held together different interests—the party leadership, the resistance, and the trade union movement—which were likely to compete against each other in the new circumstances after 1958. Apart from the rivalry of these specific groups, issues and tactics also served to accentuate conflict beyond the critical point at which a political party ceases to thrive on tension and rivalry and, instead, breaks apart. The most important issue continued to be the relationship to the king. The party leadership could easily agree that it wanted to be the dominant partner in an alliance with the monarchy. But, faced with the king's intention to retain his own powers intact, the party had to decide how to play its hand: whether cooperation with or resistance to the king was the more likely to strengthen the party. Since Istiqlal leaders, both the old guard and those who subsequently joined the UNFP, were invited to serve as ministers this tactical question was constantly alive, before and after

[1] The condemnation of the Bahais was not upheld by the Supreme Court. King Hassan played an ambiguous role which may have been intended to embarrass al-Fassi. See Waterbury, 1970, pp. 292-3 and *Maghreb*, no. 1, pp. 27-8.

the split; the more so since the palace was alert to the advantages to be drawn from it.

The Istiqlal was obviously weakened by the secession of the UNFP. On the other hand, the leadership of Allal al-Fassi was confirmed, since some of his rivals were now in the UNFP, and Ahmed Balafrej was eclipsed during the struggle for position which preceded the split. In January 1963 Allal gave the party a new programme. It retained its strongly nationalist stance, refusing to recognize the existence of Mauritania (even when the government did so in 1971) or to accept the frontier settlement with Algeria. It took a strong verbal line about the Spanish territories, modifying the volume of its oratory as circumstances seemed to require. The ninth party conference in September 1974 centred primarily on the question of the Spanish Sahara, with a clear undertone of cooperation with the king on this issue, which might lead to participation in government (its overt advocacy of a new National Front receiving a cold response from the UNFP). It also repeated formulae about the construction of an Arab Maghreb, described as stretching from the Senegal River to Sinai—a proposal which was not taken seriously by the Egyptians.

In addition to its nationalism the party acquired a more developed programme of Islamic socialism. It was firmly attached to the principles of Islam and at the same time expressed a commitment to economic independence, land reform, and economic equality. It rejected the notion of class as a basis of political action, advocating 'a classless society where social justice reigns' (Second Manifesto, 11 January 1963). At the 1974 conference the party reaffirmed its commitment to the programme of 1963. It urged: 'The reform of the distribution of the sources of wealth and of incomes to make it more equal. The increase of national production which must be based as a matter of priority on industrialization, with the intervention of the state whenever private capital proves to be inadequate.' More dramatically, it repeated the slogan, 'The land to those who work it', as the 'pivot of our struggle to liberate the disinherited *fellah* from the stranglehold both of settlers and feudal landowners'. It proclaimed the right of all citizens to health services and the duty of the state to provide them. It also advocated the nationalization of the pharmaceutical industry. It was firmly opposed to birth control, on moral grounds supposedly derived from Islam, and because it was seen as an imperialist device for limiting Moroccan (and Third World) development. Meanwhile, political issues which had relatively little part in the manifesto of 1963 were given increasing importance as government remained in the hands of the king. The liberalization of the regime and the removal of press censorship were the major demands.

There were obvious weaknesses in the Istiqlal programme and in its policy towards the palace. The degree of equality it seemed to suggest could not be taken altogether seriously, since there was no reason to suppose that the bourgeois leadership of the party would move rapidly in that direction. The demands for liberalization would probably be met by giving the Istiqlal a share in the direction of electors. The programme was well expressed in French and Arabic, but not in arithmetic; no attempt was made to calculate the cost of extension of social services or to assess the requirements of a school programme faced with the growing population which the absence of birth control produced. Not least important, the king was able to keep the initiative and introduce reforms which kept ahead of the Istiqlal's demands in several areas.

The Istiqlal thus remained in an anomalous position well described by al-Fassi: 'We are in opposition in spite of ourselves.' It was eager for office, loyal to the monarchy, and moderate in its intentions. But the king was unwilling to share power, so that the energies of the Istiqlal were absorbed in criticism of the regime. In spite of this al-Fassi's relationship with King Hassan continued to be close (as it had been with Mohammed V) as was shown when the king bore the cost of al-Fassi's medical care in Switzerland.

Allal al-Fassi died in May 1973, succumbing to a heart attack during a meeting with President Ceausescu of Romania in Bucharest and dying on the way to hospital. He was not replaced as president of the party, but Mohamed Boucetta was elected to the leading position of secretary-general.

Boucetta was born in Marrakesh in 1925 and thus does not share the Fassi or Rabat origins of so many of his Istiqlal colleagues. But like them he was educated at the Lycée Maulay Idriss at Fez, where he joined the party cell. He married a daughter of Si Fatmi Ben Sliman. Boucetta was confirmed in office by the Istiqlal party conference of September 1974. At the same time a prominent place was seen to be taken by Mohamed Douiri, who was regarded as leading a more radical wing of the party. Douiri was born into a modest family from Fez, was educated as an engineer in France, and married a daughter of Ahmed Balafrej.

The issues on which the Istiqlal had divided were not fundamental. The report which Abdullah Ibrahim had prepared for the second congress of the UNFP in May 1962 differed in its tone rather than its substance from the programme of the Istiqlal. It was more Marxist in its terminology and more abrasive in a manner that suggested a greater likelihood of its implementing agrarian reform, industrialization, and nationalization. Moreover, it acquired a different political and social base. It remained more closely linked to the armed resistance and the urban terrorism which had preceded independence; and it had the support of those social groups most opposed to the dominance of the Fassi bourgeoisie in the Istiqlal party. These included the Sussi merchants—petty tradesmen from the Sus valley, 'distinguished neither by their wealth, their learning, nor their place in the administration,'[1] but controlling the wholesale and retail trade in foodstuffs, including tea, sugar, and tobacco. The UNFP also took over the alliance with the Union Marocaine du Travail. The alliance had its limitations, and contributed to the split within the UNFP; none the less the large majority of the organized working class was linked institutionally to the UNFP, while the Istiqlal trade union organization, the Union Générale des Travailleurs Marocains, remained a minority.

Moreover the pressures to which the UNFP was subjected were acute. The party included within its ranks those who advocated a republic and those who were ready to employ violence or resort to direct action to affect change. In response, the monarch and the security services constantly harassed the party, its publications, and its members. In so far as there was any consistency in the actions of the government it was to act coercively against a threat even when it was only potential, or verbal, or intended. It not only did not limit itself to the repression and punishment of actual attempts against the regime; it used such attempts as a means of harassing those whom it judged to be associated with the accused and, beyond them, ordinary UNFP militants who suffered arrest and imprisonment *pour décourager les autres*. The Istiqlal did not escape harassment by the regime; but it suffered far less than the UNFP.

The pressure on the UNFP was such that it could neither organize nor publish freely. UNFP leaders and militants in the 1970s spoke of not less than a thousand militants under arbitrary arrest, having simply disappeared, and of men released under an (effective) promise of silence. Moreover it had difficulty in deciding on its policy with regard to direct action. The party included a small group of men who had been active in armed resistance to the French and who were willing to use similar methods after Independence. The most notable of them was Mohamed al-Basri, who had brought an important group into the Istiqlal and then into the UNFP. Convicted in his absence of crimes against the state he remained abroad, organized resistance from outside the country, and arranged for the despatch of arms.

Few were prepared to follow this revolutionary line, although there were more who were tempted to think that an element of disorder would serve the purpose of the UNFP. Equally, if not more, divisive was the possibility of using strikes for political ends—whether a strike of civil servants to force concessions from the government or a strike of workers to cause upheaval and disorder. Many who were neither civil servants nor workers saw advantages in such action; but the Union Marocaine du Travail and Abdullah Ibrahim in Casablanca were not

[1] See Waterbury, 1970, p. 133 and following pages for a discussion of the complexities of Fassi-Sussi rivalry and their political attitudes. See also A. Adam, 1968, and J. Waterbury, 1972.

prepared to jeopardize the well-being of their workers in so uncertain a venture. In 1974 the relationship of the Rabat branch of the UNFP with al-Basri and the desire of Abderrahim Bouabid to try the strike weapon were the major reasons for the split between the Rabat and the Casablanca wings of the UNFP, together with Bouabid's acceptance of the king's right to present the Moroccan case on the Sahara abroad.

Both Mohammed V and Hassan II, having an acute political awareness and operating in the small interlocking world of Moroccan politics, have been well aware of the problems confronting the political parties and have calculated their tactics with those dilemmas in mind. Mohammed appointed Abdullah Ibrahim to the premiership in 1959, thus bestowing his favours on the left wing of the Istiqlal and adding to the tensions in the party; he then dissolved the communist party and embarrassed Ibrahim by ordering the arrest of Youssufi and Basri.[1]

Outside the UNFP there continued to exist a group descending from the Moroccan communist party. Although its 3,000–4,000 adherents and sympathizers scarcely constituted a threat to the regime, the party was banned in 1959. Its activists continued to meet, however, and although only a few hundred people were directly affected by its activities, it had some importance in diffusing ideas, particularly in the UNFP and the union of students. Subsequently its fortunes varied with the rhythm of repression and tolerance followed by the regime. It was reconstituted as the Parti de la Libération et du Socialisme in 1968, but dissolved the following year, its leader, Ali Yata being sentenced to ten months in prison. However, in 1974, Ali Yata was among those opposition leaders who accepted the king's commission to take the Moroccan case on the Sahara to foreign capitals, and travelled, appropriately, to eastern Europe for this purpose. On his return he was able to announce the creation of a new party, the Parti du Progrès et du Socialisme.

The Trade Union Movement

The opposition parties are further weakened by their failure to grow roots in an organized labour movement. The Moroccan trade union movement began its life in affiliation with the French Confédération Générale du Travail (CGT); but in 1955 Tayyib Bouazza and Mahjoub Ben Seddiq (recently released from prison for their part in organizing a general strike) founded the Union Marocaine du Travail (UMT). From its inception it was nationalist, not communist, and allied to the Istliqlal. With the split in the Istiqlal it went into the UNFP camp and provided its main popular and organized support. In 1960 the Istiqlal founded the Union Générale des Travailleurs

[1] Waterbury, 1970, pp. 217–18.

Marocains (UGTM); but this has remained a dependent organization unable to compete in numerical terms with the UMT.

The political and economic climate of Morocco has proved hostile to the development of a vigorous labour movement in three important respects. The high level of unemployment makes the unions very vulnerable; they are subject both to harsh pressure and sweet blandishments from the government; and there are important divergences between trade union interests and those of the politicians. UMT offices are provided rent free, heated and lighted by the government, and many UMT officials hold government posts which they are unwilling to lose, while in 1972 the secretary-general of the UMT mining federation (Arsalane) was minister of youth and members of his union executive committee served as his *cabinet*. On the other hand, Mahjoub Ben Seddiq was imprisoned in 1967 as a result of accusing the government of being tender towards Zionists and, on his release, had lost his dynamism, while Omar Benjelloun (who since 1961 had tried to use his base in the Casablanca Post Office to initiate an activist UMT policy) was arrested, condemned to death, pardoned, arrested and re-arrested, and was sent a letter-bomb, allegedly by the security services.

In dealing with the UMT, as with the political parties, the government has used the well-tried instruments of the stick and carrot. Applied and offered with discrimination these instruments have the additional advantage of accentuating division rather than creating unity. Certainly no lasting bond has been established between the UMT and the UNFP. The first period of cooperation was vitiated by the expectation of UNFP leaders that the UMT could be mobilized in support of UNFP objectives. Mehdi Ben Barka was the most energetic in pursuit of this policy, and he made himself unpopular with UMT members in UNFP branches when he tried to organize the party accordingly. By 1962 the alliance was broken; the UMT took an independent line with regard to the referendum and the legislative elections, while the third UMT congress, in January 1963, announced its independence of political organizations and its unique dedication to the welfare of its members. In the doldrums of the next few years it renewed its relations with the Istiqlal.

The 1967 Middle East war injected a sense of urgency into Moroccan politics and Abderrahim Bouabid, in these favourable circumstances, affected a reunion with the UMT. The UNFP elected a new political bureau composed of Abdullah Ibrahim, Mahjoub Ben Seddiq (in spite of his imprisonment), and Bouabid. But the issue of the respective roles of the UMT and the UNFP in political action had only been put on ice. In March 1972 the UMT congress affirmed that militant trade unionists must also be militant politically—a resolution obviously intended to safeguard UMT interests in the negotiations the king was conducting with the political parties. Meanwhile young militants in the UNFP gained control of the administrative committee of the party which met at Rabat in July 1972 and dismissed the Bureau Politique of the party, accusing its members (especially the UMT representatives) of lethargy and inertia.

Student Agitation

Not only the UMT but also the Moroccan students' union, the Union Nationale des Étudiants Marocains, has had relations first with the Istiqlal and then with the UNFP (the Istiqlal organizing its own union after the split). Moroccan students have distinguished themselves by the high degree of their political consciousness and their leaders have suffered accordingly. A succession of students' union officers, from Hamid Berrada and Mohamed Halaoui (1963-4) to Abdelaziz Menehbi and Abdelaziz Loudiyi in 1972, have suffered arrest. In recent years the students' union has become particularly sensitive not only to 'traditional' Marxism but also to the new wave of Maoism.

In 1971-2 the student world, excited by the Skhirat *coup* and its sequel, sprang into action, the stimulus being provided by Marxist and Maoist students in touch with militants of the banned Parti de la Libération et du Socialisme or attached to the radical review *Souffles*, or participating in such groups as the Front des Étudiants Progressistes, the Association de Soutien à la Palestine, and the Front Révolutionnaire Populaire. Strikes and riots amongst university and lycée students lasted from December 1971 until April 1972. No obvious gains resulted. Student agitation proved incapable of shaking the regime; eighty-one people were placed on trial at Casablanca charged with carrying arms and 'atteinte à la sûreté de l'État', twenty-eight of them (including Ahmed Balafrej's son Anis) receiving prison sentences. (Anis Balafrej and five others were given terms of fifteen years.) The students' union was split and both the Parti de la Libération et du Socialisme and the UNFP were embarrassed by the recklessness of the activists.

The Ben Barka Affair

A particular aspect both of the split in the Istiqlal and the subsequent experience of the UNFP is to be found in the career of Mehdi Ben Barka who disappeared in Paris in 1965 and was presumably assassinated at the orders of (if not personally by) General Oufkir.[1] Ben Barka was outside the usual run of Moroccan politicians, not because of his ideas (which in any case are difficult to judge, since he was both

[1] Following the supposed suicide of Oufkir in 1972 the king denied any knowledge of Oufkir's part in the assassination of Ben Barka, which a source close to the palace attributed to the CIA.

profligate with words and very free with appealing phrases like *option révolutionnaire*) but because of his energy and vision.

Mehdi Ben Barka was born in 1920, into a modest family at Salé—son of a *fiqh* of the *zawiya* of Sidi Kacem. He thus grew up with a strong Arab culture before receiving a French education—first at the French College at Rabat, then at the University of Algiers (where he graduated in science in 1941), and finally in Paris, where he began to study mathematics for a post-graduate degree before abandoning his studies for political activity—he was a founder member of the Istiqlal. He became a teacher of mathematics at the Collège Maulay Youssef and the Collège Impérial, where Prince Hassan attended his classes. In 1951 his part in organizing violent resistance to the protectorate earned him a period of internment in the south of the country, where he distinguished himself by the political propaganda he was able to carry out among the Moroccan officers guarding him, one of whom was Lieutenant Oufkir.

After Independence he played several roles and his effectiveness in all of them resulted in his being the most serious rival to King Hassan. He showed his energy as a party man and if his objectives in organizing the Istiqlal party had been successful it would have emerged as an instrument of power which no other political grouping could rival. He was nominated by the king to membership of the consultative assembly and elected to be president of it in 1956 and again in 1957 and 1958. He showed talent as a man of government, preparing the agreement between Morocco and the FLN over zones of operation in the Sahara and opening the campaign for the return of Spanish Ifni. At the same time it is said that he was responsible for the assassination of Abbas Massidi, field commander of the army of liberation, and of Muhammad Ben Laraqi of the executive committee of the Parti Démocratique de l'Indépendance, as well as for the kidnapping of some of his colleagues.

The rupture in the Istiqlal was not of Ben Barka's choosing and it was only in the course of the dispute that he took sides with Bouabid and Abdullah Ibrahim. He became increasingly isolated and appeared to be in danger of arrest because of his relations with the activists Mohamed al-Basri and Abderrahman Youssufi. He went into voluntary exile in 1961. Then, as again two years later, he distinguished himself in a further role as one of the luminaries of the Third World as he made the tour of conferences at Dar es Salaam, Cairo, Accra, and Havana. His oratory, denouncing capitalism, imperialism, and neo-colonialism, arguing the case for positive socialism and the need to take over political and economic power, won him an assured place in the early attempts to construct African unity and cohesion in the Third World.

In the interim, from May 1962 until the summer of 1963, he returned to Morocco and campaigned actively for the reconstruction of the UNFP and against the policies of the new monarch. The obstacles in his way were made obvious by the resistance he encountered from the UMT as he tried to gain control of UNFP branches in Tangier, Kenitra, Rabat, and Salé, where the UMT was in a strong position. While the UNFP was now in vigorous opposition to the palace, denouncing personal power 'of an absolute and archaic kind', Ben Barka was particularly violent in his condemnation of the monarchy. In the legislative elections of May 1963 he was elected by 80 per cent of the votes cast in the *bidonville* Yaacub al-Mansur constituency of Rabat.

However, this limited success was immediately followed by renewed exile. Later, in July 1963 the king announced the discovery of a plot against the state and in November Ben Barka was one of those on trial, charged also with planning to assassinate the king. Ben Barka remained abroad. Outside Morocco his position remained strong, for his practical abilities resulted in his developing close ties with the parties and persons active on the 'progressive' side in the Arab cold war of the early 1960s. In March 1965 he was condemned to death in absentia for having plotted against the life of the sovereign and for having taken a position against the monarchy in the conflict with Algeria. In September he presided in Cairo over the preparatory committee for the Third World 'Tricontinental' conference to be held in Cuba the following January. Meanwhile overtures were made from Rabat bargaining for his return and it is said that he intended to do so; but on 29 October 1965 he disappeared in Paris.

His disappearance left many questions unanswered. It must be assumed that the palace regarded him as a threat serious enough to justify assassination. Predictably the manner of his assassination produced a major crisis in relations with France (where Oufkir was condemned by the French courts). But it is not certain how far Ben Barka was prepared to go in adapting to the developing pattern of Moroccan politics by returning to the fold, and whether he would have accepted the king's right to grant mercy. It is also uncertain how the balance of decision was divided between General Oufkir and the king (who has denied knowledge or complicity). Ben Barka's assassination created a sensation outside Morocco, not only within the network of Third World socialists but among western Europeans and Americans whose limited knowledge of Morocco was generally mixed with approbation or at least complacency towards Hassan's rule.

In Morocco Ben Barka's fate was a minor political event which produced no significant demonstrations or renewed political activity. He was regarded as a man who created upheaval and problems whenever he returned from abroad with plans to revitalize the party. Finally, Ben Barka's career gives little clue to the way he would have developed, had he lived. He was a man of quick intelligence and volatile thought with unusual powers of analysis, who had a wider vision of the world than many of his Moroccan contemporaries. In consequence he was torn between an intellectually conceivable pattern for the development of Morocco and an awareness of the country's pervasive conservatism. And although he wrote and talked about *l'option révolutionnaire* he never made a definitive choice between revolution or reform. (In the same way the monarch regarded condemnation for treason as a political instrument which did not require conclusive proof nor was an irrevocable judgement.)

Political Development, 1961–71

The palace had done much to change the balance of forces in relation to the political parties, developing levers which continued to assure royal power in subsequent years. At the end of 1959 the limits of tolerable criticism were shown when Mohamed al-Basri and Abderrahman Youssufi were arrested and the UNFP journal *Al-Tahrir* seized for the publication of articles questioning royal sovereignty. In February 1960 UNFP leaders were arrested, accused of being involved in a plot against the crown prince, and in May 1960 the government of Abdullah Ibrahim was dismissed, the king taking over power and appointing the crown prince as effective prime minister. Within a year, in February 1961, Mohammed V died unexpectedly during an operation. Crown Prince Maulay Hassan succeeded him in a traditional manner, receiving the *bai'a*, or affirmation of duty to obey, from the Ulema. King Hassan found himself in a strong position, and one which he was ready to exploit. He had inherited the prestige of his father and he was able to invoke the presumed intentions and purposes of his father in support of his own policies.

King Hassan proceeded to order the drafting of a constitution and to submit it to the people in a referendum. It was an effective political exercise. He took the wind out of the sails of the opposition, which had given major importance to the absence of a constitution and of an elected assembly; but he denied them the opportunity of participating in the drafting of the constitution by employing French lawyers to work quickly under his direction. When drafted the constitution conformed admirably to that part of Moroccan political culture which had changed least. The protectorate had put Moroccan constitutional development into cold storage, even though it had increased the exposure of young men to liberal and constitutional ideas from Europe. The constitution of 1962 therefore confirmed the power of the king, affirmed his authority as commander of the faithful *(amir al-mouminin)* and his responsibility for the preservation of the faith, and put into textual form his powers of appointment and dismissal of ministers.

The referendum was then organized with the full weight of traditional and modern government behind it, the orchestration being the responsibility of Ahmed Reda Guedira as director-general of the Royal Cabinet. The constitution was presented to the people on 18 November 1962—the anniversary of the feast of the throne and of Mohammed V's return in 1954; television sets and transistor radios were distributed to give the maximum immediacy to the appeal of the king: 'I believe that, as Mohammed V wished, the Constitution meets the needs of the nation. And so without hesitation, with all my heart and with all my soul I ask you to vote YES.'

The political effect was to increase the division between the Istiqlal (which advised its adherents to vote yes) and the UNFP which urged not only abstention but boycott (including active persuasion to prevent affirmative votes). In the countryside voters went to the poll as an act of allegiance to the king which justified traditional celebration of mock cavalry charges and dancing. In the cities the mould was different; but the UNFP had placed itself on a limb, to the extent that the UMT would not join its boycott and advised, half-heartedly, abstention. (The formal link between the UMT and the UNFP was dissolved the following January, 1963.) The referendum evoked an 85 per cent participation of the electorate and an affirmative vote of 80 per cent of the electorate.

Having to this extent outmanoeuvred and weakened the political parties, the palace was confronted with a problem shared by many rulers: that of developing alternative lines of communication with the political base. The successful introduction of the constitution of 1962 was necessarily followed by elections to a national assembly. Shortly before the elections a coalition was formed at the instigation of Ahmed Reda Guedira, grouping together parties in support of the monarchy. The coalition, named the Front pour la Défense des Institutions Constitutionelles (FDIC) sought to mobilize parties and men who had participated in the nationalist movement outside (even in opposition to) the Istiqlal and who would support the monarchy for its own sake or to gain an advantage over the Istiqlal. It included the following of Hassan al-Wazzani—the Parti Démocratique de l'Indépendance, which had renamed itself the Parti Démocrate Constitutionnel (PDC) when some of its members seceded to the UNFP in 1959.

The second party in the coalition was the new Mouvement Populaire. It had originated in the armed rising, led by Dr. Khatib (from Al-Jadida) and Mahjoubi Ahardane, in support of Mohammed Ben Youssef when he was deposed by the French, and also in opposition to the Istiqlal. It continued to be based on the landed bourgeoisie and to draw its support from them and from the country people under their influence. It tended to retain the support of people from these classes when they emigrated to the towns, particularly those who worked in the administration. Its loyalty to the king and its resistance to the dominance of the Fassi bourgeoisie of the Istiqlal opened the possibility of office, as the newness of the party provided opportunities for advancement in its ranks.

The third element of the coalition consisted of the liberals grouped around Ahmed Reda Guedira—few in number but aspiring to a position similar to that of the *giscardiens* in the Gaullist Fifth Republic. After the elections, in April 1964, Guedira announced, at Casablanca, the creation of a new party, the Parti Socialiste Démocrate. Its leadership consisted of the Guedira group, its president was Ahmed Bahnini, then prime minister. Its following was drawn from the bourgeoisie of the coastal towns—civil servants and professional men—none of whom subscribed to 'socialist' doctrines in any normal sense of the term.

The FDIC was a weak and hastily formed coalition; even within the coalition the Mouvement Populaire showed itself to be divided in the choice of candidates. The result was that the legislative elections of May 1963 contrasted sharply, from the point of view of palace strategy, with the constitutional referendum. As a result of Guedira's management of the elections (from his position as minister of the interior), the FDIC won the largest number of seats, sixty-nine; but this only equalled the combined total of the Istiqlal (forty-one) and the UNFP (twenty-eight) and these two parties, with 37 per cent of the popular vote, were clearly superior in popular support to the FDIC, which amassed only 24 per cent. In the constitutional referendum the monarch was able to draw maximum advantage from the authority of his religious and dynastic position; but in legislative elections the organization of the Istiqlal and UNFP carried weight while a mass of uncommitted voters who had readily participated in the referendum went unrepresented.

It can be said therefore that the palace lost the elections of 1963 without the opposition parties winning them. Moreover the representatives of the FDIC who were elected had little experience of government; their importance was as local notables rather than as members of a national governing élite, and they were more adept at defending their local and personal interests than in participating in government.

The result was that party political life lapsed into the doldrums in 1964. The parliament existed and had some importance in the politics of the country. Its members could not govern. They lacked the popular support or the institutionalized popular backing to take a stand against the monarchy. They therefore depended on royal favour for the liberties they enjoyed and were aware that they were, at least, better off than if a military *coup* should sweep the monarchy away. Their position as parliamentarians gave them a role to play. They participated in legislative discussion and were able to formulate alternative projects of legislation, even though they could not offer the force or cohesion—or authority—to provide an alternative government to that of the monarch. In a small political élite (which Waterbury described as being composed of some thousand persons) their status and activity as members of the assembly gave them an added importance.

The king found himself unobstructed by an effective opposition, but without a cohesive party to support him. The Mouvement Populaire showed the same fissiparous tendencies as the opposition. Dr. Khatib was elected without opposition at Aknoul and became president of the chamber of representatives, while Ahardane was defeated at Khenifra but was returned to the upper chamber (the chamber of councillors). But the two leaders then took opposing sides on issues concerning the formation of governments, and eventually on the suspension of parliamentary government. Without royal or government support the Mouvement Populaire risked being little more than the personal following of two men (particularly slender in the case of Dr. Khatib, given the relative unimportance of his home base, Al-Jadida). The division of the party, during and after the life of this parliament, was thus particularly illustrative of the nature of Moroccan politics.

The first period of parliamentary government was brought to an end in June 1965. In March a ministry of education circular which, it appeared, would have the effect of limiting access to higher education, proved to be a spark which started wholly unforeseen riots in Casablanca, Fez, and Rabat. The forces of order had to deploy all their energy to bring the upheaval under control; in Casablanca alone seven people died, sixty-nine were wounded, and 168 arrests were made. The response of the monarch was conciliatory: nearly all political detainees (including al-Basri) were amnestied, the upheaval was attributed to the economic difficulties through which the country was passing, and overtures were made to the political parties to form a government of national unity. Such a process would however have taken (given the normal course of affairs in Morocco) many weeks to complete and it may have been initiated by the king solely to provide a better justification for the suspension of parliamentary government, which was effected by the use of Article 35 of the constitution.

A period of five years passed without a parliament. Initially the king led the government, the post of prime minister being suspended. In July 1967 Mohamed Benhima was appointed prime minister, but the change was largely formal: power remained in the king's hands and ministers acted as secretaries with no independent authority and no collective strength as a cabinet.

A revival of political life began in October 1969 with the holding of local elections—the first since 1963. Some 782 rural communes and twenty-nine municipal councils were to be renewed by universal direct suffrage (male and female) to be followed by the indirect election of the councils of nineteen provinces and two prefectures. The powers of these councils were limited, in an administrative system which gave important regulatory power to governors and prefects and to caïds.

But they provided access to important positions of influence, the more so since they were the base for various councils, for the Crédit Agricole, for agricultural centres, and for the control of land taken over by the state and transferred to the provinces. Understandably, the initial reaction of the political parties was to express willingness to participate in the elections.

It soon became apparent that the state intended to intervene actively in the elections. It did so particularly in the choice of candidates. No electoral organization comparable to the FDIC of 1963 was brought into play (although the Mouvement Populaire played an active part); instead the state promoted neutral candidates and impeded, by a variety of means—for the most part illegal or irregular—other candidates from putting themselves forward. As a result the UNFP decided not to participate and early in September published a common communiqué with the Istiqlal. However, this striking appearance of unity in the opposition was to some extent deceptive: the Istiqlal was vigorous in its denunciation of the irregularities of the election but the leadership was aware of the desire of some members of the party to put themselves forward and ended by taking an ambiguous position, participating and yet not participating.

Moreover the Istiqlal had an advantage in that its French and Arabic newspapers continued to appear, as did the newspaper of the Istiqlali UGTM. In contrast the UNFP *Al-Tahrir* had been suspended since 1963 and the bilingual weekly of the UMT since 1967. Meanwhile radio and television (as well as newspapers of the Mas group) were fully exploited by the state, while the opposition parties were denied all access to these means of communication.

The official results appeared entirely satisfactory to the regime. Some 80 per cent of a five million electorate voted; 9,199 neutral candidates were elected, 1,472 from the Mouvement Populaire, and only thirty-eight from the Istiqlal and thirty-two from the UNFP. But the graph of statistics for 1960, 1963, and 1969 was a striking demonstration of the decline of democratic activity. The number of seats to be filled remained roughly constant: 11,167 in 1969. But the total number of candidates fell from 56,000 (1960) to 25,000 (1963) to less than 20,000 in 1969; the number of government candidates rose while that of the Istiqlal and the UNFP fell from 5,492 and 3,313 respectively in 1963 to 2,649 and 264 respectively in 1969. The meagre representation of these two parties (thirty-eight and thirty-two seats) in 1969 was catastrophic in comparison with the figures of approximately 5,000 and 2,000 in 1960 and 721 and 131 in 1963.

In the following year, 1970, a new constitution was introduced. No single event precipitated this return to constitutional government and it was suggested that the king hoped to open a new era of cooperation with political parties during a period of relative calm.

The constitution was of shortlived importance: its acceptance by referendum was followed the next year by the first of two attempts on the life of the king, and it was superseded by a revised constitution in 1972. However, the manner and the results of the referendum by which it was accepted were an indication of the way in which the mood of the country had changed since 1962. In 1970 the Istiqlal, like the UNFP, urged its supporters to vote no in the referendum on the constitution and to boycott the elections which followed. The two major political parties were joined by the trade union organizations associated with them.

In the conduct of the referendum the government availed itself of every advantage open to it. Only 290,000 new voters were registered (in addition to the lists of 1962), in spite of a disproportionate increase in the population. The state of emergency, which the new constitution was to replace, was none the less in force when the referendum was held; the opposition parties were denied radio and television time and every kind of administrative pressure was brought to bear.

The official results of the referendum of 24 July 1970 showed that 93 per cent of registered voters voted, and of these, 98·7 per cent voted yes. Among the most apt of the comments on the result was that of the king, who said that if half a million votes were taken away, the affirmative vote would still be adequate.[1]

The results showed how much support the king could command in the country as a whole, and how successfully he could evoke a parliamentary majority when the resources of his religious appeal, propaganda, and government pressure were brought to bear. But no less significant was the abstention of the Istiqlal, in contrast to its support for the monarch in 1962. The opposition, the boycott of the elections, and the readiness to form a new alliance with the UNFP (fragile and temporary as this alliance proved to be) were an indication of the pessimism which now attended the king's attempt to return to parliamentary government, in contrast to the hopes attached by the Istiqlal (and others) to a constitutional monarchy eight years previously. More dangerous was the symptomatic importance of the Istiqlal's stand, for if men as monarchist and as Muslim as Allal al-Fassi took a political stand against the monarch, others would be prepared to carry their opposition to the extent of seeking to overthrow the monarchy.

The referendum was followed by elections: the indirect elections by local authorities and professional organizations choosing 150 representatives on 21 August and the direct election of the remaining ninety representatives a week later. The elections were reduced to an almost entirely non-political exercise. The indirect election was based, almost without exception, on single lists of candidates under the etiquette of 'Economic Development' or 'God, Country, and King'. For the purpose

[1] *Maghreb*, no. 41, p. 13.

of the election a new workers' association was created, the Union Marocaine des Travailleurs Autonomes, which was as autonomous as Reda Guedira's party was socialist. For the direct elections the Istiqlal and the UNFP formed a National Front, Koutlah al-Watania, and boycotted the election, urging its supporters to abstain. The Mouvement Populaire and the Parti Démocratique Constitutionnel (the PDI under a new name) presented candidates (although al-Wazzani, the leader of the PDC, did not stand). But essentially the choice was between official candidates and their opponents.[1]

Official pressure produced (or the official results showed) an 85 per cent poll—less than the 93 per cent for the referendum. The highest percentage of abstention was in Fez, followed by Rabat-Salé.

The new parliament met, although the minister of the interior's pronouncement on 29 August that '219 of the 240 members of the chamber of representatives will support the government' augured badly for the vigour of political life. But in the event it was crisis, not *ennui*, which altered the pattern of politics once again; the next three years were marked by violent attempts on the regime and major trials, directly consequent on these abortive attempts or stemming from earlier causes.

The Coup of 1971 and its Aftermath

The first attempt on the monarchy was made at the king's summer palace at Skhirat, south of Rabat, on 10 July 1971. It had many bizarre aspects, and much remains unexplained, partly because the two leaders, General Medbouh and Colonel Ababou were killed in the course of the attempt.

The plan of the *coup* was extraordinarily unwieldy. It was to be a three-pronged attack of which the first thrust was to be against the king at Skhirat, the second in Rabat, and the third an extension into the provinces. The plan for Rabat was very conventional, consisting of the takeover, by units of the army under the immediate command of Colonel Larbi Chelouati, of the radio-television building, the ministry of the interior, and the army headquarters. But the plan for Skhirat was more baroque, since it consisted of an attack, by a force of about a thousand men drawn from the cadet school of Ahermoumou, on the king's golfing-luncheon party, for which some eight hundred invitations had been issued. The confrontation between this small army of cadet-officers trained like US marines, but given only vague and misleading indications of the purpose of the exercise (supposedly to clear out sub-

---

[1] At Al-Hoceima the official candidate, who had no connection with the region but had been under-secretary of state at the ministry of the interior responsible for *agents d'autorité*, was elected by 19,750 votes against his opponents' sixteen. His rival was a local resident. *Annuaire de l'Afrique du Nord*, 1970, p. 192.

versives), and a cosmopolitan gathering of diplomats, ministers, and golfers, under royal instruction (and gastronomic inducement) to enjoy themselves, was bound to have a greater element of unpredictability than is usual in projected *coups d'état*.

Several important personalities, and others no less mourned for being less notable, were killed or wounded in the confused and trigger-happy hours of the afternoon.[1] But the king was not among them, nor was General Oufkir, his minister of the interior. For the greater part of the afternoon (from soon after the start of the attack at about two until five o'clock) they hid, along with some fourteen others, in and around one of the groups of lavatories. They were then taken out under guard. But by this time the guard was without its top command: General Medbouh had been killed and Colonel Ababou had left to direct operations at Rabat. In these circumstances the king, with sound judgement, cool nerve, and sense of authority, converted the four soldiers guarding him into a loyal escort. From that moment he, with Oufkir as his lieutenant, took command of the situation and mastered the revolt.

The king's escape owed much to his personal qualities; but they would have been of no avail without the inexplicable carelessness of his attackers. This may have been due in part to a fatal conflict between Medbouh and Ababou who, for all that they both came from the same Berber village of Aknoul, were very different in character and, it may be assumed, in their intentions, particularly as to which of them should direct the other. It has been plausibly argued[2] that Medbouh, wanting to reform not abolish the monarchy, shielded the king from Ababou. His death followed, not from an accidental bullet but from execution by Ababou, who shot an accomplice he could not trust.

Imagination (in default of evidence) has failed to explain why Ababou did not keep the king (and Oufkir) firmly in his grasp. The monarchy was not an easy card for anyone to play, given the importance of royal and religious authority. Regicide would create problems as well as solving them; but no usurper would feel safe with the king alive (least of all a king with Hassan's intelligence). However that may be, the king and Oufkir were free to leave Skhirat and organize the counter-attack. As a result, the *coup* in Rabat scarcely had time to gain momentum, let alone spread to the provinces (where, in any case, Driss Ben

---

[1] Those killed included Ahmed Ben Souda, director of planning; Ahmed Bahnini, president of the supreme court; Abdennebi, director of the Moroccan school of administration; Abdelmalek Raraj, the first minister of public health; Mohammed Lazrak, minister of tourism; and Marcel Dupret, Belgian ambassador. General Driss M'Nichi, commander of the air force, was also killed later in the afternoon, and the air force would not join the *coup* without his orders. The king's brother, Prince Maulay Abdullah, was among the wounded. For a good reconstruction of the day's events see Francis Pedron, *Echec au roi*, Paris, 1972.

[2] See, for example, Pedron, op. cit., ch. 10.

Abdeslam had already secured the élite Brigades Légères de Sécurité and commanded Casablanca). In the limited fighting which occurred Ababou was killed; already wounded by a stray bullet at Skhirat he was hit a second time in the exchange of fire outside the army headquarters and ordered his aide-de-camp to administer the *coup de grâce*.

The failure of the *coup* was followed by retribution. Ten commanding officers were summarily condemned and shot on 13 July; in March 1972 seventy-four officers and NCOs were condemned to varying punishments and a military tribunal acquitted 1,700 men of a charge of mutiny.

But a severe blow had obviously been dealt to the regime. The myth of the loyalty of the army had been destroyed. It was assumed that General Medbouh had been drawn to the extremity of his action by revulsion from the corruption of the regime. Throughout his career he had shown exemplary military virtue. He had served in the French army in Germany, Indo-China, and Morocco, then on Independence he had become a provincial governor until he was made in turn head of the royal gendarmerie (1958), aide-de-camp to Mohammed V (1959), and director of the royal gendarmerie (1967). The last spur to action was thought to be his inadvertent discovery, while in the United States, of a request that Pan-American should pay a large bribe in order to gain a licence to build an hotel in Morocco. Neither Ababou nor Chelouati could claim the same purity. The former had enriched himself by rackets in military supplies organized in and around Ahermoumou, while Chelouati had climbed the financial and social scale by commerce in passports.

Meanwhile two other judicial processes were under way. The Skhirat *coup* interrupted a major trial at Marrakesh; and it was followed by the arrest and trial of ministers and higher civil servants on charges of corruption.

The Marrakesh trial was the culmination of a period of harassment of UNFP sympathizers and militants who had been arrested during the previous eighteen months—whether abroad (Mohamed Ajar, alias Said Bounailat, and Ahmed Benjelloun) or at home (Al-Yazighi, secretary-general of the Marrakesh branch of the UNFP). A total of 180 persons—teachers, workers, students, civil servants, tradesmen, and lawyers—were charged with 'atteinte à la sûreté de l'État'. The defence was conducted by Abderrahim Bouabid, the leader of the UNFP, who used the opening sessions to question the impartiality of the president of the tribunal and to allege irregularities in the preparation of the trial. The main witness for the prosecution was a small farmer and merchant, Monadi Brahim, who claimed to have joined the plot as an informer. His evidence did not stand up to examination by the defence and he himself was assassinated a year later. The accused disavowed statements they had made, saying that they were extracted under torture. The *procureur*, in his summing up, made a bid for forty-eight death penalties; by his standards the five death penalties inflicted (of which only one was present in the country), ranging down to fifty acquittals, was moderate. Since the Skhirat *coup* had occurred in the interim, the judgement was interpreted as an attempt on the part of the king to mend his fences with the opposition; but it none the less evoked the condemnation of left-wing groups in France, including the Association Française de Juristes Démocrates.

On 1 November 1971 the other trial opened—that of six former ministers and a number of civil servants and businessmen charged with corruption. The trial provided considerable interest, even sensation, and had the immediate effect of drastically reducing corruption. Inevitably it showed how pervasive corruption had become, and it was clear that the prosecution sought exemplary punishment for those accused and did not want enquiry pushed further than necessary for this purpose. Interest in the trial waned as the months passed and was eclipsed by the Kenitra *coup* before verdict and punishment were eventually pronounced, in December 1972. Most of the accused were convicted (Abdelkrim Lazrak, former minister of finance, was acquitted and the case against Mohamed Imani, former minister of public works, was dismissed). The heaviest penalty was inflicted on Yahia Chefchaoui, who was condemned to twelve years of prison and a fine of £1,000; he had been minister of public works and director of the mining research and development office (BRPM). Two other former ministers, Mamoun Tahir and Mohamed Jaidi, and Omar Ben Messaoud, who had been the entrepreneur of much of the business of corruption (including the plan for the Pan-American hotel), were sentenced to comparable terms of imprisonment and fines; the other penalties were less severe. The amount the convicted had collected illicitly was confiscated. Within two years the king was ready to arrange the release of his former ministers, providing this could be done without attracting attention.

During the spring of 1972, while the corruption trial was in its first flush of excitement, the king was apparently engaged in reconstructing the political order. He ordered the preparation of a new constitution, which was submitted to referendum on 1 March 1972 and he opened discussions with party leaders on the formation of a new government. In the king's strategy the two operations supported each other. Publicly he stated that: 'One obviously does not hold a constitutional referendum only to put one's feet up afterwards. . . . The referendum is simply the beginning of a series of measures which should evolve from it . . . it should create the conditions so much desired by all the live forces of the nation for participation in various areas of responsibility.'[1]

[1] Interview of 25 February 1972, *Le Matin*, 1 March 1972, quoted in *Maghreb*, no. 50, p. 41.

The opposition parties were unable to welcome the new constitution publicly, although it embodied changes they wanted. They had been given a constitution but denied a constituent assembly. And they had been caught off balance: at a moment when they thought the king was looking for their support to compensate for defection in the army, he had taken back the initiative and proposed a referendum which would demonstrate the support he enjoyed, or could command, in the country as a whole. They therefore condemned the way the constitution was drawn up, attacked the government for reducing the real problems of the country to a simple question of constitution referendum, and boycotted the referendum when it was held. This did not prevent the official figures showing 98·75 per cent affirmative votes in a poll, it was claimed, of 92·2 per cent.

But the chance of renewed participation in the government, after ten years in the wilderness was, for the opposition parties, one that must not be easily given up, either by refusal to bargain or by settling at too high a price. Negotiations therefore continued and reached the point where journalists were ready to jump the gun by publishing the list of posts which they thought would be official the next day. But at the beginning of April 1972 five months of negotiations collapsed, and the king announced the formation of a new government, essentially similar to the one preceding it.

The breakdown of the negotiations was the result of the conflict between, on the one hand, the king's intention of retaining control of the government and the direction of policy, while securing the participation of a wider range of politicians, and, on the other hand, the desire of the opposition parties to have a determining voice in government, even though they wanted it to remain a constitutional monarchy in which the monarch exercised real power. But while the king need consult only himself, the parties were bound to consider every proposal as it affected their rivals, who, temporarily, were their allies. The Istiqlal and the UNFP calculated their own future chances against each other, sections of each party looked to their own advantage, and the younger generation in each party, men of about forty, were wary of concessions which the established leadership might make. In the end, it seems, the politicians bid too high and the king decided to go his own way. The breakdown meant a loss of prestige for the politicians, and they would not readily renew the process of negotiation unless they were more confident of a successful outcome.

The Coup of 1972 and its Aftermath

The smooth course which the king no doubt hoped might now be renewed was interrupted when, in the summer of 1972, a direct attempt was made on his life. There was a significant change in the direction of the attempt, since there seems to be no doubt that General Oufkir had now become the king's assassin rather than his defender. But although the plan for the *coup* was sophisticated it included no contingency for failure and was put into operation in the belief that its success was certain.

On 16 August 1972, as the king returned from a private visit to Paris, air force fighters from Kenitra took off and attacked his plane. They damaged it badly, but were unable to press home their attack because they ran out of ammunition and because the guns of the leading plane had jammed. Under attack the king once again showed an assured authority and a cool nerve. It was reported that he calmed the crew and his fellow passengers by telling them that as they were with their king all would be well, while at the same time ordering the radio-mechanic to broadcast an SOS saying that he (the king) was mortally wounded and asking that the plane be allowed to land. With extreme skill, his pilot, Commander Kabbag (who was immediately afterwards promoted to be head of the air force) brought the plane down at the airport of Rabat-Salé. The attacking fighters, having rearmed, strafed the airport, killing eight people, but by this time the king had hidden in a neighbouring copse of pine trees. In the evening, in desperation, the attackers machine-gunned the palace at Rabat: but the king had gone to Skhirat (and would, in any case, have been very unlucky to be hit once under cover).

Commander Kouera, who led the attack, ejected from his plane and was arrested. His two accomplices, Lieutenants Amokrane and Midaoui, sought refuge in Gibraltar where they were refused admission and were returned to Morocco (an action which brought a flurry of midsummer protest in Britain). The would-be assassins claimed that they had acted on orders from General Oufkir, and during the night of the 16th the General was shot—it was said, but not widely believed—by his own hand. (Reports of the placing of the bullet wounds led to its being known as an acrobatic suicide.) It was assumed that, in the year since Skhirat, he had found excessive the task of removing disaffection in the army and had grown tired of his task of torture and purge: or that he had decided that so much effort might be turned to his own account, not that of his master. The choice of weapons, the reliance (by an infantry officer) on the untried chances of an aerial attack, and the failure to plan a second strike should the first fail, remain unexplained —unless the plan seemed so sure of success that further precautions were considered unnecessary.

Those immediately responsible for the attack were tried by military tribunal and eleven officers and NCOs were condemned to death. The opposition urged that the king should exercise clemency as a step towards national unity. But the king was not persuaded that the practice of annual attempts on his life merited clemency, and on a cold wet Saturday, 13 January 1973, the executions were carried out.

Two months later a fresh, but quite different, attack on the regime was made, in what came to be known as the plot of March 1973. Participants in the plot included activists of the Basri persuasion in addition to younger men with more radical ideas. Armed groups infiltrated from Algeria, bombs were exploded at Oujda and Nador, and placed (but disarmed in time) in Casablanca and Rabat. A group of men armed with pistols attacked an administrative post at Maulay-Bouazza (in the Middle Atlas) to capture arms, while other groups clashed with the army at Goulmina and Tinghir.

The lack of success attendant on this reckless adventure in guerrilla warfare (referred to in Rabat as Basri's Bay of Pigs) showed the solidity of the king's regime in the countryside. But the events of March 1973 were followed by a lengthy judicial and police enquiry which was equally characteristic of the regime.

Over the next two months a series of arrests was carried out, particularly among the leaders of the UNFP, who, it was said, maintained links with Mohamed al-Basri, who had been twice condemned to death, and Omar Dakhoun, who had been sentenced in absentia to twenty years in prison. The trial of the 159 accused opened before a military tribunal at Kenitra on 25 June and lasted until 30 August (almost contemporaneous with another trial, directed primarily against student activists, before the criminal court of Casablanca). On this occasion Abderrahim Bouabid was called as a prosecution witness, so that he could not be called by the defence. His testimony immediately took a political form.

The prosecution case was that those immediately responsible for subversion had been members of the Rabat branch of the UNFP (which was therefore suspended by the government) and had worked within its organization, as evidenced by tracts inciting to revolt which the police had seized. Bouabid denied any official party responsibility for the tracts and argued that those who had resorted to violence did so in response to the harassment which the party had suffered throughout its existence, in the arbitrary arrest of its members, the suspension of its newspaper, and the occupation of its premises by the police. The case of Mohamed al-Basri was to come before a national congress of the party, but this could not be held because the Rabat branch was suspended; in any case, Bouabid argued that, when considering Basri's sentence, one must take into account the fact that he, Bouabid, had been in touch with Basri, with the knowledge of the palace, during the discussions of 1971 and 1972 between the king and the party leaders, and that the possibility of Basri's amnesty had been considered.

The outcome of the trial was that sixteen of the accused, convicted of carrying arms or of placing bombs, were condemned to death; fifteen were imprisoned for life and fifty-six for shorter periods. However, this was not the end of the affair. Thirteen men who had been given light sentences—some of them peasants, others young teachers, statisticians, or electricians—were brought on the same charges before the same tribunal, differently composed. The seventy-two who were acquitted by the tribunal were immediately rearrested and disappeared from view. In February 1974 some of them were faced with new charges arising from the same events. Not all of those acquitted reappeared at this time, the surgeon Omar Khattabi and Mohamed Lyazghi, a member of the administrative committee of the UNFP, being notable absentees. Those who did appear were jointly charged in a group of sixty-nine, which included others who had been condemned in August, among them Omar Benjelloun (another member of the administrative committee of the UNFP) and a Monsieur Montadi, who alone of those condemned to death had not been executed.

It is difficult to estimate the impact of the continuing sequence of subversion and trials on the political temper of the country as a whole. The trial of 1973-4 produced such frequent allegations and evidence of torture that it began to seem a commonplace of police interrogation. However, there is no evidence of widespread public reaction against the government or the security forces; while the official condemnation of those seeking to disturb public order was broadcast over the radio (for most people the only public source of information) and no doubt carried conviction. These events created division, not unity, in the UNFP. In Casablanca Abdullah Ibrahim and his followers regarded Bouabid as having fallen into the trap against which they had warned him: failing to discourage or prevent the futile efforts at subversion by Basri's supporters he had brought penalties on innocent activists. Bouabid for his part charged the UMT, particularly in Casablanca, with being in the pay of the government. Relations between the two wings of the party were at an exceptionally low ebb. In 1975 it split, the Bouabid (Rabat) wing becoming the Union Socialiste des Forces Populaires.

The king appeared to have won all the prizes: he had reconstructed the security forces, divided the opposition, and was able to use the Sahara issue to retain the political initiative.

ARMED FORCES AND SECURITY

The Moroccan armed forces have had a role of vital importance and are to some extent an indicator of the development of the regime. Initially their growth represented the acquisition by the government of a monopoly of armed force—a novel departure from the days before the protectorate and one which corresponded, in the military sphere, to the extension of civil power from the centre and the disappearance of the semi-autonomous authority of the caïds. Not only did armed force become the monopoly of the regime but the armed forces were—

in the full sense of the epithet—*royal*; the title Forces Armées Royales implied a direct relationship with the monarch, not the ceremonial vestige which the same title has conserved in Britain. During the life of Mohammed V the armed forces were the particular responsibility of Crown Prince Maulay Hassan, so that the command of them formed an important part of his apprenticeship. The fact that the two serious attempts on the monarch's life came from within the armed forces made the king's position all the more hazardous.

If the French protectorate had an irreversible effect on the development of Moroccan administration, it also made a powerful impact on military society by drawing on the potential of Morocco for the defence of France and by opening up the possibilities of a military career, including social advancement by means of military promotion, to a substantial number of Moroccans. The same was true, to a lesser extent, in the Spanish zone. Once independence was agreed it was natural that there should be a common interest between the two countries in the development of the Moroccan armed forces. Both the French and the Spanish governments signed agreements with the Moroccans recognizing the Moroccan army and undertaking to assist its development.

The first stage in this development consisted in the absorption of semi-independent groups of fighters. Such groups had three main origins: the tradition of dissidence among the tribes; the existence of frontier armies, particularly in the south where Morocco had claims on Mauritania and the Spanish Sahara; and the armed uprising in the Middle Atlas and the Rif in support of Mohammed V against the French, constituting an army of national liberation important in itself though diminutive in comparison with that of Algeria.

In spite of the fact that the French army was at war in Algeria the French government provided as much aid to Morocco in the construction of its armed forces as the country could absorb. It assisted the Moroccans in taking over its military academy and provided places in French military schools for as many Moroccans as were able to take them up. As the central core of the army was brought into existence it became easier to incorporate men who had been active in the resistance or on the southern frontiers. By 1960 French aid was diminishing and the bases which France continued to occupy under the independence agreement were evacuated. A series of Moroccan military schools (especially for specialist officers) were to be established and the range of countries which contributed to the training of Moroccan officers was widened, although France remained preponderant. Similarly military equipment was procured from the United States (which in 1967 provided 18 million dollars of military aid), Britain, and the Soviet Union.

The result was the construction of an army, navy, and air force on a scale difficult to justify on grounds of national security, until, in 1976, the conflict with Algeria became acute again. Foreign assistance covered only a small part of the cost of the armed forces, which in 1970 absorbed approximately one fifth of national resources, its budget of 500 million dirhams running a close second to education.

However, it was obviously not the intention of the monarchy that the armed forces should be confined to the defence of Morocco, nor was this the sole claim made for them. The armed forces were intended to be a body of men dedicated to the ideals of the monarchy, aloof from politics, in the sense of being loyal to the king, and exercising a monopoly of coercive power. The intended ethos of the army was summed up in the national motto: 'God, Country, and King', and it is not normally deployed in a manner likely to expose it to political issues, although it is at hand on occasions of severe disturbance, as in 1965. For internal security the importance of the army was in its potential:

'To show its strength in order to have to use it as little as possible' might be one of the mottoes of the Palace. All those who have the ambition, avowed or not, to take power know that they will come up against a formidable force, organized and well-equipped. And if they were to succeed, by the effect of surprise or by a popular movement sufficiently important for the Royal Armed Forces to hesitate in opposition, it would still be necessary to take account of the fact that in any hypothetical new system the army, helped by the strength of its organization, would hold a key place and stand a good chance, in the last resort, of winning out.[1]

At the same time the cohesion of the armed forces appeared to be sufficient to contain the explosive effect of the abortive *coups* on 1971 and 1972 and the penalties and restructuring which followed. In any case the main lines of development of the armed forces were continued in 1973 and 1974. The image and ethos of the army which the king wished to promote can be seen in the bilingual monthly magazine entitled *Forces Armées Royales*. Virtually every number of the magazine opens with *vœux* addressed to the king, usually with the Crown Prince Mohammed in association—these good wishes being extended on the king's birthday, the anniversary of the armed forces, the feast of the throne, or a religious feast. The good wishes are addressed to the king as commander-in-chief of the armed forces and as commander of the faithful. They are customarily followed by an editorial which is written around the theme of God, Country, and King.

As an example one may cite the editorial of June 1974 relating to a youth festival to be held on 9 July (the king's birthday):

The Royal Armed Forces work for Moroccan youth, since their activities are entirely devoted to serving Morocco. In the ranks of the armed forces young

[1] J. J. Regnier and J. C. Santucci, 'Armée, pouvoir et légitimité au Maroc', in *Annuaire de l'Afrique du Nord*, 1971, p. 151.

Moroccans learn a trade, are initiated into new techniques, rediscover the great fundamental virtues of our people and the traditions of our holy religion. ... How better to serve God than in helping young Moroccans to know better the practice of these rites? How better to serve the country than by inculcating in young Moroccans the love of country and helping them to understand that for the country they must be ready for the final sacrifice? How, finally, better to serve the King than in explaining to young Moroccans the supreme function of royalty. ...

The army gained prestige as a result of the participation of two contingents in the Middle East war of 1973. Their exploits and the fact that they were decorated by the Egyptians and the Syrians were naturally given full publicity while at the same time credit was given to the king for having so managed the affairs of the country that the first contingent was in place in Syria when the war started and that a second was despatched to help the Egyptian forces in Sinai.

The army makes much of the claim that it provides training for civilian trades—as indeed it does, although it is unlikely that this aspect of its activities has as much impact as is suggested. In May 1972 General Oufkir, then minister of defence, claimed that the Moroccan system of military service was unique of its kind, since national recruits spent three months in military training and the remaining fifteen months learning some civilian employment. Thus a training school at the former American base of Benguerir trains hotel workers while the school of Sidi Slimane trains mecanographers who made an important contribution to the collection of census data. The army has its own medical research unit and succeeded in isolating a flu virus in the spring of 1972.

It is understandable that as the armed forces absorb a large part of the national revenue it should be claimed that they make important contributions to national welfare outside the military sphere. At the same time it appears that an increasing amount of attention has been given since 1972 to the material welfare of officers and, to a lesser extent, of the men. Thus the army is responsible for the construction of houses for officers, and for the provision of loans to enable them to buy their own houses. It also runs its own social service, with trained female social workers under the direction of a social welfare officer. Its services include holiday camps for children, assistance with the pilgrimage at Mecca, help with problems of re-entry to civilian life, and financial aid 'to overcome temporary difficulties'.

While the main body of the army was kept out of politics as far as possible, the security services formed either a specialized branch of the army or were dependent on the army in a manner difficult to determine. The army's special brigades, the Brigades Légères de Sécurité, were responsible for security and were of decisive importance in the *coup* of 1971. The director of national security in 1961–71 was an army officer. The king frequently paid special tribute to the work of the Sûreté Nationale in his speech on the anniversary of the foundation of the armed forces, in a manner that suggests a close relationship between the two.

In addition, General Oufkir was minister of the interior for eight years until his appointment to national defence—and to his commission to purge the army—in 1971. But the importance of this fact lay far more in the character and personality of Mohamed Oufkir than in an institutional relationship.

Mohamed Oufkir came from the Berber village of Taouz, in the south-east of Morocco, on the edge of the Sahara. His father's generation had resisted the establishment of the protectorate, but Oufkir joined the French army and distinguished himself by his bravery and ferocity particularly in Indo-China. He then returned to Morocco and began a second career in the entourage of two resident-generals, acting as go-between with the palace during the exile of Mohammed V.

After Independence he was responsible for the campaign against the rising in the Rif in 1958, where he distinguished himself by his ruthless destruction of villages to end resistance. His career in the vital years preceding Independence limited the confidence which Mohammed V was willing to place in him, but Hassan II came to depend on him and to give him free rein in the apparently difficult years immediately following his accession.

In 1965 Oufkir's notoriety increased both because of the harshness of the armed services, under his personal leadership, in the Casablanca riots and because of the kidnapping of Ben Barka. By this time he had constructed and institutionalized a system of torture renowned for its cruelty, and the Ben Barka affair clearly demonstrated the resources he could command and the extent of the network of alliances he had constructed. It has been suggested by Jean Lacouture[1] that King Hassan would have demoted Oufkir at this point, were it not that he would appear to be doing so at the behest of de Gaulle (who had indicated that relations between France and Morocco could not be normalized as long as Oufkir was in the government). Oufkir, in any case, decided to separate himself from the king; although the point at which he decided to act against the king remains unknown.

Following the defection of Oufkir the king took over direct command of the armed forces, abolishing the ministry of defence. Officers close to Oufkir were dismissed. Others were sent to the Middle East; for a

[1] See Jean Lacouture, 'Le Monarque et le janissaire', *Le Monde*, 22 August 1972. Note also the comment (ibid.) of a Taouz peasant at Oufkir's funeral: 'Les gens, dans l'ensemble, estiment que ce qu'a fait le général n'est pas bien. Le roi, c'est le roi. Il ne faut pas y toucher. Mais en même temps, ils ont eu du chagrin, parce que le général, voyez-vous, tout le monde l'aimait bien ici.' ('People, on the whole, reckon that what the general did was not good. The king is the king. He must not be touched. But all the same people are sorry, because the general, you know, everyone liked him here.')

time they were out of the way and acquired merit during the October war. Officers were no longer allowed to stay long in a single post, and the diplomatic campaign for the Sahara, being supported by military dispositions, provided an opportunity to keep the army on the move. Reserves of weapons and munitions were taken out of the control of the army and were placed under the authority of provincial governors, guarded by the auxiliary forces. Only the Brigades Légères de Sécurité, some 2,000 men under the command of Colonel Chafai, and the 1,500-strong Royal Guard under General Sefrioui (brother-in-law of Ahmed Dlimi) retained control over their own armaments.[1]

Dlimi retained his responsibilities for internal security without in any way replacing his erstwhile chief Oufkir. But the king took a direct interest in security within the army, and a new security service, with the French-inspired title of the Direction Générale de la Surveillance du Térritoire Marocain, was established in January 1973, under the direction of Driss Slaoui (until his appointment to the United Nations in August 1974).

Two years after the failure of the Kenitra *coup* and the death of General Oufkir the army was thus restructured under the king's command with renewed emphasis on its character as a non-political body, loyal to the king and Morocco, imbued with Muslim virtue, and at the same time enjoying a symbiosis with the nation, to whose welfare it was dedicated. Both its recruitment and the level of expertise necessary to handle sophisticated weapons had changed the character of its officer class so that junior officers were drawn from precisely the background of middle and lower middle class in the coastal towns where the percentage of abstention from referenda was highest. To retain the loyalty of such men it would be necessary not only to evoke a sense of dedication to God, Country, and King (although the importance of this appeal should not be underestimated), but to create, at least within the armed services, a society which rewards effort and provides good social services rather than the opportunities for corruption which incited General Medbouh to revolt.

Whatever the success of King Hassan's political disposition of the army the Saharan crisis in 1975 brought out obvious military weaknesses in relation to the Algerians. The army numbered some 65,000 men, with possible reinforcement by 50,000 para-military troops. Its tank force consisted of only 120 Soviet tanks, 25 old American tanks, and 120 light French tanks, with modernized guns. The airforce was notably weaker than the Algerian, being based on Fouga-Magisters and Northrop F-5 aircraft. The Moroccan government ordered 65 Mirages from France—an order which was finally agreed at the height of the Saharan crisis in such a way that it contributed to the political furore, although many months would pass before the aircraft were

[1] J. Gourdon, *Annuaire de l'Afrique du Nord*, 1972, p. 325.

delivered. If a conflict with Algeria were to develop the Moroccan forces would therefore depend on their experience in operating in desert conditions (for which some of their equipment was especially adapted) and on the distance which separated the better equipped Algerian airforce from the Saharan area. The Moroccan government has also ordered missile launching frigates from France and the Soviet Union.

THE ECONOMY

The economic resources of Morocco are required to meet a rapidly expanding population. Oil exploration yielded only minimal commercial output. However, the Bureau de Recherches et Participation Minières continues to receive requests for exploration concessions, and it intends to build a pilot extraction plant in the hope of realizing 30 million tons of oil a year from a shale deposit in the Middle Atlas. A refining capacity of some 2·5 million tons has been constructed in association with SNAM Progetti of Milan. In recompense Morocco has large reserves of phosphates—possibly a half of the world's reserves, and, in 1973, one-sixth of the world's output and one-third of the world's exports. It has a further advantage over the other countries of North West Africa in its water supply, which comes from the conjunction of the Atlas mountains and the Atlantic Ocean. It also has much sunshine and great natural beauty. The tourist industry has, therefore, been given a high priority in development plans, and is an important source of foreign exchange earnings.

Morocco has a natural market for agricultural products in Europe. The opportunities of this outlet are increased as the result of the most recent agreement with the EEC: a new form of association dating from January 1976 provides financial aid to the extent of $160 million over five years and makes possible the import of most goods from Morocco free of tariff. Where tariffs remain they are substantially reduced and seasonal allowances are provided to assist Moroccan producers. But while Morocco exports such agricultural products as citrus, olives, olive oil, and early vegetables it has been importing about one-fifth of its cereal needs to meet an increasing demand which outpaces increased domestic production, even in a good year.

In contrast to the population increase, the growth in the economy has been slow, without any dramatic changes of fortune (once the economic disruption of Independence was past), until the threefold increase in the price of phosphates in 1973 (coinciding, unfortunately, with increases in world prices of oil and cereals and followed by inflation in the Moroccan economy). The politics of development have not been concerned with any major upheaval of nationalization, and changes in landownership have come about in an exceptionally reformist manner.

The development of the economy and state intervention in society—internal security, education, public health, and sport—have received the attention of planners. The Conseil Supérieur du Plan drew up plans for the years 1960–4, 1965–7, 1968–72, and 1973–7. In the words of the three-year plan (1965–7) they constitute 'a programme rather than a plan', and provide an outline of the main direction of government investment. The distinctiveness of the Moroccan plans, in contrast with other national plans, lies in the modesty of the claims made for them rather than in their actual coverage. However, it must be borne in mind that they do not claim to plan monetary or pricing policy and that their attention to the growth of population is (as we have seen) marginal. The implementation of the plan is no more in the hands of the planning council than it is in any other country (the construction of an additional dam or the nationalization of foreign land being political decisions), and factors of massive importance such as the price of oil or a war in the Middle East remain outside the control of the planners.

Within these limitations the plans provide an outline of the main direction of the economy and also include a review of the achievements of previous plans, with statistics in support. They thus provide a realistic analysis of the problems of the economy which contrasts sharply with the promissory notes and obfuscations of the king and the dead dialogue of the political parties.

The Moroccan strategy of development has concentrated public expenditure on the development of agriculture. Industrial development has for the most part been left to private investments, with certain important exceptions. The tourist industry has been built with the help of major government investment, in capital and in training personnel; the phosphate industry is a national concern, but one which is relatively self-contained. Otherwise, industrial development—which is not on a large scale—receives the contribution of government in infrastructure and education and in various forms of encouragement, particularly in the direction of exports.

Agriculture

It must always be borne in mind that Morocco is a country of great geographical diversity. The variety of the countryside has been scrupulously studied by Daniel Noin, who writes:

Morocco is a land of astonishing variety since it is, like the whole of the Maghreb, a country of contact. Structural contact between the old African shield and the Alpine-Mediterranean world, so that there is a great diversity of forms of relief. Climatic contact between the temperate zone and the tropical zone, between humidity and dryness so that regions differ sharply in their atmosphere and their vegetation. Human contact also: between the world of a sedentary population and that of nomads, between the traditional civilization of an area which has been static for a long time and one which is capitalistic, with techniques brought by European colonization. It is a country of vivid contrasts and striking diversity.[1]

But while it is important to bear in mind the immense diversity of the country it is also the case that a simple division has long existed between the physically easy and climatically attractive areas of the plains and the harsher environment of the mountains and the desert. Moreover, three inter-related factors have increased the difference between the two major regions. The virtual elimination of the main epidemic diseases—plague, cholera, and malaria—has probably affected the plains more than the mountains, on the assumption that these areas were more susceptible to epidemics than the mountain areas. It was the plains and lowlands which were most affected by colonization, and it is the same areas which are most affected by agricultural development since Independence. As a result they have attracted population, although some areas, notably the eastern Rif, remain areas of heavy population (or over-population) in spite of the paucity of their resources.

The development of Moroccan agriculture since Independence has been characterized by conservatism coupled with an emphasis on technical progress as defined by the planners, rather than by social change. Certain imaginative projects have been planned—notably the development of the western Rif—and a programme of public works has been kept in movement, since no Moroccan government can close its eyes to the duality of the agricultural sector or to the obvious problems of poverty and unemployment in the under-endowed agricultural areas. But neither the personnel nor the institutions of the country have been particularly suited to the task of reversing natural trends towards inequality, and on balance agricultural programmes have favoured the already favoured areas and have given proportionately least assistance to the least favoured in those areas.

The first three development plans gave an important place in public and semi-public investment to agriculture, including the construction of dams, and the policy of building big dams has dominated plans for agricultural development. However, big dams, of which there were twenty-three in service in 1973, have an importance which is not limited to agriculture. They may provide hydro-electric power and fill urban needs for water. They also have an obvious political attraction. To harness water gives a sense of power; the distribution of water is a function which enhances the importance of the state and the administration; the ceremonial of beginning and completing construction and the naming of dams provide opportunities for important political

[1] Noin, 1970, p. 61.

occasions. It is perhaps understandable that while the plan for 1973–7 gives a relatively low priority to agriculture and includes provision for only two new dams the king announced, only two months after the presentation of the plan, that a third dam would be built.

The scale of planning for dams and irrigation can be seen from the fact that at Independence Morocco had three major irrigated areas: the Tadla, the Doukallas, and the Gharb; some 65,000 hectares were irrigated by modern methods and 200,000 by traditional methods. The government programme, instituted in 1967, was to irrigate a million hectares, and five years later the ministry of agriculture showed irrigation equipment in place for 326,000 hectares. However, the programme of dams has been repeatedly criticized, notably by the World Bank, for the delays which have intervened between the construction of dams and the development of irrigation networks and then the distribution of water to farms. The gap between the construction of dams and use of the water resources thus generated is recognized in the present five-year plan which calculates a difference of 180,000 hectares between the total area which the outlet from the dams is meant to irrigate and the total area equipped. In consequence the plan recommends:

> the completion of irrigation work ought to increase at a much more rapid rate than the equipping of canals and should therefore have a high priority, particularly in the distribution of trained personnel. In fact the continuation of an excessive advance in hydro-agricultural equipment brings not only a premature, and therefore costly tying up of capital but the absorption of limited human resources, which are drawn away from the effective bringing into service, which is the real object of the exercise.[1]

The development of dams has been accompanied by a gradual (and not always efficient) land reform.[2] The figure given for land owned by settlers in 1950 was one million hectares; according to the French embassy in Rabat there were 900,000 hectares in the possession of French citizens in 1956. The Moroccan government immediately took over the relatively small proportion of 20,000 hectares, being state-owned land recovered from settlers, and distributed it to Moroccan farmers between 1956 and 1966.

The second stage of land appropriation occurred when the government took over, by royal decree, approximately 220,000 hectares of land which had formed 'lots de colonisation'—the previous 'domaine privé' of the state which the French had distributed to settlers by selling it at very low prices. The land was taken over in three steps—in 1963, 1964, and 1965—the largest portion, some 105,000 hectares,

---

[1] *Plan quinquennal, 1973–7*, ii. 9.
[2] I am indebted to Dr. Keith Griffin for his assistance in the following study of land distribution.

being taken over last. The government maintained that no compensation was due to French settlers for this land, in view of the way it had been appropriated, but compensation was paid for assets attached to the land. Initially, this land was managed by a government company (SOGEA) set up by the ministry of agriculture for the purpose. But the company lacked the equipment and the experienced and effective personnel necessary for the job.

Starting in 1966 the land under the state farms was distributed into private ownership. The land was sold below the market price, for a sum payable over twenty years at 4 per cent. Under a law of 1966, purchasers had to be virtually landless and to belong to the area and even to the commune (by at least five years' residence) in which the land was placed. The lots into which the land was divided were designed to produce an income of 3,500 to 4,000 dirhams a year (the size therefore varying according to location, quality, whether irrigated, etc.). Thus, the beneficiaries were few in number and suddenly progressed from being landless to being in the top 15-20 per cent of rural households. Ministry figures show some 11,101 recipients of 181,197 hectares of land between 1957 and 1972; the beneficiaries being less than one per cent of the households previously owning less than two hectares. Under the 1966 law the recipients of land were required to become members of cooperatives. The ministry of agriculture has appointed directors to these cooperatives, with the intention that the cooperative shall, after a period of a few years, take over responsibility for the director's salary.

The political importance of the distribution of land is obvious. The rate of distribution increased rapidly over the years of the two attempts on the king's life (19,000 hectares in 1971 and over 90,000 in 1972). The distribution of titles was carried out at ceremonies accompanied by the colourful celebrations of the Moroccan countryside—dancing and displays of horsemanship. The king made available 6,000 hectares of his own land (probably leaving some 37,000 hectares intact). However, the opposition was able to interpret the figures the government published and the Istiqlal was quick to point out (on the basis of the 1971 figures) that 45,000 people (7,500 families) had received land since 1957 and that this represented only one-sixth of the figure of 300,000, the annual demographic increase of the countryside. But within the government no secret was made of the fact that there would never be enough land for everyone and that the intention was to avoid a division of land into small parcels, giving immediate satisfaction but destroying the rural economy (*a reductio ad limine* of political rather than rational value).

While this distribution was in progress, the third plan was contributing markedly to the prosperity of the good land within the irrigation areas—in spite of delays in their expansion. A law of 1969 provided for a concentration of expenditure in these areas; but it also provided for the expropriation of land for reasons of public utility. The intention of the law was to open the way for irrigation construction and to limit speculation. At the same time, small pieces of land were consolidated and sold in lots of not less than five hectares—on generous financial terms, with all the advantages of irrigation and technical advice, but under very strict control of cropping (including the choice of crops).

The final stage of the recovery of land in foreign ownership was begun by law in March 1973 as the major part of a programme of 'Moroccanization' of the economy. There was nothing radical in what was proposed, in contrast to the Algerian action on Independence or Tunisian nationalization of land in 1964. The government proceeded with an inventory, and in March 1974 entered into negotiations with the French government (closely watched by other governments whose citizens were involved) to agree a sum of compensation—an unprecedented way of proceeding in the Moroccan and Maghreb experience.

However, the transfer of land by legislation accounted for only a minor part of the total since the tardiness of state action gave an obvious opportunity for sale and purchase in the commercial market. Probably 100,000 hectares were sold before Independence. At Independence there were reckoned to be some 646,000 hectares of *melk* or privately owned land in the hands of French citizens; but sales between that time and the pronouncement of March 1973 had reduced the total to 260,000 hectares (in spite of the fact that the law of 1963 prohibited such sale without the prior approval of the government). However, it appeared that the amount of land actually available was likely to be less than 260,000 hectares, even when the much smaller amount of land owned by Spaniards, Belgians, Algerians, and others was added. This is because a large amount of land was in the course of being sold; some was owned by Frenchmen but farmed by Moroccans and some was owned by corporations in which a large number of shares had been bought by Moroccans. It is thus possible that of the 646,000 hectares owned by French citizens in 1956 some three-quarters —480,000 hectares, or more than twice as much as the 'lots de colonisation'—had been transferred to Moroccan hands by 1973. The effect was to strengthen the rural élite, with important consequences for subsequent agricultural policies.

Whatever the problems of development in the more favoured agricultural areas they are minor compared with those in the dry part of the country or '*zone bour*'. In the planners' definition the dry zone is distinguished from the irrigated zones. The dry zone is in turn divided for planning purposes between that part which has sufficient rainfall to permit development either with medium scale irrigation or with dry farming, and those areas with such limited rainfall that the problem is defined as being to maintain existing production intact without trying to achieve an impossible increase in production. Obviously, this classification in terms of aggregate rainfall is extremely rough as a guide to climatic conditions in Morocco. In addition, the division between zones, even between irrigated and dry as drawn in the plans, leaves a large degree of approximation in many respects.

The government's approach to the dry zone has been multiple but limited. It has instituted major projects intended to cover the greater part of the country; some of these—the 'fertilizer operation'—have had very limited success; others, notably the use of public works, have continued to operate. The government has initiated one major regional project, the DERRO (Développement Économique et Rural du Rif Occidental), covering the western Rif; and it has also undertaken a number of limited projects, intended either to serve as an example or to concentrate limited resources in a single area.

The possibility of the development of agriculture in the dry zone has not been such as to attract planners whose offices are in Rabat, and very few of whom have their origins outside the favoured areas of Fez, Rabat, Casablanca, or the mid-Atlantic area. The picture of the *bour*, with its 40 per cent landless (according to the 1968–72 plan), or its estimated 70 per cent owning two hectares or less, is a daunting one. The stereotype of the *fellah* is of a man whose mistrust and force of habit are insurmountable obstacles.[1] At the same time, there has been a lamentable shortage of trained men able to engage in agricultural extension work; and the best will and best skill can only affect, not alter, the harshness and unpredictability of the climate.

Undoubtedly, the picture has often been drawn in excessively pessimistic terms. The ingenuity and tenacity of peasants has been underestimated. The skill and industry with which the steep slopes of the Rif mountains have been brought under cultivation has been obscured by the admittedly disastrous consequences of soil erosion, and the careful calculation which has drawn produce from the limited and sporadic water available in the foothills of the Atlas has been eclipsed by the grander achievements of irrigation. The possibilities of United Nations assistance have been underestimated or used with too little effect. And there is a natural tendency for the self-interest of the landed bourgeoisie to prevail when so many reasons can so easily be found for neglecting the *bour*.

Some change is evident in the most recent five-year plan, whose authors write with considerable realism; while it can be assumed that the king is mindful of the indispensable support he has received in the countryside—where the large majority of the population is still illiterate, where agricultural production grows more slowly than population, where public health services and education are slow to develop, and there is no industry to provide wealth or employment.

[1] *Plan quinquennal, 1968–72*, ii. 23.

The present plan thus provides for a threefold increase in expenditure in the dry zone, while at the same time agricultural engineers are now completing their courses and becoming available for deployment across the country. The plan also attaches importance to livestock production which represents 30–50 per cent of the value added agricultural product.

The increase in expenditure is unlikely, however, to prevent a growing inequality between the *bour* and the modern agricultural sector. Although the *bour* is to receive 46 per cent of agricultural development expenditure, it supports 72 per cent of the population. Moreover, the experience of the previous five-year plan showed that it is more difficult to spend sums allocated to the *bour*—only 76 per cent of planned expenditure was carried out in the *bour*, compared to 103 per cent in the modern sector. Many of the causes of the shortfall seem likely to persist in the future.

The imaginative and exacting DERRO project concerns the area of the Rif mountains between Al-Hoceima and Tetuan and southwards to a line drawn from Taza to Ouezzane. The area is heavily populated (some 1,350,000 inhabitants in 1960 in an area of 18,000 square kilometres), in spite of being steeply mountainous and having a harsh climate of violent winter rain and hot dry summers. In addition, it was chosen for attention partly because it crosses the border between former Spanish and French Morocco; and partly because it affects the valley of the Sebou to the south, so that development of the area of concentration around Kenitra, Meknes, and Fez might be prejudiced if the area to the north were left untouched. A twenty-five-year programme was planned with advice from FAO and initiated in 1963.

Apparently for practical reasons, the initial programme had to be modified and the development of areas of medium irrigation postponed. This reorganization delayed the development of the project, as did differences of authority and practice between the various agencies of government involved. None the less, the DERRO project gained momentum through the period of the five-year plan 1968–72 and absorbed 89 per cent of the credits allocated to it, disbursing some 68 million dirhams (bringing the total Moroccan expenditure to nearly 110 million dirhams since 1965); 8,500 hectares of fruit trees and 9,000 hectares of forests were planted; roads or tracks were built; and nearly 6,000 hectares brought under a programme for the 'defence and restoration of the soil'. The plan for 1973–7 provides for the expenditure of 100 million dirhams with a concentration on the 'perimeters of integrated development'—integrated in the sense that a simultaneous attack is made on the improvement of crops through the diffusion of fertilizers and seeds, the improvement of livestock by better fodder and improved strains, and action to defend the soil from exhaustion and erosion.

In addition, the programme calls for the substitution of other crops in place of the much-favoured *kif* or hashish; it limits the exploitation of the land in order to reduce soil erosion; and the planting of olive and almond trees produces a return only after many years. The project thus requires the deployment of that extremely scarce resource—trained agricultural experts willing to work in harsh rural conditions and able to persuade and encourage a population not noted for its receptivity to outside influence.

Apart from the exceptional DERRO project a continuing attempt has been made to improve agricultural methods by the spreading of agricultural knowledge and by making available seeds and fertilizers at subsidized prices. Some projects have fallen by the wayside—like the 'fertilizer project', which absorbed less than half the budget allocated to it before being abandoned, in spite of the fact that where it worked well output increased by 50 per cent. In contrast, a project for soil improvement absorbed 86 per cent of the credits allocated to it, but it was available (within the agricultural investment law of 1969) only to farmers with 20 hectares or more, and was deployed over a total area of only 113,000 hectares. The retrospect which the present five-year plan casts over the achievement of the previous plan in improving stockraising is particularly negative, except in the control of animal epidemics. In the improvement of pastures, in centres for the improvement of stock, and in milk collection, government action was markedly insufficient. Yet in this area too the provision made in the new plan appears likely to provide possibilities (in the improvement of stock and artificial insemination, for example) more adapted to the needs of the prosperous farmer than to the peasants in the *bour*.

A second project is that of the Revalorisation de l'Agriculture à Sec au Maroc (PRAM) for which the United Nations has provided financial support. It concentrates on pilot projects outside the irrigation areas—in eastern Morocco, the southern Middle Atlas, the High Atlas, and the pre-Saharan region. It is difficult to know how substantial the return on this kind of experiment is, since it depends on training rural cadres who will introduce and popularize new methods of agriculture. It depends on instructors to spread knowledge in the first instance, and experience in other countries has shown that results may be limited because the extreme diversity of physical and climatic conditions renders the success of experiments hazardous and not always applicable to other circumstances.

In addition, the Moroccan government launched, in July 1961, a programme of public works designed to combat unemployment in the countryside and thereby to improve rural conditions. The programme —called the 'Promotion Nationale'—was put in the charge of a special office directly responsible to the king, but it depended in part on local initiative for the specification of work to be done. It was financed by foreign aid (notably the provision of wheat under Public Law 480) and by the national budget. By 1964 it was generating some 15 million days of work (say, 75,000 men at work for 200 days in the year). It contributed to the construction and maintenance of roads; afforestation and care of forests; schoolbuilding; improvements in local markets; minor irrigation works; and similar projects.

The programme has encountered predictable difficulties. Local initiative in identifying suitable projects has often been lacking or misguided, while the national government has failed to fill pay packets promptly so that workers have lost interest. None the less, the Promotion Nationale continued to generate work (a yearly average of 18 million days during the plan of 1968–72) and to contribute to agricultural improvement and the provision of 'infrastructure'.

Industry

Industry plays a minor part in the Moroccan economy, and this is particularly true of manufacturing industry. The most dramatic change in the industrial sector came from world market conditions in phosphates.

The discovery and initial development of the phosphates industry occurred under the protectorate. The existence of phosphate rock was first established in 1917, the Office Chérifien des Phosphates (OCP) was set up in 1920, and the first train-load of phosphates was taken out to Casablanca in the following year. There are two important deposits: at Khouribga and at Youssoufia. Casablanca provides the major outlet, three-quarters of the total export passing through its port; a secondary outlet and an important petro-chemical complex have been constructed at Safi, based on production from Youssoufia.

The OCP has remained a state company, operating commercially under a director appointed by royal decree, who is responsible to an administrative council which is in effect a government organization. The scale of the OCP's operation gives it a special place in the Moroccan economy and society. It is the most important single source of export earnings and the single most important customer of the nationalized railway and electricity industries; its dividends go to the state and are counted as revenue in the state budget. It is a major employer of labour, in spite of a marked diminution of employment with technological development, and in consequence, has important training and social programmes.

The limited size of the internal market makes the industry dependent on the world market. During the 1960s this was a buyers' market, dominated by the United States, which competed with Morocco at the top of the phosphate-exporters' table but did so with the advantage of a massive internal market. The boom of the 1970s and worldwide agricultural development produced a sharp increase in demand in 1972 —the United States' internal demand increasing by 10 per cent, in addition to a sharp increase in the requirements of developing countries. The Moroccan industry was in a position to take advantage of increased demand to become the world's largest exporter and to triple the price from January 1974. But the increase was followed by a drop in world demand, and led to an expanded world output. In the absence of a cartel like OPEC the price fell back sharply in 1975–6.

The change in world demand was also of major significance for the industrial complex of Safi. Plans for installing a phosphates industry at Safi had been developed in the 1950s; they were taken up by the Moroccan government, and realized with the assistance of the World Bank. The choice of Safi was based on proximity to raw materials and the underdevelopment of its hinterland, not proximity to the internal market. It uses phosphates from Youssoufia and iron pyrites from Kennatra (for the production of sulphuric acid) to produce fertilizers and phosphoric acid. At the time of its construction, the complex was welcomed as one of the most important ventures in North Africa from the point of view of state initiative, international financing, and foreign participation. None the less, the project languished until the world demand for fertilizer rose.

The Safi complex is the more distinctive since the Moroccan government has embarked on only one other major industrial project, the construction of a large refinery in conjunction with the Italian ENI. The Moroccan government and ENI have jointly founded the Société Anonyme Marocaine Italienne de Raffinage (Samir) with equal capital participation, and the refining capacity was brought to 2·5 million tons by 1972, using imported crude. The first Moroccan plan, that of 1957–9, gave a privileged position to a metallurgical complex at Ras Kebdena, in the province of Nador. It was dropped, revived in 1968–9, and then dropped again.

The search for fossil and mineral resources is pursued actively. The coal field of Jerada produces a small output of 474,000 tons out of a national total of 800,000 tons, and in 1972 Moroccan exports of coal roughly equalled the import of coke and good quality coal. Iron ore resources are limited, the sole important exploitation being that of Nador. With the settlement of the frontier between Algeria and Morocco, plans were agreed for the joint exploitation of the Tindouf field, which remained in Algerian territory, but these have been slow to materialize. The search for oil has not produced significant results and has moved to offshore exploration. Small quantities, sometimes low-grade, of a range of metals including manganese, lead, and copper, have been mined, and geological surveys justify the continued exploration.

Outside the phosphates industry at Safi and the oil refinery at Mohammedia, manufacturing industry has grown slowly. The state has shown no dynamism in this regard and private investment has been in the area of small and medium enterprise. The food industry (including sugar refining) is an important part of the limited industrial sector; construction has flourished; but the textile industry has not. The plan for 1973-7, in its retrospective over the previous plan, comments, 'Although industrialization was described as a necessity in the 1968-72 plan, neither the rate of annual growth achieved (5 per cent) nor the investment provided for appears to conform to the objective assigned to it. In addition the number of specific projects proposed was very modest in relation to the purpose set out.'

Meanwhile the tourist industry has made an important contribution to the economy as a whole. The objectives of the 1968-72 plan were fully realized, both in the sums invested and in the expansion of the number of beds available in a diversified system of hotels. Private capital played a major part, and may have done so the more readily since investment in hotels is relatively close to the traditionally attractive outlet in real estate. Receipts from tourism removed one half of the deficit in the balance of payments over the period 1968-72, the remainder being eliminated by remissions from workers abroad.

At the beginning of the period of the 1973-7 plan, the Moroccan economy had important statistical achievements to its credit. Gross domestic product showed an annual increase, during the preceding five years, of 5·6 per cent compared with the plan's forecast of 4·3 per cent. The 6 per cent increase in agricultural production far exceeded the plan's estimate of 2·1 per cent although this was accounted for by good harvests, of which that of 1968 exceeded all previous years. Average consumption per head had risen by 2 per cent per annum. The balance of payments was positive as a result of increased exports (including tourism) and capital transfer.

In 1973 the government proceeded to introduce (by royal decree) the 'Moroccanization' of industry, followed by a new code of investments. The Moroccanization decrees were effectively designed to increase Moroccan participation in share capital and in the direction of private industry by a limited definition of what constituted a Moroccan company. At the same time, the new code of investments is designed to encourage private investment in industry, in order to meet the investment requirements of the new plan: 26,000 million dirhams, of which it is hoped that 45·1 per cent will come from the private sector. The investment code provides remission of taxes and customs duties in connexion with approved investment projects and it also attempts to secure regional development by providing additional advantages for investment in the less developed parts of the country. The code includes and is supplemented by provisions designed to guarantee and encourage foreign investment.[1]

---

[1] Karim Lamrani, banker, former prime minister, and now head of the Office Chérifien des Phosphates, may be taken as an example of the path to prosperity in such a regime, so much so that Moroccans dub Moroccanization, 'Lamranization'.

In spite of the growth of the economy the trade balance of 1974 showed its inherent vulnerability. The export revenue from phosphates rose by 417 per cent as a result of the massive increase in price and a 16 per cent increase in output. Phosphates accounted for 55 per cent of export revenue. Other mineral exports—lead and iron ore—also increased; so did the value of fertilizer exports, in spite of a 50 per cent drop in volume. Export revenue also benefited from the general increase in the price of olive oil, and exports of canned fish increased.

On the other hand the increase in the price of imported oil to some extent balanced the increased price of phosphates, while the gain on olive oil was offset by a poor wheat harvest (the second in succession) necessitating the import of wheat. Drought also reduced the yield of citrus fruits and tomatoes. The hope that the increased revenue from phosphates would cover the cost of imports necessary for the implementation of the present plan was disappointed. There was a 70 per cent increase in the import of agricultural equipment and a 40 per cent increase in the import of metal goods for construction. The total import bill doubled and the deficit on the balance of trade was roughly the same as in 1973—$238 million.

The authors of the present plan are among the most succinct critics of economic development. It is characteristic of the qualified freedom of Morocco that their comment was included in the text of the *Perspectives générales* (after a political battle for its retention) and also that they are authors of the plan, not of policy. They comment on growing inequality in the following words:[1]

> The increase in the purchasing power of the least favoured sections of the population is thus as much an economic as a social necessity. The study of the evolution of consumption of different sections of the population over the past ten years shows that the gap between the richest and the poorest groups, far from being diminished by the economic expansion which the country has experienced, has been accentuated; even more, if the trends observed in the past are projected forward, without any mechanism of redistribution, the disparity of incomes will grow worse during the plan.

They note the argument that redistribution of income may cause a diminution in the aggregate propensity to save, but continue:

> Analysis shows that the progressive reduction of disparity of incomes has no harmful effect whatever on economic growth, to the extent that the real objective of growth is economic and social development and thus the advancement of man. In addition, saving is not an end in itself; it is only profitable to the national economy as a whole to the extent that it is invested in projects likely to bring about, by their prior and subsequent effects, economic growth; Moroccan saving, which is the product of the most favoured sections of the population, is not necessarily invested in projects of this kind, but often finds

[1] *Plan quinquennal, 1973–7*, i. 50–1.

its way into property speculation and the construction of private houses, when it is not sterilized by simply being taken out of the economic system altogether.

There is, however, no reason to expect the present plan to reverse previous tendencies to strengthen the Makhzen bourgeoisie. In agriculture the delay in land reform permitted the transfer of French estates to Moroccan purchasers; and public investment in agriculture gives the advantage to medium and large landowners. With some justification it is argued that, in a country with so slender an economic margin as Morocco, agricultural development must be achieved without the constraints on production which would accompany any attempt to foster small-scale farming. The hydraulic society which has developed as a result of dam construction links landownership to the state administration. At the same time, industrial development also gives a major role to the state—not in the construction of large state industries, but in the manner of financing investment through the banking system as well as requiring approval of investments by a state committee for tax purposes.

There is no obvious reason why the society should have developed as it has done, since it was equally propitious to vigorous entrepreneurship which would have kept the 'private' sector much more independent of the state; the wealth of Fassi merchants could have played a role similar to that of the English eighteenth-century nabobs. Instead, the state, financial institutions, industry, and agriculture, form a close circle, bound together by corruption, spoils, and family ties, but providing little outlet for a growing educated young generation and none for the unemployed and landless.

FOREIGN RELATIONS

Morocco has played an unpretentious part in world affairs. Its sympathies have been obviously (but unaggressively) on the side of the United States and western Europe against the Soviet bloc; but this has not inhibited the development of relations with the Soviet Union and eastern Europe, especially during recent years as the Soviet Union has become a more acceptable partner, both because of the support given to the Arab world against Israel and because of the détente with the United States. Relations with France have generally been harmonious and have not been coloured by comprehensive denunciation of colonialism, although the relationship was affected by the Ben Barka affair, and France was attacked for its part in the creation of the state of Mauritania. Morocco has taken an active part in both the Organization of African Unity and in the Arab League. It has played host to Arab and Islamic conferences, but without the éclat of the non-aligned conference at Algiers. Morocco has, however, been continuously concerned with the question of its own frontiers, especially the question of the Spanish Sahara.

The Soviet Union and Morocco are minor trading partners (Poland, in 1974, being a more important importer), and the Soviet Union has provided credits and technical assistance for a limited number of Moroccan projects. Traditionally Morocco has bought oil, timber, and tea from the Soviet Union and, more recently, electrical equipment. It exports citrus and minerals to the USSR, but it has not succeeded in keeping its trade in balance. Soviet engineers have provided assistance in exploration for minerals, and both technical and loan assistance has been given in a limited number of hydro-electric and irrigation projects. Diplomatic relations are friendly: King Hassan has visited the Soviet Union, and Podgorny and Kosygin have each visited Morocco (in April 1969 and October 1971) to be received with characteristic Moroccan hospitality.

But while the Moroccans may regale their Russian guests with folk dancing from the four corners of the kingdom, it is reasonable to suppose that King Hassan's enjoyment of the golf course and the liberalism of the Moroccan economy provide a readier and more natural connection with the government of the United States. The Moroccan-American relationship was constructed on a firm footing. In the years following Independence, diplomatic activity between the two countries was concerned primarily with arrangements for United States aid to Morocco and with the dismantling of the Strategic Air Command bases established in Morocco by agreement with the French government. The two series of negotiations proceeded independently; the provision of aid perhaps moderating the Moroccan position with regard to bases but never removing it from the agenda. Over the first decade of independence Morocco was the beneficiary of most types of United States aid. Public Law 480 made possible the provision of wheat and other foodstuffs. Food provided under Title II of the law was distributed through the Promotion Nationale, in the form of payment in kind. Wheat was also provided under Title I, thus generating local currency, the greater part of which was loaned for public development projects or to private Moroccan investors. The costs of the break with France at Independence were met by support loans, and USAID also made development loans and outright grants, the latter particularly to assist agricultural development. Emergency assistance on a large scale was also provided for the reconstruction of Agadir after the earthquake of 1960. The total amount of aid provided between 1957 and 1963 amounted to some 400 million dollars. As a recipient of aid, Morocco came under strong pressure from the United States to sever its trading links with China and Cuba; but aid never came to be the centre of political dispute as it did in relations between the United States and Nasser's Egypt.

Meanwhile, Moroccan pressure for the dismantling of United States bases was kept up. While there might have been some wish to follow the Libyan example of receiving rent for the bases, the government could not maintain its prestige internationally if it did so, while the political parties within Morocco readily competed with each other in expressions of nationalism. But, pressing as Moroccan demands were, the negotiations continued until the United States government could foresee the diminished need for the bases, and when President Eisenhower visited Rabat in December 1959, the communiqué announced that the bases would be evacuated by 1963. The United States bore the cost of the transformation of the bases to Moroccan use, and continued to maintain an important military mission at Kenitra.

Since that time, Moroccan relations with the United States have followed a smooth course. The United States has been a major supplier of investment funds and Morocco is a country where United States investors and businessmen are encouraged to see a reasonably attractive future, although imports from the United States amount to only 12·5 per cent of total imports, while exports to the United States are minimal. But the United States is mainly interested in the survival or continuity of stable friendly government in an area of potential strategic importance. The United States government would, therefore, be ready to use its own diplomatic and economic resources, and work through such international institutions as the World Bank in an endeavour to achieve that end. It did not follow that King Hassan was universally regarded, within the American administration, as the ideal ruler to achieve this result. Inevitably, it was suggested that the *coups* attempted against the king owed something to the United States, without any concrete evidence being brought forward.

Meanwhile, Morocco's older relationships retain their historic continuity. France remains the closest economic partner with deep cultural attachments and is the main provider of human assistance, notably in teachers and technical assistants. With Spain territorial questions remain unsettled.

The penetration of France into Moroccan society is evident in the major areas of the modern sector of Morocco: education, the economy, landownership, and even politics. For the most part the development of the relationship has followed a particularly Moroccan style. As we have seen, there was no sudden departure of French landowners or abrupt nationalization, although the departure of the French and the steep fall in French investment created sharp problems of transition. During the first decade of independence, some 100,000 French men and women stayed in Morocco, engaged in a wide variety of activities. The transfer of their interests to Moroccans came about not through political coercion or sudden panic, but in pursuit of economic gain and following enlightened calculation as to the future—an unusual sequence of events for which the term 'decolonization' might be thought appropriate. The current of thought and feeling which saw great opportunities in colonization—both national and personal—was reversed, and so landowners sold their lands to Moroccans while a younger generation of Frenchmen decided that profitable and agreeable careers were to be found in the metropolis rather than in a colony.

There have thus been two periods when relations between France and Morocco have been at a low ebb: the years immediately following Independence, and the period following the assassination of Ben Barka, which was ended by the visit of Maurice Schumann to Morocco in 1972. In spite of these interruptions, relations with France have remained close.

The Spanish relationship is of a different colour. Moreover, the struggle for independence was conducted against the French, the Spanish government appearing to observe a benevolent neutrality and readily making an agreement, parallel to the French, according Morocco full independence. Thereafter Spain pursued consistently its policy of friendship towards the Arab world. As a result, an undertone of cordiality has been maintained in the relationship between the two countries, a factor which was to be of major importance in the Moroccan pursuit of its claims to the Sahara.

None the less, Spain remained in possession of Ceuta and Melilla (and the islands off the Rifian coast) together with the Saharan possessions of Ifni, Tarfaya, and the area to the south, Seguiet el-Hamra and Rio de Oro. The legal status of these territories, and their importance to Spain, varied from one to the other. On the Moroccan side, the nationalist movement in the Spanish zone had asserted that the achievement of independence would not affect the status of the garrison towns *(presidios)*; but when independence was achieved, the Moroccan government argued that the Spanish title to Ifni, based on the treaty of 1860, was invalidated by the independence agreement with Morocco; the Moroccan nationalists turned their attention to the 'integrity' of Moroccan territory once the main object of independence had been secured; at a time when the army of liberation in the Sahara, outside the control of the Moroccan government, raided Spanish posts. Meanwhile, the importance of the territories was closely related to fishing rights; as, subsequently, the importance of Seguiet el-Hamra was enhanced by the exploitation of phosphates.

The area of contention which fell most readily before the desire of Spain and Morocco to maintain friendly relations, was that of Tarfaya, a territory of 25,600 square kilometres which Spain controlled under the treaty of 1912. The Spanish government did not resist the Moroccan contention that the 1912 treaty had been superseded by the independence agreement and Tarfaya became part of Morocco under the agreement of Cintra in April 1958. However, the cession of Tarfaya made more striking the anomaly of Ifni as a Spanish enclave in Moroccan territory, the more so since Spanish control was increasingly limited to the town of Sidi Ifni itself.

However, the question of Ifni was complicated by the readiness of Allal al-Fassi and the Istiqlal party to link together *terra irredenta*, particularly Ifni and the Mediterranean *presidios*, as well as by the government's extension of its territorial waters from six to twelve miles. But the tension thus generated, together with incidents arising from the continued activities of free-ranging groups of armed Moroccans, did not destroy the amicable conversation which was possible between the two countries: notably, King Hassan and General Franco were able to go hunting together in the Siera Morena. In 1966 Morocco's diplomatic representation at Madrid was put under the direction of General Ameziane, who had been trained at the Toledo military academy, had fought with Franco's army at the Alcazar, Madrid, and the Ebro, and served as commander of the Ceuta region and as military governor, first of Galicia, and then of the Canary Islands.

Moreover, the Spanish government was ready to pursue a course of decolonization, given, on the one hand, that it attributed an exceptional status to Ceuta and Melilla and, on the other, that it sought to strengthen its claim to the retrocession of Gibraltar by Britain. Thus, in December 1967, the Spanish delegation voted at the United Nations in support of a resolution calling for the decolonization of Ifni and the southern Sahara, and gave independence to Spanish Guinea in October 1968. Consistently with this approach the Spanish government, after secret negotiations with the Moroccans, reached agreement on the cession of Ifni, in January 1969, which was accompanied by a separate agreement permitting Spanish ships to fish in Moroccan waters (a concession which was attacked by the Istiqlal as detracting from the principle of Moroccan sovereignty over Ifni, as well as for its practical effect on Moroccan fishing). A corresponding expression of nationalist feeling in Spain took the form of an unprecedented vote of sixty-six members of the Cortes against the agreement, with twenty abstentions.

During this time the Moroccan government had tried unsuccessfully to oppose the creation of the state of Mauritania. But the agreement with Spain over Ifni was accompanied by a growing relationship between Mauritania and Morocco which led to the formal exchange of diplomatic representatives in 1970. This placed in a different perspective the Moroccan claim to the Spanish Sahara; since Morocco had recognized a rival claimant to the allegiance of the tribes who sustained themselves in the part of the Sahara under Spanish rule.

Meanwhile, the question of the Spanish Sahara had changed further by the discovery, in 1963, of a massive reserve of phosphates which the Spanish government hastened to develop through the intermediary of a public corporation (renamed in 1969 Fosfatos de Bu Craa) with the participation of foreign capital. The deposit proved to be a great prize—reserves of good quality estimated at 10,000 tons, of which an important part was close enough to the sea at Al-Aioun for Krupps to build a continuous belt for its transport there. Further south, iron ore has been located in the Rio de Oro—a resource of lesser, though none the less considerable, importance.

The importance of the reserves of phosphates may have contributed to the opening, in 1974, of an intensive phase in Moroccan claims on the Sahara. But the claims were not new, having been given formal expression by Mohammed V in a speech at M'Hamid, in southern Morocco, in 1958. The Moroccan claim was essentially historical, resting on the argument that the people of the Sahara had recognized the spiritual and temporal authority of the sultan, that Moroccan sultans had appointed caïds in the region and collected taxes. The Spanish colonization, it was argued, had thus occupied a territory inhabited by people owing allegiance to the sultan. Spain should now withdraw, since imperial rule was no longer legitimate, and the territory should become part of the Moroccan state.

The Spanish government resisted the Moroccan claim, denying that the Sahara had ever been under Moroccan sovereignty and bringing memoirs which Saharan chiefs had presented to the United Nations in support of its claims. It also declared its intention of developing the phosphates, a Spanish discovery for which Spain bore the cost, for the benefit of the local population in association with Spain.

In the 1960s the Saharan question was seen primarily as one of decolonization. In December 1965 the General Assembly of the UN passed the first of a series of resolutions concerning the Sahara. It called on the Spanish government to undertake immediate action to liberate Ifni and the Spanish Sahara from colonial domination. A further resolution adopted in 1969 required Spain to consult with Morocco and Mauritania in order to prepare the way towards a referendum. In reply the Spanish government insisted that its sole concern was the interests of the people of the Sahara, whose future was a matter for themselves and the Spanish government to determine.

As long as the issue was posed in this way the countries bordering on the Sahara—Morocco, Mauritania, and Algeria—could subordinate their separate interests in a common front against Spain. Mauritania naturally resisted the Moroccan claim to the whole of the Sahara, and was mindful of the decade which had passed before its independent status was recognized by Morocco. The Algerian government had no territorial claims of its own; but it had no wish to see its Saharan frontier with Morocco called into question, with a possible renewal of the war of 1963, and was anxious about the extension of Moroccan territory to the south. Three meetings took place between Moukhtar Ould Daddah, Boumediene, and King Hassan—at Nouadhibou

(September 1970), Nouakchott (May 1973), and Agadir (July 1973) —in an attempt to define a common position. But while there was no apparent problem in framing a final communiqué in each case, no effective agreement seems to have been reached.

In the summer of 1974 the policy of the Spanish government changed and it announced, in August, that it would organize a referendum 'under the auspices and guarantees of the United Nations' early in 1975. To regain the initiative King Hassan announced, in a press conference the following month, that he would request the United Nations to take the question of the Sahara to the International Court of Justice. A favourable decision, from the Moroccan point of view, would confirm the fact of the allegiance of the Saharans to the Moroccan sultan before the arrival of the Spaniards. The issue would then be narrowed to the rival claims of Spain and Morocco, and that of Morocco would obviously prevail.

Hassan's new move regained the advantage in diplomacy and was of great value in domestic politics. Moroccan claims to the Sahara received the warm support of all political parties. Before the press conference took place Hassan had despatched the leaders of the Istiqlal, the Rabat branch of the UNFP, and the former communist leader Ali Yata to urge the Moroccan case in foreign capitals. The army, so recently purged of its dissidents, was deployed on the southern frontier in support of the national cause.

On the other hand the intensification of the crisis sharpened the resistance of Morocco's rivals. The foreign minister of Mauritania, Ould Mouknass, proclaimed both the right of the Sahara population to self-determination and the rightful sovereignty of Mauritania, urging: 'Mauritania considers the Spanish Sahara as an integral part of its national territory . . . but it is for the populations concerned to express their self-determination in the spirit of the United Nations.' The Algerian government confirmed that it had no territorial claim on the region, and reaffirmed its attachment to the just cause of the liberation of Arab land under Spanish domination—an ambiguous statement which was correctly judged to stop short of support for Morocco.

The domestic situation in Morocco was one which Hassan could manage to great advantage. The demands of the political parties for a return to constitutional government could now be met with promises for the future, coupled with the rewards which came from participating in the national cause. Alone among the opposition leaders Abdullah Ibrahim resisted the blandishments of the government; but this did not detract from the cause since the Casablanca UNFP adopted a report welcoming 'the return of the government to our thesis concerning the towns and territories under Spanish domination'.

Moroccan politicians could thus be relied on to state and overstate

Moroccan claims while Hassan engaged in quiet diplomacy. It was
Ali Yata who denounced the 'dangerous ambiguity' of the Algerian
position (and was allowed to re-establish his party). *Le Matin* published
a map 'as documentary evidence, not as a demand' showing historic
Morocco in comparison with the present borders—making the point
that Tindouf and Reggane (quite apart from Mauritania and the
whole of the Spanish Sahara) were within Morocco's historic frontiers.
But Hassan took advantage of the Rabat Arab summit conference in
October 1974 to reach a secret agreement (the existence of which became known the following July) with Mauritania for the partition of
the Sahara—Seguiet el-Hamra going to Morocco and Rio de Oro to
Mauritania—and the joint exploitation of the phosphates.

Meanwhile the Saharan people organized themselves into political
factions. They sought the support of the interested powers, just as those
governments sought their allegiance. The Algerian government had
given hospitality, since 1973, to the Taureg Mouvement Révolutionnaire des Hommes Bleus (Morehob) but in the spring of 1975 Morehob
returned its allegiance to Morocco. The Moroccan government sponsored a Liberation and Unity Front (FLU) which held its first congress
in Agadir in September 1975. A Sahrawi National Union Party
(PUNS) accepted the patronage of Spain, although two of its leaders
defected to Morocco in May 1975. In Mauritania a movement was
organized calling itself the Front for the Liberation of the Seguiet
el-Hamra and the Rio de Oro, or Polisario. Early in 1975 it transferred
to Algeria where the government, having abandoned Morehob,
readily extended its support and patronage.

Hassan's success on the diplomatic front proved short-lived. In
October 1975 the International Court of Justice delivered its advisory
opinion. It recognized the Moroccan claim in part, for it accepted that
legal ties of allegiance existed between the Sahara and the Kingdom of
Morocco before the Spanish colonization; but similar ties also existed
with the 'Mauritanian entity', and in neither case did these ties, in the
opinion of the Court, support a claim to territorial sovereignty or override the principle of self-determination as enunciated by the United
Nations.

The Moroccan government was once again at a disadvantage. In
addition to its historic claims to the Sahara, its opposition to self-
determination was based on the assertion that any expression of option
would be manipulated by Spain, organizing and rewarding the nomadic
population to secure the desired result. But such an argument, directed
against the United Nations and the Court, did not carry conviction.
On the other hand the Spanish government was obviously in a weak
position. General Franco was ill (he died on 20 November 1975) and
no Spanish government would prejudice the possibility of a smooth
succession for the sake of the Sahara. Skilfully Hassan provided an

outlet for Moroccan emotion by organizing a 'green march' (in support of Islam) by civilians into the Sahara. A flurry of excitement surrounded the possibility of an armed clash as the Moroccan army infiltrated across the frontier. But Hassan orchestrated nationalist pressure for the return of Ceuta and Melilla and for the occupation of the Sahara, while negotiations were carried on in Madrid. On 14 November a tripartite arrangement was agreed whereby Morocco and Mauritania would take over administration of the Sahara, while discussions continued towards the joint exploitation of the Bu Craa phosphates and the rich fishing grounds of the Atlantic coast.

The agreement effectively ceded the Sahara to Morocco and Mauritania, in a manner which Madrid and Rabat hoped would leave the way open for subsequent approval by the United Nations. The Spanish government, in return for its concession, was assured that the status of Ceuta and Melilla would be frozen for the time being, and may possibly have received promises of support in its claims to Gibraltar.

But the proposed settlement met the resistance of an important part of the Saharan population, who had no wish to escape from Spanish rule into Moroccan; and it brought back to life the dormant conflict between Algeria and Morocco. The Polisario now appeared as the best organized and equipped of the Saharan political groups, and it had the active support of the Algerians. Many Saharans crossed the frontier into Algeria, while Polisario set up its headquarters at Mahbès, close to the Algerian frontier. The Algerian army crossed the frontier and a number of clashes with Moroccan troops were reported.

No doubt the Moroccan government hoped that its occupation of the territory (in concert with Mauritania) would pave the way for some form of self-expression from 'the people of the Sahara' which would legitimize the acquisition of territory. The inhabitants of the western Sahara were generally thought to number some 70,000, while there were probably 45,000 mobile tribespeople in Morocco whose nomadic movement south could be arranged to coincide with any poll that might be organized. But in the meantime Polisario established, in Algiers, a Sahrawi Arab Democratic Republic, recognized by a number of African and Asian states. Polisario forces, though scarcely a match for Moroccans in pitched battle, could cause enough damage to halt the production of phosphates.

EDUCATION

Education in Morocco has developed slowly and continues to show serious gaps, attributable in part to a certain laissez-faire attitude on the part of the government. It inherited a French system of education from the protectorate and has not succeeded either in remedying the defects of that system or in adapting it to the needs of its own society.

It has been vigorously attacked by Allal al-Fassi whose Istiqlal party has always pressed for the arabization of education. Before his death al-Fassi took the initiative in founding, under the aegis of the party, a 'school for the sons of the people' to rescue schoolchildren and students who were unsuccessful in the school system. It rapidly attracted some 500 pupils, from primary level to the baccalauréat and was promoted by the Istiqlal as a model for the national Moroccan school based on Moroccan humanism. Traditional education has remained, but cannot be said to flourish or to be intellectually alert. There were some 340 Koranic schools in 1972, with over 300,000 children studying in them. Secondary, traditional education embraced nearly 4,000 pupils and there were 748 engaged in higher education at the Qaraouiyine university.

The 'modern' educational system was characterized by a relatively low percentage of children and young people in school; a particularly small proportion of girls receiving education; dependence on France for teachers, and a low level of technical education. In 1971 there were 1·1 million pupils in state primary education and a further 15,000 in schools maintained by the French cultural and university mission (MUCF) of whom over half were French. There were in addition about 5,000 in private confessional schools and another 5,000 in the schools of Ittihad-Maroc—the successor of the Alliance Israelite which, under the protectorate, had been accorded the right to open schools for Jewish children. In 1971–2 there were approximately 300,000 pupils in secondary education, and of these less than one-third were girls. The MUCF provided a proportionately larger contribution to secondary education with 12,000 pupils—again half of them being French.

At primary level the teaching staff was entirely Moroccan, except for the 500 French teachers under the MUCF. At secondary level there were some 7,000 French teachers out of a total of 13,300, in addition to the 600 under the MCF. The French contribution to the remuneration of French teachers was 18 million francs in 1966 and rose to 28 million in 1971. It followed that while some schools used Arabic for instruction others were bilingual or entirely French. The general system of education continued to be based on a French model and produced its crop of unfortunates who failed to reach the standard necessary to progress from one year to the next. As in Tunisia and Algeria there were in consequence many who dropped out and many who were condemned to repeating the year's work in the hope of passing.

University education continued to be dominated by the faculties of law and letters, followed by medicine. In 1970 there were approximately 2,000 students studying law in French, and the same number in Arabic; 1,100 studying in French in the faculties of letters of Rabat, Fez, and Tetuan and a further 2,700 in Arabic. There were 1,163 medical students, but only 500 in the faculty of science. The numbers of students in higher technical schools (such as the National Agriculture School or the Hassan II Institute of Agronomy) was counted in hundreds. In 1971 390 students graduated from the faculty of law and 17 from the National School of agriculture.

The universities and to a lesser extent secondary schools have been subject to a continual malaise, although student disturbances have greatly diminished since the crisis years of 1971–2. As we have seen, student organizations have had clear political alignments. But without doubt the malaise is attributable to a sense of frustration and anxiety about the future, as students face a world where opportunities for employment are few in number and little related to their education.

VI
Tunisia

GEOGRAPHY AND POPULATION
Geography

No natural barrier separates Tunisia from Algeria. Its principal mountain ranges are a continuation of those which dominate the geographical structure of Morocco and Algeria. The maritime Atlas continues along the north coast, from the frontier (the mountains of Khrumerie rising to 1100 metres) to the region of Bizerte. Along the mountainous coastal section only one port, Tabarka, a former Genoese settlement, has found a lodgement. For the most part the elevation of this range is less than 800 metres; but it receives the highest rainfall in the country, averaging in places no less than 1,000 millimetres. To the south of this coastal range lies the plain of Béja and the valley through which flows Tunisia's only perennial watercourse, the Medjerda river. The Medjerda and its principal tributary the Mellègue both rise in Algeria and have their outlet in the Gulf of Tunis. The southern edge of this valley is formed by the continuation of the Saharan Atlas, here known as the *Dorsale tunisienne*. This is the most massive chain of mountains in the country, running north–east from the region of Kasserine to Cap Bon. Its highest peaks rise to 1,620 metres and it forms a barrier between the north and the south of the country. It prevents rain-bearing clouds reaching the south in winter, and it provides a barrier against the sirocco in the summer.

A second branch of the Saharan Atlas runs west–east in the region of Gafsa, stopping about 70 kilometres from the coast. This range is rich in phosphates. Finally, a smaller chain of mountains, known as the Matmata mountains or the Jabal Dahar runs north–south, between the salt depression of the Chott el-Fedjadj and the Libyan frontier. Both of these ranges provide further protection from the desert. The Jabal Dahar protects the Gulf of Gabès and the island of Jerba. The area between the Dorsal and the southern Atlas forms a second water basin. However, the water in this basin is often damaging and rarely of any great use. Its main course is the Zouroud, which is usually dry but on occasion receives torrential rainfall, collecting it from its origin in eastern Algeria and from a tributary system stemming principally from the Dorsal. It ends in the lake of Kalbia, between Kairouan and

Hammamet. With the exception of the Nebhana tributary this system is not suitable for damming; the lake is subject to rapid evaporation and so is brakish; because it is low lying it floods easily and in severe cases (as in October 1969) overflows to the sea north of Sousse, causing much damage. The roads to Kairouan are sometimes difficult to pass because of drifting sand; at other times the city is surrounded by water.

The sharpest contrast in the country as a whole is, therefore, between the north—20 per cent of the total land area, with average rainfall in excess of 400mm. on the most fertile land—and the southern 60 per cent of the land area which, apart from the coastal areas and the irrigated areas of Gabès and the Chott Djerid (famous for their dates), is desert or semi-desert. The north produces 70 per cent of the country's cereals, nearly all the citrus and grapes, two-thirds of all vegetables and milk.

In the centre lies the steppe region of the country, the interior, bounded by the two branches of the Saharan Atlas, the Algerian frontier, and the coastal region to the east. Average rainfall in the steppe country is about 200mm. and is very irregular (the steppe gives way to the coastal areas to the north and east where average rainfall rises to 400mm.). In the past the region has been used for grazing sheep, goats, and camels, and the wild esparto grass has been harvested. Cereals have been sown, but harvested only when the climate has been favourable—perhaps one year in five. One of the most important agricultural developments since Independence has been the planting of crop trees—olives, almonds, and apricots—at the expense of cereals and grazing—although drought and the failure of agricultural cooperatives (see below, pp. 383–5) have severely limited the success of this development.

A second geographical division in the country, no less important than that between north and south, is between the ribbon of coast, called the Sahel, and the interior. The long, flat and smiling coast into which the steppes and mountains descend connects Bizerte in the north with Zarzis in the south. By it the country has, from time immemorial, been laid open to influences coming from the east and from Europe. To a greater extent than its neighbours to the west its political personality has been determined by these influences. Although the hinterland of mountains and steppes resembles the rest of the Maghreb, in its physical geography it is detached from Algeria and made tributary to the Sahel by political and economic influences which the latter exerts through its dense population and many cities.

The Sahel, spread along the whole east coast, is sometimes flat and sometimes undulating: it is widest opposite Tunis, Cap Bon, Sousse, and Sfax. The sandy coast forms large bays which at intervals are prolonged by lagoons as at Bizerte and Tunis. The climate is mild and regular; from north to south the rainfall varies from 500 to 200mm.

This area is famous for the cultivation of the olive, particularly in the stretch between Sousse and Sfax to which the term Sahel more particularly applies. Farther north, around Tunis and Bizerte and on Cap Bon, the cultivation of vines and fruit trees, principally citrus, is combined with market-gardening and the growing of cereals and fodder to provide a living for a considerable European colony. It is a zone of small holdings as well as of ancient urban settlement, and innumerable big villages lurk among the gardens and olive orchards. Larger towns, famous in history, line the coast—Tunis, Sousse, Monastir, Mahdiya, Sfax and, finally, Gabès, off which lies the island of Jerba.

The total surface area of Tunisia is about 16·3 million hectares, of which 9 million are considered productive of vegetation—including mountain, forest, and semi-desert zones. The cultivation area is about 5·6 million hectares, or 35 per cent of the total surface area. Under the protectorate the cultivated area was substantially increased, at the expense of forest and grazing land. But Tunisia may now be at the limit of aggregate land cultivation and development must come from different utilization rather than an extension of the area under cultivation.

Cultivation is limited by the supply of water as well as by the availability of land. In the centre and south rainfall is insufficient, extremely variable from one year to the next and often occurs in a single brief period when at best it is useless and at worst causes soil erosion and other damage. Thus while the long term average rainfall for Sousse is 316mm., it received 760mm. in 1958–9 and only 161mm. in 1960–1; half of the exceptional rainfall of 1958–9 fell within twenty-four hours early in April, causing much damage and loss of life. The seasonal variation in rainfall is much greater in the centre and south than in the north; in these regions too the high rate of evaporation creates problems of salinity. The plan for 1973–6 recognized that much remained to be done to make effective use of irrigation channels already built; the plan for 1977–80 is likely to include further irrigation and canalization on an ambitious scale. Urbanization and the development of the tourist industry has placed an additional burden on the total water supply of the country. The water table in the Cap Bon, on which the region depends for the irrigation of citrus and vegetables, has fallen alarmingly in recent years.

In Tunisia, as elsewhere, French colonization was attracted naturally to the richer agricultural areas, so that disparities between natural geographic regions were increased. Fertile land with good rainfall was improved agriculturally; marginal land was brought into use by modern methods—notably in the extension of the olive growing area to the south and in dry-farming wheat. The Tunisian government has always declared it to be one of its objectives to redress the balance and to bring prosperity to the south. This ambition has become more practicable as a result of the development of oil and gas in Tunisia and across the frontier in Algeria. Gabès, Gafsa, and Zarzis are centres of industrial development, while Jerba is an important part of the tourist industry.

Population

The Tunisians are an old-established people, probably in essence the same Berber and Carthaginian population as inhabited the country in the time of the Romans. This population was arabized as the result of the Arab invasions of the seventh and subsequent centuries, while the Arab invaders themselves were eventually fused into the general mass. There must also be an appreciable intermixture of Europeans of Mediterranean origin, who became Muslims after entering Tunisia individually, or who arrived as refugees from Muslim Sicily and Spain. By the fusion of all these elements a distinct state came into being during the rule of the Hafsid dynasty from the thirteenth to the sixteenth centuries, though it was only under subsequent Turkish rule that Tunisia acquired her present frontiers. The continuity of settlement, the long tradition of sedentary and urban life, and the response to western and northern invasions have given Tunisia its distinctive national identity.

Historically, the Jewish minority in Tunisia has played an important role. The Jewish community came to Tunisia in a series of emigrations, the earliest, it is supposed, at the time of the first diaspora, in the sixth century B.C. Some Berbers were converted to Judaism in Roman times and in the eleventh century there was an influx of Jewish refugees from Muslim and Christian Spain. The renowned al-Kahina, some claim, was a Jewess. Kairouan nurtured an important centre of Jewish medicine and scholarship under the Hafsids.

The protectorate witnessed two changes in the population of the country. The first was the immigration of Italians, Maltese, and French —the French being, at first, in the minority among the Europeans. Other North Africans also entered the country from Algeria, Morocco, and Libya as miners, watchkeepers, or in pursuit of their traditional crafts. At the same time, the Muslim (and Jewish) population began to grow rapidly as a result of a lower death rate. Epidemics of cholera and plague and insect pests, such as locusts, disappeared. The high birth rate continued, sustained by Muslim beliefs, a natural reaction to high mortality, and pride in numbers of children. The hygienic improvements which kept a high proportion of children alive did not, however, serve to feed or house them. A survey of 1937 showed that 67 per cent of the population had less than an adequate calorie intake.

After Independence (1956), the population changed in accordance with the general pattern of the Maghreb, and, indeed, of many developing countries. It has become more homogeneous, has continued to increase rapidly, and has concentrated in the towns, while retaining the traditional distribution over the country as a whole.

There was no mass exodus of the European population as in Algeria. But at Independence civil servants were transferred, workers returned to France, and eventually farmers sold their land or saw it taken over by the state. Some 42,000 Europeans, it is estimated, remained in Tunisia in 1968, about half of them long-term residents. The Jewish community had never been persecuted by anti-Semitism, but some emigrated to Israel after Independence. Many more saw their future to lie in France rather than Israel and an important exodus occurred after the Suez war of 1956. The 1967 Middle East war provoked a rare, violent outburst against Jews (as against the British and Americans), especially in Tunis—the synagogue was attacked, but so were the TWA offices, while a fire was started in the British Embassy. A further exodus to France and to Israel occurred as a result. Only a few thousand Jews (of the 58,000 in 1956) remain in Tunisia. The *hara*, or Jewish quarter of Tunis, has disappeared and made way for new buildings and the distinctive community at Houmt Souk on Jerba is not marked by its youthfulness.

The population has continued to increase since Independence as it did under the protectorate. The death rate continued to fall. The scourges of smallpox, typhus and typhoid, and malaria had been defeated under the protectorate; tuberculosis was now defeated too and there was a decline in infant mortality. The birth rate has been maintained—one of the most active birth control programmes in the third world having relatively little effect—with the result that the net reproductive rate is of the order of 2·37 per 1,000. A high proportion of the population is young—54·7 per cent under twenty in 1966.

The process of urbanizing began under the protectorate, as a result of the pressure on land and the general attractiveness of the towns (often *faute de mieux*), even when accommodation was only to be found in *bidonvilles*. However, the growth of towns has accentuated rather than changed the existing urban pattern, and there has been no phenomenon comparable to the growth of Casablanca. The dominance of Tunis has been enhanced. The population of Greater Tunis increased from 440,000 to 667,000 between 1946 and 1966 in spite of the European exodus. The three northern governorates of Tunis, Bizerte, and Nabeul contain 32 per cent of the population and produce 50 per cent of the national wealth on only 6 per cent of the land area. Economic development, including tourism, has also increased the population of the Sahel region, Mahdiya and Monastir standing out with exceptional increases over the decade 1956-66 of 47 per cent and 61 per cent respectively, while the policy of regional development has had its most marked effect in the 33 per cent growth of Gabès and Gafsa over the same decade.

HISTORY AND POLITICS

From Antiquity till the French Occupation

The history of Tunisia is closely bound up with that of North Africa as a whole, that is to say with the destiny of the Berbers who were the earliest-known inhabitants of the country, apart from the prehistoric peoples who have left traces of themselves in the settlements of Gafsa. It was mainly through Tunisia that other races penetrated into North West Africa and in Tunisia many decisive battles were fought. Though an integral part of Barbary, Tunisia has her own individuality and forms a distinct entity.

In antiquity, Carthage was the capital city for thirteen centuries under the Phoenicians, the Carthaginians, the Romans, the Vandals, and the Byzantines. Throughout this period it owed its prosperity and fame principally to the Carthaginians and the Romans. From time to time, however, the native, Berber, population asserted their independence and succeeded in forming ephemeral kingdoms, such as those of Massinissa, Jugurtha, and Juba.

Though Phoenician Carthage has completely perished, a number of grandiose ruins have survived from the period of Roman rule, notably the Colosseum at al-Djem, capable of holding 60,000 spectators; the exquisite temples of the Roman watering-place of Dougga, and the unrivalled collection of mosaics in the Bardo Museum. Most sites, in particular Carthage, have been used as a quarry by subsequent builders; and Roman columns and marbles are to be found built into the mosques of Kairouan, Tunis, and Córdoba.

The thirteen centuries of Arab rule resulted in the country becoming Muslim in religion and Arab in language and sentiment. Berber is now spoken only by some of the inhabitants of the island of Jerba, in the Matmata, and near Gafsa, while Christianity as an indigenous religion has disappeared for many centuries. Tunisian independence has nevertheless constantly been asserted—first in the resistance of the legendary Berber heroine, al-Kahina, against the Arab invaders and then by the formation of independent dynasties of Arab culture. The first of these was the Aghlabids, who made their capital in Kairouan and who successfully undertook the conquest of Sicily. After them the Fatimids, heretical Muslims, made their capital in Mahdiya, later conquering Egypt and establishing a Shia Caliphate in Cairo. During their rule they were faced by the formidable rising of another propagandist of local heresy, Abu Yazid, 'the man with the donkey'; he was, however, finally defeated.

In the middle of the eleventh century an Egyptian Fatimid Caliph retaliated on the now rebellious Tunisians by letting loose on them two Arab tribes, the Beni Hilal and the Beni Sulaim, brigand beduin, described two centuries later by the great Tunisian Arab historian Ibn

Khaldun as 'an army of locusts'. These ravaged first Tunisia and then the rest of the Maghreb, often as allies of the local dynasties. In the twelfth century the Normans, having dispossessed the Arab government of Sicily, established a short-lived outpost on the coast of the Sahel; while the Almohads, a Moroccan dynasty of arabized Berbers, made themselves masters of the interior.

In the thirteenth century the Hafsids, a dynasty established by a rebel Almohad governor, founded a Tunisian kingdom over which they ruled for two centuries. During this period Tunis first began to benefit from the arrival of refugees from Muslim Spain; they formed an intellectual and social élite and their skill as artisans contributed greatly to the prosperity of the capital. In 1270 St. Louis of France died on the hill at Carthage during his abortive crusade against the Hafsid rulers.

In general, the Hafsid kingdom seems to have had a more specifically Tunisian character than its predecessors and may be thought of as foreshadowing the Tunisian state of today, though the dynasty, and with it the independence of Tunisia, collapsed at the end of the fifteenth century under simultaneous blows from the Spaniards and the Ottoman Turks. When Charles V was unable to maintain the base which he had acquired in Tunis, Ottoman domination was extended as far as the Moroccan frontier.

Under the Ottoman government, Ifriqiya was divided into three *ojaks* or 'regencies'—Tripoli, Tunis, and Algiers; and it is from that time that the present frontiers of these three territories became more or less definite. Turkish rule was that of a military caste which resided in the country and administered it in a rudimentary fashion, enjoying a large measure of autonomy with regard to Constantinople. The Husainid dynasty which reigned until 1957, when Tunisia was declared a republic, was founded by a Turkish agha of the janissaries, of Cretan origin, who made himself Bey in 1705. In spite of exercising absolute power within Tunisia, the country was still known as the regency till the end of the protectorate. In 1848, however, a Tunisian mission which was sent to Queen Victoria received strict instructions from the Tunisian government that it was on no account to allow any interposition on the part of the Turkish ambassador in London.[1] If such an eventuality looked like becoming inevitable, the mission was to avoid it by returning to Tunis and leave its task unfulfilled. The beylical administration continued the Turkish politico-military framework of

---

[1] By *firman* of 25 October 1871 the sultan laid down the conditions of the suzerainty of the Sublime Porte and renounced the former tribute. According to the *firman*, the Bey received the investiture of Constantinople; he must not make war, conclude peace, or cede territory without the authorization of the sultan. He could negotiate with foreigners only on internal affairs. He must coin money in the name of the sultan and put his troops at the disposal of the Sublime Porte in case of war. Internally the Bey's authority was absolute (*Almanach de Gotha*, 1881).

the state. Efforts by Tunisian liberals secured the issue of a constitution in 1856, the first of its kind in an Arab country. Though the experiment proved abortive, it is commemorated in the name Destour, or 'Constitution', in the title assumed by subsequent nationalist parties.

Certain facts stand out from this long history.

During the 2,500 years of her history Tunisia has twice been in the sphere of Semitic civilization. Once was under the Phoenicians and the Carthaginians, people who had been living in the Mediterranean basin for as long as we have knowledge of them, and once under the Arabs, people who only reached the Mediterranean from their previous desert environment a few years before they arrived in North Africa. Tunisia has also twice been in the sphere of western Mediterranean civilization, first under the Romans and then under the French. These Semitic and European influences have mingled, partly in opposition to one another, partly in fusion, within Tunisia herself. Such economic or other advantages as foreign rule may have been able to offer have never put an end to movements for independence.

Tunisia has always been a country of cities—Berber settlements, Phoenician colonies, Roman municipalities, Arab cities around their mosques. These cities have always been subordinate to the capital, to a greater extent than in the rest of the Maghreb. The individuality of Tunisia is largely the product of the city of Tunis which has given its name to the country as a whole.

Modernization and the French Protectorate

By the nineteenth century the economy was static or declining, and it was certainly declining rapidly in relation to Europe. The trade of the seaports, especially Tunis, was largely the concern of Jews and foreigners who enjoyed the protection of their consuls under capitulation treaties signed originally with the Ottoman government. Privateering disappeared, and so did the commerce associated with it. Traditional agriculture and crafts provided for exports of woollen covers, olive oil, lemons, wheat, and Moroccan leather, as well as dates, hides, wax, and soap; a notable product was the *chechia* or skull cap, made in Tunis and dyed red with the waters of Zaghouan.

This static economy and society was influenced by the ideas and forces which spread along and across the Mediterranean. From Europe came money, and the competition of European nationalism. The development of banking permitted the emergence of a group of financiers capable of mobilizing money and lending it outside Europe at high rates of interest, on terms which ensured their own reward whether or not interest or capital payments were ever made. At the same time, consuls and religious leaders came to play a new role as representatives of vigorous European nation states in competition with each other for the maintenance or extension of their regional influence and their status as great powers.

In response Tunisians sought to modernize their own society, the more so since those who governed the country belonged to the Mamluk class and were familiar with the series of reforms, the Tanzimat, begun in Turkey in 1826. Not all modernizing energies were well directed. Ahmed Bey, who ruled from 1837 to 1855, was inordinately impressed by the armies of France and Egypt; he persuaded the French to send a military mission and constructed a vast, if ephemeral, army, supplied by a textile factory and leather works created for the purpose. A sad contingent of Tunisian troops was sent to Constantinople during the Crimean war (to be ravaged by illness). The ruins of Ahmed Bey's abortive imitation Versailles still stand at Mohammedia.

The most outstanding of the modernizers was Khair al-Din, a Circassian Mamluk, educated in French as well as Arabic, who spent some years in Paris early in his career with Ahmed Bey. He returned to become minister of marine, was ousted from power by Mustapha Khaznadar in 1862, and returned as prime minister from 1873 to 1877. Forced from office again, he went to Constantinople and served for two years as grand vizir to the young Abdul Hamid.

For about twenty years Khair al-Din was the author of, or was closely associated with, the ideas and achievements of modernization. He was one of those who pressed successfully for the introduction of a constitution in 1861, and became president of the council it established. It was this constitution to which the twentieth-century nationalists, the Destour, looked back, but it was swept away in 1864, by an ill-organized revolt of the tribes, a response to increased taxes to meet the interest on loans, and an expression of suspicion of such innovations as the telegraph. He was the author of a political essay, published first in Tunis in 1867 and then in Constantinople and Paris, in which he urged the restoration of the Islamic community to its former strength, by the adaptation of European institutions. As prime minister, he tried to introduce important administrative and agricultural reforms, and founded Sadiki College—a school to train civil servants and members of the liberal professions, with a curriculum which included French and Italian, mathematics and science. Its alumni formed the core of the subsequent nationalist movement and the governing class of Tunisia after the protectorate.

Khair al-Din's efforts were insufficient—and too productive of opposition—to secure the independence of Tunisia. With its static economy, archaic political regime, and acute financial difficulties, it remained an obvious field for European expansion.

France enjoyed advantages over its rivals, Great Britain and Italy, as a result of its proximity and its occupation of Algeria. The British consul at Tunis, Richard Wood, bent every effort to increase British influence and business interests in Tunisia, but his enthusiasm surpassed that of his government and of British industrialists. The European immigration into Tunisia included a large number of Maltese; but they did not rank, in London, as the most important subjects of the Crown, while their religious and cultural needs were the concern of Italian and French clergy and religious orders—Cardinal Lavigerie the most outstanding among them. The unification of Italy posed a new danger to French influence. Tunis was an obvious prize for Italians looking for imperial expansion and Italians emigrated to Tunisia in greater numbers than French. (In 1881 there were 11,000 Italians and 7,000 Maltese, but only 700 French; and only in 1931 did French come to outnumber Italians.) See the table below.

In Paris governments of the Third Republic were thus balanced between conflicting pressures. A small group of men with political and economic interests in Tunisia pressed for action to secure those interests, for themselves and for France. The intrusion of other governments or their nationals was taken as an obvious indication that the French position was vulnerable unless assured by political control. Thus their hand was strengthened by the success of the Italian Rubbatino company, backed by the Italian government, in acquiring the Tunis–Goulette–Marsa railway from a British company after outmanœuvring the French in a legal action and outbidding them in the purchase (paying what was regarded as a grossly inflated price). Further arguments were provided by the fact that the Société Marseillaise was impeded in its purchase of the property of Khair al-Din (including the

Evolution of European Population of Tunisia, 1881–1968

Year	French	Italian	Maltese	Others	Total
1881	708	11,206	7,000	—	—
1886	3,500	16,763	9,000	—	—
1891	9,973	21,016	11,706	—	—
1896	16,207	55,572	10,249	—	—
1901	24,201	71,600	12,056	3,244	111,101
1906	34,610	81,156	10,330	2,799	128,895
1911	46,044	88,082	11,300	3,050	148,476
1921	54,476	84,799	13,520	3,320	156,115
1926	71,020	89,216	8,396	4,649	173,281
1931	91,427	91,178	8,643	4,045	195,293
1936	108,068	94,289	7,279	3,569	213,205
1946	143,977	84,935	6,459	4,178	239,549
1956	180,450	66,909	7,793		255,152
1961 (est.)	65,000	40,000	5,000		110,000
1968 (est.)	25,000	12,000	1,000	4,000	42,000

Source: L. Chevalier, 'Le Problème Démographique Nord-Africain', Institut National d'Etudes Démographiques, *Cahier no. 6*, Paris, 1947, p. 22, and later censuses and estimates.

Enfida estate) by the manœuvres of Mustafa Ben Ismail (whose instrument was a Tunisian Jew of British nationality).

At the same time, French governments were aware that colonial expansion enjoyed only limited support in the Chamber and in public opinion. Nationalist feeling was still directed towards the lost provinces of Alsace-Lorraine, the left was hostile to action in support of financial interests, and no Chamber wanted to vote additional taxes. But in 1881 the argument tipped in favour of military action—the decisive moment being reached when Gambetta, as president of the Chamber, was persuaded that failure to act would threaten France's status as a great power. Renewal of the perennial disorder of the Khrumir tribes on the Algerian frontier provided a timely pretext, and two forces were dispatched, one from Algeria towards Le Kef, the other from France, landing at Bizerte.

The invading forces encountered no serious opposition, and on 12 May 1881 Mohamed al-Sadiq Bey signed the Treaty of Bardo, which appointed the Bey head of state, under French protection, and provided for French control of foreign relations. None the less, considerable uncertainty surrounded this latest extension of French political control. The activities of Théodore Roustan before the expedition were vigorously attacked in the Chamber, and the French government— to allay international anxiety (even though both Britain and Germany had made known their disinterest) as well as to answer domestic critics —announced that its expedition was only temporary.

The speed with which this uncertainty was resolved owed much to Paul Cambon (later ambassador to England), who was appointed minister resident in 1882, and found it imperative to make French control effective if it was to exist at all. He negotiated with the consuls of Italy and Britain to terminate the International Financial Commission, and with both al-Sadiq Bey and his successor, Ali Bey (following al-Sadiq's death in October 1882), to accept the formal establishment of a protectorate under the Marsa Convention of 1883. Finally, he helped persuade the Chamber of Deputies to ratify the Marsa Convention in April 1884, in spite of the reluctance of that body to undertake a guarantee of the Tunisian debt.

The French followed the establishment of the protectorate by the development of an administrative structure through which to govern the country. The Bey continued to be nominal ruler, assisted by the prime minister and his traditional adviser, the 'minister of the pen'. But effective power rested with the resident-general, the commander of the French forces (who acted as minister of war), and the French director-general of finance. The Tunisian system of caïds, khalifas, and shaikhs was retained in local government, but French *controleurs civils* directed their actions. French courts tried cases involving Europeans. Tunisian courts were reorganized and their codes modernized, sharia law remaining for cases of personal status. Representative institutions were created on the basis of chambers of commerce and agriculture and, after the First World War, Tunisians participated in them. Municipal institutions were set up in the principal cities, although only that in Tunis was elected. An institution known as the Grand Conseil, formed of Tunisian and French sections, both elected, was given the function of voting the budget. But, essentially, government remained autocratic—a French administrative hierarchy in whose shelter and behind which the Tunisian traditional institutions enjoyed a quiet senescence.

The French in Tunisia included relatively few substantial landowners or businessmen. The majority were administrators, professional men, shopkeepers, traders, and farmers; while railways and the dockyards and arsenals of Ferryville (now Manzel Bourguiba) and Bizerte employed an important number of workers. After the First World War, Italians, Maltese, and Jews were accorded the possibility of naturalization, and the changing balance in the European population is attributable to this, as well as to limits on Italian immigration and the status of foreigners. The Italian population had a large working class element as well as a considerable number of farmers; the Maltese were engaged in trade and commerce, and to a lesser extent, in farming.

Although the protectorate took over the government of Tunisia and established a European population which was, in the last decade of the protectorate, about 7 per cent of the total, much of Tunisian society remained intact. The same was true of the countryside, where some 16 per cent of the European population lived (representing 2 per cent of the total rural population but owning one-twelfth of the productive area and one-fifth of the cultivated area). None the less, agricultural development was inadequate (and usually of the wrong kind) to sustain the increase in the Tunisian population which, through improvements in health and hygiene, nearly doubled between 1921 and 1936.

The land which passed to the French was, for the most part, taken from the public domain, from large estates—*henchirs*—owned by absentee landlords and from *habous* lands. The proportion of tribally owned land was much smaller than in Algeria and, being in the south, was comparatively unattractive. The protectorate passed legislation which made possible the acquisition of land and registration of ownership, which thereupon conferred property rights similar to those in Europe. The most important measure was the Torrens Act (patterned on Australian legislation) of 1885. Further legislation first made possible the lease of 'inalienable' lands in perpetuity, and then by means of a legal fiction, legalized their purchase.

French and other European settlers had begun acquiring land before the establishment of the protectorate; they were led by financial companies—as in the example of the Enfida estates. Legislation not only guaranteed the new owners of property but encouraged French settlers as against speculators, many of whom were Italian. The hinterland of Sfax—the *terres sialines*—was made available for purchase at a price of 10 francs per hectare. Previously, the area had included *habous* land and land belonging to the Beylicate, but was generally neglected except by the nomadic tribes, notably the Metellit, who grazed across it. It was here that large olive plantations were established and the olive oil industry developed.

The new land legislation affected the conditions of life of Tunisians who had previously enjoyed the use of *melk* or privately owned land in a variety of ways. Sharecroppers gave up the advantages and hardships of the *khammes* system and became day labourers. The customary right to graze, cut wood, and make lime, disappeared.

But private Tunisian small-scale ownership of land remained intact, and Tunisians who were sufficiently well placed could take advantage of the French land legislation. In those areas of the country which had been settled since Phoenician and Roman times—the Medjerda valley and the Tunis area in the north, Cap Bon, and the Sahel—Tunisian *melk* ownership of land remained the basis of agriculture and society, providing the same element of continuity in the villages as was to be found in the towns, descendants of Carthage or Hadrumetum.

French agriculture enjoyed success in the three crops which Tunisia could best sustain: olives, vines, and wheat. In the production of olives, the French achievement was to open up the lands round Sfax, laying out plantations of trees widely spaced and well tended to permit root growth and so take advantage of minimal precipitation. Thus, in 1881, it appears (from inadequate statistics) that there were 8 million olive trees in Tunisia, with the Sahel (Sousse, Monastir) accounting for 4 million. In 1913, there were 11·7 million olive trees, including 2·8 million in the region of Sfax, where previously there were only 380,000. Similarly, the production of olive oil was, in a good year at the beginning of the protectorate, of the order of 200,000 hectolitres and rose to 387,000 by the First World War.

Viniculture was tranformed by French and European settlement. Tunisian grapes were well known and well established. They were now overtaken by wine-grapes, producing by 1913 some 300,000 hectolitres (of which a major part was exported) from 17,800 hectares of vineyards. The vinegrowing areas remained comparatively limited. Viniculture is relatively labour-intensive and was well suited to small properties as well as to larger estates, at the opposite extreme to the vast open olive plantations of the south which are deserted except during the harvest.

Finally, the colonists were successful—although at a cost to be borne by their successors—in growing cereals by dry farming. It was in this endeavour that they benefited most from agricultural research and advice from the government. The colonists cleared scrub land and made more effective use of land on large estates which, before their arrival, had received too little, or uninformed, attention. Initially, cereals were chosen as the major crop partly because there was a shortage of labour. By 1930 there was an excess of available labour because the use of machinery grew as the population increased. But wheat was a good export crop. The variety of soft wheat known as *Florence Aurore* was particularly successful; it had been developed in France, but was not suited to the French climate. In consequence, French farmers grew an increasing proportion of soft wheat, and to some extent their example was followed by Tunisian farmers. In the years preceding the Second World War, wheat thus became the single most important plant crop in terms of the area of land devoted to it (it still accounted for about 60 per cent under annual crop cultivation in 1970), and showed a substantial export surplus. The Second World War cut off French markets, but in any case, French home grown supplies of soft wheat had increased to the point where Tunisian hard wheat became a better export.

The agricultural censuses of 1949 show the total area of productive land including forests and grazing as about 9 million hectares. Until 1915 Tunisia was a net importer of wheat; but in each of the successive five-year periods, from 1916/20 to 1936/40, there was a net export of wheat, most of it going to France, with *Florence Aurore* accounting for 60 per cent of the export. (This surplus subsequently disappeared with the growth in population.)

But the success of a strain of wheat does not create successful social engineering. The cost of French (and modern Tunisian) cereal farming was that land subject to erosion was increasingly brought into production; and the success of French agriculture was attributable to mechanization, not to the employment of labour. Whereas settlers had (in the early twentieth century) resorted to cereal production because of a shortage of labour, by the 1930s their estates became islands of well-managed farming, employing limited labour. As the population increased (the total from 2 million in 1921 to 3·2 million in 1946), young people found no outlet for their labour or their energies. It was of the 1930s that Berque (1967, p. 35) wrote:

> The most provocative symbol of the colonial epoch in the Maghreb is that of the tiled farmhouse, a cheerful dwelling standing amid vineyards. It aroused the most violent, and violently opposed, reactions from Frenchmen and the people of the Maghreb. The fact that it was surrounded by more significant forces matters little; it implied all the rest. Banks, military camps, factories and schools may have played at least as important a part, but none made so deep an impression on everyone's feelings as this French farmstead, this heraldic emblem on African soil.

The young people who grew up in these conditions did not allow themselves to be pushed to the less fertile soil of the poor and mountainous area; instead they overpopulated the towns. This was among the most important problems which the protectorate left to independent Tunisia. But it also left, relatively intact, a bourgeoisie with a continuous tradition from the years preceding the protectorate, and the burgeoning society of the Sahel from which the Neo-Destour would emerge.

Tunisian Reaction to French Rule

Once the French protectorate was established, the French took up the tasks of modernizing the administration and of constructing a minimum physical infrastructure for the country. The reforms to which the Bey was committed by the Treaty of La Marsa were in fact carried out by the French and the administration which they called for was staffed to a preponderant degree by the French. The protectorate also built roads, railways, and ports, developed phosphate mining, and modernized agriculture.

At the same time education was developed and opportunities were made available for study in France, which resulted in the emergence of a small educated class unable to find employment in the government or a career in the liberal professions. This class of young bourgeois was sensitive both to the movement for reform in the Ottoman Empire and to innovating ideas from France. The Egyptian reformer Muhammad Abduh visited Tunis in 1884 and again in 1903. His first visit alerted him to the extent of modernist Islamic thought in Tunis, and on both occasions his presence stimulated further the intellectual activity of those he met (in spite of the charlatanism and ambition which infused his career).

A small number of upper class, educated men who were receptive to reforming ideas from both the Middle East and France followed the lead of Bechir Sfar in forming an educational institution, the Khalduniya, in 1896. Its purpose was to supplement the moribund education of the Zitouna mosque (whose Ulema were strongly opposed to the innovation of the Khalduniya). A decade after its foundation it attracted an attendance of some 150 people at its lectures and counted nearly 5,000 readers in its library.[1] The Khalduniya was followed in December 1905 by the establishment of a further association, the Sadikiya, grouping together former students of Sadiki College, initially under the inspiration and leadership of a young lawyer of Turkish origin, Ali Bach Hamba. The Sadikiya, as well as forming a meeting ground for reformers, gave itself the task of popular education and followed various French examples (including that of Max Sangnier and the *Sillon*) in organizing lectures and seminars.

[1] C. A. Julien, 'Colons français et Jeunes-Tunisiens, 1882–1912', *Revue française d'histoire d'outre-mer*, 1967, liv. 119.

In this atmosphere a speech by Bechir Sfar, on 20 March 1906, gave a new impulse to the growth of reforming, and therefore nationalist, opinion and energy. Sfar held the sinecure post of administrator of the *jamaa des habous* (the archaic 'assembly of mortmain lands'). He began by regretting the policy of the protectorate towards the *habous* and then generalized his demand for the participation of Tunisians in the modernization of Tunisia, in the growth of the economy, and in the development of government and administration.

Still far from numerous, the reformers attracted sufficient attention to be dubbed Young Tunisians (after the Young Turks), a name which they officially adopted. In 1907 they started their own newspaper, *Le Tunisien*. Two years later an Arabic version followed under the direction of Abdel Aziz Taalbi—a distinctive figure in that he was a graduate of the Zitouna (not of Sadiki), although rejected by the religious élite because of his radicalism.

There thus existed, in the early years of the twentieth century, an important group of modernizers, closely unified around the Khalduniya and the Sadikiya, who published their own newspapers. The demands they put forward were for better education, combining French and Arabic cultures, and access for Tunisians to government. They varied in the emphasis they attached to Arabic and to French culture, disputing the efficacy and value of the two languages; but they all drew to some extent on the two cultures. The men who put forward these demands belonged to the bourgeois class of Tunis; they commanded no national support or mass following, and their demands were framed within the limits of the protectorate which they sought to modify but not to overthrow.

In spite of their moderation, they succeeded in alarming the French settlers and French conservatives. When seven Tunisians, including Bechir Sfar, Mohammed Lasram, and Abdeljelil Zaouche, attended the North African Congress at Marseilles in 1908 they undoubtedly provoked as much adverse reaction as they did admiration, and there were few Frenchmen who were attracted by the possibility of incorporating the energies of the Young Tunisians into the development of the protectorate. As a result their positive achievements were few. In 1912 the movement sponsored a boycott of Tunisian tramways in pursuit of equal pay for Tunisian workers and better treatment of Tunisian passengers. By the time the movement could recover from the arrests and dispersion that followed, the First World War had created a new political and intellectual world.

Some 100,000 Tunisians went to the war, either to fight or to work in France. Once outside their familiar environment, their established loyalties were disturbed. The bourgeoisie responded both to the Wilsonian ideals of self-determination and to the nationalist movements of the Middle East, particularly that of Egypt. A group of

Tunisians who had tried to send a delegation to the peace conference at Paris published, in 1921, a political tract entitled *La Tunisie martyre*. It was addressed to a French audience and claimed that the Tunisian state, as it existed before the protectorate, embodied the values to which French political theory attached most importance: the separation of powers and the social contract.

Shaikh Abdel Aziz Taalbi and a small group of friends established themselves in Paris and made contact with members of the French parliament. They began to demand the establishment of a constitution, like that of 1861, in Tunisia and transformed themselves into a Parti Libéral Constitutionnel, the Destour party. The Destourians, as Taalbi's leadership would suggest, were more deeply rooted in Tunisian society than their predecessors, the Young Tunisians. They were more religious and less attracted by secular innovations derived from France, such as the declaration of the rights and duties of man. Expressing the frustrations of the Young Tunisian movement Taalbi inveighed against the protectorate. It was alien, he argued, to the Tunisian nation as Chinese civilization to the French. With great prescience he argued that the maintenance of the protectorate would, because of its alien character, demoralize the French as well as the Tunisians. In words which have evoked Jacques Berque's comment that Taalbi's pamphlet 'is of less value for its analysis than its foresight' (Berque, 1967, p. 35), he wrote:

For one people to try to make another people—one lacking organization and being of different faith and race—accept an ideal is an exceptionally difficult undertaking; but when the society it attacks is organized (as is the case with our Tunisia), has an historic past and its own civilization; when it is, moreover, a society which reveres its own history and civilization whose richness and virtues have been well-tried; when the aggressors use brutality and oppression; then the enterprise is doomed to failure: the fury of the oppressors is aroused and translated into moral violence which, without enhancing the prestige of the aggressors, disturbs people's minds and increases, with all the horror of its sterility, the sum of crimes against humanity.

There were other initiatives, some of purely historical interest, others of more lasting importance. In 1922 the Bey of Tunis threatened to abdicate at the time of the visit of the French resident unless the demands of the Destour were granted by the protectorate, a threat that evaporated before a show of authority by the resident-general, Lucien Saint. At the other end of the social scale, one Mohammed Ali, who had previously spent only one year of his life in Tunisia, organized the dock workers of Tunis and thus provoked, in 1924, the emergence of the Confédération Générale des Travailleurs Tunisiens. The movement was suppressed by the protectorate and Mohammed Ali was exiled (he died while driving his taxi between Jedda and Mecca). His biographer, Tahar Haddad, published a Marxist analysis of Tunisia and urged the unpopular cause of the emancipation of women (at the cost of his job at the Zitouna).

Of these various initiatives the most immediately important was the growth of the Destour party. The party began to attract the support of ordinary people and to organize branches in the countryside, thus escaping the constraints of the bourgeois environment of Tunis. The atmosphere of this period has been noted by Berque (1967, p. 81):

> Let us picture a meeting of the Destour party at Mahdia in 1922. Scarcely, as yet, a 'cell', but a gathering of some twenty or thirty people, grocers, hairdressers, chauffeurs, mechanics from the harbour, a few students from the Zaituna, even a petty leader. A few years later, at Tunis in 1929, a blind baker held a meeting in his bakehouse: the cause of the excitement was the detention of Guefrash, one of the 1925 protesters, who was in prison for having demonstrated at Gabès in favour of Abd el-Krim. There was talk of imprisonments and protests and petitions. Wild hopes were raised.

In the 1920s the party was a potential rather than an actual menace. As a bourgeois pressure group it lacked the coordination and persistence to gain piecemeal reforms; and it did not yet have the force of a mass party. The leadership was weak: Taalbi himself was abroad, in France and then, from 1923, in the Middle East. The old generation of Destourians did little to capture the imagination of the new adherents nor did they provide the dynamism of a revolutionary party. But because the party was the obvious channel of protest it recruited young men who, in the next decade, took over the movement and broke away to form the Neo-Destour. In this group the most effective leader proved to be Habib Bourguiba.

Bourguiba's background and early career were typical of an important group who formed the backbone of the Neo-Destour party. He was born at Monastir, the *ribat* or monastic fortress of which was the first to be founded in the Arab west, and which enjoyed a golden age under the Aghlabids. The ground surrounding the *ribat* has a sanctity which makes it a sought-after burial place. Bourguiba's parents were respectable people, his father a low-ranking civil servant of modest income. His mother died while he was young. He was sent to Tunis and studied at the primary school attached to Sadiki College, then at Sadiki itself and at the Lycée Carnot. He went to Paris in 1924, supported by meagre family earnings, and studied law and politics. He married his first wife, a Frenchwoman, and returned to Tunis in 1927 to practise law. He was, inevitably, 'politicized' in Paris, and in a relatively short time was caught up in Destourian politics. He became one of the most successful nationalist leaders of his generation, in conflict with the French, but he kept his acquired French inheritance and established a cultural affinity between Tunisia and France. He remarried, his second wife, Wassila, coming from an important bourgeois family in Tunis.

The Neo-Destourians were drawn from a wider section of Tunisian society than the existing party. Many originated from the Sahel—a region of the country which lacked both the provincial complacency of the capital and the harsh constraints of the desert—and from the island of Jerba: 'The island where, in order to live, one has to make a fire with any wood—that is to say catch fish and fish for sponges, cultivate meagre gardens and spin wool brought by nomads from the Tunisian south or model the clay from a few corners of the island.' (Le Tourneau, 1962, p. 77.)

The political and economic atmosphere of the 1930s favoured the growth of a more vigorous nationalist movement. It drew inspiration from developments in the Middle East, where the independence of Egypt and Iraq, in spite of its limitations, provided an example to the Maghreb; while the growth of the Popular Front in France seemed to offer hope for the future. The young generation of the party, drawn from the lower middle class and upwardly mobile by reason of their literacy and education, was sensitive to external political events, although they shared with the mass of the party an appreciation of the traditions of the small towns and the countryside, in contrast to the partly French, partly Turkish, atmosphere of Tunis.

The changing character of the party and the dynamism of Bourguiba produced an historic split, which occurred early in 1934. The issue on which the split occurred was the right of Muslims who had accepted French citizenship to burial in a Muslim cemetery. Bourguiba and his friends (supported by a *fetwa* issued by the mufti of Bizerte) took their stand against such burial, thus sharpening the contrast between Tunisians and French, and showing a sensitivity to popular belief in the importance of religion in matters of birth, death, and marriage, however attractive French modernity might be in daily life. The leadership of the Destour defended the right to Muslim burial, thus allying themselves, on this issue, with the French, who persuaded the rector of Zitouna to issue a *fetwa* contrary to that of the mufti of Bizerte.

The split was followed by the first congress of the Neo-Destour, held at Ksar Hellal in the Sahel in March 1934. The party which thus came into existence proved to be a more effective mass party than any other in the Muslim world, so that when Tunisia became independent the government was supported by a popular, well organized movement which other regimes, as different from each other as the Egyptian and the Algerian, had great difficulty in creating. The formal organization of the party owed much to the example of the French socialist party; its vigour and its life were attributable to the energy of the leaders, Bourguiba first among them, who deployed immense energy in travelling throughout the country, stimulating and invigorating hundreds of branches whenever the French gave them the freedom to do so.

Twenty years passed from the formation of the Neo-Destour to the grant of internal autonomy to Tunisia by the government of Pierre Mendès-France. Bourguiba was not in a position to lead the party actively throughout that period. He was arrested in 1938 and imprisoned with a score of Neo-Destour leaders. In 1940 he was transferred to Marseilles; he was then taken to Rome, where Mussolini's government tried to negotiate with him; and he returned to Tunis in 1943. In March 1945 he quietly went to Cairo, returning to Tunis in September 1949. He was arrested again in 1952 and released when negotiations for internal autonomy began.

In spite of the varying fortunes of the Neo-Destour party and its leadership, the nationalist momentum was maintained during this period, and the structure of Tunisia as it would emerge at Independence was formed. Bourguiba's variant of nationalism, and the organization of his party, were not the only forces at work; but circumstances, combined with Bourguiba's energy, made them dominant.

The French government inadvertently contributed to Bourguiba's success. In 1937 it arranged for the return of Abdel Aziz Taalbi to Tunisia, presumably in the hope that he would either weaken the nationalist movement by dividing it, or provide a more acceptable force with which France could negotiate moderate reforms. The effect was the opposite: Bourguiba saw his leadership challenged and reacted vigorously against Taalbi, taking a more extreme position than he otherwise would have done (and so provoking his own arrest), and retaining leadership of the nationalist movement. Taalbi ceased to be an effective force, and died in 1944.

In March 1942 Prince Mohammed el-Moncef succeeded to the Beylicate and for a brief period was able to provide the leadership of a moderate nationalist movement, enjoying the loyalty attaching to the throne and giving it a new quality by the interest he showed in the welfare of his subjects and by his readiness to take a stand against the resident-general. For nearly two years Moncef Bey navigated a skilful course, modernizing the Beylicate, asserting his own moral authority, and increasing his independence among the competing forces of the French, the Germans, and the Allies. The climax was reached when, in January 1943, he appointed his own cabinet without the consent of the resident-general, under the premiership of Mohammed Chenik, and including Mahmoud Materi (Bourguiba's former colleague, who had separated from him in 1938) and Salah Farhat, secretary-general of the old Destour. This triumph for moderate nationalism and continuity was short-lived. In May 1943, with the success of the Allied invasion of North Africa, Moncef Bey was deposed by Generals Giraud and Juin, on the unjustified accusation of collaboration with the Axis. After the event the British contributed to the legend of Moncef Bey's collaboration; but the act of deposition was French, and it appears that 'the French authorities leapt at the opportunity of getting rid of a highly inconvenient partner, and at the same time placating the French in Tunisia, for whom the rule of Moncef had acquired a nightmare quality' (Le Tourneau, 1962, p. 105).

In spite of his deposition Moncef gave a lasting impetus to the nationalism of the notables of Tunisia, with whom he remained in touch until his death in 1948. His successor, Lamine Bey, endeavoured to act in the same manner although he lacked Moncef's strength of purpose; and as the French government made only limited concessions, he was, in the long run, overtaken by the Neo-Destour. Bourguiba for his part was sensitive to the continuity of Tunisian history and the importance of monarchy; his first action on returning to Tunis, both in 1943 and in 1949, was to seek audience with the Bey. But it was a continuity of which he saw himself as the embodiment and a succession of which he regarded himself as the heir. His political stance was one of dominance, and he sought no compromise (except on his terms) with the notables who would have formed the staff of an independent Beylicate *à la marocaine*, or with Neo-Destour members or sympathizers who could not accommodate themselves to his personal ambition. Men like Tahar Ben Ammar and Mohammed Chenik would have no political role in Bourguiba's Tunisia.

Nor would the extreme left. The French communist party, class-conscious in principle but opportunistic in practice, evoked little admiration or emulation in Tunisia. Moreover Tunisia produced its own labour movement under the outstanding leadership of Ferhat Hached (killed by right-wing French assassins in December 1952). Mohammed Ali's venture of the 1920s was short-lived; but in 1946 Ferhat Hached formed a new Union Générale des Travailleurs Tunisiens (UGTT), which was open in principle to workers of all nationalities but was in practice a Tunisian union. It did more than ally the labour movement to the Neo-Destour party, since it also provided a channel by which international recognition could be sought. It joined the International Confederation of Free Trade Unions, and had the support of the American labour movement. Bourguiba and Hached attended the American Federation of Labor conference in San Francisco in 1951, and when Bahi Ladgham went to New York on behalf of the Neo-Destour to establish a Tunisian Office for National Liberation, he was assisted by the AFL.

For all that he was a nationalist organizer and agitator, Bourguiba based his strategy on cooperation with France at the same time as he pursued independence. On two occasions he had reason to hope that substantial concessions would be made. The first was under Léon Blum's government of 1936, when Pierre Viénot was under-secretary of state. But Blum's government lacked the political strength and the longevity to implement reforms either in the Middle East or in North Africa. Disappointment at this setback, coupled with the return of

Taalbi, produced the violent outburst of April 1938, in Bizerte and Tunis, when government troops fired on a demonstration and killed some 122 people—the date, 9 April, passing into national tradition as Martyrs' Day.

The second period of optimism came at the conclusion of the Second World War. During the war Bourguiba distinguished himself by his rejection of Mussolini's blandishments to act on the Axis side and by his explicit support of the Allies, in their darkest hour. On 8 August 1942 he wrote to Habib Thamer:

> Give the militants the order—on my responsibility and *even over my signature* if necessary—to enter into relations with Gaullist France in Tunisia (there must certainly be some of our socialist friends, for example) with a view to joining if possible our clandestine action with theirs and leaving aside for after the war the problem of our independence.
>
> Try if possible, and through their connection, to enter into contact with the British or American agents who must abound in Tunisia. They can be sounded on the intentions of their countries towards us after the victory.[1]

But the movement of opinion which had occurred in the French government did not keep pace with the development of nationalism in Tunisia; those reforms which it proposed met with hostility from the Europeans in Tunisia and from conservatives in France. The clash lacked the intensity of Algerian politics, partly because the Tunisian Europeans did not have representation in France. But the war widened the gap between the two communities; for Muslims, it was something to be suffered, of no concern to them, while for Europeans it was a matter of national concern, however their loyalties were distributed between de Gaulle and Vichy. In addition, the French had suffered defeat in 1940. The end of the war brought the independence of Syria and Lebanon, the movement towards the independence of Libya, and the formation of the Arab League. At a meeting on 23 August 1946 (which fell on the twenty-seventh day of Ramadan) the Destour and Neo-Destour parties, the UGTT, and others joined to declare the total independence of Tunisia, just before the police closed the meeting.

In these circumstances the French policy of reform made little effective headway. It followed the obvious course of giving greater authority to Tunisians in a Tunisian government, with a view to internal autonomy in the future. But by this time there were no Tunisians likely to occupy such ministries who did not want to increase the pace towards independence. This was the experience of the Chenik government, formed in accordance with a protocol of August 1950.

---

[1] There is no means of establishing the authenticity of this letter, which was not published until after the war, and there are those who say that it would not have required publication unless there were something to hide. There exists no basis for this allegation; on the other hand Bourguiba's regime has shown no haste to exonerate Moncef Bey from the charges of collaboration brought against him.

Bourguiba at this time was abroad, visiting not only Egypt but Paris, Pakistan, Indonesia, and the United States, seeking international support for an independent Tunisia. He was not alone: when the new resident-general, de Hautecloque, arrived in Tunis in January 1952 he was affronted to find that two Tunisian ministers (Salah Ben Youssef and Badra) had gone to Paris to present their case to the UN. By this time the French government was prepared to go a step further with a proposal for 'co-sovereignty'; but it was as unacceptable to the Tunisians as it was alarming to the Europeans in Tunisia, and the Bey exploited the occasion by summoning a conference of all the major nationalist groups. De Hautecloque attempted to follow a policy of firmness: Bourguiba was once again arrested; the Chenik ministry was dismissed and ministers were placed under house arrest (apparently without the prior authorization of Paris), while the response in the country was a growing campaign of resistance and armed action. The Tunisians succeeded in keeping the interest of the United Nations where support for newly independent states was readily forthcoming.

The failure of de Hautecloque's policy resulted in his replacement in September 1953; but the decisive change in French policy came in 1954, when Pierre Mendès-France, during the brief ministry which brought the Geneva agreements on Vietnam, offered internal autonomy to Tunisia. Lengthy negotiations (in which Bourguiba played his part in the wings, having been released from prison and allowed to go to Paris) produced the conventions of June 1955. But by this time the pace of events had quickened, and the movement towards full independence in Morocco accelerated the demands of the Tunisians and the readiness of the French to accede to them. In consequence the major importance of the conventions proved to be in Tunisian politics: Salah Ben Youssef, who had gone to Cairo during the negotiations, contested the conventions, which Bourguiba had accepted. But Bourguiba overcame Ben Youssef's opposition within the Neo-Destour party in November 1955 and was thus in a dominant position when Tunisia became independent on 20 March 1956.

Politics since Independence: the Bourguiba System

Tunisia has been governed since 1957 by the presidency of Habib Bourguiba, who constructed a political system which devolves from and depends on him, so that he has taken all major decisions and directed their implementation.

Bourguiba's success derived in the first place from a sense of strategy and a clear vision of the future possibilities for Tunisia. In retrospect it is easy to discern mistakes of strategy and judgement, of which his direction of the economy and his dealings with Ahmed Ben Salah are the most important. But he has had the talent of taking a long view and the stamina to move gradually towards his objective. He has combined forceful reasoned argument with rhetorical appeals to popular audiences (with a sense of theatre from which ham is not always absent), and has combined an authoritative presence with manipulative skill in the operation of the political system.

The success of his government, especially during its first decade, was in the degree of unity which it established. This was, inevitably, at a cost, since the reverse side of the process was the exclusion of some men from public life who might otherwise have contributed to it (a sacrifice which appeared the greater as the turbulence of the early years receded into the past). But the reward was political stability, and it was achieved without the invocation of an intolerant ideology (although this was a shortcoming in the eyes of some).

The first and hardest fought contest within the party started before Independence. Salah Ben Youssef's opposition to Bourguiba stemmed from more than a tactical difference over the acceptability of the conventions of 1955. In contrast to Bourguiba, whose sojourn in the Middle East had reinforced his attachment to specifically Tunisian virtues and possibilities, Ben Youssef returned from Cairo ready to pursue the Arab cause and to urge the development of Tunisian independence within the framework of Arab advancement. More immediately, he attached importance to the independence of the Maghreb as a whole, at a time when Morocco was not independent and the Algerian war had just started.

Salah Ben Youssef was born in 1910 in Jerba and commanded widespread allegiance in the south. He joined the Neo-Destour as a young man and was appointed to the political bureau in 1937. He became general-secretary and controlled the party in Bourguiba's absence in 1945-9. He served in the Chenik government (by agreement with the party) in 1950 and then went to Cairo to seek security when de Hautecloque became resident-general. His record, his office, and his support made him a considerable person in the party and when the split occurred in 1955 Bourguiba insistently tried to achieve a reconciliation with him. When this failed he succeeded in outmanœuvring him. Although Ben Youssef's regional support was strong, Bourguiba's overall command of the party was more powerful, the more so since the mass of the trade union movement, led by Ahmed Ben Salah, supported Bourguiba. In October 1955 the political bureau of the Neo-Destour party expelled Ben Youssef from the party; the following month a party congress was called to meet in Sfax, where Jerbian (and therefore Youssefist) influence was weakest. The congress gave overwhelming support to Bourguiba.

The struggle then moved to the country, where the incipient violence that had marked the last years of the struggle for independence threatened to be transformed into a major Youssefist attempt to regain power.

But although fighting was substantial it was contained, with the assistance of French security forces. Ben Youssef fled the country and lived in exile. He was condemned to death in absentia, and in August 1961 was assassinated.

The support which Ben Salah and the trade union movement gave to Bourguiba in 1955 was of decisive importance in the conflict with Ben Youssef. During the following year the independent power of the trade union movement was curtailed, and its programme for radical social and economic change rejected, a series of events which diminished, for the time being, the influence of Ben Salah.

Tunisia was outstanding for the strength of its trade union movement at Independence. Ferhat Hached had shown as much organizing skill in this area as Bourguiba had in the Neo-Destour party, and had mobilized a membership of some 150,000. The vacuum in the leadership created by Ferhat Hached's assassination was filled in 1954 by Ahmed Ben Salah. A generation younger than Bourguiba, Ben Salah was born in January 1926 in the Sahelian village of Moknine. Like Bourguiba, he was educated at Sadiki College and in Paris, where he became general-secretary of the Neo-Destour student organization. He took his degree in Arabic and returned to take up a teaching post at Sousse. He joined the civil servants' trade union and pursued his career with vigour and ambition within the trade union movement.

The termination of the Youssefist split and the grant of independence quickly opened the way for the differences between Bourguiba and Ben Salah to emerge. Bourguiba's political objectives were to unify the party on the broadest possible base, to secure a virtual monopoly of power for it, and not to risk national unity or foreign investment by radical economic change. Ben Salah, in contrast, spoke of the nationalization of all resources and proclaimed the need for a socialist plan for development and for the deployment of the UGTT as the 'national instrument of social and economic revolution'. The disruption of the policy of gradualism, the possible danger to relations with France, and the bid for the union movement to direct social and economic policy were all unacceptable to Bourguiba, and the danger seemed the greater as the trade unions supported agricultural strikes.

However, Ben Salah's leadership of the UGTT was challenged within the movement by Habib Achour, who lacked Ben Salah's advanced education and distrusted his ambitions. Achour, who had been a colleague and friend of Hached, led the Sfax section of the UGTT and played an important part in the UGTT strike of August 1947. His consequent imprisonment made possible Ben Salah's ascent in the movement, without his having participated in the heroic days of 1947.

Ben Salah's bid for position reached its peak at the sixth congress of the UGTT in October 1956. The economic report presented to the congress was an outline project for a planned socialist economy. The congress was followed by a secession from the UGTT led by Achour, who established the Union des Travailleurs Tunisiens. In December 1956, while Ben Salah was away in Casablanca discussing Maghreb trade union affairs, an unannounced meeting of the executive of the UGTT dismissed him and appointed Ahmed Tlili in his place. In September 1957 the breakaway UTT rejoined the UGTT.

In this way the trade union movement was brought within the Bourguiba system, with a great economy of effort for Bourguiba, who had succeeded in exploiting rivalries within the movement. The victory thus achieved was demonstrated when the UGTT was forced some years later to take an independent line on narrower issues, as the devaluation of the dinar cut real wages. In 1965, while Ben Salah was minister of national economy, Achour and Tlili were manœuvred out of leadership of the UGTT and new statutes for the UGTT were devised, making clear the subordinate role which the organization was to play in the state.

Meanwhile in the first years of autonomy and independence Bourguiba established his supremacy not only in the party but also in the formal machinery of the state. Following the conventions of 1955 a constituent assembly was planned to draft a new constitution. The strength of the Neo-Destour in fighting any election was clear, and although the party had always given its support to the idea of a constitutional monarchy, the Bey and his closest supporters cannot have viewed the prospect before them with equanimity. They were accused by *L'Action* of plotting to proclaim a constitution without waiting for a constituent assembly; and the Bey was subsequently accused by Bourguiba of seeking the connivance of the French to withhold the French forces needed to combat the Youssefists. But on 29 December 1955 the Bey signed the decree for the constituent assembly and declared that the constitution would be adorned by his seal—implying his unwilling acceptance of Bourguiba's initiative. This was a significant diminution of his position since the traditional form was for laws to be submitted to the Bey for his seal, which was given at his pleasure (Moore, 1965, p. 72).

At the same time Bourguiba made sure that the election to the assembly would enhance his own authority; deputies were chosen by majority list voting, and in the Neo-Destour party the lists were drawn up by party headquarters. The effect was to strengthen the Bourguibist majority. The existence of such a majority was not in doubt; but Bourguiba had ensured that the opposition—from the old *baldi* class, from Youssefists and communists, and even from within his own party —would not be strongly enough represented even to dissipate the energies of the majority. In the election itself on 25 March 1956 communists and independents won only 1·3 per cent of the vote; Youssefist feeling showed itself, ineffectively, in a 71 per cent abstention in Jerba;

conservative and other opposition in a 41 per cent opposition in Tunis.

It took three years to draw up a constitution. The time appeared excessively long to those who saw the process merely as one of drafting a legal text; but it was a period in which constitutional practice could develop. The result was that when the text of a constitution finally emerged Bourguiba's authority was overwhelming. He first became prime minister, in succession to Tahar Ben Ammar. In July 1957 the Bey was deposed and Tunisia proclaimed a republic. The assembly designated Bourguiba as the republic's president. Meanwhile the government of the country was being carried on with little active participation by the assembly, which neither debated nor voted its measures.

The constitution of 1959 confirmed the authority of the president, particularly vis-à-vis the assembly. Both were to be elected at the same time for a period of five years. But the government was made responsible to the president, not to the assembly, and the assembly was limited to meeting for six months of the year. In the subsequent practice of the assembly its full meetings were of minimal importance and consisted largely of ratification of texts emanating from the presidency, which might have been subjected to more detailed scrutiny, although still of a restricted kind, in secret meetings of commissions.

The system which emerged has been described as a presidential monarchy, and it is indeed the case that Bourguiba had, by means of a finely sensitive political instinct, taken over the position of the Bey, while at the same time remaining at the head of a political party which, for all its limitations, remained one of the most successful in any new state. He inherited the Bey's palaces and built a new one at Carthage and another at Monastir. The long gallery of the Carthage palace is lined with portraits of the Beys. He took over some of the ceremonial practices of the Bey, such as the tour of the Medina on the night before the end of Ramadan, and he accepted the applause of the crowd in a regal manner. Inevitably his conduct and the expenditure which went with it were criticized by those who wanted independence and modernization to imply a more complete breach with the past. But in later years, when the continuity of centuries of Tunisian history regained its importance in national consciousness, Bourguiba's success in modernizing within the context of this continuity was the more impressive.

But this does not explain Bourguiba's enduring authority over the country, which exceeded anything to which the Beys had aspired. That authority derived in the first place from his determined and successful leadership of the movement towards independence. He had demonstrated courage in the defence of personal and national honour and he had been successful—qualities which command at least as much respect in Tunisia as elsewhere. He embellished and embroidered this position in a way that kept him constantly in the public eye. The presidential portrait is widely displayed. The newspapers report the unimportant and formal activities of the president, with photographs, as if they were important international news. Meetings of party or state normally pass a resolution of support for the president as part of their proceedings.

Bourguiba has kept power through manipulation and control of the political system which he himself created. From the beginning of the state, anyone who sought to set up in opposition to the president started at a disadvantage, lacking Bourguiba's prestige. Effective opposition could only be formed within the party, but a bid for pre-eminence by one person or one group would evoke the rivalry of others—rivalries based on locality (particularly between Tunis and the Sahel) or on political outlook. The forum for such political activity was not easy to find. The national assembly was of no value for this purpose; it was scarcely possible to 'capture' a party congress, given the degree of preparation which preceded such a gathering; and in both party and administration Bourguiba used his power and his extensive knowledge to move people from one post to another and so prevent the accumulation of political position. As a result there has been no bid for power at Bourguiba's expense, unless Ahmed Ben Salah's accumulation of power, in Bourguiba's shadow, be counted as such; and a single attempt to assassinate Bourguiba, in December 1962, appeared to have little political base.

Tunisian political life has been characterized by the success with which dissidents have been removed from office, even forced into exile but have later returned, to resume their part in the political life of the country.

The apex of political power has been little institutionalized. Appointments at the head of the party and to the highest offices of state have been made in accordance with Bourguiba's pleasure, and his conduct of the affairs of state has been very personal. There has been no effective cabinet and no parliamentary control, and the party has had an executive function instead of being a check on the power of the leadership. Bourguiba has appointed and dismissed, promoted or ignored, secretaries of state as he has pleased and has sought advice without the need to conciliate a formal body of advisers. But his rule long remained free of the vices which normally beset a courtly system of government. The route by which men have been able to aspire to high office has demanded intelligence and hard work—qualities without which they could not have secured the advantages of advanced education and which have been equally important in the conduct of party and state affairs.

Government and Party

Below this controlling apex, the government of the country has been carried on by a simple administrative framework, linked to the Socialist

Destourian party, which gives Tunisian politics their distinctive character. With the advent of Independence, the country was divided into fourteen (later thirteen) governorates. In each the governor became a person of obvious importance. He reported to the department of the interior, but was responsible for public order and finance in his governorate, with considerable powers vis-à-vis the representatives of national departments. Meanwhile the party structure was reformed, in 1958, and party commissioners appointed, with jurisdiction corresponding to that of the governors. The move was designed in part to change the party from an independence movement into an instrument of government. The autonomy of some forty federations disappeared with the express intention of creating 'a strong power which does not dissipate in multiple ramifications', which would give 'cohesion and efficiency' and adapt the party 'to the administrative armature of the country, so that the two structures support one another and progress in perfect harmony'.[1] It was also intended to meet a more immediate problem of organization, consequent on the sudden inflow of recruits, endangering the controlling power of the old activists. In the pursuit of these objectives party commissioners were appointed by the political bureau of the party.

The relationship between party and government occasionally gave rise to conflicts, particularly between governor and party commissioner. But as a general rule the relationship was fraternal. There was a large degree of overlap and interchangeability. The leadership of the state was the same as that of the party, not only in the presidency, but in the fact that the important ministries were headed by secretaries of state who were also members of the political bureau. The inevitable shortage of cadres in the new republic meant that party commissioners and governors alike were drawn from the same group of people, whose careers would be made in the party and the state apparatus at the same time. The party was not committed to a sharply defined ideology and owed its cohesion above all to participation in the struggle for independence, nurturing a myth which party and government men shared equally.

The development of the party and its importance in the government of the country were taken a step further by the congress held at Bizerte in October 1964. It was called the Congress of Destiny; its predecessor in 1959 had been the Congress of Victory. It was deliberately located in Bizerte, the last base held by the French. At the congress the Neo-Destour party was renamed the Socialist Destourian party—a change which was intended to show that a socialist plan of development had been chosen.

The congress showed itself to be a ratifying rather than a deciding body. Under the old party rules it should have assembled two years earlier. One of its most important contributions to the reform of party organization had been decided by a national council before it met; and its proceedings were dominated by Bourguiba. None the less, it marked

[1] Speech, 2 October 1958, quoted by Moore, 1965, pp. 113–14.

a further stage in the growing importance of the party, an institution not mentioned in the constitution of 1959, but described in the report of the 1964 congress as the 'centre of gravity of the republican regime and essential motor of the organs of the state'. It was given new institutions: a central committee and regional committees of co-ordination. The central committee was presented as an enlarged political bureau, including the existing members of that bureau, but incorporating in addition all secretaries of state not already members, all governors, and a number of persons (eighteen in 1964) elected by the congress. The committees of coordination in each governorate were to be elected by a regional council and were intended to facilitate communication and contact between governors and party commissioners, party activists, and the population.

The party structure thus constructed held a delicate balance between authority and democracy. The party has remained open to anyone who wishes to join (in contrast to carefully selected parties like the communist party in the Soviet Union), and the ethos of the party is one of democracy and participation. At branch meetings members are encouraged to speak, to voice their grievances and to offer their suggestions. The regional councils which elect committees of coordination produce lively debates, according to Tunisian press reports, and some genuine element of choice has entered into the election of members of the committees of coordination. These committees themselves meet under the chairmanship of the governor and are serviced by a secretary-general, who is a party official, but they do provide an effective consultative council. At the same time the advantages which accrue to officials in any society are particularly evident in Tunisia. Authority is expected and accepted; the details of branch business are not readily accessible to men who cannot read; there may be an element of choice, but the choice is made among the right people in a well articulated organization directed by its political bureau.

The 'National Organizations': Trade Unions and Students

The Socialist Destourian party has been an extremely effective instrument of government of a kind that exists in few states which seek popular participation while maintaining machinery for propaganda and persuasion. The work of the party is to some extent supplemented by the 'national organizations', professional bodies which lack autonomous existence. These have included the Union Nationale des Femmes Tunisiennes, Union Tunisienne de l'Artisanat et du Commerce, Union Tunisienne de l'Industrie et du Commerce, and Union Tunisienne de l'Industrie, du Commerce et de l'Artisanat. These associations exist in part to facilitate communication from the government to interest groups, in part to represent professional interests. The balance is heavily on the side of government transmission downwards; the degree of attention given to professional interests is small, and autonomy is restricted by the infiltration of the party. None of these professional organizations has either the past history or the strength of organization to play an independent role in the system.

Two other national organizations have been less easy to control: the UGTT which was finally curbed in 1965 (see p. 366), and the students' union, Union Générale des Étudiants Tunisiens (UGET). Student organization, especially in Paris, provided a valuable forcing ground for Neo-Destour activists in the days of the French protectorate, and the party expected, after Independence, to continue to recruit its élite from those who had distinguished themselves in student organization (Mohamed Sayah, who became secretary-general of the party in 1964, had served in this office in UGET in 1960). In the event the UGET, although it lacked the independent origins of the UGTT, would not comply. The relative freedom of its student membership, the ease of contact with the outside world, through the availability of foreign newspapers and publications, and via Tunisian students in Paris, combined to keep alive an independent political attitude, normally to the left of the regime. To this was added the cumulative effect of the organization of protests against shortcomings in food or accommodation, and the control of such demonstrations by the forces of order always with the risk of inflaming feelings still further.

Soon after the establishment of the republic, the UGET (although it owed its creation to the Neo-Destour) sought to follow the example of the UGTT as an autonomous organization. The attempt was resisted by party membership within the UGET. In 1964 a new Destourian student organization was formed, the Fédération Nationale des Étudiants Destouriens. Two years later, in August 1966, the two organizations were merged, in a manner that clearly ensured the dominance of the party over the UGET, which experienced the customary renewal of its administrative council and its secretary-general. Since that time the party has succeeded in keeping control of the UGET. But it has not thereby prevented student demonstrations, although they have been less frequent and less intense than in Morocco and, lacking support from other sections of the population, have never endangered the regime. Moreover, the control of UGET has been acquired at some cost, since the organization has become unattractive to enterprising students who seek an independent path and have no ambition to rise in the established order.

Starting from the dominant position they had secured at Independence, the Destourians have acquired a monopoly of political life, at the expense of autonomous bodies like the trade unions and of other political groupings. The competition which they might have faced has never been substantial, and it has been given even less place than it would have held in a free political system. The Neo-Destour party early captured the most numerous active political class—the modernizing educated middle bourgeoisie—by its ideas, its organization, and Bourguiba's leadership; thus leaving little ground for rival political organizations.

The establishment of the Destourian monopoly was at the expense of both left and right wings. The communists never competed successfully with the nationalism of the Neo-Destour nor did they make substantial inroads into the Tunisian trade union movement. The small communist party was suppressed in January 1963, an action justified by the unsuccessful assassination attempt of the previous year. In more recent years a new left wing, with its support among young intellectuals has survived the harassment of the government (the more easily thanks to the freedom and accessibility of Paris). It has attacked the regime for its lack of Marxist analysis and for not mobilizing the masses; for its close ties with France and its readiness to accept tourism and subcontracting as a means of economic development (in spite of the demoralizing and impoverishing effects which these are alleged to produce); and for its failure to oppose imperialism in world affairs. Numerically small, and without any strong alliance in the working class, this group is none the less important in offering an alternative which is attractive to some whom the government would like to recruit, and in disturbing the consciences of others, troubled by the harassment of the left.

The election of the constituent assembly showed how little electoral threat there was to the Neo-Destour party from conservatives and from nationalists outside the Neo-Destour. However, the deposition of the Bey was followed by a period in the winter of 1958–9 during which the leading members of the old order were brought to trial before a revolutionary tribunal, the high court originally set up to judge Youssefists. Trial and punishment were political, harsh, and severe. The victims were men who, as office-holders under the French, could be accused of repressing the Neo-Destour, even when in practice they had tried, in the difficult position of any office-holder in the pre-Independence period, to protect the Neo-Destour. They included men like Tahar Lakhdar and Noureddine Zaouche, who had at some time been active members of the Neo-Destour, but who had subsequently accepted the moderate reforms introduced by the French rather than continue the campaign for independence. Tahar Ben Ammar, who had been transitional prime minister and was elected a member of the constituent assembly, was condemned on spurious charges of financial corruption.

The victims were spared, by subsequent reprieves, the full weight of the sentences imposed on them. But subsequently they had no opportunity—or probably desire—to play any important political role. There was no barrier to their sons doing so, though some of them, through disenchantment, remained outside the regime or took up positions more to the left. Many of the younger generation therefore found their way into the administration. There was no possibility of the reconstitution of a wealthy upper bourgeoisie of economic or political importance. Some had suffered the loss of their property through confiscation. The socialist economy of the 1960s left little opening for capitalist entrepreneurship, and those whose incomes were large enough to allow a significant degree of saving invested in houses for themselves, or to let, rather than in industrial enterprise.

Nor did conservative religious forces constitute a serious political problem for the Bourguiba regime. Bourguiba met some resistance to his programme of reform, whether in lay legislation or in the attempt to give a liberal interpretation to Islam. The party, with Bourguiba at its head, tried to change practices which were, or by custom had become, central to Islam. The most substantial was the practice of Ramadan, with its debilitating combination of daytime fasting and nighttime jollification. In 1961 the attempt to discourage the fast, on the grounds that the battle against underdevelopment constituted a *jihad,* brought him into direct conflict with the Ulema, particularly in Kairouan. The conflict was indecisive: the regime ceased to inveigh against the fast—although it did not support it, as did the official press in Algeria—and the population went their own way, many clinging to traditional practice, others abandoning the fast, some pretending to their families that they were fasting while taking refreshment in the café. Certainly Bourguiba did not achieve his objective of preventing the loss of effective work time during the month of Ramadan.

At the beginning of the 1970s Tunisia responded to the several waves of Islamic enthusiasm which spread across the Arab world. An organization for the 'Defence of the Koran' was set up; an Islamic movement was obvious among the students, even though for the majority of students higher education was associated with a movement away from tradition. But, at least in modern times, Tunisian religious practice had not been known as especially devout, far less as fanatical, and however important religious practice might be, it did not give rise to any substantial political movement.

The Ben Salah Period

Tunisia has acquired a reputation for political stability. It has successfully passed through a period of economic and social upheaval provoked by an ambitious programme of reform directed by Ahmed Ben Salah. The crisis was aggravated by the uncertain health of the president, which stimulated competition for the succession. The system survived, but the cost was considerable.

Ahmed Ben Salah was appointed secretary of state for planning and finance in 1961—a post which was later designated a secretaryship for the national economy. In 1968 he was appointed, in addition, secretary of state for education. From 1956, when he was eliminated from leadership of the UGTT, until his new appointment in 1961, he had demonstrated his dynamism as secretary of state for social affairs. He was responsible for a systematic and successful campaign against trachoma, he improved the local production and distribution, at accessible prices, of medicaments, he reorganized hospitals, and created a system of social security.

His appointment to the secretaryship of the plan accompanied Bourguiba's decision to seek a more planned direction to the Tunisian economy as a way of escape from the stagnation which had set in after the French withdrawal. Ben Salah had much in common with Bourguiba. He was dedicated to the development of the country, which he took the trouble to know at first hand and which he sought to know better by promoting empirical, academic studies. He was no Marxist, but he was aware of the need for the participation of the people in economic development. He was ready to attempt what many thought ill-advised in creating an industrial sector, in the hope that Algerian independence would open the way to greater unity in the Maghreb, and so to larger markets.

The power which he exercised showed several of the limitations of the Bourguiba system. He steadily increased his influence within the administrative system. He built up a team of talented civil servants to devise and implement the Tunisian plans, and co-ordinated their work with those of the ministries. Agriculture was brought into his department since it was scarcely possible to plan the economy without it; education, while remaining a separate department, was added to his responsibilities to facilitate the training of cadres for the economy. His power was unchecked by the institutions of democratic government. Having the full support of the president he could use both party and press to forward his policies in a characteristic Tunisian manner— inviting discussion among party militants and at the same time mobilizing support for decisions taken at the centre. Neither a Cour des Comptes nor a Conseil d'État existed to call him to account.

On the other hand, Ben Salah did not control overall policy, which remained in the hands of the president. Not only the Bizerte crisis of 1961 but also the decision, in 1964, to nationalize French land came from the president without consultation with Ben Salah who suffered embarrassment in his dealings with the French (who did not believe him to have been ignorant of the president's intentions), and who was faced with the practical problems which the decision, and the French reaction to it, created for the economy.

Nor did Ben Salah control appointments in the governorates. Resistance to his policies, therefore, could retain support in the state apparatus and in the rural sections of the party. At the same time, his supporters calculated the possibilities of succession, particularly during the period of Bourguiba's illness, in 1968 and 1969.

In spite of the merits of Ben Salah's policies they met increasing resistance (see pp. 384–5). Faced with severe practical problems in the cooperatives, and with manifest opposition from the peasantry and from the bourgeoisie Ben Salah decided to play for higher stakes, extending the cooperative system throughout agriculture, rather than slow down the implementation of his policies. But, in doing so, he lost the indispensable support of the president. The appointment of Ben Salah's rivals to important posts in the summer of 1969 presaged the change. On 4 August 1969 Bourguiba said, in a public speech: 'The action of the leader of a political movement is ineffective when it is not supported by his troops. This means that we must look at the problem of the limits of the cooperative system, which, like any system and any regulation, is valid only up to a certain point, beyond which the balance is upset and shortcomings which have not been remedied become increasingly serious.'

In September 1969 Ben Salah was deprived of his office of secretary of state for planning and the national economy in a large-scale ministerial reconstruction. His office was divided into three departments—each with its secretary of state.

Ben Salah's disgrace was accelerated. He soon lost the secretaryship of education. He was arrested and in May 1970 tried by a special high court[1] on five charges, including 'abuse, mistakes, and irregularities in financial management, violation of the Constitution and of laws and regulations in force; actions *ultra vires*, and abuse of the confidence of the Head of State'. He was found guilty and condemned to ten years' hard labour.[2] He escaped from prison in June 1973 with the assistance of his brother and found asylum in western Europe.

The Ben Salah affair represented a serious moral crisis for the Bourguiba system. Bourguiba took shelter behind his illness, which was real, and which resulted in his absence abroad, receiving medical treatment. But neither party militants nor ordinary citizens forgot the political support and the warm personal encouragement which Bourguiba had given Ben Salah. Although there was no bid to overthrow the president, his prestige suffered severely. At the same time the country's apparatus of mobilization was seen to go into reverse. Men who had held party or state office during the Ben Salah period now busily explained that they had never really supported him: press

---

[1] The high court had been established by the 1958 constitution but special legislation had to be enacted in 1970 to extend its competence and establish its procedure.
[2] Other convictions were: for Amor Chechia, ten years' forced labour; Tahar Kacem, five years' imprisonment; Béchir Naji, Hédi Baccouche, and Mongi Fekih, five years' suspended sentence. *Annuaire de l'Afrique du Nord*, 1970, p. 274.

and radio changed direction to expose the mismanagement of funds and the coercion of peasants, when a year previously their information and their propaganda had served the Ben Salah cause.

Reconstruction of the Bourguiba System

Bourguiba's strategy to recover lost ground was to regroup his team of experienced lieutenants and to open the political system, temporarily, to free discussion. Meanwhile good fortune and good medicine brought a substantial improvement in his health and with it a reassertion of his old authority. Habib Achour was brought back into the leadership of the UGTT: Ahmed Mestiri, who had resigned from being secretary of state for defence in January 1968 in protest against excessive speed in the policy of cooperatives, was brought back into the party in April 1970 and joined the government in June 1970. Bahi Ladgham, who had served as secretary of state to the presidency since Independence, was promoted to a new office, that of prime minister; although shortly afterwards he agreed to act as arbiter in the conflict between King Hussein and the Palestinians; and in November 1970 he was replaced as prime minister by Hédi Nouira.

The climax of political activity during this period was reached at the party congress held at Monastir in October 1971. The characteristic balance between authority and liberalism appeared on this occasion to be tipping decisively towards liberalism—an appearance which subsequent events showed to be an illusion. The organization of the congress made it resemble a socialist party congress in France or Italy, a phenomenon not easily found elsewhere in the Arab world. The atmosphere was one of excitement and a sense of renewal; the limitations on free discussion seemed to be removed; and although Bourguiba's proposal for a series of seminars to discuss the shortcomings of the Ben Salah period had not materialized, the sense of investigation and discussion was real. At the same time, there was also a strange sense of return to traditional values. Abdelkader Zghal has commented:

With the sole aim of gaining the votes of the old militants and the peasants, certain candidates who occupied positions of authority at the party level and had participated actively in the politics of modernization did not hesitate, during the last party congress, to demonstrate an exuberant attachment to tradition. Half the members of the congress were over forty years old, and nearly one member in three was a peasant. By their own espousal of traditional beliefs, the modernist élite hoped to control effectively the spontaneous movement toward reactivating tradition and consequently to forestall the formation of an autonomous movement in defence of Arab–Moslem values.[1]

[1] Abdelkader Zghal, 'The Reactivation of Tradition in a Post-Traditional Society', *Daedalus*, winter 1973, p. 233.

More important was the fact that Bourguiba asserted his authority in the appointment of the political bureau. In the election of the central committee, Bahi Ladgham and Ahmed Mestiri came top of the poll, while Hédi Nouira was in fifth place. Ahmed Mestiri not only took this as a sign that the currents of liberalism were flowing fast, but said so in an interview with *Le Monde*, remarking that the congress had spoken and that Bourguiba must listen. In reply Bourguiba asserted that he retained the right to choose his closest advisers. He said that the political bureau would be chosen from a list which he would submit to the central committee; Nouira remained as prime minister and Mestiri, far from leading a liberal ministry, was once again excluded from the party and then from the national assembly (even though this latter exclusion required a change in the assembly rules to the effect that no one excluded from the party could retain his seat). Bahi Ladgham, meanwhile, returned to quiet retirement, resigning from the assembly and from the central committee of the Socialist Destour party.

It at first appeared that the appointment of Nouira might bring a new style of government, appropriate to a man described as a 'politician to his finger tips', who had a long experience of economic affairs and banking. The budget he presented to the assembly in 1970 had provoked a more serious discussion than had been known previously and indicated extensive preparatory work in committee. He had piloted through a party committee proposals for constitutional reform, giving slightly more importance to the assembly, and had seen them endorsed by the president.

But hopes of change towards political liberalism were extinguished over the next three years leading up to the ninth party congress, in September 1974, which was deliberately held in Monastir to expunge the experience of its predecessor. Bourguiba and Nouira remained in command, assisted notably by Tahar Belkhodja as minister of the interior.[1]

Together Bourguiba and Nouira confirmed their intention to command party and state together—the one as president of the party and the country, the other as secretary-general of the party and prime minister. At the 1974 party congress Bourguiba acceded to the oft-repeated suggestion that he should be elected for life. On 3 November 1974, he was re-elected president of the republic. At the same time a new assembly was elected, which duly carried into legislation the proposal of the party congress that his presidency should be for life.

The question of succession during Bourguiba's lifetime was thus settled. At the same time, the uncertainty which must follow Bourguiba's death was minimized, as far as possible, by confirmation of the

[1] Belkhodja had been secretary of UGET, became director-general of the *Sûreté*, but was dismissed from this post and expelled from the central committee of the party in 1967 for alleged abuse of authority, to be rehabilitated in June 1969.

existing provision that the president should be succeeded by the prime minister for the remainder of that presidential term (with the abandonment of the proposal, which Bourguiba had endorsed as recently as March 1973, that the prime minister should succeed for not more than forty-five days, while a new president was elected by universal suffrage).

The question of the succession had recurred repeatedly in party discussions and a series of provisions had been made to ensure a smooth transition and continuity. Inevitably it had also been a matter of constant political interest during the five years or so of Bourguiba's ill health. It was of particularly lively concern in the period of Ben Salah, while both Bahi Ladgham and Mohamed Masmoudi must have entertained hopes that, if the president were to die, it should be during their ascendancy. By the beginning of 1975 Hédi Nouira was clearly designated as the crown prince, with no guarantee against disinheritance but with the opportunity to fortify his political base.

The 1974 congress and the national assembly elections were preceded by a major purge of the party. Elections to the assembly were uncontested, since only a single party list was offered to the electorate. No incumbent deputy who had expressed sympathy for the 'liberals' of 1971, or for the Ben Salah regime, was made a candidate. Seven members of the liberal section of the party condemned the preparation of the 1974 congress,[1] asserting that the central committee elected in 1971 had not been allowed to participate in its preparation and that all the normal procedures of the party had been overridden or ignored. Ahmed Mestiri supported the declaration although, no longer a member of the party, he could not sign it. The national unity to which Bourguiba and Nouira had attached so much importance in their public speeches was qualified by the existence of an opposition—men ready to be identified as such and able to express themselves freely. Nothing in the history of the Tunisian republic suggested that they would be able to develop party institutions. Bourguiba clearly expressed his opposition to a two-party system for Tunisia when Mestiri was expelled; and Nouira understood that any 'dialogue' would be among those 'speaking the same language'.

Moreover, the years between the party congresses of 1971 and 1974 were marked by an increased deployment of the coercive force of the state. Symptomatic of the tension accompanying Bourguiba's re-assertion of authority were the trials of forty students in April 1974. The sentences imposed ranged from three to twelve months, and then a presidential pardon was given to all those convicted to mark the anniversary of the republic in July. But the demands of the students, supported by university teachers, for a freely elected UGET, remained

[1] They included Beji Caïd Essebi, former minister of defence; Habib Boularès, former minister of cultural affairs and information; Hassib Ben Ammar, former minister of defence; and Sadok Ben Jamaa, former minister for social affairs.

unsatisfied and the atmosphere of a university pervaded by police activity, with its apparatus of informers and arbitrary arrest, persisted.

A further trial opened in August 1974 when 202 young men and women (of an average age of twenty-one) were arraigned before a state security court charged with being members of left-wing groups, giving offence to the person of the president, and disseminating false information. The heaviest sentences (of twelve years' imprisonment) were imposed on eleven persons, tried in absentia. In all, 175 persons were condemned to periods of imprisonment, but 54 sentences were suspended and 81 were tried in absentia.

The increasing severity of the security measures and the known frailty of the president forfeited for Tunisia some of the prestige which it had enjoyed as a stable political order practising a form of democracy within a one-party system. But the political system had survived successive crises and showed sources of strength which would be likely to carry it through a succession in the presidency. The prime minister had won a reputation for effective government based on a clear view of the needs of Tunisian development. The administration both of government and of industrial enterprises could draw on an unusually large number of trained men. The party was directed by Mohamed Sayah who was a generation younger than the national leadership at Independence, and it succeeded in recruiting young men, even though cynicism and an eye to personal advantage may have replaced the enthusiasm of the post-war years.

THE ECONOMY

The economy of Tunisia has been that of a poor country, with a small internal market and little competitive advantage in exports, limited natural resources, and no industrial base at Independence. But its fortune changed dramatically in the early 1970s as a result of good harvests, the development of a small oil field, and increases in the price of its major exports, of which oil has become the most important, followed by phosphates and olive oil. France is its most important trading partner, the relationship having been facilitated by the Association agreement of March 1969 between Tunisia and the European Economic Community.

In January 1976, after prolonged negotiation, a new agreement was signed. It included a promise of financial aid totalling $117 million and a lowering of tariffs for the entry of Tunisian goods. The tariff on wine was to drop by eighty per cent. But this was less important than the concession made to Tunisia on olive oil, on which the Italian government had, in 1975, imposed a prohibitive levy. Under a new cooperation agreement the Italian government undertook to buy 20,000 tons of Tunisian oil at the EEC price and it was hoped that the industry would be able to regain its 1974 figure of 76,000 tons exported to the EEC.

Under the old agreement the EEC took slightly more than 60 per cent of Tunisian exports and provided rather less than 60 per cent of its imports. France has been a major provider of cultural and technical assistance. There has been a substantial emigration of Tunisian workers to France: 130,000 in 1971, whose remittances home amounted to 210 million francs. (Libya has been the second major outlet for Tunisian workers, providing jobs for some 40,000.)

The French protectorate established the basic infrastructure of a modern state—roads, harbours, railways, and public buildings—and French estates increased the output of olive oil, wheat, and wine. Independence complicated the agricultural problems which would have occurred even had the French stayed: the difficulty of competing in the French market as French agriculture and viniculture increased its output and of providing wheat for a growing but impecunious domestic market; the impoverishment of the soil, erosion, and the need for continued government interest in the agricultural section. However, the departure of the French, especially from the countryside was not sudden and precipitate as it was in Algeria. Of the French population of 180,000 at Independence 15,000–30,000 left each year until there were about 30,000 in 1962. Farmers, who farmed 850,000 hectares and owned 660,000 hectares (out of 7·5 million hectares), were slower to leave since they depended on the land for their livelihood, and relations with their employees were good.

As in Algeria and Morocco some land was sold at Independence, generally to wealthy Tunisians. The result of such sales was an increase in the outflow of capital (which the French took home). Legal restraints were, therefore, imposed both on the repatriation of capital and on the disposition of proceeds from sales which remained in Tunisia. To overcome the consequent constraint on the commercial sale of land agreements were signed with the French government, so that settlers were compensated and helped to resettle in France, while the Tunisian government acquired land from French farmers, which in many cases was then rented to private Tunisian farmers. This smooth progress was interrupted by the Bizerte crisis in July 1961. The departure of the French was thereby hastened and the remaining land nationalized in May 1964.

It has sometimes been argued that agriculture was impoverished at Independence by the French settlers' uncertainty about the future and their consequent restriction of tree planting and exhaustion of the soil for a quick return. But Dutton (1972) finds no evidence in his study of the Medjerda Valley. 'Only by 1958–9, when most farmers had stopped tree-planting, does it appear that the European farmers finally accepted that they had no long-term future in Tunisia. Only in the

1960s is there any evidence, and this by no means conclusive, to suggest that the colonists were no longer considering the long-term fertility of their land, but were motivated by a desire for short-term gain.'

Bourguiba lacked training or perception in economics, and his preoccupations in achieving independence and then establishing himself and his party in power were purely political. For five years after Independence his policy was, therefore, one of laissez-faire. The results were disappointing since the natural movement of these years was the exodus of the resources Tunisia most needed—capital and skill—as the French left.

The first major change in policy was made in 1961 when Ahmed Ben Salah became secretary of state for planning and finance. His task, having the full support of Bourguiba and the government as a whole, was to develop a planned economy, with strict economic control assuring a protected internal market as well as a fixed exchange rate and currency regulation. Ben Salah's planning department drew up a ten-year perspective, and a three-year plan, 1962–5, which was followed by a four-year plan, 1965–8 (after which further four-year plans have been devised). The objectives of the plans have been set out in the humanitarian terms of Destourian socialism: the aim of development is the welfare of man, for the benefit of all social classes in proportion to their efforts and also their needs. The first plans also set four broad objectives of economic and social development: decolonization; reform of economic structures, including industrialization; human development, including education, the training of cadres, and the fight against illiteracy and unemployment; and self-development, so that investment can come from internal resources and not be dependent on foreign assistance.

The relative success or failure of the economy over the early years is difficult to calculate with precision, since much of the investment of the period was long-term and its impact was interrupted by the upheaval of 1969–71 (see pp. 375–6). Political stability secured for Tunisia very large sums of foreign aid and foreign loans. The most advantageous part of this external financing in the short term was the provision of wheat by the United States under Public Law 480, since it was paid for partly in dinars, and the dinar funds were then made available in loans to the Tunisian government. In the longer term, technical assistance was a substantial contribution, although one that was limited in proportion to the acquisition of counterpart skills. The provision by France of teachers made possible the expansion of the educational system. But, meanwhile, the external debt increased from 77·7 million dinars in 1962 to 337·2 million dinars in 1971. Interest payments amounted to 17 per cent of average annual foreign exchange receipts over the decade. During the same period the rate of growth of the gross domestic product, in constant prices, was 4 per cent per annum.

Agriculture absorbed 18·8 per cent of the total investment in this period; but this was directed almost entirely into large projects, of importance for the future but of limited immediate benefit. Such projects included dams and irrigation, reforestation, and soil conservation. But the contribution of agriculture to the GDP fell from an annual average of 73·7 million dinars in 1960–2 to 66·7 million dinars in 1965–9 (Grissa, 1973, p. 65). There was a bad drought in 1959–62 and a second period of drought in 1965–9, ending in disastrous floods in October 1969. But the fall in output is attributable above all to the failure of the cooperatives.

New industries were developed, and the base laid for future industrialization. Tourism found an assured market and proved a growth industry earning foreign exchange. Investment in the textile industry provided some home-produced goods to substitute for imports. A refinery was constructed at Bizerte. The discovery of oil followed, with a minimal production of 615,000 tons in 1965 rising to 4·1 million tons in 1971. There was major investment in the phosphate industry, and a steel mill—the first in the Maghreb—was constructed. About 55 per cent of investment (in industry and agriculture) came from domestic sources and the remainder from external loans. Ownership and management were in the hands of major state enterprises.

The Cooperative Experiment

The most distinctive feature of the Tunisian political economy in the 1960s was the promotion and imposition of a cooperative system in production and trade. It was intended that cooperatives should play an important political and social role in the development of the country. It was also expected that the system would provide the key to a range of economic problems and would bring about a far more efficient mobilization of the country's resources. The first cooperatives were officially set up in 1960 in fishing, handicrafts, and building, together with service cooperatives in trade and agriculture. The first production cooperatives in agriculture were established in 1962. They were thus contemporaneous with the first three-year plan and with the beginning of the ten-year perspective of 1962–71 and were seen by Ben Salah as a means to achieve the objectives of these plans—an increase in the real rate of growth of GNP, self-sufficiency in cereals and other foods, a higher domestic saving ratio,[1] a surplus in the foreign trade balance, and a higher level of employment.

[1] Abdessatar Grissa regards this as one of the most important, though least publicized objectives of the cooperative policy, and reports: 'There have been profitable cooperatives, particularly in wholesale and retail trade but they rarely distributed any dividends to their members. These profits were often invested in other enterprises, such as hotels, without the cooperative members being even informed.' Abdessatar Grissa, *Agricultural Policies and Employment: Case Study of Tunisia*, OECD, 1973.)

The cooperative system seemed particularly appropriate to agriculture, where, it was hoped, it would both replace the private enterprise of the departed French farmers and provide the framework for the development of underdeveloped lands in the south. By 1965 the government had become a major landholder. The land acquired by purchase or nationalization from the French was added to *habous* land which had been brought into the public domain immediately after Independence. None of this land had been disposed of permanently, although some was rented and some had been allotted to impecunious small purchasers on an instalment plan (which the government could terminate).

The most favourable circumstances for the development of the cooperatives appeared to be in the north, where a former French estate could form the nucleus, to which smaller Tunisian holdings would be attached. The members of the cooperative would then be the former small owners whose land was attached, and the workers who had previously been employed on the estate (who rarely felt that any change had, in fact, occurred). In practice the problem of welding together small holdings and a large estate was greater than anticipated. There was no legal compulsion to join cooperatives—at the same time the movement had no roots in Tunisian popular culture and had never been the object of any spontaneous demand from the people. The creation of the cooperatives, and adherence to them, followed from government decision implemented by the administration, intermingled with the Neo-Destour party. This constituted a formidable apparatus of bureaucratic direction and pressure which obviously weighed on small rather than large farmers. Many small farmers, no doubt, joined in a spirit of compliance or belief in Bourguiba's leadership. But they were often apathetic, or when hard pressed resorted to the peasant's natural resistance to authority—non-cooperation.

Large landowners either remained outside the cooperatives, or received rent for the portion of their land which was incorporated. Much bureaucratic energy was employed and no cooperative could be started outside the government's framework or without the proper planning and technical study. But the men who formed the bureaucracy, whether of party or state, lacked agricultural skill and sensitivity to the experience and wishes of those they administered. Even more did they lack the ability and the will to enlist the support of peasants in a scheme so incomprehensible to them, when their real wages were no better than under the colonists, and there was no freedom to cultivate private allotments.

Government credit policy gave priority to loans to the cooperatives. But to the extent that this policy was successful it immobilized funds instead of using them creatively. The Agricultural Bank was the main instrument of this policy, although it was independent of the ministry of finance. Traditionally, an important part of its loans were made at seed time and recovered with the harvest. But the cooperatives ran at a loss—although this fact was never publicly admitted—so that they accumulated an increasing debt. The total outstanding debt of the agricultural sector to the banking system doubled from 5·5 million dinars in 1960 to 11 million in 1966, and doubled again to 22 million in 1969 (Grissa, 1973, p. 82). Initially (until foreign aid was sought), these resources were inevitably diverted from elsewhere in the economy; notably loans to private farmers declined from 2·2 million dinars in 1964 to 1·6 million in 1968—whether through shortage of credit, or the disincentive to large farmers caused by the threat of the cooperative system.

Meanwhile, the cooperatives often used credit to pay a full labour force even when work was not available, and lacked funds when it was; or used credit for the wrong purpose and were denied further sources. If bad management was a major factor in the weakness of the cooperatives, the pernicious practice of pretending that all was well in spite of the widespread knowledge of failure aggravated the problem. It inhibited enquiry into the source of failure and made kow-towing to the requirements of a regional government authority the most important criterion for survival in management.

From 1968 resistance to the movement began to increase. Ahmed Mestiri resigned from the secretaryship of defence in protest against the increased intensity of state direction and the arbitrariness of government associated with it and Hédi Nouira was known to be opposed to Ben Salah's policies. At another level there were manifestations among the peasants around Bou Arada and Gammouda (near Gafsa) in February 1968. Ben Salah was becoming increasingly isolated among the élite of the regime, but continued to receive the support of Bourguiba.

Ben Salah's response was to accelerate the movement, and in January 1969 a new law was passed extending agricultural production cooperatives across the whole country. This meant the extension of the policy into yet more ambitious areas. In the south of the country the cooperatives were intended not merely to improve an already efficient agriculture but to develop poor lands, reducing grazing and planting crop trees which would bear fruit (if successful) after many years of maturing. Thus the earlier policy of establishing offices with an independent budget and staff (there were three such offices, at Enfida, Sousse, and Sidi Bou Zid) had been abandoned in 1965 in favour of cooperatives and this policy was now extended across the region as a whole. It was done during a period of low rainfall and, in any case, failure in this region tipped the balance against physical survival. In other areas it meant that men of moderate property were brought within the cooperative regime, including, for example, the citrus growers of Cap Bon, and the merchant class, many of them from Jerba, engaged in retail distribution.

Meanwhile, the government had succeeded in negotiating support from the World Bank. An agreement of late 1967 with the Bank and the International Development Association provided for a loan of $18 million, and 1·5 million dinars reached the Agricultural Bank in 1968. Its initial deployment was intended, however, to restock the funds of the Agricultural Bank and provide investment funds for the cooperatives in the north. No funds were available immediately to cover the needs of the areas newly brought into the cooperative system, far less was there an increase in the supply of trained personnel. The extremities which the policy of cooperatives had produced (particularly in years of bad harvest) is shown by several different indicators. In March 1969 the government signed an agreement with the UN World Food Programme which included the provision of $21 million worth of free food products. The owner of an orange farm on Cap Bon saw his fruit trees without their chemical spray and his workers appealing to him for charity to stay alive; while in Gabès at least one Neo-Destour militant found himself powerless as he saw peasants, good Destourians, dying of starvation. The figures of livestock population show a fall from 3·2 million to 1·4 million sheep and from 590,000 to 245,000 cattle between 1968 and 1969 as peasants slaughtered their animals or smuggled them into Algeria rather than lose them to cooperatives.

At some point in the late spring or early summer of 1969, Bourguiba became convinced of the opposition case against Ben Salah's policies. It is reasonable to suppose that the active resistance of the peasantry was a major cause for this reversal, particularly when their demonstrations at Zeramdine, Touza, and especially Ouardanine were countered by the army firing on the demonstrators. In August and September the policy was reversed; Bourguiba abandoned Ben Salah, who was dismissed and later arrested.

The flood of October 1969 destroyed much of the improvement that had been carried out in agriculture, washed away newly planted trees, and flooded the phosphate mines.

The crisis was the most grievous in the history of the country. It weakened the authority of the president, diminished the prestige and popularity of the party, and brought misery bordering on starvation for many people. In the following five years, however, the economy showed marked progress, although this progress owed little to the new policies which were adopted to reverse those of Ben Salah.

The Liberal Economy

A law of September 1969 regulating the ownership of land marked the return to private agricultural property. Agriculture was still described officially as being divided into three segments: publicly owned land, cooperatives, and private agriculture. Some peasant land which had been brought into cooperatives reverted to private ownership. But much public land remained unexploited until it was sold to private purchasers; cooperatives were more like state farms than true cooperatives, in which men working the land are supposed to be responsible for direction and to share profits; while small privately owned plots could not readily recover from the upheaval of the Ben Salah period. The task of reconstruction made peasants vulnerable to the dangers of excessive borrowing, which was likely to be followed by the sale of land. The tendency of young men to go to the towns was strengthened. The link between the peasant and his land was broken, so that the demand of the rural population was often no longer for land but for work.

Recovery from the crisis of 1969–70 was enhanced by good harvests and by an improvement in the wheat crop as a result of the planting of Mexican wheat and of a new, locally produced strain, Ariana. In northern Tunisia, which is best adapted to Mexican wheat, the output of soft wheat, including high yield varieties, in 1972 (climatically a good year) was more than treble that of 1968 while the hard wheat crop was nearly doubled, with relatively small increases in the area planted (the increase in yield being from ·56 tons per hectare to 1·39 t/ha. for soft wheat, and ·46 t/ha. to 1·0 t/ha. for hard wheat).[1] The total wheat production for the whole of Tunisia in 1971–2 is recorded as 652,000 tons hard plus 262,000 tons soft. In spite of increased production, Tunisia imported 62,000 tons hard wheat and 167,000 soft in 1972 (compared to the peak import year of 1969–70 when the figures were given as 118,220 tons hard and 420,755 soft). (The objective of the 1973–6 plan is to produce the 1972 crop of wheat in a 'normal' year, by extending the areas sown with the new varieties and turning the low-yield lands to other uses.)

The 1971–2 season also produced an exceptionally good crop of olive oil providing a record level of exports—over 135,000 million tons (although other edible oils were imported for domestic consumption), and an output of citrus fruits some 54 per cent above the previous year. As a result, growth rates for agriculture as a whole were estimated as over 50 per cent in value added—in the sector of the economy which accounts for only 15 per cent of gross domestic product, but provides one half of the country's employment (with proportionate income distribution effects).

It is reasonable to expect continued growth in Tunisia's agricultural output as irrigation work is fully exploited and the European market for Mediterranean products (citrus, avocados, and early vegetables) is developed. The intention of the 1973–6 plan is to direct agricultural investment to projects and improvements likely to produce immediate benefit in production and sales rather than in a reform of structures.

The success of agriculture in recent years is in large part attributable to good climatic years, which have always been of such importance in

[1] Figures supplied by USAID from the Tunisian Office des Céréales.

North African life. The cruel vagaries of ill-timed rainfall or desert wind do not, however, affect the most important single industry created in independent Tunisia—tourism. But political and economic stability in the world as a whole does have a major impact. Hotels were empty in the summer of 1967, after the Middle East war; they substantially increased their bookings as the crisis of 1974 closed Cyprus to tourists.

A considerable effort has gone into the creation of the tourist industry and it has been well rewarded in terms of foreign exchange. The state has played a small part in direct investment and the growth of the tourist industry has been attributable mainly to investment by banks supplemented by private investment, together with a minor contribution (2·5 per cent of total investment in tourism) from foreign companies. The state has given guarantees to private investment and has also played an active role in training personnel. In 1971 tourism accounted for 47 per cent of Tunisian exports—more than oil, olive oil, or phosphates (although the increased output and price of oil had brought it to first place by 1974). The 1973–6 plan includes provision for further state investment in the tourist industry (30 million dinars financed by loans from the World Bank, IDA, and the German Kreditanstalt für Wiederaufbau), and expects private investment of the order of 100 million dinars. It is intended that the number of beds should increase from 50,000 (1972) to 85,000 (1976) and the number of jobs from 20,000 to 34,000. But the dependence of tourism on the general level of the European economy showed itself in a 13 per cent fall in the number of tourist nights from 1972 to 1973.

Phosphates constitute a major natural resource for Tunisia; they benefited temporarily from the 1974 increase in price, and they form the basis of industrial development, including that of the port of Gabès. Before the discovery of the reserves of the Spanish Sahara, Tunisia was counted as the fourth largest producer of phosphates, after the United States, the Soviet Union, and Morocco. Production was begun in 1897 by a French company, the Compagnie des Phosphates et du Chemin de Fer de Gafsa (Compagnie Sfax-Gafsa), of which the Tunisian state became majority shareholder in 1960 (owning 73·4 per cent of the capital in 1972). The phosphate mines are situated at Metlaoui, Moulares, Redeyef, M'Dilla, and Kalaa Djerda, with an overall capacity of 5 million tons a year of phosphate rock or 3·8 million tons of saleable phosphate. A substantial chemical industry has been built around the production of phosphates; there are three Tunisian firms and one with a majority Swedish shareholding, producing superphosphates at Sfax entirely for export, and the Société d'Engrais et de Produits Chimiques de Mégrine, French owned, producing fertilizers, pesticides, and fungicides for local sale.

As an earner of foreign exchange the phosphate industry has now been overtaken by oil. Tunisia's first ventures into the oil industry were limited to the pipeline from the Algerian field of In Amenas to the port of La Skhira, from which Tunisia drew rent, and the 1963 construction of an oil refinery, with Italian participation, at Bizerte. The most important oil field, at El-Borma, entered into production in 1966, and in 1972 produced more than 4 million tons while a number of smaller fields coming into production are expected to increase the aggregate output to over 6 million tons. A small gas field helps to supply Tunis, and the gas from El-Borma is taken by pipeline to Gabès, providing energy for the chemical industry.

In the industrial sector mineral wealth thus constitutes Tunisia's major asset (in addition to oil and phosphates there is a small production of iron, zinc and lead, and valuable resources of spath fluor). The textile industry has been developed to supply a major part of the internal market; the El-Fouladh steel mill was constructed soon after Independence and a number of assembly units, for cars and tractors, were also brought into production. The fourth plan aims at a higher level of investment and growth in the industrial and service sectors, including textiles, paper, chemicals, wood, mechanical and electrical engineering, and tourism.

Following the collapse of the Ben Salah experiments, the government of Hédi Nouira has adopted a markedly liberal economic policy, and Nouira has condemned the stagnation of socialist economies in severe terms. A law of April 1972 gives major fiscal advantages to foreign companies investing in production principally for export: viz. freedom to retain sales receipts outside Tunisia, tax holidays, relief from import duties, and facilities for land acquisition and for the training of labour. The law is intended both to attract new industries and to facilitate the growth of sub-contracting *(sous-traitance)*. Under these arrangements agreements have been signed with French firms for the production and export of hats, the assembly of Citroën cars, and the development of a food industry. The earlier experience of a similar arrangement with Berliet was not altogether successful, the Tunisians complaining of irregularity of orders and the French company being dissatisfied with standards.

The new policy has been introduced at an exceptionally favourable moment. Dramatic increases in the price of oil have made even the small export of three million tons exceptionally valuable; the price of phosphates quadrupled (although the new price was halved a year later); and a larger output of olive oil commands a higher price, with the result that in 1974 Tunisia had a positive balance of payments for the first time since Independence. Private saving appeared to be on a large scale, although it was not channelled sufficiently into industrial investment. A major preoccupation of the regime continued to be the creation of sufficient employment. But the continuance of unemployment and rural underemployment no doubt allayed anxieties about the rash of strikes, which Nouira attributed to the greater freedom of the trade unions and Bourguiba condemned as 'un crime contre la patrie'.

FOREIGN RELATIONS

In its external relations, Tunisia has shown a closer affinity with France, western Europe, and the United States than its neighbours have done, and greater detachment from the policies of the Middle East. The political longevity of Bourguiba and the stability of the ruling élite have ensured the continuity of a foreign policy which is consistent with their political and cultural attachment to Europe.

Tunisia's relationship with the rest of the Maghreb has steadily improved as frontier questions have been settled and the possibility of intervention in internal affairs has diminished. The theme of the 'Greater Maghreb' has been frequently repeated in the ideology of Tunisian foreign policy, and members of the Tunisian élite have inevitably looked for the advantages to be gained from the participation of Tunisia in a larger economic unit which would give Tunisia access to sources of energy and foreign exchange and would provide employment opportunities for skilled and trained manpower or even for relatively unskilled workers.

But the pattern of any such union is difficult to imagine, given the independent and distinctive manner in which the political systems of the Maghreb countries have developed. It was therefore surprising that Bourguiba and Qaddafi should sign an agreement, in January 1974, to establish a union between their two countries, and the circumstances of this abortive accord remain obscure. A year earlier, Bourguiba had expressed his scepticism concerning Arab unity during Qaddafi's first visit to Tunisia in December 1972. His intervention was particularly dramatic. Listening in the palace at Carthage to a relay of Qaddafi speaking in a cinema in Tunis, he abruptly decided to intervene and drove to Tunis to do so. He then argued:

In truth the Arab world has never been united. As soon as the Prophet was dead the wind of discord blew through the country. Of four successors of the Prophet three were killed. The assassination of Othman threw the Arab world into internecine conflict without end.

And yet across these vicissitudes of history national entities were created and affirmed their own personality. This was the case with Tunisia.

Colonel Qaddafi maintains that we ought, once independence has been achieved, to proceed towards unity. I agree on the final objective. But the great importance of the enterprise to be undertaken demands time to transform minds which for centuries have been used to thinking of our peoples as distinct entities. We must gradually reduce particularisms to restore to Arabs their common personality in a single fatherland and make a single nation of them.

Bourguiba's intervention occurred at a time when Qaddafi was at his most active and was pursuing union with Egypt. In the early months of 1973, Egyptian and Libyan diplomats and civil servants gave much energy to formulating elaborate arrangements to weld the two governments together once union had been approved by popular referendum on 1 September. The prospect of a united Arab country held little that was attractive to Tunisia; but as the date for the proposed referendum approached, the widespread scepticism that union would go beyond limited practical arrangements steadily increased. Masmoudi, as foreign minister, negotiated a series of conventions between Tunisia and Libya designed to serve Tunisia's interests as Libya moved so decisively towards Egypt and away from the Maghreb.

The September referendum never took place, the proposed Libyan–Egyptian union crumbled; President Sadat was soon accusing Qaddafi of trying to engineer his overthrow, and nothing in Qaddafi's public pronouncements suggested that he was unwilling to do so. In the meantime, Bourguiba and Masmoudi met Qaddafi on the island of Jerba and the proposed union between Tunisia and Libya was announced.

It was noticed that Bourguiba acted in the absence of his prime minister, who was in Algeria, and of Mme Wassila Bourguiba. Predictably, the union evoked vigorous opposition, both in Tunisia and in the rest of the Maghreb. The *haute bourgeoisie* of Tunis, whom Mme Bourguiba represented, found the prospect of union with Qaddafi's Libya particularly unattractive; while President Boumediene was strongly opposed to a successful merger by Qaddafi, extending his dominion to the Algerian frontier. In the following weeks Bourguiba made a diplomatic retreat and Masmoudi carried the opprobrium of the misadventure. If the union had succeeded, Masmoudi's personal ambition would have prospered and his chances in the succession stakes improved. Conversely, his failure was welcomed by those who were pleased to see him cut down to size. He was dismissed from office and from the party and went to live in Europe; he was disgraced[1] for the second time in his career but was no doubt available for rehabilitation in the future, should the Bourguiba system survive in a way to make this possible.

Libya was left isolated as a result of the failure of the union with Egypt and with Tunisia, and also by the success of Egypt in the 1973 Middle East war. The Tunisian government was free to continue to cooperate with Algeria in pursuit of their shared objective of a common Mediterranean policy. In spite of differences in domestic policies and in other foreign policy objectives, Bourguiba and Boumediene had a common purpose in seeking to strengthen their diplomatic position by creating a concert of states in the Mediterranean, or at least in its

---

[1] Bourguiba virtually accused him of accepting money for himself in the sale of Mirage aircraft to Libya.

western half. The idea was one to which Bourguiba had long given importance. He gave it new impetus in association with Boumediene during the latter's visit to Tunis in the spring of 1972. Their proposal was to transform the Mediterranean into a lake of peace by creating an association of riparian states, outside military blocs—the important European members being France (qualifying by reason of its detachment from NATO) and Spain. Thereafter the proposal was pursued with energy by the Algerian government as well as by Bourguiba, while Dom Mintoff, the prime minister of Malta, brought the foreign ministers of Italy, Libya, and Tunisia to a conference at Valetta in November 1972. But it was not clear to the European powers what advantages such a concert would bring which could not be achieved by bilateral diplomacy.

In any case, Tunisian relations with France remained close. Bourguiba's state visit to France in June 1972 appeared as the crowning point of his career, and showed the extent of his commitment to French culture. Under the protectorate he had emphasized the distinctive Muslim quality of Tunisia in opposition to France. But once independence was secure, the veil, which previously he had justified, was called a filthy rag, and legislation of European origin guaranteeing personal rights was quickly introduced. The Tunisian élite, for the first two decades of independent government, was educated in a French system of education, if not in France; access to that élite was through French language and culture; and the development of the Tunisian educational system relied heavily on French *coopérants*.

The political relationship between Tunisia and France called for skilled management in the early years of independence. Both countries intended that the independence agreement should be followed by a close relationship between them; Bourguiba's wish was to establish Tunisian independence within this relationship, securing the maximum advantage and freedom of manœuvre. Tunisia's first internal crisis was the Youssefist resistance, and Bourguiba relied on the assistance of French forces to establish his authority. The Algerian FLN and its army could carry on the War of Independence only by taking advantage of the Tunisian sanctuary. The Algerian provisional government set up in Tunis; army headquarters were established at Ghardimaou, ten miles inside the Tunisian frontier; and a large army was kept on the frontier. The unauthorized bombing of one of the camps of this army, at Sakiet, initiated the train of events that resulted in the rising of 13 May. Throughout this period, Bourguiba's task was to accommodate the demands of the Algerians while preserving good relations with France. Yet it was not his intention that those relations should be static, since the French still kept a military and settler presence in the country. Nor could relations with the Algerian FLN be taken for granted, since Tunisia hoped to win territory (possibly oil-bearing) in the south and embarked on a short, serious, though unsuccessful, military action to this end in 1961 (during the Bizerte crisis). Ideally, Bourguiba would have resolved the conflict of interests involved in relations with France and the FLN by acting as intermediary, and no doubt he tried to play this role when visiting de Gaulle at Rambouillet in February 1961. But in the event, his discussions yielded little with regard either to Algeria or to relations with France.

In 1959 Bourguiba gave a succinct account of his aims with regard to France: the achievement of formal independence and the withdrawal of the French base at Bizerte and of French property owners. It was a policy appropriate to a weaker adversary, unable to win in armed battle and in danger of losing advances already gained by being too provocative. As he expressed this policy in a speech of 2 March 1959:

> The departure of France in response to force being excluded, we shall try to bring France to leave by an act of free-will. She will naturally not agree to leave all at once. We must push her in stages; she will allow herself to be pushed if she is persuaded that the step she is taking represents the lesser evil. It is a question of bringing pressure to bear on her at the same time as we try to minimize the concessions we are seeking, in order not to frighten her. It is important that she should be convinced that in taking this step she will not lose everything, but will gain something from the exchange. This is not Machiavellian, it is a question of psychology.

But it cannot be said that this tactic was successfully applied either in the Bizerte crisis or in the recovery of French lands. Bourguiba appears to have believed that de Gaulle had, at Rambouillet, given him assurances about the Bizerte base (which remained in French hands after the withdrawal of French troops in 1958). But in June 1961, the French began to extend the main runway to accommodate new Mystère fighters. Bourguiba reacted sharply and wrote to de Gaulle, restating the Tunisian claim to border territory in the south and demanding withdrawal from Bizerte. This diplomatic action was accompanied by widespread mass demonstrations against the French in Tunisia. But the crisis escaped from Bourguiba's control. Tunisian national guards fired on a French helicopter and precipitated an outburst of fighting. French forces attacked the Tunisian barricades and barracks, took over the city, and mortared the Casbah. Some 1,300 Tunisians were killed.

Bourguiba's skill could thereafter only be deployed in recovering from an extremely weak position. The Tunisian case, taken to the United Nations in July 1961, won widespread sympathy; but Britain and the United States were more concerned with the Berlin Wall than with Tunisia; the Arab League was noisy without being very effective; and it was impossible to make common cause with the Algerian provisional government, given the existing territorial dispute. Bourguiba therefore took advantage of the first opening in de Gaulle's position to take up negotiations; conversations in July 1962 eventually led to the evacuation of the base in October 1963. At the same time, Bourguiba developed improved relations with the Arab Middle East.

The end of the Algerian war and the evacuation of the Bizerte base facilitated the development of stable relations with France, and a series of agreements were signed covering French property in Tunisia, French investments and *coopérants* in Tunisia, financial support, and the status of Tunisian workers in France. In particular, the sequestrations which the Tunisians had carried out after the Bizerte crisis were regularized and an agreement made for the nationalization of a further 50,000 hectares of land, with compensation paid in large part by France.

It seemed, therefore, that this further stage of 'decolonization' would proceed amicably, stage by stage. Instead, the law of May 1964 nationalized all remaining land owned by foreigners and required that henceforth agricultural land could only be owned by Tunisians or Tunisian companies. Compensation would be paid, but at what promised to be an inadequate rate.

Bourguiba described this action as a 'question of life or death'—a statement which appeared excessively dramatic since Tunisia had already recovered, by agreement with France, or by private purchase or sequestration, some three-fifths of foreign-owned land (370,000 hectares). Land affected by the law of May 1964 amounted to a further 300,000 hectares, of which about 240,000 belonged to French settlers, the remainder to Italians, Maltese, and Swiss. Bourguiba's action formed part of a leftward push in the economy, either to make the country appear more 'radical' in the days of the Arab cold war or to create a ferment of activity in the socialist development of agriculture. But it could not be justified by the requirements of the programme of installing cooperatives in agriculture, which already lacked resources and skilled manpower, and it was paid for at a high cost. Predictably, de Gaulle once again reacted decisively, cutting financial and technical aid to Tunisia (although only a proportion of *coopérants* were withdrawn) and suspending a commercial agreement, thus leaving the country with an unmarketed stock of wine.

However, the nationalization of 1964 did not mark a radical departure in foreign policy. The disruption caused by the withdrawal of French aid was to some extent met by assistance from the United States which, from the days before Independence, had shown as much sympathy with Bourguiba's Tunisia as was compatible with good relations with France. Within less than a year, the Tunisian government was reconstructing relations with France. Mohamed Masmoudi was re-appointed ambassador, and a series of commercial agreements were negotiated, leading up to an important financial agreement in 1968, and further protocols in 1969. By 1971-2 the French foreign ministry had a global budget of 50 million francs for assistance to Tunisia; and there were nearly 3,300 French *coopérants* in the country, most of them teachers (although the primary sector was almost entirely Tunisian), but including some 550 economists, agronomists, and doctors.

It was in these circumstances that Bourguiba made his first official visit, as president, to Paris. His major speech, on 29 June 1972, promoted the idea of a Mediterranean agreement; but it was more remarkable for the tribute which he paid to the former protectorate power, which had not only instructed him in its schools but given him time for reflection and meditation in exile and in prison. With minimal reference to Arabic culture ('If our demands borrow from Descartes and Pascal they draw as well on Arabo-Islamic culture, on the oriental soul and on treasures of imagination and intuition which Bergson would not disown'), and a total absence of Third World rhetoric, taking pride in what had been done for the status of women and for education within 'cette famille de la culture francophone', he said:

If I am the pride of Tunisia, I like to hope that I am not a disappointment for France. In any case, as I am, it is in part the product of your culture who now addresses you. . . . With what joy, with what pride, with what emotion I rediscover, in the evening of my life, France, and her friendship as I dreamed of it in my early youth. If I was the determined and loyal adversary of a certain France, it was in order to cooperate better with another, eternal France, *la patrie* of the Declaration of the Rights of Man.

It is not surprising that Tunisia should have played a distinctive, though restricted, part in the policies of the Middle East. The first decade of Tunisia's independence coincided with the great days of President Nasser. Tunisian relations with Egypt improved from the time of the Bizerte crisis, and Bourguiba made a journey to the Middle East (with surprising results) in 1965. But Bourguiba was unequivocal in his condemnation of Egypt's role in the conflict between 'radical' and 'conservative' Arab states, and he expressed distinctive and isolated views of the Israel question.

It is difficult to judge the appeal which Nasser and Nasserism held for Tunisians. It was inevitable that Salah Ben Youssef's supporters should look admiringly towards Egypt, and there was, in addition, a more widespread tendency for critical opposition to draw inspiration from Nasserism. But the attitude of Bourguiba and the ruling élite of Tunisia was well expressed in descriptions of Nasserist policies like that given by the foreign minister at the United Nations on 11 October 1966: 'a new form of interference in the affairs of a third country is that which I shall call micro-imperialism and which tends to impose on the countries by intimidation, blackmail, and calumny a certain political line, denying them all liberty of action and placing them under a foreign hegemony.'

In common with other Maghreb leaders, Bourguiba thus took an independent and critical view of Nasser's leadership. When King Faisal of Saudi Arabia proposed a summit of Islamic states as a counter to Nasser's influence and travelled across the Islamic world (and to the United States) in 1965 and 1966, he was welcomed in Tunis (as well as Rabat) in spite of the differences between the theocracy of Saudi Arabia and the lay state of Tunisia.

When Bourguiba went to the Middle East in the spring of 1965, his visit was notable for the instant development of a new Palestine policy. He went at a time of diplomatic turmoil consequent on the revelation that the German Federal Republic was planning to send arms to Israel. President Nasser invited Walter Ulbricht to Cairo—a visit which followed Bourguiba's—while the German Federal Republic dropped its plans to supply arms but established diplomatic relations with Israel and suspended aid to Egypt. Bourguiba's visit, in these circumstances, began with his taking advantage of the opportunity to cement the improvement in relations with Egypt. But he then visited refugee camps in Jordan. He was profoundly affected by the way in which the refugees were nourished on 'chimerical hopes and sterile hatred', and, in Amman, he said, 'The Palestinian affair requires a peaceful solution in which there is neither victor nor vanquished'. He pleaded for a solution 'by stages' and spoke of the existence of Israel as a 'colonial fact', an ambiguous phrase.

There were two aspects to this newly created policy. Bourguiba espoused the Palestinian cause and was outspokenly critical of the manner in which the Arab states of the Middle East treated the Palestinians. Subsequently Bahi Ladgham, as prime minister, acted as mediator between the Palestinians and King Hussein after 'Black September' in 1970 (an enterprise which also served to remove Ladgham from office), and it was a continuation of the same policy when, in the summer of 1974, he called for the abdication of King Hussein to make way for a Palestinian state.

But while Bourguiba supported the Palestinians he also urged negotiation on the question of Israel. The immediate result was a turbulent manifestation against his visit, a threatened assassination in Beirut, and the cancellation of his visit to Baghdad, where the government said that it could not be responsible for good order if he came; while Golda Meir (as Israeli foreign minister) stated that Israel would be glad to receive Bourguiba and discuss with him the means to achieve peace between Israel and the Arab states.

The affair had no immediate sequel, save to worsen relations with the Arab states of the Middle East. Tunisia alone was absent from the Casablanca conference in September 1965, and the Tunisians boycotted the meetings of Arab delegations at the UN.

The 1967 Middle East war ended this period of hostility, and

Tunisia rejoined the Arab family, promising the same support for Egypt as Tunisia had received at Bizerte. An expeditionary force was organized, although the swift defeat of Egypt meant that the only purpose served was the expression of public feeling as it marched towards the Libyan frontier. After defeat, Nasser evoked compassion rather than suspicion in the Maghreb, and warm tributes were paid at his death. Meanwhile Bahi Ladgham, the Tunisian prime minister, had played an active role in the conflict which is said to have precipitated Nasser's final illness.

The unity thus achieved was even greater during the 1973 war. In May Bourguiba once again took the initiative and, in an interview with an Italian newspaper, expressed his readiness to mediate in the Arab–Israeli dispute—an offer greeted with suspicion in Israel, until Abba Eban said that he was prepared to meet Bourguiba. The Tunisian proposal for discussions was that they should be based on the UN partition plan of 1947. It had no impact before the 1973 war, but afterwards provided a ready-made diplomatic position to urge at the UN, together with renewed offers by Masmoudi to meet Eban on this basis.

Diplomatically, the 1973 war held no complexities for Tunisia. Saudi Arabia was allied with Egypt, and France took a strongly pro-Arab position; while the old frictions with Algeria were at an end. A Tunisian contingent of a thousand men was sent to Egypt, possibly in Algerian transport aircraft, but it was in position on the canal only after the cease-fire. Tunisia provided medical supplies and cooperated closely with Algeria both in the despatch of supplies and in diplomatic activity for the Arab cause.

Throughout this period, Tunisia had maintained good relations with the United States. In 1946 and again in 1951, Bourguiba went to the United States to urge the Tunisian case for independence. The Tunisian trade union movement at the same time established close relations with the AFL. The United States and Tunisia thereafter provided mutual diplomatic support. Bourguiba refused to accept the conventional view of the United States as an 'imperialist' power in the Middle East, particularly during the intervention in Lebanon, and supported the United States position in Vietnam, at least until 1969. Tunisia became a major recipient of United States aid—18 million dollars in 1957 rising to 57 million in 1960. Unattractive as Destourian socialism was to some Americans, the character of Tunisian government, its serious concern with planning and its effective use of aid, was attractive to the United States administration so that Tunisia, with Nigeria, became one of the most important developing countries in Africa.

To some extent, the relationship with the United States was balanced by good relations with the Soviet Union. In the field of technical assistance, Tunisia showed itself to be a country with catholic tastes and received assistance from the countries of the Soviet bloc. But its attachment to France, the growing interest of the German Federal Republic in its trade and its tourist industry, and the major aid interest of the United States, made clear its western orientation. Moreover, the economic policies of Hédi Nouira confirmed Tunisia in the same direction, closely paralleling the policies of the Sadat regime in Egypt.

SOCIETY AND EDUCATION

While it is important not to underestimate the strength of traditional North African culture, it remains the case that Tunisia can claim to have adopted and adapted European culture, just as, in previous centuries, it adapted Phoenician and Roman civilizations. But this adaptation has inevitably been easier for the educated élite (which, at the same time, it has helped to perpetuate). The development of education and the democratization of society cannot be carried out without arousing conflict and tension between the two attractive poles of Europe and the Middle East (the more so since the process is under way at a time of increasing wealth and power in the Arab world).

One of the first legislative actions of the new republic was the promulgation of the code of personal rights in 1957, which passed into law over the next seven years. Its most important effect was to enhance the position of women in society. The French protectorate had never entertained the possibility of introducing a reform of this kind, having no interest in a frontal attack on the customs of the society it ruled (however disruptive colonization might be in other areas of Tunisian life). Except among those Tunisians closest to European culture, custom remained unchanged, and the new legislation was intended to have a modernizing effect, as part of a general policy of development. Polygamy was made illegal (it had always been exceptional, though permitted by law), and the law governing divorce was reformed to give women a stronger position. The consent of both partners to a marriage was required, whereas previously the father could give his daughter in marriage without asking her consent, and in 1964 a minimum age for marriage was set (seventeen for a woman, twenty for a man), where previously there had been none.

A combination of social and political circumstances: the weakness of the traditional strands of Islam, the absence of obscurantism, the enhanced position of women, and Bourguiba's leadership, have resulted in relative success in family planning in comparison with other Muslim countries, although statistics show the limits of its effectiveness.

A law of 1960 authorized the import and sale of contraceptive devices; in the same year family allowances were limited to the first child; and in 1965 abortion was legalized if it endangered the health of the mother or for other reasons if the couple already had five living children. More important, the government has developed a substantial birth control programme supported by the president and the political system. The first experimental programme was planned in 1962–3 and was begun with assistance from the Ford Foundation and the Population Council in 1964. Inexplicably, in 1966, Bourguiba reversed the direction he had given to family planning, arguing publicly that the figures of population increase did not justify any apprehension and that 'couples hostile to procreation do not fulfil their duties to the nation'. However, this change of policy was short-lived and checked the momentum of the programme only temporarily. In 1968 a department for family planning and for maternal and child health services was created. A wide range of family planning methods was developed, including the provision of contraceptive facilities, educational programmes, sterilization for women, and abortion.

At the same time Bourguiba, returning to his original position, deployed his oratory and public persuasion in support of birth control and family planning. In his traditional speech on the evening before the birthday of the Prophet he urged that the Arab and Islamic world should develop scientifically in order to be strong, and went on to advocate family planning so that the increased resources of nation and family should not be dissipated by population growth. He based his case on the Koran and the life of the Prophet and urged: 'The *Ijtihad* [legal opinion] on the matter consists in the planning of births, by spacing them reasonably, or by preventing pregnancy by methods which science indicates and religion does not forbid, or, finally, by resorting to abortion within the permitted period of time.'[1]

The obstacles to the development of the programme have been those found in other areas of government, with changes in administrative arrangements and direction, and shortage of qualified personnel chief among them. At the same time the general improvement in the position of women and the postponement of marriage (in 1956, 40 per cent of girls between fifteen and nineteen were married, in 1966 only 18 per cent) have contributed to the limitation of births. Thus it has been estimated that in 1963–8 the crude birth rate in Tunisia declined by 10 per cent or more, from about 48 to 42 or 43; the fourth plan gives a birth rate of 37 per cent.

Education

The development of education in independent Tunisia shares some problems with the rest of the Maghreb, notably the problem of language, the shortcomings of the system created under the protectorate, and the rapidly increasing population. It has been distinguished by

[1] *L'Action*, 14–15 April 1973.

the distinctive contribution of Mahmoud Messadi, who was secretary of state for education from 1958 to 1968.[1]

Under the French protectorate the provision of education was inadequate, diverse, and heavily tilted towards the French and the European population. The protectorate government was concerned with the development of schooling for French citizens and for the Italian and Maltese population, so that these should be brought into the French orbit. The Jewish population benefited from the openings available to the European population, and they also received assistance from the Alliance Israelite.

Until the last years of the protectorate, when a massive effort was made to provide more schools, only some 12 per cent of Tunisian children between the ages of six and fourteen attended primary school, and there were only 6,682 Tunisian pupils in secondary schools in 1953. Four main types of primary school covered the range from French to Arabic education. There were French primary schools, using only the French language, for French citizens only; Franco-Arab schools, also using French; modernized Koranic schools; and traditional *kuttab* schools. Secondary education was provided in French lycées and colleges, Franco-Arab schools of which Sadiki College was the most outstanding, and Muslim colleges. Higher education was available on a very limited scale, either at the Institut des Hautes Études (a first-year annexe of the University of Paris) or at the Zitouna mosque, where the Islamic university was comparable, on a Maghreb scale, with Al-Azhar at Cairo.

The standards of Islamic education suffered from conservatism, although Tunisian concern for education produced some innovation. The basic curriculum of the *kuttab* school was the learning of the Koran by heart and the absorption of Islamic tradition. The modernized Koranic schools were a great improvement on the *kuttab* schools and were the result of private Tunisian initiative and finance, with minor government assistance in the last years of the protectorate. They used French methods of teaching but Arabic as the language of instruction, although French was taught as a foreign language. On the other hand, the Zitouna showed little evidence of departure from classical Koranic education, and the Ulema were steeped in a religious orthodoxy which gave little opportunity for creative innovation. It followed that the best route for an aspiring Tunisian to follow was that of a Franco-Arab school, preferably Sadiki College, followed by further study in France. The cohesion of the Neo-Destour owed something to the fact that Bourguiba and a high proportion of the élite of the nationalist movement had followed this course. But the numbers receiving education remained small, and very few girls were educated.

[1] The section that follows owes much to unpublished papers by Pablo Foster, Mohamed Maamouri, and Robin Ostle.

Mahmoud Messadi, who was given the task of developing Tunisian education two years after Independence, is a distinguished scholar in Arabic and in French, a poet, and a dramatist. He brought immense energy to his task, and was determined to expand education along a modern, secular path which would create a cultural unity in Tunisia. The end of his tenure of the secretaryship in 1968 was followed by a period of great confusion. Ahmed Ben Salah's policy of directing education towards the immediate need for trained personnel for economic development disappeared with him in 1969. A succession of different secretaries of state tried to grapple with the problems of the next stage of development in an atmosphere of political and economic crisis.

The achievement of the first ten years is outstanding in statistical terms; and the quantitative change readily suggests to the imagination the problems which come into existence as a result. Between 1959 and 1971 the number of children in primary schools increased from 361,532 to 934,827, being an increase in the percentage of children receiving primary education from 44 per cent to 72·4 per cent. The number in secondary school in the same period rose from 35,772 to 184,125 and in university from 2,133 to 10,992. Expenditure on education was calculated at 2·8 per cent of GNP in 1960, and 7·37 per cent of GNP or 31·68 per cent of the national budget in 1970.

Primary education has been provided for children aged six to eleven on a pattern very close to that of French primary schools, with French as the language of instruction after the first two years. Secondary education has been much more diverse. It has been provided within a lycée system and in *collèges moyens*, which have replaced technical training centres. (They are attended in part by young people who have completed primary education at a very retarded age.) The diversity of the lycée system comes from the streaming of pupils which, in the Messadi system, was supposed to occur after the first year. In the most recent reforms, streaming takes place later, and by stages. University education has been expanded by the formation of the University of Tunis in 1960. It has incorporated the former Institut des Hautes Études, the Bourguiba Institute of Modern Languages, and the Zitouna university (which has been absorbed into the theology faculty). In addition, technical education has been expanded in a number of technical institutes, while at university level a series of specialized institutes follow the pattern of the French Grands Écoles.

The shortcomings of the system stem from a number of causes, some of which are outside the control of the government, while others are common to all educational systems, or at least to those in developing countries. Language provides a major difficulty. The object of educational policy has been to create a bilingual cultural unity. In practice it has proved impossible to provide sufficient teachers and enough instruction in French to produce this result, so that many young people starting secondary education still spend time mastering the French language in which they receive instruction. They also have to cope with the difficulty of Arabic, which is not a single language, but consists of (at least) classical Arabic, Tunisian Arabic, and a variant in between which Bourguiba has referred to as 'an elevated form of the *langue populaire*'.[1] The advantages accruing to the child of educated parents are thus greater if the home background is bilingual. Moreover, the demoralizing effect of the custom of repeating a year is inevitably increased as a result of language problems. In 1970-1 43 per cent repeated the sixth year of primary school while 28,000 out of 181,000 pupils in secondary school were repeating a year.

In spite of the increase in numbers in schools it proved impossible, at least until 1973, to increase the percentage of children attending school above 73 per cent, because of the increase in the population. The percentage of eligible children in school fell slightly between 1969 and 1972 in spite of an increase in numbers, while even the total numbers appear to have fallen in 1972-3. Nor has it yet been possible to provide teaching of good quality in so short a time. Although primary teaching is now done entirely by Tunisians, the country still relies heavily on French *coopérants*, both civilian and those drawn from national service, of whom there were 2,984 in secondary education and 269 in higher education in 1971. Until recently little was done to relate the subjects taught in class to Tunisian experience. (At the time of writing the Ford Foundation and the British Council are cooperating in the provision of textbooks for the teaching of English which will use intelligible Tunisian examples rather than teaching young Tunisians through the medium of French.)

In addition to the development of school education, Tunisia has made a serious effort to educate adults, having embarked, in 1966, on a programme intended to educate 150,000 adults over the following five years. It has in addition received a wide variety of grants for technical training, from France, the Ford Foundation, the United States, Holland, and the German Federal Republic among others. In so far as the results of these projects have been examined, enquiry has shown that the acquisition of skills calls for time and stamina. It is also apparent that many of the projects financed by foreign aid have their value as pilot projects which could provide vital points of development. They have not altered the cultural pattern of the country as a whole, and they have certainly not reversed the tendency of the educated, or partially educated, to seek office jobs, and of the poor to drift to the towns. Similarly, the objective of a bilingual cultural unity will take

[1] Mohamed Maamouri identifies three intermediate variants: modern spoken Arabic, educated Arabic, and French Arabic.

many years to achieve. Tunisia faces a dilemma: it is sandwiched between Libya in its present aggressively Arabic mood and Algeria, committed to arabization; yet it remains dependent on its links with Europe, which have been forged by a French-educated élite.

VII
Literature in North West Africa
(by Robin Ostle)

The Pre-Colonial Period

Ibn Khaldun's judgement on the literary heritage of North Africa was one of sad resignation: 'There have been no famous poets in Ifriqiya except for Ibn Rashiq and Ibn Sharaf. Most of the poets there have been recent immigrants. Down to this day their eloquence has inclined to the inferior.'[1] Reading the quite considerable section of *The Muqaddima* which he devotes to language and literature, one is struck by his portrayal of his own area of the Islamic world as 'provincial' in cultural terms: constant emphasis is placed on the remoteness of North Africa from the more densely urbanized regions of the Islamic heartlands, from the great centres of wealth and patronage essential to the promotion of cultural activities. A further obstacle to cultural development in his eyes is the prevalence of non-Arabic speech in the Maghreb, coupled once again with its distance from the cradle of classical Arabic and the language of Mudar.[2] One should hasten to add that although Ibn Khaldun's chapters on literature are full of interest and enlightening comments, he is not here concerned with presenting carefully evaluated literary judgements, but is making use of language and literature to support his main arguments about the forces which have controlled Islamic history and moulded Islamic society, and these remain his basic concern. The troubled and uncertain times which he himself knew in North Africa perhaps conditioned his mind against a favourable verdict on his local cultural heritage.

Yet one cannot dispute the role played by the city in the Islamic world as the focal point of literary activity, and the first notable urban centre in Muslim North Africa was Kairouan which from A.D. 800 became the capital of the Aghlabid dynasty. Prior to that it had been a typical garrison town similar to its eastern counterparts such as Kufa and Basra both in function and in the culture which it fostered: it became a centre for the study of *hadith*, grammar, and theology. The poetry of this period which has survived (mainly in fragments) has much in common with the factional verse written in the Arab east

[1] Ibn Khaldun, *The Muqaddima*, Rosenthal Translation, 1958, iii. 363.
[2] Ibid.

reflecting the religio-political struggles of the Kharijite and the early Alid parties, or inter-tribal strife such as that between Kalb and Qays.[1] These were conflicts which bedevilled the Syrian Umayyads and were not without repercussions in the province of Ifriqiya. Two of the more notable figures of this time, some of whose poetry has survived in later anthologies are al-Husam b. Dirar al-Kalbi (d. A.D. 747) and one of the early Cadis of Ifriqiya under the Umayyads, a certain Abd al-Rahman b. Ziyad al-Kairouani.

From A.D. 800 Kairouan came into its own as a cultural centre of renown as the Aghlabids began to augment their virtual political autonomy with their local prestige and patronage following a pattern to become ever more familiar in the Islamic world. Henceforth the great mosque in Kairouan became the landmark which attracted men of erudition and letters from all over the Maghreb who came to study the works on medicine, *fiqh*, Koran commentary, and other sciences produced by the new generation of scholars there. In many ways Kairouan represents a Baghdad in miniature as Ziyadatallah III (A.D. 817–38) founded his *Bayt al-Hikma* beside the mosque. There even existed the equivalent of the attempt by the ruling family to impose as official doctrine the *muʿtazili* theory of the created Koran, and the role of Ahmed b. Hanbal in Baghdad was played in Kairouan by the great Maliki *fiqh* scholar and cadi, Sahnun (A.D. 776–856). Like Ahmed b. Hanbal, he had to suffer a *mihna* or inquisition for his opposition. Apart from the works on religious, legal, and scientific topics, the prose of this period was confined mainly to letters and *khutab*—sermons or public orations by the governors, cadis, or religious dignitaries. There is little or no sign in extant literature of the *belles lettres* compositions which had become a feature of certain literary circles in and around Baghdad. Although Kairouan was a considerable city for the Maghreb, it lacked the large numbers of urbane educated bureaucrats, civil servants, and merchant classes who promoted such literature in Baghdad.

Poetry flourished in Aghlabid Kairouan, the tone being set by the encouragement and patronage of Ibrahim b. al-Aghlab, the founder of the dynasty, reportedly a man of taste and culture with a talent for versification. The same applied to one of his more notable successors, Abu'-Abbas al-Aghlabi. Perhaps the most striking feature of the verse which has survived from this period is the extent to which it was a part of the fabric of life and society in all its aspects. Apart from performing the traditional functions of eulogizing the qualities and exploits of the ruler, much of this poetry has a strongly theological content. Almost without exception, the poets of this time in Kairouan were scholars of *fiqh* and *hadith* who used poetry as a further support and medium of com-

---

[1] Rabah Bunar, *Al-Maghrib al-Arabi, Tarikhuhu wa Thaqafatuhu*, Algiers, 1968, pp. 50ff.

munication for the socio-religious values which they desired to promote. A figure whose name stands out in this early period is Bakr b. Hammad al-Zanati al-Tiharti (A.D. 816–909),[1] a man who had extensive connexions with Aghlabid Kairouan but who ended his career back in his home city of Tahert which had been the centre of the Rustamid Kharijite dynasty since A.D. 776. His career is an example of how a man of his culture and reputation could travel from end to end of the Islamic world in pursuit of knowledge, passing through areas by no means homogeneous in religio-political outlook, yet receiving honour and lavish hospitality wherever he went. From Tahert he travelled to Kairouan and sat at the feet of Sahnun and his contemporaries, widening his knowledge of the Islamic sciences and literature, and from there he travelled east to Basra and Baghdad, becoming an honoured member of court circles in the company of poets such as Abu Tammam, and Muslim b. al-Walid. On his return to Kairouan he had acquired a considerable reputation in the Islamic world as a man of learning and a poet of great skill. The range of his work pays tribute to the numerous and varied contacts he had with the cultural riches of Islamic civilization: he is a skilful composer of all manner of *madih* (eulogy), *ritha* (elegy) and *hija* (satire),[2] his role as a teacher of *hadith* and a man of religion is evident in his numerous pieces of *zuhd* poetry, verse of piety and religious asceticism after the fashion of Abul-Atahiya (A.D. 750–825), verse which is not merely moralistic and didactic but also given to flashes of profound personal introspection.

The fall of Kairouan to the Shi'ite Fatimids in 909 and the end of the Aghlabid dynasty did not signal a decline in the cultural achievements of Ifriqiya. The capital was transferred to Mahdiya which now became a new centre of patronage and artistic activity. Perhaps it was al-Mu'izz, the Caliph who eventually led the Fatimids to Egypt, who was the most renowned of their rulers in the Maghreb for his encouragement of men of letters and learning. Above all he used poetry to further the prestige of his dynasty and the Shi'ite cause, and to this end he secured the services of Ibn Hani 'l-Andalusi (937–72) as his court poet, after the latter had been forced to leave Andalusia reportedly because of his Shi'ite sympathies. The numerous eulogies composed by Ibn Hani for al-Mu'izz and other Fatimid notables, in particular his impressive descriptions of their fleets of ships, are famous in Arabic literature and earned their author the grandiose title 'Mutanabbi of the West'. After al-Mu'izz had gone to Cairo, he heard of the untimely death of his favourite poet, and he reflected sadly on how he had hoped to use Ibn Hani's talents to spread the glory of the Shiite cause throughout the Mashreq.[3]

[1] Muhammad al-Tammar, *Tarikh al-Adab al-Jaza'iri*, Algiers, 1969, pp. 32ff.
[2] Rabah Bunar, op. cit., pp. 128ff.
[3] *Diwan Ibn Hani 'l-Andalusi*, Beirut, 1964, pp. 5–8.

The poets Ibn Rashiq and Ibn Sharaf were active under the Zirid dynasty to whom the Fatimids had entrusted the rule of Ifriqiya on their departure to Egypt. Ibn Rashiq arrived at the Zirid court in Kairouan during the reign of the Caliph al-Mu'izz b. Badis, and soon became one of the leading men of science, letters, and religion in the court circle. He became the protégé of the powerful Wazir Abu 'l-Hasan Ali b. Abi 'l-Rijal who was able to promote the young poet and scholar in the eyes of the Caliph. Far beyond his own *diwan* of verse, Ibn Rashiq is rightly renowned for his book on poetry and rhetoric, the *Kitab al-Umda fi Mahasin al-Shi'r wa Adabih*, a work for which the demanding Ibn Khaldun is frequently unstinting in his praise.[1] Not only does the author treat all the usual technical problems of *balagha* or rhetoric, but he writes at length about the nature of the poet and poetry, the correct function of the poet's art, and the role played by poets and poetry in Islamic civilization. The book is a treasury of quotations and judgements on the works of Arab poets from the pre-Islamic period onwards, and has become an indispensable source for the study of medieval Islamic literature. Ibn Sharaf was also a contemporary at the court of al-Mu'izz b. Badis, and likewise a poet and critic. He and Ibn Rashiq became notorious for their bitter rivalry, vying for the ruler's favour and attention while he in turn was happy to play off one against the other. Their struggle for supremacy resembled the great poetic rivalries in the Arab east such as those between the Umayyad poets Jarir (d. A.D. 733) and Farazdaq, (d. A.D. 732?) or the protagonists of the *badi'* school Abu Tammam (d. A.D. 845) and al-Buhturi (d. A.D. 897).

The Zirid dynasty based on the Kairouan region seems to have suffered more than others as a result of the incursions of the Beni Hilal into North Africa in the early 1050s. The fall of Kairouan itself began a dispersal of its glittering circle of theologians and men of science and literature. The two arch-rivals Ibn Rashiq and Ibn Sharaf accompanied their patron al-Mu'izz to Mahdiya, and on the death of the latter they both went on to Sicily where legend has it they finally sank their differences and became firm friends. Ibn Rashiq died there at Mazara in 1064. Some of the distinguished scholars who had been at Kairouan went westwards to Andalusia, as did Ibn Sharaf, or to Egypt and the Mashreq. Sicily itself had been part of the Muslim west since the mid-ninth century and can boast some prominent writers in its own right such as the poet Ibn Khamdis (b. 1055), and the author of the geographical treatise known as 'The Book of Roger', the Sharif Idrisi (b. 1099): he worked for the Norman Sicilian king Roger II who proved as worthy a patron of Arabic culture as any of his Muslim counterparts on the African mainland.[2]

[1] Ibn Khaldun, op. cit., p. 338.
[2] H. A. R. Gibb, *Arabic Literature*, London, 1963, pp. 134–5.

After the departure of the Fatimids from Ifriqiya to Egypt various dynasties succeeded each other in different areas—Zirids, Hammadids, Almohads, Hafsids, Zayyanids, Merinids. The pattern of culture and letters proliferated but did not vary in its basic forms. Other cities in the Maghreb took over the role which had been primarily fulfilled by Kairouan and Mahdiya: Qalat Beni Hammad, Marrakesh, Fez, Tunis, Tlemsen. Particularly brilliant although short-lived was the Almohad dynasty of the twelfth century: in their cities the traditional sciences such as *fiqh*, Koran commentary, grammar, poetry, and prose flourished, and the two great philosophers Ibn Rushd (1126–98) and Ibn Tufayl (d. 1185) were made welcome at the court of Marrakesh. The latter was particularly renowned for his version of a philosophical romance entitled *Hayy b. Yaqzan*, which had originally been composed by Ibn Sina. This is a remarkable narrative of how an individual in total solitude on an island attains to the heights of wisdom and divine vision through the power of his own mind. The Almohad dynasty had been inspired in their rise to power by the theologian Ibn Tumart (d. 1130), a spiritual disciple of al-Ghazali, and the religio-political function of poetry was emphasized again by the number of poets of this time who were also men of *fiqh* and *hadith* in addition to their talents for versification. Two poets particularly, Abu Abdalla Muhammad b. Hammad (d. 1330) and Abu Abdalla Muhammad b. Yahya b. Abd al-Salam were practising cadis.[1] It was probably around the time of the extension of Almohad suzerainty into Spain that the *muwashshah* was introduced into North Africa. This was a new strophic form of writing poetry which began to appear in Spain at the beginning of the eleventh century, and after its transfer to the east via North Africa it became a conventional poetic stereotype in addition to the traditional *qasida* form. In terms of subject-matter, the *muwashshah* is almost invariably confined to amatory poetry.

The end of the Almohad dynasty and the subsequent reconquest of most of Spain by the Christians caused numerous emigrations across to North Africa, and the towns both in the interior and on the coast became cultural enclaves which maintained the continuity of some of the great traditions of Andalusia. Although geographical writing lies outside the scope of creative literature, one can scarcely avoid mentioning the name of Ibn Battuta of Tangier (1304–77), who with Ibn Khaldun himself was one of the greatest figures of Arabic letters in the fourteenth century. His record of the manners and customs of virtually every land in the Muslim world, as well as being a priceless source for cultural history, is a work of great literary merit.[2] While research into the Arabic literature of North Africa as a whole has scarcely begun, it is even more incomplete for the later period of the Hafsids, Zayyanids, or Merinids. In the case of poetry, Sufi elements became much more pronounced at this time.

[1] See Muhammad al-Tammar, op. cit., pp. 72ff.
[2] H. A. R. Gibb, op. cit., pp. 151–3.

Typical of this increasing trend is the work of Ibn Khamis, born in Tlemsen (c. 1252), who subsequently spent most of his life in Granada but without ever losing a tremendous affection and nostalgia for his native city.[1] The chronicler al-Maqqari (d. 1632), also of Tlemsen, wrote literary history in addition to his biography of the Spanish author Ibn Khatib (d. 1374), but most of his material concentrates upon Andalusia.

The Modern Period

We possess a precious record of how the short-lived Napoleonic invasion of Egypt appeared to Muslim eyes through the sober, measured tones of al-Jabarti (1756-1825), one of the latest representatives of the traditional Islamic chroniclers. A truly objective historian, he describes the end of the natural order of things and of the world which he and his contemporaries knew, but at the same time he registers his admiration for the orderly administration of the French, their efficiency, and love of science and discovery. A very different record remains of another French invasion in the writings of the Amir Abd al-Qadir al-Jaza'iri (1808-83), who led the resistance to the French after their incursion into Algeria in 1830 (see above, pp. 61-3). The atmosphere of struggle and conflict which characterizes most of his writing and poetry has remained a constant theme—if not an *idée fixe*—in the history of Algerian literature up to the War of Independence and beyond. Abd al-Qadir was a representative both typical and outstanding of that society which the French set out to conquer:[2] he was a scholar, a man of *'ilm* who was an authority on the traditional sciences of *fiqh*, *hadith*, and Koran commentary which he had absorbed from his teachers in his native land, and from the centres of learning visited as he accompanied his father on the pilgrimage. But this scholasticism was only a part of his position as a Sufi notable, a leading figure in the organizations of *turuq* which were basic components of the fabric of society and provided the framework for him to become a leader of great charisma and wide popular following, This combination of elements explains how he could be both a man of letters and learning and a militant political activist. His poetry is a faithful reflection of the different features of such a complex personality: not surprisingly a predominant theme is the battles waged against the French, or against the tribes who had made peace with the invaders. These poems are full of the old Arab virtue of *tafakhur* or self-aggrandizement almost as though the poet sees himself as a descendant of Antar and Mutanabbi. The horse, on which

---

[1] For a list of these later Sufi poets of the Maghreb, see Muhammad al-Tammar, op. cit., pp. 145ff.
[2] Muhammad Taha 'l-Hajiri, *Jawanib min al-Hayat al-Aqliyya wa'l-Adabiyya fi'l-Jaza'ir*, Cairo, 1968, pp. 31ff.

the warrior depends so much in battle, frequently forms the subject-matter of this poetry as Abd al-Qadir perpetuates a tradition of heroic poetry extending back to the *Ayyam al-arab* of ancient mythology.[1] The taking of Tlemsen back from the French occupying forces was an occasion which inspired the Amir to sing of the city as a beautiful maiden whose favours he had gained after tearing aside the veil which had been placed between them by the enemy.

Both through his deeds and his writings, Abd al-Qadir remained a considerable threat to the French as they undertook the gradual subjugation of Algeria, but finally he had to submit in 1847. He was exiled and imprisoned in France before he was allowed to return to the Islamic world, to Syria where he died in 1883. This brusque transition in his life is reflected in poetry of quite different themes and atmosphere. His odes written in exile are full of longing and nostalgia for his homeland and above all for members of his family and his friends. (Although there is little detailed similarity in their work, here one may note an interesting parallel between the career of Abd al-Qadir and that of Mahmud Sami al-Barudi (d. 1904), the Egyptian poet and politician who was exiled to Ceylon because of the leading part he played in the abortive 'Urabi revolution. The poems written by al-Barudi in exile are an early landmark in the modern literary renaissance in the Mashreq.) In this more passive meditative period of Abd al-Qadir's career, the Sufi strains from his native environment come very much to the fore. His work may be described as springing from a very old-established mould of Arabic literature. Contemporaries such as al-Sayyid Ali Abu Talib, al-Sayyid al-Tayyib b. al-Mukhtar, Shaikh Muhammad al-Shadhili al-Qusantini also produced verse and *khutab*—sermons or speeches written in *saj'* or rhymed prose—work similar in kind to Abd al-Qadir's but more often then not a fairly pale reflection of his achievements.

In nineteenth-century Algeria oral poetry in the vernacular was of great significance. As a medium of widespread propaganda and with its capacity to reach and be understood by even the remotest and humblest sections of society, this folk poetry had more practical effect than the works of Abd al-Qadir and his contemporaries written in literary Arabic.[2] Popular oral 'literature' is found in every Arab country where the literary medium coexists with the regional vernacular form, but the peculiar social and cultural dislocation caused by the French invasion and colonization of Algeria gave this folk-literature a particularly heightened importance. The wandering poet or bard could go freely from village to village, expressing himself in terms which could be understood by all his listeners.[3] The surrender of towns

[1] Muhammad al-Tammar, op. cit., pp. 267ff.
[2] Albert Memmi, *La Poésie algérienne de 1830 à nos jours,* Paris, 1963, pp. 19–38.
[3] For an Egyptian example of this figure, see *al-Ayyam,* i. ch. 1, by Taha Husain.

such as Algiers, Blida, or Constantine, figures prominently in popular poetry, as did the exploits of the Algerian resistance to the French advances. Apart from Abd al-Qadir and one or two of his contemporaries, the educated élite maintained a comparative silence, perhaps because they felt largely responsible for the defeat or because it was politically difficult for them to give open expression to their views. At all events, folk 'literature' was an essential support for popular morale. In the words of J. Desparmet, 'the Maghreb poet has assumed the mission of healing, saving and galvanizing national pride. He has been able to justify defeat, even to turn it to the glory of the defeated.'[1]

The next significant stage in the development of North African literature should not really be considered apart from the rise of journalism, and the emergence of a movement of Islamic reform in North Africa which owed much to its contacts with the Islamic renaissance in the east: Muhammad Abduh had paid two visits to Tunis, and had passed through Algiers and Constantine in 1900. His periodical *al-Manar* was read and studied in the Maghreb, and the more open-minded of the Ulema in the Zitouna and the Qaraouiyine mosques became conscious that they too could play a part in some of the more exciting movements taking place in the Mashreq. From the turn of the century, the educated Islamic élite shook off the comparative lethargy of the nineteenth century, and literary Arabic became one of the voices of liberalism and reform, to be transformed into an ever more strident nationalism from 1920 onwards. The climax of this movement of the Ulema in Algeria was the formation in 1931 of the Ulema's Association, led by Ibn Badis (1889-1940). The newspapers which made their appearance from the 1920s onwards—*al-Muntaqid, al-Shihab, al-Najah, al-Iqdam, al-Basa'ir*—were to become new and important outlets for Arabic poetry and prose. Even those who were scarcely literate could be moved by this new-found prestige of literary Arabic through their contact with students and by listening to the readings of those with more education than themselves.

Ibn Badis himself had no outstanding talent for creative literature. On occasion he wrote verse as did most of his associates, but he was renowned in particular as an orator and author of *khutab*, many of which were reproduced in the pages of *al-Shihab*: these are in *saj'* and range over a wide variety of subjects.[2] At times he railed against the injustice of imperialism, or he appealed for education and social reform. On other occasions he simply underlined the virtues of fundamental Islamic values and urged his countrymen to hold fast to their cultural and religious heritage. Altogether he encompassed a great variety of relevant issues of the time.

Muhammad al-Bashir al-Ibrahimi (1889-1965) was one of the

---

[1] Quoted in Albert Memmi, op. cit., p. 20.
[2] Abdalla Murtad, *Nahdat al-Adab al-Arabi'l-Mu'asir fi'l-Jaza'ir*, Algiers, n.d., pp. 56ff.

founder members of the Ulema's Association, and a contributor to *al-Shihab*; he was also a writer of great significance in North African literature. He was most closely connected with the newspaper *al-Basa'ir*, particularly in the second phase of its publication after 1947, when he was its editor. He himself wrote a weekly section in the paper until forced to flee the country for Egypt because of political difficulties. *Al-Basa'ir* was the most literary of all these early Algerian journalistic publications, no doubt because of the influence of its editor. His own contributions consisted of short pieces written in *saj'* under the general title of *saj' al-Kuhhan* (Rhymes of the Soothsayers). He also wrote *maqamat* in the old style, one of which was composed in memory of Ibn Badis. Both these types of composition were written in a highly ornate, difficult, and archaic Arabic style, and the sole aim of the author seems to have been to write stories without any particularly didactic aim or socio-political theme. In some respects his work is not unlike that of the Egyptian author al-Manfaluti (d. 1924), certainly in form and style, although it lacks some of al-Manfaluti's more moralistic tendencies. Al-Ibrahimi seems to have used this type of literature to assert the link with the great Islamic past. The contrast with the trenchant, highly readable prose in which he wrote his articles on social and political issues could not be more striking.[1]

A considerable advance in Arabic prose-writing is apparent in the work of Ahmed Rida Huhu (1911–65), whom some have described as the pioneer of the short story in Algeria. He departed from the ornate and archaic compositions of al-Ibrahimi and others, and produced a prose style much more of the twentieth century, having more in common with the best of political and reformist journalism. His two most important publications are *Ma'a Humar al-Hakim* (With al-Hakim's Donkey, 1953) and *Sahibat al-Wahy wa Qisas Ukhra* (Woman of Inspiration and Other Stories, 1954). The first book is based on a theme and a device already used by the Egyptian novelist and dramatist Tawfiq al-Hakim, and Huhu freely admits this derivation. In the conversations and the experiences which the author shares with al-Hakim's donkey, a large number of social and political questions are discussed. The basic concept is unoriginal, but the problems treated are specifically Algerian problems, there is effective use of humour and satire, together with extensive passages of dialogue, which combine to make this book one of the landmarks in modern Algerian prose. The second book is a collection of more traditional short stories, nine altogether, some of which had appeared in periodicals before their collection in book form. One such example was the story *Fatat Ahlami* (Girl of My Dreams) which had been published in *Ifriqiya al-Shamaliyya* in 1949. On the surface this appears to be a short story of sexual fantasy heading for a fatal descent into mawkish sentimentality, but the humorous

[1] See ibid., pp. 133ff. for examples of this prose.

twist at the end reveals the author's true intentions and the gentle irony which has been present throughout the story.

Contemporary with the activities of the Algerian Ulema's Association, historiographers such as Mubarak b. Muhammad al-Hilali 'l-Mili, Ahmed Tawfiq al-Madani, and Abd al-Rahman al-Jilani, were busy writing their various histories of Algeria and the Maghreb. This was their contribution to the fostering of an Algerian national consciousness and the bolstering of their countrymen's morale. They too were creating their versions of the golden age of Arabic Islamic grandeur in the Maghreb and were reverting to the glory of their cultural heritage in a manner different from that employed by al-Ibrahimi, but their basic objectives had much in common.[1]

Poets in the Maghreb, particularly in Algeria, from 1900 until the Algerian war, played a vital part in the revival of the prestige of literary Arabic which was a necessary accompaniment to the activities of the Islamic reformers and to the rapid, cumulative, demands of nationalism. The pages of *al-Shihab, al-Muntaqid,* and *al-Basa'ir* resounded to the sonorous verses of Muhammad al-Id, Ahmed Sahnun, and Mufdi Zakariyya. Just as in the past Arab poets had served the interests of individual rulers and dynasties, their voices now became important instruments of support raised at the festivals and gatherings organized by the Ulema's Association.[2] Muhammad al-Id (b. 1904) was to dominate poetry for most of this period: after a sojourn spent furthering his studies at the Zitouna in Tunis (1921–3), he returned to Algeria and remained active as a poet, educationalist, and journalist until the War of Independence and beyond. There was scarcely a subject of public or national concern which was not treated in his numerous poems, and one of the most frequent words in his resounding lines became *al-sha'b* —'the people'. Just as the great Egyptian Hafez Ibrahim (d. 1932) became known as the 'people's poet'—especially after his scathing attack on the British after the Dinshaway incident—so Muhammad al-Id became the champion in verse of his nation's cause. From the late 1920s onwards one can follow the gathering storm of Algerian nationalism through his exhortations to struggle, to unite, and be prepared to sacrifice all. The following lines were published in 1950, in the newspaper *al-Manar*:[3]

> Summon up your courage! Lend truth to your hopes!
>   For Time will record your deeds.
> People arise! Banish sleep from your lives.
>   For life's hours slip swiftly away.

---

[1] Ibid., pp. 177ff.
[2] Memmi, op. cit., p. 47.
[3] Abul Qasim Saadallah, *Dirasat fi'l-Adab al-Jaza'iri 'l-Hadith*, Beirut, 1966 (poem quoted on p. 41).

> Long have you borne your chains and distress. Burst
> the bonds and shatter the fetters!
> The people have groaned from tyranny, so sing of
> protecting liberty, of an Independence.

The poems of al-Id and his companions record the troubled history of Algeria from 1930 onwards. Particularly prominent are the bloodstained events of 1945 arising from the French reaction to Algerian frustration at not being able to decide her own destiny in the wake of the Second World War. Nor was the poetry confined on every occasion to events inside North Africa, as the fiercely anti-Zionist poems in support of Palestine bear witness. Ahmed Sahnun and Mufdi Zakariyya were among the most eminent of al-Id's contemporaries, but others, such as al-Amin al-Amudi, Jalul Badawi, Muhammad Salih Ramadan, Muhammad al-Akhdar al-Saihi, and al-Rabi' Abu Shama, should also be mentioned.

The stridently political nature of most of this Algerian poetry resembles the poetry supporting the Wafdist cause in Egypt in the 1920s. What is strikingly different is the lack of that quiet, contemplative, or introspective verse which became a feature of Egyptian poetry in the late 1920s and 1930s, culminating in the lyrical poetry of the *Apollo* group. Such was the Algerian atmosphere of struggle and *contestation* in the face of so many political and social causes, both internal and external, that there seems to have been no leisure for this, apart from occasional pieces by Ahmed al-Batini and Ahmed Sahnun inspired by the natural scenery and solitude of the desert.[1] The poetry discussed above was of a very public kind. Much of it was written for specific occasions, to be declaimed before an audience, and usually the poems would be printed subsequently in newspaper reports. This verse is often referred to as 'occasional' poetry—*shi'r al-munasabat*—and it is usually loud, rhetorical, and exhortatory. In form it is also highly traditional, retaining the classical metrical patterns and mono-rhyming hemistiches. The language is frequently interspersed with old poetic clichés. The themes and the audiences may have changed, but these Algerian poets are performing an age-old function in a time-honoured manner.

Algerian literature, and especially poetry, in Arabic since the early 1950s has been dominated by the themes of the armed revolution and the struggle for independence. In a situation of desperate extremity, the mere fact of expression in Arabic assumed great significance, and people avoided trying to reconcile pride in their national heritage with universal criteria of literary excellence. The *engagement* which had always been a feature of Algerian literature prior to the War of Independence became even more marked. Mufdi Zakariyya and Muhammad al-Id

---

[1] Muhammad al-Tammar, op. cit., pp. 312ff.

pursued their missions of national zeal into the war years. Even the rather unlikely subject of love-poetry was adapted to expressing the needs of war and the revolution.[1]

Poetry was not slow to reflect the intense desire for change which gripped many parts of the Arab world in the immediate post-war years. The conventional system of prosody with its complex, rigid metrical patterns which had enshrined the songs of the very earliest Arab poets gave way to the new *shi'r hurr* or 'free verse'. In most cases a basic foot was retained throughout the poem, but the habit of mono-rhyme and the regular *bayt* structure were abandoned. The era of the Algerian revolution had a similar effect on the work of poets such as Abul Qasim Saadallah and Abd al-Sallam Habib,[2] and the *fellah* in Algeria assumed the role of the heroic combatant fighting for his future and that of his country.[3]

The leading men of letters and religion from the Zitouna in Tunisia through to the Qaraouiyine in Fez were not unaware of each other's activities, and there was no lack of contact between the different groups: the period which Muhammad al-Id spent studying at the Zitouna was not an isolated and untypical case, and it was in Tunis that the first important anthology of Algerian poetry in the twentieth century was published in 1926, made up of the works of al-Id himself, Mufdi Zakariyya, and their various associates.[4] In much the same way that the members of the Algerian Ulema's Association had produced dazzling displays of old style rhetoric, albeit often 'adorned with the decadent elegance of academicism',[5] so did their Tunisian counterparts, whose names and works are recorded in the important anthology compiled by Zayn Abidin al-Sanusi in 1927-8.[6] The first poet to appear in this book is Muhammad al-Shadhili Khaznadar, described by some as the 'Prince of Poets' of the Maghreb, implying that he was the North African equivalent of the 'Prince of Poets' in the Mashreq, Ahmed Shawqi of Egypt. The comparison has been motivated by the similarity of the roles of the two poets in court life and the ruling circles of their respective cities of Tunis and Cairo, at least during the early parts of their careers. Khaznadar's verse reflects the elevated social milieu in which he moved and he belongs firmly to a tradition of court poetry extending far back into classical Arabic, although his work does not possess the same range and quality as that of Ahmed Shawqi. The other

---

[1] See the poems by Abul Qasim Saadallah quoted in Muhammad al-Tammar, op.cit., pp. 343-4.
[2] See *Masra Kha'in* (Death of a Traitor), by Abd al-Salam Habib, quoted in Abul Qasim Saadallah, op. cit., p. 43.
[3] Poem by Saadallah, quoted in Muhammad al-Tammar, op. cit., pp. 338-9.
[4] This was *Shu'ara'l-Jaza'ir fi'l-Asr al-Hadir*, compiled by Muhammad al-Hadi al-Sanusi al-Zahiri.
[5] Jacques Berque, *French North Africa*, London, 1967, p. 357.
[6] Entitled *Al-Adab al-Tunisi fi'l-Qarn al-Rabi' ashar*.

figures represented in al-Sanusi's anthology were virtually all Zitounians, and wrote verse on political, social, and religious themes, much of it highly public and 'occasional' by nature, poetry which was traditional both in style and prosodic convention. Those who belonged to this Zitounian circle (though not quite all of them graduated from there) include Abul-Hasan b. Shaban, Husain al-Jaziri, Muhammad Salih al-Naifir, al-Shaikh Hadi al-Madani, Mustafa Agha. Many of these were active as journalists as well as poets. Their work concentrates heavily on political and nationalistic themes, and they too were not unacquainted with persecution like their colleagues in Algeria (cf. Husain al-Jaziri's poem 'Wonders of Prison'),[1] but on the whole the tone of their work is more relaxed and less intense than that of their Algerian brethren, and one finds among their compositions more examples of quiet, personal, meditative poetry.

One of the Zitouna graduates who merited a place in this anthology, in spite of his youth, was Abu 'l-Qasim al-Shabbi. At the time of his inclusion by al-Sanusi he was just one member of quite a considerable group, but since his tragically premature death in 1934 posterity has recognized him as the greatest Arabic poet produced by the Maghreb in the modern period. What distinguished him from any other writer of his time was his capacity to circumvent the cultural dislocation which had hindered so many. Those who still remained closely in touch with the Arabic Islamic heritage did so with a fierce tenacity which was often too atavistic for the twentieth century, while those who through choice or necessity chose to adopt the language and methods of the colonialists often found themselves swallowed up, at the expense of their own authenticity. Al-Shabbi had received the traditional Islamic education of the Zitouna, and to this he owes his great mastery of the Arabic language. In the course of his short life (he was born in 1909), he learned no foreign language, but he had vital contacts with areas of literary activity and points of cultural dialogue elsewhere in modern Arabic literature. He was a corresponding member of the *Apollo* group in Egypt, motivated and inspired by Ahmed Zaki Abu Shadi. Al-Shabbi's poems were published in the pages of *Apollo*, and he must have received great encouragement from the praise and acclaim which he won there. Thus he took part indirectly in the literary debates and points of cultural controversy which raged among and around the *Apollo* members in Egypt. The pages of his single *diwan*, *Aghani al-Hayat* (Songs of Life), show definite evidence of influence from the *mahjar* or Syro-American school of Arabic poetry which had centred on the key personalities of Khalil Gibran and Mikhail Nuayma in New York. This school had a vital innovative influence in the main centres of literary activity back in the Arab world, and al-Shabbi, no doubt

[1] Ibid., pp. 88–92.

gleaning what he could from the relevant books and periodicals, made full use of their achievements in his own work.

Traditional in form though al-Shabbi's poetry is, his themes and style set him dramatically apart from his contemporaries. Broadly speaking he is a deeply introspective poet, but through exploring the problems of his own highly-strung existence he is capable of transcending the finite limits of his personality, and aspires to a plane which is ideal and eternal, of which life on earth is a most imperfect imitation. An image which recurs frequently in his work is that of a rebirth or redemption after life and death, usually expressed through the symbol of a new dawn breaking. He makes considerable use of nature imagery, and his language abounds with teasing ambiguous effects: he speaks of 'the smiles of distress', he describes night descending in a manner which is 'strong, overwhelming like the enchantment of eyelids, troubled and playful like melancholy flowers'.[1] Just as remarkable as the refined detail of the individual line is the care lavished on the overall construction of the poems. The last five years of al-Shabbi's life were dogged by the heart disease which was ultimately fatal, and some of his greatest poems come from this period when he is sustained by his passionate belief in the power of the spirit to rise above earthly tribulation, and his certainty of ultimate redemption. He transmits his own strength of purpose to the nation as a whole in the poem *Iradat al-Hayat* (Will to Live) written in 1933.[2]

The less extreme nature of political history in Tunisia as opposed to Algeria seems to have led, from 1930 onwards, to freer developments and more experimentation. Graduates from the Sadiki College played a role alongside their contemporaries from the Zitouna, in beginning a tradition of short-story writing, small-scale novels or *nouvelles*, and even the occasional incursion into drama, a literary form quite foreign to the Arabic tradition before the modern period.[3] Mahmoud Messadi (b. 1911), the first minister of education after Independence was the author of *al-Sudd* (The Dam) written in 1940, one of the first examples of modern Tunisian drama with a theme which strikes strong echoes in the life of a developing country: the hero attempts to bring wealth and agriculture to an arid valley by means of his dam, and tries to break through the prejudices and superstitions of the local inhabitants, but the project ends in failure. Messadi wrote a novel *Mawlid al-Nisyan* (Genesis of Oblivion) in 1944, and a collection of short stories based mainly on dramatic, episodic, incidents rather than tracts of speculative prose or deep character analysis. Other *nouvellistes* and short-story writers, particularly those of the Zitounian milieu, remained

---

[1] *Aghani'l-Hayat*, Tunis, 1966, pp. 94–7.
[2] Ibid., pp. 240–4.
[3] See M'hammed Ferid-Ghazi, 'La littérature tunisienne contemporaine', *Orient*, no. 12, 1959, pp. 131–97.

attached to the old *maqama* style. Among the more prominent writers who began their literary careers in the 1930s and 1940s are Ali al-Douaji, Muhammad Laribi, and Abd al-Razak Karabaka.

Since Tunisian Independence, this tradition of the *nouvelle* has been taken some stages further by authors such as Bechir Khraief (b. 1917), Mustafa Farsi (b. 1931), and Muhammad Larousi Metoui (b. 1920).[1] The latter is a typical example of a reforming Zitounian whose book *al-Tut al-Murr* (The Bitter Mulberry) is laden with social morality and a strongly didactic tone. One of the most interesting examples of this genre to emerge in recent years is *al-Munbatt* (Man without Roots) by Abd al-Majid Attiya, which treats a theme dear to the hearts of many modern Tunisians. Hassan, the main character, is representative of a generation of Tunisians of modest means who are educated abroad and then return to their native land. The basic problem is then to avoid the fate which befalls so many of them, that of the minor civil servant doomed to spend the rest of his life in a bureaucratic jungle. The basic conflict of the book revolves round Hassan's decision to cut himself off from his roots, to abandon his dependants, and to return to France to pursue his studies further. The cause of feminism has been espoused by Laila Ben Mami in her *Sauma'a Tahtariq* (Minaret in Flames), and her quest is to end the taboos and crippling constraints placed upon women by the conservative tendencies in Islamic society. The same spirit of challenge and dissatisfaction has been demonstrated by the journalist and essayist Izz al-Din al-Madani. His *Khurafat* (Fables or Fairy Tales) is basically an attempt to de-mysticize or make more rational people's view of the Islamic cultural heritage. At all events, the foundations of modern Tunisian prose writing (as far as the novel or *nouvelle* are concerned) are still being created, surrounded by the problems of the complex linguistic situation. Questions such as what is or is not good Arabic style or how to write dialogue in novels and short stories exercise the minds of writers in North Africa and elsewhere in the Arabic-speaking world. Valuable work has been done for the promotion of modern Tunisian literature by the articles and translations which appear regularly in the pages of *IBLA*, most frequently written by Michel Lelong or Jean Fontaine.

Perhaps the major crisis which has attended the development of literature in North West Africa during this century, a crisis seen at its most acute in Algeria, has been caused by extreme cultural polarization. Egypt in the 1920s and 1930s for example went through traumatic problems of cultural orientation as the basis for an authentic Egyptian culture was sought. Some writers found material as far back in Egyptian life as the Pharaonic era as well as in the predominant Arabic-Islamic heritage; some were more wholeheartedly in favour of

[1] See Rachad Hamzaoui, 'Thèmes et techniques du roman tunisien depuis l'Indépendance', *IBLA*, 1969, i. 37–49.

Western themes and forms in literature; while others sought to adapt whatever seemed most appropriate and authentic to the demands of the time. But at least a dialogue was taking place, and taking place in Arabic. It was often abrasive and even temporarily destructive, but it added to the corpus of creative literature in modern Egypt. In North West Africa one extreme of cultural polarization is represented by the strongly partisan Islamic historiographers referred to above, the *maqama* and *saj'* compositions of al-Ibrahimi, the *Khutab* of Ibn Badis, the fiercely strident and highly traditional poetry which orchestrated the rising tide of Algerian nationalism. The other extreme is represented by those natives of North Africa who have produced poetry and prose written in French. This gravitation towards French culture resulted not so much from a conscious desire on the part of its adherents, as from the education they had received. Malek Haddad is moved to speak of French as his 'exile', and asserts that he is less separated from his own country by the Mediterranean than by the French language.[1]

Albert Memmi gives a sympathetic and scholarly account of the major North West African writers who have written poetry in French since 1945, concentrating on Nourredine Tidafi, Malek Haddad, Kateb Yacine, Henri Kréa, and others.[2] Even more remarkable than this poetry are the French North African novels which appeared mainly in the early fifties, written by the Algerians Mouloud Feraoun *(La Terre et le sang; Le Fils du pauvre)*, Mouloud Mammeri *(La Colline oubliée; Le Sommeil du juste)*, Muhammad Dib *(La Grande Maison; L'Incendie; Au café)*, Kateb Yacine *(Nedjma)*; by the Moroccans Driss Chraibi *(Le Passé simple; Les Boucs)*, Ahmed Sefrioui *(Le Chapelet d'ambre; La Boîte à merveilles)*; and by the Tunisian Jew, Albert Memmi himself *(La Statue de sel)*. The list is by no means exhaustive. The literary merit of most of these works has been recognized in full in France and beyond. It is impossible to discuss all these books save in the most general terms: many of them dwell upon childhood experiences *(La Boîte à merveilles, Le Fils du pauvre, Le Passé simple)*, the last-named by Chraibi containing strong overtones of revolt against the family and religion in its traditional environment. Some treat the problems faced by North African emigrants in metropolitan France *(Les Boucs, Au café)*, and in most of them nationalism is never far from the surface. Almost all are anything but idealistic, full of the misery of life in overcrowded towns, in slum dwellings, the misery of unemployment or the impoverishment of the countryside, often emphasizing the backwardness of the social and religious situation. At least one commentator has been moved to describe the books as 'often irritating and

---

[1] G. E. von Grunebaum: *French African Literature*, The Hague, 1964, pp. 37–9.
[2] Memmi, op. cit., pp. 53–85.

negative'.[1] It is as though most of these writers had a morbid premonition that they might be writing in a cultural cul-de-sac, and none has expressed this more movingly than Malek Haddad who commented: 'The fate of our generation, writers or other Algerians, will have been that of a generation of transition. . . . For future generations, we shall forever remain curios, yes, real curios, in the museum of colonialism.'[2] Doubtless it was difficult for Haddad and those in his position to be anything but pessimistic about the future of their contribution to the development of North African literature, but their achievements, albeit in the language of the colonialist, must be acknowledged. History, even colonial history, will not be wiped out overnight or even in the space of ten years. G. E. von Grunebaum expresses the same opinion in more poetic terms:[3]

The suicide of French literature in North Africa would be our defeat; not because we take sides with French against Arabic, but because it would be a victory for particularism and, I am afraid, a relaxation, in an area of great promise, of that perpetual tension through which we grope farther and farther onward into the unknown.

---

[1] André Rétif, 'La leçon des romans nord-africains', *L'Afrique et L'Asie*, 33, 1956, pp. 20–2.
[2] Von Grunebaum, op. cit., p. 39.
[3] Ibid., p. 41.

Glossary

achour	Koranic tithe tax on cereals; more generally an Arab tax
aid al-Kabir	great feast, held on the last day of pilgrimage
aid al-saghir	little feast, held on the last day of Ramadan
agha	Turkish title: head man of a large area, or honorary title
arch	tribe: *arch* lands—tribal lands
azel	land belonging to the government, let out to tenant farmers
bachagha	Turkish honorary title
baraka	divine blessing, hence the beneficent influence of a man or an object
bey	Turkish title: governor of a province
beylik	government (of the bey)
blad	region
blad al-makhzen	area controlled by the government
blad as-siba	area of dissidence only sporadically under government control
cadi	judge
caïd	tribal leader: native chief, acting as auxiliary to French administration
casbah	fortress, keep: the Arab quarter of a town
douar	circle of tents, hamlet
fellah	agricultural worker, peasant
fiqh	jurisprudence, study of the law of Islam
goum	cavalry provided by Arab tribe
gourbi	shack, cabin
habous	religious foundation (*waqf* in the Middle East)
hadhra	seance of dancing and litanies
hadith	tradition of the Prophet
hadj	pilgrimage
id	feast: *see* aid
haïk	cloth piece of clothing from single piece of cloth covering a woman
haratin	non-tribal dwellers in oases in south Morocco and Mauritania
harka, harki	a military force, hence Algerians serving with the French army
imam	prayer leader in the mosque: religious functionary
jamaa	village council
khammes	sharecropper
ksar, ksour	fortress, fortified village

mahdi	leader sent by God
makhzen	government
marabout (pl. murabitin)	saint, religious person (usually of local importance)
medersa (*or* madrasa)	college, seminary
melk	private property
mokaddem	head of a religious community or *zawiya*
moudderes	teacher in a medersa
mufti	legal authority in a mosque
Ramadan	ninth Muslim month, being a month of fast
shaikh	chief, leader, elder
sharia	divine law
sharif (pl. sharufa)	descendant of the Prophet
souk *or* suq	market
tariqa	religious brotherhood
ulema	theologians, clergy
wilaya	region of local government
zakat	Koranic tax, originally on cattle
zawiya	religious institution, probably comprising mosque, Koranic school, and living accommodation around the tomb or shrine of a saint

Statistical Appendix

COMPARATIVE DATA: ALGERIA, LIBYA, MAURITANIA, MOROCCO, TUNISIA

Table 1: Demographic Data

	Algeria	Libya	Mauritania	Morocco	Tunisia
1. *Total Population*					
(a) Mid-year estimate (millions) 1974	16·28	2·35	1·29	16·88	5·64
2. *Demographic Data from Latest Population Census*					
(b) Year of census	1966[1]	1964	1964–5[2]	1971[3]	1966[4]
(c) Total population	11,821,679	1,564,369[5]	1,050,000	15,379,259	4,533,351
(d) Area (square kilometres)	2,381,741	1,759,540	1,030,700	446,550	163,610
(e) Density (population per square kilometre)[6]	4·96	0·89	1·02	34·44	27·71
(f) Total male population	5,817,145	813,386	540,750	7,518,000[7]	2,314,419
(g) Total female population	6,004,534	750,983	509,250	7,532,000	2,218,932
(h) Male population as % total population[8]	49·2	52·0	51·5	49·95	51·05
(i) Female population as % total population[8]	50·8	48·0	48·5	50·05	48·95
(j)[9] % of population under 15 years of age	47·15[10]	28·26[11]	N.A.	N.A.	46·31
% of population 15–64 years of age	48·25[10]	65·08[11]	N.A.	N.A.	50·14
% of population 65 years of age and over	4·42[10]	6·56[11]	N.A.	N.A.	3·55
(k) Life expectancy: expectation of life at birth; both sexes; 1965–1970[12]	50·7	52·1	41·0	50·5	51·7
(l) Total urban population	4,613,259	385,239	70,000	5,409,725	1,819,719
Total rural population[9]	7,208,420	1,179,130	1,043,000	9,969,534	2,713,632
(m) Urban population as % total population	39·0	24·6	6·7	35·2	40·1
Rural population as % total population[9]	61·0	75·4	93·3	64·8	59·9
(n) Total male urban population	2,277,919	201,705	N.A.	N.A.	940,124
Urban male population as % total male population	39·2	24·8	N.A.	N.A.	40·6
Total female urban population	2,335,340	183,534	N.A.	N.A.	879,595
Urban female population as % total female population	38·9	24·4	N.A.	N.A.	39·6

(o) Total male rural population[9]	3,539,226	611,681	N.A.	1,374,295
Rural male population as % total male population[9]	60·8	75·2	N.A.	59·4
Total female rural population[9]	3,669,194	567,449	N.A.	1,339,337
Rural female population as % total female population	61·1	75·6	N.A.	60·4
(p) Rate of natural increase (per 1,000 population)[12]	32·2	30·1	21·7	30·3
Crude birth rate (per 1,000 population)[12]	49·1	45·9	44·4	46·3
Fertility rate (per 1,000 female population 10–49 yrs)	173·2[13]	N.A.	173·0[14]	131·2[16]
Infant mortality (per 1,000 live births)	86·3[17]	N.A.	187·0[14]	125·0[19]
Crude death rate (per 1,000 population)[12]	16·9	15·8	22·7	16·0

Table 2: *Labour Force and Employment (census data)*

	Algeria	Libya	Morocco	Tunisia
(a) Year of census	1966	1964	1971	1966
(b) Total labour force	2,564,663	387,699	3,980,518	1,093,735
% of labour force in primary sector[20]	51·3	40·1	51·4	43·2
% of labour force in secondary sector[20]	11·8	16·0	15·5	16·5
% of labour force in tertiary sector[20]	36·9	43·9	33·1	40·3
(c) Participation rate[20]				
Labour force as % of total population	21·69	24·78	25·88	24·13
Male labour force as % total male population	42·21	45·22	44·90	44·39
Female labour force as % total female population	1·82	2·65	8·03	3·00
Male labour force as % total labour force	95·73	94·88	84·80	93·92
Female labour force as % total labour force	4·27	5·12	15·20	6·08
(d) Dependency ratio: labour force to non-employed population[20]	3·61	3·04	2·86	3·14
(e) General level of unemployment 1971 (thousands)	N.A.	1·34	26·3	52·5

Table 3: Social Statistics

	Algeria	Libya	Mauritania	Morocco	Tunisia
(a) Health services					
Year	1969	1970	1971	1970	1969
Population per hospital bed	356	256	2,727	688	405
Population per physician	8,192	2,654	17,206	13,156	7,348
(b) Education (census data)					
% of population aged 6–24 attending school	33·4	32·5	N.A.	N.A.	44·1
% of population aged 6–14 attending school	47·2	36·2	N.A.	N.A.	59·6
% of population aged 15–19 attending school	19·8	34·9	N.A.	N.A.	30·0
% of population aged 20–24 attending school	1·8	19·6	N.A.	N.A.	3·6
(c) Literacy					
% of population 15 years and over who are literate	18·7	21·6	N.A.	N.A.	23·9
% of population 10–14 years who are literate	48·8	36·5[21]	N.A.	N.A.	67·0

Table 4: Economic Data[22]

	Algeria	Libya	Mauritania	Morocco	Tunisia
(a) Year	1973	1973	1973	1974	1974
(b) Units	Billion Dinars	Million Dinars	Billion Ouguiyas	Billion Dirhams	Million Dinars
(c) Gross Domestic Product	29·7	2,193	13,043	26·71	1,386·1
(d) Gross Capital Formation as % of GDP	40·4	29·0	33·1	15·7	23·2
Government consumption as % of GDP	15·8	21·3	15·7	14·6	14·5
Private consumption as % of GDP	48·8	29·6	52·0	48·8	63·6
Exports as % of GDP	26·3	56·5	48·5	34·6	33·5
Imports as % of GDP	33·6	32·6	51·0	33·0	34·8
Net imports as % of GDP	7·4	−18·9	2·5	−1·6	1·3
(e) Central Bank International Reserves (US $ million)	1,153 (Nov. 1975)	2,053 (Nov. 1975)	66·6 (Aug. 1975)	529 (Oct. 1975)	371 (Nov. 1975)

Statistical Appendix

Table 5: Nutrition

Food Intake per capita[23]

	UK (1966–8)	Algeria (1974)	Libya (1970)	Morocco (1974)
Calories per day	3,180	2,138	2,630	2,611
% animal origin	42	10·5	11	7
Proteins (grammes per day)	90	57	66	70

NOTES TO TABLES 1–5

[1] In the Departments of Oasis and Saoura, enumeration took place between 22.xii.65 and 20.i.66. Provisional. De jure population.
[2] Estimated, provisional data based on results of sample survey.
[3] Provisional. De jure population.
[4] Excluding adjustments for under-enumeration estimated at 4%.
[5] Population is de jure: including non-Libyan nationals. Libyan national population = 1,182,194.
[6] Calculated from statistics in source (2).
[7] Estimate of questionable reliability for 1.vii.1969. From source (3).
[8] Calculated from statistics in source (2).
[9] Calculated from statistics in source (3).
[10] Data based on a 10% sample of census returns, 4.iv.66, in which total population estimated at 12,102,000.
[11] For under 18 years, 18–64 years respectively. As a % of Libyan nationals only. Libyan national population totalling 1,182,194.
[12] Estimates prepared by the United Nations Population Division for 1965–70.
[13] For 1966.
[14] For 1964–5.
[15] For 1962. Per 1,000 female population aged 15–49.
[16] For 1970.
[17] For 1965.
[18] For 1962.
[19] For 1969.
[20] Calculated from statistics in source (4).
[21] Data refer to population aged 6–14 years.
[22] Calculated from statistics in source (1).
[23] From source (2) and FAO Yearbook.

SOURCES OF TABLES 1–4

(1) International Monetary Fund, *International Financial Statistics*, February 1976, vol. XXIX, no. 2.
(2) United Nations, *Statistical Yearbook 1972*.
(3) United Nations, *Demographic Yearbook 1971*.
(4) International Labour Office, *Yearbook of Labour Statistics 1975*.

COUNTRY DATA

ALGERIA

Table 6: The Economy

	1969	1970	1971	1972	1973	1974
1. Exchange rate						
(Algerian Dinar per US $)	4·9371	4·9371	4·6440	4·5560	4·1850	3·9970
2. National accounts	(Billion Dinars)					
Gross Domestic Product	20·5	22·9	23·5	27·4	29·7	
Private consumption	11·3	12·2	12·8	14·1	14·5	
Government consumption	3·7	4·0	4·3	4·5	4·7	
Gross Fixed Capital Formation	5·7	7·6	8·6	10·2	12·0	
Increase in stocks	0·4	0·7	−0·1	0·8	0·7	
Exports	4·5	5·4	4·7	6·9	7·8	
Imports	5·1	7·0	6·9	9·2	10·0	
Net imports	0·6	1·6	2·2	2·3	2·2	
3. Government budget	(Million Dinars)					
Revenue	6,009	6,704	7,086	9,358	10,925	23,752
Expenditure	5,665	6,014	6,796	7,729	9,913	12,495
Net lending	1,340	2,680	2,043	2,545	4,144	9,223
Balance	−996	−1,989	−1,753	−917	−3,133	2,034
4. Balance of payments	(Million US $)					
Exports of merchandise f.o.b.	901	1,013	821	1,190	1,751	
Exports of services	106	98	94	96	148	
Total exports	1,007	1,111	915	1,286	1,899	
Imports of merchandise f.o.b.	952	1,078	994	1,285	2,047	
Imports of services	526	414	351	414	628	
Total imports	1,478	1,492	1,345	1,699	2,675	
Net transfers	265	255	473	293	352	
Current balance	−206	−126	43	120	−424	

Source: IMF, *International Financial Statistics*, February 1976.

Statistical Appendix

Table 7: Production

	Units	1965	1970	1971	1972	1973
1. Mining and quarrying						
Oil	Th. metric tons	26,481	47,202	36,405	49,339	49,632
Gas	Mill. cubic metres	1,754	2,838	2,945	3,390	4,745
Iron ore	Th. metric tons	1,637	1,546	1,699	1,978	1,700
Phosphates	,, ,, ,,	86	493	489	506	608
Salt	,, ,, ,,	116	100	100	108	205
Mercury	Metric tons	...	...	246	461	456
2. Agriculture						
Barley	Th. metric tons	379	570	340	720	450
Oats	,, ,, ,,	21	42	36	39	30
Wheat	,, ,, ,,	1,325	1,435	1,235	1,956	1,100
Potatoes	,, ,, ,,	233	262	274	300	300
Eggs	,, ,, ,,	9·7	11·9	12·0	12·0	12·2
Milk	,, ,, ,,	384	537	570	571	560
Citrus fruit	,, ,, ,,	402	N.A.	N.A.	N.A.	N.A.
3. Manufacturing						
Wheat flour	Th. metric tons	355	430	492	580	616
Wine	Th. hectolitres	14,026	8,692	9,247	8,360	8,700
Beer	,, ,,	365	605	612	642	N.A.
Cigarettes	Million	4,899	6,063	6,620	7,641	8,012
Tyres	Thousand	198	390	N.A.	N.A.	N.A.
Ethyl alcohol	Th. hectolitres	41	75	71	52	N.A.
Cement	Th. metric tons	739	928	967	927	1,007
Crude steel	,, ,, ,,	23	31	28	97	186
Radio receivers	Thousand	109	76	54	19	N.A.
4. Petroleum products						
LPG	Th. metric tons	66	107	112	131	245
Naphta	,, ,, ,,	...	30	58	72	434
Motor spirit	,, ,, ,,	418	514	504	507	861
Kerosene—jet fuel	,, ,, ,,	199	206	234	269	338
Fuel oils	,, ,, ,,	1,054	1,418	1,325	1,559	3,009
Bitumen	,, ,, ,,	...	...	...	12	52

Source: UN, *Statistical Yearbook 1974.*

LIBYA

Table 8: The Economy

	1969	1970	1971	1972	1973	1974
1. Exchange rate (US $ per Libyan Dinar)	2·8000	2·8000	3·0400	3·0400	3·3778	3·3778
2. National accounts	(Million Libyan Dinars)					
Gross Domestic Product	1,267	1,329	1,627	1,798	2,193	
Private consumption	376	395	469	543	650	
Government consumption	199	221	318	359	465	
Gross Fixed Capital Formation	315	243	288	437	636	
Increase in stocks	8	4	13	14	28	
Exports	788	870	975	998	1,240	
Imports	419	403	436	552	826	
Net imports	−369	−467	−539	−446	−414	
3. Balance of payments	(Million US $)					
Exports of merchandise f.o.b.	2,167	2,397	2,708	2,943	4,004	8,266
Exports of services	103	139	165	218	215	427
Total exports	2,270	2,536	2,873	3,161	4,219	8,693
Imports of merchandise f.o.b.	700	680	930	1,180	2,005	3,746
Imports of services	1,080	1,053	984	1,330	1,948	2,917
Total imports	1,780	1,733	1,914	2,510	3,953	6,663
Net transfers	−162	−158	−137	−149	−377	−206
Current balance	328	645	822	502	−111	1,824

Source: IMF, op. cit.

Table 9: Production

	Units	1965	1970	1971	1972	1973
1. *Mining and quarrying*						
Oil	Th. metric tons	58,378	159,709	132,589	119,633	104,882
Gas	Mill. cubic metres	...	4,041	4,500	5,126	5,267
2. *Agriculture*						
Barley	Th. metric tons	96	53	32	116	205
Groundnuts	,, ,, ,,	11	11	11	14	11
Wheat	,, ,, ,,	57	21	18	42	62
Tobacco	,, ,, ,,	1·2	1·6	1·2	1·2	1·0
Tomatoes	,, ,, ,,	75	136	131	170	N.A.
Olives	,, ,, ,,	101	71	5	94	N.A.
Citrus fruit	,, ,, ,,	13	20	25	27	N.A.
Almonds	,, ,, ,,	3	4	4	5	N.A.
3. *Manufacturing*						
Wheat flour	Th. metric tons	11	35	39	51	51
Cigarettes	Million	927	1,639	1,803	2,036	2,472
4. *Petroleum products*						
Naphtha	Th. metric tons	...	5	6	12	18
Motor spirit	,, ,, ,,	...	81	65	71	63
Kerosene	,, ,, ,,	...	40	43	48	51
Fuel oils	,, ,, ,,	...	310	271	304	310

Source: UN, op. cit.

MAURITANIA

Table 10: The Economy

	1972	1973
1. Exchange rate (Ouguiyas per US $)	51·250	47·080
2. *National accounts*	(Billion Ouguiyas)	
Gross Domestic Product	12,342	13,043
Private consumption	5,444	6,783
Government consumption	2,081	2,046
Gross Fixed Capital Formation	4,777	4,323
Increase in stocks	362	214
Exports	8,390	6,331
Imports	8,712	6,653
Net imports	322	322
3. *Balance of payments*	(Million US $)	
Exports of merchandise f.o.b.		119·8
Exports of services		10·7
Total exports		130·5
Imports of merchandise f.o.b.		95·5
Imports of services		36·7
Total imports		132·2
Net transfers		48·3
Current balance		46·6

Source: IMF, op. cit.

Table 11: Production

	Units	1965	1970	1971	1972	1973
1. *Mining and quarrying*						
Iron ore	Th. metric tons	3,875	5,923	5,497	6,017	6,773
Copper	,, ,, ,,	...	...	4·5	14·8	24·0

Source: UN, op. cit.

MOROCCO

Table 12: The Economy

	1969	1970	1971	1972	1973	1974
1. *Exchange rate*						
(Dirhams per US $)	5·0640	5·0288	4·7600	4·6657	4·2899	4·1548
2. *National accounts*			(Billion Dirhams)			
Gross Domestic Product	15·92	16·96	18·57	20·15	21·31	26·71
Private consumption	11·45	12·25	13·22	14·23	15·37	18·05
Government consumption	2·30	2·46	2·70	2·90	3·12	3·90
Gross Fixed Capital Formation	2·18	2·61	2·70	2·67	2·89	4·19
Increase in stocks	−0·16	−0·06	0·07	−0·07	−0·32	0·15
Exports	3·37	3·53	3·73	4·34	5·34	9·24
Imports	3·22	3·83	3·85	3·92	5·09	8·82
Net imports	−0·15	0·30	0·12	−0·42	−0·25	−1·42
3. *Government budget*			(Million Dirhams)			
Revenue	3,102	3,439	3,559	3,628	10,751	N.A.
Expenditure	3,936	4,078	4,125	4,527	N.A.	N.A.
Balance	−834	−639	−566	−899	N.A.	N.A.
4. *Balance of payments*						
Exports of merchandise f.o.b.	484	487	499	642	913	
Exports of services	189	218	246	304	389	
Total exports	673	705	745	946	1,302	
Imports of merchandise f.o.b.	522	624	637	709	1,037	
Imports of services	233	278	277	327	412	
Total imports	755	902	914	1,036	1,449	
Net transfers	69	73	109	138	252	
Current balance	−13	−124	−60	48	105	

Source: IMF, op. cit.

Table 13: Production

	Units	1965	1970	1971	1972	1973
1. *Mining and quarrying*						
Coal	Th. metric tons	400	433	475	547	N.A.
Oil	,, ,, ,,	N.A.	46	23	28	42
Gas	Mill. cubic metres	N.A.	44	48	52	65
Iron ore	Th. metric tons	567	522	433	135	214
Antimony ore	Metric tons	2,200	1,971	1,972	1,800	1,214
Copper	Th. metric tons	1·8	3·2	3·3	3·8	4·3
Lead ore	,, ,, ,,	77·8	84·5	76·6	94·9	103·0
Manganese ore	,, ,, ,,	156·7	59·6	79·8	80·3	121·9
Cobalt	,, ,, ,,	16	6	10	11	N.A.
Nickel	Metric tons	360	120	200	230	200
Silver	,, ,,	19	21	25	31	29
Zinc ore	Th. metric tons	49·5	15·8	12·5	18·3	17·6
Phosphate	,, ,, ,,	9,825	11,424	12,030	15,105	17,072
2. *Agriculture*						
Barley	Th. metric tons	506	2,572	2,466		
Maize	,, ,, ,,	154	290	368		
Wheat	,, ,, ,,	814	2,188	2,162		
Potatoes	,, ,, ,,	100	300	81		
Tomatoes	,, ,, ,,	150	250	112		
Sugar beet	,, ,, ,,	382	1,584	1,677		
Citrus fruit	,, ,, ,,	690	832	852		
Olives	,, ,, ,,	267	506	N.A.		
Dates	,, ,, ,,	90	90	N.A.		
3. *Manufacturing*						
Wheat flour	Th. metric tons	498	818	N.A.		
Tinned fish	,, ,, ,,	53	65	52		
Sugar	,, ,, ,,	334	399	424		
Wine	Th. hectolitres	3,449	1,253	1,150		
Beer	,, ,,	221	404	338		
Cigarettes	Million	3,968	4,977	6,516		
Cement	Th. metric tons	788	1,405	1,481		
Superphosphates	,, ,, ,,	160	180	N.A.		
Soap	,, ,, ,,	26	28	N.A.		
Processed lead	,, ,, ,,	17	20	18		
Tyres	Thousand	237	411	N.A.		

Source: UN, op. cit.

TUNISIA

Table 14: The Economy

	1969	1970	1971	1972	1973	1974
1. Exchange rate						
(Dinars per US $)	0·5208	0·5208	0·4807	0·4840	0·4451	0·4065
2. National accounts			(Million Dinars)			
Gross Domestic Product	679·1	746·9	861·7	1,043·7	1,117·3	1,386·1
Private consumption	437·8	495·8	559·9	674·5	736·5	881·8
Government consumption	118·1	130·8	138·1	152·9	171·8	201·4
Gross Fixed Capital Formation	148·1	149·5	172·2	196·8	237·4	321·9
Increase in stocks	5·5	4·8	9·3	31·8	...	...
Exports	149·9	166·2	212·4	270·6	300·0	464·0
Imports	180·3	200·2	230·2	282·9	328·4	483·0
Net imports	30·4	34·0	17·8	12·3	28·4	19·0
4. Balance of payments			(Million US $)			
Exports of merchandise f.o.b.	166	189	214	308	417	
Exports of services	128	143	203	250	322	
Total exports	294	332	417	558	739	
Imports of merchandise f.o.b.	257	294	334	447	625	
Imports of services	135	149	146	201	306	
Total imports	392	443	480	648	931	
Net transfers	50	58	70	85	132	
Current balance	−48	−53	7	−5	−60	

Source: IMF, op. cit.

Table 15: Production

	Units	1965	1970	1971	1972	1973
1. Mining and quarrying						
Oil	Th. metric tons	N.A.	4,151	4,096	3,975	3,878
Gas	Mill. cubic metres	N.A.	5	1	20	114
Iron ore	Th. metric tons	609	422	515	485	433
Lead ore	,, ,, ,,	15·8	22·0	20·9	19·9	15·6
Mercury	Metric tons	3	4	12	8	4
Silver	,, ,,	1	2	3	7	6
Zinc ore	Th. metric tons	3·8	11·8	11·4	11·3	8·6
Salt	,, ,, ,,	402	300	346	324	360
Phosphate	,, ,, ,,	3,040	N.A.	N.A.	N.A.	N.A.
2. Agriculture						
Barley	Th. metric tons	180	151	140	180	210
Wheat	,, ,, ,,	520	470	600	730	690
Esparto grass	,, ,, ,,	111	84	79	N.A.	N.A.
Citrus fruit	,, ,, ,,	94	N.A.	77	94	94
Dates	,, ,, ,,	54	18	39	N.A.	N.A.
3. Manufacturing						
Wheat flour	Th. metric tons	145	195	199		
Wine	Th. hectolitres	1,850	559	966		
Beer	,, ,,	198	201	280		
Olive oil	Th. metric tons	N.A.	25	90		
Cigarettes	Million	N.A.	3,286	3,549		
Cement	Th. metric tons	454	522	554		
Superphosphates	,, ,, ,,	273	382	422		

Source: UN, op. cit.

Select Bibliography

The works listed below include those which have been cited in the text, together with others in English and French which are valuable for further reading.

1. PERIODICALS

The most valuable periodicals for the study of present-day North Africa are the publication of the *Documentation Française*, which was entitled *Maghreb* from its first number (1964) to number 55 (1973) when it was expanded into *Maghreb-Machrek*, and the annual publication of the Centre des Recherches et des Études sur les Sociétés Méditerranéennes at Aix-en-Provence, entitled *Annuaire de l'Afrique du Nord*. The latter includes an exhaustive chronology and comprehensive bibliographic review of works in European languages and in Arabic. There is no comparable journal in English, but reference should be made to the *Middle East Economic Digest* for up-to-date factual information concerning the economy. The quarterly *Revue de l'Occident Musulman* includes articles of historical as well as contemporary interest. Of the journals published in North Africa the *Revue Tunisienne des Sciences Sociales* (published by the Centre d'Études et de Recherches Économiques et Sociales, Tunis) has survived most successfully the antipathy shown by most new states to empirical research.

2. GENERAL

Abun-Nasr, Jamil M. *A History of the Maghrib*. Cambridge, 1971
Adelman, M. *The World Petroleum Market*. Baltimore, 1972
Ageron, Charles-Robert. *Politiques coloniales au Maghreb*. Paris, 1972
Benachenhou, A. *Régime des terres et structures agraires au Maghreb*. Algiers, 1970
Berque, Jacques. *French North Africa*. London, 1967
Braudel, F. *La Méditerranée et le monde méditerranéan à l'époque de Philippe II*. Paris, 1966
Brown, L. C. (ed.). *State and Society in Independent North Africa*. Washington D.C., 1966
Camau, Michel. *La Notion de démocratie dans la pensée des dirigeants maghrébins*. Paris, 1971
Chouraqui, André. *La saga des Juifs en Afrique du Nord*. Paris, 1972
Clarke, J. I., and Fisher, W. B. *Populations of the Middle East and North Africa*. London, 1972
Despois, Jean. *L'Afrique du Nord*. Paris, 1964
Fisher, Godfrey. *Barbary Legend*. Oxford, 1957
Gallacher, Charles F. *The United States and North Africa*. Cambridge, Mass., 1963

Gellner, Ernest, and Micaud, Charles (eds.). *Arabs and Berbers*. London, 1973
Gordon, David C. *North Africa's French Legacy: 1954–62*. Cambridge, Mass., 1962
Hirschberg, H. Z. J. *History of the Jews in North Africa*. Leiden, 1974.
Holt, P. M.; Lambton, A. K. S.; Lewis, B. (eds.). *The Cambridge History of Islam*, vol. 2: *The Further Islamic Lands*. Cambridge, 1971
Hourani, Albert. *Arabic Thought in the Liberal Age*. London, 1962
Ibn Khaldun. *The Muqaddima*. Trans. F. Rosenthal, 3 vols. Princeton, 1967
Julien, Charles-André. *Histoire de l'Afrique du Nord*. 2 vols. Paris, 1956
—— *L'Afrique du Nord en marche*. Paris, 1972
Le Tourneau, Roger. *Evolution politique de l'Afrique du Nord musulman*. Paris, 1962
Monroe, E. *The Mediterranean in World Politics*. London, 1938
Penrose, E. T. *The Large International Firm in Developing Countries*. London, 1968
Presses Universitaires de France. *Études Maghrébines: Mélanges Charles-André Julien*. Paris, 1964
Raynal, René. *Géographie de l'Afrique du Nord-Ouest*. Paris, 1967
Université de Dijon, Institut des Relations Internationales. *Les Hydrocarbures gazeux et le développement des pays producteurs*. Paris, 1974
Zartman, I. William (ed.). *Man, State and Society in the Contemporary Maghrib*. London, 1973

3. ALGERIA

Abbas, Ferhat. *Le Jeune Algérien*. Paris, 1931
—— *La Nuit coloniale*. Paris, 1962
Ageron, Charles-Robert. *Les Algériens musulmans et la France (1871–1919)*. 2 vols. Paris, 1968
—— *Histoire de l'Algérie contemporaine*. Paris, 1966
Algeria, Republic of: *Petroleum, Raw Materials and Development*. Algiers, 1974
Aron, Robert (ed.). *Les Origines de la Guerre d'Algérie*. Paris, 1962
Behr, Edward. *The Algerian Problem*. London, 1961
Bedjaoui, Mohammed. *La Révolution algérienne et le droit*. Brussels, 1961
Bennabi, Malek. *Mémoires d'un témoin du siècle*. Algiers, 1965
Boudiaf, Mohammed. *Où va l'Algérie?* Paris, 1964
Bourdieu, Pierre. *Sociologie de l'Algérie*. Paris, 1962 (trans. as *The Algerians*. Boston, 1962)
Chaliand, Gérard, and Minces, Juliette. *L'Algérie indépendante*. Paris, 1972
Chaulet, Claudine. *La Mitidja autogérée*. Algiers, 1971
Clegg, Ian. *Workers' Self-Management in Algeria*. London, 1971
Confer, Vincent. *France and Algeria: the Problems of Civil and Political Reform*. New York, 1966
Courrière, Yves. *La Guerre d'Algérie*. vol. I. *Les Fils de la Toussaint*, Paris, 1968; vol. II. *Le Temps des léopards*. Paris, 1969; vol. III. *L'Heure des colonels*. Paris, 1970; vol. IV. *Les Feux du désespoir*. Paris, 1971
Etienne, Bruno. *Algérie: Cultures et révolution*. Paris, 1976
Fanon, Frantz. *The Wretched of the Earth*. London, 1967
Feraoun, Mouloud. *Journal, 1955–1962*. Paris, 1962
Gordon, David C. *The Passing of French Algeria*. Cambridge, Mass., 1962
Julien, Charles-André. *Histoire de l'Algérie contemporaine*. Paris, 1964

Kaddache, Mahfoud. *La Vie politique à Alger de 1919 à 1939*. Algiers, 1970
Lacheraf, Mostefa. *L'Algérie, nation et société*. Paris, 1965
Lacoste, Yves; Nouschi, André; Prenant, André. *L'Algérie passé et présent*. Paris, 1960
Lawless, Richard I. *A bibliography of works on Algeria published in English since 1954*. University of Durham, Centre for Middle Eastern and Islamic Studies, 1976
Lawless, Richard I., with Blake, G. H. *Tlemcen: continuity and change in an Algerian Islamic town*. London, 1976
Lebjaoui, Mohamed. *Vérités sur la révolution algérienne*. Paris, 1970
Lucas, Philippe, and Vatin, Jean-Claude. *Histoire de l'Algérie*. Paris. 1974
—— *L'Algérie des anthropologues*. Paris, 1975
Merad, Ali. *Ibn Badis, commentateur du coran*. Algiers, 1971
Merle, Robert. *Ahmed Ben Bella*. Paris, 1965
Ottaway, D., and Ottaway, M. *Algeria: the Politics of a Socialist Revolution*. Berkeley, 1970
Ouzegane, Amar. *Le Meilleur Combat*. Paris, 1962
Pickles, Dorothy. *Algeria and France*. London, 1963
Quandt, William B. *Revolution and Political Leadership in Algeria, 1954-68*. Cambridge, Mass., 1969
Remili, Abderrahmane. *Les Institutions administratives algériennes*. Algiers, 1968
Trebous, Madeleine. *Migration and Development: the Case of Algeria*. OECD Paris, 1970
Valensi, Lucette. *Le Maghreb avant la prise d'Alger*. Paris, 1969
Yacef, Saadi. *Souvenirs de la bataille d'Alger*. Paris, 1962

4. LIBYA

Allan, J. A., et al., (eds.). *Libya, Agriculture and Economic Development*. London, 1973
Despois, Jean. *La Colonisation italienne en Libye*. Paris, 1935
Evans-Pritchard, E. E. *The Sanusi of Cyrenaica*. Oxford, 1949
First, Ruth. *Libya, the Elusive Revolution*. London, 1974
Holmboe, Knud. *Desert Encounter; an adventurous journey through Italian Africa*. London, 1936
Khadduri, Majid. *Modern Libya*. Baltimore, 1963
Moore, M. *The Fourth Shore*. London, 1940
Pelt, Adrian. *Libyan Independence and the United Nations*. New Haven, 1970
United Nations Technical Assistance Mission to Libya. *The Economic and Social Development of Libya*, by Benjamin Higgins. New York, 1953
Wright, John. *Modern Libya*. London, 1969

5. MAURITANIA

Abun-Nasr, J. *The Tijanniya*. Oxford, 1965
Capot-Rey, R. *Le Sahara français*. Paris, 1953
Desiré-Vuillemin, G. *Contribution à l'histoire de la Mauritanie, 1900-1934*. Dakar, 1964
Gerteiny, A. G. *Mauritania*. London, 1967

Stewart, C. G., with Stewart, E. K. *Islam and Social Order in Mauritania*. Oxford, 1973
Trimingham, J. S. *Islam in West Africa*. London, 1959

6. MOROCCO

Adam, André. *Casablanca*. 2 vols. Paris, 1968
Ashford, Douglas E. *Political Change in Morocco*. Princeton, 1961
Ayache, Albert. *Le Maroc*. Paris, 1956
Barbour, Neville. *Morocco*. London, 1965
Ben Bachir, Saïd. *L'Administration locale du Maroc*. Casablanca, 1969
Ben Barka, Mehdi. *Option révolutionnaire au Maroc*. Paris, 1966
Bernard, Stéphane. *The Franco-Moroccan Conflict, 1943-1956*. New Haven, 1968
Berque, Jacques. *Structures sociales du Haut-Atlas*. Paris, 1955
Bidwell, Robin. *Morocco under Colonial Rule*. London, 1973
El Alami, Mohamed. *Allal el-Fassi*. Rabat, 1972
Gallissot, René. *Le Patronat Européen au Maroc (1931-1942)*. Rabat, 1964
Gaudio, Attilio. *Allal el-Fassi, ou l'histoire de l'Istiqlal*. Paris, 1972
Gellner, Ernest. *Saints of the Atlas*. London, 1969
Halstead, John P. *Rebirth of a Nation: The Origins and Rise of Moroccan Nationalism, 1912-1944*. Cambridge, Mass., 1967
Hassan II, King. *Le Maroc en marche* (Discours). Rabat, 1965
July, Pierre. *Une République pour un roi*. Paris, 1974
Miège, Jean Louis. *Le Maroc et l'Europe*. 2 vols. Paris, 1962
Montagne, Robert. *Les Berbères et la Makhzen dans le sud du Maroc*. Paris, 1930
Montagne, Robert (ed.). *Naissance du prolétariat marocain*. Paris, 1952
Noin, Daniel. *La Population rurale du Maroc*. 2 vols. Paris, 1970
Royaume du Maroc. *Plan de développement économique et social, 1973-1977*
Scham, Alan. *Lyautey in Morocco*. Berkeley, 1970
Stewart, Charles F. *The Economy of Morocco, 1912-62*. Harvard, 1962
Terasse, H. *Histoire du Maroc*. 2 vols. Casablanca, 1950
Trout, Frank E. *Morocco's Saharan Frontiers*. Geneva, 1969
Villeneuve, Michel. *La Situation de l'agriculture et son avenir dans l'économie marocaine*. Paris, 1971
Waterbury, John. *The Commander of the Faithful*. London, 1970
—— *North for the Trade*. Berkeley, 1972
Woolman, David S. *Rebels in the Rif*. London, 1969
Zartman, I. William. *Problems of New Power: Morocco*. New York, 1964

7. TUNISIA

Bardin, Pierre, *La Vie d'un Douar*. Paris and The Hague, 1965
Basset, A. *Initiation à la Tunisie*. Paris, 1950
Beling, Willard. *Modernization and African Labour, a Tunisian Case Study*. New York, 1965
Brown, Leon Carl. *The Surest Path. A Translation of the Introduction to the Surest Path to Knowledge Concerning the Condition of Countries, by Khayr al-Din al-Tunisi*. Cambridge, Mass., 1967

Centre de Documentation Nationale. *Histoire du mouvement national.* Tunis, various dates.
Demeersman, André. *La Famille tunisienne.* Tunis, 1967
Despois, Jean. *La Tunisie, ses régions.* Paris, 1961
—— *La Tunisie orientale, Sahel et Basse-steppe.* Paris, 1955
Dutton, R. *Wheat productivity in the Medjerda valley.* Unpublished thesis. London School of Oriental and African Studies, 1972
Duvignaud, Jean. *Chebika.* Paris, 1969
Ganiage, Jean. *Les Origines du Protectorat français en Tunisie.* Paris, 1959
Knapp, Wilfrid. *Tunisia.* London, 1970
Lacouture, Jean. *Cinq hommes et la France.* Paris, 1961
Ling, Dwight L. *Tunisia from Protectorate to Republic.* Indiana, 1967
Micaud, Charles; Brown, Leon Carl; Moore, Clement Henry. *Tunisia, the Politics of Modernization.* London, 1964
Moore, Clement Henry. *Tunisia since Independence.* Berkeley and Los Angeles, 1965
Nerfin, Marc. *Entretiens avec Ahmed Ben Salah.* Paris, 1974.
Poncet, Jean. *La Tunisie à la recherche de son avenir.* Paris, 1974
Rudebeck, Lars. *Party and People.* Stockholm, 1967
Sebag, Paul. *La Tunisie.* Paris, 1951
Stéphane, Roger. *La Tunisie de Bourguiba.* Paris, 1958
Taalbi, Shaikh. *La Tunisie martyre.* Paris, 1920 (published anonymously)
Tlatli, Salah-Eddine. *Djerba, l'île des lotophages.* Tunis, 1967
—— *Tunisie nouvelle.* Tunis, 1957

Index

Abadine, Bouyagi Ould, 240
Abbas, Ferhat, 74-5, 81 ff., 90-1, 94, 103, 104, 108, 111; and Sétif, 84
Abd Abdallah Muhammad b. Hammad, 407
Abd al-Mumin, 261
Abd al-Qadir al-Jaza'iri, *see* Abdel Kader
Abd al-Rahman b. Ziyad al-Kairouani, 404
Abdel Kader, 61-3, 141, 142, 408-10; grandfather of Emir Khaled, 72
Abdel Kader, Hadj Ali, *see* Messali, Hadj
Abd el-Krim, Mhammed, Abd el-Krim el Khattabi, 270-2
Abdesselam, Belaïd, 116, 133, 164
Abduh, Muhammad, 410
Abu Abdallah Muhammad b. Yahya b. Abd al-Salam, 407
Abu'-Abbas al-Afghani, 404
Abul-Atahiya, 405
Abu Tamman, 405-6
Abu Yazid, 346
Achour (Koranic tithe), 67
Achour, Habib, 365, 366, 367
Action, L', 366
Aghlabids, 21, 346, 404-5
Agriculture: Algerian, 79-80, 139-58; self-management in, 122, 445-50; Libyan, 202-7; Moroccan, 318-26; Tunisian, 342-3, 381-7; under French, 353-4, 380-1
Ahardan, Mahjoub, 299, 301
Ahmed Bey, 349
Ahmed, Colonel Musa, 193, 194
Aït, Ahmed, 87, 88n, 92-3, 96, 99, 112, 115
Aix-les-Bains, Conference of, 281-2, 287
Akjoujt: copper mines, 244-5
Aknoul, 305
Al-Afghani, Jamal ad-Din, 273
Al-Alawi, Moulay al-Arabi, 273-4
Alawite dynasty, 262-4
Al-Amal, and family planning, 258

Al-Basri, Mohamed, 280, 292, 293; and Ben Barka, 296; plot of March 1973, 10, 310-11
Aleg, phosphate resources, 244
Al-Fassi, Abdelwahid, 288
Al-Fassi, Allal, 49, 273 ff.; praise of Casablanca, 281; biography, 288; and Bahais, 289; leadership of Istiqlal after Independence, 290; death, 291
Algeciras conference, 265
Algeria: *see main chapter headings and headings in text*; relations with other Maghreb states, 10-11; and Mauritania, 248; Mediterrenean policy, 14, 391; Tunisia, relations with, 9, 391-2; OPEC, raw materials, 14
Algeria, War of Independence, 49-50, 52; impact on populace, 53, 151-2; land transfer, 145
Algerian statute, 82-3
Algiers: non-aligned conference (1973), 165; energy conference (1975), 166; Ottoman regency, 347
Al-Glaoui, 279
Alhucemas Bay: Spanish landing in Rif war, 272
Al-Husam b. Dirar al-Kalbi, 404
Ali la Pointe (Amar Ali), 91, 97
Ali, Mohammed, 357, 361
Al-Id, Muhammad, 412-13
Al-Kahina, 36, 344, 346
Al-Maqqari, 408
Al-Mithaq, 258
Almohad dynasty, 21-2, 57, 180-1, 261, 347, 407
Almoravid dynasty, 23-5, 56, 57, 237
Al-Mu'izz, 405
Al-Shabbi, Abu 'l-Qasim, 415-16
Al-Shalhi, Ibrahim, 189
Al-Tahrir, UNFP newspaper, 298, 302
Al-Wazzani, Mohammed Hassan, 275-6, 278; founds PDI, 287
Amar, Ouzegane, 77
American Federation of Labor, 361

Amis du Manifeste, 81-2, 85
Amokrane, Lieutenant, 309
Anual, battle (July 1921), 270
Arab conquest: Libya, 180; Morocco, 259-60
Arab invasion, 17-21, 260, 344, 346
Arab Socialist Union, 197-8
Arabic, 2; spoken in Sahara, 235; in Tunisian education, 399-401
Armed Forces: Algerian, 124, 159-63; Moroccan, 311-17
Arslan, Chekib, 74; and Moroccan nationalists, 275
Atlas mountains, 253, 254, 272, 341
Augustine, Saint, 15, 16
Aurès mountains, 49, 53, 55, 56, 85
Azrou, Berber College, 274

Ba'athist party: in Libya, 191
Bach Hamba, Ali, 355
Bahnini, Ahmed, 300
Bakr b. Hammad al-Zanati al-Tiharti, 405
Balafrej, Ahmed, 48, 273, 276, 284n, 288, 289
Balafrej, Anis, 284n
Banque Arabe Libyenne Mauritanienne, 251
Barbarossas (Aruj and Khair al-Din), 57-8
Bardo, Treaty of (1881), 351
Beaulieu, Leroy, 61
Beeley, Harold, 100
Belkacem, Chérif, 115
Belkhodja, Tahar, 377
Belouïzdad, Mohammed, 87
Ben Ammar, Tahar, 361, 367, 372
Ben Arafa, 281-2
Ben Badis, 75-7, 80-1, 173, 410
Ben Barka, Mehdi, 288; and trade unions, 294; biography, 296; disappearance, 295-7; plot of 1963, 10, 297
Ben Bella, Ahmed, 87 ff., 92, 95-6, 99, 107, 110 ff.; ousted by Boumediene, 113-14
Ben Boulaïd, Mustafa, 87, 89, 95-6
Benghazi, 175, 181, 190
Benhima, Mohamed, 301
Beni Hilal, 21, 57, 180, 238, 255, 261, 346, 406
Beni Merin, 57, 261
Beni Sulaim, 21, 180, 346
Beni Urriaguel, 270

Beni Wattas, 262
Benjelloul, Dr. Mohammed Salah, 74
Ben Khedda, 98-9, 104, 105, 107-9; supposed Tunisian support for, 9
Ben Messaoud, Omar, 307
Ben M'Hidi, Larbi, 87-9, 98-9
Bennouna, Mohammed, 48, 273
Bennouna, Abdessalem, 276
Ben Salah, Ahmed; biography, 365; trade union leader, 365-6; political rise and fall, 373-6; and cooperatives, 382-5
Ben Seddiq, Mahjoub, 293, 294
Ben Tobbal, Lakhdar, 87, 95, 99
Ben Youssef, Salah, 363-5; Youseffist following, 366-7, 373-5, 394; support for Algeria, 9
Berbers, in history, 5-6; 14-26 *passim*; in Algeria, 53-7; in Sahara, 235-8; in Mauritania, 244; in Morocco, 255, 260-2; French policy towards, 274; in Tunisia, 344, 346
Berber Dahir, 274
Berber language, 2, 15-16, 56-7, 236
Bernis, Destanne de, 123
Berque, Jacques, quoted, 354, 357
Bevin, Ernest, 186-7
Birth control, *see* family planning
Bitat, Rabah, 87-9, 99, 116
Bizerte, 342-3, 345, 352; 'Martyrs' Day' (1935), 362; 'Congress of Destiny', 369; crisis (1961), 392, 396
Blad al-makhzen, 8, 273
Blad as-siba, 8, 273
Blum, Leon, 36, 74, 80-1
Bon, Cap, 342-3, 384-5
Bouabid, Abderrahim: organized trade union movement, 279-80, 294; and al-Fassi, 288; at Skhirat trial, 306-7; at trial of opposition leaders (1973), 310
Bouadjadj, Zoubir, 87, 89, 92
Bouazza, Tayyib, organizes Moroccan trade unions, 280, 293
Boucetta Mohamed, leader of Istiqlal (1973), 291
Boudiaf, Mohamed, 87-8, 96, 99
Boukhort, Ben Ali, 77
Boumediene, Houari, 99, 105 ff.; and Algerian army, 112-13; *coup* against Ben Bella, 113-14; character and background, 114; in Algerian politics, 115 ff.; oil policy, 133; Algerian reform, 152-3; foreign policy, 164-5; and Spanish Sahara, 335-6; Medi-

Index 445

terranean policy, 390–1; meeting with Hassan (Tlemsen, 1970), 10
Bourguiba, Habib, 48; biography, 358–360; relations with French protectorate, 360–3; national and party leadership, 363–70; relations with Ben Youssef, 364–5; with Ben Salah, 365, 374–5, 384–5; prime minister, president, 366; president for life, 377; attempted assassination, 9, 368, 372; reconstructs after Ben Salah affair, 376–9; economic policy, 381; 'Greater Maghreb', 11; and Qaddafi, 11, 224–225, 389–90; Mediterranean policy, 390–1; policy towards France, 392–4; Middle East and Palestine, 395; and arrest of Algerian leaders, 97
Bourguiba, Madame Wassila, 358, 390
Boussouf, Abdelhafid, 87, 99, 105, 106
Bouteflika, Abdelaziz, 115, 133, 163, 165
Brahimi, Lakhdar, 105
Brahimi, Sheikh (Sheikh Brahimi Si El-Bachir), 76, 81, 410
Britain: refuses admission to Kenitra conspirators, 309; interests in nineteenth-century Tunisia, 350; and Algeria, 169; oil industry, 128–9; and post-war Libya, 185 ff., 222, 227
British Broadcasting Corporation, 84
British Council, 401
Bugeaud, General, 3, 40–1, 61–3
Buhamara, 265
Bureaux arabes, 63–4
Byzantines, 17, 55–6, 180

Cadiz, Phoenician, 259
Cambon, Jules, 68
Camus, Albert, 90
Caramanlis, 181–3
Carthage, in history, 14–16, 259, 356; Bourguiba's palace, 367
Casablanca, 8, 254; and French protectorate, 266, 268; importance for Moroccan nationalism, 279–81; riots (1965), 301; conference (1969), 10
Casablanca group (African states), 10
Catroux, General Georges: and reinstatement of Mohammed ben Youssef, 282; and Algerian appointment, 90–1
Ceuta, 4, 28, 269, 333, 338
Chabou, Abdelkader, 161
Chad, and Libya, 227
Challe, General Maurice, 104, 106

Chanderli, Abdelkader, 105
Chaouen, 256
Chaouia (Morocco), 253
Charles X, King, 59
Chefchaoui, Yahia, 307
Chelouati, Colonel Larbi, 304, 306
Chenik Mohammed, 360 ff.
China: and Algeria, 105, 168–70; and Mauritania, 247, 251
Christians, in Morocco, 259
Clos Salembier, meeting (1954), 87
Code de l'indigénat, 68, 69
Comité de Coordination et d'Exécution (CCE), 94, 96, 104
Comité Révolutionnaire d'Unité et d'Action (CRUA), 87
Commin, Pierre, 95
Communes, in French Algeria, 67–9, 83, 89
Confédération Générale du Travail (French), and Moroccan trade unions, 279, 293
Colonization, of Algeria, 40–1, 63–4, 66, 139–45; Italian, in Libya, 184–5; of Morocco, 268–9; of Tunisia, 350–3
Cominor, 245
Communist parties: in French Algeria, 77–8, 81; Algerian CP and FLN, 91, 94, 114–15; Moroccan, 293; Tunisian, 361, 366–7; French, and Messali, 73; and Algeria, 91
Compagnie Mauritanienne pour l'Armement, la Pêche, l'Industrie et le Commerce, 246
Complex Minier du Nord (Cominor), 245
Conseil National de la Révolution Algérienne (CNRA), 93–4, 96, 99
Conseil Supérieur de l'Algérie, 69
Constantine, 55, 75
Constantine Plan, 103, 122–3, 138
Constitution: Moroccan constitutions, 286–7; of 1962, 286–7; of 1970, 302–3; of 1972, 307–8; Tunisian, 366–7
Cooperatives: in Tunisia, 382–5
Córdoba, 24
Corsica: in May 1958, 102
Corruption trial, Morocco (1971), 307
Crémieux Decree (1870), 65
Cyrenaica, 174 ff.

Dahlab, Saad, 98–9
Dakhoun, Omar, 310
Debaghine, Lamine, 88, 105
Delbecque, Leon, 101–2

Delcassé, 265
Délégations Financières (Algerian), 69
Delouvrier, Paul, 103
Derro, 324
Destour Party, 357
Diagana, Sidi Mohamed, 241n.
Dib, Mohammed, 418; quoted, 139-40
Didouche, Mourad, 87-8
Diocletian, 259
Djerba, *see* Jerba
Dlimi, Ahmed, 316
Douiri, Mohammed, 275, 291
Doukallas, 320
Doukkali, Bonachib, 273, 274
Dra, 254, 255, 256

Education: in French Algeria, 68; in independent Algeria, 123-4, 170-3; in Libya, 232-3; in Mauritania, 241; in Morocco, 338-40; in Tunisia, 397-401
EEC: and North Africa, 12-13; and Algeria, 12; and Morocco, 317; and Tunisia, 379-80
Egypt: and Algerian war, 91-3, 97; and independent Algeria, 167; and Libya, 191-2; projected union with Libya, 199, 223-4; asylum for Abd el Krim, 272; support for Moroccan nationalists, 276, 279; decorates Moroccan officers, 314; and Tunisia, 394
El-Bachir, Sheikh Brahimi Si (Taleb el-Bachir), 76, 81
El Khattabi, *see* Abd el Krim
El-Moqrani, Mohammed el-Hadj, 65-6
El-Obeidi, Abdel Ati, 233
El-Okbi, Sheikh Taieb, 76
El-Oummah (Algerian newspaper), 73
El-Senussi, Mohammed Ali, 62, 182
El-Senussi, Sayid Idris, 184 ff.; *see also* Idris, King
Entente Mauritanienne, 239, 240
Essaouira, 256
Étoile Nord-Africaine, 73-4
European Economic Community, and Mauritania, 247
Evian, conference and agreement, 107-9; and oil industry, 128-9

Faisal, King, visit to Tunis and Rabat, 395
Family planning: in Algeria, 166, 173; in Morocco, 257; in Tunisia, 397-8
FAO, and Rif development, 324
Fatimids, 180, 346-7, 406-7

Faure, Edgar: North African policy, 281; and Algeria, 89
FDIC, *see* Front pour la Défense des Institutions Constitutionelles
Fédération des Élus, 74, 80-1
Feraoun, Mouloud, 109
Ferry, Jules, 61, 68
Fez, 8, 253; and Roman times, 259; Islamic kingdom established, 260; and Dilaids, 262; in Rif war, 271; Sultan's visit (1934), 48, 275; Nationalist agitation, 276; riots (1965), 301
Fez, Treaty of (1912), 266
Fezzan, 181 ff.
Fishing, Mauritanian, 246
Ford Foundation, 398, 401
France: impact on North Africa, 2; exodus of nationals from N. Africa, 4; relations with Algeria, 169-70: over oil, 125-35; over armed forces, 159-160; over education, 171-3; and postwar Libya, 185 ff.; and independent Libya, 190, 229; and Mauritania, 248-9; and Morocco, 330, 332-3, 339; and Tunisia, 380-1, 391-4, 401
Francis, Dr. Ahmed, 94-5, 104
Front de la Libération Nationale, 88 ff., 118-19
Front pour la Défense des Institutions Constitutionelles, 299-300

Gabes, 343, 345
Gafsa, 345
Gara, Djebilet, 9-10
Gas, in Algeria, 121, 125-35; nationalization (1971), 133
Gaulle, Charles de, Constantine speech (1943), 82; (1958), 103; and events of 13 May 1958, 100-3; Algerian policy, 103 ff.; and peace initiatives, 106-9; and Moroccan nationalists, 277-8; and Bizerte crisis, 392-3; Tunisian land nationalization, 393
Genseric, 180
German Federal Republic: and Algeria, 169; and Tunisia, 397, 401
Germany: and Morocco, 1905-11, 275-6
Gharb (Morocco), 253, 320
Ghardimaou (Algerian HQ), 104
Gheris, 254
Ghozali, Ahmed, 116, 133
Giraud, General, 361
Giscard D'Estaing, President, 169-70
Gouvernement Provisoire de la République Algérienne (GPRA), 104-6

Granada, 27–9
Graziani, Marshal, 184–5
Grévy, Albert, 67
Guedira, Ahmed Reda, and constitution of 1963, 287; founds FDIC, 299–300, and PDI, 300
Guillaume, General, 50, 279
Gypsum, in Mauritania, 244

Hached, Ferhat, and Tunisian trade-unionism, 361; assassination, 361; death stimulates Moroccan nationalism, 280
Haddad, Malek, 418–19
Haddad, Tahar, 357–8
Hafsid dynasty, 21–2, 26, 181, 346–7
Haratin, 244, 255
Hassan II, King: and Allal al-Fassi, 291; and Moroccan politics, 293, 298 ff., 308; attempted *coups* against: 1971, 304–6; 1972, 308–11; meeting with Boumediene at Tlemsen (1970), 10; reconstructs armed forces, 316; visit to Soviet Union, 331, and Sahara question, 336–8
Hawwaz, Colonel Adam, 193, 194
Health, public, in Morocco, 258–9, 319
Herriot, Édouard, 72
Huhu, Ahmed Rida, 411

Ibn Abdullah, Sidi Muhammed (1757–1792), 263
Ibn Badis, *see* Ben Badis
Ibn Battuta, 407
Ibn Hani 'l-Andalusi, 405
Ibn Khaldun, 19, 346–7, 403–4
Ibn Khamdis, 406
Ibn Khamis, 408
Ibn Nafi, Sidi Oqba, 56, 260, 288
Ibn Nusair, Musa, 260
Ibn Rashiq, 406
Ibn Sharaf, 406
Ibn Tashufin, Youssef, 25, 260
Ibn Tumart, 260, 407
Ibrahim, Abdullah, 288, 291–3, 296, 298
Ibrahim b. al-Alghlab, 404
Ibrahimi, Sheikh, *see* Brahimi, Sheikh
Idjil (Fort Gouraud), iron ore, 245
Idris, Moroccan ruler, 260
Idris, King, 184, 188 ff.; deposed (1969), 191
Idrisi, Sharif, 406
Ifni, 4, 333
Ifrane, Algerian–Moroccan treaty (1969), 10

Ifriqiya, 21–2
Igueriben, attacked by Abd el-Krim, 270
Imani, Mohamed, 307
Independence: of Algeria, 108; of Libya, 187–8; of Morocco, 282; of Tunisia, 363
International Bank for Reconstruction and Development, 385
International Development Association, 385
IRA and Libya, 229
Iran, and Libya, 228
Iron, in Mauritania, 245
Islah (National Reform) party (Spanish Morocco), 276; National Front with Istiqlal, 278
Islam, 5–6, 18–19; in Moroccan constitutions, 287; in Tunisia, 373, 397
Israel, effect of creation of state, 4–5; and Libya, 225–7; Bourguiba's policy towards, 395
Istiqlal: established (1944), 277; and Sultan, 278; National Front with parties of Spanish zone, 279; organization and finance, 288–9; UNFP secession (1959), 289; programme and part in Moroccan politics, 290–2, 299–304; and trade unions, 293–4; attitude to Mauritania and Sahara, 10n.; and family planning, 258
Italian settlers, exodus from N. Africa, 4; in Tunisia, 350–2, 399; in Libya, 184–5, 222
Italy: limited impact on North Africa, 2; and Libya, 183–8

Jabala (Morocco), Spanish advances, 269
Jalloud, Abdesselam, 199, 201; foreign policy, 224 ff.; visit to Soviet Union, 230; condemns terrorism, 226
Jeunes Algériens, 69, 72–3
Jeunes Tunisiens, 355n., 356; model for Jeunes Algériens, 72
Jerba, 5, 341, 343; Jewish community on, 345; birthplace of Ben Youssef, 364; Jerba agreement (1974), 201, 389–90
Jews, 4–5; in French Algeria, 65, 81, 141; in independent Algeria, 52; in Libya, 177, 222; Jewish revolt (A.D. 115), 180; in Morocco, 256; in Tunisia, 344–5, 351, 399
Jordan: and Libya, 227
Juba II, 259
Jonnart, Charles, 61, 68

Juin, General Alphonse, 50, 360
July, Pierre, minister for Tunisian and Moroccan affairs, 281

Kabbag, Commander, 309
Kabyle, Kabylia, 6, 53; Mograni revolt, 65, 85; in de Gaulle's options, 103, 151
Kaëdi, phosphates, 244
Kairouan, 8, 19, 21, 341-2; resistance to Bourguiba, 373; Aghlabid cultural centre, 403-6
Kaïd, Ahmed, 115, 117, 149, 153
Kassim, Mouloud, 72-3
Kenitra, attempted *coup*, 308-11
Kerkoub, Ahmed Ould, 240
Khair al-Din, 349, 350
Khalduniya, 355, 356
Khaled, Emir, 72-3, 82
Kharijites, 5, 56-7, 260
Khatib, Dr., 299, 301
Khene, Abderrahmane, 166
Khider, Mohamed, 87, 88n., 92, 96, 99, 111-12, 116
Kosygin, visit to Morocco, 331
Kouera, Commandant, 309
Koutlah al-Watania (Moroccan National Front), 304
Krim, Belkacem, 88, 95-6, 98-9, 105, 107-9, 112, 116
Ksar Hellal, Neo-Destour Congress (1934), 359
Kufra, 203

Lacoste, Robert, 91, 96-7
Ladgham, Bahi, 361, 377; prime minister (1970), 376; and Palestinian crisis (1970), 396
Lagaillarde, Pierre, 100-1
Lakhdar, Tahar, 372
Lamine Bey, 361
Land nationalization, 4
Land reform, in Algeria, 117, 152-8; Morocco, 320-3
Larbi, Tayebi, 115, 148
Lasram, Mohamed, 356
Lavigerie, Cardinal, 350
Lazrak, Abelkrim, 307
Lebjaoui, Mohamed, 92
Leo Africanus, 31
Le Tourneau, Roger, quoted, 74, 79
Libya: *see main chapter headings and headings in text*; proposed union with Egypt, Tunisia, 11, 199-201, 223-5, 389-90; relations with other Maghreb states, 11-13; with Algeria, 231;

Mauritania, 248, 250-1; with Morocco, 227-8, 232
Local government: Algeria under France, 63, 67-9; independent Algeria, 117-19
Louis Napoleon, 63
Lyautey, Marshal Hubert (1854-1934): as imperial ruler, 43-4, 48, 266-8; weaknesses, 269; and Rif revolt, 271
Lyazghi, Mohamed, 311
Lyazidi, Mohammed, 273 ff.

Maaqil, 255
Maghreb: Maghreb unity, 11-13; Tunisian view, 389-90; strategic importance, 13-14
Maghreb Unity Party, 276; National Front with Istiqlal, etc., 278
Mahaichy, Major, 193, 200
Mahdiya, 21, 180, 343, 346, 405-6
Mahroug, Smaïl, 116
Mahsas, Ali, 87, 115
Malta, 391; and Libya, 231-2
Maltese, in Tunisia, 350-1, 399
Manifesto of the Algerian People, 81-2
Maraboutism, in Moroccan history, 263-4; and Moroccan nationalism, 273
Marçais, William, quoted, 56
March decrees (Algeria 1963), 111, 122, 145
Marrakesh, 8, 26; trial (1971), 306-7
Marsa, convention (1883), 351
Mas, Yves, 273; newspapers, 302
Masmoudi, Mohamed, 378, 396; and union with Libya, 390
Massu, Jacques, 97, 101, 104
Materi, Mahmoud, 360
Maulay Abd Al-Aziz, 264-6
Maulay Abd al-Hafidh, 266
Maulay Abd al-Rahman (1822-59), 263
Maulay al-Hassan (1873-94), 263-4
Maulay Hassan, Crown Prince, meeting with Roosevelt, 277; and Ben Barka, 296; *see also* Hassan II, King
Maulay Idriss, 256
Maulay Ismail (1672-1729), 263
Maulay Rashid (1660-72), 262-3
Mauley Sulaiman (1792-1822), 263
Mauritania: *see chapter headings and headings in text*; relations with other Maghreb states, 9-12
Mauritania Tingitana, Roman province, 259
Mauritanian Fishing Company, 246

Index

Medbouh, General, 304–6
Medeghri, Ahmed, 115, 117
Medjerda, river, 341
Meknes, 253; and Roman times, 259; riots (1937), 275–6
Melilla, 4, 28, 269; Phoenician, 259; in Rif revolt, 270, 333, 338
Melun, peace initiative, 106–7
Memmi, Albert, 418
Mendès-France, Pierre, North African policy, 281; and Tunisia, 359–60, 363; Carthage speech on Tunisian autonomy (1954), 50; and Algeria, 89 ff.
Merinid dynasty, 261, 407
Messadi, Mahmoud, 398–400, 416
Messali, Hadj (Hadj Ali Abdel Kader), 73–4, 75, 78, 91, 103, 109; and First Muslim Congress, 80–1, 85–6
Mestiri, Ahmed, 377–8; ambassador to Algiers, 9
Midaoui, Lieutenant, 309
Miferma, 245
Mining, in Morocco, 327
Mintoff, Dom, 391
Miske, Ahmed Baba Ould Ahmed, 240
Mitadja Valley, self-managed farms in, 148–50; land reclamation, 157
Mogador, 259
Mohamed Al-Sadiq Bey, 351
Mohammed V, King (Mohammed Ben Youssef), 48; meeting with Roosevelt, 277; deposed by French, 50, 279–280; reinstated, 282; and politics following Independence, 288, 293; claim to Sahara, 335; and arrest of Algerian leaders, 96; death, 298
Mohand ou El-Hadj, Colonel, 112
Mollet, Guy, 89, 93, 97–9
Monastir, 343, 353; birthplace of Bourguiba, 358; party congress (1971), 376
Moncef Bey, 360–1
Montagne, Robert, quoted, 49
Moors, 259
Moqrani, 141
Morehob (Mouvement Révolutionnaire des Hommes Bleus), 337
Morice line, 100
Morocco: *see chapter headings and headings in text*; relations with other Maghreb states, 9–11; before French occupation, 44; establishment of French protectorate, 43–5, 47; relations with Libya, 227–8, 232; Spanish rule, 47–8, 276–7, 282; *see also* Rif war

Moujahid, 93, 94, 99, 151
Mouvement Démocratique National (Mauritania), 242
Mouvement National Algérien, 91 ff., 99–100
Mouvement Populaire (Moroccan), 300–302
Mouvement pour le Triomphe des Libertés Démocratiques (MTLD), 85 ff., 89, 91
Mozarabs, 27–8
Murphy, Robert, 82, 100
Muluya, 254
Muslim Congress, First (1936), 80
Mussolini, Benito, 184; and Bourguiba, 362
Mzabites, 5, 103

Nabeul, 345
Naciri, Mekki, 276
Naegelen, 85
Nanda al-Wattaniya al-Mauritanniya, 240
Napoleon III, 63–5, 75
Nasser, Gamel Abdel, influence on Qaddafi, 192, 223; and Tunisia, 393, 394
National Charter, Algerian, 173
National Congress Party (Tripolitanian), 188
National Front (Moroccan Koutlah al-Watania), 304
Nationalism: in North Africa, 48–9; in Algeria, 69 ff., 80; Sétif, 84; under Boumediene, 115; in Tripolitania, 187–8; in French Morocco, 273 ff.; in Spanish Morocco, 276; Moroccan nationalism as foundation for independent state, 284; in Tunisia, 355–363
N'Diaye, Sidi el-Moukhtar, 240
Neo-Destour, origin, 358
Noin, Daniel, quoted, 318
Nouadhibou, fishing at, 246; meeting on Sahara (1970), 10, 335–6
Nouakchott: as capital city, 239, 242; gypsum deposits, 244; development plans, 247; meeting on Sahara (1973), 336
Nouira, Hédi, prime minister (1970), 376, 377–8
Numidians, 15–17, 54

Office National de la Réforme Agraire, 145

Oil: in Algeria, 121, 125–35; nationalization (1971), 133; in Libya, 208–16; in Morocco, 317; in Tunisia, 387–8
OPEC (Organization of Petroleum Exporting Countries): Algerian role in, 164–6; and Libya, 211 ff.
Oqba, Sidi, *see* Ibn Nafi
Organisation de L'Armée Secrète, 107–8
Organisation des États Riverains du Sénégal (OERS), 249
Organisation pour la Mise en Valeur du Fleuve Sénégal, 249
Organisation Secrète (OS), 86–7
Organization for African Unity (OAU), and Algeria, 165, 168
Ottoman Empire, 3, 29–33, 347; over Algiers, 57–9, 61; over Libya, 181–3
Ouezzane, 256
Oufkir, General: biography, 315; and Ben Barka affair, 295–8; and Skhirat, 305–6; and Kenitra, 309; death, 309
Oujda, 265; French capture (1907), 266, 268; Algerian HQ, 104; Oujda group, 115, 117
Ould Amar, Ismael, 244
Ould Amar, Mohamed, 249
Ould Babana, Horma, 239, 240
Ould Daddah, Ahmed, 247
Ould Daddah, Moukhtar, 239 ff.; and Mauritania's relations with France, 247–9; Sahara question, 336
Ould Mohamed Salah, Ahmed, 241n.
Ould Mouknass, Hamdi, 241n.
Ou Musa, Ba Ahmad, 264

Palestine Liberation Organization: and Algeria, 167; and Libya, 227
Palestinians, possible early settlement in Morocco, 256; Algerian support for, 166–7; Libyan support for, 225–7
Paris, Convention of, establishes Tangier Statute (1923), 267
Parmentier, rue (Tunis), meeting at, 105
Parti de la Justice de Mauritanie, 242
Parti Démocratique de l'Indépendance (PDI), founded (1946), 287
Parti du Peuple Algérien (PPA), 74, 85
Parti du Peuple Mauritanien, 241–3
Parti du Progrès et du Socialisme (Moroccan), 293
Parti du Regroupement Mauritanien, 240
Parti Libéral Constitutionnel (Tunisian Destour Party), 357
Parti Socialiste Démocratique, founded (1964), 300
PDI, *see* Parti Démocratique de l'Indépendance
Pélissier, Marshal, 64–5
Pétain, Marshal Philippe, 81
Phoenicians, 3; in Libya, 179; in Morocco, 259; in Tunisia, 344, 346
Phosphates: in Algeria, 139; in Mauritania, 244; in Morocco, 317, 326; in Sahara, 336–8; in Tunisia, 387
Pineau, Christian, 95
Piracy, *see* Privateering
Plan, Algerian, 124–5; Libyan, 216–17; Moroccan, 258–9, 318 ff.; Tunisian, 386–8
Plan of reforms (Morocco), 275
Podgorny, visit to Morocco, 331
Polisario, or Front for the Liberation of the Seguiet el-Hamra and the Rio de Oro, 11, 337–8
Population: in French Algeria, 79–80; in independent Algeria, 151; Algerian policy, 166; Libyan, 176–9; Mauritanian, 235–7; Moroccan, 255–7; Tunisian, 344, 354; European immigration, 350
Portugal, 27, 29 ff., 253
PRAM (Projet de Revalorisation de l'Agriculture à Sec au Maroc), 325
Privateering, 29–43 *passim*; from Benghazi, 181; from Tunis, 348
Promotion Nationale (Moroccan), 325
Punic civilization and language, 15–16
PUNS (Sahrawi National Union Party), 337

Qaddafi, Muammar, 191 ff.; biography, 192; political leadership, 194–5; political ideas, 195–7; Zouara speech (1973) and cultural revolution, 198; Green Book, 200; foreign policy, 222 ff.; and Tunisia, 11–12, 389–90; Israel and Zionism, 225
Qaraouiyine University, 276, 284, 288, 339, 414

Rabat, 8, 27, 254; Roman, 259; riots (1965), 301; meeting on Sahara (1972), 10
Rahmaniya Order, 65
Ramdane, Abane, 88, 96–100
Randon, General, 64
Referendum: on Algerian independence (1962), 108; on Moroccan constitu-

tion (1962), 298-9; (1970), 303; (1972), 307-8
Religious Brotherhoods, 61, 65, 76, 79
Rif Mountains, 252-3, 254; Spanish advance, 269; development of, 319, 323-5
Rifian Republic, 270-2
Rio de Oro, 4, 337
Riqaibat tribes, 236, 240
Roman Empire, 16-17; modern European occupation compared to, 47; in Algeria, 54-5; in Libya, 179-80; in Morocco, 259
Roosevelt, President Franklin D., meeting with Sultan of Morocco, 277

Saadi, Yacef, 91-2, 97, 98
Saadian dynasty, 262
Sadaki College, 355, 358, 399, 417
Sadakiya, 355, 356
Sadat, Anwer, 223-4, 390
Sadawi, Bashir, 188
Sahara: climate, 234-5; population, 235; tribes, 235-6; in Evian negotiations, 107-9
Saharan crisis (1975), 10-11; relative strength of Moroccan-Algerian forces, 163, 316-17; and Libya, 228, 232
Saharan dispute, 335-8; and Algerian army, 124; and Moroccan army, 316-317
Sahel, Tunisian, 342-3, 353; and Neo-Destour party, 359
Sahrawi Arab Democratic Republic, 338
Sahrawi National Union Party (PUNS), 337
Sahnun, 404, 405
Sahnun, Ahmed, 412-14
Sakiet, 100; importance for Tunisia, 391
Salafism, in Morocco, 273
Salan, General Raone, 101-4
Salé, Portuguese in, 29; Phoenician, 259; and Dilaids, 262; reaction to Berber dahir, 274
Sall, Abdul Aziz, 241n.
Sanhaja, 56, 75, 260
Sanusi, 43; rising (1916-17), 238; in Libya, 183 ff.; in Second World War, 185; under King Idris, 189; *see also* El-Senussi
Saudi Arabia, and Libya, 224, 226
Sayah, Mohamed, 379
Sebha, 192-3
Sebou, river, 276
Seguiet el-Hamra, 4, 337

Senatus-consulte (1865), 65
Senegal, trade with Mauritania, 243, 245
Senegal, river: agriculture, 243, 247
Senoussi, Abdullah Ben Driss, 273
Septimius Severus, 16, 180
Sétif, 53, 75, 139; Sétif conflagration, 83-4
Sfar, Bechir, 355-6
Sfax, 8, 342-3; party congress (1955), 364
Shalhi, Colonel Abdul Aziz, 193
Sharifian Empire, early library, 262-5
Sicotière Report, 61
Sidiya, Souleyman Ould Shaikh, 240
Sirte, Gulf of, 3, 174, 175
Skhirat, attempted *coup*, 304-8
Socialist Destourian Party, 368-72
Société des Frigorifiques de Mauritanie (Sofrima), 246
Société des Mines de Fer de Mauritanie (Miferma), 245
Société Nationale Industrielle et Minière (SNIM) (Mauritania), 244, 246-247
Sonatrach, 129 ff.; as example for Mauritania, 244
Soummam conference (1956), 93-5
Sousse, 8, 342-3, 353, 384
Soustelle, Jacques, 89-90, 94
Soviet Union: and Algeria, 9, 105, 168-170; oil industry, 131, 172; armed forces, 159, 163; and Morocco, 331; and Tripolitanian trusteeship, 187; and independent Libya, 190, 230-1; Tunisia, 396-7
Spain: Arab empire in, 22-30; outposts in N. Africa, 253; and Rif revolt, 270-272; and Moroccan nationalism, 276, 278; relations with independent Morocco, 33-4
Spanish Civil War, Moroccan troops in, 276
Spanish Sahara, 4, 10-11, 334
Student Movements, in Morocco, 295; in Tunisia, 371-2
Sudan, and Libya, 228
Suez expedition (1956), 97
Suidani, Boudjemaa, 87
Sus valley, 253, 291
Syria: and Algeria, 167; union with Libya, 223; decorates Moroccan officers, 314

Taalbi, Shaikh Abdel Aziz, 356-8; and Moroccan nationalists, 275

Tacfarinas, 17, 55
Tadla, 320
Tafilalt, and Alawite dynasty, 262; French conquest, 272
Tafna, treaty of (1837), 61–2
Tahir, Mamoun, 307
Tangier, 4, 28, 29, 252, 254; visit of Emperor William II, 265; Statute governing (1923), 267; Spanish rule, 269; speech by Sultan Mohammed (1947), 278
Tarfaya, 333
Tawfik, El-Madani, 94, 104, 105
Taza, 265
Terbouche, Mourad, 92
Tetuan, 254
Thamer, Habib, 362
Tillion, Germaine, 61, 85, 89
Tindouf, 10
Tizi-Ouzou, 53
Tlemsen, 8, 56, 58, 139, 261; Boumediene–Hassan meeting (1970), 10
Tlili, Ahmed, 365, 366
Tocqueville, Alexis de, 61
Torrens Act, 352
Torres, Abdel Khalek, 276
Tourism: in Algeria, 124, 139; in Morocco, 317; in Tunisia, 343
Trade Unions: Algerian, 119–20; Mauritanian, 241; Moroccan, 293–4; Tunisian, 361, 365–6, 370–2
Tripoli, 28, 175; Ottoman regency, 30, 32, 347
Tripoli Congress (1962), 110–11, 151
Tripolitania, 174 ff.
Tunis, 8, 22, 28; Ottoman regency, 30–32, 343, 345, 347–8; 'Martyrs' Day', 362
Tunisia, *see main chapter headings and headings in text*; relations with other Maghreb states, 9–12; Saharan crisis, 11
Tunisie martyre, La, 357
Tunisien, Le, 356
Turkey, and Libya, 231

Uganda, and Libya, 227
UGTA, *see* Union Générale des Travailleurs Algériens
UGTM, *see* Union Générale des Travailleurs Marocains
UGTT, *see* Union Générale des Travailleurs Tunisiens
Ujda, *see* Oujda
Ulema's Association, 76, 80, 94, 104, 410–14

Um er Rebia, 254
UNFP, *see* Union Nationale des Forces Populaires
Union Démocratique du Manifeste Algérien (UMDA), 85–6, 94
Union des Travailleurs Tunisiens (UTT), 365–6
Union Générale des Étudiants et Stagiaires Mauritaniens, 242
Union Générale des Étudiants Tunisiens (UGET), 371–2, 378–9
Union Générale des Travailleurs Algériens (UGTA), 119–20; and land reform, 153
Union Générale des Travailleurs Marocains (UGTM), 293–4
Union Générale des Travailleurs Tunisiens (UGTT), 361, 365–6, 371, 376
Union des Travailleurs Mauritaniens (UTM), 242
Union Marocaine du Travail (UMT), 288; and UNFP, 292–5, 299
Union Nationale des Forces Populaires (UNFP), 284; secession from Istiqlal (1959), 289; political fortunes, 291–3; and trade unions, 293–5; and Ben Barka, 296–7; political activity, 299–304; and plot of March 1973, 310–11; Sahara question, 336–8
Union Nationale des Musulmans Nord-Africains, 73
Union Nationale Mauritanienne, 239–40
Union Progressiste Mauritanienne, 240
Union Socialiste des Forces Populaires (USFP), 311
Union Socialiste des Musulmans Mauritaniens, 240
United Nations: and Algeria, 104–5; Algerian raw materials policy, 165; Libyan independence, 186–8; Mauritanian membership, 239; Ifni and Sahara, 344
United States: historical relationship with North Africa, 38–40; relations with Algeria, 13, 168; oil and gas industry, 130, 135–6, 172; and Libya, under Caramanlis, 182; Libya after Second World War, 187; Libya after independence, 189–90, 230; and Morocco, 13, 330–32; and Tunisia, 13, 396–7
Urbain, Ismaïl, 64–5

Valetta conference (1972), 391
Victoria, Queen, 347

Viénot, Pierre, 361
Violette, Senator, 80
Volpi, Giuseppe, 184
Volubilis, 8, 16, 259

Waterbury, John, 257, 284-5
Wergha, river, in Rif war, 271-2
West African Monetary Union, 247
Wheat, 7-8; in Algeria, 143, 157; in Tunisia, 386
Wilaya, during and after war of independence, 94, 96, 110-11, 113; as local government units, 117-18
William II, Emperor, 265
Wine, Algerian, 143-4
Woolman, David, quoted, 272
World Bank, 385
World War (1914-18), impact on Algeria, 66, 69-70, 142
World War (1939-45), impact on Algeria, 82; on Libya, 185; on Morocco, 276-277; on Tunisia, 359-61

Yata, Ali, 293; Sahara mission, 336-7
Yaoundé Agreement, Mauritanian signature, 247
Yazid, Mohamed, 92-3, 95, 97, 104
Young Tunisians, 356
Youssufi, Abderrahman, 296

Zakariyya, Mufti, 413-14
Zaouche, Abdeljelil, 356
Zaouche Noureddine, 372
Zenata dynasty, 56-7, 261-2
Zghal, Abdelkader, quoted, 376
Zionism, condemned by Qaddafi, 196, 225
Zirids, 21, 181, 406-7
Zirout, Youssef, 87-8, 95
Zitouna (mosque and university), 75, 356, 399-400, 414-16
Ziz, 254
Zouerat, 241

NORTH WEST AFRICA

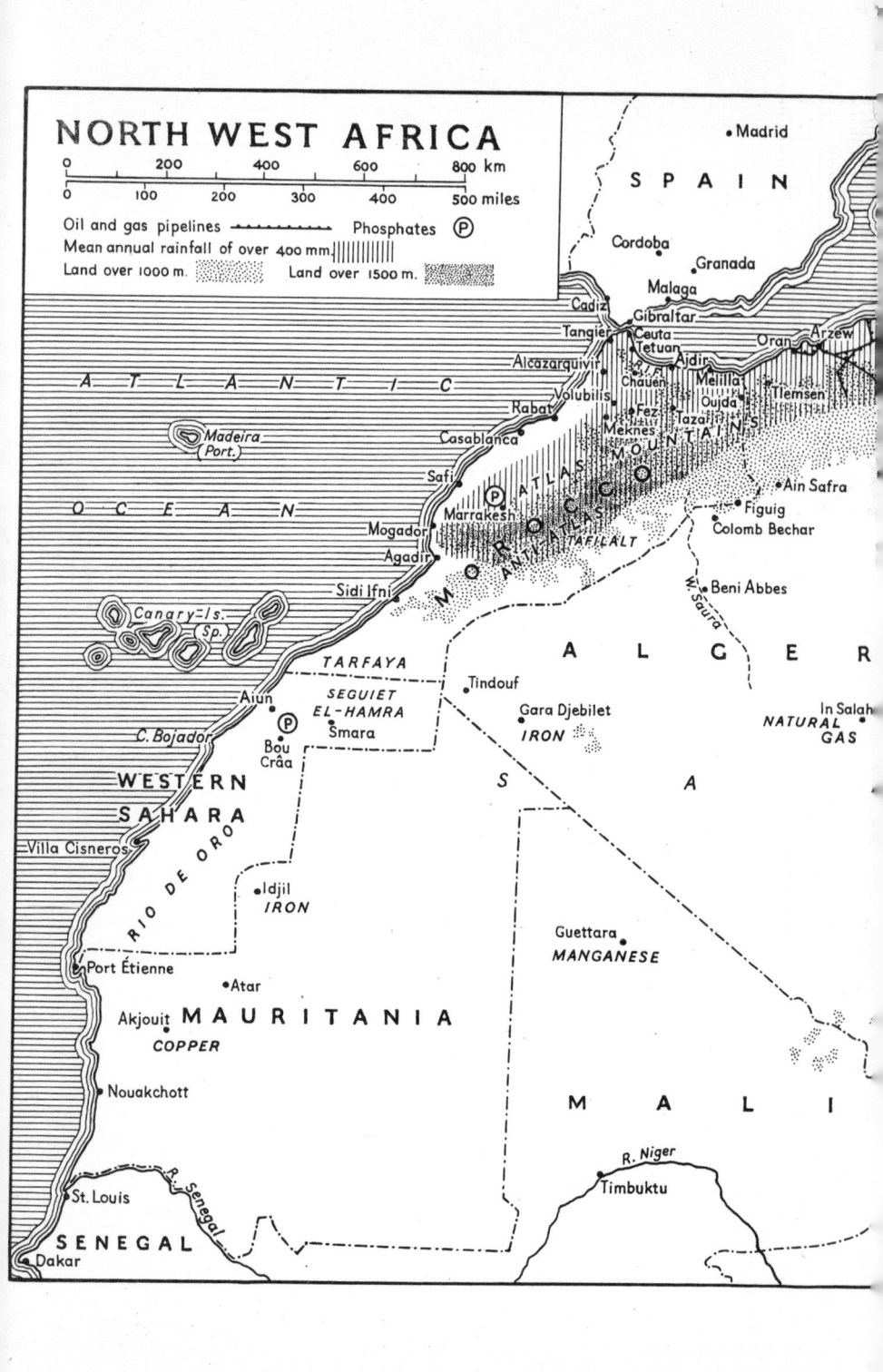

0 200 400 600 800 km
0 100 200 300 400 500 miles

Oil and gas pipelines ———————   Phosphates ⓟ
Mean annual rainfall of over 400 mm ||||||||
Land over 1000 m. ░░░   Land over 1500 m. ▓▓▓

- Madrid

SPAIN

- Cordoba
- Granada
- Malaga
- Cadiz
- Tangier
- Ceuta
- Gibraltar
- Tetuan
- Aidir
- Oran
- Arzew
- Alcazarquivir
- Chauen
- Melilla
- Tlemsen
- Volubilis
- Rabat
- Fez
- Oujda
- Meknes
- Tazai...
- Casablanca
- **ATLAS MOUNTAINS**
- Safi
- ⓟ
- Marrakesh
- Ain Safra
- Mogador
- **ANTI ATLAS**
- Figuig
- Colomb Bechar
- Agadir
- TAFILALT
- Sidi Ifni
- W. Saura
- Beni Abbes

ATLANTIC OCEAN

- Madeira (Port.)
- **MOROCCO**

- Canary Is. (Sp.)

- TARFAYA
- Aiun
- Tindouf
- **ALGERIA**
- C. Bojador
- SEGUIET EL-HAMRA
- Gara Djebilet
- IRON
- Bou Craa ⓟ
- Smara
- In Salah
- NATURAL GAS

WESTERN SAHARA

- Villa Cisneros
- RIO DE ORO

- **S A H A R A**

- Idjil
- IRON

- Port Étienne
- Atar
- Guettara
- MANGANESE
- Akjoujt
- **MAURITANIA**
- COPPER

- Nouakchott

- **MALI**

- R. Niger
- Timbuktu

- St. Louis
- R. Senegal
- **SENEGAL**
- Dakar